D1437160

Good Housekeeping

THE
COMPLETE
BOOK OF
PARENTING

Good Housekeeping

THE COMPLETE BOOK OF PARENTING

Everything you need to know to care for your child,
from before birth to adolescence

EBURY PRESS
LONDON

First published 1996

1 3 5 7 9 10 8 6 4 2

Text copyright © Ebury Press Limited 1996
except chapters 1 and 3 text copyright © Ebury Press/Nikki Bradford 1996
and chapter 13 text copyright © Dr Nicola McClure 1996
Photography and illustrations copyright © 1996 Ebury Press Limited

Nikki Bradford has asserted her right to be identified as the author of chapters 1 and 3 of this work.
Dr Nicola McClure has asserted her right to be identified as the author of chapter 13.

All rights reserved. No part of this publication may by reproduced, stored in a retrieval system, or transmitted
in any form or by any means, electronic, mechanical, photocopying, recording or otherwise, without the prior
permission of the copyright owners.

The expression Good Housekeeping as used in the title of this book is the trade mark of The National Magazine
Company Limited and The Hearst Corporation, registered in the United Kingdom and the USA, and other
principal countries of the world, and is the absolute property of The National Magazine Company Limited and
The Hearst Corporation. The use of this trade mark other than with the express permission of The National
Magazine Company Limited or The Hearst Corporation is strictly prohibited.

First published in the United Kingdom in 1996 by Ebury Press
Random House · 20 Vauxhall Bridge Road · London SW1V 2SA

Random House Australia (Pty) Limited
20 Alfred Street · Milsons Point · Sydney · New South Wales 2061 · Australia

Random House New Zealand Limited
18 Poland Road · Glenfield · Auckland 10 · New Zealand

Random House South Africa (Pty) Limited
PO Box 337 · Bergvlei · South Africa

Random House UK Limited Reg. No. 954009

A catalogue record for this book is available from the British Library.

ISBN 0 09 179042 5

Good Housekeeping Consultant : Linda Gray
Editors: Anne Yelland, Nicky Adamson

Design and Art Direction: Martin Lovelock
Photography: Jo Foord
Photographic Stylists: Hilary Guy, Kay McGlone
Illustrations: Raymond Turvey
Colour origination by Colorlito Rigogliosi, Milan
Printed and bound in Spain by Graficas Estella

FOREWORD

'When will *Good Housekeeping* bring out a baby book?', readers have been pleading for years. Well, I'm delighted to announce that *Good Housekeeping*'s new baby has arrived. This is a childcare book with a difference, because it recognizes that parenting does not end when your child starts school. Packed with practical advice, sensitively given, this is the one book you need to take you through pregnancy and those all-absorbing months with your new baby, to nursery age, schooldays, adolescence and beyond.

Written by a panel of leading specialists in health and child development, it combines a wealth of up-to-date information (including an invaluable A-Z of child health which you will refer to again and again) with an emphasis on your child's emotional needs. What you will not find anywhere is an unrealistic emphasis on perfection. Being a 'good enough' parent is all that is required and all that any child needs. I hope this book will help to make that easier and more enjoyable for you.

LINDA GRAY, ASSOCIATE EDITOR, *Good Housekeeping*

THE CONTRIBUTORS

Nikki Bradford (Pregnancy / Your Baby at Home) was formerly Health Correspondent for *Good Housekeeping* magazine. She is the Honorary Secretary of the Guild of Health Writers and her previous books include *The Well Woman's Self Help Directory*, *Pain Relief in Childbirth* and *Men's Health Matters*.

Dr Dorothy Einon (Giving Birth / The First Year / Toddlerhood and Beyond) is a lecturer in Psychology at University College, London. She also contributes to a range of newspapers and magazines and has broadcast on radio and television. Her previous published books are *Creative Play*, *Parenthood* and, with Jane Asher, *Time for Play*.

Dr Jane French (Schooldays) pursued an academic career for some years, lecturing at New College, Durham and the University of York. She now works as a journalist and has written for many national newspapers including the *Guardian*, *The Independent* and *The Times*. She is the author of *The Education of Girls: A Handbook for Parents*.

Sue Hubberstey (The Teenage Years) is a journalist specializing in parenting and childcare. She was editor of *Nursery World* magazine and has written for many publications including *Parents* and the *Guardian*.

Fiona Hunter (Healthy Eating) is a qualified dietician and since 1989 has been the nutritionist on *Good Housekeeping* magazine. She writes on food and health issues and appears regularly on radio and on television.

Jennie Lindon (Learning Through Play / Help with Your Child) is a chartered psychologist who works as a freelance consultant. Her previous books include *Help Your Child through School* and *Child Development from Birth to 8 Years* and she has written for many magazines.

Dr Nicola McClure (Your Child's Health / General medical editor) is a GP in a busy West London practice. She was the medical consultant and main contributor to the *Good Housekeeping Family Health Encyclopedia* and her other publications include *The Century Book of Pregnancy and Birth* and *A Baby's Story*.

Janice Parrock (The Teenage Years) was formerly editor of *Young Mother*. She is now a freelance writer who contributes to newspapers and magazines such as the *Guardian*, *Parents* and *Our Baby*.

June Thompson (Your Baby's Health) is a medical journalist who is also a qualified nurse, midwife and health visitor. Her freelance work has included the preparation of professional handbooks and research reports for the Department of Health and the Health Education Authority. She is the author of numerous childcare and parenting books.

Heather Welford (Feeding Your Baby) is a freelance journalist and author who has written for a wide range of newspapers and magazines including *Parents*, the *Guardian* and *The Times Educational Supplement*. She is an NCT breastfeeding counsellor and tutor. Her previous books include *The Illustrated Dictionary of Pregnancy and Birth* and *Feeding Your Child from 0-3*.

Contents

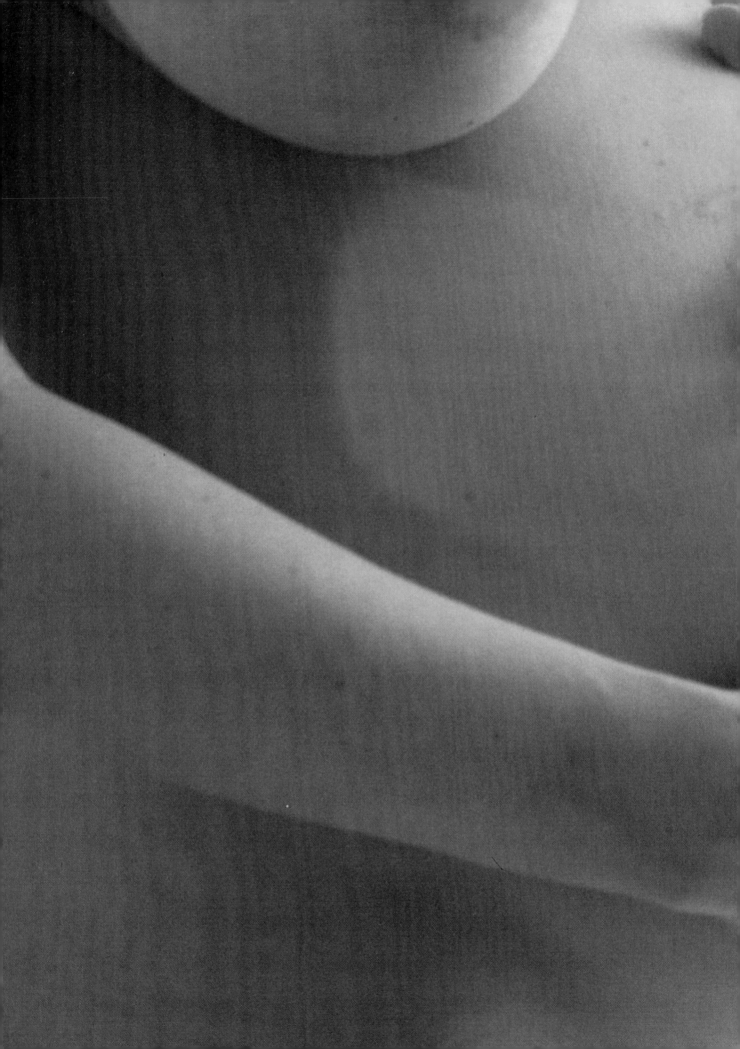

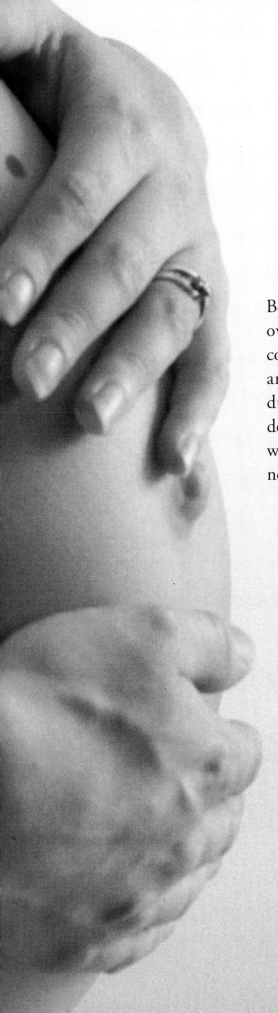

CHAPTER ONE

Pregnancy

Becoming pregnant, particularly for the first time, is an overwhelming and thoroughly absorbing experience, colouring every aspect of your life and every moment you are awake. This chapter details what you can expect during a normal pregnancy, how the baby grows, the decisions you will have to make and the items that you will need to acquire to make the first few weeks with a newborn easier.

Before your baby's birth

Having a baby can be so fulfilling that it can be hard to find words to express how you feel. It gives your life a whole new focus – from now on, you have somebody else to think of, somebody who affects almost everything you do. But along with the excitement comes a certain amount of apprehension. Will I love my baby? How will we cope? Will the baby be all right?

The good news is that mothers and babies are healthier and birth is safer than ever before. And although that is partly due to the ability of doctors to intervene in difficult or premature births, it is also due to increased knowledge of how babies develop in the womb, and to a better understanding of the importance of pre-conceptual care.

BEFORE YOU CONCEIVE

Most doctors now believe that it is important for both partners to be as fit and healthy as possible to maximize their chances of having a healthy baby. Being fit before you try to conceive increases your chances of doing so (one in six couples in the UK has trouble conceiving) and of carrying the pregnancy to term. Estimates suggest that as many as half of all pregnancies end in miscarriage (although often so early that you're aware only of a late period); 25 per cent of confirmed pregnancies are miscarried before the end of the twelfth week.

Ideally, you should both start planning for pregnancy at least three (preferably six) months before you want to conceive. It is important you both do so, because a healthy baby results from a healthy sperm fertilizing a healthy egg – a healthy egg fertilized by unhealthy sperm increases the risk of miscarriage – and it takes up to three months for new sperm cells to be made.

What you can both do

Give up smoking

Many studies suggest that tobacco reduces both men's and women's fertility. An American study found that female non-smokers were more than three times more likely to conceive than smokers; a Finnish study that smoking affected the speed at which sperm moved, making it move more slowly.

This advice applies to recreational drugs, in addition to tobacco.

Give up alcohol

Alcohol affects sperm production, not depressing the amount the body makes but increasing the proportion that is dead, damaged or in some way deformed. It has also been implicated in early miscarriage and is thought to affect the action of the cilia – the tiny hairs lining the fallopian tubes, the action of which helps the passage of the egg from the ovary to the womb.

Check for infections

Ask your GP to test for symptomless genito-urinary infections, as these can make both miscarriage and premature labour more likely. Chlamydia, in particular, is important to detect since it can affect a newborn baby.

Reduce your stress levels

Trying to become pregnant – especially if it takes longer than you hoped it would – can become stressful in itself.

In women, stress is believed to induce spasms in the fallopian tubes, which can interfere with ovulation, affect the womb lining and inhibit egg implantation. In men, stress hormones are known to affect sperm production.

Eat a healthy diet

Eat as much fresh food, raw food, wholegrain bread and cereals, lean meat and pasteurized dairy produce as possible, to ensure that you get plenty of vitamins, minerals and essential fatty acids. Iron-rich foods, such as red and white meat, fish, lentils, green leafy vegetables and beans are also important. Try to eat a varied diet to be sure you do not miss out on anything you need.

Make love often

Although timing affects whether you conceive or not, the regularity with which you make love can be as important. Making love regularly two or three times a week will maximize your chances of conception. There is a 'window' of three or four days in the middle of your cycle when conception is likely, so don't feel you have to make love on the day you ovulate – this can become stressful in itself.

Monitor drug use

Always tell your GP if you are trying to conceive since some prescriptive drugs can affect fertility. These include certain antibiotics and steroids for asthma in men; others may harm a developing embryo.

Try to avoid over-the-counter drugs for three months before trying to conceive, and during pregnancy.

What men can do

Keep your testicles cool

Their optimum temperature is a degree or two cooler than the rest of your body. Avoid tight briefs and trousers and sitting for long periods with your legs crossed; turn the central heating down.

What women can do

Stop taking the contraceptive pill

You should stop taking the pill at least three months before you plan to conceive and use a barrier method of contraception in the meantime.

Check your immunity to rubella

If you have never had German measles, ask your GP to give you a blood test to check that you are immune. If you are not, ask to be immunized and wait at least three months before trying to conceive.

Take extra folic acid

The demand for folic acid – which is used in building cells' DNA – is very high when foetal tissue is being made. Insufficient folic acid can increase your chances of having a baby with spina bifida or other neural tube defects. At least three months before you plan to conceive and during the first three months of pregnancy, the Department of Health recommends that you take 400 mcg a day. Most women are taking about half this amount. Folic acid is found in dark green vegetables, beans, peas, pulses, bananas, grapefruit and oranges; some breads and cereals also have folic acid added to them (check the label). You can also buy folic acid supplements.

Wear gloves when gardening

This can reduce the risk of toxoplasmosis, a disease caused by an organism sometimes found in cats' faeces which can cause miscarriage and birth defects. Similarly wear gloves when handling cat litter trays and wash your hands thoroughly afterward.

Take regular exercise

Do not start anything new and strenuous, but keep up any exercise you are taking and try to walk or swim more often (see also pp. 25–7).

Avoid X-rays

Do not have an X-ray of your lower back, abdomen or pelvis if you are or are planning to become pregnant. Tell your dentist if he or she wishes to give

How long will it take?

Women are at their peak fertility in their mid-twenties, after which it starts slowly to decline. This decline is accelerated after the age of 35. Men's fertility levels remain unchanged until their fifties, and men are biologically able to father children into their eighties.

As a general guide, about half of all couples trying to conceive do so within six months, a further 35 per cent within a year. The remaining 15 per cent may have problems.

If you are in your early thirties and have not conceived after a year of trying, ask to be referred to a fertility clinic.

you an X-ray: this should either be postponed or you should be given a lead-lined apron to place over your abdomen. If you are not, ask for one.

Watch what you eat

Infections such as listeria which in non-pregnant people cause food poisoning, can result in miscarriage or birth defects if you eat affected products when you are pregnant. Avoid if you can: raw and partially cooked meat and fish; unpasteurized milk and cheeses or yogurt made from it; soft, mould-ripened cheeses such as Brie and Camembert; soft-boiled eggs; pâtés; soft, whipped ice-cream from machines; and ready-made, prepacked salads and sandwiches. Women are also now being advised to avoid liver since veterinary feeds contain large quantities of vitamin A, which builds up in animal livers. High levels of this vitamin can cause foetal abnormalities. And caffeine prevents the absorption of certain vitamins and minerals.

When you cannot conceive

Infertility affects one British couple in six at some time, but the good news is that new fertility treatments and approaches to preconceptual care have made it more likely than ever before that they will become parents.

If you have not conceived within a year of trying, you can ask to be referred for infertility treatment. Since in 40 per cent of cases the 'problem' involves both partners, you will both be examined and interviewed, together and separately, in order to find out if the problem might be associated with your lifestyle – if you are smoking or drinking too much alcohol, for example – or whether further medical investigation is called for. Once the problem is identified, treatment can be carried out.

Often changes in your lifestyle are all that is needed; in other cases minor surgery or treatment with drugs may be required; if the problem is more serious, IVF (in vitro fertilization) or GIFT (gamete intra-fallopian transfer) may be considered. Take heart if you are having trouble becoming pregnant – more than half of all couples treated professionally for infertility do become parents.

WHAT HAPPENS IN CONCEPTION

For most couples becoming pregnant poses no problems and results in a normal, healthy baby. Looked at in detail, however, the process is complex and if anything goes wrong along the way, there will be no pregnancy. Knowing what happens when will help you to do the best for yourself and your child.

Successful pregnancy

Pregnancy depends on the following events happening in the right order and at the right time.

- The man must produce healthy, normal sperm and ensure that they are placed by the entrance to the woman's cervix (neck of the womb). From here the sperm must get through the barrier of mucus which protects the cervix from bacteria and viruses. Around the middle of the woman's menstrual cycle, the mucus is watery so sperm can swim through it more easily. At other times of the month, it is quite thick.
- The woman needs to have ripened and released a healthy egg from one of her ovaries. This travels down one of her two fallopian tubes, stroked along its length by the tiny, finger-like cilia fronds which line the tubes.
- Sperm then swim past the cervix, through the womb and up into the fallopian tubes to meet the descending egg. Eggs can live about 24 hours and sperm may live for two to three days, so they need to find each other within this fairly brief period.
- Several sperm may reach the egg at about the same time, but one needs to be able to break through the egg's protective shell and get inside.
- Once this has happened, the nucleus of the sperm fuses with that of the egg and the egg's wall becomes impenetrable to other sperm. The egg spends the next two or three days passing down the remainder of the fallopian tube, then reaches the womb cavity, where it floats free for two or three days. Conception has now taken place.
- Inside the fertilized egg, the combined ball of egg and sperm nuclei have been dividing, first in two, then four, eight, sixteen and so on, to develop into a cluster of cells called an embryo.

Boy or girl?

When a sperm cell fuses with an egg cell, the result is a ball of their nuclei. Sperm and egg both donate 23 chromosomes, making a set of 23 pairs in all. These form the genetic blueprint for your future baby, and cover everything from hair and eye colour to blood group.

It is the father's chromosomes that determine the sex of the baby, so there is no such thing as a woman's inability to produce boys. Women's cells have two X chromosomes; half of men's sperm cells contain X chromosomes, half Y. It is the Y chromosome that results in a male baby. If an X-carrying sperm fertilizes the egg first, the baby will be a girl.

- The embryo embeds itself in the blood-rich lining of the womb. You are now technically pregnant. However, it is believed that as many as 40 per cent of pregnancies are lost at this stage because the embryo does not implant itself properly.
- The womb lining is kept in place (rather than being shed in a normal monthly period) by extra progesterone produced by your ovaries. It is the major upsurge in the amount of this hormone in the body that makes many pregnant women feel nauseous in the first few weeks of pregnancy.

This entire process, made to look so easy by couples who conceive quickly, or accidentally, is very finely balanced throughout. It is thought that perhaps as many as 20 per cent of embryos which do implant are lost in what seems to be a late period.

Finding out you are pregnant

Some women know almost immediately that they are pregnant – they simply feel it, especially if they have been trying to conceive for some time. Others appear to be having periods and retain fairly flat tummies and are oblivious, in the most extreme cases for several months. It is possible to continue to bleed a little for a couple of months after you conceive. This is because your body may be producing enough progesterone to maintain most of your thick womb lining and the embryo in it, but not enough to prevent a little of it being shed.

The first signs

Early signs that you may be pregnant include:
- A missed period, or one which is lighter than usual.
- Tender, larger or tingling breasts, perhaps with darkened nipples.
- Nausea and vomiting.
- Changing tastes and a heightened or altered sense of smell.
- A need to urinate frequently.
- Feeling more emotional.
- Constipation.

Pregnancy tests

Most pregnancy tests are done on a sample of your urine, by checking for increased levels of one of the hormones produced in pregnancy called human chorionic gonadotrophin (HCG). Hospitals and some specialist clinics can do a more sensitive test on a blood sample.

Your GP may no longer do free routine pregnancy tests; many GPs who continue to offer tests charge for doing so. You can also get a test done for a fee by your local pharmacist. Or you can buy a home pregnancy testing kit. These can generally be used from the first day after your period should have started. Manufacturers claim such kits are 99 per cent accurate, but you must follow the instructions to the letter. It is worth doing a back-up test a day or so later.

How do you feel?

Emotional reactions to a positive test can vary enormously. Obviously if you had not planned to become pregnant, you will probably feel shock, surprise and, perhaps, disbelief. Even if you have been trying for some time, you may – along with the delight – feel panic, relief, anxiety, or even have second thoughts. Some people want to rush out and tell the whole world immediately; others want to take some time to get used to the idea themselves (it can be difficult keeping a secret like this from prospective grandparents, particularly if they have been waiting a long time for a grandchild). Often, several conflicting emotions are at work, until one or two start to dominate. Whatever you feel is perfectly natural.

Your partner's reactions are also likely to vary widely. Disbelief, pride and anxiety are all common.

Many men are surprised by the almost immediate change in their partners who, long before there are any visible signs she is pregnant, may prefer not to drive to a dinner party and sit up talking half the night, but stay at home and get an early night.

If there are no physical signs of pregnancy, you may find the first few months rather unreal. Often it is seeing the baby move on a scan (see pp. 23–4) that brings the reality that you are going to have a baby home to you. And if you are nauseous almost from the start and working outside the home, perhaps in a situation in which you do not want everyone to know immediately, the first few weeks can make you feel so wretched that you have almost no time for any real thoughts about the fact that you are going to be a mother and your partner a father.

Broadly speaking, there are three areas where you are likely to find your outlook changing.

Finance

Babies and children are expensive. No one believes the surveys that compute the cost of raising a child to the age of 18, until they have a child of their own.

Going it alone

Whether you intended to have a child on your own or not, you are likely to go through the same emotions as other women. Do not feel, because you do not have a partner, that you need to face everything alone. Groups such as Gingerbread and the National Council for One-Parent Families (see Useful Contacts, pp. 390–3) may have local support groups – people in your area who can share their experiences of single parenthood with you. Your health visitor (see pp. 152–3) is there for you, as is your GP. You have the same rights as anyone else to have a partner of your choice – friend, relative – with you at antenatal appointments and classes, and during the birth (see p. 21).

Bringing up a baby is not easy, even when two share the care and the responsibility. There is no doubt, however, that it is less difficult to raise your child alone than to do so with an uncooperative, uninvolved – or perhaps even hostile – partner.

One of you may lose some or most of your income for a few months, and even if you return to full-time employment while your baby is still small, there are the costs of child care to consider (see Help with Your Child, pp. 230–47).

Security

Women often feel very vulnerable when pregnant, not only is your body changing – at times almost on what seems like a daily basis – in a way over which you have no control, but you may feel sick and tired, and your emotions may be haywire. A warm, stable relationship becomes of paramount importance in such circumstances.

Responsibility

You and your partner are going to be completely responsible for another person, in a way that neither of you has been before. This can be a tremendously exciting and thrilling prospect; it can also be unnerving and even frightening.

Many parents are glad that pregnancy lasts 40 weeks – it gives you plenty of time to sort out your feelings about moving into a radically different phase of your life. There is no rule that says you must be delighted on day one and have worked out how you will manage to cope with a tiny baby on top of everything else in your lives by day two. The overwhelming majority of parents simply sort it out as they go along.

YOUR PREGNANCY WEEK BY WEEK

Pregnancy is measured from the first day of your last period, so that although you are four weeks pregnant, it is only two weeks since conception. Pregnancy usually lasts for 37 to 42 weeks from the first day of your last period: the average is 40 weeks.

In the early weeks of pregnancy, the developing baby is referred to as an 'embryo'; from about eight weeks, the term 'foetus' (meaning 'young one' is used). Technically, the foetus is not called a baby until birth. However, once your abdomen starts to bulge and you feel the baby's movement, it is almost impossible for you to think of the foetus as anything other than your baby.

Weeks 4–5

Your baby

This period ends with the implantation of the fertilized egg in the womb lining (see p. 13). The outer cells of the egg link up with the mother's blood supply. The inner cells form into two, and later into three layers, each of which will become a different part of your baby's body. One forms the brain and nervous system, skin, eyes and ears; another the lungs, stomach and gut; and the third the heart, blood, bones and muscles. At around 4–5 weeks your baby's heart starts to beat.

You

This is about the time that you will miss your first period but you may not even realize you are pregnant, although you may have some of the early signs.

Weeks 6–7

Your baby

All the major organs are now in place, although they are still rudimentary. Your baby's facial features are beginning to form and the first movements are being made. The heartbeat may be seen on a transvaginal scan as a pinprick of light blinking on and off. Your baby is now around 25 mm (1 in) long.

You

You may feel more tired than usual, or nauseous, or you may vomit; you may feel none of these. A test will confirm that you are pregnant.

Weeks 8–9

Your baby

Fingers, toes and tear ducts are present and the face is recognizable with eyes (which have some colour), nose, mouth (with tongue) and ears. The soft cartilage of the skeleton begins to turn to bone.

You

There is a rapid rise in the production of hormones from the placenta and ovary to adapt for pregnancy, so you may feel nauseous and/or vomit. Your womb is sufficiently large for a doctor to confirm that you are pregnant by an internal examination.

Sex in pregnancy

In a normal pregnancy, there is no reason why you should not continue to make love as often or as little as you wish. Many pregnant women report a higher libido than at any other time of their lives; others – particularly if they are tired and nauseous – don't. Both are perfectly natural.

If you have had a previous miscarriage, ask your GP for advice. Some doctors think it safest to avoid penetrative sex in the early months in these circumstances.

You may need to experiment with different positions for lovemaking, since what is comfortable at one stage may not be a few weeks later. Be assured that whatever you do cannot harm your developing baby. Later in pregnancy, an orgasm may set off contractions, but these will pass if you relax.

Finally, you should avoid sex once your waters have broken because of the risks of introducing infection (see p. 46).

10 weeks

Your baby

Eyelids and fingernails have formed, as have the external genitalia so that it is possible to tell whether you will have a boy or a girl. Your baby is now about 56 mm (2¼ in) long.

You

You may start to notice that you are putting on weight, and your breasts in particular may be getting heavier. Buy a good support bra (see p. 33).

12 weeks

Your baby

Limbs, hands, feet and internal organs are fully formed. Your baby is now feeding via the umbilical cord and placenta and moving around, although you will not be able to feel this yet. She can swallow and move her upper lip in an early sucking reflex. She will also react if her forehead is touched, by turning away and frowning. At this stage, she measures some 87 cm (3½ in) long and weighs more than 30 g (1 oz).

You

You have now missed two periods and have no doubts that you are pregnant. You may notice increased skin pigmentation in various parts of your body (see p. 36) and a brown line may appear up the midline of your abdomen. You may still be nauseous and vomiting, although this will start to subside over the next couple of weeks.

Your first antenatal appointment (or 'booking in', see pp. 22–3) will probably take place around this time. Make enquiries, too, about antenatal classes (see p. 25) so that you can be sure of a place at the ones you want.

16 weeks

Your baby

Now weighing around 150 g (5 oz), your baby is some 150 mm (6 in) long. There is fine, downy hair, known as lanugo, all over her and a greasy white substance (vernix) is beginning to cover the body; vernix is believed to protect the unborn baby's very thin skin. Your baby can suck her thumb.

You

You may well be offered a routine ultrasound scan at around this time (see pp. 23–4).

This is also the stage of pregnancy at which many tests for abnormalities are carried out (see p. 24). All morning sickness will normally have disappeared as you enter the stage at which most women start to feel

and look their best, with clear skin, glossy hair and a renewed sense of energy and well-being.

Your pregnancy may now start to show, although if you have good abdominal muscles and are on the small side, it may be another couple of weeks before your pregnancy is obvious to strangers. Your tightest-fitting clothes will no longer fit.

20 weeks

Your baby

Her skin is now a deep reddish colour and the head is approximately half the size of the body. The limbs are still very thin but growing stronger and bigger and your baby may be able to hear your voice.

You

If this is your first pregnancy, you will probably feel your baby move for the first time (you will notice these movements a couple of weeks earlier with subsequent babies, largely because you know what to expect). Initially this is like a fluttering or bubbling sensation, but as your pregnancy progresses, these movements become definite kicks and you will be able to tell whether the elbow, bottom or foot is doing the 'kicking'. Tell your midwife or GP when you first feel a movement – this can also help in dating the pregnancy.

Your breasts, which have been changing in size and shape since you were first pregnant may now have reached their final, pre-breastfeeding size.

Foetal development

Although as your pregnancy becomes more advanced, the changes in your body are increasingly apparent, it can be difficult to visualize how your baby is developing. Broadly speaking, babies' vital organs and body parts form early in pregnancy, after which the baby grows in length and weight. From around week 32, most are head down all the time.

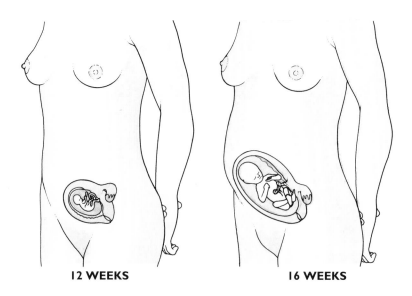

12 WEEKS   **16 WEEKS**

24 weeks

Your baby

Her skin is now translucent and pinkish-red and her eyelashes and eyebrows are recognizable. Simple behavioural experiments suggest that your baby is capable of learning; certainly she reacts to loud noises by kicking or jumping. She is swallowing tiny amounts of the amniotic fluid in which she is floating and passing small amounts of urine back into the fluid. She may hiccup, which you will be able to feel. She is now about 225–250 mm (9–10 in) long and weighs about 450 g (1 lb).

Some babies born at this age have, with skilled medical care, lived and thrived.

You

Your abdomen is getting progressively larger and you may start to develop stretch marks. A doctor may be able to hear your baby's heartbeat with a foetal stethoscope – ask to listen.

The increasing size and weight of your womb will also affect your posture, and you will throw back your shoulders and stick out your bottom, arching your lower back. To avoid back problems, try to tuck your bottom in and relax your shoulders. It also helps if you have been taking regular exercise.

This is the time when you gain weight most rapidly and your feet and ankles may start to feel the strain. Make sure that your shoes are comfortable and try to spend some time each day with your feet up.

26 weeks

Your baby

Your baby will respond to bright light from outside the womb: she will know, for example, if you are sunbathing in a bikini. Experiments suggest that she will also respond to music, remembering after birth themes played repeatedly.

Her eyes are now open and blue; although a few babies are born with brown eyes, the majority have blue eyes which remain blue until a few weeks after birth. She also has fingerprints.

You

Your heart and lungs are now doing 50 per cent more work than they did before you were pregnant. Make sure that you are eating well (see pp. 27–8).

28 weeks

Your baby

Now 350 mm (14 in) long and weighing about 900 g (2 lb), your baby has a 75 per cent chance of survival if born at this stage. She would cry weakly and breathe with difficulty. Subcutaneous fat gives her skin more of a flesh tone than previously.

You

You will probably start having antenatal appointments every two weeks from now on. This is the earliest at which you can begin your maternity

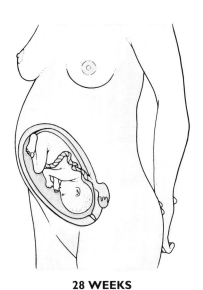

28 WEEKS

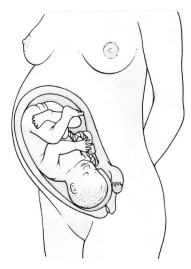

36 WEEKS

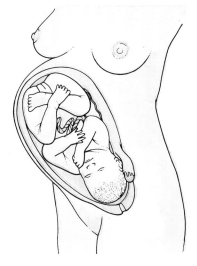

40 WEEKS

leave, if you work (see Your rights and benefits, pp. 28–30). Consider when you might want to stop working: remember you must give 21 days' notice.

If you wish to travel by plane, from now on you will need a letter from your doctor stating that you are fit to do so.

Make sure that you are getting plenty of rest and enough sleep.

30 weeks

Your baby

If she is born now, your baby has an 85–90 per cent chance of survival. She is around 400 mm (16 in) long and weighs about 1.5 kg (3½ lb). Her head is now more in proportion to the rest of the body, but she is still very wrinkled and thin.

You

You will probably start attending antenatal or parentcraft classes about now. Do not put off any of the larger purchases you intend to make for the baby or your home much longer – you may soon be too tired to shop.

32 weeks

Your baby

Most babies have now turned head down and are likely to stay that way since there is more room in the upper womb for the bulkier bottom and legs.

You

The upward pressure on your diaphragm may make it more difficult for you to breathe properly.

If you have other children, make arrangements now for their care while you are in hospital. Even if you plan a home birth, someone must be on hand to care for them, and it is best to be prepared in case something goes wrong and you have to go into hospital.

34 weeks

Your baby

The kidneys and lungs are now fully mature, she is some 430 mm (17 in) long and weighs around 2.5 kg (5½ lb). If she is born at this stage, she has a 95 per cent chance of survival.

You

Kicks and punches will now be very clear. If you have stopped work, spend the time relaxing – read a book, go for a walk, rest. Make sure you get plenty of sleep and eat well.

36 weeks

Your baby

The head may now have 'engaged' – dropped down into the birth canal, which eases pressure on your diaphragm. Do not worry if the head does not engage: some don't until nearer 40 weeks, others until well into labour.

You

The pressure of the head on your bladder may make you want to urinate frequently, including at night, so that getting a good night's sleep may be difficult. Try to catch up by resting during the day.

You will not be permitted to travel by plane, even for a short, internal flight. From now on, your antenatal appointments will be every week. Pack your bag for hospital (see box opposite) and keep important phone numbers – hospital labour ward, midwife – handy. Make sure you can always contact your partner if you need him. You may now feel quite strong contractions of your abdomen. Known as Braxton–Hicks contractions, these occur throughout pregnancy, but it is only in the last few weeks that you become aware of them. It is a good idea to practise your breathing techniques on them.

38 weeks

Your baby

She is now fully mature, with a rounded plump body. Most of the lanugo has dropped off although the hair on her head may be up to 40 mm (1¾ in) long. Finger and toe nails reach the ends of her fingers and toes.

40 weeks

Your baby

The birth may be at any time, but only 5 per cent of first babies arrive on the due date, so don't be anxious. Her movements decrease as space gets more limited, but you will still be able to see and feel kicks and jabs.

You

Get plenty of rest; cat nap during the day to make up for lost sleep at night. If you feel up to it, walk or swim. If not, try a relaxing bath. Many women get an overwhelming urge to 'spring clean' – tidying out cupboards, cleaning windows and so on – as the time for the birth nears, which has been attributed to a 'nesting instinct'; others do not.

If you do have a surge of energy, use it profitably but sensibly. Don't stand on ladders to reach high windows or top shelves, and if you have not finished decorating the baby's room, ask someone else to do so or leave it (the baby will not notice!). Similarly avoid kneeling or sitting on the floor working on low cupboards for any length of time – you may find yourself unable to get up again. It is a good idea, however, to stock up on necessities for when you come out of hospital – nappies (if you intend to use disposables) and other baby essentials such as wipes, cottonwool, soap or babybath and cream, washing powder and other cleaning materials, toilet rolls, sanitary pads. Avoid lifting anything heavy.

If you like cooking and find it relaxing, make some meals to freeze so that neither you nor your partner has to think about shopping for the first few days.

YOUR ANTENATAL CARE

Although the physical and emotional aspects of being pregnant can be overwhelming, with all the changes that are happening to you and to your relationship with your partner, there are a number of practical decisions to make too: what type of antenatal care would you like? what sort of birth? It makes sense to think about these and other practicalities as early as possible so that you have ample time to investigate your options.

Where to have your baby

You can choose to have your baby at home or in hospital (not necessarily the closest to your home), and you have a right to maternity care, whatever you choose to do. Take the time to look into the choices with your partner, with a midwife and with your GP. Ask other mothers in your area where they had their babies, and what sort of care they received.

Some women feel more comfortable in a hospital where emergency equipment is to hand, others are happiest in their own home, where they are able to feel in control. It is up to you.

Packing your bag for hospital

It makes sense to do this well before you will need it in case your baby arrives suddenly.

- wash bag and towel
- small sponge (for sips of water and sponging your face) and a larger one (to sponge you down)
- two clean nightdresses, with front openings
- dressing gown, slippers
- underwear, including nursing bras if you intend to breastfeed
- money or a card for the telephone
- earplugs (to block out the sound of other people's babies)
- bran tablets (constipation is uncomfortable and if you have had stitches, painful)
- a child's inflatable swimming ring (if you have had stitches it can help to sit 'in' one of these and there are rarely enough in hospital)
- glucose or dextrose tablets (you may need the energy)

- a tennis ball in a sock (for backache in labour)
- socks, shawl or cardigan (in case you start to shiver)
- something to wear in labour (if you don't want to give birth in a hospital gown)
- clothes to wear home (something that fitted when you were about six months pregnant should be about right)
- clothes and nappies for the baby to wear home
- a book, cassettes and personal stereo, writing paper, knitting, needlepoint (or anything else that relaxes you)
- camera and film
- pillows or cushions for the car

At the last minute, add:
- food for your partner
- ice packs (keep them in the freezer until you are ready to go)

Giving birth in hospital

Depending on where you live and where your health authority has contracts for its deliveries, you may be able to choose between different local hospitals, all within reasonably easy reach of your home.

Most women today have the majority of their antenatal care with their GP or community midwife and you may only visit the hospital once or twice during your pregnancy. It is becoming more common for the 'booking in' appointment – the first antenatal appointment that 'books' you a place for delivery (see pp. 22–3) – to be done at home. You are likely to have most of your care at the hospital if there is any problem with your pregnancy, since you may need to see a consultant obstetrician regularly; if a problem develops while you are pregnant, you will also probably be asked to see the consultant too.

The majority of babies – even if they are born in hospitals – are delivered by midwives. Normally doctors only intervene if forceps are needed or if a caesarean is necessary.

There are a number of issues which might affect your choice of hospital or decision to choose home rather than a hospital. All hospitals now say that they treat every mother and baby as individuals and they are anxious to get away from the idea that procedures take precedence over a mother's wishes. You may, however, want to ask specific questions to reassure yourself that you will be welcome to express your preferences (see also Making a birth plan, opposite).

The Patient's Charter

The Department of Health has a free leaflet entitled Maternity Services, which sets out the standards and rights included in the Patient's Charter regarding maternity services. Among your rights are:
- the right to a named midwife
- the right to see and keep your records
- you should be given a time for antenatal appointments and seen within 30 minutes of that time
- the right to keep your baby with you at all times, unless there are medical reasons not to.

Your GP or midwife should be able to give you a copy of this leaflet.

Some mothers prefer to give birth in a midwife-led unit or, in the few areas in which these are available, a ward or wards called a 'community' or 'GP unit'. Many of these are in fact attached to maternity hospitals, but staffed separately.

Consider the following questions:

- Can you have a domino delivery? This means that the community midwife comes to your home and stays with you until she thinks it is time to go to hospital. She then takes you to hospital, delivers the baby and takes you home a few hours after the birth. She will continue to visit you at home.
- Will you have the chance to meet the midwives who are likely to deliver the baby? Some hospitals operate a team midwifery system which means that the same midwives look after you before, during and after the birth. Most no longer have separate teams in the antenatal clinic and on the labour ward.
- If you prefer a woman doctor, will it always be possible to see one?
- Can your birth companion be with you at all times if that is what you want?
- Can you talk over your birth choices and have a record of them put in your notes?
- Will you be able to move around in labour and is there a variety of equipment so that you can give birth in the position that you find comfortable?
- Can you use a water pool during labour (and the birth) if that is what you would like?
- Do you have a choice in the way your baby is monitored?
- How long might you be expected to stay in hospital after the birth (you can discharge yourself whenever you wish, but it may help to know the average length of stay)?
- Is there good breastfeeding support?
- What are the visiting hours?
- Will there be a chance to talk about the birth afterward with the midwife who delivered your baby and ask any questions about the birth?

Having a baby at home

You can arrange for a home birth through your GP, or via your local community midwives. Many GPs are reluctant to support first-time mothers in having a home birth, because there is no way of telling how difficult a birth is going to be (your experience the first

Making a birth plan

Wherever you choose to have your baby (including at home), it is a good idea to talk through your options for care and any treatment, preferably with at least one of the midwives who is likely to be with you during labour. This discussion can then be formalized into a birth plan, which is written down and held with your notes.

Some hospital maternity departments have their own forms for birth plans but you do not have to stick to theirs if you don't want to. In any case your midwife is likely to point out that it is best to be flexible: your birth plan does not commit you to anything and circumstances and preferences can change even at the last minute.

The birth plan is really an aid to communication between you and your carers and it is better to compile it with a midwife than to present her with one that you have already drawn up. She may well think of issues you have missed, and will know what facilities are available in your area (not all hospitals have facilities for water births, for example).

- **Who do you want with you?**
  You may want to choose from your partner, a friend or relative, or your antenatal teacher. You may want more than one person, or no one. If you do not want anyone you know, but do not

want to go it alone, ask for someone to be with you: a midwife or student midwife will be happy to be there for you, while her colleague delivers the baby.

- **What sort of position might you find comfortable?**
  Ideally you should give birth in a room that offers a range of options: cushions, chair, bed, a covered area on the floor, so that you can move between them as and when you feel like it.
- **Can you opt for an epidural at any point?**
  This may become particularly important if you need a caesarean. A general anaesthetic takes effect more quickly, but not all 'emergency' caesareans need to be done immediately.
- **Do you want an electronic foetal monitor all or some of the time?** See p. 48.
- **Do you wish to avoid an episiotomy? Or induction? Other intervention?** See pp. 53–4.
- **Do you want your waters broken or would you prefer them to go naturally?**
- **Do you want your birth companion with you at all times, including when you are being examined?**
- **How long might you have to stay in hospital?**
- **See pp. 51–4 for options in pain relief.**

time gives some indication of the ease with which you will give birth subsequently). However, if you have young children at home already and do not wish to disrupt them, or feel that the birth will be more relaxed at home, you may decide that this is for you. You have the right to a home birth if that is what you want.

Your GP may be able to offer you antenatal care. If not, contact your local FHSA for the address of a GP who has an interest in childbirth. And contact your local supervisor of midwives who will arrange your antenatal care, delivery and postnatal care.

You will see the community midwife for all your antenatal checks, and she is the one to call when you think your labour has started. She will stay with you through labour and, perhaps with another midwife, deliver the baby. She will call a doctor or ambulance if you need to get to hospital in an emergency.

Antenatal appointments

In order to ensure that you and your baby are fit and that the baby is developing as she should, throughout your pregnancy you will have regular check ups under the care of either a hospital antenatal clinic, or your GP or a community midwife. Who looks after you depends largely on where you are going to have the baby. If the baby is going to be born in hospital, your antenatal appointments are likely to be split between the hospital antenatal clinic and your GP or community midwife (this is known as 'shared care'). If you are having the baby at home or in a community or GP unit, your GP and community midwife will look after you throughout your pregnancy, although you may be asked to go to the hospital for a scan.

When is it due?

You can assess when your baby is due from the chart on the right, although it is important to remember that very few babies actually arrive on the date on which they are technically 'due'. This is because due dates are calculated on the basis that women have a regular 28-day menstrual cycle, and that conception takes place right in the middle of that, neither of which is necessarily true. Most doctors agree that pregnancy lasts between 39 and 41 weeks; induction will normally be advised if your pregnancy has lasted more than 42 weeks.

The important date to remember is that of the start of your last menstrual period. These are given in pink in each column. The date at which your baby can be expected is given in blue.

January / October	February / November	March / December	April / January	May / February	June / March	July / April	August / May	September / June	October / July	November / August	December / September
1 8	1 8	1 6	1 6	1 5	1 8	1 7	1 8	1 8	1 8	1 8	1 7
2 9	2 9	2 7	2 7	2 6	2 9	2 8	2 9	2 9	2 9	2 9	2 8
3 10	3 10	3 8	3 8	3 7	3 10	3 9	3 10	3 10	3 10	3 10	3 9
4 11	4 11	4 9	4 9	4 8	4 11	4 10	4 11	4 11	4 11	4 11	4 10
5 12	5 12	5 10	5 10	5 9	5 12	5 11	5 12	5 12	5 12	5 12	5 11
6 13	6 13	6 11	6 11	6 10	6 13	6 12	6 13	6 13	6 13	6 13	6 12
7 14	7 14	7 12	7 12	7 11	7 14	7 13	7 14	7 14	7 14	7 14	7 13
8 15	8 15	8 13	8 13	8 12	8 15	8 14	8 15	8 15	8 15	8 15	8 14
9 16	9 16	9 14	9 14	9 13	9 16	9 15	9 16	9 16	9 16	9 16	9 15
10 17	10 17	10 15	10 15	10 14	10 17	10 16	10 17	10 17	10 17	10 17	10 16
11 18	11 18	11 16	11 16	11 15	11 18	11 17	11 18	11 18	11 18	11 18	11 17
12 19	12 19	12 17	12 17	12 16	12 19	12 18	12 19	12 19	12 19	12 19	12 18
13 20	13 20	13 18	13 18	13 17	13 20	13 19	13 20	13 20	13 20	13 20	13 19
14 21	14 21	14 19	14 19	14 18	14 21	14 20	14 21	14 21	14 21	14 21	14 20
15 22	15 22	15 20	15 20	15 19	15 22	15 21	15 22	15 22	15 22	15 22	15 21
16 23	16 23	16 21	16 21	16 20	16 23	16 22	16 23	16 23	16 23	16 23	16 22
17 24	17 24	17 22	17 22	17 21	17 24	17 23	17 24	17 24	17 24	17 24	17 23
18 25	18 25	18 23	18 23	18 22	18 25	18 24	18 25	18 25	18 25	18 25	18 24
19 26	19 26	19 24	19 24	19 23	19 26	19 25	19 26	19 26	19 26	19 26	19 25
20 27	20 27	20 25	20 25	20 24	20 27	20 26	20 27	20 27	20 27	20 27	20 26
21 28	21 28	21 26	21 26	21 25	21 28	21 27	21 28	21 28	21 28	21 28	21 27
22 29	22 29	22 27	22 27	22 26	22 29	22 28	22 29	22 29	22 29	22 29	22 28
23 30	23 30	23 28	23 28	23 27	23 30	23 29	23 30	23 30	23 30	23 30	23 29
24 31	24 1	24 29	24 29	24 28	24 31	24 30	24 31	24 1	24 31	24 31	24 30
25 1	25 2	26 30	25 30	25 1	25 1	25 1	25 1	25 2	25 1	25 1	25 1
26 2	26 3	26 31	26 31	26 2	26 2	26 2	26 2	26 3	26 2	26 2	26 2
27 3	27 4	27 1	27 1	27 3	27 3	27 3	27 3	27 4	27 3	27 3	27 3
28 4	28 5	28 2	28 2	28 4	28 4	28 4	28 4	28 5	28 4	28 4	28 4
29 5		29 3	29 3	29 5	29 5	29 5	29 5	29 6	29 5	29 5	29 5
30 6		30 4	30 4	30 6	30 6	30 6	30 6	30 7	30 6	30 6	30 6
31 7		31 5		31 7		31 7	31 7		31 7		31 7

Bottom headers: January / November · February / December · March / January · April / February · May / March · June / April · July / May · August / June · September / July · October / August · November / September · December / October

Medical checks

Your first major antenatal appointment – the 'booking in' appointment – is done at home, at the health centre or at the hospital antenatal clinic, usually when you are between 8 and 14 weeks pregnant. You will be asked questions about your general health, your family history, any medical problems, any previous pregnancies and how you feel that this pregnancy is going. You will be asked the date of your last period so that the baby's due date can be worked out (see chart above). Your heart will be listened to for signs of its overall health and your blood pressure may be measured. Routine internal examinations are no longer common, unless there are doubts about the duration of your pregnancy, but you will have a cervical smear if you have not had one in the last three years.

You will be asked to give a blood sample, which is then sent to the lab for testing. The lab identifies your blood group; checks your haemoglobin levels (to make sure you are not anaemic); looks for signs of immunity to rubella; and checks whether you have been exposed to hepatitis B or syphilis. If you live in a high-risk area (usually classed as the metropolitan areas, and in particular London and Glasgow), you may be asked if you wish your blood sample to be tested for HIV antibodies. This is done routinely and anonymously at certain hospitals which are part of a national programme to measure how widespread HIV is in the community – if your hospital is part of the scheme, you will be told. If you are not asked, but would like an HIV test, request it. Whatever the result, DoH guidelines lay down that you should be told face to face.

If your pregnancy is going well, the usual routine is for your antenatal checks to take place every month until you are 28 weeks pregnant, then every two weeks until 36 weeks, and once a week thereafter. Local practices vary, however, so you may be seen less frequently; you will be seen more often if you have problems, if you have had a previous pregnancy that was complicated, or if your GP or anyone at the clinic feels that it is appropriate for you.

Routine checks

The same checks are made at each appointment, wherever the appointment takes place.

Urine
You will be asked either to bring a sample with you or to produce one at the time. This will be checked on the spot for signs of infection, diabetes and pre-eclampsia (see p. 38).

Blood pressure
Raised blood pressure is one of the telltale signs of pre-eclampsia.

Weight
Research has shown that monitoring your weight is an inefficient way to tell whether the baby is growing as she should and is a poor indicator of your general health. As a result, you may not be weighed, although it is still common practice in many areas.

Abdomen
The midwife may measure your girth and she will check (by feeling) the position of the baby and the height of your uterus.

The baby's heartbeat
This will be felt using a stethoscope, or – depending on hospital policy – using a foetal monitor.

Your legs, feet and hands
For swelling (another sign of pre-eclampsia) or varicose veins.

It is a good idea to use your appointments to bring up any questions or problems you have (write them down in advance so that you cover everything you want to). If you prefer, sit up so that you can talk to your doctor or midwife face to face – having a conversation is difficult when you are lying down and someone is feeling your tummy. If you have something sensitive to talk about, ask if you can have time after your examination to do so when you have your clothes back on.

SCANS

You will have an ultrasound scan in early pregnancy. You will be asked to make sure that your bladder is full, so that your womb is more clearly visible, then a scanner is passed over your abdomen. Ask for help in 'interpreting' the picture.

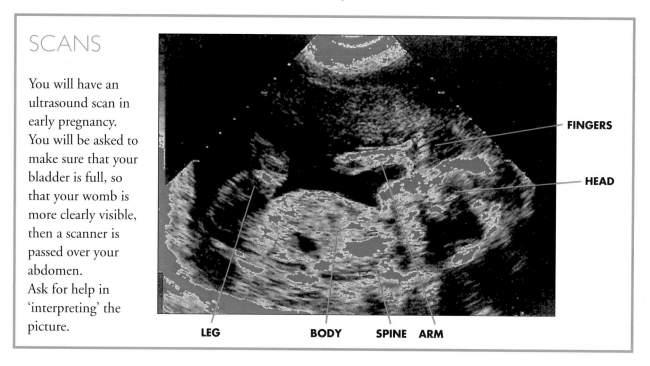

FINGERS

HEAD

LEG   BODY   SPINE   ARM

You may also be asked to go to the hospital to have an ultrasound scan. It is very common for a scan to be done in early pregnancy (around 16 weeks) with perhaps another later on. The main reasons for a scan are: to help date the pregnancy; to check for more than one baby; to check the baby's growth and development; to monitor the placenta; and to look for some abnormalities, notably spina bifida and Down's syndrome. Practices vary, but if you want your partner there he should be able to accompany you, and you may be offered an instant photograph of the scan. If you would like one, ask if this is possible. A skilled scanner operator can see a baby's genitals and therefore sex: if you want to know, ask; if not, say so.

Other tests

Depending on your age and your family's medical history, you may also be offered other tests. If you are not, and would like them, ask.

The AFP (alphafetoprotein) test

This is done at 16–18 weeks and involves taking a sample of your blood and checking it for high levels of AFP, which can be associated with disorders of the nervous system such as spina bifida. Lower than normal levels may suggest Down's syndrome. If problems are suspected, you will normally then have an ultrasound scan or amniocentesis.

The triple test

Sometimes called the Bart's test or serum screening, this is done at about 15 weeks. A sample of your blood is tested for two or three chemicals. Their presence, plus your age, help to calculate the risks of Down's syndrome or spina bifida. Depending on the results, you may then be offered amniocentesis.

Chorionic villus sampling (CVS)

This is done at around 10–11 weeks and involves removing a tiny frond of the tissue that forms the placenta and examining it for chromosomal abnormalities, especially Down's syndrome.

Amniocentesis

Carried out at around 18 weeks, amniocentesis involves having a needle inserted in your abdomen to draw off a sample of amniotic fluid. The sample is then checked for abnormalities, especially Down's syndrome, but also spina bifida, muscular dystrophy, cystic fibrosis and haemophilia. It will also determine the sex of the baby: if you do not want to know, say so.

None of these tests is perfect. Both CVS and amniocentesis carry a small risk of miscarriage and any test could increase your anxiety (although, since the results usually show that there is nothing to worry about, some women are more reassured by them). Routine ultrasound also has its critics who feel that not enough research has been done to offset any supposed benefit against the risks. None of the tests offers a totally certain diagnosis.

If a test shows that your baby is likely to have an abnormality, you may want to consider a termination. You should be given a chance to talk this through before you have the test (contact SATFA for advice, see Useful Contacts, pp. 390–3). Even if you know you could not consider a termination, you may want the time to prepare for having a baby with special needs.

Depending on where you live, your ethnic origin and family history, you may also be offered other, less common tests. You should be given the chance to discuss the associated risks and benefits before you decide whether to go ahead.

The risk of Down's syndrome

Down's syndrome is an abnormality that affects a baby very soon after conception. Affected children have a characteristic appearance: a flatter than usual face, slanting eyes, snub nose and a large and protruding tongue. They may suffer from heart disease. The degree of learning disability varies enormously. All children with the syndrome are mentally and physically affected, but most will learn to speak and many can read and write. Down's children are usually loving and affectionate.

The risk of having a child who is affected rises sharply according to the age of the mother.

At 25 years	1 in 1,500 births
At 30 years	1 in 800 births
At 35 years	1 in 300 births
At 38 years	1 in 180 births
At 40 years	1 in 100 births
At 45 years	1 in 30 births

Antenatal classes

Many maternity units and health centres run classes for expectant parents. They may be called antenatal classes or parentcraft classes. These classes are free and usually taken by midwives and health visitors with perhaps one class including a contribution from a hospital doctor, probably about pain relief, caesarean section or special care facilities for babies who are sick or premature.

The major non-NHS classes are run by the National Childbirth Trust (see Useful Contacts, pp. 390–3), with courses taken by their own specially trained teachers in most areas of the UK. There is usually a charge for NCT classes, although in some areas subsidized places are available for those who cannot afford to pay.

NCT classes are often less formal than NHS ones, with teachers concerned to encourage class members to support each other and to use the class as a safe, welcoming environment in which to explore feelings and fears, as well as a forum for information giving. NHS classes vary enormously – some are excellent, others patchy – but there is usually not the same emphasis on group support. NHS classes usually offer you the opportunity to visit the labour ward and the special care baby unit (although you can always ask to do this if you intend to have your baby in hospital, even if you do not attend the classes).

A typical course of antenatal classes consists of between seven and ten two-hour sessions and you can expect to start going when you are around seven months pregnant. Good classes cover:

- what to expect during labour and birth and afterward, with time for questions and discussion so that you go into the birth confident that you are making the right decisions for you
- you may be shown a video of childbirth
- options in pain relief (see pp. 51–4)
- relaxation techniques to help with pain in labour
- exercises to keep fit and to help in labour
- advice on caring for your baby
- advice on looking after yourself after the birth.

If you know other women with children, ask them which classes they found most useful. You may also be influenced by the timing and location of classes. Some classes are primarily for couples, others for women only. You can of course go to more than one set. Local classes (particularly if you have not been working locally) can be a good place to meet other mothers-to-be with whom you can perhaps stay in touch after your baby's birth.

Ask your community or hospital midwife about the availability of classes; in some cases you may have to book in advance.

Exercise in pregnancy

If you are wondering whether you should exercise while you are pregnant, the answer is an unequivocal 'yes'. If you are fit, you are far more likely to get through the tiring last weeks of pregnancy and cope more easily with the hard work of labour than if you are not. If you are used to regular exercise, keep it up as long as you feel able. You will probably be advised at antenatal classes to avoid sports that carry a risk of falling or rough contact with other players, such as martial arts, squash, skiing or riding. If you are not used to exercise, pregnancy can be a good time to start, as long as you do it gradually.

Whatever you do, be responsive to your own body and do not push yourself too far. Total, physical exhaustion is not a good idea. Stop and rest more than you would normally. Also, avoid taking on anything strenuous when it is hot – you are more likely to faint or become dizzy – and be sure to drink plenty of fluids to avoid dehydration. If you attend exercise classes of any sort, tell your instructor that you are pregnant: she may suggest that you miss some exercises out, or do them in a different way. High-impact aerobics involving heavy bouncing are best avoided, since all your muscles and ligaments are softer in pregnancy (so that they stretch to enable you to give birth). This means that they are more easily damaged than at other times. Your extra weight could also mean that you put undue strain on your back.

Swimming and walking are great exercise and suitable right to the end of your pregnancy. In some areas aquanatal classes – which combine swimming with body toning and stretching to focus on the muscles used in pregnancy and childbirth – may be available. Some antenatal classes include toning and stretching exercises. If you do not usually exercise, try to choose antenatal classes that include a simple fitness programme.

Pelvic floor exercises

You will hear several times during your pregnancy and afterward how important it is that you do your pelvic floor exercises. The muscles of the pelvic floor support the internal organs, including your womb, bladder and back passage. Keeping these muscles in good tone will, therefore, help you during and after the birth – as they have to stretch sufficiently to allow your baby to come out and then go back to their normal state afterward. If these muscles are weak, you run the risk of stress incontinence – leaking of small amounts of urine from your bladder when you cough, run, laugh or sneeze. This can occur in the last few weeks of pregnancy (see p. 35) but is more common after the birth.

The basic pelvic floor exercise is very simple and you can do it anywhere, sitting, standing or lying. For most women, the problem is remembering to do the sequence often enough. You need to tighten the muscles of your front passage as if you were trying to hold on to urine when you are 'bursting' to go. Keep tightening, first vaginal area, then rectum, hold for four seconds, and then relax. Repeat several times, and repeat the whole sequence several times a day.

Relaxation techniques

If you have already tried yoga or other meditation techniques, you will find that they are particularly useful in pregnancy. If you have not, learning basic relaxation will help you while you are pregnant, during the birth and afterward.

The easiest way to start learning to relax is to make space in your day for 10 minutes' uninterrupted, quiet time. Lie down, and starting at your toes and feet, alternately tense and relax each part of your body, right up to your head. Don't forget your shoulders, arms and hands, or your face (frown, screw up your face and then let it go). Keep your eyes gently closed as you are doing this. Some people find it helps to have some soothing music playing; others to focus on a beautiful image. In time, you will be able to use this technique whenever you feel stressed to help you regain your physical and mental equilibrium.

This technique is particularly useful in childbirth. Coping with contractions is easier if you are relaxed; it also conserves your energy.

Of course, there are other ways to relax. Simply making some time for yourself, even once a day, is

Antenatal exercises

Regular exercise, including stretching, in the months before you become pregnant and in pregnancy itself, will stand you in good stead to face the hard work of labour. The exercises illustrated here will all help with labour and delivery, but are no substitute for a structured session of antenatal exercise, either as part of your antenatal classes, or on the advice of your local sports centre or gym. Warm up before you begin.

Sit with your feet together and forearms along your inner calves. Gently press your knees toward the floor. Hold for 10 seconds.

Stand with your feet shoulder width apart and slowly ease down into a squatting position. Repeat as often as you can.

Squatting is not easy if your muscles are tight and you may find it helps to support yourself on a chair or the end of the bed.

important. In late pregnancy, you may be advised to rest with your feet up to help combat mild oedema (swelling or puffiness). You can even do this at work in the middle of the day. Take some time to have a proper lunch break, away from your desk, rather than rushing around the shops and grabbing a sandwich. Ask your partner to do the shopping.

Take care to look after your other physical needs. Many women find their skin and hair look better than ever before in pregnancy – especially from about four or five months. If you have a tendency to oiliness, this is likely to lessen while you are pregnant to give you that healthy bloom that makes you look and feel good. If you find that your skin is dry, add oil to your bath and be generous with the moisturizer. Treat yourself to a good haircut shortly before the baby is born. It may make you feel better in the days immediately after the birth if your hair looks good, and you will find it difficult to make time for an appointment for weeks afterward.

Don't be afraid to ask for help, particularly in the later stages. If asking a neighbour to pick up your toddler from playgroup – when he or she is probably going for their own child in any case – gives you ten minutes to put your feet up, then do so. Most people are only too willing to help. Remember that toddlers do not always need to be running around: after a busy morning at playgroup or with friends in the park, she may be quite happy to cuddle up on the sofa with you while you look at a book or watch a video or TV programme together.

What to eat

Good-quality food, low in sugar and high in carbohydrate from a variety of sources should be the basis of a healthy diet at all times, not only when you are pregnant. Opinions differ as to how many extra calories you actually need when you are pregnant (certainly you should not be 'eating for two'), but the metabolism does change at this time – both to cope with the extra demands on your heart and lungs, and later while you are breastfeeding – so it is likely you will feel hungrier than usual once any morning sickness has passed.

Follow your appetite, without heading for instant 'junk' foods. Snack on fresh and dried fruits if you are hungry between meals, and drink plenty of water. As

Lift your right shoulder forward and up, then back and down. Repeat with your left arm.

Aerobic fitness helps you cope with the extra demands on your heart. Try rhythmic marching.

When you have a good marching pace, lift your right knee and touch with your left hand.

Repeat right hand to left knee. Try to keep the pace even, and aim to get your knees high.

a general guide, most women gain 10–12.5 kg (22–28 lb) during pregnancy and, although it is difficult to get rid of excess weight after the birth, it is usually more of a worry to your GP and midwife if you put on too little rather than too much weight while you are pregnant.

Make sure you have plenty of fresh fruit and vegetables, carbohydrates such as bread, cereals, pasta and rice, plus proteins such as eggs, pulses, meat and fish. A high-fibre diet, with plenty of fluid, may help combat constipation, which is common in pregnancy. Milk is a convenient source of many nutrients, including calcium and protein but if you do not like it, it is not essential. Everything found in milk can be obtained from other foods too.

There have been few studies into the effects of alcohol on foetuses after the first 13 weeks, when all the major organs have been formed. As a result, there is no recommended 'safe' limit on the amount you can drink without harming your baby. For this reason, many doctors advise you not to drink alcohol at all while you are pregnant. Equally, there is no real evidence that the odd glass of wine or beer does any harm. But binge drinking and heavy habitual drinking do harm babies. See also p. 10.

WORKING IN PREGNANCY

Many mothers-to-be work until quite late in pregnancy and feel fine doing so. It is normal, however, to want to reduce the pace of your working life, particularly during the most physically demanding times. For many women, this means the first three months and the last six to eight weeks.

In early pregnancy, sickness and tiredness may mean that you want to avoid the rush, fumes and pressure of early-morning travelling. Think about negotiating a later start time in return for a later finishing time. Later on, the sheer exhaustion of being heavier and more uncomfortable can make travelling stressful. Again, try to change your hours, even temporarily, to suit how you feel. If you anticipate that your employer might be un-sympathetic, ask your GP or the antenatal clinic to back up your request.

You have certain rights regarding hazardous working conditions (see below). If appropriate, ask to move to a non-smoking area and make sure you sit in such an area in the canteen. Don't skip lunch – you and the baby both need it. If you do not feel like sitting, go for a walk or swim, but do take a break.

Standing for long stretches of the day can cause tiredness, backache and swelling. If your job involves long periods of standing, see if you can sit for some of the time (in a chair that is comfortable and supports your back). Again, if you anticipate problems, ask your GP for support.

Your rights and benefits

There are three broad classes of state benefit to which you may be entitled: those for which everyone can apply as of right; those for parents or their partners on low incomes; and those which apply if you are (or have been) in employment.

Benefits for all
- Free dental treatment and prescriptions for you during your pregnancy and for a year afterward, and for your child until she is 16.
- Child benefit: a weekly tax-free flat-rate benefit paid directly to the mother for every child until she is 16, or 19 if still in full-time education.
- One-parent family benefit: a weekly tax-free flat-rate benefit which is paid directly to you if you are a single parent.

Benefits if you are on a low income

You may be entitled to some of the following benefits as the size of your family increases; amounts usually vary and are dependent on several factors, including income, savings, size of your family, whether any member of your family has special needs and whether you or your partner is working. Call the DSS free telephone enquiry line for up-to-date information on benefits to which you may be entitled.

Income Support
This is payable to anyone who does nor have enough money to live on. Income Support 'tops up' earnings and other benefits so the amount to which you may be entitled varies. If you have a mortgage, Income Support may help toward your interest payments, which may be paid direct to your mortgage lender.

Family Credit

This tax-free benefit is payable to working families on low incomes (at least one partner must work 16 hours a week and you must have one child).

Maternity payments

A flat-rate payment to help you to buy things for the baby; you must claim within three months of the birth.

Housing Benefit

Amounts vary, but Housing Benefit is paid direct to the council if you are a council tenant and to you if you are a private tenant.

Council tax

You may be entitled to help with paying this tax; amounts vary but you could get your whole bill paid.

Free milk and vitamins

If you are entitled to Income Support, you will get tokens for a pint of milk a day for you and each child under five (they can be exchanged at the baby clinic for formula for under-ones); vitamins are available free at baby and child health clinics for you while you are pregnant and breastfeeding, and for your children until they are five.

For working women

If you are pregnant and in employment, you have certain legal rights to time off and, sometimes, to pay during that time. Current rights are detailed below, but it is advisable to contact the DSS Helpline, your trade union, the Citizen's Advice Bureau, local law centre or the Maternity Alliance (see Useful Contacts, pp. 390–3) for up-to-date information and advice as early in your pregnancy as possible. Some benefits depend on your telling your employer your intentions before a certain stage in your pregnancy.

Classes and appointments

You are entitled to time off without loss of pay to attend antenatal appointments and antenatal classes, including relaxation and parentcraft classes. Your employer is entitled to ask for a letter from your GP, midwife or health visitor to say that these classes are necessary and has the right to ask to see your appointment card.

The nature of your work

If you cannot do your job while you are pregnant, have given birth in the past six months or are breast-feeding (if it involves heavy lifting, for example, or working with X-rays), your employer must offer you a suitable alternative, if one is available; if not, you are entitled to be suspended on full pay. If you refuse a suitable alternative, you lose the right to full pay.

Unfair dismissal

You cannot be dismissed because you are pregnant, nor can you be dismissed during your maternity leave. If your employers wish to make you redundant, they must wait until you apply to return to work after the birth.

Maternity leave

You are entitled to 14 weeks off work, regardless of how many hours a week you work, or how long you have worked for your employer. You must write to your employer at least 21 days before you intend to start your leave. You can start your leave up to 11 weeks before the baby is due, or work right until the due date. If you return after 14 weeks, you do not have to give your employer any notice that you are returning; if you want to go back before 14 weeks have elapsed, you must give your employer seven days' notice. You should return to your own job.

Benefits for fathers

Fathers tend to get a raw deal. There is no statutory requirement on employers to offer paternity leave, although some employers do. Most give time off for you to be at the birth, but that apart, many insist that extra leave is taken from your holiday entitlement, so that you may well find that you are expected to take a holiday to cover the period when the baby comes home.

It is, however, important that you are there for as long as possible. If your partner is in hospital for a few days, try to work then so that you can be at home when mother and baby come out.

As well as the practical support that you can give, changing nappies, bathing, spending time with the baby while your partner rests, shopping and so on, you need time with your partner and baby, simply learning to be a family.

Maternity leave does not count as 'time off', so that pension rights, holiday entitlement and company car are unaffected by this break.

Extended maternity leave

If you have worked for your employer for two years by the 12th week before your baby is due and your employer has more than five employees, you are entitled to additional maternity leave to your 14 weeks, until the end of the 29th week after your baby is born.

To qualify you must notify your employer 21 days before you leave that it is your intention to return; you must also notify your employer at least 21 days before you intend to return to work. Your employer is entitled to write to you at any time after 11 weeks from the start of your leave, asking if you intend to return, and you must answer within 14 days. If you are not sure at this stage, follow the procedure until the final stage (21 days before your return).

Other benefits

Statutory maternity pay (SMP)

If you have worked for your employer for at least 26 weeks by the end of the 15th week before your baby is due, you are entitled to statutory maternity pay.

SMP is paid for any 18 weeks between week 11 before the birth and week 11 after the birth. For the first six weeks, you get 90 per cent of your average pay; for the next 12 weeks you will get the basic rate SMP. To qualify you must write to your employer claiming SMP 21 days before you stop work.

Maternity allowance

This is paid to women who are not eligible to receive SMP (including the self-employed); to qualify you must have paid NI contributions for 26 of the 66 weeks before the week the baby is due. Like SMP, this is paid for 18 weeks. If you are unsure whether you are eligible to claim, do so: the DSS will work out whether you are entitled or not.

Sickness benefit

If you have paid NI in the last three years, but have not paid enough contributions to claim maternity allowance, you may be entitled to sick pay, paid from six weeks before the baby is born to two weeks after.

WHAT YOU WILL NEED

It is a good idea to get most of the basic equipment and clothes for your baby before she is born. Shopping for major purchases will be difficult once she is with you. But try to resist the temptation to rush out and buy lots of clothes and bedding, especially if you have generous family and friends, and have friends with children who may pass outgrown clothes on to you.

Choose machine-washable items only and avoid anything with long, trailing ribbons and trimmings that could come loose.

The list here is of the basic items you will need for the first few weeks. Gifts will still be welcome, since this is the minimum – you will be washing very frequently if this is all you have.

Somewhere for the baby to sleep

This could be a cot, carrycot or crib. You might find it easier to use a pram top, carrycot or cradle as your baby's sleeping place for the first few weeks, since all are portable and can easily be carried from room to room and even up and down stairs. Check that the mattress fits correctly. Depending on how quickly she grows, you will need a proper cot within around six months.

You will also need two or three sets of bedding – sheets and machine-washable blankets (see pp. 168–9).

Transport

Your pram or pushchair is one of the most expensive single purchases of your baby's first year, so it makes sense to take time over choosing one.

Full-size, traditional 'coach-built' prams are extremely hard-wearing, beautiful-looking and very warm and comfortable for your baby. They are, however, very expensive (although they seem to keep their value secondhand, even if you have used them for more than a couple of children of your own). Sometimes they cannot be used inside shops, they take up a lot of room and it is impossible to travel with them by car or public transport.

Many parents today opt for a pram which comes in two parts – a fold-down frame and a top which can be used as a carrycot with handles. It's difficult to get this on a bus (although you can on most trains), and

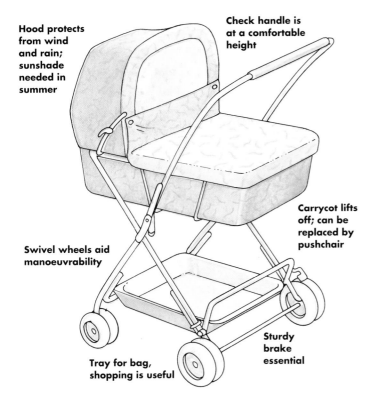

Hood protects from wind and rain; sunshade needed in summer

Check handle is at a comfortable height

Carrycot lifts off; can be replaced by pushchair

Swivel wheels aid manoeuvrability

Sturdy brake essential

Tray for bag, shopping is useful

folding it down after separating top and frame, then carrying the frame and baby is often a two-person job so it cannot be used on escalators. Most car boots and hatchbacks will hold both frame and top.

A popular alternative is a pushchair which folds flat, with a seat that tips into different positions from lie-flat to sitting. (You may find this comes as an extra to a frame and carrycot model, so that you use the carrycot when the baby is small, then graduate to the seat, keeping the same basic frame.) Buggies which fold up like an umbrella are lightweight and easy to handle, excellent if you are on and off buses a lot. These are, however, not really warm or sufficiently well sprung for a tiny baby and are best for toddlers who need less support.

You may also want to buy a rain cover, sunshade, shopping basket or tray for the pram or pushchair.

Car seat
Read the advice on car seats given on p. 172.

For bathing
You can bath your baby with you in the ordinary bath, as can your partner, but it may not be convenient at all times, so a baby bath or large washing-up bowl is a good idea. You will also need toiletries (baby soap and shampoo) and two towels.

Clothing for a newborn
- two shawls or wraps
- four vests
- four stretchsuits
- two cardigans or matinee jackets
- one outer garment, such as a snowsuit
- socks (unless all your stretchsuits have feet)
- a pair of mittens
- a hat (against the sun or the cold, or both, depending on when the baby is born)

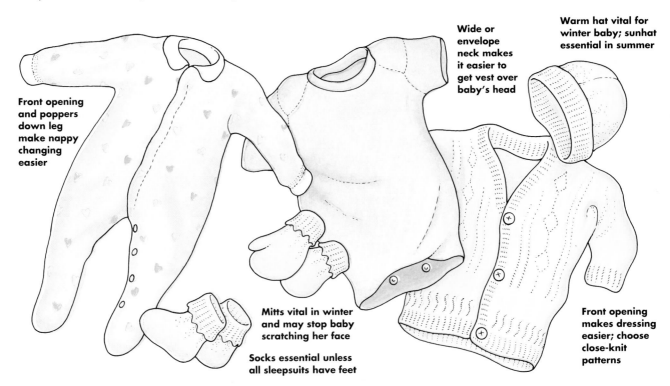

Front opening and poppers down leg make nappy changing easier

Wide or envelope neck makes it easier to get vest over baby's head

Warm hat vital for winter baby; sunhat essential in summer

Mitts vital in winter and may stop baby scratching her face

Socks essential unless all sleepsuits have feet

Front opening makes dressing easier; choose close-knit patterns

For changing

You can change a baby on a waterproof sheet over an old towel, but a plastic changing mat with raised edges is a good idea. It is safest to put the mat on the floor; if you want it at waist weight, keep one hand on the baby at all times. You will also need:

- nappies (new babies get through at least six a day, see Nappies, pp. 93–6)
- baby lotion and cottonwool balls, or baby wipes
- barrier cream
- (if you are using terries) a bucket with a lid

For feeding

If you are going to breastfeed:

- two nursing bras (these are not essential, but they are comfortable and convenient)

If you are going to bottlefeed:

- bottles
- sterilizing kit
- formula milk

You may also want to buy a breast pump (although expressing by hand is a useful skill, see p. 77) and breast pads (or cotton hankies). You will also need sanitary pads for up to six weeks after the birth.

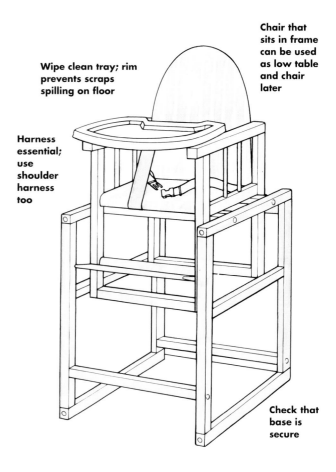

Wipe clean tray; rim prevents scraps spilling on floor

Chair that sits in frame can be used as low table and chair later

Harness essential; use shoulder harness too

Check that base is secure

You may want to add these items:

Baby chair

▶ Some of these double as car seats, others consist of a fabric seat on a lightweight frame which hold your baby in a semi-upright position. Both are ideal for when your baby is awake but don't put them on a raised surface. Babies love being able to see what is going on, which is impossible in a carrycot.

Baby carrier

◀ Choose one that supports the baby's head if you are buying one for use from birth. This is an essential if you have to use public transport a lot, and a good way of keeping your baby close to you. Many fretful babies are soothed by the contact and movement they get in this way.

Later on in the baby's first year (remember to budget for these items), you will need:

More clothing

Babies grow out of first clothes by the time they are three to four months old.

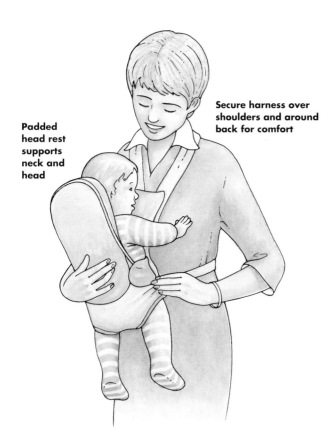

Padded head rest supports neck and head

Secure harness over shoulders and around back for comfort

Feeding chair

◄ This will be useful from about four months. Feeding chairs do not have to be 'high'. You can buy chairs which fit on to your table, which are also useful for when you are out and about. Some high chairs convert later into a low chair and table, which can prolong their usefulness. If space is short, consider a foldaway chair, but choose and site carefully – some are not as stable as more traditional models. Think carefully about how easy a chair is going to be to keep clean: some look beautiful but collect food scraps in impossible crannies.

You will also need a safety harness, bibs, feeding utensils and, of course, food.

Larger car seat

Stage One seats only last until the baby is around eight months (see also Buying a car seat, p. 172).

Toys

Babies appreciate colours, textures and sounds from very early on; most can hold a rattle by around six to eight weeks and a small cuddly toy in the cot or crib may quickly become a trusted friend.

And, if you are using disposables

More and more nappies (see pp. 93–6).

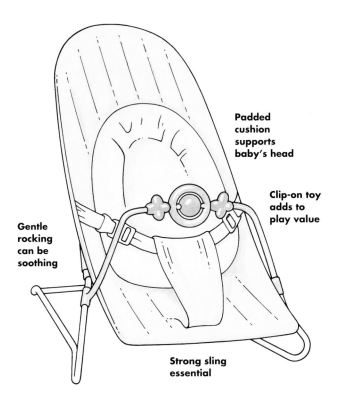

Padded cushion supports baby's head

Clip-on toy adds to play value

Gentle rocking can be soothing

Strong sling essential

Buying secondhand

Accepting hand-me-downs and buying large items secondhand makes sense as long as you are happy with the safety of the item. The exception to this is a car seat, since any impact can cause perhaps invisible damage (see also p. 172). Check prams, pushchairs and cots carefully for loose bolts, nuts and fixings, torn fabric or chipped paint.

Avoid anything that looks very old, even if it appears to be in good condition – it may have been made before modern manufacturing standards ensured a high degree of safety.

Clothes for you

Depending on your usual wardrobe, you may be able to wear your ordinary clothes for the first five or six months of your pregnancy, although obviously if you generally choose tailored suits or tight jeans, these will not fit for that long. It does not make sense to buy lots of new clothes for just a few months' wear, but a couple of new outfits can be a morale booster and will be useful after the birth (remember it can take several months to get into all your pre-pregnancy clothes again: some women never do).

The most important factor in choosing clothes to wear while you are pregnant is comfort. Avoid anything tight or restricting, including belts, and tights and socks with tight ribbing. Baggy tops, trousers and leggings with drawstring waists and loose pinafore dresses are all ideal. Natural fibres such as cotton are preferable to synthetics. Tops with low front openings may make breastfeeding easier, though teeshirts and sweaters will do just as well and may be more discreet when you're out.

A well-fitting bra is a must: by the end of your pregnancy you may be at least two cup sizes bigger than usual. In the last month, if you intend to breastfeed, you will need to buy a couple of nursing bras (take them into hospital with you, in case you are still there when your milk 'comes in').

High heels are not a good idea, neither are flat shoes. Choose styles with a small heel to avoid putting strain on your back and ankles. After about seven months you may find bending down to tie laces difficult.

DISCOMFORTS IN PREGNANCY

You may go through pregnancy having never felt better in your life, but most women feel at least some twinges now and then. Many of these discomforts come and go, so you are unlikely to be uncomfortable with any one of them throughout your pregnancy. In almost all cases, too, there is something you can do about it.

Pregnant women are still entitled to free prescriptions, so it makes sense to go to your doctor, rather than buy over-the-counter preparations.

Anaemia

- Have a blood test to check that you are anaemic and not tired for any other reason.
- Eat iron-rich foods: eggs, whole grains, lean meat, kelp, wheatgerm.
- On your GP's advice, take iron supplements in conjunction with vitamin C (iron on its own is not absorbed well).

Backache

- Take care when lifting and bending – bend your knees and keep your back straight. This is particularly important when you lift your other children (see p. 37); it is all too easy to swing them up, which can cause problems.
- If your feet don't reach the floor when you sit, sit with them on a couple of heavy books.

- Ask the hospital physiotherapist for advice about your posture.
- Discard your high heels, but wear shoes with a small heel for support.
- Swim regularly to strengthen your back and also to take the stress off it for a time.
- Try yoga and do some gentle stretches.
- Place a cushion in the small of your back when you are sitting or driving.
- Try a maternity panty girdle for extra support.

Bleeding gums and gum disease

- Dental care is free on the NHS while you are pregnant and until your baby is a year old. Make the most of it.
- Use a softer toothbrush than normal.
- Rinse with an anti-plaque mouthwash before brushing your teeth.
- Floss your teeth daily.

Breathlessness

- Take slow deep breaths.
- Sit as straight as possible.
- Prop your head and shoulders with several pillows at night (see below).

Cramps

- Massage and flex the affected area.
- Make sure you get plenty of calcium in your diet: milk, cheese, leafy green vegetables, nuts, seeds, peas, beans and pulses.

How to lie

Increased weight and your expanding waistline mean that some of the movements you make on a day-to-day basis are uncomfortable or difficult, particularly as your pregnancy advances. Often a change of position or the addition of some cushions for support is all that is needed.

You will find it uncomfortable to lie on your front, so sleep or rest on your side or back. A cushion under your thigh prevents you rolling on to your tummy.

Feeling faint, or fainting

- Eat protein- or carbohydrate-rich snacks mid-morning and mid-afternoon (unsalted nuts, banana, rice cakes).
- Lie on your side with your feet raised, or sit with your head between your knees.
- Avoid lying on your back, prolonged standing and tight clothing.
- Tell your doctor.

Fluid retention

- Spend at least 15 minutes twice a day lying on the sofa with your feet raised slightly higher than your head.
- Avoid long periods of standing; do not wear tight socks or elasticated hold-up stockings; avoid salty foods (read food labels for added salt).
- Try lying on your left side.
- Massage the affected areas regularly.

Frequent urination

- Avoid diuretic drinks such as tea and coffee, but do not cut down on your overall fluid intake.
- Always empty your bladder fully.
- Empty your bladder last thing at night and before you go out.

Haemorrhoids

- Eat a high-fibre diet and drink plenty of water so that you do not become constipated. If you do, try a small bowl of prunes, a drink of prune juice or nibble dried prunes.
- Avoid very hot baths. Soaking in a warm bath can help ease discomfort. Alternatively apply an ice pack for about 10 minutes.
- Ask your GP to prescribe a cream to shrink them.

Heartburn

- Eat little and often.
- Avoid hot, spicy foods.
- Eat your evening meal at least two hours before you go to bed.
- Try antacid tablets – ask your GP for advice.

High blood pressure

Your blood pressure will be measured at all your antenatal appointments and any abnormality monitored and treated where necessary.

- Take regular daily naps, or complete bed rest, depending on what the doctor suggests.
- Try gentle exercise such as swimming.
- Do relaxation exercises, or go to yoga or relaxation classes. If these are not specifically for pregnant women, tell the instructor that you are pregnant – you may need to make some movements differently from other class members.

Incontinence

- Do your pelvic floor exercises (see p. 26).
- Empty your bladder frequently.
- Avoid lifting on a full stomach.

Lying well propped with pillows and cushions may make you more comfortable.

To get up from lying, roll on to your side, and use your arms to push yourself up.

Insomnia

- Take a warm, relaxing bath before bed. Add a drop or two of lavender aromatherapy oil.
- Relaxation techniques or a massage, again with soothing oil, before bed may help.
- Try sleeping with a pillow supporting your stomach, another supporting your back and one under your knees.

Morning sickness

This is inaptly named since it can occur at any time. It is caused by the upsurge of hormonal activity in your body and affects four out of five women.

- Eat a plain biscuit or slice of dry toast before you get out of bed in the morning.
- Do not rush about, especially in the morning.
- Ginger capsules or drinks may help. These are available from health food shops; follow the directions for preparation on the packet.
- Eat small meals every two to three hours.

Pelvic pain

- Rest with your body supported on a pillow.
- Try a warm bath, or hold a warm hot-water bottle over the painful area.
- Gently rock to and fro.
- Call your doctor or midwife if the pain is intense and/or persistent. In early pregnancy, it could be the start of a miscarriage (although it is more likely to be caused by the ligaments of your womb stretching); later it may be that the baby's head is pressing on your pelvic nerve; toward the end of pregnancy, it could be a sign of early labour.

Skin darkening

- Avoid strong sun and sunbathing – use a sun block or a face-shading hat. The pregnancy hormones cause more melanin to be produced by the skin (this is the pigment that gives you a suntan). In pregnancy, this can be deposited under the skin in a, literally, butterfly shaped mask over the cheeks and nose. It disappears after delivery.

Stretch marks

- Try not to put on too much weight.
- Rich oils may help, although there is no proof that they do (likewise expensive stretch mark creams are not scientifically proven to work).
- Consult a qualified aromatherapist over which essential oils to add to the oil – some should not be used during pregnancy.

Thrush

To prevent thrush:
- Keep your vulva area cool, wear cotton underwear, and skirts rather than trousers. Avoid tights.

How to sit

Sitting cross-legged can aggravate varicose veins and should be avoided while you are pregnant. Make sure any chair you sit on regularly (in an office, for example) supports your back – use a cushion if necessary – and allows you to place both feet flat on the floor. Try to avoid lounging unsupported, even in an armchair.

Sitting with your back straight, shoulders back and legs apart is good for the spine and stretches your inner thighs.

Sit cross-legged with your back straight and shoulders back to gently stretch your inner thighs.

- Wipe your bottom from front to back.
- Wash your vulva with a cool, gentle shower spray after lovemaking.

If you get it:

- Sitting in a warm bath gives temporary relief.
- Consult your GP and ask for a prescription for a fungicidal cream or pessaries.

Tiredness

- Rest whenever you get the chance.
- Delegate as much housework as possible.
- Eat little and often.

Varicose veins

- Wear support tights.
- Raise your feet higher than your head as often as possible. Always read or watch TV like this.
- Avoid standing for long periods.
- Swimming and low-impact aerobics improve the circulation, which may help.

How to lift

It is even more important than usual to keep your back straight and bend your knees when you are lifting. Take special care when you lift children, who tend to 'hurl' themselves at you. Try to make sure his weight is evenly distributed and do not move him from side to side. Avoid heavy shopping bags altogether if you possibly can.

MORE SERIOUS PROBLEMS

Most pregnancies progress completely normally but occasionally there are complications. Thanks to thorough antenatal checks, any difficulties can usually be detected early, which means that they can either be put right, or at least, managed effectively.

In early pregnancy

Early pregnancy is classed as referring to the first 12–14 weeks.

Bleeding

This is very common and may have a completely harmless cause, such as the slight bleeding or spotting which occurs due to erosion of the ripe cervix. It may, however, also suggest more serious problems and is one of the signs of miscarriage.

Don't panic, or assume that you are having a miscarriage. Phone your doctor straight away. He or she may suggest you go to hospital as a precaution.

Ectopic or tubal pregnancy

This is the term used when the embryo has implanted itself outside the womb, usually in one of the fallopian tubes. Many such pregnancies cause no special problems – the embryo dies at six to eight weeks and is reabsorbed back into the body.

In other cases, however, the pregnancy stretches and finally ruptures the tube wall, causing sudden and severe abdominal pain. This is an emergency, which may cause heavy haemorrhaging. You will need surgery straight away.

Gestational diabetes

This affects about one woman is 25 and simply means diabetes that develops while you are pregnant and disappears after the birth (you will be checked for signs of this at each antenatal appointment). It can be very mild or more serious.

If you have a slight predisposition to diabetes – if someone in your immediate family suffers from it, for example – pregnancy can tip the balance. One of its effects can be to make the baby put on weight which makes a caesarean more likely (if you have already delivered a baby of 4.5 kg/10 lb, you will be monitored especially closely).

Depending on its severity, you may initially be given a high-fibre diet to follow. If that does not control it, or if it is severe, insulin tablets will be prescribed.

The overwhelming majority of babies born to women with gestational diabetes are healthy and normal, although there is a higher risk of prematurity.

Rhesus incompatibility

The red blood cells of most Caucasians contain a substance called the Rhesus factor and are said to be Rhesus positive (+). If you do not have it, you are Rhesus negative (–). Problems only arise when Rh– women with Rh+ partners carry Rh+ babies. Routine blood tests reveal your status and if there is any risk your partner will be tested too.

Difficulties in first pregnancies are rare. In subsequent ones, however, some of the first baby's Rh+ cells, which entered the mother's body during delivery, can cause the mother to produce antibodies to fight them.

If this is left untreated, during a second pregnancy these antibodies cross the placenta and start to damage the red blood cells of a Rh+ baby, leading to rhesus haemolytic disease. Amniocentesis will show the degree to which the baby is affected. If he is too young to be born, he can be given a blood transfusion from around 22 weeks. He may need others before the pregnancy comes to term. If he is sufficiently mature to survive, delivery is induced or a caesarean carried out. He may need another transfusion at birth.

Problems later in pregnancy

Once the first 12–14 weeks are over, most pregnancies are relatively problem free. The most common difficulties are listed here (although rest assured that all are rare).

Bleeding

This may be minor, but could have more serious consequences. Let your doctor know immediately if you start to bleed. In later pregnancy, bleeding may be caused by problems with the placenta. The two most common are:

Placenta praevia

This means that the placenta is attached at the bottom of the womb, either partially or wholly blocking the baby's way out. As the baby gets bigger, it takes up more space and the bottom of the womb, in particular, stretches to accommodate the extra growth. If the placenta is low down, it may start to peel away from the wall of the womb, which causes it to bleed intermittently.

If placenta praevia is suspected you will have regular scans to monitor its position (it can edge its way up the side of the womb, out of the way). If it stays at the bottom of the womb, it will cut off your baby's food and oxygen supply once labour starts so you will usually be given a caesarean.

Placental abruption

This is when a normally attached placenta starts to detach itself from the wall of the womb. If this happens with one or two tiny sections, it causes no problem, but in some cases as much as a third can come away. In mild cases no treatment is necessary; in moderate cases, you will probably be admitted to hospital to rest for the remainder of your pregnancy. In severe cases, you may need a transfusion and your baby will be delivered by caesarean.

Pre-eclampsia

The symptoms of pre-eclampsia include raised blood pressure, headaches, swelling and water retention in the feet, legs, face and hands, and protein in the urine. If it is left unchecked eclampsia (convulsions) can result, but regular antenatal checks mean that it can be detected early and treated, or monitored and kept under control.

Treatment includes rest and drugs to control blood pressure. Depending on the seriousness of pre-eclampsia, it may be necessary to deliver the baby early by caesarean.

Polyhydramnios

This means having too much amniotic fluid, so that your abdomen feels like a balloon tightly filled with water. It is at best uncomfortable and can be extremely painful. This may develop slowly at any time between 22 and 32 weeks, or it may come quickly at the end of the pregnancy.

Treatment usually involves rest (not necessarily in hospital), draining of small amounts of fluid with a syringe and, if the condition causes a great deal of pain, sedation.

HAVING TWINS

Twin – or supertwin – pregnancies are becoming more common, a fact that is usually attributed to the use of fertility treatments, particularly the use of drugs to stimulate ovulation. About one in 80 pregnancies results in a multiple birth; as recently as 15 years ago, the figure was one in 100.

You may sail through a multiple pregnancy – there are no medical reasons why you should not. Carrying two babies is, however, harder on your body and the births will be subject to closer medical supervision. Your doctor is unlikely to agree to anything other than a hospital birth.

Twins can be fraternal, resulting from two different eggs fertilized by two different sperm, in which case they are no more alike than any other siblings. If they are the result of a single, fertilized egg splitting in half at a very early stage, the babies will be identical.

Around a third of twins born in Britain are identical, evenly divided between boy and girl pairs. About half of non-identical pairs are boy and girl; the remainder are equally split between dissimilar girls and dissimilar boys.

Your pregnancy

If you carry twins or triplets, you are likely to gain weight more rapidly than a woman carrying a single baby, and to gain more since you have the weight of two babies, two placentas and two amniotic sacs. Your total gain may be up to half your normal weight. You will feel very cumbersome toward the end of your

The likelihood of twins

The chances that you will have twins increase if:

- you are taking fertility drugs
- you have several children already
- you have a family history of twins
- you are in your early 30s: the likelihood increases to 35, then starts to fall
- you are of African origin (you are twice as likely as a European to have twins)

pregnancy and may also experience what in other women are minor discomforts, such as nausea and tiredness, far more acutely.

Multiple pregnancies are, however, usually shorter than single ones, at around 35–37 weeks and the average weight for each baby is lower (some 2.5 kg/ 5½ lb as opposed to 3.1 kg/7 lb).

What you can do

- Get as much rest as you can. Sleeping, particularly from around six months onward can be difficult – you cannot find a comfortable position. Nap little and often.
- Think carefully, well in advance, about how long you want to carry on working. At 30 weeks, you may have gained as much weight as a woman pregnant with a single baby at 40 weeks. Try to negotiate reduced hours if at all possible, and be prepared to be flexible about when you start your maternity leave.
- Try to exercise – swimming is excellent since your extra weight is supported, as are aquarobics, if you can find a class at your local leisure centre. Yoga is also good exercise.
- Be sure to do your pelvic floor exercises (see p. 26) – these are even more important if you are carrying two babies. If you find it difficult to do them standing as your pregnancy advances, lie on the floor with your feet up on a chair to 'tip' the weight of the babies and your womb off your pelvic floor.
- Take extra care when lifting; follow the advice on p. 37. And try to stand properly – avoid arching your back as far as possible. Always roll on to your side when getting up from lying down (see p. 35).

How twins lie

In the womb, twins usually lie so that either both are head down (or vertex, below left) or one is vertex and one breech (below right).

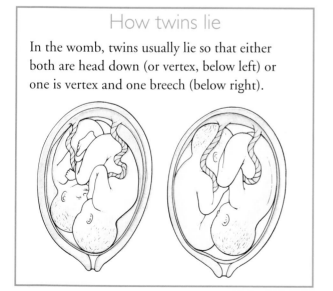

- Go to all your antenatal checks. You will probably be asked to attend more frequently than for a single pregnancy (perhaps weekly from 30 weeks), and not be able to have shared care for as long. It is important to keep appointments, however, so that any problems can be monitored effectively.
- Go to antenatal classes. Hospital classes tend to be geared to single births which are, by and large, straightforward: twins are more likely to be premature or delivered by caesarean or both. It is still, however, worth going. Your local twins support group may be able to help you find the most suitable classes. Tell the course leader that you are expecting twins. You should also arrange to attend classes earlier than normal, otherwise you risk not completing the full course if your babies arrive early.
- Eat well: two babies need more food than one. Eat regularly and get lots of fresh foods. Women carrying more than one baby can be prone to anaemia (see p. 34), so get plenty of iron-rich foods such as spinach and other leafy green vegetables, lean red meat (but not liver), dried fruit and nuts. Drink plenty of water to help combat constipation.
- Contact your local twins or superbirth support groups (see Useful Contacts, pp. 390–3).

Potential problems

Some problems are more common in twin pregnancies, but good antenatal care should mean early identification and effective treatment.

- One baby may grow more slowly than the other, perhaps because one placenta is working more effectively than the other.
- High blood pressure is more common in twin than single pregnancies, as is pre-eclampsia.
- Reabsorption of one embryo can happen: a scan shows twins, but later there is only one baby. This presumably has always happened but in the days before ultrasound was common, women did not realize they were carrying twins until much later in pregnancy than they do today.
- Premature birth is common: technically babies born before 37 weeks are premature.
- Miscarriage involving the loss of one baby while the other continues to term may occur.

What you will need

Twins, obviously, need more clothes and equipment than single babies. In most cases, double up on what is suggested on pp. 30–3.

- **Sleeping**
  You may prefer to buy one cot for them to sleep in together to start with, then add a second as they grow. If not, you will need two cribs, carrycots or Moses baskets.
- **Transport**
  A double carriage pram is costly. A double pram with two carrycots, which converts to a double pushchair, is a good alternative. (If your babies are sleeping in the carrycots at night, check the mattresses are suitable – some are not.) A double folding buggy is useful later, but not stable or warm enough for newborns. You will need two car seats.
- **Clothes**
  Later on, it helps twins to see themselves as individuals if you dress them differently. That may not be possible when they are tiny, when the most important thing is a clean, dry sleepsuit, regardless of colour. But try to keep at least one outfit personal to each baby.

The birth

How straightforward the birth of twins is depends on two factors: their maturity at birth and their position in the womb.

Pre-term twins and triplets can be very small and need careful handling during birth. This often means a caesarean which, if planned, can be done by epidural so that you are awake, but does not put them through the trauma of being pushed into the world. They may still need time in a special baby care unit.

It is not easy for both twins to get into the correct position to be born. In only 50 per cent of cases are they both head down so that they can be born normally. Often one twin is head down and one breech, but sometimes one is lying transverse, blocking the way out. In this case, your obstetrician may try to turn the baby, but usually you will have a caesarean. The more complex their positions, the more likely that they will be delivered by caesarean.

THE BABY THAT WAS NOT TO BE

Miscarriage is the loss of a pregnancy before the end of its 24th week; the loss of a baby after that date is classed as a stillbirth.

If you have suffered three miscarriages in a row, you will be investigated and treated. If this does not happen automatically, contact the Miscarriage Alliance for advice (see Useful Contacts, pp. 390–3).

Many factors are known to be involved in miscarriage, but in only about half of all miscarriages can a specific and almost certain cause – usually a chromosomal abnormality – be identified. If you have suffered a miscarriage, take special note of any information the hospital can give you when you plan a second pregnancy.

Are you miscarrying?

Signs that you may be about to miscarry include:
- bleeding, from spotting to a period-like flow
- passing clots of blood
- cramping, period-like pains
- backache
- feeling generally unwell.

You may have no symptoms at all; on the other hand, having any of the above symptoms does not mean that you are about to miscarry. Do not panic, but contact your doctor or midwife immediately.

Coming to terms

It is important that you are allowed to grieve for the loss of your pregnancy. It can help to cry as much as you feel you need to, and talk about what has happened as much as you wish, with anyone who will listen kindly. Some people find that it helps to know as much as possible about the miscarriage. Can your doctor give you a reason why it happened? What sex was the baby? After a couple of weeks, write down all the questions you would like to ask and arrange to go and see the gynaecologist who was caring for you.

After a stillbirth, many parents find it comforting to see and hold their baby. Even if there was some deformity, it is seldom as marked as you might have imagined. If you do not want to see the baby, most hospitals take photographs of the baby, which you can ask to have to keep (later if you do not want them straight away). Naming her and having a blessing, memorial service or burial may all help you to acknowledge your baby as special, as an individual.

Facing the future

The stages of recovery tend to follow a pattern: shock or denial; intense distress; feelings of loss, loneliness, guilt; and depression, for varying periods of time. You may find the date that the baby should have been born difficult to get through for a couple of years at least.

If you are feeling well there is no medical reason why you should not try to become pregnant again after you have had your first period following a miscarriage. But obviously emotionally you may need more time. Don't rush it if you are not ready.

Termination for abnormality

If your unborn baby is diagnosed as having an abnormality, you face a difficult decision. Do you continue with the pregnancy and care for a child with special needs, or do you have the pregnancy that you were so happy about terminated?

If you are more than 14 weeks pregnant (and many test results do only come through after this time), you will probably undergo an induced labour which could be long and painful. The baby, though small, is likely to be fully formed.

- Do you want to know as much as possible about the baby and the diagnosed disorder?
- Talk to the staff about tranquillizers, pain relief, epidurals, anything that might help you.
- Tell them what you want of the delivery. This should take place with dignity. Would you like a photograph of the baby? Do you want to see and hold her? Either, or both, may help you come to terms with her individuality and death.
- A post-mortem can help determine what went wrong. Consider asking for one since results can be valuable for genetic counselling when you are deciding about another pregnancy.
- A blessing, burial or memorial service can be comforting. Speak to the hospital chaplain.

If you have to consider, or have undergone, a termination in such circumstances, contact SATFA (see Useful Contacts, pp. 390–3) for information, advice and support.

CHAPTER TWO

Giving Birth

Giving birth is one of the most fulfilling experiences of a woman's life, and the ultimate experience for a couple of 'togetherness' – both working in unison to bring the tiny person they have created into the world. In this technological age, it can be easy to lose sight of those two facts, but the technology is there to ensure that every birth experience is as problem-free as possible.

Birth and your newborn baby

BECOMING A PARENT

It is surprisingly difficult to think beyond the actual birth to parenthood. It is as if you need to know what the baby looks like before you can fit him into your dreams. You take out the layette and try to imagine how your baby will look in the clothes you have bought, but the reality of parenthood is elusive. It is hard to believe that the physical aspects of giving birth or nursing a child will ever seem insignificant. But they will.

Because most couples prepare for birth rather than parenthood, getting the birth 'right' seems important. But really it is not. The older and more organized you are, the more likely you are to want it to go to plan. It is easy to lose sight of the fact that birth is just day one of parenthood. There are thousands more days to follow. The most important aspect of giving birth is to deliver a healthy child as safely and as easily as possible. Plans should be flexible.

A month before

During the final month before your expected delivery date, you should:
- Make sure you and your partner know how to get to the hospital and where you can park your car.
- Put the telephone number of the hospital and a taxi company by the phone. You will usually be entitled to call an ambulance in an emergency, but it may not be possible (you may not feel up to driving yourself). Keep the taxi fare handy.
- If you don't have a phone arrange with neighbours to use theirs. Check which local pay or card phones are in working order. Remember that you may have to call the hospital or taxi company at night. Keep some change and a phonecard handy.
- Make arrangements to keep in touch with your partner. If you cannot always contact him by phone, make sure he can contact you. Pagers and mobile phones can be hired for short periods of time. Check advertisements in child-care magazines for details.
- Pack your bag (see p. 19).

If you are having a home birth
- Keep your midwife's and doctor's telephone numbers pinned up permanently beside the telephone.
- Make sure you have all the equipment you need at home ready well before time (discuss this with your midwife in good time – she will supply quite a lot of the equipment herself, see below).
- As with a hospital birth, in the month before the baby is due, when your partner is not at home, make sure you know exactly where he is going to be at all times.
- Make sure you have a close friend or relation who can come round quickly to be with you until your midwife or partner arrives if you go into labour when you are on your own at home.

Your bed for a home birth

Your midwife will discuss the layout of the room in which you give birth with you – she will need to have access to both sides of the bed, for example. As soon as you are sure you are in labour, make up the bed with clean sheets, then cover the whole with a large sheet of strong plastic. Cover that with newspapers, then clean, old sheets. After the birth, you can strip off the soiled sheets and protection to leave you with a clean, fresh bed.

WHAT HAPPENS IN LABOUR

Labour is the hardest work known to man or woman (save the superhuman efforts needed to face disasters). Your body will be working for hour after hour but you cannot stop or pause for breath. It is easy to feel out of control, especially if you are unprepared for labour or do not understand what is happening to you.

How you give birth

If you pucker your lips to whistle, your mouth is in a similar position to the cervix before labour begins. If you open as wide as possible it is in the position reached at the end of labour.

To whistle, the lip muscles are small and tight. They have contracted. The cheeks are long and thin because the muscles are extended. You can feel this if you put a thumb in your mouth and a finger on your cheek and pinch.

Now open your mouth as wide as you can. Look at and feel the change in the muscles. The lips have narrowed and expanded. The cheeks have bulged and

The end of pregnancy

Towards the end of your pregnancy, some of the following may occur:

- Lightening or engagement: 2–4 weeks before birth the baby begins to descend into the pelvis thus lightening the pressure on the diaphragm.
- Groin pain and cramp (this is rare in first pregnancies).
- Loss of about 0.9–1.3 kg (2–3 lb) in weight.
- A change in energy level, either up or down. You may feel an overwhelming urge to clean all the kitchen cupboards or alternatively a sudden feeling of being utterly fatigued.
- Increase and thickening of vaginal discharge.
- Strong and more frequent Braxton–Hicks (see p. 18) contractions.
- Diarrhoea (this is often a sign labour is just about to begin).
- The loss of the mucus plug – a pinkish 'show'.
- Backache.

Above: The end of pregnancy is a time for physical closeness and relaxation, sharing the last few days of being a couple, before you are transformed into a family.

shortened. As you force your mouth to its widest possible position, you can feel the tightness extending far beyond your lips. Now move your lips from the whistling to the fully wide position. See how much the cheek and neck muscles must work to achieve the open position.

At the beginning of labour the cervix is closed and low in the vagina like lips which are puckered to whistle. By the end of labour it is wide open. In the course of labour, you will feel the tugs of each contraction as they pull the cervix open. Like the feeling in the neck and cheeks as you begin to open your mouth, the sensation of those early contractions is some distance from the opening: in the lower abdomen and back.

What to do if your waters break

Membranes can tear at any stage of pregnancy. If this happens some amniotic fluid will be lost. Sometimes there is a gush of fluid, at other times there is just a trickle. You may think you have wet yourself – many women experience stress incontinence during the latter stages of pregnancy (see p. 35) but amniotic fluid can be distinguished from urine by its pale straw colour and sweet smell. Because amniotic fluid is constantly replaced, unless there has been an almost complete loss, the baby continues to be bathed in fluid. Babies whose heads are engaged will act as a plug to the flow of amniotic fluid, so you may only be conscious of a slight leakage.

If your waters break you should:
- If it is just a trickle, inform your midwife, doctor or the hospital; if it is a gush – which is unmistakable – go straight to the hospital.
- Avoid sexual intercourse.
- Do not swim.
- Do not take a bath.
- Keep the vaginal area as clean as possible.
- Use a sanitary towel to absorb the flow.
- Be especially careful to wipe front to back after using the toilet.
- If the fluid trickles and then stops the membrane may simply have torn and repaired itself, but you should tell your doctor.
- If the fluid gushes or continues to flow, contact the hospital. Provided you are near term, labour is normally induced if it does not begin within 24 hours of the membranes breaking.

Recognizing that labour has started

With a first baby, in particular, it can be quite difficult to determine whether this really is 'it'.

You are probably *not* in labour if:
- The 'show' was brown.
- You feel contractions in the lower abdomen.
- Foetal movements increase with contractions.
- Contractions are irregular.
- Contractions do not increase in severity.
- Contractions do not increase in frequency.
- Contractions die down if you walk about.

You probably *are* in labour if:
- You have a pinkish 'show'.
- The membranes rupture, particularly if they gush.
- Your contractions feel as if they start in the lower back and spread to the lower abdomen.
- Contractions feel more or less the same whether you sit or stand.
- As time passes contractions become more regular.
- As time passes contractions become longer.
- As time passes contractions feel stronger.

When to worry

The following symptoms could indicate serious problems for you or the baby. Try not to panic, but do not ignore them.

Cord prolapse

If the waters break, the umbilical cord occasionally drops into the neck of the uterus or out through the vagina. Because pressure on the cord can cut off the baby's oxygen supply, you must act immediately.
- Get on your hands and knees and remain there (this reduces the pressure).
- Support any cord which protrudes from the vagina with a warm wet sanitary pad.
- Avoid any pressure on the cord. Do not try to push it back.
- If you are travelling by car, get on your hands and knees in the back seat.
- Call your hospital, doctor or midwife straight away – if possible get someone else to do this for you. If there is no one available, call an ambulance to take you to hospital.

Greenish brown liquid leaks from your vagina

Occasionally amniotic fluid is greenish brown because it contains meconium. This is present in the gut of all babies at birth. Passing meconium, which then leaks from your vagina prior to the birth, may be an indication that the baby is in distress.
- Ring the hospital immediately.

Vaginal bleeding

The early stages of labour are often accompanied by slight spotting or bleeding. Bleeding can also occur after lovemaking.

- Heavy bleeding should never be ignored. Call an ambulance or get someone to rush you to hospital at once.
- Pinkish or red-streaked mucus (a 'show') which does not persist should be reported at your next appointment, but otherwise can be ignored. If it is accompanied by contractions, ring the hospital: labour has begun.
- Brownish-tinged mucus or slight spotting which occurs 24–48 hours after intercourse or vaginal examination and then stops is quite normal. Tell your doctor at the next examination. If it persists call the doctor.
- Bright red bleeding or persistent spotting can indicate problems with the placenta. Call the doctor or go to hospital at once.

THE THREE STAGES OF LABOUR

Birth has three stages. In the first stage (which is sometimes itself divided into three phases) the cervix is opened, in the second the baby is pushed out of the womb. In the final stage the placenta is detached from the wall of the womb, and like the baby is pushed out through the cervix, vagina and perineum (the area between the anus and the vagina). All of these stages are under hormonal control. At the beginning of labour hormones, released into the mother's bloodstream, set labour in motion; as labour advances hormones maintain it.

The first stage

For most women labour begins with the onset of fairly regular and widely spaced contractions. These continue until the cervix is fully dilated and the baby born. The early stages of labour may be marked by nothing more than odd twinges or strong Braxton–Hicks contractions (see p. 18). More typically contractions occur at increasingly regular intervals. Women often describe them as similar to cramps, period pains, or twinges of backache. Sometimes a tightening feeling starts in the back and moves around to the lower abdomen then stops. Typically contractions occur once every 20 minutes and last about 30 seconds. Between contractions there is no discomfort.

Over the next hours contractions intensify until they last about 45 seconds, occur every five to ten minutes and have quite distinct peaks. As labour progresses the tightly puckered cervix relaxes and a gap opens up. At the end of the first phase labour has usually been in progress for two to six hours but the gap is only about 3 cm wide. Now things begin to move faster. The next 4 cm of dilatation takes only two to three hours on average, although all these phases tend to be longer for first babies. Contractions feel more intense and are more predictable. The space between them shortens. They feel as if something is being pulled hard, then harder, then unbelievably hard before it is slowly relaxed. Contractions dominate, taking your entire attention and making you feel increasingly uncomfortable. It becomes harder to relax or keep up the breathing exercises. Labour begins to feel endless.

Transition

Any remaining feelings of being in control are likely to disappear as the final or transitional phase is entered. A lucky few cope; for the majority, the best that can be said of transition is that it is usually short. There is a sudden speeding up of contractions which can now tumble together in an endless stream. The last 1–3 cm of dilatation can take less than 15 minutes. Most women now feel irritable, and exhausted.

The slow, steady building of contractions during the early stages of labour gives many the confidence to cope without drugs. For some transition is no more than a speeding up of these contractions. For others a range of problems arise which undermine confidence and undo all preparation. You may find it impossible to predict when or if a contraction will subside or whether there will be a pause before the next.

In addition, you may vomit and/or your body temperature may begin to go haywire. You may run a temperature, sweat and thrash about restlessly. You may feel cold, shiver and tremble uncontrollably. You may do one, then the other. As if this was not enough the flow of oxygen to the muscles of the cervix can often leave the brain a little short. When this happens you feel befuddled, irritable and sleepy.

Toward the end of this phase the baby's head begins to press down on the back passage and lower back. This causes some women to soil themselves which can be distressing but is normal. Your midwife will be quite used to dealing with it so try not to be embarrassed. As the cervix is pulled back to its full extent blood vessels are broken and vaginal bleeding which has previously been slight may increase.

Not coping in these circumstances is understandable. If you scream, shout and swear you will not be the first. Coping is a matter of luck, not simply preparation.

The second stage

In the second stage the baby passes through the fully opened cervix, into the vagina and out through the perineum. This takes about an hour with a first baby, rather less with subsequent children. If the second stage seems to be extended the doctor may feel that it is necessary to monitor the baby's health electronically. (Practices vary: in some hospitals, electronic foetal monitoring at intervals or even constantly throughout labour is normal. If this means that your movement is restricted and you are not happy, say so.) If all goes well the baby can be delivered vaginally even if the second stage is two hours or more. If however the baby shows any signs of distress the delivery will probably be assisted by forceps or suction (see pp. 54–5). If you are having your baby at home and your midwife or doctor feels that labour is delayed you will be admitted to hospital for an assisted delivery.

The second stage usually begins with an urge to start pushing. Although pushing or bearing down

Stages of labour

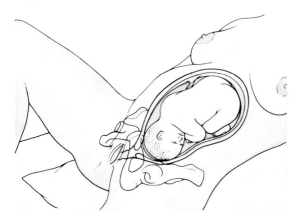

In the first stage of labour, the cervix thins, and the cervical canal is eliminated, or fully effaced. At that stage, further contractions dilate the cervix.

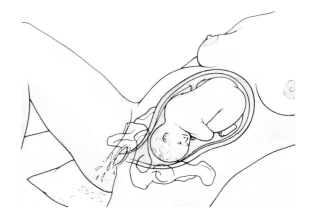

When you are 7 cm dilated, the midwife can feel only the front and sides of the cervix round the baby's head. When it has disappeared, you are fully dilated.

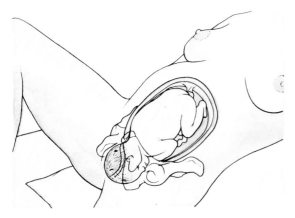

You are now ready to start pushing the baby down the birth canal. With each contraction, the head moves nearer to your vaginal opening.

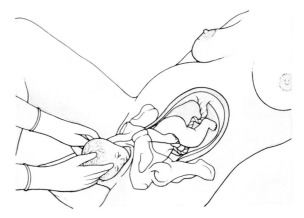

As the anus and perineum bulge, the vaginal tissues are stretched so thin that the nerves are blocked. The baby's head finally emerges.

helps to expel the baby, most of the work is still done by the contractions. The more upright you are, the easier it is to push the baby out. If you lie on your back the route is uphill, if you squat it is straight down. Most hospitals are now flexible about birth positions, and have birthing stools, cushions and floor mats so that mothers can choose what feels most comfortable. Your antenatal classes (see p. 25) should include advice on this, since support helps to avoid excess pressure on the perineum and unnecessary tearing.

The contractions at this stage are more widely spaced, often less intense and last from 60 to 90 seconds. In one of these contractions the baby's head first comes into sight. It will slip back from the vulva before reappearing in the entrance at the next contraction. Watching the head through the vulva gives the impression of a battering ram pushing, retreating, pushing, and retreating once more. This is basically what is happening. Each time the head comes forward the vulva opens a little wider, and stays wide until the head approaches again. The feeling has been described as like trying to pass a large melon when you're extremely constipated! You feel the baby move into the birth channel, then forward and back with each contraction. The pushing continues until the head can squeeze through the wide open vulva.

As the head is crowned you may feel a stinging sensation if you have not had local anaesthesia such as an epidural block (see p. 54). As soon as you feel this you should stop pushing and pant. (To get an idea of how the stinging feels try pulling your mouth wide at the corners until it hurts, and then pull wider still.) Once the head is born the rest is easy and quick. Your midwife will turn the baby's head to the side and ease out first one shoulder then the other. In two or three contractions the baby is born.

The third stage

The final task is to deliver the placenta. The birth has pulled it from the uterine wall, and contractions (helped by bearing down once more) push it quickly out through the cervix. Many doctors administer an injection of a synthetic version of oxytocin (the hormone which induces contractions) just after the birth of the baby to speed up the delivery of the placenta. There is controversy about whether this is always necessary, and many natural birth proponents

recommend putting the baby to the breast immediately after the birth as the same hormone, oxytocin, is involved in the 'let down' reflex – the release of milk into the milk sacs behind the areola (see p. 71). The contractions of the third stage can be felt, and are very similar to severe period pains or cramps. But they do not last and most women do not find them at all troublesome. If you have had an episiotomy or have torn, you will be stitched.

WHAT TO DO DURING LABOUR

In the first phase of dilatation you should:
- Call your partner.
- Pack your bag if it is not already packed.
- Keep moving about.
- Time your contractions.
- Practise your breathing: even if you do not need it yet, it makes sense to remind yourself what to do.
- Unless contractions have obvious peaks, have a drink and a light meal (it may be ages before you eat again).
- Try to urinate at least once an hour.
- Call the hospital.
- Have a warm bath (but not if your waters have broken – if they have, take a shower).
- Try to relax. It will speed up labour.
- Make a snack to eat after the birth. Put champagne on ice.

In the second phase of dilatation you should:
- Keep up your breathing pattern.
- Go to hospital.
- Try to stay relaxed.
- Try to keep moving for as long as possible.
- Use your partner, the midwife or the wall for support during contractions.
- Do not eat or drink.
- Try to urinate if you can, on the hour every hour. Get your partner to remind you.
- If you need pain relief, ask for it. It gets worse before it gets better.

In transition:
- Hang on.
- Try to relax between and during contractions.

How long does labour last?

First stage: dilatation of the cervix

- The first 3 cm: dilatation starts slowly and imperceptibly. The first 3 cm can take days – even weeks. You are unlikely to be aware of any sensations that this is happening until the last two to six hours (perhaps the last 1 cm), but significantly longer for first babies.

- From 3 to 7 cm dilatation: some women remain unaware of labour for much of this stage too, although toward the end there is no doubt of what is happening. For most it lasts two to three hours during which contractions get longer, stronger and more frequent.

- From 7 to 10 cm: about 15 minutes to one hour of strong and frequent contractions – longer for first babies.

Second stage: birth of the baby

- 15 minutes to one hour; occasionally it can take up to two hours, but any longer is rare – most doctors intervene to avoid a long and tiring second stage.

Third stage: birth of the placenta or afterbirth

- About 10 to 15 minutes, or up to half an hour, depending on whether an injection has been administered or not.

- Adjust your breathing pattern to find one which helps you at this stage. Abandon them all if they do not help. Try to distract yourself from pain.
- Don't worry if you cannot cope: very few can.
- Take deep breaths between contractions: but don't hyperventilate.
- Say exactly what you want.
- If you feel like pushing, pant and hold back until the midwife has checked the cervix is fully dilated.

In the second stage:

- Push with your pelvic floor muscles during contractions.

- Stop pushing and pant when the midwife tells you to. Pushing once a contraction has finished is a waste of effort – save it for the next one.
- Do not worry if you feel as if you are soiling yourself – or if you do.

What your birth companion can do to help:

- Time contractions.
- Stay calm.
- Keep a sense of humour.
- Help to distract her – watch a video, play cards, go for a walk. Try to remember the names of all the shops in the High Street, the counties of England,

Comfortable labour positions

If you want to bear down before the cervix is fully dilated, kneel and lean forward on your hands to slow the baby down.

In the early stages, keep upright with your back straight and knees apart. It often helps to use the back of a chair for support.

the states of the USA, the hit songs of 1990 – anything which will keep her mind off labour.

- Offer reassurance, support and comfort and mediate with the medical staff.
- Just be there.
- Breathe with her if it helps. Remind her if she forgets. Massage if it's needed. Hold her hand.
- Stop all of the above if she asks you to.
- If she shows signs of hyperventilation (dizziness, numbness, becoming light-headed) cup your hands over her mouth and get her to take a few shallow breaths. Breathe with her if it helps.
- Never criticize. Stay calm even if the medical staff irritate you.
- Remind her to urinate every hour, give her ice to suck (take it with you) or moisten her lips with a damp sponge.
- Use a cool flannel to wash her when she is hot. Cover her up if she feels cold.
- Take the photos and open the champagne when it is all over.
- Stay as long as you can after the birth.
- Phone everyone and let them know.
- Prepare for the homecoming.

COPING WITH PAIN

Most women interpret the huge muscular effort their body engages in during labour as pain. Some feel pain in the earliest stages of labour. Others do not make this interpretation until much later.

There is nothing fixed about feeling pain. It is known for example that those involved in road accidents can be unaware of their own serious injuries while they fight to save the lives of others. Pain catches up with them as soon as the emergency has passed.

Those who do research into how we perceive pain suggest that between the body and the brain there is something rather like a gate. This gate is usually partly open. When pain signals arrive only a few can get through at a time. If there is an emergency we can almost shut the gate. This blocks out most of the pain. At other times (when we are on the look out for danger) we can open it very wide and we become sensitive to the smallest pain.

This makes a lot of sense. In a real emergency no one wants the pain from a small cut to interfere with survival. At other times the exaggeration of pain might add a necessary note of caution. Although for the vast majority of women painless childbirth is a myth, managed pain is a possibility.

Pain control in childbirth

The following methods of pain control are often used by women in labour. One or more may work for you.

Relaxation

Tension makes pain feel worse but relaxation raises the threshold for pain. The more relaxed you feel, the less something hurts. Women report that the following help them to relax in labour:

Use your partner as a support as much as you want to. If you sit on the end of the bed with your feet on a chair (far left) and lean into him, you take some pressure off your lower back and have a feeling of closeness. If you prefer to stand (left), let him take your weight. Try to stay upright, but if you need to rest, do so.

Partners who assist in this way are also able to monitor signs of tension and help to reduce it before it becomes a problem.

Emergency delivery

If you think that the baby is coming quickly and have no time to get to hospital, this is what you should do:

1 Call 999 for an ambulance.

2 Pant and avoid bearing down for as long as possible.

3 Find someone to help.

4 Wash your hands and the perineal area.

5 Spread some clean towels or newspapers on the floor and lie down. Raise your buttocks with cushions or pillows to slow the birth down.

6 If the baby starts to arrive, move your buttock support. Sit in a semi-upright position or crouch. Push with each contraction. Pant or blow as the head appears. Let it emerge gradually. Never pull. As the head emerges, you (or a companion if you have found one) should reach for the baby and feel whether the cord is around the neck.

7 If it is round the neck, hook a finger under the cord and gently work it over the baby's head. Pant as this is done to avoid pushing.

8 Stroke the baby's nose downward and under the chin upward to help expel mucus.

9 Your companion should take the head gently in both hands. As the next contraction arrives, push as your companion presses the baby's head slightly downward while the first shoulder is delivered. As the arm appears lift the head slightly to free the other shoulder.

10 Quickly place the baby on your stomach and cover both of you with something warm. Do not tug the cord.

11 If the placenta arrives wrap it in newspaper; check you have all the bits: throw nothing away.

12 Keep the placenta higher than the baby but do not cut the cord. Leave that to the experts.

- Keeping moving for as long as possible.
- Being at home for as long as possible.
- Instruction in relaxation techniques (see p. 26).
- Having a birth companion.
- Music and soft lights.
- Foot massage.
- A warm bath.

Breathing exercises

Drawing in breath rapidly makes you tense; doing so repeatedly can make you hyperventilate. Controlled breathing, on the other hand, lowers tension and helps maintain a feeling of relaxation. To help:

- Take classes; they are run in most areas (see p. 25).
- Deep slow breathing, concentrating on the out breath will help relaxation in early labour.
- High chest breathing (blow as if trying to bend a candle flame without blowing it out) helps at the top of a contraction.
- By concentrating on breathing out during contractions, you can avoid clenching your teeth and taking a swift intake of breath.

Delivery positions

Squatting is an ideal position in which to give birth, since gravity helps, but most Western women find this difficult unaided. Let your partner take your weight in his arms (right). Alternatively, sit in between his legs (far right). He can feel contractions coming in this position and you can lean back on him and relax between pushes.

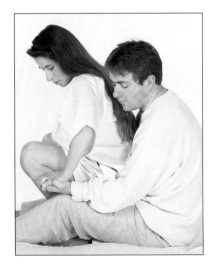

Distraction

Having something to do while in pain reduces its perceived intensity.

- Tap out a rhythm or sing a song.
- Recite a poem.

Gas and air (Entonox)

Entonox is a mixture of anaesthetic gases and air, breathed in through a face mask. It takes about 30 seconds to work. It works well during transition because not only does it reduce pain, it can also return a sense of being in control. Grabbing the mask and putting it to your face feels as if you are doing something to help.

TENS

This is not available at all hospitals, so it is worth asking beforehand if you would like to try it. TENS stands for transcutaneous electrical nerve stimulation and is believed to work by stimulating the body to produce endorphins, its own natural painkillers. Electrodes are taped to your back, connected by wires to a hand-held battery-powered stimulator. As you feel the need, you press the stimulator, giving yourself small amounts of current. There are no side effects on you or the baby.

Some women find TENS does lessen the pain; others that it makes no difference.

Pethidine

This is an analgesic, usually given by injection, which has the effect of continuing your present mood. If you are feeling good it will make you feel better. If you are feeling bad it makes you feel worse. Many women find it does not help with pain. Some like the woozy feeling it gives. It can be passed to the baby, making her sleepy and slow to respond after the birth.

Epidural

See box on p. 54.

Episiotomy

This is a small cut in the perineum, usually made under local anaesthetic, to ease the passage of the baby's head. It does not hurt at the time it is made but can be painful afterward. The cut is made along the midline toward the anus or slanting to one side. The intention is to prevent tearing, but this is controversial: some doctors feel it increases the likelihood of tearing and the healing process is slower and can interfere with lovemaking. As a result the practice of giving routine episiotomies has declined. However, they are needed for forceps deliveries and when babies need to be removed from the vagina quickly.

Cuts have to be stitched after the birth under local anaesthetic. Each layer of the perineum must be stitched separately, which is why it takes so long.

If you want to avoid an episiotomy, tell the hospital that you do not want one unless it is essential and ask your partner to make this clear when you are in labour. You can also reduce the risk of tearing or episiotomy by stretching your perineum in the last months of pregnancy. To do this, first wash your hands thoroughly. Take some cocoa butter or oil and massage your labia, vaginal entrance and perineum

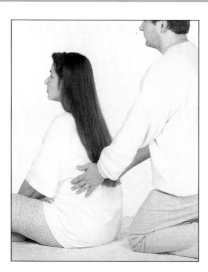

Breathing

Practise breathing for labour with your partner beforehand – he must be able to feel the different effects on your body of deep and shallow breaths. At the beginning and end of contractions, breathe deeply so that your ribcage expands (far left); at the height of contractions, take shallow breaths, just enough to raise your shoulder blades slightly (left).

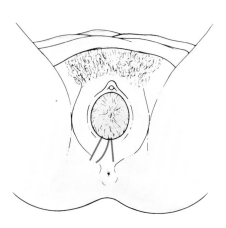

Episiotomy is a cut in your perineum, usually from the back of the vagina out to the side; it can also be made toward the anus, or a combination of the two.

until the oil is absorbed. Then, put more cream on your fingers and insert them into your vagina and stretch the outer lips. Continue until you feel the burn and hold at this point for a few minutes. Your aim is to be able to open the vagina to about 7–8 cm (2¾–3 in) before the burning begins. It takes about a month to work up to this point. Regular pelvic floor exercises (see p. 26) will also help. This procedure, however, is not recommended for anyone who is at risk from miscarriage.

SPECIAL CASES

Not all births are straightforward, but fortunately few problems these days are life threatening to the mother or child. Here is a list of the most frequent problems. If you are reading this before you go into labour do remember that they are all the exception rather than the rule.

Forceps delivery

Since the 16th century forceps have been used to turn babies who are poorly aligned with the birth canal or who need lifting out of the vagina because the second stage of labour fails to progress quickly enough. Forceps look like a pair of shiny coal tongs which can be separated. They are used to:

- Protect the baby's head from the pressure of the vaginal wall.
- Enable the baby's head to be manipulated.
- Enable the baby to be gently manipulated and then lifted from the vagina – the baby is definitely not pulled or dragged out.

Epidural and other nerve blocks

Nerve blocks are local anaesthetics injected along the course of a nerve. They deaden sensation. The two most often used in labour and delivery are the pudendal block and the epidural block.

The pudendal block is used for forceps deliveries and stitches to the perineum. An anaesthetic is injected into the vagina. Once the area is deadened, you will feel pressure but not pain.

The epidural block is used for vaginal and caesarean deliveries. It is the only means of ensuring a completely pain-free labour. A very fine tube is inserted beside your spine. Anaesthetic is delivered into the tube and topped up as required. You will still feel pressure, but not pain. Very, very occasionally after an epidural women suffer from severe headaches which can persist for a couple of days. Even more occasionally numbness is felt in the legs for a few days.

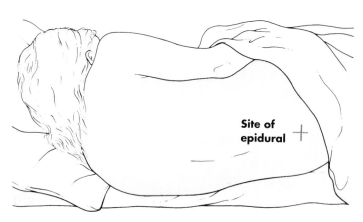

Site of epidural

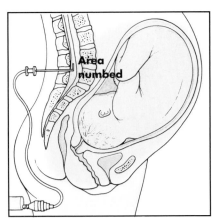

Area numbed

What happens in a forceps delivery

- Your legs will be put into stirrups.
- A local anaesthetic will be injected into the vagina.
- An episiotomy will be cut.
- One by one the two curved blades of the forceps will be slipped into the vagina and placed on either side of the baby's head and locked into position.

After a forceps delivery

You will have a certain amount of bruising and also stitches to contend with. The soreness should not last more than a week.

Ventouse

Sometimes a vacuum extractor is used instead of forceps (usually according to the doctor's or hospital's preference). A vacuum cup is attached to the baby's head by suction. (It is a bit like placing a hand over the pipe to the vacuum cleaner.) The head is then drawn out in much the same way as it would be by forceps. The suction cup often leaves a bump on the head, which may look alarming but the swelling is superficial and should disappear within a week.

Breech delivery

Many babies spend much of pregnancy in an upright position. Most are, however, born head first and facing backward. If a baby is still upright (in a breech position) at 32–34 weeks an external cephalic version (ECV) may be carried out. The doctor will attempt to turn the baby by the use of gentle pressure. Few babies turn after 36 weeks.

There are three breech positions:

- A frank breech is most common. In this position the baby's legs are folded flat up against his body, so that they touch the face or tuck under the chin. Babies enter the birth channel in this folded position. A frank breech is the easiest of breech deliveries. Many will be delivered vaginally and without major complications.
- In a complete breech the baby's feet are tucked up beside the bottom.
- In a footling breech one leg is extended downward from the breech position so that the foot is born before the buttocks.

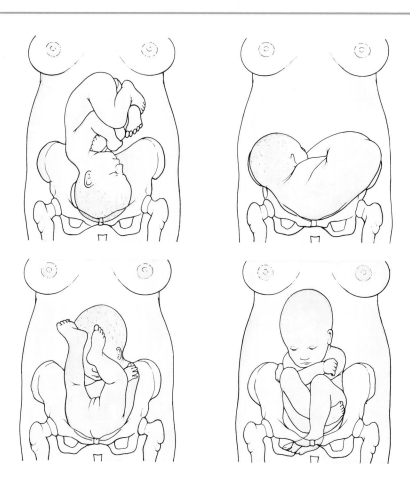

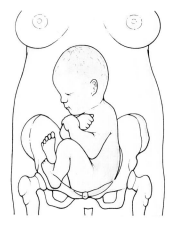

How babies lie

Most babies are head down by the end of pregnancy (top left) and delivered vaginally. Others lie across the exit (centre). A complete breech (above) occurs when the baby 'sits' across the exit. In a frank breech (far left) the baby's bottom, but not legs, is first into the birth canal; in a footling breech, one foot appears first.

Vaginal delivery of breech babies

This is usually only possible if:
* The baby is expected to weigh less than 4 kg (8½ lb)
* It is a frank breech.
* There are no obstetric complications.
* The presenting part is engaged.
* The baby's head is tucked down toward the chest.

* Both complete and footling breech babies are difficult to deliver. An elective (a planned) caesarean section is normally carried out.

Coping with a posterior birth

Most babies are born facing your back, and during labour the baby's bottom is pressing on the abdominal wall. Occasionally the baby is the other way around. This does not necessarily make labour more difficult but it can mean that there is pressure on the mother's back, which produces painful backache throughout labour. Babies born face first may progress rather slowly in the second stage.

Do not lie on your back during labour. Keep walking for as long as possible and then crouch or squat. You might find that getting down on all fours is the most comfortable position. If you feel you must lie down to rest, lie on one side and keep your back well rounded.
* A hot-water bottle soothes the back.
* An ice pack numbs the pain.
* Strong counter pressure or fairly aggressive massage applied to the lower back helps ease the pain. Your partner can use his knuckles, the heel of his hand or a tennis ball wrapped in a sock. The pressure needs to be quite intense in order to work. Expect bruising! Some women find that direct pressure works best, others that a firm circular motion brings more relief.
* Apply strong finger pressure just below the centre of the ball of the foot. This is the acupuncture point for backache.
* A forceps delivery is more likely, after which most women are sore. The baby's head may also be bruised and temporarily misshapen.

Birth by caesarean section

A caesarean section is a safe and quick operation. The actual birth only takes about five minutes, but stitching the wound is a longer process, and can take 15 to 20 minutes. In the past a caesarean was carried out under general anaesthetic, but today most are carried out using epidural anaesthesia. This is safer for mother and baby and makes recovery more straightforward. A planned caesarean under epidural is less dangerous than having your tonsils out.

Watching your baby born by caesarean section is not as alarming as it seems: you do not see the cut being made or even have to watch the baby being lifted out. Your view is blocked by a screen.

Reasons for caesarean section

Caesarean sections are usually performed in the following circumstances:
* Breech births, especially a complete or footling breech (see p. 55).
* Problems associated with the placenta (placenta praevia or placental abruption, see p. 38) or cord.
* Women who have had one or more earlier sections.
* Where the maternal pelvis is too small for normal delivery (this is rare).
* Where the baby's head has not lined up correctly in the birth channel.
* Where pre-eclampsia has not responded to treatment (see p. 38).
* If there are complications. These include active vaginal herpes; maternal diabetes (see p. 37); hypertension or kidney disease; pre-term maternal or foetal distress.
* If a foetus is more than two weeks overdue and/or placental function has diminished.
* If labour has failed to progress after 16 hours.

What happens during a caesarean section

Before the operation your pubic hair will be shaved, a catheter inserted into your bladder and a glucose drip inserted into your arm. If you are having a general anaesthetic the smallest dose possible is used to avoid any anaesthetic passing to the baby. You will be unconscious for a very short time.

If you have an epidural the needle will be inserted into your lower back. You will feel numb from the waist down, but you will feel pressure during the procedure. A screen is put up so you cannot see the operation taking place.

A small cut is made in the lower abdomen (at about the bikini line). You will feel this being made but it will not hurt. A second cut is then made in the lower part of the womb. The membranes are ruptured and the waters drained. (This sounds as if someone is eating soup rather noisily.) Next the baby is eased out by hand, or hand and forceps. You will feel a pulling or tugging sensation as this is carried out, but again it will not hurt. You will then be given an injection of the hormone oxytocin to help the womb contract.

Next the placenta is removed, and the cord cut and the surgeon will stitch you up. Because each layer is stitched separately, this takes a little time. You will hear the suction tubes draining blood and fluids before the abdominal wall is closed.

The surgeon should explain what he or she is doing at each stage of the operation and may warn you how it will feel. In many hospitals a partner can watch the operation. You or your partner can hold the baby while you are being stitched.

There will be a paediatrician in attendance at the operation, and most babies delivered by caesarean section spend the first hours in intensive care. Do not be alarmed. This is standard procedure in many hospitals and does not mean anything is wrong.

Twins

About one in 80 pregnancies results in a multiple birth – most of them twins, but about one in 90 multiple births are triplets. Carrying more than one baby puts both mother and baby under strain so there is a higher incidence of birth complications and prematurity among twin births. The risk of delivering prematurely is highest between 28 and 32 weeks and mothers should be particularly careful at this time. Rest is vital and you should avoid lifting. Once past 32 weeks the likelihood of premature delivery declines, but in any case few twin pregnancies go to full 40 weeks' term.

The actual delivery need be no more complicated than the delivery of one baby. Twins may both lie head down in the normal birth position, or one or both of them may be breech (see p. 39). Birth is most straightforward if both enter the world head first. If the second baby is breech, forceps are generally used to lift this baby out after the normal delivery of the first. Both babies are normally delivered by caesarean section if the first-born baby is breech.

Because twins are more likely to be small (either due to prematurity or because they are small for dates) there is a higher probability that they will both spend the early weeks in intensive care. Sometimes the way they lie in the uterus means that one twin has taken the lion's share of the nourishment. As a result, one baby comes home and the other remains in intensive care, which can be particularly difficult for you and your partner.

Coping with two babies is difficult, especially if they are both small. You will need plenty of help in the early weeks and you may need to review your priorities. Remember, babies do not have to be breast-fed, or bathed every day, and it is also perfectly acceptable to leave them in the same clothes for 24 hours occasionally.

THE FATHER'S ROLE

Today, most fathers are present at their child's birth and many describe it as among the most joyous experiences life has to offer. At the time, however, that joy may be clouded by anxiety. It is hard to watch someone you love in pain, especially when there seems to be so little you can do about it. However, women are almost unanimous in saying that having their partners there helped. Pain is a movable feast: our perception of it depends on so many things that we do not fully understand. Sharing the birth with her partner makes a woman feel more secure and reduces the anxiety of giving birth in a strange place. Because it reduces anxiety, it almost certainly reduces the perception of the pain of childbirth too.

Being at the birth may be an anxious time for men, but the anxiety is not reduced by waiting outside. It is easy to imagine the worst. Where studies have been carried out men seem to be more anxious if they wait outside, and whereas a man's anxiety is reduced by seeing and holding the child he watched being born, the absent father's anxiety seems to persist for longer. Once he stops worrying about his partner he starts worrying about the child. A newborn baby looks rather alarming when you have not observed the blood and gore of birth!

Men who attend the birth feel more united with their partners and more in tune with the caring side of their natures. But watching the birth also may make them feel more physically vulnerable. Men's view of their vulnerability is at odds with women's views of them. Those whose partners were present at birth are more likely to see their man as strong, competent and dependable.

Men who are absent from the birth are often those who see children as badges of their manhood; women whose partners choose not to attend the birth are more likely to see them as someone to worry about rather than depend upon. (If your partner will not be there, choose another companion, see p. 21.)

Birth changes the dynamics of a couple's relationship. The shared experience of childbirth reinforces the feelings of being a couple as well as a family. It undoubtedly brings those who share the experience closer together.

FIRST IMPRESSIONS

Your baby can begin to breathe before his body is completely born. Most breathe within two or three minutes of birth though some need their airways cleared first, and others need the stimulation of a slap. Not all babies cry; some gasp or splutter into independent life. It does not matter how they start as long as they are breathing well within the first couple of minutes.

The condition of your baby is assessed at birth according to a checklist known as the APGAR score (see box). You may be unaware of staff doing this.

Babies make breathing movements before birth, but it is amniotic fluid rather than air which is drawn in and out at this stage. Without air the lungs remain flat and sticky. They need the first breath of air to inflate them. They expand and stretch with each breath like a shrivelled-up plant given water. As the lungs expand blood rushes into the capillaries which surround the spongy tissue. The blood gathers the oxygen and transports it to all parts of the body. A new and separate life has begun.

The first minutes

In those first minutes most babies are alert. His eyes are open, his face serious. He may seem smaller than you expected, puffy eyed, rather red, with an oversized head, large genitals, a round abdomen and rather puny looking arms and legs. He is of course beautiful. You will smile, look your baby in the eye and tentatively put out a finger to touch. Then hands begin to explore, and words of endearment are

APGAR scores

SIGN	POINTS		
	0	1	2
Appearance	Pale or blue	Body pink extremities blue	Pink
Pulse	Not detectable	Below 100	Over 100
Grimace (reflex irritability)	No response to stimulation	Grimace	Lusty cry
Activity (muscle tone)	Flaccid	Some movement of extremities	A lot of movement
Respiration (breathing)	None	Slow irregular	Good (cries)

Babies who score 4–6 often need resuscitation; those who score under 4 need life-saving techniques. A score of 7 or more at five minutes is a good prognosis. Not all babies who have scores lower than this have later problems but some do.

interspersed with questions and comments on how the baby looks. Greeting the baby, parents often behave rather like lovers do after a separation.

In the first minutes mothers often comment how similar the child is to the father. It is as if they wish to draw the father into the relationship but it is rarely necessary. Although some men are nervous of holding the baby and may be at a loss how to behave, most describe watching the birth of their child in a way that shows something is too deeply felt and personal to be put into words: they say things like 'amazing' or 'unbelievable'. For both of you, the exhilaration of birth is overwhelming.

The alert baby

In the first hour most babies are wide awake. You may notice that he looks closely at your face, focusing on your eyes. He may pull faces, poke out his tongue and make little snuffling noises. More alarmingly he may shiver and shudder and may even suddenly stop breathing for a few seconds. All this is quite normal, as is the sleepiness that follows. Having viewed the world most babies curl up and retreat from it. It may be days before he has that look of wide-eyed wonder again. Most babies spend the first few days sleeping.

A small baby's breathing is very soft and shallow, and poor circulation makes him appear very pale. Often it will seem as if he is not breathing at all, which is why many new parents wake their tiny babies to check they are alive. Circulation and breathing matures as he grows, and you will get used to how a baby looks when asleep. Some babies continue for some months to be very pale and still when they sleep.

Is he all right?

'Is he OK?' is often the first question parents ask, even before 'Boy or girl?'. But, in most cases the question does not need to be asked. If something is wrong the medical staff caring for you quickly take over.

About 1 in 25 babies has a congenital abnormality. Half of these are minor – an extra finger, a loose hip, a couple of webbed toes. About 1 in 50 is more serious. Some of these are inherited, some due to damage at birth or soon after (often associated with prematurity). Many have no known cause.

Worries about newborn babies

Major problems are rare, but few babies are born without the odd bump, spot or waxy secretion. The most common are normal and will soon disappear.

The head
The skull of a baby is squeezed by labour and delivery. Because the bones of the skull have not fully fused together, they are free to move, which protects the brain but can leave the head looking a little odd. When the bones have returned to their normal position and swellings gone down, the head will look normal.

A bump on the back of the head is caused by the baby pressing on the cervix before it was fully dilated. Bumps on one or both sides are caused by the pressure of the cervix and vagina and/or by forceps. Bumps disappear within a few days. Dents or grooves caused by forceps also disappear in the first week.

The fontanelle
This is the pulsating soft spot on the top of the head. There is no need to be afraid of touching the fontanelle, nor does it need special care. If you notice that it is taut and bulging, or has shrunk away from the skull, contact your GP or take your baby to hospital.

Jaundice
Jaundice gives the skin a yellowish tinge and can make urine darker. Mild jaundice is common and treated by giving extra fluids and exposure to ultraviolet light; it disappears in a few days. It can make a baby rather sleepy and you may have to wake him for regular feeds. Serious jaundice is usually due to an infection or rhesus incompatibility.

If after returning home jaundice seems worse, give your baby boiled water and call the doctor at once.

The eyes
Most babies are born with puffy eyes, and many have bloodshot eyes. Both conditions soon disappear.

A newborn baby often does not have control of the muscles of his eyes and may have difficulty in focusing, which can make him look as if he is squinting. If it persists beyond three months, a squint should be checked (see pp. 165 and 370).

Watery eyes are common. Usually the cause is a blocked tear duct which will correct itself; it can be treated if it persists. A discharge from the eye may indicate infection and should receive attention straight away. Many infections can be avoided by cleaning your baby's eyes correctly each day (see p. 98).

The mouth

White spots which rub off are milk curds; those that cannot be rubbed off may be thrush (see p. 166).

Babies' tongues are small and they cannot stick them out very far, which often makes them appear to be tied by a membrane attached to the lower jaw. Most are not. A truly tied tongue does not affect feeding or speech.

Very occasionally a baby is born with one or two teeth. These should not affect breastfeeding.

Very pale face

The top of your baby's body may be pale, his trunk red and his limbs blue. This is due to immature circulation and poor temperature control. Keep him in an even temperature – heat the bedroom in winter to about 21° C (70° F) and take care he does not become overheated in summer. Undo or remove outer clothing if you spend time in heated shops or cars.

Spots on the skin

Urticaria neonatorum looks as if the baby has fallen in a bed of nettles. It only lasts a couple of days.

Milia are tiny white spots on the bridge of the nose and cheeks caused by a temporary blocking of sweat glands (see pp. 164–5).

White pearl spots on the body are caused by the mother's hormones and soon disappear.

See p. 341 for other birth marks.

Skin coverings

Lanugo is the downy hair which covers a baby's body in the uterus. An early baby may have some lanugo and premature babies have a significant covering. It disappears in the first few days after the birth.

Vernix caseosa is a waxy substance which covers all babies in the womb. How much is left at birth depends on your baby's maturity. It may seem unsightly but it is safer to leave the vernix in place as it may give the baby protection against infection.

Very occasionally a baby is born with some of the membranes still covering his head and body. So-called caul is traditionally thought to be a sign of good luck.

Other skin problems

Flaky skin is common in newborns, especially on the hands and feet. It is usually caused by the baby being overdue and rarely lasts more than a couple of days.

A wrinkled skin, caused by a long pregnancy, also disappears in the first few days.

Bat ears, or flattened ears

Ears are so soft at birth they can easily be squashed out of shape if your baby lies on them. They are no indication of later size and shape.

The genitals

Boys' and girls' genitals often seem out of proportion with their bodies. As soon as the mother's hormones have passed out of the baby's bloodstream the genitals look more normal. Girls may have milky vaginal secretions or a little vaginal blood, and boys spongy testicles for the same reasons. These also disappear.

Swollen breasts

This happens in both boy and girl babies. Sometimes the breasts have a little milk, also caused by maternal hormones. The milk and swelling soon disappear.

Dark green stools

A baby's first stools are dark green and sticky; this is meconium, digested mucus from the glands which lubricate the bowel. Most babies pass meconium gradually over the first three or four days.

Arms and legs

Extra fingers and toes are common, usually just tiny flaps of skin which are easily removed. Minor bends and twists of the arms and legs usually right themselves once the baby is active. All babies have bow legs.

Girls often have clicking hips, caused by an excess of hormones – it may affect other joints too. Clicks may need treatment (see Your Child's Health, p. 356).

Hernias

An umbilical hernia occurs when a loop of intestine pokes through a weak area of the abdominal muscle and lies under the skin. It usually rights itself in the first few years of life; there is rarely need for surgery.

A bulge above the scrotum in boys is also a hernia and can cause obstruction to the blood vessels; it can be corrected surgically.

YOUR CHANGING BABY

Newborn babies' looks can change quite dramatically in the first months.

Size

Small women have small babies – even if their partners are large – but some of these children grow as tall as their fathers. Early plumpness (or skinniness) can be deceptive. A baby born two weeks early will be thinner than one born a week late, but both may weigh the same at six months. Girls tend to be smaller than boys.

Skin colour

The skin colour of many babies darkens in the first months. Mixed race children are often fairer at birth than they will be later.

Eyes

Caucasian babies have blue eyes at birth. Many darken later. Brown-eyed parents may have blue-eyed children, but the children of two blue-eyed parents remain blue. Dark-skinned children are born with dark eyes.

Nose

A baby's nose looks quite prominent at birth. Sucking develops firm cheek muscles and within weeks he will have a more typical baby face.

Hair

The first hair is often different from later hair both in colour and texture. Early hair falls out gradually over the first months. It can take up to two years for the permanent hair to start to thicken; timing is no indication of later thickness.

Baby skills

At birth a baby will:
- Turn to a voice.
- Prefer high-pitched sounds.
- Move in time to his parents' speech (although the movement is too small to see).
- Recognize his mother's smell (within days).
- Recognize his mother's voice (within a week).
- Prefer salt to sweet (this quickly changes).
- Spend most of his day sleeping, and most of that sleep dreaming (he is dreaming when his eyes move).

At birth a baby will not know:
- That he can make things happen.
- Where his body stops and the rest of the world begins.
- That his mother exists when she has left the room.
- That his mother is not a different person every time he sees her.

At birth a baby cannot:
- Focus on very near or very distant things.
- See anything which is small.
- See colours very well.
- Move fingers independently.
- Remember anything for very long.

See The First Year, pp. 122–49.

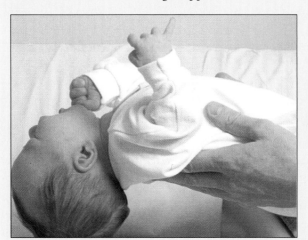

Newborns have no muscle control, so heads 'flop'.

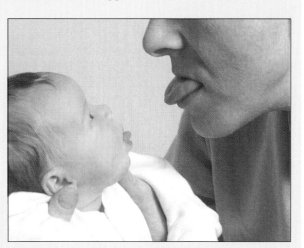

Within days, a baby mimics a repeated action.

BONDING

It is sometimes claimed that cuddling and holding a baby in the first few hours after birth is essential for parental bonding to occur. If this were true some fathers and grandparents would never bond to children, but they do. So do those who adopt children. There is no time limit to bonding: it happens when you love and care for a child. In fact up to 70 per cent of mothers say they were not really interested in their baby immediately after the birth, especially if labour was long and tiring.

The word 'bonding' implies something sudden and complete like an application of superglue which quickly sets. While this description will seem absolutely right to about 10 per cent of parents, it is not how most parents describe the growth of love. For them love develops gradually over the first weeks of the child's life.

The growth of love for a baby is no different from the growth of love for any other person. Few sensible people expect to fall instantly in love, nor fear that a relationship is doomed because it began with rather negative feelings about each other. Love for a baby is sometimes instant, at other times it grows.

Being with the baby helps the bonds to grow. Separation in the early days is certainly not good but it is not an insurmountable obstacle to love. A baby that is ill is rarely from your thoughts. Love can grow even though the baby is not with you. A photo of the child will help.

REFLEXES

A reflex is a response which is triggered automatically by a particular stimulus. Whenever the stimulus occurs, the baby makes the response. Adults also have reflexes – the knee jerk which doctors test by tapping just below the knee is one example and there are many more. Some, such as blinking when a puff of air is blown into the eye, are present at birth and remain throughout life. Others that exist at birth are less important as babies grow and disappear with age.

Certain reflexes are checked by your paediatrician or doctor soon after birth, and may be looked at again before you leave hospital, because abnormal or absent reflexes could be a sign of neurological damage.

Rooting, sucking and swallowing are probably the strongest reflexes at birth, since they are vital for your baby's survival.

Rooting reflex

If you touch a baby's cheek he will turn his head to the side touched. He also opens his mouth as he turns and searches for something to suck. If you have difficulty getting your baby latched on to the nipple, you can use this reflex.

Sucking reflex

When he gets his mouth around something – a nipple, teat, or even your finger – a baby lowers his tongue to create a vacuum and then automatically begins to suck.

Newborn reflexes

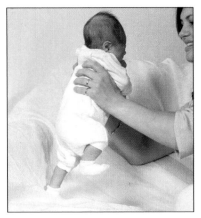

When his feet are placed against a firm surface, a newborn will bend his knees and 'step'.

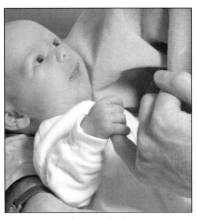

The grasp of a tiny baby is strong and automatic, in both his fingers and toes.

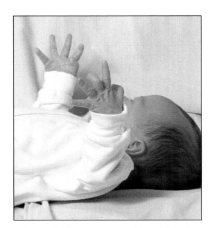

If your baby is startled by a loud noise, he will throw out his arms and legs and open his hands.

Swallowing

Babies have a swallowing reflex from birth but it takes time to learn to co-ordinate this with breathing. Don't worry if your baby splutters and coughs when your breasts are very full (see p. 73).

The grasp

Babies automatically close their fingers when something touches their palms. Toes work in the same way. Stroke the sole of his foot and your baby will spread then curl his toes. This is called the Babinski reflex. The grip of the hand is strong enough to support the baby's weight at birth and even stronger in premature infants than full term. The grip weakens and is lost from the toes at about three months. It finally disappears from the hands at about seven months, when babies learn to poke and prod and use their fingers independently.

The step

If you hold a newborn baby in an upright position with his feet touching a firm surface he will 'walk'. If you hold him so his feet touch the edge of a solid surface – such as a table – he will lift his leg and step up. Most babies stop walking like this as their legs become plumper, since they do not have the strength to lift heavy legs. Such movements keep the joints from seizing up. Until the baby is mobile the joints are kept flexible by kicking – which is exactly the same movement.

The crawl

When placed on his stomach, a newborn baby will curl up with his knees tucked under his body. In this position he can sometimes creep along. Before it was realized that sleeping on the stomach increased the possibility of 'cot death' (see Your Child's Health, p. 371), many babies were put down to sleep in this position and over the course of a few hours often crept to the top of their cribs.

The Moro or startle reflex

A startled baby spreads his arms and legs with fingers outstretched and back arched. After the stretch he will curl, clenching fingers and toes and bringing arms and legs into his body. Your baby is likely to respond in this way if he is frightened by a sudden loud noise or jolt.

BABIES WITH PROBLEMS

Some babies are born with profound difficulties and will have special needs for the rest of their lives (see Children with special needs, pp. 173–5). Others, for a variety of reasons, may spend time in a special baby-care unit. Finding your baby taken to intensive care does not necessarily mean there is a permanent problem, but it may well be a precaution to make sure specialist staff are on hand at all times to monitor your baby's health.

Low birth-weight babies

A baby whose birth weight is less than 2.5 kg (5½ lb) is considered in need of special care. Some are small because they are born too soon, others because they have grown too slowly in the womb. About 8 per cent of all babies are premature, a smaller percentage are small for dates and many of these will be twins.

Premature babies

The skull of a premature baby is not hard enough to provide good protection for the brain during birth. The passage through the cervix may be so easy and rapid that the baby may arrive at the perineum before it has stretched so the fragile head comes up against the tight perineal muscles and skin. The impact can cause bleeding inside the skull, which damages the brain. Even if the baby escapes such problems it may be too immature to cope with the very different conditions outside the womb, with the result that some premature babies are doubly damaged. Technological advances in the care of such babies now give them the best possible start in life, particularly if they are cared for in one of the up-to-date neonatal intensive care units. Babies born before 24 weeks of gestation or weighing less than 1 kg (2¼ lb) are at greatest risk but many do come out of it unscathed – each case is different.

Small for dates

Some babies are small because they are underfed in the womb. The placenta may not have functioned well, one twin may not have received its fair share of nourishment or the mother may have smoked heavily.

Such babies are small and skinny with few fat reserves and wrinkled, dry and peeling skin.

Because small-for-dates babies have spent longer in the womb, their skull bones are harder and lungs more mature than those of premature babies, so they have fewer problems at the birth. However, the liver is often very small and jaundice is common. They can have quite low levels of blood sugar.

What happens in intensive care

There are many reasons why your baby may be taken to intensive care.

Resuscitation
At birth tiny babies often need resuscitating. All attention switches to them and you may be left without an explanation. It is difficult, but trust the staff – their major concern at this time is your baby.

If a baby does not breathe properly once the nose and mouth are cleared of mucus, he will be given oxygen through a mask. If this does not work a thin tube will be passed into the baby's lungs and oxygen blown in directly. This nearly always succeeds in inflating the lungs and the baby will soon begin to breathe by himself.

This is always an anxious period for new parents. The paediatrician or doctor will be too busy with the baby to explain what is going on, and you may be left in ignorance. Once the immediate crisis is over, it is a good idea for your partner or birth companion to ask for a reasoned explanation to reassure you, as you will be in a highly emotional and anxious state.

Hypothermia
A tiny baby cannot easily control his temperature. If he becomes cold, he cannot easily warm up because he cannot shiver or move about easily. To avoid hypothermia the baby is rapidly removed to a warm incubator. If he has become cold during resuscitation he may be wrapped in foil so that he can warm up gradually as rapid warming is dangerous.

Respiratory distress syndrome
Very small babies often have difficulty breathing because their lungs are immature, a condition known as respiratory distress syndrome. This is treated by increasing the concentration of oxygen in the incubator. Respiration is always monitored electronically with an electrode attached to the baby's chest. An alarm will sound if the baby fails to take a breath and he will be resuscitated. This can happen more than once but the staff in the intensive care unit are trained to act quickly in this situation.

Feeding
If a baby is not mature enough to suck, a tube must be inserted directly into his stomach and small amounts of milk passed down this tube. Sometimes you will be encouraged to express your own milk to feed the baby with, but if the baby is very small and premature, he will may well be given a special formula (see p. 75).

Exchange transfusion
Most premature babies suffer from jaundice because their livers are not mature enough to cope with breaking down the byproducts of foetal blood. These seldom rise high enough to cause concern, but very occasionally the baby may need an exchange

Hospital security

Most hospitals today are open places, with visiting hours – particularly in the postnatal wards – largely unrestricted. The majority of new parents want the freedom that this brings: fathers can be there when they want to be, and friends and relatives can drop in at convenient times. The downside of this, however, is that it is impossible to make hospitals secure.

Although cases always make headline news, baby snatching is very, very rare. But it does make sense to follow some simple guidelines.

- Don't allow anyone to take your baby anywhere without you. If you are told he needs a test, insist on you or your partner going too.
- Don't leave your baby in an empty room. If you are taking a bath or shower, ask one of the other mums to keep an eye on him, or wheel him into the bathroom with you.
- Every member of the hospital staff should have a security badge (not simply a name badge). If anyone approaches your bed without one, ask to see it.

transfusion during which his blood is completely replaced (see Your Child's Health, p. 359).

Getting to know a tiny baby

Getting to know a baby in an incubator is difficult. You will be encouraged to visit often and to stay with the baby but this may not be possible if you have young children or live some distance away. Beds in special-care units are not easy to find, and the one that can accept your baby may not be near your home. If you cannot see your baby every day have a photo (or better still a video) of him and look at it frequently. The staff of the unit will encourage you to touch, hold and feed him as soon as it is safe to do so (you may also be able to express milk for him, see p. 75).

If you find this time stressful (and you would be unusual not to) talking may help. Contact your health visitor, or one of the support organizations – they can almost certainly put you in touch with someone who has been through what you are going through now and come out the other side.

FIRST DAYS

In the days following birth, babies spend most of the time sleeping. This is obvious to all those who have a second baby but not perhaps to those with their first. Life with a first baby is one endless string of things started but never finished and at the end of each day it is hard to say if anything was accomplished or quite how the time was passed.

It is never possible to explain to prospective parents how it feels to be responsible for a baby or why it is so difficult to switch off. If the baby sleeps you check his breathing. If he is in his crib you go to the door and listen. If he sleeps more than four hours you pick him up to make sure he is alive. All of this is supremely tiring, achieves little and leaves no time to get on with the 101 things which must be done, but it is also a perfectly normal reaction of first-time parents. Even reading a book is difficult at first – you are simply too engrossed in the baby. It takes time to learn how to put the baby out of mind while you get on with other things but parents do eventually learn to switch off. Within months you will wonder how on earth a newborn baby could have taken up so much of your time.

First days for the father

Pregnancy and labour may be the mother's show but at the moment of birth it is the father who has the better view. In those first moments, first-time parents are on equal terms with each other as neither knows much about babies, but the equality is fleeting. He goes home to an empty house, you stay with the baby, holding and cuddling him. You soon learn how to pick him up, dress and change him. Your baby smells your smell, hears your voice and feels secure with them. The father is a stranger who has yet to learn any of these skills.

The demands made upon families today are inconsistent. Both parents are expected to work. Both parents are expected to share the care and res-ponsibility of children. Yet there is little possibility of parents spending the night after the child's birth together, unless the birth is at home or discharge is after six hours, which rarely happens for first babies. However, while a mother may appear to have a head start in parenthood, it is important for both parents to accept this and find time at home to allow the father to get to know his baby. If your partner is returning to work after just a short break then this becomes even more important.

Mothers need to relinquish the baby's care to their partner to enable this to happen; fathers need to keep in mind how tiring as well as totally absorbing the care of a new baby can be and gently relieve you of that care when he is at home.

First days for the mother

After labour, mothers need rest but this is not always easy in a room full of other people's babies, or at home with older children or a stream of relations coming to visit. Hospitals used to confine mothers to their beds for two weeks and send babies to the nursery between feeds. In the night babies had bottles while mothers slept. Of course, it is essential to have your baby with you, but if you had a long and difficult labour you may regret that women cam-paigned so hard for change!

In most of the world tiny babies spend the night in their mothers' arms. When hungry they latch on to the breast and often neither wakes. If you breastfeed, you will find it much easier to combine feeding with a full night's sleep if the baby sleeps in the bed with you or his crib is next to your bed for the first couple of months. You need not be anxious about rolling on your baby while you are asleep – this does not happen, although it is important that you have not been drinking alcohol or taken a sleeping pill. Sleeping with your baby during the early weeks and months does not produce long-term problems providing you teach him to sleep in his cot at other times (see pp. 104–8).

Breast is best but not at the expense of your total exhaustion. A depressed mother can have far more serious implications for her child's development than the occasional bottle. If you are becoming overtired and overwrought the occasional bottle can actually help the establishment of breastfeeding: you will be less anxious if you have allowed your partner to feed the baby while you sleep (with earplugs) in a separate room. Expressing some milk before you go to bed and after the morning feed will ensure that your milk production does not drop. If sleep removes tension, this will also help your milk production. As long as you sterilize bottles, the baby is in no greater danger of illness. The immunity passed to the baby in breast milk does not miraculously stop because you give the occasional bottle (see Feeding Your Baby, pp. 70–83).

Older mothers

A late baby may mean a late conversion to mother-hood. Some converts go a little overboard. You don't need to be a perfect mother – good enough will do.

There is no physical reason why women in their 30s or even early 40s should find labour or parenthood more tiring. Many women choose to start their families later so that their careers are properly established before they contemplate taking maternity leave. Most so-called older mothers are in fact more relaxed and better organized than younger mothers – they have already achieved something in their lives and can afford to take time out to enjoy parenthood. However, when problems arise it is often because mothers who have had a structured career expect to achieve something every day. At 20, most women (and men for that matter) are more laid back about the fact that days go by without anything being completed. At that age you are also less set in a method of working which encourages you to concentrate your undivided attention on one topic. (How many 30-year-olds can work with the TV on, as most teenagers do?) At 30-something, however, partners and friends are engrossed in careers. They, like you, find it hard to understand why you cannot even make time to read the newspaper. If you find yourself worrying about this, remember that a baby is a human being and not a machine that can be programmed to work to your preferred schedule. It does help to try to accept this and not to become too anxious about systems and routines.

Before you come home

A preliminary examination of your baby's current health and prospects for the future is carried out at birth (see p. 58). If any problems are suspected the baby will be taken into special care for observation. Babies who are premature, in distress during delivery or born by caesarean, normally spend the first hours in the special care unit where they can be observed more easily. If a baby is very small or if there are potential problems, he will remain in special care.

Before you take your baby home from hospital, the paediatrician will check that all bodily functions are in working order. If you had your baby at home, your family doctor will carry out the checks about five or six days after the birth, and your baby will be checked again at six weeks of age (see pp. 116–17).

Your baby's appearance
The doctor will check whether your baby has a very large or very small head, whether his backbone is normal and if there are signs of Down's syndrome. He or she will check muscle tone, the mouth and eyes. Common problems usually have recognizable signs. You will be told if an abnormality is suspected, and further tests will be given to confirm the diagnosis.

Listening to heart and chest
Some heart problems are evident at this stage; some are discovered later. If the baby remains blue, additional checks may be carried out.

Urine and faeces
The doctor will check that the baby has passed urine and had a bowel movement. Tests will be carried out to check that these are normal. If problems are suspected

further tests will be given. Together these indicate that the digestive and urinary system are working well.

Feeding

You will be asked about how your baby is feeding so that the doctor can assess if everything is satisfactory.

Reflexes

His reflexes will be tested. Some problems associated with the nervous system can be detected this way.

Minor abnormalities

He will be checked for jaundice, loose hips, twisted limbs and hernia. If necessary, appointments will be made to recheck these in a week or so.

Infection

The doctor will check that the baby has no obvious signs of infection in the eyes, mouth or ears.

Growth in the first six weeks

At birth the average boy is 52 cm (20½ in) long and the average girl slightly less than that, 50 cm (19¾ in). Both grow by about 2 cm (¾ in) in the first six weeks.

Babies and children do not grow by a fixed amount every week. They grow fastest in the month after birth and slowest just before puberty. The rate of growth declines throughout childhood.

It takes six weeks to gain the first 2 cm (¾ in), then 12 weeks to gain the second 2 cm (¾ in), and 24 weeks to gain the next 2 cm (¾ in). This doubling rule holds until puberty, although growth spurts (see p. 125), obviously, mean that the progression may not be smooth.

In the first week all babies lose weight. By the second week they have usually regained those losses and begun to increase in weight. By six weeks they have usually put on about 900 g (2 lb). As a very rough guide babies gain about 150 g (5 oz) per week. Girls take roughly five months to double their birth weight and about 13 months to triple it. Boys put on weight rather faster, doubling their weight in about four months and tripling it in about 11.

Testicles

The testicles of a baby boy should have descended into the scrotum.

Weight and size

Your baby's initial weight and size, including his body length and head circumference, will be measured.

PKU test

A blood sample taken from a heel prick on about the third day after the birth will be tested for PKU (phenylketonuria). PKU is a treatable disorder of the metabolism which, if unchecked, can produce severe mental handicap.

Vision and hearing

Visual and hearing tests are sometimes carried out at this stage. More normally they will be carried out when your baby is six to nine months old.

As well as these formal tests, the hospital staff will simply observe your baby. If they suspect abnormality they will carry out further checks. Similar checks will be carried out at six weeks (see pp. 116–7).

The good-enough parent

No one needs to be perfect. No one should even try. What child could cope with perfect parents? Good parenting is a compromise, a balancing of the needs of all family members – and that includes mothers. If you are a first-time parent, it may help to remember the following points:

- Babies do not need constant attention.
- Babies do not need endless stimulation.
- Babies do not need their nappies changing at night unless they are soiled or sopping wet.
- Babies do not need burping.
- Babies can sleep in your bed.
- Babies can have dummies.
- Bottlefeeding does not mean you have failed as a mother.
- Babies can be topped and tailed two days in a row.
- Your partner can (and should) be left in charge.
- Some babies actually like wet nappies.
- Small babies do not miss their parents if they go out for the evening.
- Competent babysitters can look after babies.

CHAPTER THREE

Feeding Your Baby

Holding a tiny baby in your arms as you feed her is one of the most emotionally fulfilling experiences of parenting a young child. Watching her grow and thrive is one of the most rewarding. How to feed your baby, however, is one of the most loaded issues. This chapter presents the facts about breast- and bottlefeeding so that you can decide how you want to feed your baby.

Breast or bottle?

The best way to feed your baby is the way that feels right for you. Breastfeeding is best for the health of your baby, but if you are uncomfortable about the whole idea, forcing yourself is going to help neither you nor her. So, how do you decide whether to breastfeed, or to give your baby formula milk in a bottle? For many mothers, there is no choice: they feel very strongly that they want to do one or the other, and cannot imagine even trying the other way. But if you are undecided, or genuinely wonder which method would suit you and your baby best, there are some points you need to know.

BIRTH TO SIX WEEKS

The first six weeks of your baby's life are when feeding becomes established. Most problems – if any – are usually resolved by the end of this time.

The facts about breastfeeding

It would be wrong of anyone to try to persuade you to breastfeed if you have deep feelings against it. But health professionals, and books such as this, do well to present the facts so that whatever your choice, you are making it on the basis of good information.

Breast milk has health advantages
This is unsurprising as breast milk, like all mammals' milk, is species specific – it has been 'designed' to offer optimum nutrition for baby humans. Formula milk is usually cow's milk, modified in the factory to make it more digestible for a new baby's system.

Breastfeeding offers significant protection against gastroenteritis, respiratory disease and ear infections in babyhood. In the longer term, it helps protect against the development of childhood diabetes and some childhood cancers. It may have a role in the prevention of allergy, and offer some protection against cot death. There are indications that it promotes intelligence, too.

It is not always understood why breast milk 'works' in these ways, but it is known to contain valuable antibodies which protect the baby in the first few weeks and help build up her immune system.

Breastfeeding is good for you
Mothers who breastfeed have less chance of pre-menopausal breast cancer. When breastfeeding is going well, it feels good. It promotes the secretion of hormones which help you relax while you feed – and many mothers derive great satisfaction from seeing how their babies thrive when fed on their breast milk.

Breastfeeding and medication

If your doctor advises you not to breastfeed because of your medical condition or because of medication prescribed for you, you may want to seek a second opinion. In very rare instances, breastfeeding may be ruled out. In other cases, your medication can be changed, or suspended or the dose may be altered to make breastfeeding possible. Some mothers with conditions such as epilepsy, for example, can learn to time their medication, and their feeds, so that the drug is not present in the milk when the baby feeds.

This, of course, takes organization and motivation, and plenty of support. If you know in advance that your medical history may be a problem to breastfeeding, discuss the whole issue with your health visitor or a breastfeeding counsellor, so that you can make an informed decision.

Breast milk is made independent of your nutritional status. Unless you are truly and consistently undereating, your breast milk will always be high quality, and suited to your baby's stage of development and growth. You will have enough breast milk, too – as few as 2 per cent of all women, according to World Health Organization estimates, have real underlying physiological difficulties in making enough milk for their babies.

Breast milk is, however, far more than a way of getting top-quality nutrition into a baby's stomach. Breastfeeding in modern Western society is not always easy, and understandably many women give up and turn to bottlefeeding. It is true to say that most problems are caused by avoidable factors and with help and support can be overcome.

Breastfeeding and your feelings

Your breasts may be linked in very powerful ways to your feelings about your body. You – or your partner – may be embarrassed by breastfeeding and may find the prospect of feeding in front of other people unwelcome – even though this can be done very discreetly (see box).

How breastfeeding works

You will make breast milk whether or not you intend to breastfeed. At first, the breasts produce colostrum, a highly concentrated fluid, rich in protective substances, that appears toward the end of pregnancy and for the first few days after the birth. This then changes to breast milk, under the influence of the hormone called prolactin which is secreted after delivery. This process is known by many as the milk 'coming in'.

You may feel this surge of milk production as a fullness, although it is possible you will not, especially if your baby has fed well from the start, in which case she will deal with the extra as it is made. Some mothers experience engorgement: when the breasts are so full of fluid – not just milk – they are truly uncomfortable (see p. 73). Your breasts may leak milk, in which case put breast pads or clean cotton handkerchiefs in your bra. If you do not want to wear a bra at night (you may be more comfortable if you do), you may find it helps to sleep on a towel. After the first few days, breast milk is made in direct

Discreet breastfeeding

It is worth thinking about your attitude to breastfeeding your baby in front of others before she is born, and to discuss them with your partner. If you find the idea unwelcome, there are ways around it.

- Choose clothes with care. Some tops have zips which enable you to undo one breast at a time in such a way that no one can see anything. Most loose tops and teeshirts enable you to feed your baby without your breasts being visible and a shawl or wrap hides everything.
- Go to a different part of the room, or a different room altogether. Alternatively, lie on the sofa with the baby in front of you.
- Find out which stores, restaurants, gyms and so on have parent and child rooms: local NCT branches and other organizations may have information. Some of the chain stores, especially those which specialize in baby clothes and equipment, have good facilities for breastfeeding mums.

Remember that a baby being discreetly fed is less noticeable than one who is crying because she is hungry. Once your baby is feeding well, breastfeeding her is likely to feel so natural that you will probably be able to feed her in almost any situation, regardless of how you thought you might react.

response to the baby feeding so this excess is less likely to be as great a problem. This process is twofold:

- the baby's suck stimulates the hormone oxytocin, which works on the storage areas inside the breast, and causes the 'let down reflex', pushing the milk down into the ducts and toward the nipples; and
- the removal of milk from the breast stimulates the hormone prolactin, which makes more milk to replace the milk taken away by the baby at that particular feed.

Prolactin levels remain high at first, which is why mothers continue to make milk for some time even if they are bottlefeeding. But the only way to ensure a good milk supply is to feed your baby as often as she wants, so that you pass on the right 'orders' to your body. Frequent feeding is normal initially.

What to expect

Feed your baby as soon as you can after delivery. If you are both well, there is no reason to delay it, and your baby can make use of that alert period straight after birth to come to your breast and to start learning about your taste and smell. Not all babies want to feed at this stage, but it is a good idea to give yours the opportunity to do so. In any case, the oxytocin produced as a response to your baby's suck stimulates the uterus to contract, which assists the delivery of the placenta.

For the first couple of days, babies vary. Some seem sleepy and uninterested in feeding, others feed very often – every two hours or more – and there are many other normal variations in between. When your milk comes in, however, your baby is likely to want to feed often. Between six and a dozen sessions at the breast in 24 hours are quite usual. This pattern may seem unpredictable, and time-consuming, and confusing – you may never be quite sure when your baby is likely to want to feed again, and may not always know when she has finished. But it tends not to last. If it did, no mothers of more than one child would manage to breastfeed their babies as well as getting

breakfast for their older children and taking them to school – yet many do.

As long as your baby is showing signs of contentment and satisfaction some of the time, this feeding pattern simply indicates that she is establishing your milk supply, learning to feed and to adjust to the world outside. If she shows frustration, crying and she has frequent unsettled bouts of misery, it could mean that your feeding technique and management need some adjustment. Don't struggle on. Get help – see p. 74.

By three or four weeks of age, many babies are already a good deal more settled in their feeding behaviour, although there may still be occasions when they feed more often than the day before.

Night feeds

Your baby is likely to need feeding in the night for some time. One or two night feeds are normal for the first few weeks, and some babies need more. Very few babies sleep through the night before they are about 12 weeks (many take considerably longer). You can, however, expect your baby to have her longest sleep during the night. If she shows signs of having her

How to breastfeed

In order to breastfeed successfully, make sure that both you and your baby are comfortable before you begin. Choose a comfy chair that supports you well. If your baby is crying she may feed better if you soothe and calm her first.

If your baby is not well latched on, you can get sore or cracked nipples and it can be difficult for your baby to stimulate a good milk supply.

Make sure that she remains close in to your breast; if she is slipping off the breast, she is not properly latched on. Many babies take themselves off the breast after a good feed, tired and delightfully full: this is not the same as coming off in frustration because

she cannot get at the milk waiting in your breast.

If your breasts are heavy and floppy, support them from underneath, but don't press on them from above.

Breast milk is food and drink in one. It even becomes more watery in very hot weather, so you do not need to give your baby any other fluids to satisfy her thirst. Giving other drinks, whatever they are, can interfere with the supply–demand production of breast milk. There is certainly no good reason to give anything else, nor is there any evidence that water, herbal drinks, or specially formulated baby fruit juices helps with wind or colic.

Sit or lie comfortably (see p. 74). Hold your baby on her side, so that she is chest to chest to you, with her mouth close to your nipple. She should not have to twist, turn or bend her head to feed and you should not have to slot your nipple into her mouth. You may need patience at first.

days and nights mixed up, and is awake more often at night than during the day, try changing her pattern by waking her up during the day.

Keep night feeds low key, to make them easier for yourself and to help your baby settle back to sleep as soon as she feels full. Do not change her nappy unless you have to: if it has leaked, for example, or if she has a sore bottom that could be irritated by a wet or dirty nappy. Keep the lights low, and try to rest yourself while you are feeding her.

You can feed your baby in your bed, and many mothers find this is the easiest way to doze off and conserve their energy. Lie down with your baby next to you. Make sure she does not get too hot under your bedclothes – it is safest to have a shawl or sheet over her, rather than slipping her under your own quilt.

Coping with problems

Although breastfeeding is the most natural and time-honoured way of feeding babies, at times it can feel anything but that.

Many mothers give up breastfeeding after a short time, and never reach the stage where they can really enjoy it, relishing the facts that it is quick, easy, convenient and cheap. Surveys show that mothers rarely give up because they feel they have breastfed long enough, or as long as they planned to. Far more common are reasons such as sore nipples, or anxiety about whether or not they have enough milk for the baby. Most problems can be overcome, often quite quickly, with the right information, encouragement and support.

Engorgement

This is most common in the first days, although it can happen at any time. Engorgement means that the breasts are uncomfortably, even painfully, swollen. If your baby is feeding well, the problem is likely to go by itself after a short time. If it does not, gentle expressing (see p. 77) to take off just enough milk to soften the breasts will help.

Sore and/or cracked nipples

A certain amount of tenderness as you and your baby learn about breastfeeding is normal. But soreness that gets worse rather than better, and that is painful rather than tingling or uncomfortable, needs dealing

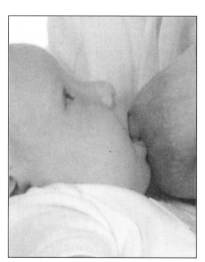

When she opens her mouth wide, bring her on to your breast. If she is taking the breast correctly, her tongue will be forward and out, pushing her lower lip so that it rolls over. Her nose and chin will be touching, or almost touching, your breast. This is known as latching on.

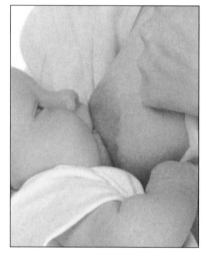

If she is correctly positioned, there should be more of your areola showing above her top lip than below. Don't press on your breast – this could inhibit the free flow of milk through the ducts. Short, quick sucks at the start of the feed are normal with deeper glugs as the feed gets underway.

When she has finished one breast, offer the second. Some babies have one breast at each feed, others both; or one sometimes and two at others. If you need to take her off the breast for any reason, break the suction by inserting your finger into the corner of her mouth.

Help with breastfeeding

If you find it difficult, or if you are slightly concerned or puzzled about anything, seek help from someone who knows and understands about breastfeeding. If you are still in hospital, midwives there will help you. Some maternity units have a specialist adviser, usually a midwife with an interest in breastfeeding. At home, contact a community midwife, or your health visitor or one of the breastfeeding support groups. The National Childbirth Trust has a network of breastfeeding counsellors. You do not need to be a member to make use of this service. Look up local members in your phone book or contact the national headquarters (see Useful Contacts, pp. 390–3). La Lèche League also helps mothers who want to breastfeed (see pp. 390–3).

with straight away. Do not just grit your teeth, curl your toes and tell yourself to put up with it.

The most common cause of sore nipples is poor positioning of the baby at the breast (see pp. 72–3).

In fact, if you are sore and have never had any period of pain-free breastfeeding, you can be sure your baby's position needs changing. It is likely that she is sucking too close to the end of the nipple and does not have enough breast tissue in her mouth. The result is that the nipple rubs against your baby's hard palate as she sucks, or she pinches the nipple in order to keep it in her mouth.

Ask a breastfeeding counsellor or health professional to help you check the way your baby takes the breast into her mouth and how she sucks once she is there. If you need to break the suction for any reason once your baby is latched on, gently insert your finger into the corner of her mouth.

If you have had a period of pain-free feeding, then become sore, thrush may be the cause (see p. 166), although positional soreness can exist alongside thrush. You need medication for you and your baby from your GP.

Creams and lotions recommended for soreness do no good if the positioning of the baby at your breast is not corrected, although you may find that they soothe already-sore nipples, while the healing process takes place and the baby latches on in a different way.

Comfortable breastfeeding

In the early weeks you may spend a great deal of time breastfeeding; if you are not comfortable, not only will you find it more difficult to relax and enjoy feeding, but you also run the risk of backache and a stiff neck and shoulders.

Try out different positions and different chairs until you find the one that suits you best. If you prefer to sit, you may find an armchair or the sofa does not offer you enough support and, perhaps surprisingly, you will be more comfortable on something firmer. Make sure that both your feet reach the floor – put them on a box or a couple of thick books if they don't. A cushion in the small of your back may also help you feel more comfortable.

As your baby gets bigger and heavier, supporting her on a couple of cushions on your lap may reduce strain on your back.

Finally remember that what works best at one stage or even one time of day may be less comfortable at others; be flexible.

Breastfeeding may be easier if you lie on your side with your head propped up comfortably. You may find a cushion helps. You can lie on the floor, bed or sofa, but if you choose the latter make sure it is wide enough – you cannot relax if you are worried about you or the baby being too close to the edge.

Nipple shields – used to protect a sore nipple – cut down on the milk available to the baby, and confuse her suck. Some babies become hooked on the shield and cannot then feed from a breast without them. If you use a shield, bear all this in mind and try to get rid of it as soon as you can.

Mastitis

Mastitis is an inflammation of the breast which can be, though it does not have to be, an infection. Mastitis usually begins when a duct (one of the pathways that take milk to the holes in the end of the nipple) becomes banked up with milk. A plug of milk blocks the duct, and starts to leak into the surrounding tissue, causing redness, and possibly swelling, tenderness and pain. It can be extremely uncomfortable to feed from the affected breast, but it is important that you do not just stop. If it is left, mastitis can become infected and a breast abscess – which may need hospital treatment to drain – can result.

Gentle massage, hot and cold compresses, feeding the baby first on the affected side can all help shift the plug. See your doctor or midwife if these measures do not begin to help straight away.

Not enough milk

While mothers almost always have the physiological ability to nourish their babies fully on breast milk alone for the first four to six months of life, not producing enough milk is a real phenomenon. If milk production is not stimulated well enough at the start, it is more difficult to build up a satisfying supply.

Giving bottles of formula in the early days and weeks fills the baby up, stops her being hungry for the breast and fools your body into thinking that breast milk does not need to be made. And if the bottle teat confuses her suck and makes it harder for her to get used to the breast again, there will be even less stimulation of the breast.

Poor positioning can also lead to a poor supply, as can trying to restrict the times and frequency of feeds.

If you think you may have a problem with your milk supply, check your positioning and let your baby feed as often and as long as she wants, staying on the first breast until she comes off by herself before offering the second. And try to fit in more feeds for a day or so.

It is also possible that your worries about not having enough milk are groundless. If your baby is

Feeding pre-term and special care babies

Babies who are born pre-term or who need special care after the birth can still be breastfed, although very tiny or sick babies may need tube feeding with expressed breast milk at first. It is a good idea to start expressing as soon as you can (see p. 77) to stimulate milk production. At first you may produce only a few millilitres, but this can still be used and is especially valuable to special care babies since they are more vulnerable to infection. As soon as your baby is well enough, hold her close to your breast so that she gets to know your smell and taste – even if she is not breastfeeding yet.

It is more and more common for special care babies to be given expressed breast milk from a little cup, once they move on from tube feeding, instead of a bottle and teat, which could teach them the wrong sucking action.

gaining weight well enough according to your clinic (even if the weight gain is erratic, as it often is in breastfed babies) and appears to be thriving, the chances are that there is nothing wrong with your supply. Seek support from other people who are confident about breastfeeding, and do not feel that every squeak from your baby is a sign that she might be hungry. A breastfeeding counsellor (see box opposite) will be able to help you decide about supply and what is and is not normal.

Baby fails to latch on/fights at the breast

Some babies just do not latch on easily at the start, and seem to get cross and frustrated; others seem to get ever more reluctant and even hostile to the breast. Often, the background of these babies indicates they have been handled roughly at the start of feeding, perhaps by someone who has tried to ram their head toward the breast. The situation can be compounded by the use of bottles and/or nipple shields (used to try to get the nipple into a shape the baby can grab or to draw out an inverted nipple).

If your baby feeds like this, and every feed seems to be a battle, you may need a lot of patience and skilled help. Your baby needs to learn that breastfeeding is easy, pleasant and rewarding, and the sooner you can get help and support, the more likely it is that you will overcome this hurdle. If it is a slow process, express your milk (see opposite) and give it to your baby by letting her sip it from a cup (this is better than giving a bottle of expressed milk, as a cup is less likely to condition her sucking wrongly).

Your baby is sleepy

Some babies are reluctant to feed, and sleep rather than make the effort to rouse themselves sufficiently. This may be only temporary, often the result of a long and tiring birth, or a side effect of drugs used during delivery. Be patient, and try not to resort to a bottle – which is easier to give, as the teat can be pushed into the half-open mouth of a drowsy baby – unless you are given a medical reason why your baby needs formula.

What you need

Looking after yourself, primarily by resting and eating well, is often considered crucial to the success of breastfeeding but, in fact, mothers all over the world breastfeed under adverse physical and dietary conditions. The breast milk produced is inevitably of high quality, and as long as the baby feeds unrestrictedly, the quantity is sufficient, too. It is, however, important to look after your health while you are breastfeeding, for your own sake. You will feel better, and have more energy to care for your baby, if you eat regularly, and listen to your body's needs when it comes to sleep and rest.

You do not need to eat anything special when breastfeeding, or to avoid any foods. Occasionally, mothers report that eating a certain food seems to

Breastfeeding twins

If you want to breastfeed twins, and these are your first babies, be prepared to spend a good deal of your day and night breastfeeding until it is well established. Once it is underway, however, you will produce milk in response to your babies' needs and there will be plenty for both. Ask your health visitor or a counsellor for help and advice in establishing feeding.

When your babies are very tiny, you may be able to cradle them both in your lap. Sit well supported, either crosslegged on the floor, or on the bed.

Sit well supported with each baby on a cushion in front of you. Tuck the babies' legs under your arms and cradle their heads with your hands as they feed.

A combination of the first two options may suit you best. Tuck one baby under your arm, supporting her head with your hand, while the other is cradled in your lap with her head supported on your arm.

Even when feeding is established, it may be still be easier to hold both babies in your lap. Use pillows and cushions to support yourself and them. Alternatively, you could lie back with them on top of you – this makes night feeds easier.

As long as one baby is prepared to wait, separate feeding may be easier. Sit on the sofa. Cradle the feeding baby in your lap and lie or prop the second one so that you can play with her. Try not to feed the same baby first each time.

Expressing milk

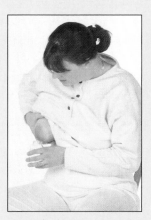

If you want to continue giving your baby breast milk but want the occasional few hours away from her, it is worth learning to express your milk. It can be difficult at first, but once your milk supply is established, it gets a great deal easier. Hand expressing is one way; the alternative is to buy a hand pump. (If your baby is pre-term or spends time in a special care baby unit, you will be asked if you want to express your milk using an electric pump.)

There are different pump designs on the market, but all work in a broadly similar way; simply follow the directions for use with the pump. Always sterilize it before use.

A breastfeeding counsellor or your health visitor can show you how to express by hand.

1 Wash your hands and sterilize a feeding bottle or large bowl. Support your breast in one hand and start to massage toward the nipple. Gently work your way all round the breast, at least half a dozen times to encourage the milk flow.
2 Stroke downward toward your nipple several times with your fingertips, but avoid pressing on your breast tissue. Press gently on the area behind the areola with your thumbs and fingers.
3 Press your breast tissue back while squeezing your thumbs and fingers together. Drops of milk should begin to flow through your nipple. Do this for a couple of minutes, then repeat the whole process with your other breast.
4 Keep massaging and squeezing alternate breasts until the flow slows down or until you want to stop.

Expressed breast milk keeps, covered and in a sterile container, for up to 24 hours in the fridge and for about three months in the freezer. It is quicker to defrost if you store it in ice cube trays – you can also match what you need to your baby's appetite.

result in a lot of crying or windiness in their baby and, although it is difficult to prove, it is possible that traces of some foods affect the breast milk. There is no case for deliberately cutting out fruit, fruit juice, sprouts, curry or anything else you may hear is bound to affect your breast milk, until you are sure it always causes a problem. There is some evidence that dairy products can cause colicky crying in babies, but the research is contradictory. If you have a baby who seems to cry a lot, consult your health visitor or doctor before cutting out anything major from your diet. If you do this permanently, you may have to adjust other parts of your diet to compensate.

It is normal to feel thirsty while you are breastfeeding, especially at first. Drink according to your thirst. Making efforts to increase your fluid intake – some books suggest litres a day – over and above what you want to drink, is pointless.

Limit your alcohol intake, do not take up smoking again and consult your doctor or pharmacist before taking any medicines while you are breastfeeding.

Bottlefeeding from the beginning

If you have made the choice to bottlefeed, either from the very start, or in the first few days before breast-feeding has really got underway, you do not need to wind down your breast milk supply. Although you may be uncomfortable for a few days – your body makes milk simply as a result of pregnancy and delivery, whether or not your baby uses it – this fullness should disappear as the supply is not stimulated by the baby coming to the breast (if you change your method of feeding at a later stage, you may need to introduce bottles more gradually, see pp. 84–5). Wear a well-supporting bra during this time.

The only non-human milk suitable for a young baby is a recognized infant formula, most of which are based on cow's milk. A few babies are unable to digest the protein in cow's milk, and milk based on soya is usually recommended for them. There are also formulas made from goat's milk, but what advantage these may have over cow's milk formula is not clear.

Formula manufacturers change the composition of their milks from time to time, in line with both research and the cost of raw ingredients. Your midwife should have up-to-date knowledge of the main differences between the various products on the market. However, there are two main types of formula – whey based and casein based. This refers to the major source of protein in the milk. Whey-based milks are sometimes branded as 'stage one' milk, and marketed as 'closer' to breast milk with the result that most babies start off on a whey-based formula. Mothers often make the change to a casein-based formula later on (see p. 86), although there is no nutritional reason for doing so.

You can expect your new baby to need several small feeds in a day at first – about six to eight is typical. Because formula milk takes longer to digest than breast milk, bottlefed babies tend to feed rather less frequently than breastfed ones. After the very first days, she may take up to 100 ml (3½ fl oz) of formula at a time, although it may well be more or less so be guided by her appetite. As she gets older, she is likely to have more milk, in five or six feeds, and take about 200 ml (7 fl oz) at a time.

In hospital, you will probably use ready-to-feed formula, in pre-sterilized bottles. These bottles are useful standbys and ideal if you are out and about, but they are expensive to use every day (you can also buy ready-to-feed formula in cartons). At home, powdered or granulated milk, which you mix with water and give in bottles you sterilize between each use, is more economical.

What you need

Modern bottles are made of plastic, marked to show fluid levels. You will need at least six 200 ml (7 fl oz) size bottles as a basic, and perhaps the same number of 100 ml (3½ fl oz) bottles to use at first. Teats are made of silicone or latex rubber. Silicone teats last longer; latex ones are softer. Most babies can use either, and there is no advantage in choosing one over the other. Generally speaking, small holes in the end of the teat are used for younger babies, who then progress to using teats with larger holes as they grow. (You can always enlarge existing holes with a razor blade. Do not make holes too large, however, or your baby may splutter and choke.)

'Orthodontic' or 'natural shape' teats are sold as being 'closer' to the shape of a mother's nipple. This may be so, but sucking on them does not imitate breastfeeding, as the baby's mouth and tongue are in a different position entirely. Some babies do, however, develop a preference for one shape over another, probably because they get used to it.

Crying and feeding

Crying is one way – and the major way – in which your baby can show you that she is hungry. This is not a problem in itself if she is feeding well, and the feed – whether breast or bottle – comforts and satisfies her. Frequent feeding is normal in the early weeks. However, if you feel she often cries with hunger because the feed does not fill her up, or leaves her happy for only a short period of time, speak to your health visitor or midwife. This may be no more than the erratic, unpredictable behaviour associated with newborn babies getting used to the world and a new way of feeding, but it may also indicate a problem that needs dealing with now.

A bottlefed baby may need more formula than the guidelines for weight and age normally suggested; a breastfed baby may simply need to be fed more frequently than you were expecting, perhaps only for a short time to build up your supply. Alternatively, she may be poorly positioned and not getting a good, satisfying feed. Poor positioning can lead to the baby crying with frustration and – possibly – hunger, after a breastfeed, yet refusing the breast if it is offered again, or taking it for only a few seconds before turning away.

Some breastfed babies take what they need in a comparatively short time, particularly as they get older. Your baby may cry simply because she does not want any more, and does not want you to keep trying to keep her on the breast.

Persistent crying is not a trivial problem, whatever causes it – seek help for you and your baby (see also Babies and crying, pp. 101–4).

Making a bottlefeed

When you buy a bottle, you will also usually get a cap (this fits inside the teat holder and allows you to cover the bottle for storage in the fridge without a teat) and a teat holder which screws on the neck of the bottle. Most bottles also come with a cover, which allows you to place the teat on top of the closed bottle for transportation without leakage or spillage.

You will also need tins or packets of dried formula (or – if you only give the occasional bottlefeed – cartons of ready-to-feed formula), plus sterilizing equipment. Always wash your hands before you start.

If you have used chemicals to sterilize the bottles, rinse them with cooled, previously boiled water to get rid of the taste.

All formula packs have instructions on them. You must be as accurate as possible when measuring out the milk; use the measuring scoop provided, rather than your own measure, and do not pack the milk down into it – you could dramatically increase the amount of milk that way.

You may find it easier to make up a whole day's feeds at a time. Made-up formula is safe to use for 24 hours as long as it is stored in the fridge, either in closed bottles with the caps on, or a lidded jug (but choose a jug with an accurate measure on the side and be sure to sterilize the jug too).

If you store a bottle in the fridge before giving it to your baby, you may find that she prefers it warmed. To do this, stand the bottle in a jug of hot water for a few minutes. Microwaving is not safe – the heat-through may not be even, and hot spots in the milk could scald your baby. Check the milk by shaking a few drops out on to your wrist. It should feel warm but not hot.

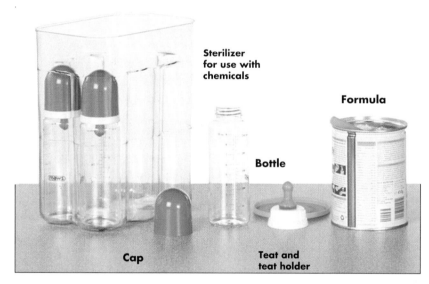

Sterilizer for use with chemicals

Formula

Bottle

Cap

Teat and teat holder

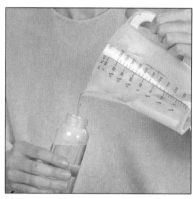

1 Boil the water you are going to mix with the milk powder. Pour the water into the bottle or jug up to the required level.

2 Add the right quantity of milk powder to it. Use the scoop provided, levelling off excess powder with a knife.

3 Shake or stir well so that the powder dissolves. If you are giving the bottle straight away, cool it under cold running water.

4 If you are storing it for later, cover with the top provided and keep in the fridge. Transport cold in a cool bag.

Keeping it all clean

Bottlefed babies do not have the protection against gastroenteritis that breast milk gives them, and warm milk, of any sort, is a great breeding ground for bacteria, so it is vital to be careful about cleanliness when you are bottlefeeding.

After each use, wash the bottle thoroughly in hot water with detergent. Make sure the inside and the thread of the screw neck are free of all traces of milk. Wash the teats inside and out, and wash the screw-on teat holders that fix on the neck of the bottle. Keep a bottle brush just for your baby's bottles to help you do all this properly (if you buy a complete feeding set, one should be included). Rinse everything in clean water, then sterilize using one of three methods – boiling, chemicals or steam.

The sterilizing routine is a chore until you are used to it, but you need to do it until your baby is at least nine months. It is easier to sterilize several bottles at a time, and keep them aside ready for the next feed.

Giving a bottle enables fathers to feel close to their small babies and play a real part in this basic aspect of their care.

- Boiling is useful if you only give the occasional bottle, but it is tedious to boil six bottles, teats and so on every day, as you may need more than one pan load. To sterilize in this way, boil a large pan of water and put everything you want to sterilize into it. Keep the water boiling and all items immersed (with no trapped air bubbles) for 10 minutes.
- Steaming is convenient and quick. Do it in a purpose-made electric steam sterilizer, which stands on your kitchen worktop and is designed to hold a day's worth of equipment. If you have a microwave oven, you can buy a steam sterilizer for use in this, for even quicker results.
- Chemical sterilizing uses cold water with sterilizing fluid or tablets made for baby feeding equipment. You immerse the items in a special tank, or other suitable container (such as a large plastic bowl) and leave them for the specified time. You need to use a fresh solution every 24 hours. Rinse off all traces of sterilizing solution with cooled, boiled water when you remove the items from the solution.

Once your feeding items are sterilized, you can keep them covered and away from any potential germs, and use them when you need to.

Giving the feed

Hold your baby close, and always tilt the bottle so the teat is full of milk to prevent your baby swallowing a teat full of air as she sucks (she is bound to swallow some air). Every so often you will have to remove the teat from her mouth so that the teat resumes its former shape: teats tend to collapse with sucking, and this stops the milk flowing through. Your baby will probably need to stop once or twice during the feed, and after it, to let any wind come up as a burp.

Do not insist that your baby finishes the feed if she has clearly had enough; let her appetite be your guide. And do not keep left-over milk from one feed to another. Throw it away.

Other needs

In hot weather, a bottlefed baby may need a drink of water to satisfy thirst. Boil the water first and then cool it before giving it to your baby. You need to boil the water, even if it is bottled mineral water, to make sure any bacteria are killed. Any mineral water you give your baby should be labelled as safe for babies – some types are very high in sodium or other salts.

SIX WEEKS TO FOUR MONTHS

After the first few weeks, both breast- and bottle-feeding tend to get easier and you and your baby get more used to a routine.

Breastfeeding

By the time your baby is about six weeks old, you are likely to be reaching a point where breastfeeding is easy, comfortable and enjoyable – even if you have had problems earlier on.

Your baby may still have times when she seems to need feeding more often – this is reflected in her growth, which will probably not be a smooth incline up the graph. This is normal; if you feed her as often as she asks, it is highly likely that your baby will revert to her previous pattern in a couple of days or so. It is usual for a baby of around three months to have six breastfeeds in 24 hours, with one of those feeds at night, and the others spread at fairly regular intervals through the day and evening.

Changes you will notice

Your baby may take less time – often dramatically less time – at the breast. This does not mean that she is 'going off' breastfeeding, so do not try to get her to stay on for longer than she wants. If she feeds when she wants, and comes off the breast happily by herself, the chances are that she is getting what she needs – even if she seems to you to be feeding for no more than a few minutes.

The major reason for this change is that you are producing more efficiently, and the let-down reflex is working beautifully, and your baby's skills in getting herself positioned correctly first time, and in sucking and swallowing have developed, too.

There is still likely to be at least the occasional feed which your baby likes to linger over – and times when she wants to be on and off the breast for an hour or two, especially in the evening when she is winding down to go to sleep. These are all normal variations, and unless your baby seems constantly or frequently unhappy, or shows signs of frustration, or appears to be unable to feed, these patterns do not indicate poor feeding or a feeding problem.

Coping with wind

Bottlefed babies, in particular, swallow a lot of air as they feed. This may make your baby uncomfortable; it could also make her feel full temporarily, but leave her hungry a short time later. When your baby – whether breast- or bottlefed – pauses, give her the chance to bring up any wind that may be trapped, without getting obsessive about waiting for a burp before you let her continue.

1 Place a cloth over your shoulder. Hold your baby so that her head is on your shoulder (support her head when she is tiny) and gently rub her back.

2 Alternatively, lie her across your knees and rub her back. You may need to put a cloth on your knees or on the floor since she will bring a little milk up too.

3 Once your baby is able to sit for short periods, cuddle her in your lap and rub her back gently so that any trapped air is released as a burp.

Changing your mind

It may be possible to build up your milk again after a period of bottlefeeding: this is known as relactation. Putting your baby to your breast often may be enough to start things up. A device called a nursing supplementer can give formula at the same time as the baby is on the nipple – a breastfeeding counsellor will help you to obtain one. Think carefully before you embark on relactation, though. It depends on having a baby who is happy to co-operate, and it takes time, energy and a lot of commitment. Remember: there is nothing to stop you putting your baby to the breast whenever she needs comfort and closeness, even if you have stopped feeding her in this way.

The other major change is one that may happen to you. At some stage, you may notice your breasts feel softer than they were when breastfeeding was just becoming established. You notice less of a dramatic change from the way your breasts feel full before your baby comes to you for a feed, and the much emptier feeling afterward. There may be times – for example, first thing in the morning if your baby has managed to sleep through the night – when your breasts do seem rather uncomfortable but, in the main, they now look and feel rather more like your breasts did before you became pregnant.

This does not mean you have run out of milk; quite the reverse. In the early weeks, the breasts are prone to overproduce. Now that feeding is well established, your breasts have replaced the fat that used to give them their fullness with milk-producing and storing tissue, which is not as bulky. And you are now making milk efficiently and in response to your baby's needs, without too much excess. Levels of prolactin (the milk-producing hormone) gradually fall during the first months after delivery, with the result that milk production becomes much more dependent on the baby's sucking action and the amount she takes at each feed.

You can still have problems breastfeeding a baby of this age, just as in the early days (see pp. 71–6), but as before, the right information and advice should sort them out.

Bottlefeeding

Bottlefed babies are likely to be more settled and predictable in their feeding habits by about six weeks, but it is still common for mothers to change formula in response to what they perceive as a lack of satisfaction in their babies. You may find that, although your baby is feeding more regularly than she did as a newborn, she still cries between feeds and perhaps after them. In such circumstances many mothers assume that their baby is not 'settled', and the maternal response is to change the feed, usually to a 'stage two' or 'follow-on' casein-based formula (see p. 86). Casein is thought to take longer to digest in the stomach than whey, and therefore fills a baby more effectively, but there is no real evidence that it makes a great difference. But if you are keen to see if a change of diet could make your baby happier, there is no nutritional reason why you should not switch. Ask your health visitor for her opinion before you make a final decision.

By the time they are four months old, most bottle-fed babies have gradually increased their intake to be taking 200 ml (7 fl oz) at each feed.

Changing to bottlefeeding

If you are changing to bottle feeding after a period of more than a couple of weeks of breastfeeding, the first thing to do is check that this is your only option. The right help with breastfeeding, plus encouragement from those close to you, may mean that you can continue to breastfeed if you want to. Nevertheless, if that help has come too late for you, or if you feel the whole thing is a struggle you would rather abandon, then a switch may well be the right thing.

Don't feel guilty

When you switch to bottles you may feel relief, or that it's a practical solution. But if you're doing so reluctantly, you may feel regret, disappointment, sadness and even anger. All are understandable; guilt, however, means you feel you are to blame that feeding has not worked out the way you wanted. You are not.

Cut down gradually

Top up each breastfeed with a small amount of formula, which you increase each day, as you take your baby off the breast before she falls asleep full. Alternatively, replace one breastfeed every couple of days with a bottle feed, so within 10 days to a couple of weeks you are fully bottlefeeding. If you have already been using bottles, you may find your supply decreases more quickly than this.

Do not make a sudden change

Your breasts will take a few days to learn not to produce milk, and if you suddenly stop breastfeeding you will feel extremely full – and possibly get engorged, blocked, and perhaps suffer a bout of mastitis as a result. If you feel your breasts are uncomfortable while you are trying to make the changeover, express very gently (not too much, as this will encourage more milk) to reduce your discomfort.

INTRODUCING SOLID FOOD

Solid food may be anything but solid. The term refers to foods other than milk, introduced to a baby who has until fairly recently been fed on a milk-only diet.

Babies do not need anything other than milk until they are about six months

old, the age at which they are assumed to require more iron than is available from either breast milk or formula. Since the first teeth are also starting to come through at about this age, it would seem nature is giving a clue as to when a baby can begin to cope with non-milk foods.

It is usual, however, to give solid foods rather earlier than six months. This is partly a cultural phenomenon, to do with the way parents feel they should be pushing their baby on to the next stage of growth and development, and reducing their baby's dependence on them. It is also done partly in the belief that solids will fill the baby up so that she will sleep through the night. (Studies have shown it makes no difference overall, although some babies may coincidentally start sleeping through at the time they begin on solids.)

It is advisable to introduce solid food no earlier than four months, which is still rather later than many families tend to do. The major reason for waiting is that younger babies are more susceptible to

Left: An interest in food and time for a 'chat' while he is eating help your baby appreciate the move on to solid foods.

Baby rice

Baby rice is a manufactured product and, as it is 'ready' almost instantly, it is very handy. It is an ideal first food. Mix it with water (boiled and cooled), expressed breast milk or formula, and serve it by itself or mixed with other foods such as fruit or vegetable purées.

A major advantage of baby rice is that it is gluten free. Coeliac disease, in particular, is an inability to digest the protein gluten, found in wheat. The incidence of coeliac disease has fallen, probably because babies are not introduced to wheat as early as they used to be.

given foods their digestive systems cannot cope with. In addition, solid foods inevitably take the place of at least some of the milk in the baby's diet, and young babies need a mainly milk diet for most of the first year.

Do not rush to begin solids. Once your baby is four months, these signs indicate that she may be ready.
- Does she show an interest in the food you are eating?
- Is she restless after milk feeds?
- Does she seem to enjoy the occasional bit of food off your plate, if you hold her while you are having a meal yourself?
- Is she starting to be able to grasp things?

- Is her weight levelling off?

Speak to staff at your baby clinic about introducing solid foods. They will help you to decide if now is the right time.

Take it slowly

Some babies are very keen on solids; others are reluctant at first. Let your baby set the pace. Begin by offering small tastes on the end of a spoon, and stick to bland food, one or two new tastes at a time, so that you can easily isolate any food to which your baby has an adverse reaction.

Give solids after or in the middle of the milk feed so that your baby has the chance to take the milk she needs, with solid food as an extra as far as possible. Offer solids once a day, building up to twice and then three times a day over a period of weeks. The later you start solids, the quicker your baby is likely to increase her appetite for them. A six-month-old baby is probably keen enough to move on to three meals a day in three or four weeks. A four-month-old may take five or six weeks. It does not matter how long your baby takes if you are going at her pace.

Try to arrange it so that your baby has her meals at the same time as you and the rest of the family. This makes eating a social occasion, and one she will enjoy for your company and the shared experience of it all. It is also more convenient, on the whole, for you.

Giving solids

A high chair is not essential, but even a small baby can sit propped up in one and it makes it easier and more sociable if she sits with the rest of the family for meals. Make sure she wears a harness.

Be prepared for mess. A good deal of the food your baby feeds herself is likely to miss her mouth and some will inevitably end up on the floor – you may find it helps to put a sheet of plastic on the floor under the chair.

Make sure the baby is wearing a bib, then help her feed herself.

Begin by feeding the baby a couple of spoonfuls yourself, as long as she is happy to take it from a spoon.

She may not be interested in feeding herself but if she is, give her a spoon. Keep one yourself so that some food goes in.

First foods

Suitable first foods include baby rice, puréed or mashed fruit, and puréed or mashed vegetables.

Keep foods smooth in texture and do not season.

Foods to avoid

Some foods are unsuitable for a young baby's digestive system and may cause adverse reactions. They should be avoided until she is about six months.

- eggs
- wheat and wheat products, including bread and breakfast cereals
- dairy products, including fromage frais, yogurt and cheese, unless their milk content has been modified
- citrus fruits
- fatty or fried foods; if you offer meat trim off all fat
- nuts
- strong or spicy vegetables, such as onions, peppers or okra

Second foods

When your baby is a little older, make her food rather lumpier and introduce different foods so that you increase her repertoire. By six to eight months, most babies can have most foods you have, apart from nuts (although ground ones are all right). Egg yolk should be hard-boiled until after her first birthday.

Solids and weight gain

If your baby does not appear to be gaining weight as she should, do not automatically assume that she needs solid food before the recommended age. It may be better to offer more breastfeeds, having checked that everything else concerned with breastfeeding (such as positioning) is going well, or to give more formula in some bottles if you are bottlefeeding.

Weight gain is only one indication of health in young babies – albeit an important one. If your baby is alert, responsive and contented, she may naturally be a 'slow gainer'. Some babies' weight levels out for a week or so without there being any problem, but talk to your health visitor if you are at all concerned.

Trim off all fat from meat and check fish for bones, then grill, bake or poach. Peel fruit and vegetables and remove pips. Mince or mash (and as she gets older chop) as appropriate.

What to drink

Breast milk is best throughout the first year and beyond. As a drink, formula is the next best thing up to a year, although your baby can have small amounts

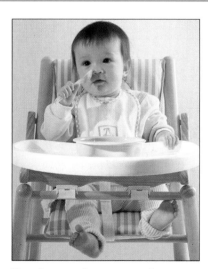

Practice at using a spoon is important for your baby – the more she tries, the easier she will find it to reach her mouth.

Finger foods are ideal, since your baby is probably used to finding her mouth with toys and other objects (see p. 137).

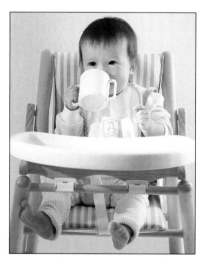

A cup with a trainer spout, firm lid and two handles enables your baby to help herself to a drink when she wants one.

Food hygiene

You do not need to sterilize the serving dishes, utensils and preparation equipment you use for your baby's food. Washing in detergent and hot water and then rinsing (or washing in a dishwasher) is perfectly adequate. However, it makes sense to continue to sterilize your baby's bottles and teats and her spouted drinking cup for two reasons:

- traces of warm milk are excellent breeding grounds for bacteria; and
- it is more difficult to see just how clean these items are and to clean them effectively in the normal way.

Once your baby starts to put all manner of things in her mouth, it is usual to relax your cleanliness standards a little, but continue to sterilize bottles and cups until your baby is nine months to a year old.

of whole pasteurized milk mixed with other foods from the age of six months. Whole milk has the fat-soluble vitamins and calories that your baby needs; these are not present in skimmed or semi-skimmed milk.

Follow-on milk is marketed as suitable for babies from six months, as an alternative to whole pasteurized milk, mainly because it is higher in iron. There is no real reason to change to it, as it is no better for your baby than ordinary formula or breast milk. It is sold more as a 'marker' that your child is getting beyond the young baby stage: buying it is a consumer rather than a nutritional decision.

You can also give your baby plain water – there is no need to boil it after about six months – or well-diluted fruit juice. Avoid sweetened drinks or syrups, which can have a very bad effect on teeth, especially if they are drunk from a bottle.

Finger foods

Give your baby the opportunity to feed herself. She will enjoy it and feeling food with her hands before she eats it offers a valuable learning experience. She will make important judgements about colour, texture and taste far more easily than if you are spooning food into her.

Chop up food into bite-sized pieces and put it on her tray for her to pick up and handle. Bananas cut in half lengthways are good finger foods, though a bit sticky and messy, and you can give bread and bread sticks, carrot sticks and small chunks of peeled cucumber, slices of apple or pear, and anything else that is not naturally sloppy in this way. Most babies cannot manage a spoon themselves until well after their first birthday. Always stay with your baby when she is feeding herself, in case she chokes.

Baby food – bought or home-made?

Almost all babies have some pre-packaged foods in their first year. Most parents appreciate the convenience of giving their baby something suitable when they are not eating themselves, when there is something baby-unfriendly on the menu, such as an extra-spicy chilli, or when you are out and about and cannot be certain of finding anything suitable. Bought baby food is quick to serve, and liked by babies: each recipe is consumer-tested to make sure you will buy the product again and again, after all. The meals are consistent; all such foods today are prepared without artificial additives.

To give your baby nothing but jars, packets or tins is, however, very expensive, compared with home-cooked food. In addition, the fact that brand X cauliflower cheese always tastes the same may not necessarily be a good thing – home-made is always a little different in taste and texture, and as babies do need to start eating 'real food' at some stage, learning that things are not always smooth, lump-free and identical with the one before is important.

Your own home-cooked food is likely to be higher in quality than a lot of bought products. If you read the labels on baby food, you will see that many are bulked out with thickeners (these are responsible for that particular gloppy texture which makes them easy to spoon out of a jar or can). These ingredients are not harmful to babies, but they may mean that the food is poor value, both nutritionally and financially. It is not surprising that good baby foods with a high proportion of quality ingredients tend to cost more.

Remember that many of the foods you eat because they are 'instant', or almost-instant, are also suitable for babies: satsumas, bananas, raw vegetable sticks, bread and bread sticks, for example.

CONTINUING TO BREASTFEED

If you want to carry on breastfeeding your baby, do so. Worldwide, mothers continue to breastfeed well into toddlerhood and even beyond. The World Health Organization recommends breastfeeding for two years (though with a range of solid food as well).

In the West, breastfeeding for this long is not common and because it is not often seen, it is easy to assume that it does not happen at all. That, however, is not the case.

You may find that as breastfeeding becomes more established and easier and easier, you and your baby enjoy it. Stopping is just not an issue: why bother ceasing something that both of you find rewarding?

Meeting both your needs

Mothers who work (see p. 88) may find the feeds they enjoy at the beginning and end of the day and at weekends are a special way of staying close to their babies. It is not difficult, either, to get into a feeding pattern that suits you and your baby, as your baby grows – and as feeds for an older baby often last no more than a few minutes, they fit into even a busy day very well.

The exception to this 'few minutes a feed' is the evening or bedtime feed, which may well last longer. This may be a highly efficient way of winding your baby down for the evening, and it helps ensure smooth settling as your baby falls happily asleep. (The downside of this is that some babies can only easily get to sleep for the evening if you are there, which may be a problem if you are involved with even the occasional early evening activity.)

Do not believe the old story that your milk 'goes off' or becomes inferior the longer you feed. Breast milk is always a nutritious drink, and its infection-fighting properties remain (although as your baby gets older and can fight infection herself, these become less significant). Mothers of older babies are often thankful they have continued to breastfeed when their babies are ill: breast milk is often the only thing they are willing to take.

Once you have been breastfeeding for a few months, it is possible to keep the supply going with

Menstruation and ovulation

It is normal for your periods to cease while you are fully breastfeeding, because the breastfeeding hormones suppress ovulation, and therefore menstruation. Once your baby starts to take solid food, or to space her feeds out, or to reduce her number of feeds, your periods may return. On the other hand, they may not return until you have completely stopped breastfeeding.

Breastfeeding is the most commonly used contraceptive method in the world, but it is not considered reliable in the West, largely because so few women breastfeed as often as is necessary to prevent ovulation (at least every four hours; for some women, as often as every two hours). Also, since ovulation can happen before you have a period, it is hard to monitor accurately enough, so you can be fertile without knowing it.

very little stimulation. There is always some milk in the breasts, and as time goes by, breast milk is made more and more directly in response to the baby's sucking, almost immediately she feeds. The result is that mothers can keep breastfeeding on just one feed a day, without finding their supply dwindles to nothing. (This is not the case in the first days and weeks when the breast milk production system simply shuts down.)

Supply also becomes more flexible. It is possible to feed an older baby erratically, with more on one day than another, as you may do if you are away from your baby in the day from Monday to Friday. At first your breasts may feel uncomfortable as they adjust to this, and they may start to feel rather fuller after they have had some 'extra' demands placed on them, but this stage passes.

Coping with hostility

There are social reasons which make some women feel uncomfortable about breastfeeding; there are also some people who seem to disapprove of the whole notion of feeding babies this way. This attitude is even more prevalent with older babies. You may come across comments such as 'You're not still doing that, are you?', or 'She doesn't get any benefit from it now, you know'. Some people may even imply you are imposing breastfeeding on your baby because of some sort of selfish motives to do with wanting to be needed. The good thing is that having breastfed for some time, you are likely to be feeling a lot more confident about the whole process than you might have been in the beginning, and also about your abilities as a mother. You can see for yourself that your baby is thriving.

Biting and resistance

If your baby starts to bite at the breast (some do, once their teeth begin to come through), simply take her off, with a firm 'No'. This usually stops her. It is not a sign that your baby is starting to become vicious, or deciding she does not want to be breastfed any more.

A few babies under a year do voluntarily wean themselves, and show you by fighting, and refusing to suck, that they have had enough. Do not take this first sign of reluctance as a permanent refusal if you do not want to. Your baby may well come back to breastfeeding, given the chance, if you keep offering over a few days.

Working and feeding

If you are keen to continue breastfeeding when you go back to work, you have a number of options:
- arrange your hours and breaks so you can carry on giving your baby a breastfeed at her normal times
- combine breast- and bottlefeeding with formula
- combine breast- and bottlefeeding with expressed breast milk
- combine breastfeeding with cup feeding with expressed breast milk or formula

The one you choose may depend on the age of your baby. Babies under five months or so are just learning to take a cup, and are unlikely to be able to get all the fluids they need in this way. It is more difficult to combine breast and formula until your breast milk supply is well established, which can take as long as three months. Your choice may also depend on whether you can express breast milk and store it at work. Not expressing could leave you uncomfortable (though after a time this passes), and also means that you must spend a lot of time at home expressing your milk. If you want to express your breast milk (see p.

77) at work, you will need a private place and a clean fridge to store it. Transport it between your workplace and home or childminder's in a cool bag.

Don't feel you need to get your baby used to a bottle long before you have to leave her. A baby who is used to being breastfed may have a bit of a struggle learning to suck on a teat, but she will manage. If she finds the struggle too much, hold a cup of expressed breast milk or formula to her mouth and 'tip' it in (the vast majority of babies do not need this).

Using a cup

Babies can start using a cup from birth although this is normally only suggested if there is a problem with the way the baby sucks, or as a transition stage between tube-feeding a sick or pre-term baby and breastfeeding. It is also occasionally done as a supplement to breastfeeding, to avoid conditioning and confusing the baby's suck.

If you use a cup for a young baby, she will lap or slurp, rather than drink, but once she is about four or five months old, she may be able to start learning to drink 'properly' from a cup. This is a useful skill, as it means your baby can begin to have fluids other than breast milk or formula.

At first, think about choosing a spouted cup. Some babies are about seven or eight months before they can manage these well, and you may need to try a few different shapes and lengths of spout before you hit on one your baby can use easily. A double handle is useful at first, too.

You can of course use an ordinary cup from the start, but your baby will need help to hold it steady and to tip it up at just the right angle to avoid empty-ing the contents all over her face.

Offer a cup – whatever sort you use – with every meal, to encourage your baby to reach for it. Offer a drink of water, milk or diluted juice in a cup once or twice a day between meals, too.

It does not matter if your baby still prefers the breast or bottle for months, and even rejects the cup. Keep the cup on offer, and visible, and she will eventually come round. It is also not worth worrying about how much your baby drinks – she will not voluntarily stay thirsty. As long as the drink is there, and she has a breast- or bottlefeed when she 'asks' for one, she will take the fluid she needs.

WEANING

As your baby eats more solids, and at the same time as you do, you can expect her to join in family meals, and to have more or less the same food as you and the rest of the family. Do not add salt to your baby's food, and avoid heavily salted foods. She can have eggs, but make sure they are still hard-boiled until her first birthday. Whole nuts remain on the 'no' list until your child is five. Your baby will tolerate and chew lumpier food, and in fact it is a good idea not to concentrate on the smooth purées you may have started her on: babies can develop conservative food habits and start to dislike and refuse all food with any sort of texture. Make mealtimes fun, and sociable.

Once she is well established on solids, you may want to stop breast- and bottlefeeding.

Stopping breastfeeding

To make the changeover as smooth as possible, you may find some or all of these strategies useful.

Distraction

Start by distracting your baby about the time of, or just miss out, the feed(s) you feel she is least attached to. Offer a drink of something else, or simply take her out in the pram or buggy. Do not drop more than one or two feeds every few days, or your breasts could start to feel uncomfortable.

Keep the feeds your baby seems to enjoy the most until the other feeds have gone. You could drop your daytime feeds, for example, before you stop feeding at bedtime, or perhaps first thing in the morning.

Flexible babies

Babies under a year are more flexible – and can 'forget' about breastfeeding more easily – than older ones. Your baby may take quite happily to being put to bed without a breastfeed if your partner or a trusted babysitter puts her to bed, for example, or if you swap a story or a cuddle for the feed. If you leave it until she is older, you may have to think of more complicated strategies if your baby remains keen on the breast (you may end up feeding, as well as reading a story and having a cuddle), but she may also settle if someone else gives her milk in a cup.

Stopping bottlefeeding

The sound argument for phasing your baby's bottles out by the end of her first year is the risk of dental decay. Babies who suck anything other than plain water through a bottle teat are bathing their new teeth in potentially decay-causing fluid. This is less of a problem if bottles are restricted to mealtimes, as saliva can counteract the effect. However, older babies can hold their bottles themselves, and enjoy doing so. They can get very attached to them, to the extent that they have them for much of the day, with an all-day bottle of juice or milk for instant swigging.

Encourage a cup

A cup rarely gives the sucking comfort of a bottle, so offer that during the day. And try to prevent your baby from falling asleep with the bottle in her mouth, which might mean she needs to suck on a bottle in order to settle at all.

Comfort sucking

Older babies get a lot of comfort from sucking a bottle, especially at bedtime, and seem to need it to wind down after a busy day. If you find yourself relying on the bottle to help your baby go to sleep, try offering a dummy instead.

Weaning older children

You can breastfeed through a second pregnancy, but it is only fair to both children to wean the older off the breast well before the younger arrives. When you decide the time has come to wean your older child off the breast, you have a number of available strategies.

- Drop all feeds but the one to which your child is most attached (usually the bedtime one).
- At bedtime, settle your child down to sleep without offering your breast. Be prepared for several evenings of protest, but stay firm. If you give in, you are not being consistent or fair.
- Avoid situations or places where you know your child will want to feed: if you always fed her curled up on the sofa, sit somewhere else.
- Distract your child at times you think she may want to feed: offer her a drink or a snack instead.
- If your child is older, explain that big children do not have breastfeeds, they have cuddles instead.

CHAPTER FOUR

Your Baby at Home

Getting to know a newborn in the first few days and weeks at home is a thrilling experience, which reaches far beyond caring for his daily needs. In this time, he is learning about you and the rest of his family, and getting used to his surroundings. He is starting to learn about his home, in particular, and the rest of the world in general.

First days with a newborn

If you have had your baby in hospital, bringing him home when he is a few days old is an exciting milestone. But it can also be a bit unnerving. In hospital, there was always someone to turn to if you had a problem, and you did not have to worry about getting a meal, cleaning or any other domestic chores.

For the first few days, or even weeks, after you bring your baby home, life can seem to be an endless round of caring for his needs with little time for those of other members of the family, including the new mother. You will find that you spend entire days without achieving anything, and yet the baby may be sleeping up to 16 hours a day. The reason that you seem to do little else but attend to him is that his needs have to come first. If he cries, you have to pick him up because you are not sufficiently in tune with his cries to know whether he is genuinely miserable or simply a little grizzly (see Babies and crying, pp. 101–4). Nor is his feeding pattern likely to be so well established that you can judge when he is likely to need feeding again, particularly if you are breastfeeding (see chapter 3). And, you may be feeling tired, sore, weepy or simply very different now that the baby is finally here and your body is readjusting back to normal. All of these factors make it difficult to get any pattern to your days or nights – which is particularly frustrating if you were used to a job with a structure.

What you can do

In the first few weeks after your baby comes home, expect to spend 24 hours a day looking after him.

- Be flexible. Newborn babies do not run to a schedule, and you will only wear yourself out for no reason if you try to get yours to.
- Get as much rest as you can. It may seem alien to you to sleep in the middle of the day, but you probably did not get woken twice a night before the baby was born either.
- Forget about housework as far as possible. If you can get help here, try to do so, perhaps by getting someone to pick up a bag of ironing or clean for a couple of hours.
- This may be the time to buy a microwave, if you don't already have one, so that whatever time you manage to find for a meal, you can have something hot if you want. And if someone likes cooking, ask them to cook some dishes that can be frozen and reheated.
- Try to get some exercise, even if it's only pushing the baby round the park in the pram.

TAKING CARE OF YOUR BABY

In days when families were large and geographically close, older children took some of the responsibility for caring for younger siblings or cousins so that few children (and, especially, few girls) grew up unable to give a baby a bottle or change a wet nappy. Today, even these routine tasks can be daunting for many first-time mothers whose first experience of handling a tiny baby may be when the midwife puts him in her arms after the birth. Add to that, the lack of perhaps family or friends nearby to whom you can turn for advice and what should be a special time of nurturing and bonding can be worrying.

It helps to remember that this period does not last. Within weeks, feeding and nappy changing may take half the time they do to begin with and bathtime ceases to be an occasion to worry (will I drop the baby? will he slip out of my arms?) and starts to become a relaxing, sociable occasion.

Nappies

Changing a nappy is something you will do around 40 times a week in the first few weeks if you take sole charge of it, so try to share it out as much as possible (new parents spend seven hours a week on this task). It is important to change your baby's nappy every time it is wet or soiled to prevent soreness or nappy rash. The major causes of nappy rash (see pp. 96 and 163–4) are not changing your baby's nappy often enough so that urine and faeces remain in contact with his skin. Check your baby's nappy before and after a feed, unless you have just changed it.

Types of nappy

Today, you have more choice than ever before, but while you may be certain which type you want to use, it is worth considering the options.

Disposables

Used by about 70 per cent of new British parents, disposables are increasingly being made with the same type of technology as sanitary protection towels. This means disposable nappies have progressively more slimline and absorbent designs, and are often treated with a gel that draws fluid in to contain it within the nappy centre, away from the baby's skin.

PROS: Disposables are very convenient to use; simple to put on; are unlikely to leak; and are claimed to make nappy rash less likely. They also do not need washing or drying, which may be a bonus if you do not have a washing machine and/or tumble dryer, or anywhere to dry washing.

CONS: They are expensive – your baby is likely to get through 4,000 to 5,000 nappies before he is potty trained; there are also ecological concerns about their disposal. Disposables are not truly 'disposable': they go out with the domestic refuse into land fill sites that have to accommodate some 9 million soiled nappies every day. The plastic these nappies contain takes generations to biodegrade, especially if the nappies are wrapped in plastic sacks, and then in plastic bin liners as well. It is possible (although there is no proof) that viruses in the faeces many of these nappies contain may contaminate ground water supplies.

Disposables also contain wood pulp, which has caused a steep rise in the number of trees felled to cope with demand; also chlorine was used in the bleaching process (most manufacturers have stopped or switched to low chlorine bleaches). Chlorine produces dioxin, which damages wildlife and humans. YOU WILL NEED: A packet of 36 a week and some nappy sacks to wrap up soiled ones (alternatively, keep supermarket plastic and paper bags).

Shaped cloth nappies (reusables)

They are shaped to look like disposables, but made from soft, padded, often patterned cotton. Usually available in three or four sizes, these are a compromise between terries and disposables.

PROS: They are quicker and easier to put on than terries, since they fasten at the sides with velcro; they are more environmentally friendly than disposables since they do not use wood pulp, bleach, gel or take up space in landfill sites; they are less bulky than terries (some makes even come with a waterproof shell so do not require plastic pants); they are cheaper than disposables over a couple of years although the initial outlay is high.

Choosing disposables

Manufacturers are continually developing nappies that are more absorbent, better fitting and generally more comfortable for your baby. Most produce several sizes from those for premature babies through newborn, up until your child weighs around 25 kg (55 lb). Buy the size that is most appropriate – a nappy that is too big may leak and one that is too small may be uncomfortably tight.

Apart from those for very tiny babies, there are different nappies for boys and girls: boys' have more padding at the front than girls'. Many manufacturers have also now introduced 'trainer nappies' for toddlers, which can be pulled up and down like pants so that children have the security of a nappy, but can start to register that they may need to use the toilet (see also Toilet training, pp. 189–90). For older children, too, special night-time nappies, which are thicker and more absorbent than those for use during the day, may be worth considering if your child cannot seem to rid himself of his night nappy.

Changing your baby's nappy

Always have everything you need ready to hand before you start. Wash your hands.

- changing mat
- clean nappy
- warm water or nappy wipes
- cottonwool
- barrier cream
- talcum powder (optional)

Unless you are changing the baby on the floor, keep a hand on him at all times. Even tiny babies can twist off a changing table when your back is turned. If your baby is older and tends to wriggle, try putting a mobile above the changing mat.

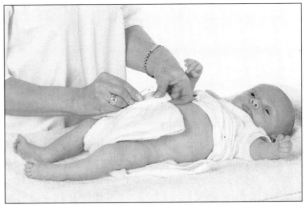

1 Take off trousers or leggings and socks and open the legs of his sleepsuit or vest and roll it up to around chest height so that it is well out of the way. Undo the nappy.

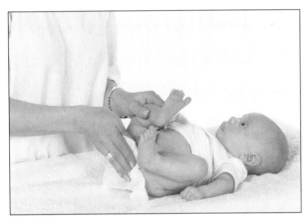

2 If the nappy is dirty, try to keep as much inside as possible. Fold it up and put it in a sack. Using cottonwool and warm water or a wipe, clean his bottom thoroughly. Clean girls from front to back. Dry the baby thoroughly with more cottonwool.

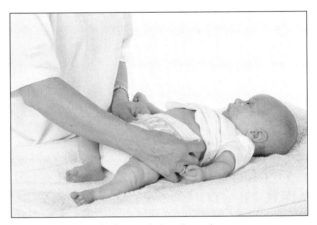

3 Let him kick for a while, then slip a new nappy under his bottom. If you want to use a barrier cream, do so, but wipe your hands thoroughly afterward: if you get cream on the tapes of a disposable, they won't stick.

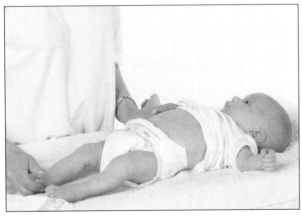

4 Open the tapes and stick them down. Get the baby dressed again. Roll his vest or bodysuit down and fasten, then replace sleepsuit or leggings. Wash your hands.

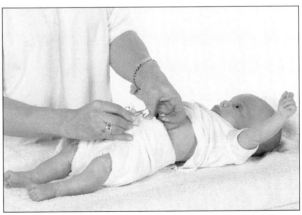

5 If you are using a terry, slip a nappy and liner under the baby, then pin carefully through all layers. Put on waterproof pants, then dress the baby. Wash your hands.

Cons: Like terries, they require routine disinfecting, soaking, washing and drying; they may not be as absorbent as ultra disposables; you may need to try a few before you find the ones that suit your baby best; they are more expensive than terries.

You will need: About 15 reusables should be enough, disposable nappy liners, plastic pants, a lidded bucket, and nappy solution or vinegar for disinfecting soiled nappies. You will also need a washing machine and – possibly – a tumble dryer.

Terry cloth nappies

Traditional terry nappies are used with or without soft liners. (You can use muslin squares instead of terries for newborns, but use a liner with these.)

Pros: These are cheaper than disposables, even taking washing machine use and powder into account; one size fits all; they are also kinder to the environment (but obviously you use more energy in washing them and tumbling them dry).

Cons: They take longer to put on than disposables and also have to be folded and pinned (traditionally, midwives used to learn eight different ways to fold and pin, and even learning one can take a bit of practice); they are bulkier than both disposables and reusables, both for the baby to wear and for you to carry spares when you are out and about (and you must carry a soiled one home); they may also be less absorbent than the best disposables; and they need laundering (unless you use a nappy service).

You will need: About 24 nappies, nappy pins, disposable nappy liners, plastic pants, a lidded bucket, and nappy solution or vinegar for disinfecting soiled nappies. If you do not use a nappy service, you will also need a washing machine and – possibly – a tumble dryer.

Nappy services

If you are using terries, it is worth considering a nappy service, an idea imported from the United States. These companies supply you with clean nappies and a bin for dirty nappies, which they collect when they deliver fresh nappies to your doorstep, usually once a week. The costs are slightly lower than if you use disposables, but you do not have to do anything, even buy the nappies. Contact the Association of Nappy Services (see Useful Contacts, pp. 390–3) for your nearest one.

Folding a terry nappy

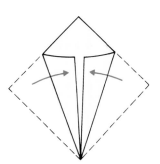

Lay the nappy flat, then fold in opposite corners at an oblique angle.

Bring the triangle at the top in to meet the other corners.

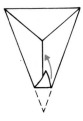

Fold the two layers at the bottom point in toward the middle.

Adjust this fold to make the nappy the right size for the baby.

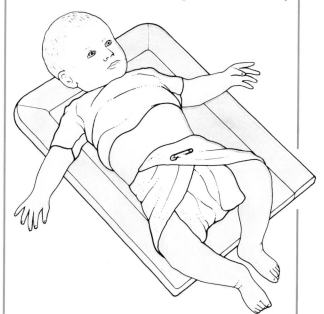

The kite fold (above) is one of the simplest to master, suitable for both girls and boys, and enables you to lengthen or shorten the nappy to make it fit your baby. It is a good idea to fold a few nappies at a time so that there is always one ready for use.

Do terries cause nappy rash?

Reusables and terries are often said to cause more nappy rash than disposables. It seems likely, however, that both the waterproof plastic pants babies wear with reusable nappies and the plastic layer of disposables can create ideal damp, warm conditions for bacteria to produce ammonia, which is the substance that causes nappy rash. If nappies are changed often enough, this tends not to be a problem.

Reusables and terries are not as absorbent as disposables. You can, however, use additional nappy liners, change more frequently during the day and try double nappying at night.

Points to remember

- Whichever type you choose, it is worth having a few disposables for when you are out and about.
- Many hospitals no longer supply you with nappies while you are there. It is worth checking beforehand and taking some disposables with you when you go in.
- Shop around for the best and most effective buy and, as long as you have storage space, purchase disposables in bulk (some companies and large department stores deliver free).
- Do not buy too many 'newborn' nappies, as babies grow out of this size quickly.
- All babies are different. Help find out which type of nappy suits your baby best by taking advantage of free sample packs and swapping a few of your nappies with different brands from other mothers.
- Advice on reusables, from making washing easier to finding a stockist, is available from WEN (see Useful Contacts, pp. 390–3).

Points about changing

- Put the mat on a surface at upper chest height, so you do not bend your back (most changing tables are not made at back friendly heights). Raise yours up if necessary.
- If you are changing the baby on the floor, squat or sit so that your back remains straight, rather than hunched over.
- Beds, especially hospital beds unless you can manage to crank them up, are usually at a bad height for nappy changing.
- Keep cream well away from your baby's hands and feet. A wriggly baby can knock a pot over, which makes a terrible mess.

How to bath your baby

Have everything ready before you start. You will need:
- bath
- baby soap or bath-care liquid
- cottonwool
- bowl with boiled, cooled water
- baby lotion or wipes
- two towels
- apron and/or towel to keep yourself dry
- clean nappy
- barrier cream
- clean clothes

1 Fill the bath. Undress the baby and wrap him in a towel, then wash his face as if you were topping and tailing (see p. 98). Hold your baby's head over the bath and gently wash his hair, using water from the bath and babybath or baby shampoo.

2 Rinse his hair with water from the bath and towel dry it. Unwrap your baby and carefully lift him into the bath with both hands, supporting his head and shoulders with your arm and gripping his outer arm with one hand and leg with the other.

KEEPING YOUR BABY CLEAN

Cleanliness and good hygiene are essential throughout your child's early months and years because babies and young children are more vulnerable to vomiting and diarrhoea than older children or adults, and these illnesses can have much more serious consequences (see pp. 163, 167, and 375). Developing a habit of cleanliness is a good idea – you may feel you are already quite fastidious but it is surprising how many people do not always wash their hands before handling food, for instance.

Bathing your baby

The first bath is often an anxious occasion for first-time parents as they learn to handle their vulnerable new baby in water. Usually you will be given a chance to bath your baby under the supervision of a midwife at the hospital or at home when he is anything up to a week old to give you confidence.

It is not really necessary to bath a baby every single day, especially as some small babies don't enjoy the bath in their first few weeks. Others find it obviously enjoyable and bathtime can be a relaxing event for both baby and parent(s). Find a time that suits you and your baby best – it is a good idea to do it during a period of natural wakefulness before a feed, but not when he's really hungry, which may or may not be in the early evening. This often helps to settle a baby down for the evening, allowing parents a quiet time for themselves, and can be a relaxing part of a coming-home routine if one of you is working. If you have older children, however, you may find it easier to bath the baby in the morning perhaps when children are at school or nursery so that the bath can take place without distractions.

Bathing safety and hygiene

- Choose a warm room (it does not have to be the bathroom) without draughts.
- Make sure the bath is on a firm surface at the right height for you; you should not have to hunch over.
- Wash your hands thoroughly before you start and make sure the bath is clean.
- Assemble everything you need beforehand and make sure all is within easy reach.
- Pour the cold water in the bath first, then add hot. There is a risk of scalding your baby if you put the hot water in first. The water should feel warm to the touch on your wrist or elbow, not to fingers which can withstand much hotter temperatures.

3 Let him get used to the sensation of the water on his body for a few minutes while you continue to support his head and arm with one hand. With your free hand, start to gently wash his body, taking special care with all the creases.

4 If he enjoys it and the water and air temperature are still warm, let him kick for a while as you 'chat' to him. He may like having his tummy gently splashed with water, or prefer to have a toy to hold and play with. Be guided by him.

5 When you sense he has had enough, or runs the risk of getting cold, lift him out carefully with both hands. Remember that he will be slippery. Wrap him immediately in a towel and cuddle him close. Sit comfortably and dry him on your lap.

Topping and tailing

On days when you are not bathing your baby you can simply 'top and tail'. As with bathing, find a time when you and your baby can be fairly relaxed about it; it is sensible to do it after your baby has had a long period of sleep as this is likely to be the time when his nappy area will need thorough cleaning.

How to top and tail

Collect all the equipment together and wash your hands before you start.

- cottonwool
- boiled, cooled water in a bowl
- baby lotion
- soft facecloth or sponge – use for face only; keep a separate cloth for your baby's nappy area
- bowl of warm water with bath preparation
- small towel
- clean nappy
- clean clothes (as necessary)

You can 'top and tail' in a warm room on your lap or on a changing mat laid on a firm surface. Never leave your baby alone on a changing mat on a high surface – even when he is very tiny he is capable of rolling off it.

Protecting your back

Make sure that you bath, change and top and tail your baby at a comfortable height for your back. Baby-bath stands and changing tables are often not at the right level.

Stand at a changing table before you buy. If you are buying a bath, make sure it has a plug in the bottom, so you can stand it in your bath to use it, then easily let the water out, or place the baby bath next to the adult bath or sink for easy emptying. Heaving a full baby bath off its stand and carrying it across the room to empty it is one of the easiest ways to damage your back.

The umbilicus

After the umbilical cord is cut at birth, the remaining stump is clamped; it takes between a few days and a couple of weeks to dry up and come away completely, leaving a typical 'tummy button'. Your midwife will show you how to clean the area around the clamp in the first days after the birth. The hospital or midwife will also supply you with surgical spirit swabs and antiseptic powder with which to clean and dust the umbilicus to prevent infection. It is safe to bath your

Topping and tailing

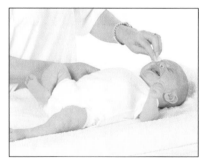

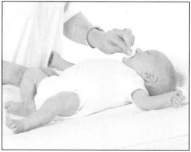

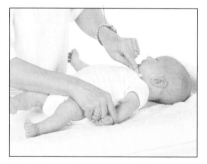

1 Take off all clothes except his vest or bodysuit and wash his face using boiled, cooled water – there is no need to add soap or babybath to the water for his face – and cottonwool. Wipe the eyes gently from the inside corner to the outer edge, using a separate piece of cottonwool for each eye. If there is a lot of dried mucus, repeat. (Your baby may not like this process.)

2 Carefully wipe any dried mucus away from his nostrils with separate pieces of cottonwool. Do not poke inside your baby's nose with cottonbuds (or anything else) – this is unnecessary and may damage the delicate skin inside. There is no need to clean inside your baby's mouth until his teeth appear, but wipe the outside with a clean piece of cottonwool.

3 Clean the creases of his neck gently with warm, boiled water and cottonwool (do not use soap). Pat dry with the corner of a towel, making sure that the neck creases are not left damp. If there is any ear wax visible in the opening of the ear clear this away with a cottonbud. But don't push a bud right into the ear – this is unnecessary and dangerous as it could damage the ear drum.

Unhappy bathers

Some babies love baths from the start, others take longer to get used to them. Some like having a bath, but cry at hairwashing and vice versa. If your baby really does not like being bathed, top and tail him as far as possible, while you investigate ways to make bathtime more acceptable.

- If your baby does not seem to feel safe or comfortable in a baby bath, try lying him on a large, 'cut out' sponge (available from the baby departments of major stores, and specialist baby equipment shops). This also works well in a big bath.

- Consider taking him into the big bath with you and hold him close to your breast while you wash him gently. Make sure the water is much cooler than usual, have a nonslip mat in the bath and take extra care getting into and out of the bath while you are holding the baby. (The first couple of times you do this, try to have someone else in the room with you.)

- If your baby is not happy with any of these options, try taking his clothes and nappy off, wrapping him in a soft towel previously warmed on the radiator, then gently flannel bathing him with warm water bit by bit, cuddled on your lap. Use a different flannel (or wetted piece of cottonwool) for his bottom, and the rest of his body and use a separate piece of cottonwool for each eye.

baby before the umbilicus has healed or the stump has dropped off, provided you dry the area thoroughly afterward.

You may be a little nervous of cleaning behind the stump as it will look a little sore, but this is important. If any redness develops or the umbilicus area 'weeps' or any pus appears, contact your doctor at once as this is a sign of infection.

The foreskin

A baby boy's foreskin cannot be pulled back at birth, so do not try to do so or you could tear the skin,

4 Wipe his hands with a sponge, cloth or piece of cottonwool and dry them with a towel. If the room is warm and he seems happy, you can leave him in his vest while you clean his nappy area (see p. 94). If not, put the top half of a clean sleepsuit or a cardigan or jumper on him before you continue. If he is unhappy, play for a few minutes or give him a toy to hold and look at.

Cutting your baby's nails

A young baby's nails are very soft and flake off easily, but can still scratch – so keep an eye on the length of your baby's nails. Some parents find biting off 'hang nails' simpler than using scissors as it is easy to catch the skin on tiny fingers even with baby nail scissors.

Sit your baby in your lap. Using small, round-ended nail scissors, cut the nails straight across when they have grown beyond the fingertip.

Cut toenails in the same way. If you find it difficult to hold and cut, try cutting them when he is lying on his changing mat or while he is asleep.

causing later scarring. It could also introduce infection if the area becomes soiled with faeces. The foreskin separates from the glans of the penis during childhood; in the meantime it actually protects the tip of the penis from infection and from any irritation caused by wet nappies. Occasionally it may become sore and inflamed if nappy rash has already developed (see pp. 163–4); apply plenty of barrier cream in this case. However, if soreness or redness persists or you are worried, contact your doctor or health visitor who may recommend a suitable antibiotic cream to help the healing process.

Getting your baby dressed

Choosing clothes wisely for your baby in the first place makes dressing him easier than it might otherwise be.

- Make sure that anything that must go over his head has a broad, 'envelope' neck or buttons along the shoulder line. Otherwise, avoid over-the-head designs as far as possible.
- Nappy changing is easier if you choose suits that have poppers right down the legs.
- If you buy trousers, make sure that they are loose and have firm but stretchy elastic waists.
- Avoid anything with lots of tiny buttons.

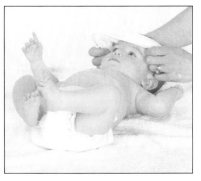

1 Stretch the neck of his vest and slip it over his head, supporting his head as you do so.

2 Holding one sleeve open, take your baby's hand and gently guide it through.

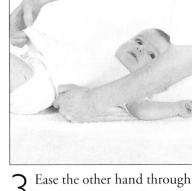

3 Ease the other hand through the armhole and pull the vest down. Do up the poppers.

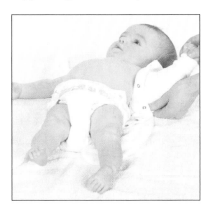

1 Lie your baby on the stretch suit. Scrunch one sleeve up, and guide the baby's arm through.

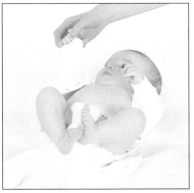

2 Scrunch up the other sleeve in one hand; with your other hand, ease the baby's arm through.

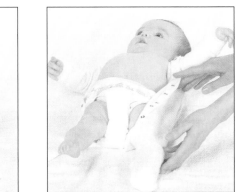

3 Gently bend your baby's leg at the knee and ease it down into one of the legs of the suit.

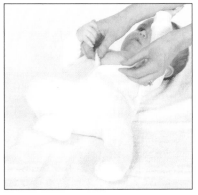

4 Do the same with his other leg, then do up the suit. Put on a cardigan if necessary.

BABIES AND CRYING

Babies cry in all sorts of ways, from a small amount of grumbling (perhaps just before they go to sleep) to screaming loudly for several hours. Naturally, when your baby cries, you will be disturbed and distressed.

Babies also cry for all sorts of reasons. When they are very tiny, it is the only way they can communicate their needs. It can be something of a matter of trial and error when your baby is small to determine what he needs, but among the most common reasons for crying are:

He is bored or frustrated
Some babies seem to need more attention and activity than others and hate being left on their own. Try to keep your baby company as much as possible.

He is feeling lonely
He may want to be cuddled, talked to or carried, or propped up in a baby bouncer or pram where he can see you as you work around the house.

He is uncomfortable
Perhaps he is too hot or too cold (see pp. 106 and 128), his nappy may be too tight, or soiled, or the clothes next to his skin are irritating him.

He is tired
If he refuses to sleep in his cot but you sense that this is the problem, take him for a walk in the pram, or put him in a sling and go for a walk, or strap him in his car seat and go for a drive.

He is hungry or thirsty
Feed him or give him cooled, boiled water. The comfort of sucking may help, even if he is not hungry.

He is unwell
If the crying persists and/or you are at all worried, contact your GP. Doctors always take potential illness in small babies very seriously and prefer to see small babies sooner rather than later.

He is in pain
This may not be from anything major – colic and wind both cause real pain (see also pp. 104 and 162).

Above: Crying is the most obvious way in which your baby can let you know that all is not right with his world. In time, you will recognize the significance of his different types of crying.

He is alarmed
Many things might make him nervous or startle him, including such routine happenings as being bathed. There is also evidence that even the tiniest babies may experience bad dreams or relive their births for a while: if so, cuddling and your soothing voice are the best remedies.

He needs more peace than most
Some babies have a relatively low sensory threshold and do not enjoy a lot of handling and stimulation.

He had a difficult birth
A baby is likely to cry more than average for a couple of weeks after a birth that involved complications. If compression of his head was a problem – if he was a forceps delivery, or his head looks misshapen – some mothers have found a cranial osteopath helpful (see Useful Contacts, pp. 390–3). Some pain-relieving drugs given to mothers during labour seem to affect certain babies more than others, making them more irritable and generally harder to settle for the first few days or weeks.

He was premature

The nervous systems of premature babies may still be slightly immature, and after the bright lights and noise of a special care unit, many initially dislike the relative peace of home. Light and white noise in the background – say a radio tuned off station – can help, as can music played at a low volume, until he gets used to his new environment.

He has an allergy

This is unusual, and if your baby is allergic, there are usually additional symptoms such as diarrhoea or skin rashes. See pp. 160–1.

He is a high-need baby

Some babies are just high-need or extra-sensitive, crying a good deal not because there is anything especially wrong but because this is simply the way that they are. Such babies naturally need more attention and nurturing than other babies to keep them happy.

When all else fails

If your baby is inconsolable and you cannot bear his crying any longer, but you are sure there is nothing really wrong with him:

- Wrap him up and get out of the house with him in the pram.
- Get help: for immediate help, ring a telephone helpline. Then talk to your GP or health visitor. If you really seem to be getting nowhere, keep asking.
- When you really cannot bear any more, put your baby gently in his cot and go into another room for 10 minutes. Do not feel guilty about this. You have your needs too.
- The fact that your baby cries more than most does not mean you are not such a good parent as someone whose baby sleeps all day. Whether you have a calm or a high-need baby is a matter of luck.
- Experiment with the package of suggestions, talk to other parents about what helped them, and follow your instincts: you will almost certainly be right.
- Remember – it really does get better.

Your idea of excessive crying may differ from somebody else's, but you are not alone if your baby does seem to cry a great deal: about 1 in 10 does. Crying really is not due to any incompetence on your part (except in the most obvious cases – you have stuck the nappy tape to his tummy, for example, or put it on too tight).

If crying is caused by colic, your baby will have stopped by about three months; most other types of crying peak between about two and nine months, and decline fairly rapidly after that.

Crying is not something to feel alone with. Organizations which can help include CRYSIS – which has trained telephone volunteer helpers who themselves were the parents of crying babies – and Parentline (their trained volunteers also are parents themselves). Both can offer a sympathetic ear at the moment you may need it most and practical advice (see Useful Contacts, pp. 390–3).

Remember, crying really does get better. And with a bit of help, you can either find the best coping strategies around – or see the situation improve faster than you had dared to hope.

What you can do

You know your baby best, so if he is not generally a crying baby and starts, or if he is often irritable but this is more than usual, check these factors first and take the appropriate action. If you are at all concerned, contact your health visitor or GP.

Is he hungry?

Breastfeed or bottlefeed.

Is he thirsty?

Breastfeed or offer previously boiled and cooled water in a bottle or on a spoon.

Is he in pain?

Try massaging his tummy (see Colic, pp. 104 and 162) or place a warm (not hot) hot-water bottle covered in a cloth on his tummy and hold it there, or cuddle him upright against your shoulder, so the bottle is gently sandwiched between his abdomen and your chest.

You could also try carrying him around in a sling, rocking him or cuddling.

What fathers can do

It is almost traditional for fathers to feel left out of the very close physical and emotional bond between a mother and her new baby. They may also have mixed feelings about breastfeeding. It can help to not only talk to each other about this as much as possible, but to share the tasks of caring for the baby.

Fathers who are allowed to build up their own strong, loving bond with their babies are less likely to feel jealous and left out of the mother–baby relationship.

Actively encourage him to feed (if the baby accepts a bottle), bath, change, burp, cuddle, sing to, walk around with and generally have the baby near him as much as possible. Babies of all ages like watching or just feeling their father's presence nearby while he is working, gardening, cooking or painting, reclining and reading or looking at the TV, while the baby lies on his chest, or is rocked to and fro in his pram by his foot.

Fathers do not do things the way mothers do. But unless the baby is clearly uncomfortable, a

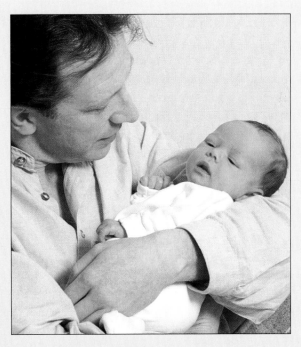

father's way is just as good as a mother's. Most fathers initially feel helpless and under-confident around small babies. If they do not become physically involved with them, these feelings remain, as do the resentments. Allow your baby the comfort of a loving father.

Breastfeeding or offering a bottle may help, although if he is in real pain, he may be uninterested; you could try gripe water or a dilute herbal remedy such as camomile tea.

Ear infections cause persistent, miserable crying, occasionally punctuated by silence as the baby falls asleep exhausted, which then starts again as he shifts position and wakes. If this pattern fits, suspect an ear infection and contact your GP immediately. On his or her advice you may be able to give Calpol (liquid paracetamol) until you can see the GP who will almost certainly prescribe antibiotics.

Always call your GP if your baby:
* seems to be getting no better
* actually appears worse
* has a temperature (sponge him with tepid water in the meantime)
* is crying in a different way than usual
* seems very lethargic
* does not seem to know you.

Is he uncomfortable?

Check his nappy is not wet, dirty or on too tight, or leave him to kick without a nappy for a while (put him on a towel to protect the carpet or bed). Check his temperature (see pp. 106 and 128). If he seems hot, remove some clothes or take him out in the pram; if he feels too cold, wrap him in a shawl or clean towel pre-warmed on the radiator and cuddle him close, or put on a hat, socks or mittens.

Check for clothing rashes and nappy rashes.

If your baby is lying down, see if he prefers to be propped up, or placed in a different position.

Is he extra sensitive?

Handle him quietly and talk to him gently and try to keep visitors to a minimum. Ask siblings to be gentle around him.

Do not overwhelm him with sights, sounds, movements and other stimulation, and try to get into a routine so that feeds, baths and outings happen at roughly the same time each day.

Is he tired but fighting sleep?

Offer breast, dummy or bottle; or rock him in your arms or in the pram. Try moving him to a quieter room or a noisier room, perhaps putting on a baby cassette with some gently soothing music or leave a clock with a regular tick in his room.

Walk up and down with him in a dimly lit room, at a pace of one step per second, patting him very gently on his back at the same speed.

Leave him to cry for a short time but if the crying does not diminish from loud to sniffling within five to ten minutes, cuddle again and rock.

As a last resort, wrap him up, strap him in his seat and take him for a car ride.

Is he generally irritable?

Carry him in a sling on your back or front, put him in a bouncy chair and rock it with your foot or take him out in the pram.

Rock him in your arms or the pram, gently talking or singing to him. Dance to gentle music, holding your baby in your arms or up against your shoulder. Try a change of scenery – a different room, the garden, balcony, having a warm bath, or gently massage his back, feet or head.

If he is irritable for more than a few hours and nothing seems to be working, consult your health visitor or GP, or a suitably qualified practitioner of complementary medicine.

Colic

Colic is characterized by regular attacks of piercing screaming, which tend to occur at the same time (or times) each day – usually early evening. While these attacks last, it is extremely difficult to comfort the baby for more than a few minutes at a time. Both the crying, and the difficulty of soothing the baby, can be exceptionally upsetting for you too.

Your baby is likely to have colic, rather than be crying for another reason, if:

- the crying is accompanied by your baby drawing up his legs as if in pain;
- there are loud rumblings from his abdomen, he is burping and/or passing plenty of wind;
- he is temporarily soothed by feeding, but this seems to make it worse in the long run. See p. 162 for advice on coping with colic.

SLEEPLESS BABIES, EXHAUSTED PARENTS

Definitions of what constitutes a 'sleep problem' vary, but basically if your baby's sleeping patterns are causing a definite problem for him – or you – then he has a sleep problem. Such problems cannot generally be said to exist until your baby is around six months old: before that age, most babies wake at least once in the night because they are hungry. After this time, however, problem sleepers usually fall into three categories:

- the won't go to sleepers
- the repeated night wakers
- the very early (4 am to 5 am) risers.

The effect on your baby

Whichever category fits your baby, the chances are that his lack of sleep will have few noticeable effects on him. He may suffer a little short-term irritability the next day, but if he is tired from his antics in the night (and some babies seem not to be), he will probably nap for a little longer than normal in the day to compensate.

As there is no specific research on the long-term effects of lack of deep sleep on babies and young children, it is difficult to know whether this may cause long-term problems. But it is believed to be better for them to sleep properly; if they do not, they may be missing out on the deep sleep that fosters optimum growth and physical or mental development.

How much are babies meant to sleep?

Babies' needs vary enormously, but as a rough guide (including naps) your baby may sleep in the region of:

Week 1	16½ hours
1 month	15½ hours
3 months	15 hours
6 months	14½ hours
9 months	14 hours
12 months	13¾ hours
18 months	13½ hours

The effect on you

If your baby falls into one of these categories, the effects on you may be profound. They include:

- continual tiredness, with the result that you become obsessional about sleep
- your parenting skills may be affected
- you may feel inadequate as a parent
- your relationship with your partner may suffer
- your other children may suffer from your lack of energy for parenting
- clinical depression is strongly linked to long-term exhaustion and sleep deprivation
- you may develop negative feelings for your baby, and the guilt associated with them.

Babies' sleep problems can turn a loving, rational parent into an exhausted wreck. Human beings cannot function properly on insufficient sleep. It can put terrific strain on relationships within families and has even been cited as a cause of marital breakdown and child abuse.

Some sleepless nights are inevitable with young babies, and bearable. But continual interruptions two, three or four times a night, leading to deprivation of sleep for months (even years) are not. People whose children did not behave in this way naturally have no idea of the distress and potential damage it causes.

Below: Cradling a tiny baby in your arms as you talk quietly to him may make him sufficiently relaxed to fall asleep.

They tend to dismiss it as an exaggeration on the part of the sufferers or even an indication that they are not doing a very good job, which can be almost as up-setting as the lack of sleep itself.

Parents used to be told simply to wait until their child grew out of sleep problems. Now a greater understanding of this type of problem has produced a broad range of potential solutions and coping mechanisms, ranging from baby behavioural training and drugs to support networks involving other parents.

The good news is that, today, it is almost always possible to find the combination of factors – or the one thing – that works for you and your baby. Do not despair, and do not try and struggle through on your own. Get help.

The facts about sleep

Babies should be sleeping through the night (at least six hours) more nights than not by the time they are around six months. If yours is not, something in his routine, or response to his night waking, needs adjustment. If he wakes and wants to be fed, it is now likely to be more of a comfortable habit than a necessity. (Specific sleep disorders, such as sleep apnoea, can also be solved with the help of a specialist doctor, see Useful Contacts, pp. 390–3.)

Babies have more potential for waking up at night than adults. This is because people sleep in a series of cycles. At the end of each cycle, most people stir slightly, stretch, wake briefly then fall asleep again. The brief waking happens every 90 minutes to adults – but every 60 minutes in babies. Not only that, but adults have developed the ability to put themselves back to sleep when they wake. Babies and infants need to learn this skill. If, however, babies are automatically picked up or fed each time they wake, it is arguable that they may be slower to learn how to put themselves back to sleep and remain reliant on you for (repeated) help at night, for longer.

Physical problems

It is worth checking that your baby is not waking repeatedly because of a physical problem which needs treatment, or an environmental one which can be easily resolved. Check:

- Is his room too hot or cold?
- Is he too hot or cold: check blankets, sleepsuit and so on.
- Is he kicking off his bedclothes at night and waking up cold? Try a warm sleepsuit with only light bedclothes.
- Is his night-time nappy – and undersheet – repeatedly sopping? Perhaps cut back a bit on late night drinks, or consider double nappying or putting an absorbent pad inside the nappy.
- Might the washing powder you use for his night-clothes and bedding irritate his skin? Try a very gentle brand, and double rinse in the machine each time.
- Is he nervous of the dark? Try leaving a dim night light on by his bed.
- Is the room too light at night, and disturbing him? Try it darker.
- Is he bored or lonely in his cot at night? Try adding a musical toy or two that he can operate

by pressing, or pulling a string on the side of the cot, cuddly toys, an interesting mobile, pictures stuck to the inside of the cot.
- Has there been an emotional upset in the family recently, has either you or your partner had to go away for a while, have you moved to a new home? Is there some trouble at home?

Your baby could also have an underlying medical problem that is preventing him sleeping well. These can include:
- Mild eczema, which can be sufficiently uncomfortable as to keep him awake at night. If so contact your GP and National Eczema Society (see Useful Contacts, pp. 390–3) for prompt help and advice.
- A mild recurring ear or bladder infection.
- Recurrent nappy rash. This may begin to sting in the small hours as a nappy becomes soggy with urine. See Nappy rash (pp. 163–4) and put on a great deal of cream at night as both prevention and treatment.

If none of these seems to be causing a problem, ask your GP to give your child a full physical check up.

What you can do to help yourself

- Ignore parents whose babies sleep right through the night.
- Cat nap whenever your baby sleeps, and go to bed when he does, even if it is 7.30 pm – anything to get a full, uninterrupted three- or four-hour sleep.
- Take turns to be on night duty with your partner – again so you can both get an uninterrupted few hours at least once a night. Sleep in separate parts of the house if necessary. If you are breastfeeding, express some milk so that someone else can give one feed. After the first few weeks, this will not affect your milk production (see p. 77).
- Do the same with any friends or relatives prepared to help, rather than just offer advice.
- Ask for and accept help of all types (baby minding for a couple of hours, shopping, cleaning) to conserve what energy you have.

What you can do to help the baby

Although you cannot expect him to sleep through the night until he is six months old, there are things you can do from the start to promote good sleep habits later.

- Try not to feed, rock or cuddle your baby until he is sound asleep, and then lay him in his cot. This may make him develop the habit of only being able to go back to sleep if he has been suckled, rocked or otherwise had attention from you.
- Make a clear distinction between night and day.
- Have a set bedtime routine as soon as possible, so that your baby has plenty of cues to recognize that bed is coming. These may include: a warm bath, dim lights, a feed, a cuddle, a particular comfort blanket or soft toy, and/or a special song or tune from you or played by a tape or mechanical toy. Round off with 'goodnight' and a kiss. (This is seldom practical for the first few weeks as very new babies tend initially to show no pattern or routine, but it becomes easier after about two months.)
- Avoid anything noisy, or exciting in the hour before bedtime. This includes boisterous play, loud music, or evening visitors who want to hold and play with the baby. If siblings want to play with him, it has to be low key.
- If you need to feed the baby at night, keep the lights dim, or do not switch them on at all; talk in a calm, low voice or do not talk at all. Do not change his nappy unless it is very wet (rather than slightly damp) or soiled. Keep the baby warm and comfortable – perhaps feed him cuddled inside your dressing gown. Wind him gently. Alternatively take him into your bed and feed him there.

Many parents find that sharing their bed with their baby, or with the cot placed flush next to their bed, perhaps with the side adjacent to you down, works well. There is no danger of you rolling over and squashing your baby, as long as you have taken no sleeping or recreational drugs or any alcohol. (If your baby shares your bed, he will receive the warmth from your bodies so only needs to be dressed lightly. A fluffy sleepsuit would make him far too hot.)

Changes in sleeping patterns

If your baby was a good sleeper and suddenly starts to wake up again at night, there may be an obvious cause. A bad cold or earache, or other minor health problem may make him sufficiently irritable to disturb his usual pattern. Holidays, too, upset normal routines with perhaps later nights and later starts in the morning, and can throw babies out of gear.

Some babies have problems when their first teeth start to come through, then when the molars make their appearance between 12 and 18 months. Preparations such as Bonjela and Teejel, and homeopathic teething powders (available from your pharmacist or homeopath) may help, as does Calpol (liquid paracetamol).

Once you have tackled all the obvious causes of sleeplessness, you may find gentle behaviour modification works. Do not try to use this technique until your baby is at least six months. Babies are increasingly receptive to such techniques from six months onward.

The checking routine

This technique is used by many parents who contact CRYSIS for help, with largely positive results. If you are thinking of trying it with your baby, consult an experienced health visitor, your GP or speak to CRYSIS first for fuller details. You may also initially need some support from them if you decide to try it.

Before you start:

- Make sure that both you and your baby are well.
- Choose a time when you have no major commitments or pressures.
- Try and clear four or five days – or begin the routine on a Friday night, with, if possible, the following Monday off.
- Discuss what you are doing in detail with your partner, your health visitor, GP and any relevant help organization.
- If you have not already done so, establish a clear bedtime routine first.

How checking works

If your baby cries after being put to bed, allow him to do so undisturbed for a set time – between 3 and 10 minutes. Return to his room and 'check' on him. Avoid eye contact, but tuck him in gently, say goodnight and leave within 30 seconds. Do not pick him up, cuddle or feed. Do this as many times as it takes before he falls back to sleep. Remain gentle, but firm.

Your baby may cry for some time (anything between half an hour and several hours) but continue to return, check and leave. This will reassure your baby that he has not been forgotten or abandoned, but that nothing enjoyable like a cuddle or a drink is forthcoming. He will conclude that it is not worth the effort. However, be prepared for a battle of wills.

You may find a noticeable improvement in a couple of days; it may take longer. The success rate of the approach (in that it brings at least a substantial improvement, or sleeping through the night properly) is about 90 per cent.

Making it work

Checking does not work if you (or your partner) cannot stay firm. Keep a sleep chart of how long your baby is awake and how long he cries: improvements may give you the impetus to carry on.

It is upsetting to listen to your baby cry. Consider ear plugs, going to another room and watching TV or playing music for the time between checks. And, think positive. Go through all the things you will be able to do again if you can get some more sleep. Try not to feel guilty. Interrupted sleep is preventing you from functioning properly, and it is not especially good for your baby either. The whole family will benefit when you can sleep through the night.

WHAT ABOUT YOU?

While you are busy getting used to caring for your baby's everyday needs, in the six weeks immediately after your baby's delivery (often referred to as the puerperium), your body gradually starts to return to its pre-pregnant state. Although a woman's body is never exactly the same as it was before the birth of a baby, the changes you can expect in this period include the following:

- You will be losing blood through your vagina. Known as lochia, this is coming from the raw site on the wall of your womb to which the placenta was formerly attached. It helps to wear soft, thick, comfortable sanitary towels (rather than the harder very slimline ones) and wash the area regularly with cool water, then pat it dry with toilet paper to prevent it remaining constantly moist and sticky. For the first 24–48 hours, this bleeding is normally quite heavy, but if it seems to you to be excessive, ask advice from your midwife or doctor. After a couple of days, the blood loss slows, gradually becoming reddish-brown, then brown. It should fade completely within four to six weeks. If it starts to become red again after fading away, consult your doctor as this may be an indication that there is still a piece of placenta remaining. If so, it will have to be removed.
- Your breasts begin to swell considerably with fluids, including colostrum and blood, between the second and fourth days after delivery, as you begin to produce milk.
- Between two and six days after the birth, you may develop some measure of temporary postnatal 'blues' (see box on p. 120). The symptoms include weepiness, anxiety and irritability. This feeling is partly due to the profound changes in hormonal levels your body is undergoing – those hormones which maintained your pregnancy and fuelled your labour plummet, while those that produce breast milk rise rapidly. Nine out of 10 women who experience the blues find they pass within a couple of days. If they do not, let your GP, midwife or health visitor know.
- Your uterus gradually shrinks back to its normal compact size. Immediately after birth, it weighs some 1.2 kg (2¾ lb), a week later 500 g (1 lb),

and after six weeks have elapsed, it has returned to its non-pregnant weight of around 70 g (2½ oz).

- Your cervix, which during delivery opened up so that the small hole in its centre – the os – measured 10 cm (4 in) across, closes up again. It may now be a slightly irregular shape, and the os is a slit rather than a dimple in the middle.
- Your blood volume returns to normal after about three weeks; during pregnancy this increased by around 50 per cent.
- One in eight women is ovulating and able to become pregnant again as early as six weeks after the birth; this proportion rises to one in three after three months.

Temporary discomforts

It may be a relief to no longer be pregnant, but you may suffer discomfort during this postnatal period. Some problems, such as those caused by stitches from tearing or episiotomy, do not affect everyone; others such as vaginal bleeding are common to all newly delivered mothers. The good news, however, is that most discomforts can be significantly reduced quite easily and all are temporary.

Afterpains

You may feel pain as your womb slowly contracts back to its former size. So-called afterpains last for up to a week and range from being uncomfortable (like a mild period pain), to almost as bad as labour pains. You may not be conscious of them at all with your first child, but they tend to become progressively sharper after the birth of subsequent babies.

Afterpains are especially noticeable if you are breastfeeding because the hormone stimulated by your baby's sucking helps your womb muscles contract. They may be particularly uncomfortable if you had your baby by caesarean.

WHAT YOU CAN DO Strong painkillers may be the only effective treatment. If you are in hospital, ask for them; if you are at home, ring the doctor and ask for a prescription. Do not exceed the recommended dose.

You could also try placing a warm hot-water bottle against your lower abdomen, as the heat can have a comforting, muscle-relaxing and mildly analgesic effect. And any breathing or relaxation techniques you learned to use in labour may help.

Blood clots

You may pass blood clots after the birth, usually when you urinate, although they can sometimes be left on your sanitary towel. If they are substantial or you have passed two or three, tell your midwife or doctor. If possible, show them one as it may be a piece of retained placenta. If it is, you may need minor surgery to remove it before it causes an infection.

A raised temperature, pale skin, rapid pulse and very tender abdomen can all be signs of such an infection. Report them to your doctor immediately as you may need antibiotics in addition to minor surgery to remedy the problem.

Bruising and soreness

You may feel sore and bruised just about everywhere, as labour is usually a hard physical effort and demands the full co-operation of muscles you may not have known you had.

WHAT YOU CAN DO Try soaking in a warm or hot bath for at least 20 minutes. And persuade someone to massage you afterward, when your muscles will be more relaxed and easier to work on.

Soreness around the coccyx (which moved back out of the way during delivery) and sore swelling around the perineum and vulva can all be soothed with ice packs. Use a small packet of frozen peas or sweetcorn (which can be endlessly re-frozen) on the area for 10 minutes at a time. Wrap a thin tea towel or scarf around the pack so the frozen surface does not come into direct contact with your skin as it could give you ice burns.

Pain on urinating or emptying your bowels

If it hurts passing urine, the measures suggested under stitches (see p. 110) are all helpful.

Avoiding constipation is one of the best self-help measures. Drink as much plain water as you can (avoid tea and coffee, which are both diuretic and may make matters worse) and eat plenty of fresh fruit (ask a visitor to bring a bowl full). Grapes are especially good as they are easy to graze on throughout the day, and are ideal in the hot, dry hospital environment. Try also to move around as much as is possible, even a short careful walk several times a day will help.

Straining to open your bowels will not burst your stitches, but if you are worried, hold a soft sanitary pad against the stitches. A glycerine suppository can gently help get any waste matter in the rectum moving, and lubricate the passage to make things easier and less painful. An enema may be suggested if by the fourth or fifth day after delivery you are still unable to open your bowels: if you do not want one, you should say so.

Stitches

Perineal stitches may be the result of a tear, or of an episiotomy. They usually heal quite quickly as the blood supply to this area is very rich. A tear or episiotomy should be noticeably better after a week and may give little trouble after 10 to 14 days or so (the stitches will dissolve after about a week). If yours still trouble you months after your baby's birth, mention the matter, forcibly if necessary, to your GP and request that you be referred to a gynaecologist to find out what the problem is.

WHAT YOU CAN DO Keep the area very clean and dry. Change your sanitary towel regularly, wash the area in warm water and pat it dry with toilet paper after urinating or opening your bowels. Stitches heal better when they are dry, and the drier they are, the less likely they are to become infected.

Ice packs (as for general bruising) may help, as do Epifoam – a mildly anaesthetizing foam containing a steroid to reduce inflammation, which is sprayed on – or lignocaine, a gel which also contains a local anaesthetic. Both of these are only available from the hospital or on prescription from your GP.

Ultrasound may help heal this type of soft tissue damage: ask whether this is available from the hospital's physiotherapy department.

You could also try bathing in warm water with antiseptic liquid added, although this can make the bath rather slippery. Salt baths – add enough salt to be able to taste it in the water – or lavender baths – add 10 drops of good-quality lavender essential oil – may also help.

A herbal infusion of one handful of uva ursi, one of shepherd's purse and one of comfrey, boiled together and left to steep for 30 minutes, then added to the bath may ease discomfort, or put a few drops of Hyper Cal, a homeopathic tincture, on to a soft sanitary pad.

If you find it uncomfortable to sit, use a child's inflatable swimming ring as a cushion and carry it about with you. If your stitches sting when you

Stitches that persist in hurting

If the stitched area is still hurting months after it has technically healed, it may be that:
- the edges of the tear or cut were unevenly sewn together, in which case an operation is needed to make a clean incision over the same place and re-sew it very carefully;
- an excess of scar tissue has developed into a sensitive lumpy area; this is known as keloid scarring and it can often be treated with injections of cortisone, or (failing this) another incision and additional careful stitching;
- there may even be a small nerve trapped in the area – an experienced gynaecologist should be able to diagnose this.

Do not put up with pain that lingers. Talk to your GP and get help.

urinate, pour water over them as you do so. Or pass water at the end of your bath or shower, and clean (or get someone else to clean) the bath or shower stall thoroughly with disinfectant afterward.

Piles and haematoma

Piles (haemorrhoids) are enlarged varicose veins in the spongy walls of the anus. They can appear during pregnancy for the same reason as varicose veins in the legs – because of the rise in progesterone which relaxes all muscle tissue, including that of the vessels of your circulatory system. They can be tender, especially during a bowel movement, itchy and may bleed after a bowel movement too. You may also find they prolapse – push out of their surrounding tissue – after a bowel movement and need to be tucked back in with your fingers each time.

Haematoma are small sacs filled with clotted blood. They feel like tender lumps under the perineal skin and tend to appear after the strenuous pushing of labour. If they persist, fibrous tissue may develop around them, this in turn can form scar tissue and they may become infected. These can be treated by your doctor.

WHAT YOU CAN DO Haemorrhoids can be soothed by holding an ice pack (as for general bruising) against the skin, or ask your GP for a prescription for a haemorrhoid shrinking and soothing cream. It also helps to avoid constipation, as straining to empty your bowels makes piles worse (see Pain on urinating or emptying your bowels, p. 109). Minor surgery may be advised if piles persist.

Haematoma need professional treatment under anaesthetic, usually only considered once six months have elapsed since the birth. Talk to your GP or ask to be referred to a gynaecologist.

Sore breasts

Your breasts swell considerably during this time because hormonal changes are preparing them to feed your baby – whether you actually wish to do so or not. The result is an influx of fluid (including blood) to the area which makes your breasts very full and taut. The stretching of the breast skin can become uncomfortable, the breasts tend to become hard, hot and tender to touch.

WHAT YOU CAN DO Wear a comfortable, supporting maternity bra day and night. You can also try warm baths deep enough to soak your breasts in, and either warm or cool flannels over each breast (try both to see which you find more comfortable). A traditional remedy – reputed to be very soothing – is to place a leaf of washed, dark green Savoy cabbage inside each bra cup so it curves around the breast.

If you do not wish to breastfeed, your breasts should go down to their usual size within about a week. If you wish to discourage milk production, you could bind your breasts gently but firmly with a soft, wide crêpe bandage (you may need to insert a breast pad over each nipple as they will tend to leak a little colostrum). Bromocriptine, available on prescription only, also inhibits milk production but it can have unwanted side-effects such as nausea.

See pp. 73–6 for advice on dealing with dis-comforts related to breastfeeding.

The blues

The blues often coincide with the milk coming in to your breasts, the initial euphoria induced by the hormones released during and after labour wearing off, and your becoming aware of the full impact of any physical discomforts – everything seems to be either leaking or hurting.

These feelings usually disappear within two or three days. See Postnatal illness, p. 120.

WHAT YOU CAN DO No treatment is usually necessary for the blues since they disappear on their own. But it helps to have peace and quiet to bond with your baby, and support to get feeding well established.

Practical help with domestic chores and caring for other children can help, as does the emotional support of your partner, friends and relatives.

Getting back into shape

Along with the pleasure at looking down to see your feet for the first time in months, you may feel some alarm at the flabby tummy, perhaps complete with stretch marks, that greets you after your baby's birth. Internally, too, your body is far from normal. Among other changes, the muscles of your abdomen, which are usually aligned and close to one another, stretched to accommodate the growing baby, and may well have parted company with each other. And those of the pelvic floor have been stretched to the limit during the birth. Fortunately there is plenty you can do – almost from birth – to help the changes which are naturally occurring to restore your body to normal.

Apart from eating sensibly and getting as much rest as you can, the most important factor in getting back to normal is exercise. Postnatal exercises are at least as important as antenatal exercises: they result in strong abdominal muscles to protect your back from the demands of lifting a baby, good pelvic floor muscles (see p. 26) to prevent stress incontinence (see p. 35) and good thigh muscles to keep your knee joints flexible. The better you feel, the fewer problems you will have with the everyday demands of caring for a new baby.

The earlier you begin to exercise after your baby's birth, the easier you will find it to get into a routine, and the faster you will notice the effects on your body, which in itself can be a good boost to keeping the exercises going. But remember that immediately after the birth your ligaments will still be softer than normal due to the effect of the pregnancy hormones, so you must take it easy. An obstetric physiotherapist will almost certainly visit you on the postnatal ward – if you are in hospital for all but the briefest of stays – and give you advice on what is suitable for you. It is particularly important to get advice on exercise if you have had a caesarean.

Remember, too, that it is never too late to start. If the first couple of weeks after your baby's birth seem

POSTNATAL EXERCISES

In all the excitement of giving birth and having your baby at home with you, it can be difficult to remember that mothers, too, have been through a demanding experience. In caring for your baby, it can be easy to overlook that your body is not going to return to its pre-pregnant state in terms of muscle control and tone, unless you actively take steps to ensure that it does. Postnatal exercises are vital and the more you can do, the better.

Curl ups

These help to draw your parted abdominal muscles together and generally firm and tone them.

1 Lie on your back with your knees bent and feet flat on the floor. Place your hands on your thighs. Pull your abdominal muscles in and tighten your buttocks.

2 Breathe out as you slowly tuck your chin in to your chest and lift your head, then your shoulders, off the floor. As you do so, slide your hands along your thighs toward your knees.
   When your head, shoulders and upper back are off the floor and your hands have reached your knees, hold for a count of three, then slowly lower yourself back to the floor. Repeat the whole sequence.

Leg slides

This exercise strengthens your abdominal muscles and closes the gap that the growing baby caused to open between them.

1 Lie on your back on the floor with your elbows bent and hands under your head. Bend your left knee so that your foot is on a level with your right knee. Keep your foot flat on the floor.

2 Breathe out, pull your abdominal muscles in firmly and raise your head, tucking your chin in to your chest.

3 Keeping your head into your chest, change legs: slide your left leg so that it is flat on the floor and bend your right knee. Now lower your head. Repeat the whole sequence.

Waist twists

The skin around your middle and your abdominal muscles stretched enormously to accommodate your growing baby. If you could see your vertical abdominal muscles, before the birth they resemble parallel lines of muscle; afterward, they can be an ox-bow shape. This exercise helps to pull your waist back to its 'normal' state and improves the range of movement in your upper body.

1 Sit on a chair with your back straight, knees apart and feet flat on the floor. Fold your arms at about chest height. Keeping your buttocks on the chair and your abdominal muscles pulled in tight, twist slowly to the right. Hold for a count of three.

2 Twist back to centre and without relaxing your abdominal muscles, twist as far to the left as you can. Hold for a count of three, then return to the centre. Only then should you relax your abdominal muscles. Repeat the whole sequence.

Outer thigh lifts

This exercise works on your abdominal muscles, but also increases the strength and tone in your thighs.

1 Lie on your left side, with your head on your left hand. Place your right hand on the floor in front of you for balance. Pull your abdominal muscles in and keep them tight throughout the exercise.

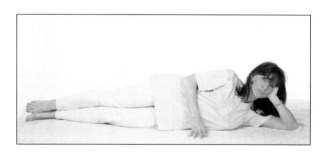

2 Raise your right leg as high as you can, while keeping it as straight as you can. Hold for a count of three, then lower back down. Repeat six times then turn on to your right side and do an equal number, raising your left leg. Repeat, working both sides equally.

to pass in a blur, start exercising when you can. It helps to try to do a set of exercises at the same time each day, simply so they become part of your routine, but if you do not have a routine to begin with – and most new parents do not – do them when you can. If you are too exhausted one day to do them at your normal time, do them later, after you have had a rest. If you feel full of energy one day do an extra set, but take it easy and do not overdo it.

All these exercises work on the muscles that have been most affected by your pregnancy. In each case, start by repeating the sequence six times and gradually increase as your muscles return to their former strength and flexibility.

Where to go
You may find it easy to exercise at home. The exercises given here, together with many antenatal exercises (see pp. 26–7) will give you a good basis on which to work. Alternatively, consult a book on post-natal exercise – the hospital obstetric physiotherapist will be able to recommend one.

Some hospitals run postnatal exercise classes, and if you attend antenatal classes there it is worth asking what they can offer. Or, try your local leisure centre which may run classes for new mums, or your nearest NCT branch which may be able to give you advice on what is on offer locally. Your health visitor or GP's surgery should also be aware of what is available in your area.

CARE AFTER A CAESAREAN

One in every seven babies in Britain is born by caesarean. Although this is a safe, common operation, it is still (rightly) classed as major surgery since both the abdominal wall and womb are opened. Additional aftercare and help are therefore necessary after a caesarean birth.

Depending on how much help there is at home, how you are feeling and on the hospital's policy, you may spend up to ten days in hospital.

Immediately after a caesarean

- The incision area – usually a bikini cut from side to side just above the pubis – is covered by a light dressing. This will be painful at first, and you will probably need strong, effective pain relief for at least 48 hours afterward.
- A drain, which draws off any excess blood and fluid from the incision site, stays in place for the first few hours only. (It may not be necessary to have a drain at all.)

After the first few days

By the time you go home from hospital, you should be feeling far more mobile and no longer need strong painkillers. But you should still take care, limiting the amount you do to ensure that your body heals as quickly as possible.

Energy
Many people lack energy for several weeks or even months after major surgery of any type. Take it easy.

- Avoid heavy lifting during the first six to eight weeks. This is easier said than done if you have a toddler as well as a new baby to care for. Try to get as much help as you possibly can, and also try: crouching down without bending to cuddle a toddler instead of lifting him; using a step-up (pillows, a cushion, a cardboard box) to help him on to the sofa next to you, or on to your bed. To feed a toddler, sit on the floor on a cushion and put his meal either on a low table or in the low version of a convertible high chair so that you do not have to lift him in and out.
- Avoid any housework that means you need to stretch, pull or push for six weeks – this includes hoovering, ironing, changing beds and carrying shopping or laundry.
- You should not drive for two to six weeks after a caesarean. Ask the hospital for advice.

Exercise

Many of your pelvic floor exercises are similar to the ordinary postnatal exercises done after a vaginal birth (see pp. 112–113) but you should do them slowly and gently, at your own pace. Others, because you have had major abdominal surgery, are rather different. The hospital physiotherapist should see you before you go home, and will give you full details and a sheet of exercises. If you do not get to see her, ask to do so.

Alternatively, contact the Association of Chartered Physiotherapists in Obstetrics and Gynaecology (see Useful Contacts, pp. 390-3).

Feeding

Your incision site will stay sore for a while, so whether you are bottle- or breastfeeding, it helps to keep the baby's weight off the area.

If you have a vertical scar (which is uncommon these days), feed sitting up with pillows across your stomach to absorb the baby's weight. Alternatively, lie on your side with the baby next to you. It may take a bit of practice at first to get the baby at the right 'height' to breastfeed in this way, but once you get the hang of it, this is very comfortable, especially if you are feeling tired, or have taken the baby into bed with you to feed him at night.

If you have a bikini scar, lie the baby on a pillow 'tucked' underneath your arm, so that his head is facing your breast or a bottle and his body is under your arm (see Feeding twins box on p. 76). Or, sit up with a cushion or pillow supporting you on either side, and put the baby's head on one pillow and his feet on your thighs.

Infected incision

This is the most common problem following a caesarean. Signs that the wound may be infected include a raised temperature, a red, inflamed and weepy wound, hard lumps developing behind the scar, increased pain in the whole area and the wound opening slightly.

Such infections can be quickly and easily treated with antibiotics.

Pain and soreness

If pain persists, ask the hospital for milder but effective pain relief tablets to take home with you in case you need them. Make sure they know if you are breastfeeding so that any drugs they give you do not harm the baby. If you hired a TENS machine for the birth, know how to use it, felt that it helped, and do not yet need to send it back, this can be very useful for relieving pain (see p. 53).

Warm baths can also have a very soothing, slightly analgesic effect, although you may still need some help getting in and out of them. Don't bath when you are alone in the house, or lock the bathroom door.

Scar pain

The initial pain should wear off within a couple of weeks. After that you will probably feel some discomfort in your scar area, especially when you bend, lift or push – or at night when lying in a particular position may pull on it. If you experience more than the occasional twinge months later, or if the pain is worsening rather than diminishing, go and see your doctor.

Scar appearance

Over time your scar will change from red to pink, and finally to silvery white. In most cases, the scar from a bikini cut will be hidden when your pubic hair regrows. You may, however, find that the area is itchy for months afterward, or that the flesh on either side feels numb for some time.

Tiredness

You have had a major operation, so while you may feel fine within a few weeks, you may well feel more tired than a new mother who has given birth vaginally for several months. If getting as much rest as possible means letting any household chores go for a while, then do so.

Get as much help as possible, from your partner, a parent, friends, neighbours. If there are no volunteers and you can afford it, spend money on cleaning and cooking help, or help with any other children you may have. Ask your health visitor too what sources of state help may be available to you, especially if you are a single parent.

What to wear

Soreness from the incision site will fade away to itchiness and tenderness before it disappears altogether. Try to wear waist-high cotton pants if you have a bikini scar, and loose clothes – either dresses or baggy cotton leggings with teeshirts or sweatshirts over the top – while you are healing. Flattish shoes or trainers will help your posture and prevent you from tipping forward or off balance.

Making love

Unless you had a caesarean after a trial labour involving episiotomy, you may be ready to make love a couple of weeks after the birth, as long as you use positions that keep any pressure off your scar site. Equally you may not feel like having any sexual contact for several months. Both reactions are perfectly normal. You may feel less attractive than before the caesarean, although your pubic hair will hide the scar almost completely. If you feel this way, buy the most attractive new nightdress you can find and wear it to make love in until you feel confident enough to take it off.

If lovemaking is still physically uncomfortable for you two or three months later, tell your GP, since this could indicate a lingering infection around the incision site which needs treating.

If you or your partner do not feel emotionally comfortable with the idea of lovemaking because of the caesarean, try to talk it over together; if this is difficult, contact Relate or the Caesarean Support Network (see Useful Contacts, pp. 390–3), which may be able to put you in touch with other couples who experienced similar feelings.

Emotional recovery

Caesarean birth can be a very positive, fulfilling experience, especially if it was planned in advance, properly discussed with you, you were kept well informed throughout, and the operation was handled sensitively by the hospital staff. In many cases, emotional recovery can be very rapid. But some women who give birth by caesarean do feel very distressed indeed by the experience (especially if it was an emergency procedure), and for them, emotional recovery may take far longer. In general, it can be described as a four-stage process:

- physical and emotional shock
- denial (there is nothing for me to get upset about)
- sadness, and anger
- acceptance of what happened and coming to terms with it.

However just as every woman's reaction to vaginal birth is different, there is a huge variation in the reactions of individual mothers to caesarean birth. It is not unusual for some sadness and anger to appear after many months of positive feelings about the birth. If you feel there are any issues about your caesarean which remain unresolved, discuss them

fully with your doctor at your six-week postnatal check-up (see below). Particularly if it was an emergency procedure, you may want to discuss the reasons why it happened more fully, and the chances of your needing a similar operation if you have another baby (there is often no reason why you cannot give birth vaginally after a caesarean). It can also help to talk to one of the help and support organizations (see Useful Contacts, pp. 390–3).

THE SIX-WEEK CHECK

Whether you had your baby at home or in hospital, you will be given a date on which to see your GP, or return to the hospital, for a postnatal check-up. This usually takes place around six weeks after the baby's birth. There is nothing especially magical about six weeks, but after this time, most new mothers have recovered from the immediate after-effects of the birth and most babies – who are also looked at – are settled into some sort of feeding and sleeping routine, and smiling with delight at the sight of their parents.

Voicing any concerns

The six-week check is an ideal opportunity to discuss anything that is worrying, concerning or has simply crossed your mind about your baby's health and development and your new role as a mother. It is a good time to talk about contraception (see p. 119), diet and exercise (pp. 111–14) and anything else that may be troubling you (lack of sleep, for example).

You can also ask about the changes you can expect to see in your baby, and when (see also Chapter 5). The range of 'normal' behaviour for babies is enormous, so do not worry that anything is going to be too trivial. No one is going to think you silly, no matter what you ask. It is far better to be told that there is nothing to worry about, than to fret at home later, when you should be resting or enjoying your baby. Worrying is a natural, positive and necessary part of being a parent: you would not be a 'normal' mother or father if you did not worry.

The six-week check does, however, have considerable psychological significance. It marks your final signing off from the usual obstetric services (at least as far as this pregnancy is concerned – another pregnancy is classed as a separate patient 'episode') and completes your health record for this pregnancy and delivery. It also provides a good opportunity to talk to the doctor about anything that might be worrying you (either from your own point of view, or about the baby) and to have a general health check.

Checks for the mother

- Urine test, blood pressure, examination of the site of any stitches.
- Breast check to ensure that there are no problems, such as blocked ducts or any infection, and – if you are not breastfeeding – that you are not still producing milk.
- The doctor will feel and palpate your abdomen and will do an internal examination to check that your uterus has contracted back to its normal, non-pregnant size and that all is well with your cervix and vagina.
- You may be offered a blood test for postnatal anaemia. It is worth accepting, if it is offered, since if you are suffering from it, you may have no symptoms other than tiredness, which you may be putting down to the unavoidable fatigue of new mothers. Undetected anaemia can persist for months and leave you drained of energy. If you are not offered a test, but do feel exceptionally tired, ask for one. If you are still exhausted after three months, go back and ask for a test to be done.
- You may be offered a smear test, if this was not done at your booking-in appointment (see p. 22–3) and you have not had one in the last four years.

Checks on the baby

Some of these checks are repeats of those done at birth or shortly afterward. They include:
- He will be measured
- He will be weighed (naked, which he may not like)
- His skin colour will be looked at
- His or her genitalia will be examined
- His hips will be checked for 'clicky hip' (see Your Child's Health, pp. 356–7).

Registering your baby's birth

It is the law in England, Wales and Northern Ireland that you must register your baby's birth before he is six weeks old (this must be done before he is three weeks old in Scotland). The address of the local registry office will be in the phone book. If you live in a different district from the one in which the baby was born, you can register at your local office, but the registrar will then send the details on to the 'birth district' and the birth certificate will be sent to you by mail.

If you are married, either parent can register the birth, with both mother's and father's names on the certificate. If you are not married, the mother can register the birth alone, but if the father's name is to appear on the certificate, he must go along in person.

At the same time as you are given your baby's birth certificate, you will be given his National Health Service number. This will enable you to register him with a GP (see p. 153).

In addition, the doctor or health visitor will check your baby's skills in the following areas.
- **Motor development**
  The measure of control a young baby has over his body, even at this age, will be looked at, perhaps by holding him up to see his degree of head control, or by lying him down on his stomach and noting whether he lifts his head and tries to turn it from side to side.
- **Hearing**
  The doctor will ring a bell or shake a rattle out of his range of vision to see if and how he reacts.
- **Sight**
  A bell or rattle will be moved across your baby's line of sight to see if he follows it with his eyes.

Don't worry if your baby cries during these checks, and/or refuses to look or listen to the rattle. These are not tests which a baby passes or fails, but general indicators of his well-being. It is undoubtedly true that doctors prefer a baby that screams healthily to one who lies back placidly and is unresponsive to everything around him. You can always ask for these checks to be redone at any time at the baby clinic if you are worried.

SEX AND CONTRACEPTION

Traditionally, women wait until after the six-week postnatal check-up (see pp. 116–17) before starting to make love again. But apart from the risk of sexual intercourse introducing infection into the vagina, there is no reason why you cannot have sex as soon – or wait as long – as you both feel is right.

Why sex may be difficult

There are scores of reasons, some specific (continued soreness after stitches, for example), some more general (overall fatigue), why you may not wish to make love after the birth of your baby.

But many couples do acknowledge that their sex lives improved after the birth: some women say they have a better body image, are less inhibited and have more powerful orgasms than before. Many couples feel that because they make love less frequently, both partners made more effort to make it special.

Nonetheless, the physical demands of being a new parent often mean that given the choice between an hour of peace for making love or an hour's un-interrupted sleep, you tend to choose the latter. You may find yourself caring for your new baby 24 hours a day for many months, unless he rapidly learns to sleep through the night. Fortunately this phase does not last, and there are many different strategies you can adopt to make sex begin to seem like a pleasurable option once more rather than something you feel you ought to be doing but for which you cannot quite summon the energy. These include both physical problem solving, and practical arrangements.

Body image

Feeling that you are unattractive because your body is not as it was before you became pregnant can inhibit your sexual response or your desire to have any sexual contact at all.

WHAT YOU CAN DO Talk to your partner, honestly, about how you feel and try to accept his reassurances at face value. And carry on, as long as possible, with your postnatal exercises (see pp. 112–14), both for your pelvic floor (see p. 26) and for the rest of your body. The easiest time to lose the extra weight you put on during pregnancy is the eight weeks after childbirth. If you can, take up gentle all-over toning exercise, such as swimming once or twice a week. And even if you cannot lose all the extra weight – white women are on average 4.5 kg (10 lb) heavier after childbirth, Afro-Caribbean women up to 8 kg (18 lb) – remember that bigger, toned bodies are more sexually attractive than slim, flabby ones.

Stretch marks fade, but if you are unhappy, buy a beautiful new nightdress. This also helps to obscure your larger postnatal contours while you reduce them.

Have a professional massage – several if you can afford it. When you feel ready, try some massage with your partner, taking turns.

Breastfeeding

Breastfeeding can cause vaginal dryness; it can also make you feel differently about your sexuality. The sensual and emotional aspects of breastfeeding can be so satisfying that you have little desire for sex. You may also feel that your breasts temporarily 'belong' to your baby and that it is inappropriate for them to be erotic zones as well.

Because breastfeeding affects your oestrogen levels, it can also reduce your sex drive. Your libido fully returns when you stop breastfeeding – providing you are not still very tired, or sore.

Sexual stimulation often also stimulates milk flow, which can be disconcerting.

WHAT YOU CAN DO Try to make love soon after feeding your baby so that your breasts are empty, or press the heels of your hand firmly against your breasts for half a minute if milk begins to flow from them during lovemaking.

Soreness

Sex after childbirth can often be uncomfortable at first, and it may take time, an understanding partner and many gentle attempts before you feel completely happy about making love again. Give yourselves time to become sexual beings again, after a period of being affectionate, rather than erotic, with each other.

WHAT YOU CAN DO You may feel happier with non-penetrative sex, including sensual massage and gentle oral or manual stimulation, for a while.

If you have had stitches, the area may remain sensitive to pressure or friction for a few weeks, even months. If it continues to be a problem, see your GP and if necessary ask for a referral to a consultant gynaecologist, or go to a well-woman clinic at your nearest family planning centre. You may not have healed well, which can be treated by injections.

Experiment with different positions for love-making, to find those which put the least pressure on any area which is still sore.

If your vagina feels sore and tight, try KY gel or contraceptive cream smoothed around your vagina, labia and your partner's penis, before penetration. This may be a problem if you are breastfeeding since breastfeeding causes a temporary reduction in your levels of oestrogen, which affects vaginal lubrication. Also ask your GP about oestrogen cream (available only on prescription), which can help to rehydrate and lubricate the vaginal tissues more effectively.

Your vagina

Although the vagina stretches to allow your baby to be born, it returns to its former size afterward. As long as your pelvic muscles are toned, it is virtually impossible for a partner to tell the difference.
WHAT YOU CAN DO Keep up your pelvic floor exercises (see p. 26). These have three important effects: they strengthen the sling of your pelvic floor to keep it strong for any future pregnancies; they help in treating or avoiding postnatal incontinence or prolapse of the womb later in life; they strengthen the vaginal wall muscles themselves, so they can grip a partner's penis firmly. If you did not bother to work on your pelvic floor muscles before you were pregnant, you may well find that they are better toned after birth than they were before.

Postnatal contraception

Contraception is usually the last thing on a woman's mind when she has just had a baby. But if you resume lovemaking fairly soon after the birth and are bottle-feeding, a combination of breast- and bottlefeeding, or simply not breastfeeding sufficiently often (see box on p. 87) you can be fertile and therefore pregnant again as early as three weeks after your baby's birth.

Try to sort out contraception as soon as possible after your baby's birth. Do not wait until you have had your first period because you will be fertile before that. You may want to wait until your six-week postnatal check-up, which gives you the opportunity of being in

your GP's surgery, to discuss contraception. But if you want to make love before then, make an appointment with your GP or family planning clinic; your midwife or health visitor can also advise you on which method(s) you may find most suitable.

Which method to choose?

You have the same basic choices in method of contraception after the birth as you did before you became pregnant and it is a good idea to discuss your options with your GP or at the family planning clinic. There are, however, a few factors which you should take into account after the birth of a baby.

- The combined pill is not suitable if you are breastfeeding, as it reduces the amount of milk your body produces.
- The progestogen-only pill (or minipill) does not affect the amount of milk you produce, although some traces of progestogen will enter your milk. What effect this has on your baby is uncertain. This pill is also less effective if you weigh more than 70 kg (11 stone).
- If you start taking either pill more than 21 days after the baby's birth, it will not be reliable for the first seven days, so you should use something else too (such as a condom).
- The female condom (or Femidom) may be uncomfortable if your cervix and vagina are still bruised or sore.
- If you used a diaphragm before you became pregnant, it will not fit any longer. It is vital to get a new one fitted and to change again each time you lose or gain 3 kg (7 lb) in weight.
- An IUD cannot be fitted until after your postnatal check-up, when your womb has returned to its normal size.

A time and a place for partners

The combination of tiredness and little or no free time may put considerable strain on your relationship with your partner, leaving little opportunity for enjoying much time together.

However, it is important for you both as parents and lovers to get at least a little regular time on your own together, if only for a couple of hours a week. Many new parents try to make this an unbreakable weekly date, no matter how tired they are and say that

Postnatal illness

Feelings of sadness and depression after childbirth can vary widely from the baby blues, which last only a few days (see p. 111), to postnatal depression which without treatment might last for many months. Postnatal psychosis requires admission to hospital. Postnatal illness of any type is not common; half of all mothers experience no problems at all. Of the rest, between 50 and 80 per cent feel some degree of the blues and between 10 and 15 per cent experience some degree of postnatal depression. As few as 1 in every 1,000 recently delivered mothers develop postnatal psychosis.

If it happens to you, don't panic. Do not feel you will never get better – because you will. Call the Association for Post Natal Illness (APNI, see Useful Contacts, pp. 390–3) and talk to some of their helpers, all of whom have experienced postnatal illness and recovered fully. You are not unbalanced or weak in some way. It can, and does, happen to any woman. It is not your fault if it happens to you. (If you are the partner of someone who you believe to be suffering from PNI, you may have to call on her behalf. Be very persistent with your GP or your partner's gynaecologist to get yourself heard.)

it was this 'time out' together, with as much mutual support as possible, which kept their relationship strong – even when one was surviving on three hours' sleep a night and the other was doing the housework and cooking each night after a day out at work.

You have needs too, both for each other's company and (especially if one of you is at home all day with the baby) for that of adults in child-free surroundings. You also need a little time and space to nurture your own physical relationship. Although it can seem to require so much organizational effort as to be off-putting, you will find that you have more emotional and physical energy to spend on being a parent if you allow yourselves some private time (see also Taking a break, pp. 231–3).

But if your new baby is temporarily sharing a room or a bed with you, you may find his presence simply too inhibiting.

What you can do

- Try making love somewhere other than your bedroom for a while.
- Arrange one night or afternoon every week when a trusted babysitter, friend or relative has your baby in their home for a while.
- Ask the sitter to come over to your house to babysit. If you feel embarrassed about both retiring to your bedroom, say you are having broken nights and badly need some sleep.
- Ask the sitter to take your baby for a long walk.
- Opt for frequent cuddling rather than sex. The most important thing is that you are comfortable with your relationship.

If you feel the quality of your sexual relationship – or lack of it all together – is a problem or that it could quite easily turn into one, now is a good time to tackle it. Contact Relate or a psychosexual counsellor at a large family planning clinic or a well-woman organization (see Useful Contacts, pp. 390–3) before unwanted patterns become well established.

GOING IT ALONE

In Britain, there are currently 1.3 million single parents bringing up 2 million children. One in five British families is headed by a lone parent, 90 per cent of whom are women. And there is no doubt about it, it is much harder work to bring up a baby on your own than if you have a helpful partner.

Single mothers are placed under a good deal of stress. Single parents of both sexes suffer far more ill health than those with partners. Whether you chose to have your baby alone, or whether the situation was thrust upon you, and regardless of your feelings during your pregnancy, the effect is about the same.

The most common pressures include:
- Being the one person who has to try to carry out all the parental roles in your baby's life for most of the time.
- Shortage of money: only one in three absent fathers pays any maintenance; you may find child care takes a large proportion of your pay, if you have paid work outside the home. Research suggests that 9 out of every 10 lone mothers without jobs would return to work if suitable, affordable child care was available.

- Housing problems are far more common for single parents than for those with partners.
- Keeping in contact with the baby's father, if both sides are willing, can bring difficulties of its own, as well as benefits.

You may need extra support in certain areas either at specific times during your baby's or child's life, or on an on-going basis or both. Among the organizations which can help you are Gingerbread, The National Council for One-Parent Families, The Maternity Alliance, Parentlink, Exploring Parenthood, Homestart, MAMA and Parents At Work (see Useful Contacts, pp. 390–3).

Coming home with your baby

If at all possible, try and arrange beforehand for someone to be there when you return with your new baby, perhaps your mother, sister, a friend or neighbour who can either come and stay or pop in regularly. Emotional support and practical help in the form of cooking, shopping, cleaning and even short periods of babysitting take the pressure off you so you can concentrate on your baby.

Money

You may be entitled to one or more different kinds of financial benefit. To find out, phone the local DSS (see the phone book, or your local Post Office can give you the number). If you need further advice or find the often complex DSS forms hard to work out, try the Citizen's Advice Bureau or any of the organizations mentioned above.

If you have a room in your house that might be rented out to a lodger to provide you with an income, seek advice from the help organizations – and other single parents – before you do so. It can work out well, but a parent – especially a woman – alone with a child is also quite vulnerable.

Housing

If you are homeless with a young baby, currently the local council is obliged to offer you one potential place of accommodation. This does not have to be what you – or any other parent – might consider 'suitable' and the council only has to offer you one, which could be a hard-to-let flat in a high-risk area. If you turn an offer down, the council is not by law obliged to offer you anywhere else.

Financial aid is often available to help with payment for existing rented accommodation. If you already have your own place with a mortgage, a contribution toward payments should be made for you by the council if you are on Income Support.

Back to work

A major hurdle in trying to earn a living can be finding good, affordable child care. Single parents – and even today, single mothers more than single fathers – may find they are little better off financially if they do go out to work. However, as a single parent who wishes to work, you should be given priority for any assisted or free creche and community nursery places available.

You may need to be persistent about this, so begin asking about it and going to see nurseries concerned very early on. Again, local Gingerbread groups will have information on what is available in your area, and perhaps know which the best ones are. Your local authority Social Services department will also have a list of nursery addresses, though they cannot make specific comments on their suitability.

Back up

All parents need extra back up, single parents doubly so. Networks of other single parents in your area can be exceptionally supportive and helpful; also, try to collect people who offer to help with anything whatsoever, from the odd bit of shopping when they do their own to giving you a couple of hours off once a week. Sort out which ones really mean it, and take them up on their offers.

Try to cultivate at least two people (apart from any childminder you may have, although a good childminder will almost certainly know other local minders who may be able help in times of need) whom you and your baby like and trust. There will definitely be times when you need them. Even if you do not call on them, knowing they are there helps to reduce the pressure on you. See also Chapter 9: Help with Your child, pp. 228–47.

CHAPTER FIVE

The First Year

Being the parent of a small baby is about far more than looking after her physical needs, although they can seem overwhelming. It is also about watching a tiny person make sense of the world around her, learning to move through that world and interact with it. The first year of a baby's life is an unforgettable time for the whole family.

Your baby's development

At birth an average baby weighs about the same as three bags of sugar and is about as long as the distance from your elbow to your fingertip. By one she will stand about as high as the kitchen table and by two she will be half her eventual adult height. As she grows up, she also grows out. In the first six months your baby will probably put on 550–800 g (20–28 oz) in weight and grow about 25 mm (1 in) every month.

Babies do not just grow: they grow up. If you pick up your one-year-old the fact that she now weighs as much as a dozen bags of sugar is of minor significance compared to the other changes that have taken place. Between six weeks and one year almost everything about a baby changes. At birth her muscles are weak and literally watery. Her bones are bendy and the brain in her tiny head is small. She is not very good at controlling her temperature, blood pressure or breathing. She can do almost nothing and understand even less.

By her first birthday her bones and muscles have changed in structure, her heart beats strongly, she can control her breathing, and her brain has grown considerably. What you see is the effect of all these changes. She now walks around the furniture, draws in a breath before she shouts long and loud, says 'pss-pss' when she sees the cat, plays pat-a-cake and almost always stops when you say 'No'.

This chapter traces the changes you can expect between six weeks and the end of an average baby's first year, and when you can expect them. Development is not a race, however, and being a month ahead is of no significance. Girls develop a little faster than boys, and Afro-Caribbean babies a little faster than European. There is no correlation between how soon a baby walks or talks and later sporting prowess or intelligence. If your one-year-old is still sitting on her bottom saying nothing it is reassuring to know that Albert Einstein did not say a word until he was two (he also had early learning difficulties, but his name is still synonymous with prodigious intelligence).

Average means in the middle. Half of all babies are ahead of the average and half behind. Most (some 60–70 per cent) are close. It is those babies at the very bottom (or sometimes the very top) of the scale who give cause for concern. Not those who walk late, but those who walk last. Not those above average weight, but those in the top 5 per cent. If your child was

One year of growth

Height: Adds 25–30 cm (10–12 in) by her first birthday.

Weight: Doubles birth weight by four to five months; trebles birth weight by 12–14 months.

Brain: Fastest growing organ in the baby's body.

Skeleton: Bones are quite flexible at birth, but flexibility declines with age.

Muscles: Muscles start off weak and watery, but change in size and composition with use.

Circulation: The heart becomes much stronger and more efficient and blood pressure decreases.

Digestion: Food is only partly digested, with possetting (bringing back a small amount) common; this should decline by six months.

Immune system: The baby slowly produces her own antibodies to replace those passed to her by her mother while in the womb; her mother's antibodies are also passed in breast milk.

Lung capacity: Increases and the lungs become sensitive to irritation; the baby gradually becomes able to combine breathing and moving.

Teeth: Erupt between six months and three years.

premature, she will take a long time to catch up; when you are looking at her development, start from her 'due date' and add a bit to that. If she was a very premature baby, do not expect her to reach the usual developmental milestones at around the same time as her peers until she is about three. It really does take a long time.

Babies who are damaged at birth will also be very slow to begin. Their rate of progress gives a better indication of future potential than their age. Specific disabilities can have quite wide ramifications in the first years: a blind baby, for example, will be slow to walk and to communicate.

YOUR BABY'S GROWTH

For years doctors assumed that children grew at a uniform rate, with babies considered to grow about 0.5 mm (⅕ in) a day. When a group of babies was measured, however, it was found that often they did not grow at all for several weeks, then suddenly there was a spurt, with some growing as much as 12 mm (½ in) in 24 hours. Growth charts, by their very nature, only give averages. This unevenness in her rate of growth will be particularly apparent to you when your child starts wearing shoes. One size might last for six months and the next for only six weeks. Nor are these stops and spurts confined to measurable growth. Children do not learn to do one new thing every day. They learn eight things in two days and then nothing at all for a couple of weeks. If you keep a diary of your child's achievements in the first year you will find that some weeks are full and others quite empty.

Measurable and developmental growth both take energy, which is one of the reasons why babies have such plump bodies. They need to stock up on fuel for the spurts in increased height or weight, and in achievements. Both sorts of growth spurt will probably make your baby tired, hungry, fussy and 'out of sorts'. Being out of sorts or even regressing to more babyish behaviour generally precedes a physical and mental 'milestone' like starting to walk. This fussiness is often attributed to the frustration of not quite being able to do what she wants to do.

Before a 'leap' your baby may be particularly easy. As the leap begins, she becomes difficult and demanding. She then 'grows up', and gradually settles back to her old self. You will find her baby- and childhood peppered with these settled and more difficult times, which can last for weeks, or even months. Fortunately the good times in between are usually longer.

Is she ready?

Babies can only do things if their bodies are ready. No amount of practice will make your baby walk unless the parts of her brain which control her posture and balance are working, and the parts of her brain which allow her to decide which muscles of her legs and trunk she wants to move have developed. Even then she will not walk unless the structure of her muscles has changed so that they can now support the weight of her body, and her bones have hardened and become less flexible so that they can support the movement of strong muscles. In short she walks because her body and brain have grown up. The practice you give her at walking into your arms is the icing on a cake she has already baked.

There is nothing you can do to speed up this development. Early walking runs in families, as does late walking. It is more or less true to say that your baby will walk on the 'appointed day' whatever you do to encourage her.

Your baby's brain

The reason babies are born so helpless and grow to be able to do so much is that their brains grow. The brain controls everything from talking to breathing, from reading books to running races. Because a baby's head needs to pass though her mother's pelvis, it has to be small. Inside the small head is a small brain, only 25 per cent of which is functioning. Since brain cells do not get bigger, as hands or leg bones do, this means that at birth 75 per cent of the brain's functions are missing. During the first three years of life the brain grows faster than any other part of a baby's body.

Present at birth The bottom or lower part of the brain grows and matures first (while the baby is still in the womb). Those parts next to her neck and above the roof of her mouth are all functioning at birth. The lower part of the brain is concerned with automatic actions such as breathing and circulating the blood. At birth your baby can control breathing, heart rate, blood pressure, digestion, arousal, waking, sleeping and elimination. She can also attend to things and recognize that something is familiar. In fact your newborn baby can do all the things she needs to do.

Still to grow The upper parts of the brain are concerned with organizing movement, deciding to move, and all manner of skills from writing to carving statues. They govern making plans, interpreting what is seen, heard and felt, thinking, speaking, reasoning, and committing things to memory.

This area also deals with finding your way around and locating where things are in space, understanding other people, communicating with them and predicting what they might do next. In short, the upper parts of the brain are concerned with everything that tends to be labelled 'human' and all those things that adults, unsurprisingly, do considerably better than babies.

Below: Toward the end of his first year, your baby is almost unrecognizable as the tiny newborn you brought home.

Although many of the higher centres of the brain are in place at birth most other systems have a lot of growing to do. It is because the brain grows so fast that your baby's abilities improve at such a phenomenal rate. Compare how a baby changes in the first two years with how a teenager changes, for example.

The brain matures in a certain order, with the result that the body does so too. Inputs into the brain are better developed than the outputs from it, so your baby finds it easier to see the rattle you are holding out to her than to organize a hand to reach out and touch it. Control of the upper body also develops before the lower body, so that your baby will sit before she stands and be able to reach for a ball before she can kick one.

The higher centres of the brain start to grow and expand between three and six months. As this happens your baby will become better able to control what she is doing now, will begin to remember what she did before, and develop the ability to organize what she will do next.

What you can do

Love her. Nothing grows unless it is fed and watered, but after birth (in contrast to before birth when it is vital) good nutrition is probably less important for the growth of your baby's brain than loving care and the stimulation such care brings. Babies need cuddles and they need talk. They learn because they are happy and they learn best when helped by people who love and care for them.

Babies need to touch, taste, feel, hear, smell and see things and at first are thoroughly dependent on you to show them how to do this. They need to get excited and laugh and jabber, which they do if you jabber back to them. Between times they need to stay quiet and lie still.

Because you love to see her laugh you show her things and play games that make her smile. You also know when she has had enough, so you stop. Then she likes to 'cuddle in' while you hold her close and talk to her. This is just as it should be. Your baby is programmed to know what she likes and what she needs: you are programmed to love her. The things your baby needs to see, feel and touch are the same things that make her happy. She needs them for as long as she remains interested.

YOUR BABY'S BODY

The changes in your baby's body in her first year are phenomenal; almost everything about her changes in size, and composition.

Bones

At birth babies have soft bones made mostly of cartilage, which makes them very flexible. After birth minerals are deposited in the bones which cause them to harden, a process called ossification. It begins before birth and continues to the end of adolescence, happens faster in girls than boys, and in black babies than white ones. This is one of the reasons why girls walk a little sooner than boys, and why black babies are physically more advanced than white.

Muscles

Babies are born with a complete set of muscles, but like everything else these have to mature. They do so in the same order as the nerves which control them: starting at the neck, working down the body and out toward the fingers. As they mature their structure changes. Mature muscles contain less water and more protein and minerals than immature ones, which gives them added strength and stamina.

Digestion

If babies were fed as nature intended, they would probably be breastfed more or less exclusively for at least two years. Until then their digestive systems are immature. This is demonstrated through examination of babies' stools: in the first year many things pass through undigested. Some do not even pass through, since most newborn babies bring back part of their feed. So-called possetting declines with age and normally stops by about six months. Digestion is helped by 'friendly' bacteria which take up residence in the gut in the first few weeks.

Temperature

If you get too hot you sweat and blood moves into the small blood vessels below the skin (making you turn red). The evaporation of sweat from the skin

Hot or cold?

Since babies have such poor control over their temperature, it is important that you do what you can to help her.

She may be too hot if:
- she is red in the face
- she appears to be sweating
- she feel too hot to your touch

She may be too cold if:
- she seems unusually pale
- she looks blue
- her breathing has slowed dramatically.

As a rule of thumb, when you go out wrap her as if you knew you had to stand at a bus stop for a good while. Remember she is not moving to keep herself warm as you do. Indoors, if the central heating is on, take off her outdoor clothes (even if she is asleep). At night, heat her room, or dress her more warmly than you dress when you sleep alone in an unheated room.

then cools you down. You can also help matters by moving into the shade or reducing your level of activity. If you are cold you do not sweat, and your blood moves away from the surface to the centre of your body which is warmer. You shiver, become active and do things which conserve heat like huddling close to others or putting on extra clothes.

Babies are not very good at any of these things, which is why they cannot exert control over their temperature until they are 12–18 months old. The smaller your baby, the poorer her control.

Breathing

If you compare how a very young baby breathes with how you breathe you will see two differences. The first is obvious: the baby uses her stomach muscles, you use your chest and diaphragm. The second is more subtle. Adults have two breathing systems, one automatic and controlled by the nature of the gases (oxygen and carbon dioxide) in the lungs. This is what prevents you from holding your breath until you are dead. When the oxygen falls below a certain level, you have to take a breath. Everyone has this system. The second system is voluntary and can to some

extent override the automatic. This is what enables you to breathe in before you speak or take a deep breath before you dive into a swimming pool. It enables you to eat without things 'going down the wrong way' and to speak without running out of breath in the middle of a sentence.

Newborn babies do not have this system. They cannot co-ordinate breathing with eating, so they splutter when feeding and if they cry may gasp for breath. In general they breathe in slowly and breathe out quickly. By 6–12 weeks of age they begin to take some control over their breathing and the pattern changes, so that they take in a breath quickly and let it out slowly. You will notice how this alters the way she cries, with her crying becoming more melodic. As she begins to mesh breathing and action she will begin to kick for longer periods. (If you remember how difficult it was to swim a width before you learned how to combine breathing with swimming you will sympathize with babies who have not learned to breathe in before an activity and pace the activity with their breathing pattern.)

This may seem simple, but it underlies your ability to speak and move. Babies are believed to learn the 'in quick out slow' pattern by following your pattern as they cuddle in to your chest. Later they practise breathing and moving as they kick in their cots.

Teething

There are 32 adult teeth but only 20 baby teeth. One baby in 1,500 is born with a tooth, rather more do not have any teeth until after their first birthday. Early or late teething runs in families, but most babies cut their first tooth between five and seven months. The others follow in fairly rapid succession. For some time before they erupt you will see the baby's teeth as little white patches underneath her gums. Just before they break through, they form pale bumps on the gums.

Whenever a baby is 'out of sorts' teething tends to take the blame but since there are only 20 teeth it is not usually at fault. Apart from the short period when the tooth breaks through the gum, there is no reason to suppose that a tooth growing is any more or less painful than a bone growing. Since, at puberty, teenagers often feel 'growing pains' – and are equally out of sorts – it is much more likely that babies are out of sorts because they are growing rather than teething.

Being miserable is one thing, but being ill another. Illness in babies can get out of hand very quickly and should never be ignored. Teething *does not* cause fever, diarrhoea, sickness or convulsions. Such symptoms should not be dismissed as 'teething' (see A–Z of Baby Health, pp. 165–6).

The dos and don'ts of tooth care

It is never too soon to begin to look after teeth – you do only get two sets, after all. Instilling good cleaning and care habits from the start with milk teeth is far easier than trying to establish them when your child is older. If your child loses a first tooth too early, the adjoining teeth may fill the gap, so that when the permanent tooth is ready to emerge, there is nowhere for it to go. This can cause the second teeth to come through irregularly and badly positioned, and lead to problems such as overcrowding, or crooked teeth.

Tooth decay is caused by plaque, which covers the teeth with a sticky bacterial substance. When the bacteria comes into contact with sugar it produces an acid which attacks the teeth. As soon as your baby's first teeth appear, they are at risk from decay, so start cleaning them as soon as they erupt.

- Keep to a good diet during pregnancy.
- Tell your doctor you may be pregnant if medicine is being prescribed, and avoid tetracyclines.
- Make sure that your baby has plenty of calcium (milk, cheese and yogurt are good sources, after six months, see p. 85).

- Make sure she gets vitamin D (egg yolk, oily fish, dairy products, vitamin supplements).
- Limit sweets, cola and ice cream to special times and clean teeth afterward.
- Do not add sugar to drinks or cereals.
- Do not dip dummies in anything sweet.
- Do not let your baby go to sleep sucking a bottle of milk or juice; give her a dummy or bottle of water.
- Give chocolate, cake or biscuits in preference to chewy sweets or sweet drinks because they do not stay on the teeth quite so long.
- Dilute juice is better than squash.
- An apple is better than apple juice.
- Watch for hidden sugars – glucose, sucrose and honey are all sugars.
- Wipe gums (and later teeth) with a soft cloth and a small amount of fluoride toothpaste; ask your dentist's advice on fluoride tablets (see p. 166).
- It does not matter how children clean their teeth as long as they do!

Soothing your teething baby
See pp. 165–6.

Gumming

Babies 'gum' everything, which does not necessarily mean they are teething. The mouth is used for exploring objects. All four- to six-month-olds 'gum', even those who do not get teeth until after their first birthday. See From hand to mouth, p. 137.

The teeth

Typically a baby cuts her first tooth between five and seven months, the rest follow in the order indicated. Your baby should have cut all her teeth by the age of around two and a half.

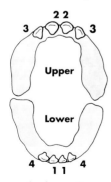 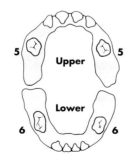 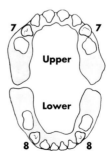 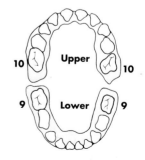

1 lower incisors; **2** upper incisors; **3** upper side teeth; **4** lower side teeth;

5 first upper back teeth (molars); **6** first lower back teeth;

7 upper 'eye' teeth (canines); **8** lower 'eye' teeth;

9 lower second molars; **10** upper second molars.

YOUR BABY'S PHYSICAL DEVELOPMENT

When babies are tiny, it is easy to wish their lives away. A baby, especially a first baby, always seems to be about to reach the next milestone. It can sometimes be a race with the baby next door. Naturally you want yours to win, but motor control is largely genetically programmed. Whether she walks at 10 months and 4 days or 16 months and 10 days depends on the programme she inherited. Some families walk earlier than others. It signifies nothing at all about your child. All the evidence suggests that early walkers are no more likely to be athletes or dancers than late ones. Nor is a child who walks at nine months likely to do better at school or preschool than one who does not walk until she is 16 months.

The only thing that early walking tells you about your baby is that she is likely to reach other milestones early too.

Practice seems to have very little effect on the timing of any motor-control skills. At best a baby walker can advance when your baby walks by a day or two. Researchers watching more than 100 pairs of identical twins noticed than in almost all cases the motor skills of one twin matured at the same time as the other. But weight makes a difference. A child with heavy arms and legs needs more strength to get going.

'Tables' can only give indications of the order in which skills develop. Some children never crawl, some crawl as soon as they can sit and others sit for a long time before they try to crawl. Most children can stand before they are able to walk and walk before they can run. A few run on tiptoe before they can stand still or walk slowly – they need the speed to keep balance!

Your baby's progress in one area is a better guide to her physical skills than her age. A walking baby should be able to pick up a pea between her fingers and thumb; a crawling baby should be able to pass things from hand to hand.

Milestones in head control

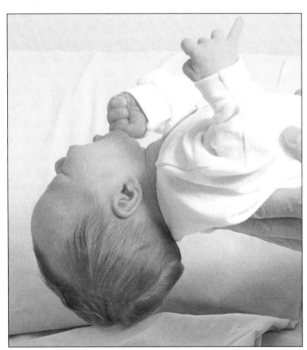

Weeks 1–4: No head control at all

1–4 weeks If you pull your baby by her arms from a lying to a sitting position, her head lags completely behind her body.

8–10 weeks If you pull your baby by her arms from a lying to a sitting position, her head still lags a little behind – but not completely.

Weeks 16–20: Head only slightly lags behind rest of body

16–20 weeks By now, her head lags only slightly behind; if you hold her upright, she can turn her head in all directions.

24–28 weeks Your baby lifts her head spontaneously when you pull her into a sitting position, tucking her head into her chest.

Learning to sit

Sitting gives your baby a better view of the world, and gives you a better view of her. The major advantage a sitting baby has over one who is still lying down is the level of interaction sitting makes possible. People tend to ignore a baby lying on her back and she is confined to looking at the sky and the occasional tree when you are out walking. Once she can sit, she can see everything you can, and 'talk' to and smile at people.

For this reason, sit your baby in a bouncy chair or a car seat indoors, and choose a buggy that allows her to sit propped up if she is not tired.

Milestones in becoming upright

1–14 weeks Your baby is quite passive if you pull her up past a sitting position.

16–24 weeks She begins to push up by raising her buttocks but cannot sustain this position.

36–44 weeks If you raise her up, she will lower her legs and begin to push down; she becomes somewhat more erect.

48–52 weeks She stands erect, but movement is still an effort.

Learning to move

Being able to move changes your child's interaction with the world and with other people because she can find new things to explore and new things to do. Babies who can crawl can also follow their parents and siblings around the house. In cultures in

Milestones in sitting

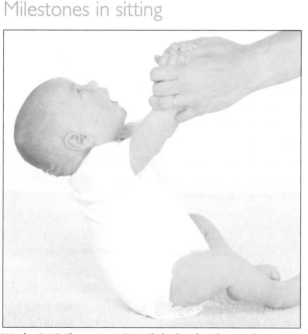

Weeks 8–12 She cannot sit until she has head control

1–4 weeks If you support your baby in a sitting position, her back is uniformly rounded and she has no head control.

4–6 weeks If you support her in a sitting position, her back is rounded but she holds her head up intermittently.

8–12 weeks Supported in a sitting position, her back is still rounded, but she now can raise her head and flex her knees; she can sit for as long as 10–15 minutes if her back and sides are wedged or propped with cushions.

Week 36: She can sit alone for long periods

16–20 weeks Her back is now straighter and she can hold her head erect without any sign of wobble; she can sit for 30 minutes if she is well supported.

20–24 weeks She sits with slight support and can pull herself up to sit; she sits well balanced on a chair.

28 weeks She sits alone steadily if briefly; can push herself into a sitting position.

32 weeks She sits alone, can move and bounce while sitting.

36 weeks She can sit for long periods of time.

40 weeks She can lower herself to sit from standing.

which babies are put on the floor to play, crawling increases the amount of time the child spends with her prime carer. No one leaves a crawling baby alone in a room: you take her with you when you leave. A mobile child cannot be trusted to sit and play quietly.

Not only can a moving baby find more to see and more to do, but this movement and activity are accompanied by chatter. Because you must watch a mobile baby, you look at her and catch her eye more often. You will comment on what you are doing, and are likely to name the objects she touches. 'What have you got there?' you may say, 'Have you got a sock?' with emphasis on 'there' and 'sock'. If she touches something she should not you say 'No' and move her

away. You start to use phrases like 'Down you come' or 'That's naughty' in consistent ways.

When you talk to your mobile baby, you make the meanings of words clear. The words you use to comment on something your baby is doing make the association between the sound and the object or action increasingly obvious. And this, of course, is how your baby will learn to talk.

What you can do to encourage crawling

Your baby will not crawl until she is ready, although you can encourage her to creep forward by putting her on her tummy to play and by calling to her when she is on her hands and knees. A nice soft surface also

Milestones in crawling

Weeks 1–14: Makes crawling movements.

Weeks 26–28: Rolls over, and can turn head to side.

1–14 weeks When lying on her front, your baby makes crawling movements, moving the arm and leg on the same side of her body; she is unable to turn from her front to her back and vice versa; turning her head has no effect on the rest of her body.
16–20 weeks She rolls from stomach to back; lying on stomach, can push her hands and flex her knees.
26–28 weeks She turns her head to the side and toward the back, raising her shoulder and curving her spine; her legs and arms move to the side; she manages to roll from her back to her stomach; she lies on her stomach and pulls herself ahead with her arms; if she is placed on her hands and knees, she rocks.

From creeping to crawling
28–30 weeks She creeps forward rather unsteadily on her hands and knees; pivots from side to side on her stomach.
34–38 weeks She starts to roll intentionally (but – beware – she has no realization that she can roll off the bed); she may move by a combination of rolling and stomach pivoting; creeping and crawling become better coordinated.
48–52 weeks She begins to roll intentionally to get into a sitting or crawling position; she shows some sign that she can adjust to her whereabouts; she is less likely to fall off the edge of the bed or attempt to crawl downstairs.

helps – the fact that today's babies crawl much sooner than babies used to probably has a lot to do with the fact that they have warm carpeted floors, while 100 years ago they had to contend with cold rough slabs.

Crawling babies love to play hide and seek games. Try chasing her behind the settee or round and round an armchair. Drape a cloth over the kitchen table and let her crawl underneath. Keep peeping or crawl under yourself. Such games increase the level of activity and encourage boisterousness and teach her to expect, anticipate and plan (skills which are the basis of so much later learning). Most of all they are good, loving, social fun.

Once your baby starts to crawl, if you have not done so before, you must 'baby proof' the house (see Is your child safe?, pp. 168–72).

Milestones in walking

Weeks 18–24: Supports her weight in your lap

Weeks 26–30: Cruises around the furniture

1– 14 weeks If you support your baby under the arms, her posture is limp; she steps with high knees when her feet touch a sloping surface; she kicks using the same movements when she is excited or upset.

18–24 weeks If you support her under the arms, she holds her head in line with her body; she supports most of her weight when standing on your lap; she may stamp or push down with her foot; she will begin to hold a posture as she moves; if she steps, she holds out her arms or turns to adjust her balance.

26–30 weeks Her postural adjustment improves; she can now support her weight when she holds on to the furniture; may pull herself up, and be able to move her feet when standing; begins to 'cruise' around the furniture holding on and adjusting her balance with each step. At first she clings with both hands, then uses one to hold and the other to explore. Barefoot walking promotes strong feet, ankle and leg muscles; using walkers for too long can damage hip sockets.

40–48 weeks Stepping and postural adjustment are more obvious; she can lean out to reach something while she is standing; she pulls herself up and sits down again with confidence; she can walk if you hold both her hands; she can lift one foot when standing.

50–58 weeks She can stand by herself and walks if you hold one of her hands; she may soon begin to walk alone, but she loses balance if she stops suddenly and falls often.

18 months She can walk forward, sideways and backward; she is able to pull a toy behind her or push one in front; she can use a sit-and-ride bike; she may be able to run but still falls easily.

Choosing a walker

There are two basic types of baby walker: those that babies sit inside and those that they push. The first are for immobile babies, the second – which are often like little carts or convert into sit-and-ride bikes – are for babies who are already beginning to walk around the furniture.

A baby walker is not an essential item, and many health professionals feel that the dangers of using one outweigh their advantages. If you do buy one:

- Ensure a walker cannot tip, especially if your child can push a sit-in walker against the furniture. Ordinary push-alongs are not safe to use as walkers and should be confined to children who can get into a standing position without any help.

- A tray or a few inbuilt activities adds to the play value of a sit-in walker.
- Fence off stairs: walking aids give babies speed before they have sense. Remember they can (and do) push themselves down steps and stairs (including the slightest change in floor level) and into radiators, glass cupboards and other dangers. Before putting a young baby in a sit-in walker, baby-proof the room (see pp. 170–1) and make sure that sharp edges and doors have protective corners (babies do not always look where they are going at speed).
- Do not leave your child in a walker for too long. A walking baby sits down when her ankles are tired. Babies left in sit-in walkers for long periods can damage their ankles.

What you can do to encourage walking

For some while before they walk, children pull themselves up and walk around the furniture. Make this more fun by arranging the furniture for her. Once she can walk the length of the settee put a chair near enough for her to cross to it. Once she can manage this, move it a little further away. Remove all unstable furniture such as rocking chairs (once she starts to pull herself up, she will try to do so on anything which is the right height). Tablecloths can also be dangerous – she may pull both cloth and anything on top of the cloth down on to her head.

Although there is not much evidence that baby walkers speed up learning to walk, there is evidence that they can bring babies some of the advantages of mobility. Babies who scurry after their parents in baby walkers do get closer contact, more social interchange and more language training. It is not clear, however, whether this has any long-term advantage. Such babies may be quicker with their initial understanding of language but they may not maintain this advantage. Those left to sit and play soon catch up.

Whether you buy a baby walker or not is a matter of taste. If your baby is creeping at six to seven months or quite happy to sit and play, there is probably little point in buying a sit-in walker. A crawling baby has far greater opportunities to explore with her hands than one imprisoned by a baby walker. If your baby is demanding and frustrated by her inactivity or cries if you leave the room, a walker is worth considering. Any child who is not mobile by 9–11 months will probably enjoy the freedom that scooting about brings.

Once she can walk intermittently a push-along walker can give her more freedom to explore, which many children enjoy, but choose models for stability (see box above).

Left: Some time between his first birthday and 18 months, your child will walk confidently.

HOW YOUR BABY'S SENSES DEVELOP

The overwhelming majority of babies can see and hear at birth, of course, but in the first year of your baby's life, her reactions to what she sees and hears, and the way she builds on these primary senses to shape her understanding of the world around her develop and change.

Learning to see

Your newborn baby spends about 5 per cent of her waking time scanning the environment for something special to look at; by the time she is two, this will have increased to 35 per cent. And, of course, her waking time has considerably increased.

Milestones in seeing

Birth The pupil of the eye adjusts to light; baby blinks; she can focus for a moment on an object held about 20–25 cm (8–10 in) away; if her head is moved to the side, her eyes follow slowly.

4 weeks She is very interested in faces; recognizes her mother's face; can cry tears.

6–12 weeks Can see 'out of the corner' of her eyes; her eyes work together and move to focus; she looks at edges and corners.

12–20 weeks She knows when things are familiar; she looks at her hands; and focuses on her reflection in a mirror.

20–28 weeks She develops hand–eye co-ordination; she prefers looking at complex things; she pats her image in a mirror and adjusts her posture to get a better look; she can see 800 times better than she did at birth.

28–44 weeks She can focus on very small objects; she likes to look at new things; and she registers depth.

45–52 weeks She can follow a rapidly moving object; her vision is almost as good as yours.

What do babies look at?

If you show a month-old baby a square she will look at the edges and the corners, and hardly bother about the pieces in between. When she looks at your face she does not meet your eye but concentrates on your chin and hairline – the bits that she 'recognizes' when she sees you. At first, babies tend to focus on one characteristic of an object at a time. They probably do not notice the differences between a red circle and a red square.

By two months, your baby shows more interest in the features of a face and the relationship between them. She likes your eyes to be open; she prefers you to turn so she can look into both your eyes at the same time. As you meet her eyes she shows interest and excitement and her gaze moves between your eyes and from your eyes to your mouth and back. She probably only glances at your hairline. By five months, she can differentiate those faces she has seen before from those she has not.

What you can do

Show her things with clear lines and choose dark or brightly coloured objects (babies generally prefer red and blue) or things that glitter and sparkle and catch the light. Until about three months babies seem to prefer movement and find it easier to 'latch on' to things that both move and make a noise.

- Mobiles – especially musical mobiles – are an obvious choice, but buy one that gives your baby the best view. Cardboard shapes look very pretty as you enter the room but may be unimpressive for a baby lying flat on her back. If the mobile does not make a sound, add a few tinkling bells (available from pet shops).

- Babies are especially interested in pattern, texture and depth, which are the factors that enable them to learn to recognize objects and understand what certain things have in common. A cup, for example, can be all sorts of colours and quite a few shapes and vary in brightness depending on the light, but it always has the same arrangement of handle and container (pattern), the same glossy surface (texture), and an open top and closed base (depth). Until she knows what cups have in common she cannot begin to fit a name to them.

- Until she is old enough to grab, attach all manner of things to your baby's cot. Very young babies enjoy familiar things and variations on a theme. Watch while she looks at the shapes. If she likes some better than others look for things which are similar. If she likes a mitten she may love a glove. Fix a pole across the cot and hang things from short pieces of wool.

● The stage beyond looking is swiping. Once she starts to kick and wave her arms, tie some toys where she can accidentally hit them. The movement of the toy will excite her further and she will kick and flail even more. If she hits the toy again it will move again, and so on. It is in these simple games that your baby comes to realize that she can actually make things happen and starts to gain the motivation to learn how to do these things for herself.

Milestones in hand control

**Weeks 22–30:
Keeps eyes on hand when reaching**

**Weeks 32–36:
Catches a ball rolled toward her**

**Weeks 36 onward:
Palmar grip develops**

0–8 weeks Hands predominantly closed.

8–12 weeks Hands still usually closed, but can be held open; holding objects is a reflex action; her grasp is haphazard. By three months her hands are usually open; she grips objects but does not look for one she drops; dropping is not deliberate. Nor is reaching deliberate, but if she accidentally swipes an object tied to the bars of a cot and it excites her, she may repeat the action.

12–16 weeks Clasps her hand round an object; watches her hand; is distracted if it comes into view.

16–20 weeks Her hands are usually open and she may begin to reach out and touch, bringing her hands together deliberately. Cannot grasp an object until it touches the palm of her hand and grasping involves only closing her fingers. If you offer her a toy, she will look back and forth from hand to toy, focusing attention on one then the other.

22–30 weeks She uses her eyes to help her reach an object, keeping her eyes on it while she reaches for it. She begins to grasp objects by cupping her whole hand around them and using her thumb. By seven months she can move her hand to reach for a noisy object in the dark; she uses her thumb to oppose all her fingers; and she can use both hands together.

32–36 weeks She can catch a suspended object or ball rolled to her; she uses her hands separately; passes an object from one hand to store in the other. One hand becomes the active hand, the other the passive. Toward the end of this period the 'palmar' grasp is clearly developed: when grasping, your baby uses the palm of her hand and her fingers together, rather than simply closing her fingers over anything that happens to be in her hand.

36 weeks–15 months The palmar grip develops and matures; she moves her thumb to oppose her fingers. Begins to anticipate; her hand moves into a grasping position before touching the object she intends to grab and will be 'lined up' correctly; moves her hand down and reaches from the top; she begins to use a pincer grip, picking things up between her thumb and forefinger.

By 9–10 months she begins to drop things deliberately and to poke and prod with her fingers; she may also point. She can hold a crayon and feed herself little sandwiches or peas.

Tests

Vision, hearing and movement tests are all part of regular developmental checks (see Chapter 6). Always tell someone if you are worried that your baby is not developing as you think she should and make sure that your concern is taken seriously. The sooner a possible defect is noticed, the better it is for your baby.

Seeing her hands

In her first weeks your baby does not see her hand or know that it belongs to her. One day she might reach out with one hand and find the other. The touch probably interests her, so this new hand becomes something to play with. She does not realize that it is part of her body. If her hands make a noise (because they contain a rattle) she will like them even better. At this stage a wrist rattle or a wrist band with a little bell attached will encourage her to watch her hands. The noise helps her to 'connect' what she sees, what she hears and the movements her body makes.

By 12 weeks, she will sit or lie and watch her hands waving in front of her eyes. By now she has probably also learned how to hit out and make something move and to put out her hand to touch a noisy toy. She does not watch how she does these things: they are reflex responses. Babies are born with a capacity to reach for the place noise comes from or where they see movement. When she first begins to reach for objects rather than respond automatically to a noise she is totally distracted by her hand coming into view. She sees the object, moves her hand toward it, sees her hand and then forgets what she intended to do. Slowly she learns to ignore her hand.

It is tempting to keep putting the toy she reaches for into her hand, but if you do she does not learn to reach. If she is having a lot of difficulty move the toy nearer but let her do the last bit.

Rattles with a narrow stem are easiest to grab, and those which are well balanced easiest to hold. A dumb-bell-shaped rattle or a light ring is ideal.

Reaching is a complex skill

You prepare your hands before reaching, taking into account the object you are reaching for. You judge if you need one hand or two to clasp. You turn your hand to line it up with the object. You open your hand wide enough to grasp the object and extend your arm to the correct place. You decide whether to use your hand like a cup or your fingers like crab claws. You are not aware of doing any of these things. Babies have to learn how to do them all.

From hand to mouth

By five months your baby is likely to be ready to reach out fairly directly to take objects from you without making intermediate adjustments. When she has something in her grasp she will begin to take it to her mouth. She can hold a teething ring with shapes on it, lollipop-shaped rattles, soft bricks and chewing shapes and the interest an object has for her tongue is as important as its shape or colour. Rough and smooth surfaces, things that crackle when chewed or feel both warm and cold to the touch are all stimulating for her.

Babies are not teething when they put things in their mouths: they are exploring. Until she can use her hands to explore or move her fingers at will to poke and prod, stroke and feel, she uses her lips and tongue. These also magnify how things feel (this is why a tooth feels so big in your mouth). Babies explore with their lips, gums and tongues until their hands have matured enough for their fingers to take over. After this they put things into their mouths less often.

The gape test

When your baby takes things to her mouth, she is aiming to get her fist to her lips. In doing so, she can push anything she is holding into the back of her throat or poke herself in the eye. All toy manufacturers have to ensure that their products pass a 'gape' test so that they cannot be poked deep into the throat, and that they do not have sharp edges or corners that could cut or harm the eyes.

To make a gape tester for yourself, cut an oval hole in a piece of card the size of your baby's mouth at its most open. Any object, or part of an object, that goes through the hole is potentially dangerous.

You may think that you will not take your eyes off her, but you will: the phone rings, you smell the potatoes burning, you hear a commotion outside. It only takes a couple of seconds.

Making sense of the world

The human eye is often likened to a camera, but what you see is infinitely more interesting than a photograph. The camera transfers a world which has depth to a flat surface; a photograph is and looks flat. Things nearer the lens seem bigger than those further away because they take up more of the picture.

The world you see with your eyes is not like a photograph: you see that some things are close to you and others further away and take this into consideration when you are judging their relative sizes. This 'interpretation' applies to shapes too. Square table-tops always look square and round plates always look round whatever angle you view them from, but if you are trying to draw the table and can see the legs you do not draw a square top, nor do you draw the plate round, you make it oval. Scientists call this phenomenon 'constancy' because you perceive objects as having the same constant size and same constant shape (and constant colour and brightness).

Babies do not have too many problems in interpreting the world because they move (or are carried) about. When you stand up, all the world below eye level changes shape. When you sit down again it goes back to the way it was. When you walk toward the bus stop, everything gets bigger but the relationship between objects stays the same: children are still smaller than adults, and adults are still shorter than the bus stop sign.

Perceiving depth

By the time they can crawl and walk, most babies are able to perceive depth. In experiments in which a glass barrier was placed over a hole, babies did not crawl out on to it. Some very early crawlers ventured on to the glass, although they were uneasy once they had done so. This suggests that babies both see and respond to depth by about eight months.

Constancy

They respond to constancy a little sooner, at about five months. Babies who are very interested in something suck hard on their dummies. When they are bored they stop sucking. The way constancy is tested is to show a baby one object and then move it so that she looks at it from a different angle. If she starts sucking the dummy after the object is moved, she thinks that she is looking at a new object; if she does not, she realizes it is the same one. At three months most babies suck, at five most do not.

Understanding that things exist

A baby needs to know that her mother is the same person every time she sees her and she needs to know that she continues to exist even if she cannot see her. Psychologists call the first skill object identity and the second object permanence. Babies develop object identity at about five months: your baby knows there is only one mother. Before five months there is a new mother every morning.

Learning that people and things continue to exist even when they cannot be seen takes longer to absorb. Babies play with this idea for about a year, which is why they love games in which things are seen and then disappear. Most toys aimed at children between 9 and 18 months have something that can be used to play hide and seek – Jack-in-the-box, shape sorters, stacking cups and toys with little doors and hidey-holes are obvious examples – and she will also love 'peek-a-boo' and collecting things in little bags.

At about nine or ten months babies begin to behave as if their parents exist even when they cannot see them. Your baby will cry and fuss if you leave the room and remain miserable for some time after you have gone. (Previously she would have stopped crying once you were out of sight as if she had forgotten all about you.) About the time she gets this sorted out, your baby will probably become fearful of strangers. Once she knows that people continue to exist when she cannot see them she becomes perturbed by those she has not seen before, including close relatives who visit infrequently. She may have beamed and gurgled at Grandma last time she visited, but now she screams and cannot be induced to go to her.

In the early months you could take toys away from her quite easily and if she dropped something she never looked for it. At about the same time she becomes clingy and fretful if you try to leave her, you will notice that she begins to look for the things she has dropped and to lift a cover you place over a teddy to hide it from view. This is a precursor to throwing something from her cot or high chair deliberately so she can look at it on the floor. (Because it gets a response from you, this soon becomes a highly social game as beloved – by the baby – as 'peek-a-boo'.)

Regardless of all the practice and all the games she plays it will be months before your baby works out the complexities of inside, outside, under and over. Until then she will play endlessly: putting one thing inside another, looking at it inside and then taking it out; gathering things in a bag, emptying the bag and then putting everything back; looking for dogs under flaps in books and pictures under puzzle shapes; and taking the car keys to hide in her trolley.

Milestones in perception

0–20 weeks Does not look for an object she drops; soon settles if you leave her; if something is hidden behind a screen she will look surprised if the screen is lifted and there is nothing there, but is not surprised by a change of object.

20 weeks Watches an object go behind a screen and looks for it emerging on the far side; does not look surprised if a new object emerges (if you cover a teddy with a cloth and remove the cloth to reveal a toy train she does not seem surprised).

26 weeks Watches if she drops an object; looks for a partially hidden object.

32–40 weeks Moves one object to reach another hidden from view; looks for objects dropped from cot (and plays the game incessantly); looks for an object where it usually is – not necessarily where she saw it last; clings when you leave; is afraid of strangers.

12–14 months Looks for object where she last saw it; plays lots of hide-and-seek games; enjoys shape sorters, hidey-holes, and 'swag' bags (see p. 211).

Learning to hear

All babies are different. Some sleep through almost anything, some wake at the slightest sound. The same baby may be interested in a rattle when she is happy and distressed by it when fretful. There are, however, some general guidelines:

- When they are alert and awake babies are more interested in gentler sounds. Your baby will become more alert when she hears approaching footsteps, a rousing signature tune or water running from the tap.
- Slow rhythmic sound calms babies, especially when they are ready to sleep. It changes the baby's breathing and heartbeat from a pattern typical of waking babies to one associated with sleep. A

steady hum such as a fan, the vacuum cleaner, or the engine of a car can have the same effect. A fretful baby can often be soothed by strapping her to your back and vacuuming the house.

- Babies like female voices most of all. Most people take this preference into account when they talk to babies – children as young as four raise the pitch of their voices.

Babies are born with the ability to hear low- and high-pitched sounds, and to locate them approximately in space. From a very early age they link hearing with seeing and look to see what is making a sound. They also reach out and grab for the sound-making object. At first they are not good at locating a sound that comes from above, behind or to one side, particularly when they are lying down, but if a baby is propped up she can look around and turn her head to explore the world; she will also look up when you call. If you are off to one side she may turn but may not be able to find you.

By eight weeks she will look in the right general area, by 12–16 weeks she will look in exactly the right place. Within another month she will be able to locate something above her head or behind her back.

Milestones in hearing

Birth Startled at a noise; turns toward a voice; moves very slightly in time to speech (this is called the language dance); quietened by low-pitched sounds.

4 weeks Can distinguish sounds such as 'p' from 'b' and 'dah' from 'tah'; prefers complex sounds; likes to be told stories even though she cannot understand them.

8–12 weeks Turns her head to right or left in response to a sound from that direction.

12–16 weeks Can locate where a sound is coming from; looks to see.

16–24 weeks Can find a sound made above or below head level; can distinguish more complex sounds like 'baba' from 'bagay' and recognize a sound hidden in a string (in other words, she can recognize the 'ba' in 'kobabo'); she can tell tunes apart; and distinguish individual voices.

24–32 weeks Responds to her own name.

32–52 weeks Responds to simple commands such as 'give me', 'show me', and 'no' and to the names of familiar objects such as 'dummy' or the names of familiar people.

When to worry

About 85 per cent of deaf babies are born to hearing parents. Early detection of deafness is important. Although all babies occasionally fail to respond to sounds, one who consistently fails to respond, or turns only to certain sounds, or in the direction of one ear should have a hearing test.

You can carry out some simple tests if you are worried about her hearing. Call from different areas of the room. Shake a rattle from left, right, top and bottom and see if she responds. Can she also do it if you ring a bell? If you are not reassured by such tests ask the clinic to check her hearing (see p. 155). Even if she does seem to respond you should remain vigilant and continue to report your concerns. She may have some hearing loss.

What you can do

It is natural to call your baby's name and wait until she catches your eye, or walk into her line of vision, or show her a rattle, shake it to attract her attention, wait until she turns to find it and then shake it again. In all these things, you are helping her to improve her ability to locate where sounds are coming from.

Expectation

By about three months a baby will begin to expect certain sounds to accompany certain activities. A toy duck is expected to squeak so if it barks she may cry. By four months she will cry if she hears a recording of your voice coming from one side of the room while you stand on the other. By six months she can match voices and faces, and remember sounds. This is essential before she can begin to understand language.

LEARNING TO TALK

There is a lot more to language than speaking the words. Although babies do not begin to understand what is being said until the end of the first year, they make preparations long before this by engaging those around them in conversation. Babies are especially tuned to speech. Within hours of birth they are dancing in time to language and turning to the sound of voices. You will not see this first phase of the dance because the movements are very small (researchers record them on film).

From soon after birth you can look directly at a baby and pull a face, perhaps poke out your tongue or raise your eyebrows. If you keep doing this and smile and talk as you do so, your baby will probably make the same face (see p. 61). You do it, she copies, you do it back. This is the turn-taking of a conversation.

By the time she is 4–6 weeks your baby will probably be moving her mouth in answer to your questions. These movements look exactly like speech, and they may or may not be accompanied by sounds or bubble blowing, but she certainly breathes as she would if she were speaking, drawing a breath in quickly and letting it out slowly. As she does this, you will automatically stop and wait. When she has finished and you take your turn, she stops all activity to listen to you. She may raise her eyebrows in answer to your questions. You may see her hands joining in this conversation from as early as three weeks; certainly by eight weeks she will be clearly waving and moving her hands when it is her turn to 'speak'.

Milestones in language

4 weeks Responds to the human voice.

8 weeks Moves mouth as if talking; makes noises and 'talks' back.

12 weeks Babbles and coos when spoken to.

16 weeks Cooing changes pitch and volume; talks to objects and faces; talks more when happy; makes sounds h, n, f, p, b.

20 weeks Babbles become more elaborate and sound more like speech.

26 weeks Combines sounds; says something like 'kibee'; varies pitch and rate of speech; talks to toys or her mirror image; calls to you.

30 weeks Repeats syllable, such as 'numnumnum', 'dadada'; tone of her babbling rises and falls like adult speech.

34 weeks Shouts for attention; shows emotion through sounds; responds to 'no' and 'bye bye'; may say 'pss, pss' when she sees the cat.

38 weeks Says one meaningful 'word' or has one meaningful sign; it could be 'dog' or something of her own like 'num, num' for food, or lifting her arms for 'pick me up'; babble now sounds like speech (as if she is speaking a language of her own).

44 weeks Says 'No!' or 'Hi!' and begins to understand more words.

48 weeks Says two or three words or has two or three meaningful signs; uses 'babble' as if she knows it means something.

52 weeks Says three words or has three meaningful signs; points; jabbers; understands more complex requests such as 'bring your shoes here'; may have one word for a whole class of objects, so, for example, all animals are 'pss, pss', all men are Dada.

Taking turns

Turn-taking is the basis of all social interaction. You speak, she listens. She smiles, you watch and listen, and then answer her with a smile and a compliment or question. When you talk to your baby, use sounds, smiles, gestures and words. She will reply with sounds, smiles, facial expressions, kicks and arm waving. What is said is unimportant, but the way it is said is vital. You must both take turns, since the art of conversation has as much to do with being a good listener as it does with being an interesting talker.

Not all parents are good conversationalists. If you go on speaking without offering your baby a turn, or smile without breaking off for her to smile back she will look away. She will also look away if you start again before she has finished. If you continue to smile she will cry. Repeated time and again, poor conversations can teach babies to withdraw or to become over-demanding. In both cases they develop poor conversational skills.

When you talk to a baby exaggerate what you would do when talking to an adult. Make your voice particularly high pitched, and your eyebrows disappear into your hairline and leave your mouth open wide as you wait for her response. Once you have drawn her into the conversation, let her take control. She will decide when she has had enough.

Babies like imitation: initially at least your baby will respond best when you return the noises, facial expressions, smiles and hand movements she makes to you. Toward her fourth month this will begin to change, as she takes charge. If you ask her how she is, she may look away to find something to watch. You will notice and comment on it. Then and only then does your baby respond. Having learned how to have a conversation, your baby is now looking for something to talk about.

Understanding you

By nine or ten months your baby will begin to read your intentions and seek your approval by observing your face and listening to the tone of your voice. Before going to the cupboard she will look at you, make sure you have understood what she is going to do, then crawl over. She will not necessarily obey spoken or unspoken commands.

Your crawling baby may wait for you to say 'No' before starting on some task and recognize some ambiguity in your response. She crawls toward the cupboard. You know this is fun. She knows this is fun. You say 'No', lift her away and you both laugh. Yet when you say 'No' as she crawls toward the fire, she stops. By the end of her first year your baby takes your response into consideration. Naturally she can do something 'just to annoy you' and will. But this development gives a reason for language, something to talk about and share. The look on her face as she crawls to the cupboard says 'What do you think?'

From 'coo' to 'dada'

Speaking involves moving the mouth, lips and tongue in quite precise ways and also controlling breathing.

At birth your baby is poorly equipped to do either of these things. She breathes by taking air in slowly and letting it out in a rush and the muscles of her tongue are not formed for speaking. At about the time that the vocal muscles are developing for speech, your baby will begin to coo and babble. In the early months she makes all the sounds used in all the languages in the world, not only those she

Right: Babies chat to beloved toys, as well as people – getting a reply is less important than practice in making sounds.

hears. In fact hearing sounds has nothing to do with the sounds she makes because deaf babies produce the same sounds.

By four months these cooing sounds change pitch and volume to sound more like the language(s) she hears around her. She concentrates on the sounds h, n, k, f, p, b, babbling repeatedly whenever she is on her own.

Within a month she will have added vowel sounds to say a, aa, e, ee, i, aye, o, oo, u, and will incorporate these sounds into 'conversations' with you. Within another month she will begin to combine vowels and consonants, to say ka or pa and repeat sounds to say 'papapa pa' or 'numnumnum num' and later 'papanumga' and other combinations. By six months she will be more selective, concentrating on the sounds she hears around her and putting them into long speech-like sequences. As she gets older these sound more and more like real speech. It sounds so real that you may find yourself asking 'What did you say?' or assume that she understands what she is trying to communicate. Sometimes she may. Most families have stories about a child asking something like 'Gumga, pi cacifna?' and when she received the answer 'Yes' going to find her coat.

At around seven months your baby will start to copy the sounds you make. You may find that she answers you with an echo. These sounds will not be complicated – the favourites are naturally 'Dada' and 'Mama'. She will not attach any meaning to these sounds; at this stage she is simply perfecting her sound production. Meaning is, however, not far away.

Words and sentences

In the beginning babbling is simply vocal play, only later do the sounds begin to have meaning. They may not be generally accepted words but you, your child and the rest of the family will understand them. She will babble less once she can produce real words, but children as old as two may revert to babbling when they are excited or when playing. Baby talk is positively good for your child: do not discourage or be afraid to let her know you understand – she will use the 'proper' word when she is ready.

Once children know the sounds and patterns of their native language they begin to attach meaning.

The language of signs

By the time she is seven or eight months old your baby will have one or two meaningful signs. Some are obvious (right), others more subtle. A child who has watched her older sister sing 'The wheels on the bus' may wave her hands every time she sees a bus. Often she accompanies signs with sounds, to draw your attention to the fact she is making them. The best response is to tell her in words what she is telling you in signs: 'It's a bus', 'You want more'.

A child who can make signs may not yet understand spoken words but she has begun to understand why and how language is used. Telling her you understand reinforces this. She may put out her hand for more, or turn her head away, for 'no'.

Your baby lifting his arms imploringly skyward is the clearest way he has to tell you that he wants you to pick him up.

When he sits on your lap, his persistent raising of his bottom tells you his intention: 'Jog me up and down.'

Seven per cent of children say one word at about eight months and about two per cent do not attempt to say a word before they are two. The rest fall in the middle. Again this is not an indicator of intelligence. Late talkers probably have problems in producing, rather than understanding, language. Children who speak later often have a detailed understanding although they say nothing. Those who start early sometimes do not understand anything they cannot yet say. If your child understands and follows instructions there is probably nothing to worry about – but do ask the doctor or clinic to check, just in case.

What you can do
- Talk even though she does not understand.
- Give her a turn; wait for her response.
- Create opportunities for conversations.
- Comment on things when she does them.
- Name the things she picks up.
- Show her books, give names to the things you look at together.
- Encourage sign language: stroke the picture of the cat, kiss one of the baby, smack the big bad wolf.

Language in deaf babies

Deaf babies cry, coo and babble and initially sound exactly like hearing babies. They also communicate with smiles, gestures and sounds. At some point though they seem to lose interest in babbling – perhaps because they cannot hear themselves doing it, or because they cannot perfect their sounds. At this age it is difficult to teach a deaf child to communicate by making noises. It is, however, quite easy to teach deaf babies sign language. Those who have done so say that deaf babies progress to becoming skilled language users just as quickly (and in some cases more quickly) than hearing children.

- Say things simply.
- Reinforce her efforts: if she lifts her arms say 'You want to be picked up'; if she says 'num num' say 'You want numnum. You want dinner?'
- Sing to her, read nursery rhymes, play games like 'This little piggy'.

Helping with language

Asking your baby to point to objects shows you that he has understood what you asked and 'knows' the word for an object, even if he cannot say it yet.

You can take this further, by saying something like 'Where is the ball? Can you give it to me?', to encourage language skills and interaction.

LEARNING ABOUT RELATIONSHIPS

Whatever happens between you and your child now or in the future, she has the power to break your heart. This bond between you is generally known by the rather bland word 'attachment'. Attachment can happen suddenly in the first moments after your baby's birth or more slowly over the first weeks of her life. Her attachment to you happens more slowly and many believe it forms a model for all the close relationships of her life.

Love and consistency are vital for 'good' attachment. Firmness or indulgence are probably less important than the fact that if you love your child and treat her consistently she will know what is expected of her and know that her love and security will not suddenly be undermined.

How attachment develops

When your baby is less than six weeks old, everyone is her friend. Although she prefers the smell, voice and sight of her mother, this is a small preference. Over the next months people become less equal in her eyes and it is soon clear that she prefers her main carer. She smiles more, laughs longer and watches more carefully when he or she is around. The warmer, more caring and responsive the carer, the more firmly does the baby become attached. By six to eight months her preference is pronounced: her face lights up, her arms go up for a cuddle and she calls out in delight.

Fear of strangers

Once your child can recognize you, she can recognize that other people are not you and will scream when she sees them. The only way to deal with this is to approach strangers very gradually. Hold your child firmly, cuddle her in your arms and do not make her look at the stranger (even if it is Grandpa). Sit together without placing any stress on your child and she may come round, but do not assume too much. Looking from the safety of your arms is not the same as sitting on Grandpa's knee.

Babies form attachments to all of their family and those who regularly care for them. They love those who give them time, love, care, comfort and consideration. They also love teddies, bottles and blankets. Since they frequently spend time alone in bed, it is not surprising that babies find security in the things that surround them as they sleep. A love object can comfort a child who is upset, hurt or afraid.

About half of all Western children form these attachments and keeping the blanket clean, or finding it when it is lost can challenge even the most resourceful parent. You will not be the first who has had to scour the shops for an identical teddy – only to be told it does not smell right – or searched the garden with a torch at midnight.

Attachment to objects is a good thing. It gives a child confidence and helps her to deal with difficult situations. Even adults need to 'psych' themselves up to face potentially difficult situations. Children use comfort objects to give themselves courage and often cope better with new situations for doing so. This can hold true for children as old as ten (although they will change the object to which they are attached for something more suitable for their age).

Separation

As early as four months some babies like to have something familiar nearby. Anything that 'puts you in mind' such as an old jumper will help. Most children spend some time separated from their loved ones. How well they adjust depends on how long the separation lasts and how old the child is at the time. Children under six months, for example, adjust quite well to their mothers' returning to work because out of sight is out of mind. At eight months they may scream persistently because they miss *you*. At this age, and later, long-term separation – if your child has to go into hospital, for example, and you cannot go too – is almost always difficult and disturbing.

This obviously can cause problems if you return to work at this time. When a parent who has always been there disappears a child assumes that he or she has gone for good, and cries or screams and clings to those she knows. But, be reassured: as long as you have handed her care over to someone who is going to love her in an environment that is going to offer the sort of stimulation she knows, she will settle.

Milestones in relating to others

0–4 weeks Watches your face intently as you talk to her; settles better when with someone familiar; imitates facial expressions.

8 weeks Smiles; takes turn in a 'conversation'.

12 weeks Very interested in surroundings; stops crying when you enter the room; recognizes familiar people; aware of strangers and strange situations.

16 weeks Demands attention by fussing; bored if left alone; enjoys people; anticipates feeding when she sees bottle; shows excitement by squirming, squealing and laughing; shows interest in strange people and places.

20 weeks Smiles at herself in the mirror; pats bottle or breast with both hands; subject to rapid mood changes; people make her laugh and kick with excitement; makes noises to show her pleasure; can tell strangers from those she knows.

26 weeks Begins to fear strangers; holds out arms to be picked up; laughs when you play 'peek-a-boo'; excited on hearing footsteps, door opening, and so on; imitates more complex behaviour; has definite likes and dislikes.

30 weeks Begins to look for things she drops; fear of strangers increases; frets when prime carer disappears; imitates simple actions; plays 'peek-a-boo'; expects certain things to happen. Bites aggressively; keeps mouth closed if she does not like food. Tries to attract your attention; may have a few simple signs.

34 weeks Increasing anxiety when prime carer leaves; fear of strangers and strange places; may dislike being dressed; may become quite disturbed when you are away from home.

38 weeks More dependent on prime carer; increased interest in pleasing prime carer; afraid of being left alone even in familiar places; puts up hand to avoid

Clapping games such as 'pat-a-cake' give hours of pleasure from around 10 months.

being washed; uses prime carer as a safe base.

44 weeks Stops when someone says 'no'; waves bye-bye; imitates actions and expressions; offers toy but does not let go; looks around a corner, or out from behind the sofa; repeats actions if someone laughs; pulls at your clothes to attract attention; plays 'pat-a-cake'; reacts to your moods; cries if scolded; becomes independent; wants to put on shoes; tests your patience; looks at books; looks at you to check your expression before doing anything.

48 weeks Experiences joy when she achieves something; shows her frustration especially if stopped from doing things she wants to do.

52 weeks Understands simple requests; anticipates – she is, for example, ready to be tickled when you play 'This little piggy'; shakes head for 'no'; covers her face to play 'peek-a-boo'; may also show jealousy, affection, anger and fear; explores away from you; clings; needs her dummy, teddy or security blanket; points to show you things.

Left: At 20 weeks, she laughs and kicks for the sheer pleasure of doing so.

Being a warm family

The first thing a child recognizes is what psychologists call the emotional tone of her family. It is hard to say exactly what warmth is because different people express it in different ways, but a warm parent cares, responding sensitively and with understanding. He or she can put herself in the child's shoes, often puts the child's interest first, expresses affection and shows enthusiasm for the child's activities. A hostile parent does none of these things. The message he or she gives is one of rejection. Children from warm families:

- have higher IQs in preschool;
- are more secure;
- have higher self-esteem;
- show more understanding of others;
- are nicer to others, helpful and responsive to their distress.

What you can do

You may know you love your baby, but to a baby love that does not show might as well not exist. Even if you are not the sort of adult who touches and hugs other adults you should cuddle and hug your baby as much as you can.

If you give your baby lots of love she will know how to demonstrate love later on. Be guided by her: some babies squirm to be put down, some cuddle in as if by keeping still you might forget they are there. If you enjoy cuddling her, and she enjoys your cuddles, do it, but do not force yourself when you do not feel like it. Pretending does not fool a baby who is tuned to your emotions.

Nobody can give all the time nor do all the things they would like to. Life with a baby or small child is always a compromise between her needs and those of the rest of her family – and that includes her parents. If your baby knows she is valued whether laughing or crying, sweet or sour she will return the compliment. A child who knows that love is always the bottom line does not need you to be constantly happy or constantly attentive to her wants, needs and games. She will know instinctively that your current distraction or preoccupation does not mean she has lost you for ever.

LEARNING ABOUT FEELINGS

Some babies are easy-going, adaptable and sunny. Some are easy-going when you get to know them but cautious about accepting new people or new things. Others are difficult.

In the same way that grown-ups do not fall into neat categories, babies vary enormously, but some differences seem to be there from birth. 'Easy' babies have regular habits from the start. They quickly settle into a feeding schedule, a sleep pattern and even have bowel movements at the same time each day. They take new places, foods and people in their stride. If things go wrong they do not over-react. An easy child whimpers if food is delayed: she does not scream. Most of all she is sunny, smiling and easy-going.

All this may sound great news for you, but because an easy baby is so good and makes so few demands she may receive less attention from her parents. A study in America showed that the middle-class parents of easy infants tended to leave them to fend for themselves more often than did the parents of more difficult babies. Easy babies tended to fall behind the achievements of more difficult children.

Children who are slow to warm up are less regular, show more caution, need persuading to take new food or enjoy new places and are slower to smile. Difficult children are irregular. Even at ten years of age she may not have a regular sleeping pattern and when she has not had enough sleep she is likely to be bad tempered and weepy. She is difficult to wean and will remain picky about food. Disasters are always around the corner. A line wrong, a word misspelt and she flies off the handle. She gets homesick.

Difficult babies make demands. They face more stress (much of it of their own making); life is never straightforward. In certain situations they fare better, surviving times of stress; they also however make up the majority of individuals who need counselling as adults.

Milestones in expressing emotion

Birth Has a 'windy' smile, shows that she is startled, distressed or disgusted.

4 weeks Develops a social smile.

12–16 weeks Laughs; shows anger, surprise, sadness.

20–28 weeks Shows fear.

24–32 weeks Shows shame and shyness.

Smiling and laughing

Babies smile in a 'windy' way almost as soon as they are born, but the smiles have nothing to do with wind. A young baby's smile is not a big broad beam but rather a pulling back of the lips, sometimes on only one side of the face. These first smiles only occur when babies are falling into a deeper sleep or coming from a deeper to a lighter sleep. Later she will smile in her sleep if she hears certain high-pitched noises.

You will see (and be able to recognize) her first real smiles when she is four to six weeks old, depending on her maturity at birth. Those born before the due date are likely to be older when they first smile. Blind babies smile quite readily at this stage but by six months most have stopped smiling. If you want your baby to smile you need a high-pitched sound and a nodding head; later she will want to look at your moving smiling face; finally she will smile directly at your still face. By the time they are five or six months old, babies smile most frequently at the faces of people they recognize.

Laughter is a more intense emotion than smiling, but just as infectious. Babies begin to laugh at about three to four months. At first laughter is produced by a combination of speech and physical activity, such as tickling, and is deep and hearty. Laughter is entirely social and is about anticipating and sharing. The more you laugh with her, the more she laughs back, although you will not be as successful at making her laugh as her older siblings.

What makes her laugh?
0–2 weeks Falling asleep or beginning to wake.
2–3 weeks A high-pitched sound while she is asleep.
4–8 weeks Smiles when awake; a high-pitched sound; a nodding head; things that move and make sounds; your moving talking face.
10 weeks Your still face.
20–24 weeks Familiar faces; laughter.
4–6 months Someone laughing or talking.
6–12 months Social games like 'peek-a-boo'; being jogged on your knee; games involving anticipation such as 'This little piggy'.
12 months Unexpected things like you wearing her hat; as a response to things she has done such as knocking over bricks, or making the Jack-in-the-box jump; anticipation of events.

Shape sorters and other toys involving hidey-holes improve your baby's perception, the ability to remember what goes where and manual dexterity.

LEARNING TO REMEMBER

A child cries because she is hurt; because something has caused her to be afraid; and because she wants attention. The first sort of crying is unlearned. The second two are learned.

Young children quickly learn that one thing leads to another, so uncoupling your bra precedes a feed, the sound of running water precedes a bath. They can also learn that being in their bed precedes sleep and nappy changing precedes a game. The learning process is simple – event A usually precedes event B.

Babies learn by trial and error that they can make things happen. Your baby would like the mobile to move but does not know how to make it happen. She looks at it ... she waves her arms ... nothing. Then one day when she is kicking at the side of the cot the mobile moves. When she stops kicking it stops. She has learned that if she kicks the bars of her cot, the mobile moves. By the same process she learns that she can make you come when she cries, and that people will play with her if she smiles and laughs.

Your baby does not only learn what you want to teach her. She learns about emotions, beliefs, attitudes and roles. Coming home precedes relaxation; getting into the car precedes tension. If you always draw her away from dogs, she will learn to be wary of dogs. She can also learn that being good makes her loved, or that when she is good, she is ignored.

Try occasionally to stand back and look at the messages you are giving your children. If you are giving the wrong messages, remember that what has been learned can be unlearned. The child who has learned that A is followed by B can also learn that A is no longer followed by B. And a child who has learned that crying always brings her mother to her side can learn that in some instances it will not.

What babies know

In the first weeks of life, most of the things babies can do are 'built in', or reflexes (see chapter 2). Your baby automatically turns her head and opens her mouth when her cheek is touched; she cannot choose to keep her mouth shut. Nor can she open and close her mouth to see how it feels, since such voluntary actions are beyond her capability. By two months, she is beginning to replace reflexes by voluntary actions. She can choose to reach for the teddy tied to her cot. Until she is about three months she can only control one voluntary action at a time. She can choose to cry or to reach but cannot reach and cry at the same time. She can kick and cry because kicking automatically goes with crying. If she does two things only one of them can be of her choosing.

By about six months she can do two things at once, suck her thumb while she plays and bang a drum while she shouts. She can also use one of these actions to produce another, so she can press a button to make the Jack-in-the-box jump and repeat such activities. One of the two 'things' she does can be to have an intention, the other to act, so that she realizes she needs her mother and knows how to summon her.

In the first months babies hold all toys in their hand and bang them on the table or put them in their mouth and gum them. As she begins to be able to do two things at once, she can push something because she remembers that pushing makes it move, and can hit something to knock it over.

By the time your baby is about 10 months old, she begins to co-ordinate and plan more complex actions. Now instead of being limited to two 'thoughts' or actions, she can integrate several: remember that a toy is in the cupboard, go to the cupboard to get it and take it to the sofa to play, for example. She can look, shout and crawl while grasping a spoon in her hand.

In the early months babies live in the moment, reacting as if nothing went before and nothing is coming after (this is why your baby drops a toy but does not look for it, see pp. 138–9). At around 10 months they begin to act as if they can remember what went before and can predict what might come after. When you take off her sock to play 'This little piggy', she is already prepared to laugh. When you show her a book she waits for the picture of the dog (and knows if you have missed out the page with the dog, and gone to the picture of the cat).

Paying attention

Grown-ups can do more than one thing at a time. As you read, you can hear the clock ticking, the traffic moving, someone in the room may be watching TV. You are aware of all of these things, but they are not the focus of your attention: you focus on the words you are reading. If you are asked a question you can switch your attention, answer and then go back to reading. Babies cannot do this. They can only concentrate on one thing at a time. They are easily distracted and once distracted cannot return.

If your child sees a toy car on the far side of the room she will crawl rapidly to it. It is the centre of her attention. But if she notices a half-eaten biscuit on the floor as she is passing, she stops and starts eating, and forgets that she was heading for the car. She can only hold one thought at a time. Only if she happens to notice the car again will she return to the first activity. As children grow up they become better able to focus their attention, and can look away and then return to an activity.

How memory develops

Your baby's ability to remember changes as the first year progresses. Tiny babies do not consciously remember the past. They only know that something is familiar.

If you change something your baby has just looked at (take a car from the table and put it in the drawer), she notices. If you show her something she has seen before (the car in the drawer), she remembers; she cannot, however, do both things at once. By seven months she can. If a car was in the drawer the last time she looked, that is where she will search for it first on the next occasion that it is missing.

Intelligence

Measuring infant intelligence has always been controversial, not least because it is unreliable. It is possible to say how old the average child will be when she can sit without aid or when you can expect her to say her first word. This really does not predict how well she will do when she starts school. Children who seem a little slow at one stage may be top of their class later on. What the scales and charts can do is identify children with potential problems. A child who is consistently late at reaching milestones may have an unrecognized problem.

In infancy play and cognitive development are always closely related. When a baby plays she is both practising and learning. Watching her gives a very clear view of what she can do and how she understands the world.

Avoiding superbaby syndrome

- Remember that she has a right to her childhood.
- Be realistic and reasonable.
- Make any learning fun.
- Play down the competition; most children cannot and do not win – the child in line for 13th best might as well try something else.
- Guide but do not push. Recognize what she wants and what you want and do not confuse them: if you want to play the violin take lessons yourself.
- Do not insist.
- Take your cue from your baby: pushing when she is not interested is pressure not stimulation.
- Do not be afraid to let your child have fun: 'All work and no play makes Jack a dull and stressed superbaby.'
- Give her a choice: jumping on the beds is just as good an exercise as learning to swim.
- Babies only need loose timetables and free time is at least as important as 'quality time'.
- A child who is entirely organized may never learn to organize herself.
- It is the effort that counts, not the end result.

Too far too fast

Obviously you want the best for your child, but the line between encouraging and pressurizing is very fine. Some American parents worry that their two-year-olds will not pass the entrance exams for the 'best' preschool and there are reports that some spend 50–60 hours a week cramming two- and three-year-olds to help them get ahead, to ensure their child's place in the competitive market.

Researchers have watched hurried babies become bored toddlers and unmotivated and stressed schoolchildren. Doctors have seen more and more overstimulated children develop headaches, stomach upsets and sleep disturbances. Psychologists have monitored the development of behavioural problems. The situation has become sufficiently serious in the USA for the American Academy of Pediatrics to issue guidelines to help pediatricians recognize what has been dubbed the 'superbaby syndrome'. Do not push too hard: your child deserves the luxury of a childhood.

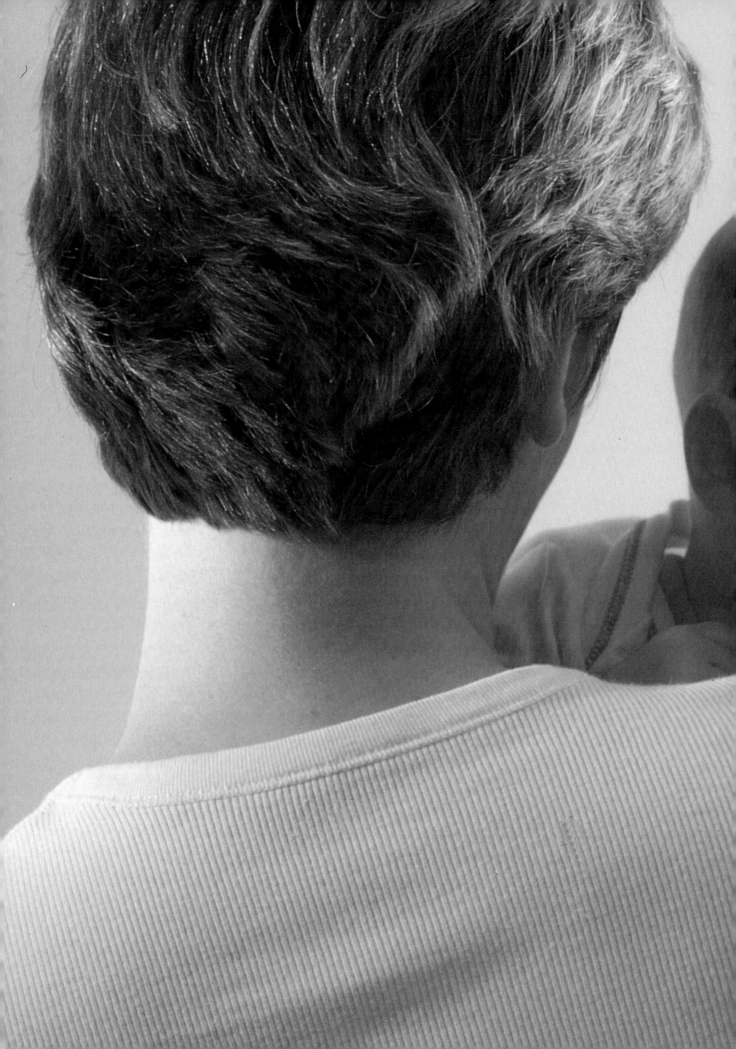

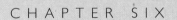

CHAPTER SIX

Your Baby's Health

Parents worry, often unnecessarily, about their babies' health and safety. For most of the time, babies are well, and commonsense precautions and careful choice of what you buy for your baby will keep him safe. There is, however, a network of health professionals to consult about your baby's well-being; these people will also ensure that he is developing as he should.

Your baby's well-being

As well as the joy and pleasure that a new baby brings, you may – like many other parents – also experience feelings of panic or apprehension about caring for him.

These days, many people do not live near their immediate family, and you may be the first of your friends to have a child. It is easy in these circumstances to feel alone in caring for your baby. And, even if you do have family and friends with children close by, you may well receive conflicting advice about what to do if your baby does not want to feed, sleep or stop crying.

As you get to know your baby you will gain more confidence as parents, and will be able to spot more easily when something is wrong. You will begin to recognize your baby's cries and know when he is hungry, sick, or just needs a cuddle. But there is also a team of professionals there to help and advise you on the care of your baby, and to keep a check on his health and development.

WHO CAN HELP?

All parents of young children can call upon the services of an individual, named health visitor, your GP and the child-health or well-baby clinic.

Your health visitor

Health visitors are part of the National Health Service community health services. All are registered general nurses who have undergone further training, and have experience in child health and development, preventive health and health promotion. Health visitors work closely with GPs, and may be based at your GP's surgery or at a health centre or child-health clinic. The overwhelming majority are women.

Every family with a child under five has a named health visitor. You may have met yours when you were pregnant, but if you did not, she will be notified of your baby's birth, and should visit you at home when your baby is around 11 days old – get in touch with your GP's surgery if she does not. At this visit, in addition to talking to you about your own health and that of your baby, your health visitor will explain the health care system in your area to you. This information may include, for example, the days and times of your nearest baby clinic, and the immunization programme. She will usually then visit you at intervals throughout your child's first five years, more frequently in the first year and if you have any special problems. In addition you can see your health visitor at the child health clinic, you can telephone her for advice, or you can ask her to visit you at home.

Your health visitor is there to listen to you and to help and advise you in all sorts of situations. She is not there to check that you are bringing your baby up correctly, or to impose her own views on you. She is, however, the person you can turn to for advice on any aspect of your baby's health such as feeding, colic, crying, teething, rashes or immunizations. She can also advise you on minor illnesses and their treatment. Together, you and your health visitor can monitor your baby's developmental progress, and if there is any concern she can arrange for your baby to be seen by a doctor or paediatrician. She may also carry out some of your child's developmental reviews either in your home or at the clinic.

What else can she do?

Your health visitor is not just there for your baby. She is also there for you and your whole family.

- She can advise you on other matters which affect your health and well-being such as child-care facilities, local support groups and networks, caring for elderly relatives, relationships, relaxation and healthy lifestyles.

- She can let you know what welfare benefits you may be entitled to claim and can put you in touch with other agencies such as social services, if that is what you wish.

Try to treat your health visitor as a family friend and do not be afraid to talk to her if you are feeling depressed, unable to cope with the baby or are having other difficulties. Sometimes just talking about a problem can help you to put it into perspective. She will not be shocked by anything you say or be in the least censorious.

Your family doctor

Your GP is a second key person who can help you to look after your family's health. If your baby is not well he or she will make a diagnosis and reassure you or prescribe any necessary treatment. Your GP will also refer your baby to a hospital specialist if necessary. GPs are increasingly doing developmental checks too.

If you think that your baby is ill or suspect that something is wrong, phone your doctor or take your baby to the surgery. Do not be anxious about bothering the doctor with what may be something trivial: most doctors prefer to see a sick child early, and are pleased to reassure you if all is well. If you are really not sure about seeing the doctor, phone the practice nurse or your health visitor and ask for her opinion first.

Most doctors now immunize those babies who are on their lists, although vaccinations can also be done at your local NHS trust or health authority clinic. Your GP may also run a well-baby clinic, and do some of your child's developmental reviews.

Except in an emergency, you must be registered with a GP before he or she can treat you. When your baby is born, register him with your own GP and if you move house, register with a GP as soon as possible. It helps to choose a doctor within easy reach, but ask neighbours with children whom they recommend – some are infinitely better with small children than others. Alternatively, visit one or two practices before you decide to register, ask for the practice leaflet describing the services on offer, talk to

the doctors and look around you. Are there toys in the waiting room, for example, and is there an easy-access toilet?

The child-health clinic

The well-baby or child-health clinic is a free service, provided by your local health authority or NHS trust, or by your GP, for children under the age of five. You can attend a well-baby clinic whenever it is open – an appointment is not necessary.

At the clinic you can discuss any worries you may have about your baby with your health visitor, and have your baby weighed. Always take your child health record book with you so that information about your baby and any advice given can be noted. The clinic is also a good place to make contact with other mothers. Go as often as you want to: most parents of new babies attend weekly for the first few weeks, then fortnightly, then monthly for the first year. But, initially at least, if it is a hassle to get there, do not force yourself (remember you can ask your health visitor to see you at home). Developmental reviews or checks and immunizations will also usually be done at the clinic, although probably at a different time from the well-baby sessions, and you will be sent an appointment for these (if an appointment is not convenient, ring and change it).

The other services that these clinics offer vary according to where you live. Some also run postnatal groups or mother and toddler groups and offer other facilities such as dental sessions. The physical location

Your child's health record book

You will normally be given a personal child health record book, also known as a parent-held record, either when your health visitor makes her first visit to you, or at your first clinic appointment. This is for use by yourself and health professionals, and helps you to keep track of your child's progress, immunizations, and any illnesses he may have had, until he leaves school. Try to remember to take it with you whenever you take your baby to the clinic, to see your doctor or to the dentist. Remember, this is for your use and can be filled in by you as well as professionals.

of such clinics also varies enormously: in some areas you will find the clinic in a purpose-built health centre, in others a church hall, your doctor's surgery or even a mobile caravan. In theory, you can choose to go to the clinic which is most convenient for you, but changes in the NHS may make the choice more limited in some areas. If you are unhappy with facilities in your area, it is worth getting together with other parents and approaching your CHC (Community Health Council) and FHSA (Family Health Services Authority) – the numbers are in the phone book.

Health is a partnership

Caring for your baby's health and monitoring his progress should be a partnership between parents and professionals, so make any decision about your baby's health in consultation with the health professionals. Professionals do not have all the answers and you undoubtedly know your own baby best. Ask questions if you feel you are being kept in the dark about any aspect of your child's health or development, and do not be afraid to disagree if you think a doctor or health visitor is mistaken. Ask for a second opinion if necessary.

If you are not happy

It sometimes happens that for some reason you and your health visitor or doctor do not hit it off. Or misunderstandings arise which need to be talked through. If these differences cannot be resolved, try visiting the clinic on another day when there is a different health visitor or doctor there. If there is more than one health visitor in your doctor's practice, ask to change to one with whom you feel more comfortable. If you wish to change your doctor, go to a new GP and ask to be taken on to his or her list.

What the law says

You are entitled to refuse entry to a health professional who has no legal right to enter your home. Taking your baby to the clinic, having developmental checks and having your child immunized are all voluntary. However, if for any reason the health or social services have grounds for serious concern about your child's health, development or well-being, you may be asked to allow your child to be assessed by a health professional. This could be done by your family doctor or by an independent professional.

If you refuse to co-operate with a proposed voluntary assessment, the social services department can apply to the court for a child assessment order, so that an assessment can be made.

REGULAR HEALTH CHECKS

In addition to attending the well-baby clinic for general advice on your baby's health and progress, you will also be invited to take him for routine health and developmental reviews or checks at certain ages, under the child health surveillance programme (these may also be called developmental assessments, or screening tests).

Although not compulsory, these reviews are important. Their purpose is to detect any problems such as developmental delay, or hearing or vision impairment as soon as possible so that any necessary treatment can be started early. They also give you the opportunity to sit down with the health visitor or doctor and discuss any concerns you may have about your child's health or behaviour or simply to be reassured that everything is 'normal'.

Even if you have no worries about your child, the review is still worth having – some problems such as a hearing impairment or a congenital dislocation of the hip are not always apparent. The developmental review also gives you a record of your child's progress at certain ages, so if problems do develop later, you have a useful reference to look back on.

The age at which your baby has a developmental review and even the content of the review, varies slightly in each area. Most areas, however, tend to follow the recommendations made by a Department of Health backed team of experts, including paediatricians, GPs and health visitors. In most parts of the country, therefore, you will asked to take your child for a developmental review between the following ages:

- Six and eight weeks
- Six and nine months
- 18 months and two years
- Three and four years
- Four and a half and five and a half years (often referred to as the preschool check)

These reviews are carried out by your GP, health visitor or both, and may take place at your doctor's surgery, at the child-health clinic or in your home.

There are wide variations in the rate at which babies and children develop (see Chapters 5 and 7), and each child develops at his own pace. So the developmental reviews are not 'tests' that your child passes or fails, but an indication of his overall progress. If he was premature, he should be assessed from his expected date of delivery, rather than his actual date of birth. So a baby who was eight weeks premature, for example, will be assessed at eight months as a six-month-old baby.

See Chapter 4, pp. 116–17 for the six-week check.

Six to nine months

This is the age when most babies are learning to communicate, sit and have increasing visual alertness. It is also the best age to check your baby's hearing.

The examination is usually carried out by the health visitor on her own, or by the health visitor and doctor together. The review includes:

- A general look at your baby's progress; whether you have any concerns about his health or growth, teething, feeding and sleeping problems and so on.

- An assessment of his motor development; whether your baby is starting to sit, roll or perhaps beginning to crawl.
- A check for congenital dislocation of the hips; even though your baby will have been tested earlier for this, it can sometimes be missed.
- Observation of his learning and communication skills: whether your baby is alert and responsive, is making a variety of sounds and is able to grasp objects.
- His head circumference, length and weight may be measured (this is not always done).
- A check for a squint and any vision defects; you will also be asked if you have noticed a squint or whether there is any family history of squints or vision defects; the examiner will also check that your baby is visually alert and able to focus on objects.
- (For boys only) A check that the testes are descended into the scrotum.
- A hearing test will be done by two people, one to distract your baby, the other to make various sounds behind your baby to see if he can hear them; if your baby fails to respond to this test, you will be asked to return in three to four weeks so that it can be repeated.

Six to nine months

This is a good age to test many of your baby's reactions and skills. Remember that some babies reach milestones earlier than others; this review simply gives a general impression of his progress.

Your baby's movement will be observed. It will be noted if he can crawl, or if he is showing signs of doing so soon, by rocking on all fours, for example.

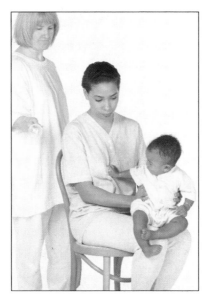

While you distract your baby, a rattle will be shaken outside his field of vision to see whether he reacts to it, and whether he turns in the direction of the sound.

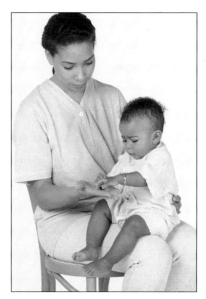

Your baby's manual dexterity will be checked, to see whether he can pick up a building block, and how well his palmar grip is developed (see p. 136).

If your baby still fails to respond, you will be referred to an audiology clinic where more sophisticated tests can be carried out. Do not be alarmed if your baby does not respond to all the sounds first time. He may be tired or bored, or might have had an ear infection.

18 months to two years

Children of this age can be difficult to evaluate in a clinic and this review may be carried out by the health visitor in the more relaxed atmosphere of your home. Again, your health visitor will review your child's progress with you and discuss any problems you may have. Management problems such as food refusal, sleep disturbance and temper tantrums are common at this age. You may also want to discuss potty training. Other important parts of this review are your child's walking and language skills.

Specifically, your health visitor will:

When to worry

Before your child reaches the age of five, any major developmental or health problems should have been picked up. But you know your child best. Draw to your health visitor's attention any concerns you have over:

- Speech: if your child stutters or lisps badly, or has difficulty with certain sounds, for example
- Vision: if he cannot see his friend at the other side of the play area, or consistently misses a ball rolled to him
- Hearing: if he seems not to hear when you are to one side, or directly behind him
- Social behaviour: if he is unduly anxious about starting school, and is shy
- Understanding: if he does not seem to understand what you are saying, even when you rephrase a question.

You are not wasting anybody's time in asking for any aspect of your child's development to be checked, more than once, if necessary. The sooner a problem is identified the better.

If you have any concerns about your child when he is at school, raise them with the school nurse or doctor (see p. 268), or your GP.

- Check that your child is walking normally: by the age of 18 months, 97 per cent of children are walking, but those who 'bottom shuffle' may not be, especially if late walking runs in your family.
- Ask if your child is saying several words and understands simple commands such as 'shut the door' or 'give it to me'.
- Monitor his hand–eye co-ordination, seeing whether, for example, he can pick up tiny objects such as crumbs from the carpet using his finger and thumb, or build a tower of about three bricks.
- Measure his weight and height (not all health professionals do this at this review, and not all children are co-operative).

If she is concerned about any aspect of your child's development, your health visitor may ask you to return for a further check, or refer you to your doctor or another health professional such as a speech therapist for a second opinion. In some parts of the country, children at this age may also have a blood test for anaemia.

Three to four years

This review may be carried out by your health visitor or doctor or both, and in some areas is regarded as the preschool examination. The aims are to ensure that your child is physically fit and there are no medical disorders or problems with development, language or behaviour which may have educational implications. The doctor will carry out a physical examination, such as a general check of your child's heart and (for boys) testes. (If in your area the preschool examination is carried out between the ages of four and a half and five and a half, a physical examination may not be done at this review.)

The health visitor may do a formal assessment of your child's developmental progress by, for example, asking him to build a tower of bricks or do a simple jigsaw. Or she may assess him informally by watching him play and run around. However the review is done, the health visitor or doctor will discuss your child's progress and any concerns you may have about his health or behaviour. In addition, your doctor or health visitor will usually:

- Check for vision or hearing problems (in some areas, the doctor or health visitor may do a formal vision or hearing test).

- Check your child's thinking skills, for example, his ability to understand and reason.
- Check his language and ability to communicate: does he know a nursery rhyme? can you understand him clearly when he speaks?
- Check his motor skills: can he ride a bicycle? can he jump up and down?
- Check his social maturity, his ability to cope with unfamiliar situations, for example, and whether he is shy.
- Check his weight and height.

Four and a half to five and a half

This may be called the preschool entry review, or it may take place once he has started school. This may include a physical and vision and hearing test, his immunization status will be checked, and he will be given his preschool booster injection (see p. 159).

IMMUNIZATION

When your baby is in the womb, and while he is breastfed, antibodies (substances which attack bacteria and viruses) are passed to him by his mother, with the result that new babies have some immunity to infection (although not whooping cough). After a few months, protection against diphtheria, tetanus and polio wears off, and by the time your baby is about a year old, he will also have lost his immunity to measles, mumps and rubella. Because these antibodies are not replaced, it is necessary to protect children against these infectious diseases, by immunization.

What is immunization?

Vaccination or immunization means introducing a substance into the body to stimulate immunity to a particular disease. The vaccine works by giving the child a tiny amount of the particular bacteria or virus which causes the disease. The body reacts by producing its own defence against the disease, so that it can fight the infection if it encounters it again. For maximum protection the full course of immunizations is necessary. If enough children are immunized (at least 90 per cent), the level of disease in the community is reduced, leading to so-called herd immunity.

Immunizations given

Your child should receive five sets of vaccines. Some come in three doses and others in one, but each vaccine protects against a specific disease (see table, p. 159). Most immunizations are given by injection, usually in the upper arm or outer thigh. Polio vaccine is given by drops placed on the baby's tongue.

Diphtheria, Tetanus and Pertussis (Whooping cough)

Known as DTP for short, this is a triple vaccine that gives protection against all three diseases.

Diphtheria is now rare, but outbreaks still occur in some countries. It is a serious disease which starts with a sore throat and a low fever. A 'membrane' develops which blocks the nose and throat, causing choking and breathing difficulties. A severe attack can kill.

Whooping cough (*Pertussis*) is a dangerous and distressing disease, particularly in the first year of life. It starts with a runny nose, fever and cough, which are followed by bouts of coughing in succession in the same breath, ending with a 'whoop' as the child gasps for breath. During such fits, the baby may turn blue from lack of oxygen.

Is immunization necessary?

Although many of these diseases for which your child will be immunized are now – because of widespread immunization – rare, they still exist, and outbreaks can occur both in Britain and in other countries you may visit. They can all make your child seriously ill, can have severe complications and may even cause death.

Serious side effects from immunization are very rare, and research has shown that the risks of harmful effects from the diseases are far greater than that from the immunizations. In the years between 1978 and 1989, 118 anaphylactic reactions (where the child has a severe and sudden reaction to the injection, see Allergy, pp. 160–1) were reported out of approximately 25 million childhood immunizations.

If the figures do nothing to allay your fears of possible side effects, discuss immunization with your doctor or health visitor before making the decision to have your child immunized or not.

These coughing bouts can occur up to 50 times a day for several weeks, with vomiting common after coughing; this may lead to dehydration or weight loss. Complications from whooping cough can include convulsions (fits), pneumonia, bronchitis, hernias, ear infection, brain damage and even death.

Tetanus is not an infectious disease, but it is still dangerous. It is caused by germs from soil or dirt getting into an open wound (especially if this is a deep 'puncture' wound) or a burn. It then attacks the nervous system causing muscle spasms which can affect breathing, and may be fatal. Although tetanus is quite rare because of immunization, the germ spores which cause the disease are always present in the soil.

Hib (Haemophilus influenzae type b)

These bacteria can cause a serious form of bacterial meningitis in under-fours; a severe form of croup known as epiglottis; pneumonia; blood poisoning and infections of the bones and joints. Before Hib immunization was introduced, one in 600 children under five developed some form of Hib-induced meningitis, which resulted in 65 deaths and 150 cases of brain damage every year. Hib immunization only protects against one form of meningitis; a vaccine to protect against another type is being tested.

Polio

Polio attacks the nervous system and paralyses the muscles in any part of the body. Permanent paralysis can result if it attacks the legs; if it attacks the respiratory muscles, artificial help in breathing may be needed and the child may even die. Polio has technically been eradicated in Britain because of immunization, but it can still be caught abroad, and may then be re-introduced. Also, the virus can be excreted in a baby's faeces for up to six weeks after immunization, so adults who have not been immunized may catch the disease from changing a newly immunized baby's nappy. If you have not been immunized against polio, ask your doctor about having it done, and wash your hands after changing your baby's nappy. Because there are three types of polio virus, the vaccine is given three times to ensure full protection.

Measles, mumps and rubella (MMR)

This immunization is given as a triple vaccine.

Measles is often considered a mild childhood disease, but it is not only unpleasant for your child, it can also be dangerous. It starts like a bad cold with a cough, runny nose, watery eyes and rising temperature. A blotchy red rash then appears on the face and body. Complications from measles can include encephalitis (inflammation of the brain), which may cause brain damage, convulsions, ear and eye infections, croup, pneumonia, bronchitis or death.

Mumps causes headaches, fever, dry mouth and difficulty in swallowing, with swelling below the ears and/or in front of the jaw. Although it is usually a mild disease, it can have serious consequences. Mumps can cause deafness and encephalitis and it is the most common cause of viral meningitis in under-15s (see Your Child's Health, pp. 361–2). It can also cause inflammation of the testes in boys, and a painful infection of the ovaries in girls.

Rubella (*German measles*) usually starts with a cough, sore throat and runny nose before a bright pink rash appears. Although it is normally a mild disease, if a woman who is not immune catches it in the first four months of pregnancy, there is a risk that her child may be born deaf, blind, or with heart or brain damage. Rubella immunization is important for all children: both boys and girls may pass the disease on to pregnant women.

Tuberculosis (TB)

TB can affect the lungs and other parts of the body. Not so long ago, it was a serious disease that required months of treatment; it was also a major killer. Good public health measures and prevention by vaccination meant that TB was virtually wiped out in Britain, but as routine immunization was stopped, it has recently started to make a comeback. At present, the policy on

Alternatives to immunization

Some parents choose to have their children 'immunized homeopathically'. There are, however, no proven, effective alternatives to immunization and, in fact, the Council of the Faculty of Homeopathy strongly supports the immunization programme. The Council recommends that immunization be carried out using the conventional tested vaccines as long as there are no medical reasons not to do so.

giving protection against TB varies in each area. If your baby is thought to be at risk from the disease, or you live in a high-risk area, he may be offered BCG protection at birth. Elsewhere, schoolchildren may be tested for immunity against TB (the mantoux test) and if necessary, immunized. If you are travelling to a country where TB is common (check with your GP), your baby should be immunized.

Side effects of immunization

After an injection your baby may be a little irritable or have a slight fever, or he may have side effects such as pain, redness and swelling. These effects are normally only temporary and you will usually be advised to give your baby a dose of liquid paracetamol to relieve any pain and bring down a temperature. If your baby screams briefly after an injection, this is probably due to pain or fright; if, however, his screaming is high-pitched or prolonged, it is likely to be due to a reaction. If this happens, or your child has a high temperature, or seems very unwell, contact your GP for further advice.

Reports of permanent brain damage after the whooping cough part of the DTP vaccine have probably been the single most important factor in dissuading parents from having their children immunized against any diseases at all. However, neurological illnesses which can cause this type of damage can develop from a variety of causes in the first year of life in both immunized and unimmunized children. There has been a lot of research into the whooping cough vaccine, but no conclusive evidence has been found to show that this causes permanent brain damage. Whooping cough, however, can cause brain damage, and the risk of being damaged by the disease is infinitely greater than that of being damaged by the vaccine injection.

When not to immunize

If your child is unwell, immunization may be postponed. Your health visitor will discuss any contra-indications with you, but these may include:
- A severe reaction to a previous injection
- A severe allergic reaction to eggs (MMR injection only)
- If your child has a malignant disease such as cancer.

The immunization timetable (0–5 years)

Vaccine	How given	Age
Diphtheria	One injection (DTP)	2 months
Tetanus		
Whooping cough		
Hib	One injection	
Polio	By mouth	
Diphtheria	One injection (DTP)	3 months
Tetanus		
Whooping cough		
Hib	One injection	
Polio	By mouth	
Diphtheria	One injection (DTP)	4 months
Tetanus		
Whooping cough		
Hib	One injection	
Polio	By mouth	
Measles	One injection (MMR)	12–15 months
Mumps		
Rubella		
Diphtheria	Booster injection (around school entry)	3-5 years
Tetanus		
Polio	By mouth	

There is usually no reason to delay immunization if:
- Your baby has the 'snuffles'
- There is a family history of convulsions
- Your baby has epilepsy
- There is a family history of adverse reactions following immunization
- Your baby is premature, or has a disability
- Your baby is being breastfed
- Your baby has asthma, eczema or allergies
- Your baby has had one of the infectious diseases
- Your baby is on antibiotics or steroids (unless he is ill that day)

A–Z OF BABY HEALTH

The overwhelming majority of health problems experienced by babies in the first year of life are minor, shortlived and easily treated, although some – such as allergy – can continue to be a problem into adulthood. The most common problems experienced by babies are listed here in alphabetical order.

Allergy

An allergy is an abnormal response by the body to a substance or 'allergen' which does not affect non-allergic people. Allergies can affect even very young babies, and in the first year of life children are particularly susceptible. The proportion of young children affected by allergies appears to be increasing. There may be several reasons for this. Firstly, allergies are more often diagnosed than they were in the past. Secondly, potential sources of allergens such as the house dust mite, pollution, food additives and chemicals have become more widespread in recent years. In addition, breastfeeding, which may have protected some babies from allergens in the past, has declined.

The term 'atopy' is sometimes used in place of allergy. Technically, atopy is an inherited tendency to develop allergy. Atopic may also be used as an adjective to describe an allergic condition, such as atopic eczema (that is, eczema to which you are genetically disposed).

Common allergens

Almost any food or substance can produce an allergic reaction, but the most common are:
- Non-food: house dust mite; pollens (grass, trees, flowers); moulds; animal fur and feathers; chemicals; medicines
- Food: milk; eggs; wheat; fish; oranges; nuts; pork/bacon; food additives, colourings and preservatives (see also p. 252).

Types of reactions

Reactions to allergens may be immediate, such as an asthma attack or (rarely) a severe reaction such as swelling and difficulty in breathing, the first time a food is eaten (this is known as an anaphylactic reaction). Alternatively, the reaction may be delayed and occur 12–48 hours after exposure to the allergen, as in the case of a food. A delayed reaction, usually vomiting or a rash, can make it difficult to pinpoint the cause of your child's allergy.

Food allergies

Intolerance of or allergy to a food is controversial, but there is no doubt that certain foods can cause adverse reactions in young children. Food allergy can cause or contribute to many conditions such as eczema, rashes, hay fever, bronchial asthma and gastrointestinal problems. Coeliac disease is caused by an allergy to the gluten in wheat, rye, oats and barley (see pp. 83–4). To reduce the risks of food allergy:
- **Try to breastfeed**
  Where there is a family history of atopic disease it is best to breastfeed your baby for four to six months, longer if you can.
- **Do not wean too early**
  Weaning foods should not be introduced before four months of age. Allergenic foods such as wheat or eggs should not be included in your baby's diet until he is at least six months old. Cereals given to babies under six months should be gluten free, such as rice or maize.
- **Give one new food at a time**
  Where there is a strong family history of allergy, introduce one new food at a time so that you can pinpoint any food that causes a problem.

Is allergy inherited?

A general tendency to allergy or atopy does run in families, although children may not necessarily inherit it (if you have identical twins, both will be atopic but only one may develop an allergy). If your child is atopic, this may appear in a variety of ways, for example, as eczema, asthma or food allergy. The risks of your child developing an allergy are:

Both parents have the same allergy	60–80 per cent
Both parents have a different allergy	40–60 per cent
One parent has an allergy	20–40 per cent
Neither parent has an allergy	10 per cent

Cow's milk intolerance

Intolerance to cow's milk can be due to an inability to digest the lactose (sugar) in milk, or a reaction to the protein in milk (see p. 77). About 2 per cent of children under one year are thought to suffer an adverse reaction to cow's milk protein. This is usually shortlived, and your child may well grow out of it by the time he is around three or four years old.

Symptoms of this type of allergy are:

- Gastrointestinal, such as vomiting, diarrhoea, colic, abdominal pain, abdominal distension
- Dermatological, such as atopic eczema, or rashes
- Respiratory, such as asthma or runny nose
- Behavioural, such as excessive crying and general irritability

Not all these symptoms are due to cow's milk allergy, however, and it is important that you seek professional medical advice before you eliminate cow's milk from your child's diet.

If cow's milk allergy is confirmed, depending on the age of your baby and his degree of sensitivity, special infant formula will be prescribed. This may be a milk based on hydrolysed milk protein or on soya. Soya itself can cause an allergic reaction in some babies so, although soya formula is available over the counter, it is important that you talk to your health visitor or doctor before introducing this into your baby's diet. Goat's milk and sheep's milk are low in vitamins and minerals and should not be given to babies under the age of one (you can give it once your baby reaches this age, but you must use pasteurized milk and boil it first).

Asthma

Although asthma attacks in children under one are often set off by viruses, they can also be triggered by allergies. Symptoms include wheezing and coughing (see also p. 339). As it is difficult to treat asthma in young children, precipitating or trigger factors should be avoided as far as possible.

- Cigarette smoke is especially harmful. Do not smoke anywhere near your child – preferably not in the house at all – and insist that others do not. Try to avoid smoky atmospheres completely. (If you plan to have another baby, you and your partner should both stop smoking during pregnancy to reduce the risk to your next baby.)

Preventing allergies

If allergies or atopy runs in your family, it makes sense to try to minimize your child's chances of developing them, by taking preventive measures in his first year of life. This is not always easy, but the following measures may help:

- Try to breastfeed for four to six months or longer.
- Avoid weaning before the age of four months.
- Do not smoke, or let anyone else smoke, near your child.
- Keep pets such as cats, dogs and birds out of the house for his first year.
- Keep your house well ventilated and try to avoid damp.
- Do not use irritants such as spray polishes, perfumed cleaners or air fresheners.
- Try to keep your baby away from high traffic areas, particularly when he is in a pushchair.
- Try to keep house dust to a minimum. It is difficult to eradicate the house dust mite completely, however thoroughly you clean your house. In particular it thrives in places such as carpets, bedding and soft toys. Your child will, however, probably have a washable cover on his mattress and will not be using a pillow, so the problem will not be so severe in his first year.
- Consider replacing the carpet with cork tiles or linoleum.
- Wash bedding at 55–60°C to kill the mite.
- Wash soft toys regularly, or put in a plastic bag in the freezer for 24 hours once a week.

- Pets (both animals and birds) can cause allergic asthma in babies. In particular, exposure to cats in the first year of life can cause hypersensitivity to cat fur in later life.
- House dust mites are responsible in some cases; try to reduce the number in your home.
- Food allergies can trigger asthma; if you think that food is a trigger, ask to be referred to a specialist before cutting anything from your baby's diet.
- Polluted air, particularly at pushchair level – the level of car exhausts – may trigger asthma; do your best not to stand near cars emitting fumes when you are waiting to cross the street.

Colic

Infant colic, also known as evening colic or three-month colic, is thought to affect between 15 and 40 per cent of young babies between the ages of two weeks and three months. Although a baby with colic is not ill, colic will distress him and you.

Symptoms

In a typical attack of colic, a baby who has been his normal self during the day, will suddenly start emitting shrill, piercing screams at around 5 or 6 pm. His face may become red and congested and he will draw his legs up and down. His tummy may be hard and distended and you may hear it rumbling.

The crying bouts can last from about two to 20 minutes and occur at regular intervals throughout the evening. Your baby will be inconsolable, and finally fall asleep, exhausted, at about 10 or 11 pm, by which time you will be exhausted too. A baby with colic will not have diarrhoea or vomiting, and will have normal stools, a normal temperature and continue to gain weight normally.

Causes

Many theories have been put forward to explain colic, but the cause remains unknown. Rest assured, however, that it is not your fault. The most likely cause is thought to be gas trapped in loops of the bowel. This then builds up into bubbles and causes spasms in the bowels, resulting in abdominal pain. Continual crying, during which your baby swallows air, compounds the problem.

What you can do

If your baby has colic, he will continue to thrive, and the condition will eventually get better. Picking him up and cuddling him can help, and you are not 'spoiling' him by doing so. For temporary relief, try:
- Giving him a dummy to suck.
- Massaging his abdomen.
- Rocking him.
- Placing him on your knee and rhythmically massaging his back.
- Driving him around in the car.
- Giving him infant colic drops before a feed (these have a progressive effect and may take up to five days to start making a difference). Or try gripe water.
- Giving small amounts of camomile or fennel tea (make a weak solution using a herbal tea bag) or try camomile colic drops.

Do not automatically put your baby's crying during the evening down to colic. Always check other causes (see pp. 101–4). If he seems to be ill or has vomiting and diarrhoea with abdominal pain, this is not colic and you should consult your doctor.

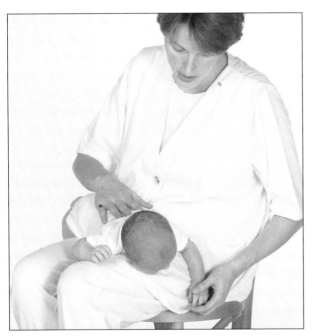

Above: Lying your baby with his tummy against the warmth of your body while you gently and rhythmically stroke his back may help relieve the misery of colic.

Constipation

Since babies tend to open their bowels infrequently, and go red in the face and grunt when they are filling a nappy, parents worry that their baby is suffering from constipation. The number of times a baby opens his bowels varies enormously, however, and grunting is normal for babies. Only if your baby's stools are hard and compacted and he passes them with difficulty or appears to be in pain, should you suspect constipation.

Causes

Babies may become constipated when changing from breast- to bottlefeeding – breast milk is more watery in hot weather than formula, which is the same consistency all the time – or if they are simply not having enough fluid. Occasionally constipation may be due to a congenital disorder.

What you can do

If your baby is constipated, check that you are making up his feeds correctly, and try giving extra boiled water or well-diluted fruit juice between feeds. If your baby is more than four months, try giving him puréed fruit and vegetables once or twice a day, in addition to extra fluids. If the constipation is severe or these measures do not work, consult your doctor.

Coughs and sneezes

Sneezing is very common in newborn babies and does not mean that your baby has a cold. The lining of a baby's nose is sensitive to substances such as dust and sneezing is your baby's way of clearing out his nasal passages. Frequent sneezing can also occur if your baby has a cold as he cannot blow his nose to clear any congestion. If your baby's nose seems blocked, tickling his nose with a teased cottonbud to make him sneeze will help him clear it. Coughing in babies may have several causes, including a cold, measles, bronchitis, or whooping cough (see pp. 157–8).

What you can do

If your baby develops a cough or wheeze and seems unwell, or vomits after coughing, consult your doctor. Never give 'cough mixture' unless it is prescribed by your doctor. To ease a cough, give your baby extra fluids, such as boiled water. During the day sit him up in a baby chair. At night raise him up slightly by putting a book or pillow under his mattress.

Cradle cap

Thick, greasy yellow or brown scales on the baby's scalp are known as cradle cap. This can occur soon after birth and is not usually seen after the first year. Although cradle cap can look very unsightly, it does not cause your baby any distress, nor does it stop him eating or sleeping. Do not pick the scales off.

What you can do

Gently shampoo your baby's scalp daily with a mild baby shampoo, using tepid water. If the scales are not easily removed, massage some warmed olive oil or arachis (peanut) oil into the scalp. Leave the oil on for an hour or overnight before shampooing it off. You may need to repeat this for several days.

If the scalp still remains scaly, massage aqueous cream (from your pharmacist) into your baby's scalp and leave it for several hours, then wash it off. (Aqueous cream can also be used instead of soap for dry skin and as a moisturizing cream.) Repeat this treatment until your baby's scalp is clear.

Diarrhoea

Most babies have occasional loose stools and it is important to distinguish between these and true diarrhoea which can be dangerous in young babies. Diarrhoea is the passing of loose, watery, foul-smelling stools which may contain mucus and which may be brown, yellow or green. Your baby may also appear to have abdominal pain. Diarrhoea accompanied by vomiting (see p. 167) is called gastro-enteritis (see Your Child's Health, p. 353).

Causes

Acute diarrhoea is usually caused by an infection. Chronic diarrhoea in babies could be a symptom of a problem such as cow's milk intolerance (see p. 161) and further investigations will be needed.

What you can do

How soon you should consult your doctor depends on your child's age (if your baby is only a few weeks old, the risk of dehydration is greater than in older babies), whether he is continuing to take fluids, and the severity of the symptoms.

Treatment also depends on these three factors. You should continue to breastfeed, and may be advised to give cooled, boiled water or an oral rehydration solution after feeds. Bottlefed babies should continue to be given normal feeds and an oral rehydration mixture. You can also continue to give solid food. Do not give any anti-diarrhoea mixture.

Eczema

See Your Child's Health, p. 350.

Nappy rash

Nappy rash is common in young babies and can range from a slightly red bottom to an angry inflamed rash with broken skin and blisters.

Causes

Contact with ammonia in the urine and bacteria in the baby's stools can irritate the skin and cause nappy rash, as can reactions to irritants such as washing powder, or some bath products.

Nappy rash may also be caused by thrush (*Candida albicans*, see p. 166) or seborrhoeic eczema. Suspect thrush if the rash does not clear up after treatment and if the skin is a shiny, brick red colour, with white or yellow pustules around the edges. In this case your baby will need to be treated with an antifungal cream.

What you can do

Change your baby's nappy as frequently as possible, and clean the skin each time with a gentle non-soap cleansing product which does not irritate (do not use wipes – which contain alcohol – or harsh soaps). Then apply a cream to protect your baby's bottom and heal the rash; there are a number of these on the market and you may need to experiment to see which one suits your baby best. Whenever you can, let your baby spend as much time as possible without a nappy.

Regurgitation

Also known as possetting, regurgitation is the spontaneous bringing back of some of the contents of the stomach. Milk regurgitation is very common in babies immediately after feeding, and can occur as the baby brings up wind. This is not the same as vomiting (see p. 167) and is not projectile. Babies who regurgitate are usually fit and healthy, and it is not normally a cause for concern (the biggest nuisance is usually the mess a baby who regurgitates can make over his or your clothes). He will eventually grow out of it.

Spots and rashes

Skin does not fully mature until adolescence. Because the oil and sweat glands are immature, they do not

Giving your baby medicine

The two most common forms of medication for small babies are medicine (such as antibiotics and liquid paracetamol) and drops, for conditions such as earache, blocked up nose (which can make feeding difficult), or sticky or infected eyes.

Medicine
Sit your baby in your lap with his head back and hold his free hand with yours. Place the spoon on his lower lip and when he opens his mouth, gently tip the medicine in. Try to get it as far back in his mouth as you can.

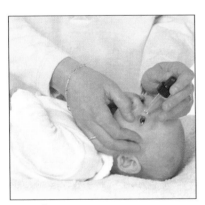

Eye drops
Gently pull down your baby's lower lid and squeeze the drops into the gap between the white of the eye and the lid.

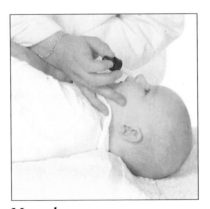

Nose drops
Lie the baby on a flat surface and tip his head back a little. Squeeze the drops into each nostril in turn, trying to get them high inside.

Ear drops
Lie the baby with his head on one side with the infected ear toward you. Squeeze in the drops and try to keep him still for a minute.

work properly, so a baby's skin is affected more by the environment and is more prone to dryness and irritation than an adult's. It is, therefore, a rare baby who does not have some type of spot or rash in the first few months of his life. These can include atopic eczema, seborrhoeic eczema and nappy rash (see p. 163–4). If you are concerned about your baby's rash or it appears infected, consult your doctor or health visitor. Most rashes are temporary, do not need any treatment and soon clear up; the most common are miliaria and milia.

Miliaria

This is a red rash with raised bumps, caused by in-flammation of the sweat glands due to the baby getting too hot. Miliaria is also known as a heat rash or prickly heat. Keep your baby dry and cool.

Milia

Also known as 'milk spots' (for their appearance), milia are tiny white or yellow spots usually on the cheeks, the nose and creases at the side of the nose and the forehead. They are caused by blocked glands on the skin and no treatment is necessary – they disappear within three to four weeks.

Squint

A squint is a condition in which the two eyes do not look in the same direction at the same time; it is the most common eye problem in young children. Squint occurs because the muscles attached to the eyeball are not balanced correctly.

There are several types of squints and their cause is not always known, although they can run in families. A baby may be born with a squint (congenital squint) or one may develop later. Some babies have an intermittent squint but by the time your baby is three months old his eyes should be co-ordinated and always move together. Pseudo squint is used to describe the condition in which a wide bridge to the nose and folds of skin from the nose to the eyebrows combine to give the impression of a squint.

What you can do

If you think your baby has a squint, always mention it to your doctor or health visitor. Never ignore it or think that he will grow out of it. Squints can lead to

poor vision and even very young babies are treated early these days. Treatments include surgery, glasses, eye drops or patches.

Sticky eyes

Sticky eyes usually refers to yellow–green discharge from a young baby's eyes which gums the lids together, especially after sleep. It is common, and usually due to a mild infection, although the cause may be a blocked tear duct. If this is the case, your doctor will give you drops or cream to clear it up.

What you can do

To clean sticky eyes wipe each eye separately with a clean cotton wool ball, soaked in cooled boiled water, starting from the inner corner and working outward (see Topping and tailing, pp. 98–9).

Teething

Some babies cut their teeth without any problems at all. Others may be a little irritable or fretful, dribble, gnaw hard objects or chew their fingers. Some babies also have flushed cheeks, and red or sore gums where the tooth is coming through. Some babies have problems with some teeth, but not with others.

If your baby seems to be suffering when teething, extra cuddles and plenty of drinks of cool boiled water will help, as may one or more of the following.
- Try giving him something hard to chew on, such as a piece of crust or carrot or a chilled (not frozen) teething ring. *Never* leave your baby alone while he is chewing food, in case he chokes.
- If your baby's gums are red and sore, gently massage them with your fingers or a tiny piece of ice (but be careful – babies can get frost bite). Try applying a little sugar-free teething gel.
- If he seems to be in pain from teething, liquid paracetamol may help. Always use sparingly and in the correct amount for your baby's age. Never give a child under 12 aspirin.
- Dribbling may cause a rash (sometimes called a 'teething rash') or sore patches on or under your baby's chin. Protecting the skin with petroleum jelly or a barrier baby cream can help.
- Cuddle and comfort. Put him in a sling and walk about. Go for a ride in the car.

Fluoride supplements

Fluoride is a mineral which makes tooth enamel more resistant to acid attacks from plaque, and so helps to prevent dental decay. It is found in water in various amounts, and is added to most toothpastes. Fluoride supplements can be given to babies from the age of six months if the level of fluoride in the water in your area is low.

Many children, however, tend to 'eat' toothpaste and giving fluoride supplements can result in overdosing, which causes brown stains, a condition known as fluorosis. For this reason, current dental thinking is that fluoride supplements should not be given as a matter of course, unless there is a high risk of dental decay (for example, if childhood dental decay runs in your family, or if your child has special needs). Instead, take the preventive measures outlined on p. 129 and clean your child's teeth with a children's formula fluoride toothpaste. (The level of fluoride in adult formula fluoride toothpaste is too high for children, and these toothpastes in any case taste too strong for small children.) If you think your child needs fluoride supplements, consult your dentist before giving them.

Going to the dentist

It is never too soon to start looking after your baby's teeth (see p. 129). You can register your baby with a dentist soon after birth. Dental treatment and preventive care are still covered by the NHS and are free for children. Your dentist can also give you further advice on caring for your baby's teeth.

It is also a good idea to take your baby to the dentist as soon as his first teeth come through and when you yourself go for a check-up. In this way your baby will get used to going to the dentist as a normal part of his life, and learn that there are plenty of occasions when he goes to the dentist and does not need to have treatment.

Children with special needs

A child with special needs is at particular risk from such dental problems as decay, periodontal (gum) disease, dental injuries and malocclusion (improper fitting together of the upper and lower teeth). Good dental health is, therefore, especially important for these children. Dental infections or extractions can also have serious consequences for some children, including those with heart disease or haemophilia. For some children, the teeth may be very useful for holding special aids as they get older. They are also needed to ensure that your child can eat a good diet.

Gum disease can be a particular problem for children with Down's syndrome whose teeth may be abnormal in size and number, and for children with epilepsy, for whom some medicines may cause gum overgrowth. Because of these problems, in addition to taking extra care with your child's dental health, you may also be advised to give a child with special needs fluoride supplements, since concerns about staining may well be outweighed by the benefits in other areas.

If your child has a chronic illness, ask about sugar-free medicines. If cleaning your child's teeth is difficult, special dental aids are available, again your health visitor, doctor or dentist should be able to help. Some community dentists also specialize in the dental care of children with special needs. Ask your health visitor or the FHSA for the address of your nearest specialist dentist.

Thrush

The yeast-like fungus *Candida albicans*, which causes thrush, is naturally present in most people's bodies and does not usually cause any harm. Babies are particularly susceptible to a thrush infection as their immune system is not fully developed, and some can catch it from their mothers at birth. Thrush can occur in both breast- and bottlefed babies.

Always check his mouth for thrush if your baby cries when he is feeding. (Thrush looks rather like milk curds but cannot be wiped off.)

What you can do

Your baby will be prescribed an antifungal cream or drops. If you are breastfeeding and your baby has thrush, you will also need to treat your breasts. If you are bottlefeeding, take extra care to sterilize your baby's feeding bottles and teats, and his dummy if you use one. Never put your baby's dummy in your mouth in case you are carrying the infection which you can pass on to your baby. Thrush can also appear as a nappy rash (see pp. 163–4).

Umbilical problems

Babies' umbiliduses or navels vary greatly in shape and size. Umbilical hernias are also common and usually heal spontaneously by the time the child reaches the age of two.

The stump that is left after the umbilicus is cut usually shrivels and drops off in about a week to 10 days. Your midwife will clean this for you, and advise you on keeping it clean and dry. Once the stump has fallen off, your baby's navel should only need cleaning as part of your general routine when you bath or top and tail him (see pp. 97–9). Slight bleeding is usually nothing to worry about, but if the bleeding is heavy or the umbilicus looks red, swollen or inflamed, contact your doctor or community midwife.

Vomiting

There are several causes of vomiting in young babies, including infection, overfeeding, food intolerance or a sign of a disorder such as pyloric stenosis.

What you can do
Consult your doctor if:
- Your baby vomits two consecutive feeds.
- He cannot keep any fluids down.
- He has diarrhoea with vomiting.
- He is ill or feverish.
- He appears to be in pain.
- The vomit contains blood or is brown.
- The vomiting is violent or is 'thrown' across the room (so-called projectile vomiting). Projectile vomiting is immediately obvious – if it is not thrown a good distance, it is not projectile.

Vomiting accompanied by diarrhoea (see p. 163) is called gastroenteritis (see p. 353). The treatment of vomiting depends on the cause and the age of your baby. In general, you need to replace the lost fluid by giving sips of an oral rehydration mixture to prevent dehydration. Oral rehydration mixtures, which can be bought from the pharmacist, contain a balanced mixture of salt and sugar to be mixed with water. You should also continue to breastfeed.

Teeth and teething

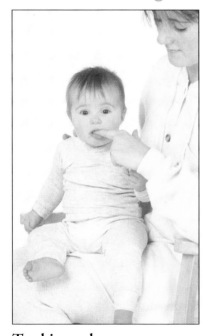

Teething gel
Sugar-free gels can soothe sore gums. Their effect is not very long lasting, so this remedy may work best just before bed, giving relief until the baby falls asleep.

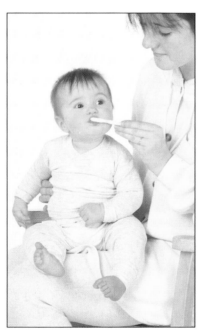

Brushing first teeth
It is never too soon to start cleaning your baby's teeth. As soon as the first one is through, use a soft brush and baby toothpaste to gently clean.

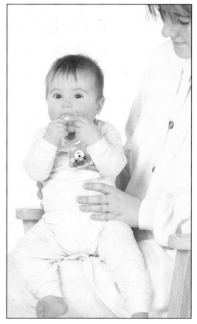

Teething ring
A cooled teething ring can soothe aching gums temporarily and give the baby something hard to gnaw. Put the ring in the sterilizer when it is not in use.

IS YOUR CHILD SAFE?

Children under the age of five run the greatest risk of having an accident of any age group. Every year some 600,000 children have to go to hospital because of an accident in the home. Accidents are also the most common cause of death among children between the age of one and five.

But exploring his environment is an essential part of your child's development, and he is naturally curious. With the best will in the world you cannot keep your eyes on your child for 24 hours a day. Taking adequate safety precautions around your home to prevent accidents is, therefore, vital.

Accidents can happen even to the youngest child. So right from your baby's birth you will need to think about how to protect him from various dangers in and around the home. Following are the major sources of potential danger in the home: keep these in mind as your child grows.

Unsafe equipment

When you buy anything for your child's room, any electrical appliance and any toy, check to see whether it carries a British Standards (BS) number, Lion mark, Kitemark or CE symbol (see box). All toys should carry the BS 5665 or BS 3443 and should be appropriate for the age of your child.

If you buy secondhand equipment, make sure that it complies with safety standards. Check that safety harnesses and straps are firmly attached and not worn, and that toys do not have sharp edges or small, loose pieces that your child could swallow.

Choking and suffocation

Choking and suffocation are the third most common cause of accidental death in preschool children.

Feeding
- Don't leave a young baby alone with a propped-up bottle. Not only does your baby need the security of your arms, but he could inhale milk and choke.
- When your child starts on solid foods, do not leave him alone with finger foods such as bread, carrot or apple – if a lump breaks off, he could choke.

What to look for

The kitemark indicates that an item conforms to British Standards for safety and quality. It should be accompanied by a BS number.

The new 0–3 sign replaces written warnings that a toy may be unsuitable for children under 36 months because of small parts.

The Lionmark can only be used by accredited toy manufacturers and is an indication of quality and safety.

The CE mark is used on toys and indicates that a toy conforms to European Union safety standards.

- As he gets older, do not give him large, hard sweets or let him run around with food in his mouth.
- Do not give whole nuts to under-fives; peanuts are especially dangerous as they can be inhaled into the lungs, and contain an oil which can damage them.

Dummies
- Do not tie a dummy around your baby's neck with ribbon – this could strangle him.
- Only buy a dummy made to BS5239, and check it regularly for wear and tear.

Bedding
- Make sure that cot bumpers are securely tied and that ties are well out of your baby's reach.
- Remove the polythene cover from a new mattress to avoid the risk of suffocation.
- Do not use a pillow until your baby is at least a year old. Pillows should conform to BS 1877.
- Make sure that your baby's cot and mattress conform to BS 1753 and that the mattress fits the cot properly. A gap of more than 40 mm (1½in)

anywhere round the mattress could trap your baby's head – a smaller gap could trap his fingers. Carrycots should conform to BS 3881; buy a safety mattress if your baby is sleeping in the carrycot.

- A baby nest should meet BS 6595; do not use a nest as somewhere for your baby to sleep. Always wash the nest in detergent powder, as soap can clog the fabric and stop air passing through.

Clothing

- Do not let your child wear clothes with ribbons or cords that can be pulled tight around the neck.
- Avoid open-weave clothes or blankets in which tiny fingers can be caught and trapped.

Other items

- Keep polythene bags and plastic away from babies and small children, and teach children never to put these over their heads.
- Check that there are no small parts on toys which a child could swallow and take care that your child does not pick up tiny items such as beads, buttons and coins. Button batteries are especially dangerous as they may contain mercury that can leak if swallowed. If your child swallows one, take him to the nearest accident and emergency department at once. Call an ambulance if necessary.

Scalds, burns and drowning

These can happen at any age, but young children are vulnerable as they learn to crawl, climb and walk.

- Never carry a hot drink when you are carrying your child. Hot water can scald for half an hour after it has boiled.
- Do not leave a hot-water bottle in your baby's cot as this could cause burns, and do not leave an electric blanket on when your baby is in the cot.
- Put cold water into the bath before adding hot, and test the water with your elbow – your fingers can stand much greater temperatures – or a bath thermometer before you bath your baby.
- Do not leave your baby or small child alone in the bath even for a moment. A baby can drown in just a few centimetres of water. If the telephone or doorbell rings, ignore it or get the baby out.
- Do not leave buckets or bowls of water where a baby or young child could fall into them.

Falls

Falling over is common when children are learning to walk and run, and one or two bumps are almost inevitable. Injuries sustained from a fall from a height or on to a hard surface can be much more serious.

- Babies learn to roll at a surprisingly early stage. If you change your baby on a high surface, keep a hand on him. Don't leave your young baby asleep on the sofa or bed, unless he is firmly tucked in.
- Sit-in baby walkers (see p. 134) have tipped babies into fires and down stairs.
- Babies usually love bouncing chairs and they can be a great help in rocking a fretful baby, but never put one on a high surface or a vibrating machine. Even a small baby can make them move, and if the chair falls, your baby may fracture his skull.
- Fit a harness conforming to BS 6684 to your pram, pushchair and highchair and use it every time you put your child in the pram or highchair.
- Make sure that the bath and shower have slip-resistant surfaces or a slip-resistant mat. The bath should have a safety grip handle.

Upwardly mobile

Before your baby starts crawling and walking – which will be sooner than you think – go around your house with this checklist looking for the danger zones.

- Glass in and around doors and low cupboards can break or splinter if your child bumps into it, and may cause serious injuries; replace it with safety glass or plywood if possible, if not cover it with safety film.
- Fires, whether open, gas or electric, should be shielded by a fireguard fixed to the wall; guards should conform to BS 6539.
- Fit locks to windows; make sure that your child cannot open them more than 10 cm (4 in), but that you can open them easily in case of fire.
- Move furniture away from in front of the window so that your child cannot use them as stepping stones in order to get up on to the windowsill.
- Floors should be non-slippery; avoid scatter rugs on polished floors.
- Furniture must be stable and not tip over easily. Sofas and chairs should be made of fire-resistant material; anything purchased since 1988 should

have been treated with a fire-retardant material, but if you are buying secondhand be extra vigilant since there are no guarantees.

- Fit protectors on sharp table corners and put small objects and ornaments away out of reach.
- Fit safety gates at the top and bottom of the stairs once your child starts crawling.
- Check that your child cannot fall through, crawl under, climb over, or get his head, hands or legs stuck in, banisters or landing rails (block them in with hardboard if necessary).
- Bunk beds are generally not recommended for children under six.
- Wires that could trip your child, or entangle and strangle your baby should be secured.
- Fit proper locks to the washing machine, fridge, freezer and video. A clip-on video cover will not put off a determined child for long.
- Fit finger protectors to doors that are heavy or that slam shut easily.

Smoke alarms

Despite intensive government campaigns promoting the fitting of smoke alarms, not every home has one. Fit one before your child is born in a place where you will be able to hear it all over the house. Follow the manufacturer's recommendations on siting and installation.

Test it by holding a recently snuffed out candle beneath it. Every six months, check the battery in the same manner.

Once a year, remove the cover and vacuum clean the alarm and change the battery.

- Sockets should have safety shutters or covers.
- Cupboards and drawers should have locks fitted. Childproof catches do not stay childproof – every tug weakens them further. If you really want to keep him out, fit a proper lock.

In the living room

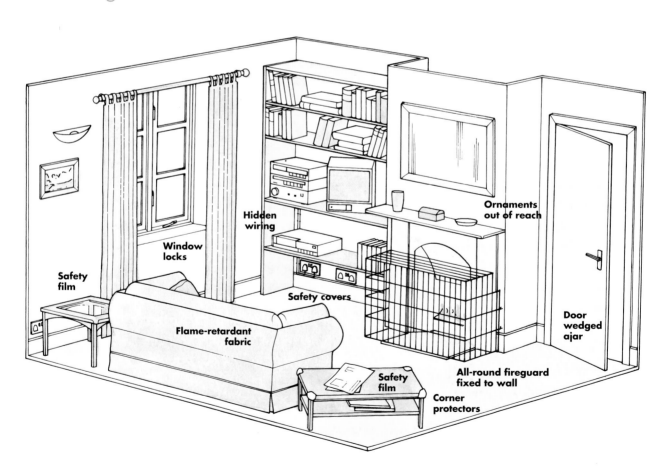

The kitchen

The kitchen is one of the most dangerous places for your baby. Not only is there a risk of accidents such as scalds, or poisoning from cleaning products, but babies can easily get under your feet when they are crawling or walking about.

- If your baby is in a chair, put it where you cannot trip over it and your baby cannot grab anything.
- Keep trailing iron and kettle flexes well out of your baby's reach; use curly flexes or cordless appliances wherever possible.
- Make sure that saucepan handles do not stick out ; use the back burners or fit a cooker guard.
- Put tablecloths away until your child is older; keep hot drinks and dishes out of pulling distance.

Poisoning

A crawling baby will be into every cupboard and treat everything he finds as a potential toy.

- Lock chemicals, medicines and cleaning materials away or place them where your child cannot climb to reach them – children are excellent climbers!
- Buy products with child-resistant tops, but remember they are only child-resistant, not child-proof.
- Do not transfer chemicals to other containers.

Out and about

When you visit other people's homes (especially those without children), look for cupboards containing chemicals or tablets lying about. When you take your toddler out on the streets, use reins or a wristband to keep him securely by your side.

Electronic devices, which can help you locate your child if he wanders off and strays out of transmitter range, are now available. These are, however, no substitute for keeping hold of your child and as he grows up teaching him about safety (see pp. 297–9).

In the kitchen

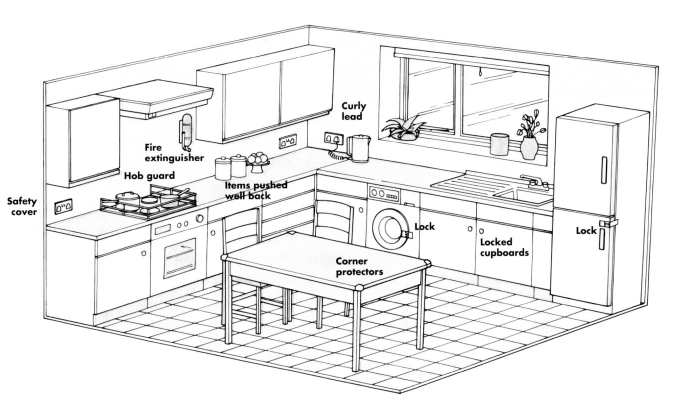

In the garden

Like the house, this can be a potential danger zone.

- Make sure that gates can be locked and that fences are secure, so that your child cannot wander off.
- Fit electric lawnmowers, strimmers and so on with circuit breakers.
- Keep sheds or garages which contain chemicals or equipment locked and the keys well out of reach.
- Some plants can cause unpleasant symptoms in children. Teach your child never to eat anything from the garden. If you suspect plant poisoning, go to the nearest accident and emergency department.
- Fence off ponds and pools.

In the car

No car journey is safe. Making sure that your baby is securely strapped into the appropriate and correctly fitted car seat for his age and weight, however, reduces the likelihood of injury in an accident by two-thirds.

The law says

- Children under the age of three travelling in the front seat of a car must be in an approved child restraint appropriate to their weight. In the back seat, a child restraint must be used if available.
- Children aged 3–11 years (and under 1.5 m/5 ft tall) must use an appropriate child restraint if one is available; otherwise, an adult belt must be worn.

Buying a car seat

Purpose-built child restraints to suit children of all ages and sizes are now widely available and the new EC44 regulations are designed to make car seats easier to fit and use. When buying make sure that:

- The seat carries the Kitemark or CE mark and is correctly fitted by a professional if in doubt.
- It is appropriate to your child's weight and size.

Stage 1 *Birth to 9 months old or 10 kg/22 lb*
These fit, rearward-facing, in the front or the back of the car although they must not be used in the front of a car fitted with air bags. They are safer than carrycots.

Stage 2 *9 months to four years or 9–18 kg/20–40 lb*
These seats are larger and heavier than stage 1 seats, and may be combined with stage 3 seats.

Stage 3 *Four to 11 years or 15–36 kg/33–80 lb*
These bring your child up to the level where he can be secured safely with an adult seat belt.

If you need a seat for a child with special needs, ask your local road safety officer for advice. If you are carrying three children in the back, get a shoulder harness fitted in the centre of the back seat. Check your baby regularly to make sure he is not too hot or cold. Never leave your child alone in a car.

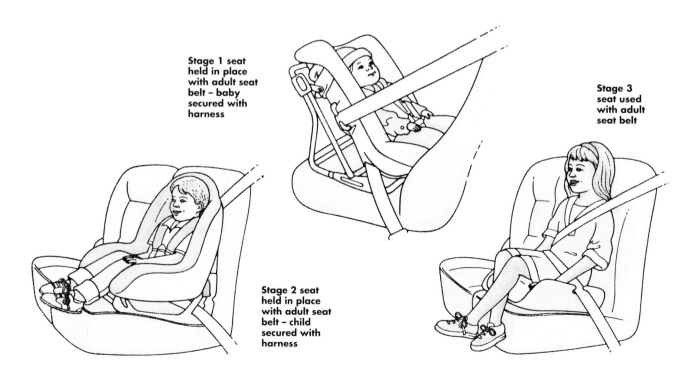

Stage 1 seat held in place with adult seat belt – baby secured with harness

Stage 2 seat held in place with adult seat belt – child secured with harness

Stage 3 seat used with adult seat belt

CHILDREN WITH SPECIAL NEEDS

Every parent wants his or her child to be physically and developmentally perfect. 'Is everything all right?' is usually the first question a mother asks when her baby is born, ahead of even 'Is it a boy or a girl?' Sometimes, however, everything is not 'all right'. Some children have a temporary or permanent physical or mental disability. In the past, children who had a disability such as a developmental delay or cerebral palsy were labelled 'mentally' or 'physically handicapped'. This kind of labelling, which only focused on the child's disability and not on him as an individual, is no longer used. Children who have a mental or physical disability are now described as 'children with special needs'.

It is estimated that one in five children has special needs at some time in his childhood. These can range from a severe developmental problem or a rare congenital syndrome, which are permanent and lifelong conditions, to a minor speech difficulty which will respond to help within a few months or years. Problems such as a cleft lip and palate (see Your Child's Health, p. 344) can cause considerable distress and require treatment over a number of years, but the outcome is usually good.

Identifying special needs

The discovery that a child has special needs may occur immediately at birth, or soon after (you may even have discovered while you were pregnant and chosen to go ahead and have your baby). A neural tube defect such as spina bifida, for example, or a cleft palate or Down's syndrome are obvious from the start. On the other hand, a learning difficulty or hearing impairment may not be detected until your child is a few months or even a few years old. Sometimes the disability may be discovered during a routine developmental check, or you, your GP or health visitor may suspect that all is not well with the baby after observing his progress over a period of time.

Depending on your child's problem, he will be referred to the appropriate specialist. If he has a hearing impairment, for example, he will be referred to an audiologist. If you or a health professional suspect that your child is not progressing as well as he should be, then he is likely to be referred for assessment to a paediatrician. After assessing your child, the paediatrician may – depending on the problem – then refer him to another specialist.

In some areas, your child may be referred to a child development centre. Here a multi-agency team of professionals including doctors, therapists, psychologists, health visitors and social workers work together to identify the specific needs of your child, and to offer the appropriate treatment, advice and support. As your child gets older, educational, psychological and psychiatric assessments may be made if necessary. If you do not understand anything, ask for it to be explained again; if you are still not happy with anything, make a fuss and ask for a second opinion.

Coping with your feelings

Parents' reactions to the realization that their child has a mental or physical disability depend on several factors: the seriousness of the problem; the way in which they are told of the diagnosis; and, often, their own personalities. If you have strong religious beliefs, you may feel you have been given a special child to care for. If you know someone with a child with a similar problem, you may feel more able to cope than if you are totally ignorant of its implications. If you have been worried about your child, having an actual diagnosis may give you a sense of relief. Most parents, however, experience shock, disbelief and guilt and, if their child has a severe or permanent disability, an overwhelming sense of loss.

When you suspect all is not well

You may well be the first people to suspect that all is not well with your baby. So if you are worried, ask your doctor or health visitor to check. If you are not satisfied, ask for a second opinion from a specialist such as a paediatrician or audiologist. Remember, you know your own child best, so follow your instincts, and do not be afraid to make a fuss if you have to. The earlier a diagnosis is made, the earlier treatment can be started and the more likely treatment is to be successful.

Your feelings may resemble those of the bereaved, including all or some of the stages of grief such as denial, anger, blame, despair, bargaining and acceptance. Having all, or any of these reactions, is perfectly normal. You are, after all, grieving for the loss of your 'normal' child, and need time to come to terms with your feelings.

You may also experience a mixture of feelings toward your child – protectiveness, resentment, love and dislike. Again, these feelings are perfectly normal. You need time to work through them, before you can start to accept your child as he really is.

Getting help

It is important that you and your partner talk to each other and share your feelings, and that you do not bottle everything up. You may also find it beneficial to talk about how you feel to an outside person such as a health professional or a member of a voluntary organization or support group, or to go to a counselling service.

Services are also available to support you in caring for your child, and to help your child reach his full potential. These are provided by health and social services and by voluntary organizations. Unfortunately, accessibility to and availability of some of these services are not uniform, and depend to some extent on where you live.

What the law says
Under the Children Act, local authorities have a duty to provide services designed:
- to minimize the effect on disabled children in the area of their disabilities; and
- to give such children the chance to lead lives which are as normal as possible.
By law, children with disabilities must be treated first and foremost as children with particular needs, and are entitled to the same general level of social services as other children in need, to enable them to live as normally as possible.

Professional and statutory services

Your GP, health visitor, paediatrician and social worker can all give you general advice and support in caring for your child. In some areas, specialist health visitors are available to give extra help and to act as a liaison between hospital and home. You may also have a paediatric community nursing service in your area which can provide a nurse to visit you at home and help in managing your child if he has a severe handicap, chronic illness or was born prematurely. Your health visitor, GP or local hospital can tell you more about this service.

Depending on your child's needs and age, other specialist help includes: physiotherapists, occupational therapists, speech and language therapists, psychologists, nurseries and family centres. Always ask what is available in your area and make a fuss if you have to in order to make sure that you and your child get the help to which you are entitled.

Home learning service
If your preschool child shows signs of developmental delay, you can be helped to teach him new skills through home-visiting schemes such as Portage, which is run by the local education authority. Through this scheme, a home visitor will visit you on a equal basis and together with you decide what new skills to teach your child. These may include simple skills such as holding a rattle for a young baby or showing him how to play with bricks, to toilet training and early reading as your child gets older. Voluntary organizations such as Kids may also provide home learning teachers (see Useful Contacts, pp. 390–3).

Voluntary organizations
Whatever condition or syndrome your child has, there is likely to be a voluntary organization or a parents' group to offer you help and support. Often too, the best person to talk to is another parent whose child has the same difficulties as yours, and who has been through similar experiences.

Some organizations are familiar. They include Scope (formerly the Spastics Society) for people with cerebral palsy, the Down's Syndrome Association and the National Deaf Children's Association. If your child has a rare condition or syndrome which no one else seems to have heard of, try Contact a Family. This organization not only supports a large network of self-help groups covering all disabilities, but also maintains a network of national groups specializing in rare syndromes (see Useful Contacts, pp. 390–3).

What you can do

Once your child's condition has been diagnosed, try to learn as much as possible about it. This will help you to feel more in control about the management of your baby, so do not be afraid to pester people if necessary. If you do not understand anything a professional tells you, ask him or her to explain again. It is difficult to take everything in at first. If your partner is unable to be with you when you see a specialist or your child has an assessment, ask a friend or relative to go with you to help you remember what is said. Write down any questions you want to ask before you go, so that you do not forget to ask anything important. Remember too, that even if your baby has a disability, he will also have similar needs to other babies. So he will still need cuddling, talking to, playing with and to be treated as an individual. As he grows up, he will also need the discipline you give to your other children.

- Encourage ability – praise, stretch, present him with things he can do and things you think he may be able to do.
- Be sure to praise progress even if it is only a very small advance.
- Encourage independence. It is so easy to teach a child that he 'cannot', but he can learn and should be encouraged to try.
- Treat him normally and do not be afraid to discipline him or sometimes to put yourself, your partner and your other children first.
- Try to look beyond his special needs to a child who must grow up to face a real world which will not always make allowances for his disabilities, and try to fit him for that world.
- Accept his frustration. Things are not easy and he should feel free to say so.
- Do not deprive his siblings in a misguided attempt to treat your children equally: they should be allowed to do things he cannot do and deserve as much of your time as you can give.
- Explain as much as you can as honestly as possible to his siblings; remember that they too need time to adjust to the fact that their new brother or sister is not 'normal'.
- Encourage his siblings to take some responsibility, but do not be unreasonable in what you ask them to do.

Play

Even if your baby does not seem to respond to you, it is important that you play with him. Play is important for all children, and can enhance the learning skills of children with special needs. Depending on your child's condition, he may need extra encouragement to play, and may take longer to acquire new skills. Toys should match your child's mental age and ability (but if an older child is using a toy made for a younger one, make sure that it is strong enough). All toys should be bright and colourful, and offer action and stimulation. Again, a charity or support group will have members who can tell you how to adapt a toy for your child and where to find toys suitable for children whose bodies are older than their minds, and vice versa.

There are a number of excellent books aimed at encouraging play in children with various different needs and which offer solutions to problems such as keeping toys within reach. These should also help you to understand how to stimulate your child and how to play to his abilities, rather than concentrating on what might be seen as his problems.

A child who is blind or partially sighted will need toys with an interesting texture to offer some tactile variety, and with sound or music. If your child has a hearing impairment, the toys should vibrate when they are shaken. Further advice on suitable toys for your child can be obtained from the National Association of Toy and Leisure Libraries, which can also tell you where to find your nearest toy library (see Useful Contacts, pp. 390–3).

Educational provision

Local education authorities have a statutory duty to ensure that special educational provision is made for pupils with special educational needs. This includes making an assessment of your child's needs if he is over two (or under two if you request it).

Financial help

If your child with special needs takes a lot of looking after, you may be entitled to financial help, such as the Disability Living Allowance. For further information about this, ring the Benefit Enquiry Line, or ask at your local Benefits Agency. You may also be entitled to help from the Family Fund (see Useful Contacts, pp. 390–3).

CHAPTER SEVEN

Toddlerhood and Beyond

The years between one and five are often those that parents remember with most affection. Between these ages life itself is an adventure, and it seems that hardly a day goes by without your child mastering a new skill, speaking a new word, understanding a new concept, or playing a new game.

The preschool years

It is hard to say exactly when a baby becomes a toddler, but you will find the transition quite sudden. At some point between about 9 and 18 months you will realize that your child is not really a baby any more. Yet in many ways her progress is gradual. She pulls herself up and cruises around the furniture, so you expect her to walk. But she does not. It may be six or eight more weeks before she walks alone. It is because she progresses on so many fronts at the same time that the movement from baby to toddler seems like a sudden leap, but lots of little things have added up to that big step out of babyhood.

Walking is one, obviously, but in spite of calling them 'toddlers' this is not the most obvious difference. The main thing which distinguishes a baby from a toddler is that your toddler shares her experiences with you. She communicates her excitement and her fears. And, more subtly, she looks up to you and smiles as she plays. She understands. She lifts her arms when you ask and stops when you say 'No!' Her movements are more fluid and she gives the impression she has a clear intention. She knows what she wants, although cannot necessarily work out how to get it.

The whole is still, somehow, more than the sum of all these parts. Each new skill you write in her baby record emphasizes that she is not a baby. In some small sense she is now your companion. What you do together is partly on her terms: and from now on this will always be the case.

GROWING UP

Your baby's development in her first year (see chapter 5) was almost certainly characterized by periods of transition in which she learned a new skill, followed by periods of consolidation in which she practised and perfected it. There are three major periods of change in the first year: the first is birth, the second happens at about six to eight weeks when she begins to interact with the world and the third happens at about nine months. There is another major transition between 18 months and two years as she begins to exert her will more strongly and enters 'the terrible twos'. There is a smaller one between about three and a half and four when she becomes able to understand other people's points of view, and another major change at six years when she begins to think more logically. Finally there is the major transition of puberty (see Chapter 12).

At each transition children become more difficult. At six weeks there is an increase in the level of crying.

Letting go

Babies are wonderful. Every smile, movement, gesture is guaranteed to overwhelm you, make you feel amazed at your ability to produce such a miracle. And a baby's vulnerability brings out the protectiveness many parents did not even know they possessed and adds an unimagined dimension to their feelings for each other.

It can be difficult to accept that your baby is growing, that with each day that goes by, she needs you just a bit less, can do just one more thing herself. This is often made worse by the fact that as she takes each step on the road to independence, she may pass through a phase of being particularly difficult.

Don't be afraid to let go. Your children need you in different ways throughout childhood and even adult life. Each stage of their development brings its own charms and rewards, in addition to its own problems.

At nine months children start to cling, moan and/or wake at night. At 18 months children become more wilful and may have temper tantrums. At three and a half they are often disobedient and quarrelsome. At six they bicker with you and their siblings and at 13 all hell may break loose. But during the periods of consolidation – which last much longer – children are easier and happier.

How well your child weathers each transition depends partly on her underlying temperament and partly on her relationship with her main carers. An easy child may sail through despite indifferent caring. A difficult temperamental child needs sensitive parenting to see her through. 'Growing up' may reflect changes in the way she thinks or in what she can do, but whichever it is, you will find that, afterward, the old patterns of parenting do not work. Something new must evolve.

Getting it right

There are no simple formulae which ensure that you get parenting 'right'. In this century alone, advice to parents has wavered from the extreme indulgence of the flower power era to the 'spare the rod spoil the child' mentality that was a throwback to Victorian times, and every shade in between. The reason for this variation is that applied consistently most systems work. You can beat children into compliance (though few would now advocate this), but between the firm and free it is clear that no one has all the right answers. Nor can one set of principles be applied to all behaviours or at all ages. To live in society your child needs to acquire self-discipline and the best way to teach discipline is to apply it consistently. But, so that she is not down trodden by the stronger members of society she must also learn to be assertive of her own needs. Allowing her to unfold, to know she has her say, is the best way to teach this. Getting the balance between these two is one of the most difficult tasks you face as a parent.

- All children need opportunities to unfold, and sometimes their needs should come first. They should be able to put their point of view and you should listen even if you overrule the request.
- Although complete freedom is unrealistic, allow your children to do things for themselves even if they make mistakes.

- Your family is your child's first model of society. If you want her to grow up to consider other people (and have a society which does this), you have to teach her that her parents and siblings also have those rights. Sometimes she must do the washing up while you are having a few minutes' peace.

There is probably a series of things – bad behaviour, rudeness, running into the road, expecting to be waited on, refusing to settle down to sleep – that you (and every other reasonable parent) want to stamp out. Sometimes you can change things by discussion and understanding; at other times you have to insist. How you balance the two is a matter of taste. There is no right and wrong way. There are no rules that are suitable for all children or for the same child at every age. Decide on your family message, your way of doing things, and do it consistently.

What kind of parent are you?

There are shades in every parent and probably no one fits a category exactly, but there are general trends in the way all parents behave.

Accepting permissive

You are warm and loving to your children and create a democratic environment. Your children's needs are considered and their views treated with respect. You are permissive about most things and your children are free to try new things.

RESULTS: Children tend to be independent, outgoing, active, assertive, popular and democratic.

DANGERS: You can be so permissive that your children grow up unable to control impulses and since they lack self-control, they lack maturity. You may raise an individual who expects everyone to fit in with her: self-indulgent, self-centred, selfish, rebellious and disobedient.

Being permissive about the wrong things, such as aggression, can lead to increased aggression and a lack of care for the feelings and property of others.

Accepting demanding

You accept your children and are warm and loving toward them but nevertheless exert a great deal of control over them. You know your children and are not afraid to confront them.

RESULTS: Well-behaved, but often submissive, children who are polite and obedient. They may, none the less, have high self-esteem and outperform children from more permissive homes (this is particularly true of children with learning difficulties and other special needs).

DANGERS: Overprotected children can become too dependent on others. They may not be able to stand up for themselves and may be insecure without the controls you exert.

Rejecting permissive

You do not show love and concern, nor do you control your child's behaviour.

RESULTS: Disobedient, and sometimes delinquent, children who show little concern for other people. They can be quarrelsome and aggressive and may become bullies.

Rejecting demanding

You are demanding and at the same time hostile toward your children. You put forward a strict set of rules and require unquestioning obedience and punish if it is not forthcoming.

RESULTS: Socially withdrawn and often sullen children who may be quarrelsome and shy. Such children often turn the aggression they feel toward others inward upon themselves and may become the victims of bullies.

FROM BABY TO CHILD

These are the changes you can expect to see in your child and the ages at which you can expect to see them, all of which contribute to her transformation from baby to toddler to child. But remember all children are different and develop at different rates: yours may be earlier or later in one or more of these areas.

If you are concerned that your child is continually below the average in several of these skills, consult your doctor or health visitor.

9–12 months

Physical skills

Mobile: most children crawl or walk around the furniture, some walk independently. Becomes increasingly confident when upright.

Uses her hands to manipulate and explore; passes an object from hand to hand; holds an object with one hand, explores with the other; she pokes, prods, strokes and twists to unscrew.

Thinking

Knows that an object continues to exist even when she cannot see it; can solve simple problems.

Shows persistence in doing things and makes connections (pressing the button will make the Jack-in-the box pop up); she can pay attention quickly to anything that interests her.

Can look away from what she was doing and return to it; she can put two ideas together to make a plan (like wanting a biscuit and crawling to the cupboard to get one). This gives the impression that behaviour flows, since she does not simply react to the moment.

Language

Understands simple commands like 'No!'

Understands and may produce one or two words; communicates with sounds and actions.

Can imitate sounds.

Matches a face to a voice, looking for someone she knows when she hears them speak.

Can discriminate between different facial expressions.

Social skills

Has formed a central attachment to one person and is dependent on him or her.

Looks for approval and disapproval.

Clings and cries if left with strangers; likes to be near you or carers at all times; may have a comfort object.

Communicates her intentions.

Follows your gaze, looking where you look or point.

Initiates and plays games with you; understands social signals and imitates what you do.

Self-awareness

Knows her own name; touches her image in a mirror but does not recognize herself.

Emotions

Delighted to see you; calls to you in the morning and needs to be told when you are going to leave; less promiscuous in her affections; afraid of strangers and attached to her immediate family and carers – parents, siblings, grandparents, childminder and babysitters.

12–18 months

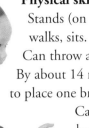

Physical skills
Stands (on one foot with support), walks, sits.
Can throw a ball.
By about 14 months, she may be able to place one brick on top of another.
Can twist her hand and feed herself; she can use a sit-and-ride, push a trolley and carry an object.
Can scramble up and down stairs.

Self-awareness
Knows her own abilities.
Can show you her shoes if you ask her to.
'Into' everything.
Teases.
Wants her own way; protests when she does not get it.
Does not forget immediately.
Less clinging, moving further away from you.
Likes to watch herself in the mirror.

Thinking
Unwraps parcels; takes the lid from a box.
Can put simple shapes in a puzzle board.
Names some objects and understand names of others.
She explores and is generally more purposeful and persistent.

Emotions
Shows preferences.
Expresses emotions: affection, anxiety, fear.
Likes to be with other children.

Language
Jabbers and uses between five and 20 words.
She makes lots of signs and generally tries to communicate.
She understands more than she can say.

Social skills
Plays pat-a-cake.
Responds to requests and stops when told to.
Focused on main carers: parents, nanny, childminder.
Likes other children; may offer a toy but does not play (although she will play with an older sibling).

18 months to two years

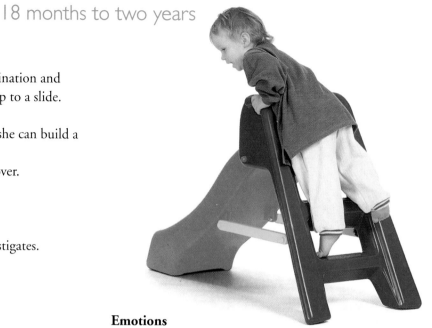

Physical skills
Climbs on to a chair; runs with co-ordination and climbs stairs; climbs on to a frame or up to a slide.
Pushes toys and pulls them behind her.
Hand co-ordination improves, so that she can build a tower of many blocks.
Stops to pick up a toy without falling over.

Thinking
Names familiar objects.
Plans activities; explores, watches, investigates.

Language
Says 50–200 words.
Starts using two-word sentences.
Uses 'me' or 'I' and 'you'.
Follows verbal instructions.
Listens to simple songs and stories.

Social skills
Scribbles.
Likes to play with your possessions and mimics what you do; likes 'adult' toys such as kitchens and lawn mowers.
Follows simple directions and orders people about.
Tests, fights, has tantrums and says 'No!' often.
At 18 months plays in parallel with other children but by two years may begin to interact with children she knows well.
Begins to imitate your intentions rather than simply your actions.

Self-awareness
Recognizes body parts of teddy or doll.
Recognizes herself in a mirror.
Challenges your wishes.
Wants to 'do it myself' and make her own choices.
High sense of self-importance.

Emotions
Wants independence and may react forcefully if she does not get her own way. Laughs and gets very excited.
Has tantrums and screaming bouts.
Likes to please and may be very loving but also quite aggressive; she may bite, kick and hit parents, siblings and other children.
May hurt herself on purpose to gain attention.
Likes to solve problems but is easily frustrated.
Delighted by own achievements.

From two to three years

Physical skills
Jumps and hops.
Walks up and down stairs.
Knows what is safe and dangerous.
Begins to dress and undress himself.

Thinking
Names many objects.
Begins to understand the concepts of 'one'
and 'lots'.
Memory span grows.
Begins to give reasons and solve problems.
Makes comparisons ('that cake is bigger
than mine').
Knows some colours.
Respects rules.
Interested in 'why' and asks often to keep
you talking.

Language
Communicates thoughts and ideas.
Uses language to express social and
affectionate relations.
Enjoys talking.
Understands 'up',
'down', 'later', 'now'.

Social skills
Tests limits, saying
'no' but doing it
anyway.
Enjoys being with
people and plays
with other children.
Likes to 'be like'
an adult.
Likes to race
about but also to play simple pretend games such
as cooking dinner for teddies.

Self-awareness
Contrasts himself with others.
Expresses preferences.
Expresses pride.
Possessive about his things.

Emotions
Strives to master skills and tolerates more
frustration.
Accepts substitutes.
Independent; seeks to do things for himself.
Less aggressive.
Uses language to express wishes and feelings.
Shows beginnings of a sense of humour.

From three to five years

Physical skills

Runs, starts and stops suddenly and dodges; gallops, skips, hops and jumps, raising feet high and taking strain as he lands.

Walks up and down stairs with alternate feet.
Uses his hands to manipulate small objects.
Throws and can catch a large ball.
Dresses himself, but may still have some difficulty with laces, small buttons and zips.

Thinking

Talks fluently and questions frequently.
Begins to understand what numbers mean.
Can give and discuss reasons and solve more complex problems.
Makes frequent comparisons and can put some things in order.
Names many colours.
Begins to show sympathy and empathy for others; cries at sad stories.
Understands that you do not see what he sees and will explain things to you. Pretends to be someone else, talking for his toys and instructing himself as he plays.

Language

Communicates thoughts and ideas fluently using the past tense as well as the present. Uses language to express feelings; enjoys talking.
Distinguishes between reality and the pretend world; says 'Pretend that you are the Mummy and I'll be the Daddy'.

Social skills

More obedient and less testing with you, but more likely to quarrel with both siblings and other children.
Most children have stopped having tantrums.
Enjoys being with other children, but can sit quietly by himself.
Likes to race about, especially with other children.
Gets bored and tells you so.
Shows glee.
Begins to tell jokes but does not understand what makes something a joke.
Acts out roles based on TV or films; imitates other children.

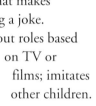

Self-awareness

Concerned about what others will think, so may refuse to wear shorts or insist on wearing pink.
Contrasts himself with other children and what they have and are allowed to do. Says who and what he likes.
Likes to do 'grown up things' such as choosing and paying for things in the shop.

Emotions

Independent, may insist on trying things for himself.
More dependent on other children.
More aware of how he should act and influenced by the culture of other children in ways you may not approve (for example, boys should not cry and girls should be good) and may start to conform to that culture.
Does not always tell you his thoughts and feelings as he used to.

Influences on development

A child's development is influenced by biological factors – her heredity, the fact that she may have been damaged at birth, and by sickness and/or health. But environmental factors also play a part – the love and stimulation she receives; what happens to her; where she grows up; and how her family and others relate to her. The sort of child she is also influences her development: her temperament, security, confidence and how easy or difficult she is to love.

An attractive lovable child may draw attention and stimulation in ways a more difficult or less attractive child might not.

Heredity

Some aspects of development are more strongly influenced by inheritance than others. Physical development generally happens to a set timetable. As long as the environment and nutrition are within the normal range, it progresses along its pre-ordained road. Identical twins, who have exactly the same genetic inheritance, usually sit and walk within days of each other.

Language also emerges more or less regardless of what you do. The amount you talk to your child influences how many words she will say and how rapidly she learns, but most children learn how to communicate by the time they start school. Unless a child is severely neglected or has some specific language disability, she will know how to ask questions or speak about things in the past tense by the time she is four or five.

Becoming an intelligent adult, however, does need parental input. No child can reach her true intellectual potential without the love of her carers and a stimulating environment.

Your child's personality

Although babies seem pretty much alike, as children grow up they become more different from each other, their individuality and personality go with them into every situation. Some children always look before they leap: others invariably leap before they look. When faced with something new one child looks carefully before she reaches out to touch; another rushes in. The way a child interacts with the world tends to remain fairly stable. Impulsive toddlers were probably impulsive babies and may well in turn grow up to be impulsive adults, although this tendency may be overstated.

Being reflective is more likely to endear your child to her teachers and, initially, at least, your reflective child may do slightly better at school, but it is not as big an advantage as it might seem at first sight. Impulsive children are used to getting it wrong. They are more willing to 'have a go' and less likely to have their confidence undermined by what people think.

Your child's temperament

Sunny babies tend to be sunny children, and miserable babies tend to grow into miserable children (although if the cause of their misery is discovered and remedied, they will not). Extreme children make their parents fit in with them: you tiptoe around your child if you know that she might otherwise scream for an hour and a half. She then learns to use the threat of her temper to manipulate you. At the other extreme a sunny baby probably learns how to manipulate with her charm.

How children who are less extreme turn out is less predictable. 'In between' children probably learn more than one 'trick'. Sometimes they charm, sometimes they demand. One may realize that charm works best, while another finds confrontation far more successful.

HOW CHILDREN GROW

Throughout her preschool years, your child will grow about 50–75 mm (2–3 in) taller and put on around 2.6 kg (6 lb) each year. Fat peaks at about nine months, after which she should start slimming down, although many children remain more 'stocky' than they will be as adults.

Bones

Your child's bones will continue to grow and since her limb bones grow faster than those in her trunk, her proportions change. The small bones of her wrist increase in number (there are nine bones in an adult wrist, but only three in a baby's). By the time she is two her fontanelle (the membranous space between the bones of her skull) will have closed.

The brain

The power of the brain comes from the thousands of interconnections between the different brain cells. The word 'cell' gives the wrong impression of brain cells which are in fact more like trees, with branches that reach out to communicate with other cells. If you imagine all the large branches, small branches and twigs of a large tree, and then all the veins of each leaf you will get an idea of how much each cell reaches out to influence other cells. Each little vein finds a connection. If you then consider all the roots and root hairs you will get an idea of how many other cells reach out to interact with the brain cells.

Although most brain cells are present at birth they are not well connected. Nor are they all in the right place. First they move to the right place and then they start to make connections. In forming the connections, the brain increases in weight from 350 g (12 oz) to 1.35 kg (3 lb), most of it in the first two to three years of life. As well as making connections, the brain also starts to break some of those it no longer needs. When your child is about two, her brain will start pruning out these connections.

Myelination also occurs. Myelin is a fatty sheath which covers the nerves, in much the same way that electric cables are covered with a plastic sheath, insulating them so that impulses can pass along them more quickly. (Appreciating that multiple sclerosis is a disease in which myelin breaks down gives some idea of its importance.)

Milestones in physical skills
13–14 MONTHS Walks without help
18 MONTHS Goes up and down stairs without help
TWO YEARS Runs, walks backward, picks things up without overbalancing.
TWO AND A HALF Balances on tip-toe, jumps with both feet.
THREE YEARS Balances on one foot; goes up and down stairs by stepping and then bringing both feet together on one step; hops; and runs with a flat-footed action. She cannot change direction when running, shuffles if asked to skip and is unlikely to crouch or bend her knees when jumping.
FOUR YEARS Walks up and down stairs by placing one foot on each step; runs in a controlled way; can start, stop and turn suddenly, but may not be able to change speed without stopping first. She can hop about eight hops, climb up and down on the climbing frame and take alternate steps when walking on a wall. She skips with a flat-footed step if at all. Most children can now do hurdle jumps.
FIVE YEARS She can skip with both feet alternating; gallops starting with either left or right foot; runs, dodges, changes speed and direction without stopping first. Hops ten or more hops. About seven out of ten children can climb a rope ladder or a 'firefighter's pole'. She jumps smoothly using an arm thrust and crouch to take off and absorbing the impact by bending her knees.

What you can do

Everything your preschooler learns she learns by watching somebody else and then by doing. She keeps on trying until she succeeds. Once she has the basic skill, she practises. Most physical play is practice for the things she has already learned to do. There will come a stage where she loves to jump off the stairs on to a pile of cushions or walk along a wall while you hold her hand.

- **Encourage walking**
  Go for walks without the pushchair – you do not have to go far (remember her stride length when planning walks). Walking after dark when the street lights are on is a great treat.
- **Encourage running**
  Most children need little encouragement to chase and run around to music. Games like 'statues' enable children to practise running and standing still; chasing games encourage dodging, starting and stopping.
- **Walk backward**
  Can she weave backward through a maze of cushions? She can certainly walk to them and then fall over. Can she walk backward with her coat on backward?
- **Help her balance**
  How fast can she pick up her toys? Can she get them all before the music stops? Can she run around the garden filling a small bucket with leaves? Make stepping stones across shark-infested water (paper plates across the carpet), or let her 'walk the plank'. Balance two shelves across two piles of books.

- **Jumping**
  Play horses galloping over the 'jumps' (piles of cushions are probably the best choice for these). Most children enjoy skipping or running as fast as they can.
- **Hopping**
  Hopscotch is an obvious game, but you could also try 'Simon says "Stand on one leg". He also says "Hop around the room".'
- **Climbing**
  The sooner a child learns to go up and down stairs by herself the sooner she learns caution, but do not assume she has sense – she may try to carry something big like a bicycle up or down stairs. Climbing frames and slides offer practice. Check that they are sited on a safe surface and watch children as they play.
- **Make obstacle courses**
  Even small children can climb and crawl around an obstacle course. Make a tunnel behind the sofa, stepping stones with cushions, climb on to the coffee table. Obstacle courses for bike riders encourage spatial skills and teach them to weave and stop and start.

Using her hands

By her first birthday your child could probably move her thumb at will and curl her hand up so that she could wrap it around an object. Once she can twist her wrist, she places objects by holding them from above, and turns her hand to line objects up before she places them.

What you can do

Providing opportunities for skilled hand movements is the best way to develop your child's skills in this area. This does not need elaborate toys. Turning pages; finger painting; feeding dollies; spreading jam on bread; ripping paper into long strips, rolling it into balls and throwing it; posting shapes in shape sorters; building with bricks – the list is endless. You may also want to try some of the following ideas.

Construction kits

Fit the kit to your child's ability rather than the age on the box. A toy is useless unless she plays with it. The easiest kits, such as Stickle Bricks, fix together without a great deal of precise wrist movement. Once she has mastered these, offer something chunky such as Duplo which requires a little more precision. If your child enjoys building, she can be drawn forward if you gradually increase the difficulty of the task you set her.

Jigsaws

Some children love jigsaws; others hate them. When you buy a puzzle look carefully at the pieces. In a well-made puzzle it should be possible to see what is depicted on each piece.

Encouraging movement

Exercise need not be formal. Watch children coming out of the classroom into the playground: they explode into activity. All children need to let off steam. They need a time to race about, jump on their beds, roll down grassy banks, turn windmills or dance wildly to music. If they have other children to do it with, so much the better. Silly games are not as silly as they seem. Through them children make friends. They also practise spatial skills: those they absorb through playing with building bricks are as nothing compared with those they learn by riding a small bicycle through an obstacle course. Chasing and catching a child who is ducking and dodging requires even greater skill.

You cannot teach your baby to swim, ride a bike or dance, but you can provide the atmosphere in which she can learn, by taking away her fears and showing her the pleasures. Dancing involves using a physical skill to interpret music and express feelings and since toddlers are not much good at either of these, formal lessons are out of the question. But toddlers do enjoy moving to music. Since they particularly enjoy doing this with other children, early 'dance' classes can be great fun. Similarly children who are much too young to start formal training in gymnastics get a great deal of pleasure jumping and climbing their way around a baby gym.

Painting and drawing

At first children just scribble. Give your child one short fat crayon. Try this variation. Mix two or three tablespoons of cornflour with a little water to make paste that flows. Add a drop of food colouring. Put it into a cake tin and let her 'draw' in it with a blunt pencil. The lines will be clear for a moment and then close over so she can start again.

Dressing dolls

Putting on dolls' clothes – and taking them off – requires good hand–eye co-ordination.

Cutting

Trying to cut out pictures is difficult, but you can make long thin strips of paper and let her snip across them to make confetti.

Unskilled hands

Providing games is one thing: getting your child to use her hands is quite another. Some children love jigsaws, dressing dolls, construction kits and drawing. Others would far rather race about on bikes or sit and watch videos. The problem with many children is getting them to sit still long enough, so the obvious solution is for you or her carer to organize your preschooler's day – much as a nursery school would. Make a timetable. Morning and evening is the time to let off steam. In the afternoon there is a time for silly, noisy or messy games. Between times find slots for her to do some housework, baking, drawing, go for a walk, read, play quietly with toys and watch TV. Not only will such organization help her to fit into the structured environment of school and nursery, it will make her feel secure.

If you need to add a little bribery to that organization, get her to do the things she does not like as a condition for doing the things she prefers. Washing down the table before playing at the sink. Make things more fun. Pick up all the toys and put them away before the music stops. Then make an attempt on last week's record.

Getting dressed

Girls tend to be a little more competent than boys at dressing themselves. Whether this is motivation or practice is not really known: girls after all do need partly to undress every time they go to the toilet. Easy dressing is rarely compatible with children's fashions. Doing up fly buttons and zips, dealing with dungarees, shirts with buttons, or shoes with laces, is quite beyond the scope of a two-year-old. Many five-year-olds still find these difficult.

Vests, teeshirts and dresses

If your child looks at the front of a teeshirt or dress before she puts it on, it is then the wrong way around when she picks it up, so she puts it on back to front. Select clothing with pictures or buttons on the front and show her that these have to 'hide' before she picks them up.

Manual dexterity

Initially your child will simply cut pieces from paper; the ability to cut out a shape comes later.

Finger painting is messy, but all children love making pictures in this way.

Jigsaws can be great fun for children who take to them. Start with a few pieces and build on that.

Dressing dolls and teddies is excellent practice at manipulating small objects.

Getting clothes over her head can be problem, so choose those with wide necks. Show her how to burrow in from the bottom. Again, it helps to put the vest down with the neck furthest away from her. Teach her to put her arms through the sleeves before putting her head in.

Pants and trousers

Avoid buttons and bibs until your child is skilled at dressing herself: they are too difficult for two-year-olds. Elasticated waistbands enable a two-year-old to pull trousers and knickers on quite easily, but tights remain a difficulty throughout the second year, and often beyond.

To get trousers the right way round, the front has to be facing upward before she starts, so lay them out with the front up and waist closest or – better still – select trousers which do not have a specific back and front. Try to select pants in which the leg holes are clearly different from the waist hole.

Coats

Place the coat on the floor button side up and tell your child to walk around to the head end and put her arms into the sleeves. She can then raise her arms up high, sweeping the body of the coat over her head.

Socks and shoes

When you put out your child's socks, place them with the heels touching each other to reduce the possibility of the heel ending up on top of your child's foot. Or, better still, buy socks without heels.

The easiest way to get shoes (and wellington boots) on the right feet is to step into them from the stairs.

Toilet training

Most parents can predict when their one-year-olds are likely to move their bowels: they may be quite regular in their habits, and may strain or go red as they pass stools. If you always sat your one-year-old on the potty at the right time, you could probably go for several days without a soiled nappy, but that would not mean that your child could control her bowels. Children can only do this when they have developed the necessary muscle and sphincter control, which for most is some time between the ages of 18 months and two and a half. However hard you try to train her,

your child is unlikely to be dry day and night until she is around two and a half and many children are considerably older than this.

In these days of disposable nappies, washing machines and dryers, and plastic mattress covers, it is easy to be relaxed about potty training. Leave it until your child is ready, and it will happen quickly.

Before you start

- Are you free from family stress?
- Are things normal – no holidays, illness, visitors and so on?
- Can you make light of accidents?
- Does your child have quick release clothes? If in doubt, wait.

Is your child ready?

You cannot train a child who is not physically ready to cope. She must be able to stand and walk; to sit on a low chair and get up again without toppling over; and pull her pants up and down easily (a child with jeans with zips or buttons, or dungarees is not going to learn).

Showing signs that she knows she is about to go or telling you afterward indicate that she may be ready to learn, as does going for a couple of hours between wet nappies. Finally, make sure that she knows the words your family uses ('wee', 'pee', 'pooh' and so on).

What to do

- Draw attention to any signs she makes that she may be about to go; ask 'Did you do a wee then?'
- In summer let her spend time without a nappy on, so that she feels what it is like to wee without one.
- Buy some quick-release pants.
- If she shows signs of needing to go, sit her on the potty for a couple of minutes; if nothing happens, get her off.
- Suggest she sits on the potty at 'likely' times: before her bath, before bed, when she wakes up.
- Let her know when you want to go and take her with you.

Making it work

- Praise her when she gets it right; tell her she is grown up.
- If she does not seem willing or able, put it all off for a week and try again.

- If she manages to use the potty, let her help you empty it, wipe her bottom from front to back, flush the toilet and wash her hands.
- If she asks to use the potty, praise her even if it is too late. Be ready to move quickly – at first she will give little warning.

What not to do

- Don't force the pace or compare her with other children – girls usually manage sooner than boys.
- Don't scold, punish, get emotionally involved or make a fuss.
- Don't be surprised if she wants to look at or play with the contents of the potty. Let her look.
- She may also want to play with the water in the toilet or dip toothbrushes in it: don't leave cleaner in the bowl overnight.
- Don't show frustration or expect her never to make a mistake again.
- Never hold her on the potty.

Night times

Some children 'crack' potty training in one go, others take a year or more before they are dry at night. Some children continue to make mistakes well into their school years. If you or your partner had problems with bed wetting, your child is also likely to.

There is no rush. Leave off a night nappy when your child is often dry in the morning; take off the plastic sheet when she always is (see also pp. 93 and 363).

THE DEVELOPING SENSES

At one year children see almost as well as adults. Their hearing is also acute and in the higher ranges they hear better than adults do. Your child will use her hands to feel, screw up her face at unpleasant smells and delight in those she enjoys. She may still, however, blow down her nose to smell rather than sucking air into it. She is also ready to explore a range of tastes.

Learning to see

If you had puzzle books as a child you may remember pictures in which you were asked to find objects hidden in a landscape. From such puzzles, psychologists identify two types of people: field dependent, who find it difficult to ignore the background; and field independent, who find it much easier. Generally speaking children become more field independent as they get older. But individual differences remain.

Children who are able to ignore the background tend to be good at manipulating and building things. Those who are more distracted by (or appear to take greater notice of) the background tend to be more socially skilled.

Drawing

Your child's first pictures are likely to be round scribbles which she makes without taking the crayon off the page. With practice she progresses to lines and dots and perhaps a small squiggle. The broad sweeps become her drawings and the little squiggles her writing. At first she does not intend to draw. She draws first and looks to see what it is later. One day her round swirls and dots look like a person, so she draws like this again. When she draws a person she basically draws a head. Even when she later adds arms and legs the head remains the focus of her picture, bigger and more detailed than the body. When children start to add fingers and eyes their first concern is to add, the second to add the correct number and only then to get them in the right place. Even at seven she may be unconcerned about relative size: the proportions of the various elements in her pictures will be wrong.

When children add eyes or fingers to a person or windows to a house they do not necessarily count how many there should be. The important thing is that people have fingers and because they are important they are also very big, perhaps as big as an arm. The way she draws reflects the way she looks at the world. Children rarely notice a change in size or position but do notice whether things have disappeared. They focus on one thing at a time, not the relationship between them. When they are thinking about fingers they are not comparing the size with the head, arms or body. They are drawing something new and important.

Children's drawings improve because they practise, which is why elderly people who have not drawn since childhood may produce the naive drawings of young children.

Milestones in drawing

18 MONTHS TO TWO YEARS A picture may look like scribble but the lines are not aimless and the pattern is well balanced: something on the left is usually balanced by something on the right. Drawings are not meant to be anything, simply patterns.

TWO TO TWO AND A HALF YEARS Your child will still not set out to draw anything in particular, but because you ask her what it is, she tells you what she has drawn. This is the stage when children make good circles which can and do stand for anything: ask two days running and the answer may well be different.

TWO AND A HALF TO THREE YEARS It becomes more obvious that children see their drawings as representing something and your child may well tell you what she intends to draw before she starts (although she will depart from the original plan if she thinks it is looking like something else).

THREE TO THREE AND A HALF YEARS Gradually you will notice circles, squares, crosses and combinations of these elements. Children start to enclose things within some circles. You may see a cross within a circle, or dots and lines. Lines radiate out from the circle too, as your child draws a sun. It is probably in these shapes that she notices she has drawn a person and thereby makes her first representational drawings. She sets out to draw a person and she does. Sometimes she puts things in the wrong place. The eyes may be in one corner of the face or even in the stomach. It is more important to get the parts in the picture than to get them in the right place.

THREE AND A HALF TO FOUR YEARS Positioning becomes more important; she places the eyes in the face. The body may still be missing but the legs come out of the bottom. She may use circles for the head, the eyes, the nose and the mouth.

FOUR TO FIVE YEARS Children are more skilled. They add more details, so that people have arms as well as legs and little details such as buttons and hair. Pictures become 'busier': there may be a plane in the sky or a tree by the house.

From now until your child is about eight years old, her drawings are symbols of the objects drawn not pictures of reality. 'My house' has a chimney, four windows – two upstairs and two down – and a central door, even if you live in a flat. Drawings include what should be there, so if she draws a dog side on, it will still have four legs, lining up underneath. Faces of animals turn to grin full face; cats have whiskers, cars four wheels.

Drawings also include things that are not normally seen, a baby inside a mother's stomach, for example, while a picture of a man sitting in a chair will include all the man and all the chair.

Learning to listen

Although preschool children can only sing a few notes, they like to dance, sing and clap along to music. It soothes and it excites them. A love of music is best fostered by encouraging your child to listen and join in. Because music is made up of lots of little sounds, listening for small background noises can improve a child's 'ear' and helps her to develop musical skills. Stop and listen to the silence, birds, ticking clocks or distant traffic. As she gets older, try listening out for one particular instrument or repeated theme in a recording.

Learning about taste

Children know what they like to eat and it is usually sweet and bland because most of the food they are given (including breast milk) is bland and sweet. Baby food – especially pre-packaged baby food – tends to be very bland indeed. Like all young animals, children are naturally conservative about foods. This is sensible: sorting out good from harmful foods is not something to do by trial and error, so children rightly treat all new foods with caution. They accept what they know and slight variations on that theme but will not take more than a mouthful or two of a new food.

Different cultures have different basic foods but the principle in expanding the number of foods your child will accept is the same. To go from carrots to spinach add gravy to the carrots and then a little spinach to the carrots and gravy. Once she accepts this, gradually reduce the carrots and then the gravy. Once accepted, spinach can then be paired with a little cheese. And so on.

LEARNING TO TALK

Most children say their first word between 10 and 17 months. The average is about 14 months. The first word is usually a noun like 'dog' or a simple verb like 'go' or 'eat'. By 20 months, most children can say about 50 words. Like Goldilocks, children go for nouns that are 'just right'. When they see a poodle they don't say animal (that is too big a category) nor poodle (that is too small) they say dog because dog is just about the right compromise between too broad and too precise.

How children learn

Your child's first word may well be 'Dada', but that does not necessarily mean her father. It means man. In the same way that 'woawoa' means all small animals. By the time they are 16 years old most young people have a vocabulary of 40,000 words; if you include names and idiomatic expressions the number doubles to 80,000. That means they have learned about 100 new words in every week of their childhood. Children with large vocabularies may acquire words at twice this rate. The only workable learning strategy is to grab the word, and to work out the precise meaning later. You can help by correcting mistakes and telling her when she is right: 'No, that's not a horse. It's a zebra' or 'Yes. That is yellow.'

Whatever language they learn to speak, most children do things in the same way. They refer to the things they see and can point to. They learn lots of nouns and then a few verbs. (Of the first 50 words about 40 are nouns and about 7 verbs.) However there are always a few children who do it differently. Instead of pointing and saying 'bus' their first words are things like 'you', 'me' and 'please', and words they run together like 'do-it' or 'go-way' and 'love-you'. Rather than commenting on objects, they comment on social relationships, needs and feelings.

Children learn to speak by listening for the emphasis in a word. This is why they call an elephant an 'efant' but can say 'helicopter' – where the emphasis is more evenly placed – clearly. Help her by talking about what you are doing, by pointing and naming, and by looking at the things you are talking about. Your child will also begin to follow your gaze at about the time she begins to understand language.

Her pronunciation may remain immature because vocal apparatus does not fully mature until a child is about six years old. But although children often mispronounce words, they know how words should be said. She may say 'bo' for bottle but will expect you to say 'bottle'. You may not because you find her words endearing: there is nothing wrong with this. Children who hear two languages learn to speak both. Calling a bottle a 'bo' will not slow her development.

What you can do
- Talk to her frequently.
- Listen to what she says.
- Pronounce things clearly for her. You do not need to correct what she says: just let her hear the correct word.
- Speak clearly, emphasizing the words she understands. 'That is DADDY's SHOE.'
- Look at books together (choose those with simple clear pictures of familiar everyday objects).
- Put pictures on the wall and look at them and talk about them together – murals of familiar animals or household objects are good.
- Sit down together for a game of point and name: Where is her foot? Her nose? The cup? Mummy's nose?
- Talk as you shop. 'Here are the beans'; 'Let's get some apples.'
- Let her know you understand what she says; the best way is to expand for her. If she says 'Shoe' answer, 'It is a shoe.' If pointing at the shoe she says 'Daddy' say, 'That is Daddy's shoe.'
- Songs and rhymes are good sources for early words, since the tunes often help her make longer sentences than she might otherwise manage (see Fun with music and song, pp. 218–20).

Making sentences

Putting words together to make a meaningful sentence happens at around 21 months. Sentences are more than strings of words: they have structure, and a meaning that comes from the way the words are arranged. Her first real sentence will be preceded by word-gesture sentences. 'Biki' she says, putting her hand up to the tin. She is asking with her hand outstretched, 'Can I have a biscuit?' When she points to the coat and says 'Mummy' her hand is in a different position. It is a different sign. She cannot yet say 'That's mummy's coat' but between her hand and her one word she can express the meaning.

Most children know about 200 words before they begin to speak in two-word sentences. The sentences they use are rather like the gesture-words that went before, short, simple and telegraphic: 'Want biki' and 'Mummy coat'.

In her early sentences, your child will:
- Make statements: 'That house', 'It ball'.
- Note possession: 'Daddy book', 'Mummy shoe'.
- Note location: 'Teddy bed', 'Cat table'.
- Describe action: 'Car go', 'Eat dinner'.
- Make demands: 'Come here', ''nother book'.
- Describe: 'Big dog', 'Red ball'.
- Ask questions: 'Where ball?', 'That hat?'.

Rhymes with simple, repeated words and a good rhythm to clap along with are an excellent way to help your child learn to talk.

Children use words in the same order each time they make a sentence because in English word order expresses meaning. 'Teddy is in bed' means something different from 'Bed is in Teddy'. If you say 'I can see a bed with Teddy in it', your child will say 'Teddy bed'. She is selecting the part of the sentence you emphasize as you speak, not simply copying what you say or putting two words together at random. She is arranging words to convey a specific meaning.

Language is creative. She may take her cue from you but she can create sentences she has never heard before. If you tell her a puppy is a 'baby dog' she may create a new sentence by calling a lamb a 'baby sheep'. Even when she has started to say two-word sentences, she will continue to use gesture to clarify meaning.

What you can do

- Expand sentences so that it is clear to your child that you have understood what she said.
- Use short simple sentences.
- Repeat what you have to say in a number of ways: 'It is a dog'; 'It is a small dog.'
- Talk about things she can see and hear.
- Talk about what she is doing.
- Talk about what you both see in her books.
- Ask her to fetch things for you.
- Talk as you feed, change, dress and bath her: early sentences are often about familiar activities.
- Talk about possessions.
- Sit down every day for a cup of tea and a chat.
- Speak in a higher pitched voice and at a slower pace than you do normally.
- Pause for longer at the end of sentences.
- Use short grammatical sentences (adult speech contains long and unfinished sentences and is frequently ungrammatical).
- Use very simple and basic grammar ('Where is Teddy? Can you see Teddy? Teddy is there. Look, there is Teddy').
- Repeat your child's sentences, recasting what was said, so 'Mummy shoe' becomes 'Yes that is Mummy's shoe'.
- Talk about what you can see and point to and select the word you think your child will understand.
- Stay in touch with your child's language; know what she is saying and keep one or two steps in front so that you draw her forward.

Absorbing grammar

From two-word sentences, your child will move on to grammar – such as adding 's' to make a plural, and 'ed' to indicate the past tense – and prepositions (such as 'on') and articles (such as 'the'). The earliest example you will probably hear is 'I playing' or 'I crying'. Soon after, you will hear prepositions in sentences like 'Cup on floor' and plurals like 'cats'. She starts putting 'a' and 'the' into her sentences. So she will say 'This a pig', or 'Where the cat'.

Children do not just learn the words they hear. They learn how to express things by working out the rules which underpin language. So they do not just learn to say cars and bikes, they learn that in English the plural is made by adding 's'. She starts by learning a few examples, such as 'sweeties' and 'cars', then once she uses the rule will apply it to everything. She may previously have said 'feet' and 'sheep', but now will say 'foots' or 'feets', and 'sheeps'. Similarly, with verbs, she may say 'goed' for 'went' and 'comed' for 'came'. By the time she starts school, she will know all the common tenses and know when to add words like 'to' (as in 'going to bed'). She may even be able to say things like 'We went to the circus, didn't we?'

Children also use language to monitor their own behaviour. As she tries to put the wrong shape into her shape sorter, she may say 'No, not there'. Using language in this way is common in two- to three-year-olds, peaks at about five or six years of age, then goes 'underground'. Some children practise what they want to say: a string of loosely related ideas such as 'Teddy here. Teddy in cot. What colour Teddy? What colour blanket? Blanket here ... ' is typical.

LEARNING TO THINK

Before their first birthday babies often repeat those things they discover by chance, but rarely take them further. As your child approaches her first birthday, she begins to experiment, testing and trying to see how various actions affect outcome. In her high chair she takes a spoonful of potato and drops it. She spills her juice on to the floor. She drops her cup. She watches as things go splat, splosh or bounce and roll away. She dips her hand in water and then she dips her sleeve and examines the difference.

When to worry

The fact that a neighbour's child chatters away and yours says almost nothing may be of no significance whatever. But, if you are worried, tell your doctor or health visitor and ask for a hearing and developmental test. Telltale signs that she is experiencing difficulties include:

- If a hearing test suggests that she may be having problems.
- If you suspect she is having hearing problems.
- If she is saying nothing at all at 21 months.
- If she does not seem to understand one word at 14 months or any language at 18 months.
- If what she says is very unclear, even at three.
- If she starts to stutter.

If your child needs speech therapy, the sooner she starts the better.

As she experiments she learns that the harder she throws, the bigger the splat and that some things get wet and stay wet, and other things get wet and can be dried. By 18 months she can think of things she cannot see, and imitate things she has seen in the past.

Seeing is believing

By the time she is 8–12 months old your child will search for something where she expects it to be (see pp. 138–9). By 12–18 months, she watches to see where you put a toy and searches for it in the last place she saw it. She only looks for something where she has seen you putting it. She only believes her eyes.

As she approaches her second birthday your child can ignore what she sees and imagine where an object might be. Once she is able to imagine things which are not in front of her, her thoughts do not have to be the same as her actions. She can think about one thing and do something else.

If the door to the kitchen is closed and she wants to carry a cup of juice to the lounge, she puts the cup down to open the door. She may put it in the path of the door but then realizes the door will knock the cup over. Before she tries to open the door, she moves the cup out of the way. A younger child cannot imagine how the door will move. She will only realize she has to move the cup when the door bumps into it.

Concept-forming

A three-year-old may have strange ideas about the world around her. If you give her a pile of objects and tell her to pick out all the ones that go together she might pick two cars, three blocks and a scarf, and explain that 'The cars go together because they are cars. The blocks go with the blocks because they are the same. The blocks go with the cars because you can build a bridge with the blocks for the car to drive under. The scarf goes with the blocks because they are all red.' Small children put one and one together and do not think beyond those two. Tomorrow, her choices – and the reasons for them – could be different.

Working one step at a time leads children to jump to conclusions. If mummy came out of hospital with a baby, Grandad must get a baby if he goes into hospital. If she flew to Spain on holiday and her friend flew to Greece, Spain and Greece must be in the sky.

What you can do

- Buy model cars, farm animals and coloured bricks which can be arranged in various ways. Can she pick out all the baby pigs? All the red bricks?
- In the kitchen can she separate the onions from the carrots? The tins of beans from the tins of tomatoes? Her socks from Daddy's socks?
- Look for puzzles which show a progression of pictures from small to large. Arrange tins of food, toy cars or plastic animals in the same way.
- Read books which emphasize big and small, in and out, thick and thin, under and over.
- Play lotto or picture dominoes which match pictures and numbers or colours. When she is a little older, try work books which ask her to put objects into groups and to match things which look alike.

Theory of mind

One of the nicest things about toddlers is that they believe you can perform miracles: you can make the blanket tuck in, the sock go on straight and stop the bricks falling over. Children believe that a teddy can miss them when they are at playschool and that a statue by the hotel door can look after their bucket and spade. Nor are things simply alive: they also know everything that she knows.

Three-year-olds do not allow that your experience is different from theirs, but around three and a half, they are able to understand that you have thoughts and feelings that are separate and hidden from them, and they have thoughts and feelings which are separate and hidden from you. Psychologists call this 'theory of mind' and it marks an important stage in your child's development. Until she has a theory of mind she cannot fully understand why hitting her brother should be so naughty. She knows her brother cries, but because she does not feel the pain herself she cannot empathize. If she is upset it is because you will be cross with her. Because she does not know you see and think differently from her it is difficult for her to deceive you or lie convincingly.

Make believe

The best way in which a child learns to understand that other people have thoughts and feelings which are unlike her own is by being someone else.

The preschool years are the time of make believe. As children pretend they manipulate ideas, thoughts and emotions in games. They pretend to be other people, and that the things they are playing with are not what they seem to be. A teddy is in hospital. An empty cup is full of tea. Playing pretend games becomes more and more important as your child approaches three and for some years afterward.

What you can do

You play a pivotal role in encouraging pretence in your child, from buying the right toys and reading the right stories to joining in her games. Throw a blanket over the table then ask her if she wants her tea in her house. Refer to her dolls as babies.

- **Books and stories**
  Young children are introduced to the idea that other people have feelings and experiences when they sit on your lap with a book. The words tell them something is happening, but the pictures do not fully support the story. The story tells more than she can see. She knows that the fox is dressed up as Grandma, but she also knows that Red Riding Hood does not know.
- **TV and videos**
  When young children pretend, all the players need to know the story. They need to hang role-play games on a well-understood story line. So they play

house, Mummys and Daddys, shopping and driving cars. To step outside the domestic story, they use the shared experience of TV or video.

- **Little worlds**
  At home children do not always have friends to take part in pretend games, so they need props. Tea can be made for the soft toys; little people can be taken to the shop in a car. They learn the rules and the story by playing the game with you.
- **Soft toys**
  Small families can never provide all the players for an elaborate game and even if they could there would be some dull parts nobody would want to take. Here soft toys come into their own. They can be the sick children in the hospital, the naughty schoolchildren who cannot go out to play and the extra passengers who have to stand on the bus.
- **Friends and family**
  Familiar friends are good partners for pretence and siblings are better still. A good family pretend game can be taken out like a favourite toy. Children with shared experience understand. If both children go to hospital to visit their grandmother, they know about the lift, they both saw the flowers, the charts and the beds. A schoolfriend would not understand 'those papers hanging on the bed' because she did not see the nurse looking at them and your child does not understand enough to explain.

Attention and memory

By the end of their first year children begin deliberately to focus their attention, but they do not do it well. If several things compete for a child's attention, she concentrates on how something looks. So she quite literally watches TV and may ignore the words or music.

Because her store is so limited a preschooler often has to 'clear her mind' by doing what she is thinking about first. When playing 'Pairs', she finds it impossible to think where two cards might be hidden at the same time. Holding the thoughts about one card displaces thoughts about the other from her memory. Most of the time this store is filled with more important things than card pairs, so adults resort to making notes. A small child cannot do this, which is one of the reasons she finds it so hard to think logically. It is also the reason why small children talk in short sentences. To think logically, or construct a long and complex sentence you have to be able to 'hold on' to more than one idea at a time.

What you can do

Children do not begin to think logically until they are about six or seven, when they begin to rehearse things they want to hold in their 'working' memory and can remember enough to be able to sort out simple ideas. But long before then, you can help your child by laying the groundwork.

- Explain things simply and answer her questions.
- Encourage her to determine how things work by letting her explore sand, water and building materials (see pp. 217–18 and 210–11).
- Listen to her explanations of how the world is.
- Play board and card games.
- The age when children begin to think logically is also the age of 'collectables'. Between four and seven most children have a collection of some sort. Collections help them to think about things in more than one way. A card is a football player, a goalie and a member of Manchester United. It is also a 'swap' because she already has two.
- Know your child's likes and dislikes and tailor activities, toys and speech appropriately.
- Encourage her to talk and listen.
- Provide something to see and do. Label the world for her by telling and showing her what things do.
- Talk often but when she is engrossed let her concentrate on what she is doing. Remember that she has difficulty listening to you and getting on with the task in hand.
- Encourage her to try.

LEARNING WHO SHE IS

Self-awareness is the sense of being you, the knowledge that when you wake tomorrow you will still be you. Children are not born with an idea of self. If you put a small smudge of lipstick on to a six-month-old baby's nose and then sit her in front of the mirror, she looks at the reflection but does not show any interest in her red nose. By 12 months she would reach out and touch the mirror and may even touch the reflection of her red nose. Sometimes she may even look for the little girl behind the mirror. But she does not know that the baby with the red nose is her. At 21 months a child with a smudge on her nose will look at her reflection and rub her own nose.

Somewhere between one and two years children become aware of themselves, but this awareness is not the same as your awareness of yourself. Your child knows herself by contrasting herself with others, by what she can do and what she possesses. She is the girl with the red coat and the girl who can jump off the second step. It is only when they reach about eight that children start to talk about themselves in terms of their personal history, hopes, feelings, personality, experience and belonging to a family or culture group (although they have memories of the past before this).

Girl or boy?

From a very early age children are interested in the sex of other children. By the time they can say the words 'boy' and 'girl', children know which sex they belong to, although they do not necessarily understand that they always were and always will be the same sex.

At three your child may insist she is a girl now, but assume (if all the babies she knows are boys) that she was a boy when she was a baby. Boys may talk of being 'a mummy'. By four children usually know that they started off as a girl, are now a girl and will grow up to be a woman. But it still might not be entirely clear. By six they have sorted this out and know that dressing up changes nothing.

Almost as soon as they can say the words, children tell us Daddys drive tractors, Mummys do the washing, boys are naughty and girls are good. By two they know about sex roles and their views are always traditional in the extreme. Toys, too, have become more rather than less sexist. And yet children see both parents working, fathers doing the washing and pushing prams and women driving fast cars and joining the army and the police. Children ignore the evidence of their own eyes because they need sex roles to define what it is to be a man or a woman. For a girl to understand that she will grow up to be a woman she has to know what being a woman means, which is more difficult than it was in the past. And it is equally difficult for your son to know what being a man means.

As the 'real world' roles of men and women have become less distinct, children have turned more and more to fantasy worlds to define things.

LEARNING TO FEEL

Infants cannot say how they feel: you imply your baby's emotions from her reactions and expressions. As children enter their second year, they begin to be capable of angry moods and petulance, although such moods rarely last long. By 21 months, their growing sense of themselves as individuals means they are able to think about what they want, and contrast this with the rules you set for them and your expectations of their behaviour. They are capable of defiance, start to feel shame and to feel pleased and proud of themselves.

By two your child can make people cry intentionally, by two and a half she may be afraid of things she imagines. She begins to offer simple explanations of why other people feel certain emotions, so she will say, 'Daddy cross. I broke cup.' She knows which actions should go with which feelings, so she might say, 'I not cry now. I happy.' She also knows how her actions can affect others. She might say 'I cry. Mummy pick me up.'

Between about two and a half and four children begin to understand how emotions work. They know that facial expressions 'match' certain emotions. They know that people calm down and that the initial intensity of emotion always subsides. They begin to realize how their thoughts and feelings can be related to certain consequences and that their emotions can be used to manipulate others. Your three-year-old might say, 'If you go out, I will cry.' She knows that you and others use emotions to manipulate her. She will say, 'He cried 'cause he wanted me to give him the car.'

This understanding of their own feelings and the experience of other people's emotions and actions gives children the capacity to feel social emotions such as guilt, concern, responsibility, jealousy, hostility, in addition to feeling miserable, resentful and horrified.

Being helpful

As babies become toddlers and toddlers preschoolers, they become more and more co-operative and helpful. This is partly because they copy you and others who are helpful toward them, but they also like and enjoy being helpful. They are pleased with themselves when they have watered the plants or washed the table.

Problems arise because Western society values competition, so children are praised for winning. By the time they are in junior school competitiveness has

Life and death

Children worry about things that they do not understand. As she begins to realize that she always was the same person, and always will be, she begins to think about ideas of life and death. She is aware of the fact of death but too young to understand what it means.

Preschoolers worry about death without really understanding what it means. It is not real. They cannot understand that death is not transitory and reversible. At the same time they think that all sorts of things will make them die – from stepping on the road without holding your hand to eating a worm. After the cat dies they may expect it to come home as usual in the morning. After Grandad's funeral they expect him back again.

Children are equally worried by the beginnings of life. 'What was I before I was born?' is a difficult question for you to answer and a worrying concept for a child. Even though you explain about the baby growing 'in your tummy' she does not really understand. 'What was I before I was thought of?' she asks.

A child faced with death is forced to come to terms with the reality of its permanence. The loss of a loved one is often reflected in withdrawal. Talking about death helps understanding. Children have long used a favourite psychological technique for dealing with their fears. They think about worrying things when they feel most happy and relaxed. This is why they play monsters, ghosts and games in which people die in endless crashes or hospital beds. A child who has nightmares about monsters can come to terms with her fears by fishing for monsters, or escaping from them in gleeful screams when chased by her pals at playschool. She can laugh as she imagines the monster chasing her. If she does it often enough, the fear will go away.

driven out some of children's natural helpful tendencies. Seven-year-olds are less co-operative than they were before they started school and find it quite hard to work together. The obvious reason for this change is that they see competition all around them and are praised when they do better than others.

What you can do

Some cultures are far more competitive than others. City children are on the whole more competitive than those brought up in rural areas; boys tend to be more competitive than girls. Competition leads to quarrels and fights; try to tone the competition down.

- Encourage co-operation, but set an example: children will not co-operate if what they see all around them is competition. Competitive parents have competitive children.
- Create a 'we' environment. Encourage your children to help you and each other not as a favour but as a matter of course. Do things together.
- Love your children uniquely for who and what they are. Never say 'I love you both the same' instead say 'You are the best Lauren in the world' and 'You are the best Paul there could ever be'.
- Selecting two toys of exactly the same value and worth for two children is impossible. Buy Lauren the book when you see one you know she will love. Buy Paul a treat next time you go shopping. If you are always 'even handed', children spend their time looking for which one got the bonus. Everything they do, all the time you spend with them gets embroiled in life's great competition.

LEARNING RIGHT FROM WRONG

Preschool children know right from wrong. They can say something is naughty and something is good, but they tend to think that rules are fixed by nature rather than by communal decisions. It is only after she starts to play with other children and finds that the rules of a game can be agreed among her friends, and varied sometimes, that your child begins to understand what rules mean. A five-year-old tends to think that the deed rather than the intention is important. Accidentally breaking six glasses is much naughtier than deliberately breaking one glass.

Tantrums

Most children have tantrums. In any population of two-year-olds, rather more than half are having tantrums on a more or less daily basis. A few start earlier, a few later. Some have tantrums for years, most have them for a couple of years, some children never have a tantrum. The average child who has tantrums has one a day and the average tantrum lasts about five minutes. But some children have more than five a day, and some tantrums last more than an hour.

Tantrums start with shouting or crying. There is usually a note of protest ('No!'; 'Won't!'), and a demonstration of anger (slamming the door, hitting, kicking, stamping the floor or screaming). When the tantrum gets underway children wave arms, kick legs, stamp feet, arch their backs and fall to the floor. They go red in the face and cry and scream. They may deliberately kick you or the furniture. They throw things and may hurt themselves. Your child may bite her arm until it bleeds, or bang her head until it is bruised. Such behaviour is alarming but common.

Most children grow out of self-mutilation just as they grow out of tantrums. Not all children show all of these behaviours. Not all tantrums are severe.

Tantrums have definite phases. Before the crying or screaming starts, children seem to be 'spoiling for a fight'. They are contrary, and easily frustrated. Sometimes they seem to provoke the tantrum on purpose, by asking for something they know they cannot have, or asking in a way that you will not be able to understand. They then have a tantrum because whatever it was they wanted is not forthcoming.

Once the tantrum is underway, the early part is invariably intense. Your child will shout, scream, kick and flail. This phase may be followed, particularly in older children, by a quieter phase when she is sad and sorry. Sobbing replaces screaming and she may come and sit or stand beside you. This sadness then gives way to a period of forgiveness when she may need to be cuddled, in spite of which she may still be angry and in a bad mood afterward. The older the child, the more likely that the anger and bad moods persist.

Very young children blow their tops quickly. The tantrum comes from nowhere and disappears as rapidly, almost as if nothing at all had happened. The older the child the more complex the tantrum and the more sorry and upset she is afterward.

Why do they happen?

Tantrums almost always occur when your child is with you or another major carer, rarely when you are not there. About half of all the children who have tantrums when alone with their mothers also have them when alone with their fathers. Very few have them with nursery school teachers or playgroup leaders. Children who spend most of the day with a childminder may only have tantrums when at home.

Most tantrums occur at home, usually when you are trying to do something from which your child is excluded. Children have more tantrums when you are upset, down or ill. They also have them when they are ill, tired, frustrated or fastened into a chair. And for no obvious reason at all.

Tantrums are nevertheless about relationships: love, attachment, security and anger. Just as you lose your temper with those you love most, so your child loses hers with you. Just as you shout and cry more easily in the safety and security of your home or car, so does she.

What you can do

There are no easy answers and what works one time may not work again, but some people have found one or more of the following to work.

Head off

It is sometimes possible to head off an impending tantrum by simply distracting your child. Read a story, engage in a boisterous activity or play a very silly game. If she is spoiling for a fight, try to find something out of the ordinary to do.

Left: Hugging a child in a tantrum may make the tantrum less severe, or last for less time.

Ignore

Once the tantrum is underway, walk out of the room and leave her to it. Tantrums do not occur in a vacuum: they occur within a relationship. If you are not there to witness it, she will stop.

Be consistent

If your child knows your 'bottom line', she is less likely to fight against it, and will be less frustrated by your 'no'.

Hug

Hugging tightly by gathering her up and trapping her in your arms, 'squeezing' the tantrum out more quickly. Opinions differ as to whether to look her in the eye as you hug, or look away. It is worth trying both.

Cuddle

Children who are cuddled when they become sad and sorry have fewer tantrums than ones who are left to fend for themselves.

Talk

Talking about the causes of the tantrum, and how to avoid them in the future seems to reduce their frequency, especially in older children.

What not to do

Try hard to avoid:

- Slapping, which seems to increase the frequency and duration of tantrums. It is also associated with more violent tantrums.
- Giving in, which enables your child to manipulate you through her temper. If she gets what she wants by having a tantrum, she will have more tantrums because it is worth it.

SPREADING HER WINGS

One-year-old children are almost always self-absorbed. They may like to look at other children or be with their siblings, but it is always a case of the older child playing with the baby. Babies are invariably more social in the months after their first birthday when they begin to extend those skills they learned with you and other members of the family to a wider circle.

The importance of play

Play launches a child in the wider social world and toys lure children to play side by side. Learning how to play on an equal footing is an ability perfected over many years and can only happen when she spends time with other children. It is easier for children with siblings. If she is dependent on playgroups, personality will ease the task, out-going children develop social skills sooner than shy children, as do attractive children. A conventional name helps too!

Relationships with adults or older children are no substitute for play with children of the same age. Adults make allowances for immaturity and clarify their intentions in a way that peers cannot do. When talking to another two-year-old she has to learn to make herself understood. She must also understand the imperfect communication of her friend.

Broadly speaking, children do not play together until they are two to three years old. They usually talk to the assembled company rather than an individual and what they say is likely to be a comment on their own behaviour – 'Me make castle' rather than 'You make castle'. Nor do they comment on what others might have said.

This does not mean that they do not react with others. One child may shout and another then laugh and the sequence may be repeated to the great delight of both children. Or one child may pass something to another, but they do not share games or take turns with toys or have discussions. If there are older children in the circle a two-year-old may watch to see how they interact. She will not try to join in and may turn away or cry if you try to make her do so. She is happy to watch from a distance.

The role of language

When she starts to try and play with other children, she often eases her way into the social group with a few words. She might go up to the children in the sand pit and say 'I've got a kitty' and if one of them then answers 'I've got a ginger cat' or 'My Daddy's got a new car' she has her invitation. When children first start playing together, the conversation and the game are often quite separate. They may exchange statements about their pets or garden toys while sharing the cups and teapots at the water table. Once they have mastered the basics, toddlers begin to play interactive games, like throwing and catching balls, chasing and being chased, follow my leader and so on.

As language blossoms between the ages of two and a half and three, social interactions take on a new richness. What children actually say to each other may make little sense to you – conversations follow the 'Red bike' 'Red bike' 'Yep' 'Go there' 'Red bike' 'Yes' pattern – but the children are communicating. Good friends share activities, they look at each other, smile, laugh and shout together. If such a game starts in the nursery, other children may join in. By three most children are taking turns, sharing toys and games. Popular children tend to be leaders because they have the social skills necessary to manage other children without dominating.

By the time they have passed their third birthdays the majority of children's talk while they are playing is likely to be about the game they are sharing.

Making friends

Friendship is fuelled by familiarity, but you cannot make children be friends. It is not easy to pinpoint what turns two toddlers into bosom pals: similarity of temperament, developmental stage and behavioural style are almost certainly factors. Friends meet because they gravitate to the bikes, the library or the house corner. They start to talk together because they are the ones who often sit at the top of the climbing frame. There is a special joy in being with friends for which time with her parents and other grown-ups is no substitute. Nothing makes a child laugh quite so much as jumping off the step or running in and out of the sprinkler with her best friend. Happiness and laughter are shared with the family but to be really full of glee she needs a sibling or a friend.

From babyhood, children direct distinct kinds of behaviour toward you and other children. By your child's third year, you are there to talk to and provide security: her peers are her partners. Opportunities for playing with other children are important for her social development. These days, most preschool children only make friends if you make the opportunities for them to do so (see pp. 244–7). While other children practise their social skills, your child will lag behind if you do not make an effort now, and you may hamper her ability to settle into nursery and school quickly.

Getting ready for school

You can prepare your child for school intellectually, through the skills she develops and learns through her play (see Chapter 8, pp. 204–27) that lay the groundwork for later reading, writing and number work. You can also prepare her socially, by providing her with opportunities to be with other children (see pp. 244–7). And you can help her emotionally, by making sure she can manage without you.

If you do not want to send your child to playgroup or nursery, make sure that you take time to instill some of the skills she will need at school.

- Encourage her to sit still.
- Encourage her to work through a problem (or finish a painting) without constant reassurance.
- Encourage her to plan.
- Have friends around to play and encourage her to mix with other children – and try not to interfere if one of them tries to take over.
- Make sure she understands what coming second or third feels like.
- Do not let her first day at school be her first day without you.
- Let her have a really big hug of her comfort object before she sets off.
- Make sure she understands what all day means.
- Make sure she understands that she cannot stop going to school; even if she hates it (don't suggest she might), she has to go tomorrow.

HAVING A SECOND CHILD

Obviously, it is up to you whether you have a second child. Only children can have clear advantages in later life, so long as they grow up in an environment in which they are encouraged to make friends. If you do not want a second child, don't have one and don't feel pressurized by talk of the 'an only child is a lonely child' variety.

But a child growing up with other children gains a great deal of social knowledge and usually finds it easier to get on with other children. A young child can be drawn into games much earlier than she could construct activities for herself. An older child has a better playmate than a teddy bear. They have more to love and a wider base for security.

There is no ideal age gap between children. Those born close together may be good friends, but they can equally be good enemies. If you have them further apart, you may find it easier to treat each child uniquely. The best gap tends to depend on the personalities of the children: they can be close in age without feeling they have anything in common; they may be four or five years apart and very close. How well children get on together is a matter of luck.

Coping with jealousy

Jealousy is natural: you will not be the first parent to feel a pang of jealousy and resentment when your child runs to her childminder or says she wants Grandma to put her to bed. A child's jealousy of a new baby is inevitable and you should probably worry more if it does not happen, than when it does.

- **Let her voice her feelings**
  Don't dismiss negative feelings about a sibling. If she regresses into more babyish behaviour, understand that at the moment life may well look more rosy for a baby than a two-year-old.
- **Be on her side**
  Let her know you understand; don't be afraid to say, 'I know sometimes you wish she would go back into my tummy'.
- **Accept that she is unsure**
  Don't tell her how nice it will be once the baby is big enough to play with her: she cannot think that far ahead and in any case it may not be true.
- **Love her**
  Love her differently from the baby. Make sure she knows that she is the very best Claire in the world.
- **Allow her aggression**
  Aggression arises from frustration and jealousy, so find ways for her to vent and express her feelings. Invent a bad-tempered child she can 'play' at being, and let her be that child, throwing a teddy on the floor or stamping and shouting. If she shows aggression toward the baby, stop her.
- **Make time for her**
  Find times to put her first. If the baby wakes in 'her time', then the baby may have to cry. Listen to her when she talks to you. Even when physically dealing with the baby, you do not need to shut her out. If you say 'just a minute', make sure that you do then come back to her after the minute is up.

Sibling rivalry and love

It should be easy to anticipate how your children will behave toward one another. If you have siblings you may remember the mean and nasty things you did to each other at various times. Why then are all parents shocked at their children's capacity for meanness?

Siblings quarrel because they know each other so well. A child who has lived all her life with another knows exactly how to needle, exactly how to get you on her side in any argument, how to put her sibling in a bad light. Rivalry for your affections, for the larger piece of cake, for your attention, rivalry about anything and everything fuels feuding.

If you can understand negative feelings you will make life easier for yourself. Show you understand. Say, 'I can see why that would make you cross' when you are trying to handle disputes.

- Encourage children to talk and listen by showing them how to express anger to each other. Get your children together and let one tell the other, 'I get angry when you use my toys without asking.'
- Try to avoid labels. Whatever the reason for the initial quarrel, children can both revel in the after-effects. If you shout at the aggressor, she gets your attention (and a sure means of claiming it in the future). Her brother learns that she will get into trouble if he can needle her into hitting him. Next time he wants to be one up on her he knows exactly what to do. Labels have a way of sticking. If children are fighting physically it is better to ignore the aggressor and give your attention to the injured party, but try not to blame or take sides.

How to handle disputes

- The best way to handle bickering is to ignore it. Leave the room.
- If the bickering is serious, acknowledge the anger and describe what you see from each child's point of view. Express confidence in finding a solution: 'I think you could sort it out if you tried.'
- Handle fighting by trying to describe it: 'I see two children who are going to hurt each other.' Then separate the children, send them to different rooms to calm down.

CHAPTER EIGHT

Learning Through Play

Children love playing. To your preschooler, anything can be a game, as long as he has the tools and materials he wants, or the company and props he needs. You have only to be there, encouraging and ready to get involved if he asks you to, for your child to start to learn about the world around him through his games and other activities.

The importance of play

All children want to play. From the early months parents do not have to persuade their babies to learn through their playful actions; the babies are poised and ready to go. Babies and children are fired up with enthusiasm to discover, to find out and explore. Long before your child will be asking the questions in actual words, his behaviour will show you that he is keen to find out answers to a whole host of questions: 'What's that?', 'What does that do?', 'What going to happen if … ?', 'Can I get there?', 'Can I do what he's just done?', 'Can I poke this … drop that … climb into that?'

Very young children are avid watchers of what is going on around them. They are keen to copy the actions of the adults' world and older children they meet. You will see your toddler copy your actions when he goes round the garden with his own watering can, because he wants to do the flowers like you. You will hear your voice and your words as your children put their dolls and teddies to bed or organize a pretend tea party. And through all this imitation you will also see your child's own individuality flowering and realize that your child, as much as he is learning from you, is nevertheless also developing a very personal way of going about his play.

Younger children want to be able to do what adults and older children are managing. They are highly motivated to start the long road of learning everyday skills that will make them independent. Their play is the vehicle for practice and trying out skills in many different ways. But although you do not have to push children into playing, it is possible to discourage them and prevent their learning as much as would otherwise be possible.

The essence of children's play is that they are enthusiastic about it and satisfied with the outcome – whether they have made something in particular or have simply had a good time and not been bored.

Children sometimes take their play very seriously, yet, if you watch them, you will see how some kinds of play are also for the sheer pleasure in using physical skills – watch your toddler in the garden when he first learns to pedal his own tricycle or do a forward roll – or the power of their voices. Listen to the interminable imaginary dialogue between teddy and dolly, or the words of a favourite song sung over and over again.

Play can be the way children learn to concentrate and see a task through, even when it gets difficult. They often need the help and support of an adult to get them over the more difficult patches. Children can also put a great deal of mental effort into their play through planning, thinking out how to do something, remembering what they have seen or heard before and puzzling out why something is not working, or on occasions why it is working.

As a result children's play does not always go smoothly and it sometimes ends in tears of frustration or fury, which need your helping hand or calming approach. But overall children's play will be a great source of emotional, as well as intellectual, satisfaction to them.

HOW CHILDREN LEARN THROUGH PLAY

You can help your children to learn through the play of their early years when you understand how children learn.

Learning is a continuous process

Babies and young children have a breathtakingly large amount to learn. All their skills and their growing understanding of how the world works, including people's reactions, are built up from many different experiences. You may notice that your child reproduces your ways and phrases. Often you will not even have been aware that your child was watching or listening. So no single playtime and no one toy, however well designed, is going to ensure that a child learns all he needs to know about a physical skill, how to engage someone in conversation or the meaning of abstract ideas like number, colour or shape.

Understanding through doing

Children learn a certain amount through quietly watching and listening but they cannot learn how to do things properly unless they have a chance to try them for themselves.

The most effective learning for children involves activity – trying something out, making sounds, exploring something that has caught their interest. Young children have a particularly pressing need to do it for themselves and some find great difficulty in staying still for long. So their particular kind of doing is often being on the move between places and objects of interest. They will also vocalize constantly – play is accompanied by a running commentary, much of it imaginative and fanciful. Here play is helping them develop their use of language.

If you need special help

If your child has special needs, all the ideas in this chapter still apply. However, depending on the pattern of his disabilities, you may find that some specialized play materials will help. Sometimes, children's disabilities mean that they are progressing at a slower rate of development, so that it becomes important to have a wide range of materials and possible activities suitable for their current interests and skills – if you do not, children get bored (see also Children with special needs, pp. 173–5). It is worth getting advice from specialist professionals in your area (see also Useful Contacts, pp. 390–3). They will also know of toy libraries and other resources you may find useful in helping your child with his play.

Play is a good guide to a child's development so if your child does not play, plays in a strange way or has difficulty in physically manoeuvring a range of toys and games, ask your health visitor or GP to investigate.

Children need plenty of practice which gives them the opportunity to use similar skills in different ways. They need to make links between different skills and what they have learned.

What you can do

It is not enough to give your child a range of play materials and expect him to 'get on with it'. Some children are happy to play alone for short periods, but that does not mean that you should not be involved. There are many ways in which you can help your child get the most from his play.

Look through your child's eyes

Children cannot always work out why they cannot do something or understand an idea. This is where you can use your broader perspective to try to grasp what your child has understood so far and what is confusing him at the moment. Adults can offer hints and suggestions, useful short-cuts and guidance, without taking over completely.

If you relax and are responsive to your child's stage of development, without trying to hurry him in to the next, you can enjoy the freshness of discovery with him. One of the delights of playing and talking with your children is that they can surprise you with their questions and their discoveries.

Make allowances

Your child has a lot to learn. You have lived with a wide range of skills and chunks of knowledge for so long that it is easy to forget that all this was learned. Nobody is born knowing that eggs dropped on the floor smash, and stay smashed. Your toddler may have safely dropped all sorts of other things, and some even bounce back up again, so the smashed egg has to be chalked up to everyone's experience.

Be physically close

You cannot support your child in his play from a distance – if you are in different rooms (this just leads to, 'shouting' and 'interfering'!) or across a large room or the length of the garden. If you are not actually involved already in what your child is doing, then you need to be close enough to move easily to look at something and to hear and reply to his conversation or questions. This is equally true of your carer, if you are at work. If you are a working parent, try to be with your child as much as is natural, without upsetting his normal routine.

Help when help is wanted

As an adult you have a much broader base of knowledge than your child. However, in order to be truly helpful, you need to make the effort to recapture the feelings and perspectives of a child who is still finding out about life. Adults who stand on a pedestal of superior years and supposed wisdom come across as impatient and critical know-it-alls, and children learn to avoid them.

It is fun to find out, so children do not want some adult spoiling the surprise of discovery. But on the other hand they do not want to be left struggling when you, another adult, or even an older brother or sister, could give them a clue or show them a more reliable technique.

If you tune in to your child, you can offer guidance and suggestions that go with the flow of what is interesting him today, though it is important not to take over your child's play. You can communicate through actions as well as words.

Be close enough to offer help when help is wanted, and join in your child's games sometimes.

What you can do

- Show him how to turn around a shape so that it fits through the hole in his posting box. What you mean will be much clearer through action than just explanatory words.
- Start a little tower of bricks for your toddler and offer him a brick to add on top.
- Play alongside your child in a way that he can copy, for instance in putting teddies to bed.
- Demonstrate to your child another way of holding his paintbrush that may work better. Showing and offering can be very effective and works especially well with very young children. Of course, you do not have to be silent – use words as well.

WORD PLAY

It is a good idea to say something simple as you show your baby how the rattle works or your toddler how to put together the simple pull-apart car. Naturally, it is not helpful to talk so much that it comes out like verbal wallpaper, and it is very important to leave a pause for your child to reply.

Talking about play

You can describe in a simple way what you are doing or comment on what your child is doing. For example: 'This brick's too big – I'm looking for a smaller one'; 'You're trying some blue in your picture now? That's a lovely bright blue'; 'You've got the firefighters in their fire engine. They all look ready to zoom off.'

Some questions have an obvious 'Yes' or 'No' one-word answer but you can often just as easily ask open-ended questions that encourage your child to think further. These kind of questions can start in several different ways. For instance: 'How did you make that lovely shape in your painting?'; 'I wonder if your boat can take another brick? Or will it sink?'; 'What's going to happen if we … ?'; 'Can you think of another way to do it … ?' 'I'm afraid I can't make this work. How did you do it … ?'; 'Now where are we going to find a … ?' 'I bet you can tell me all about … ' Encourage communication.

ENCOURAGING YOUR CHILD

Children blossom with encouragement. Throughout your family life together you will have to tell them off and tell them 'No' many times, so it is important to balance this up with positives. There are many ways that you can act so as to encourage your child as you play together. When he feels that he is included in your activities with pleasure – regardless of what you are doing – it counts as play for him.

Showing your pleasure

You show on your face, particularly by your smiles, that you are pleased with what your child has done, which can encourage him to keep trying on those occasions when an activity is not going easily.

When you play with babies, you show your interest and enjoyment by your physical closeness, an excited or pleased expression on your face or by actions like clapping with pleasure. Once your child has started to understand more language, he will understand the meaning of what previously was communicated just through your body language.

Voicing your pleasure

Toddlers are delighted to be told 'Well done!' about their brick tower, their finished dinner or the fact that this time they made it to the toilet before they wet themselves. Children are encouraged if you notice and comment on what they have done.

Try not use the same words every time. If you always react to any drawing or model by saying 'That's nice', your children will start to wonder if you really mean it – after a while it will not sound sincere. Ring the changes with other phrases that are natural for you to say and suitable for the age of your child.
- 'I do like that.'
- 'Is that for me? Thank you.'
- 'Isn't it long/colourful/unusual/ enormous…?'
- 'Well done.'
- 'You've done a lovely job on that.'
- 'Just look what you've managed.'
- 'Oh great! You've made it work.'
- 'That was difficult, wasn't it? But you kept going.'

Remembering the past

Four- and five-year-olds have a sense of themselves as individuals with a past in memories, a present of the here and now and a future of plans. When your child is having difficulty with something in play you may be able to encourage him through it or to keep trying by reminding him of what he has managed before. You can boost your child's confidence by pointing out how far he has come and what he can now do that was still difficult for him even a few months ago.

Showing your interest

When you are not closely involved in your child's play for the moment, show your interest and admiration by stopping what you are doing and taking a close look at what he has made or listening with your full attention to his story or account of what he has done.

Try to have somewhere that you can fix up his drawings or put his models on display, if only for a short while. And make sure that no adults, or disdainful older siblings, make fun of his efforts.

PHYSICAL PLAY

Children need active physical play. Not only does it use up energy but also enables them to benefit from the opportunity to practise skills and improve physical co-ordination.

Enjoyable physical exercise

Babies, toddlers and children need plenty of practice if they are to be confident in their existing skills and learn new ones. Join in their physical games, such as:
- Crawling, including speedy crawling for sheer fun and crawl-and-chase.
- Walking and running about. You do not have to go anywhere in particular, simply run about for the enjoyment of it. Vary this by chasing and hiding.
- Jumping and hopping.
- Climbing up, round, over and through things. A good play park is extremely useful but a tolerant adult is also an excellent prop. You may get the odd bruise until children recognize that adults can feel pain too.

- Clambering up and sliding or jumping down.
- Spinning round or twisting in circles.
- Dancing to all kinds of music.
- Wrestling and rough and tumble. This is a very natural use of children's physical skills, but take care that it does not get too rough and that smaller or less physically strong children are not getting hurt or squashed.
- Splashing in the swimming pool. Time in the shallow end of a pool can be very enjoyable for your child long before he has learned to swim so long as you or another adult is within reach.

Playing with equipment

Playing with balls, bats, bikes, ropes and similar equipment help children develop their hand–eye co-ordination and use their whole bodies. Once children are about three they begin to appreciate simple rules which come with the concept of taking turns (see p. 227). Sometimes children play happily together but your child will need some help initially to learn how do any of the following:

- Carrying and dropping big balls.
- Rolling balls to each other.
- Throwing and then catching big and small balls or bean bags.
- Jumping rope and trying to skip.
- Playing with balls and wide bats.
- Kicking balls.
- Pushing along wheeled toys, dolls' prams or buggies.
- Riding push-along bikes or sit-in cars, tricycles and then bikes with stabilizers.

It is up to you to decide what you do or do not allow children to play with or do in your home. If space is restricted then you should make sure that your child has access to safe outdoor space for these activities. Apart from any other considerations, the level of traffic and the speed at which it travels on minor as well as major roads means that it is not safe to let under-fives out to play unsupervised.

If you do not have a garden, take your children out to local open spaces – commons, parks, recreation grounds. Even if you live in the country look for stretches of public space, since a lot of the open land in rural areas is not suitable for play or does not have public right of access.

Exploring and building

To your child, the whole world is a playroom and every object he encounters a toy. It is only through looking at and playing with everyday things that he can start to make sense of the world around him.

Playing with everyday objects

Toddlers like a wide variety of objects, not all toys, that can be explored and used in different ways. Parents can get exasperated with under-twos because they are 'into everything'. Yet toddlers do not pull clothes out of low drawers or dive into cupboards or waste bins precisely in order to be naughty. They are utterly fascinated by the contents of mundane parts of your home and they want to explore. The trick for you is to offer toddlers access in a safe way.

Look at the rooms in your house carefully before your baby is mobile (see pp. 169–71).

Toys that last

The range of toys available is vast and their quality and play value vary from excellent to minimal. Think carefully about what your buy: often the least expensive items are the ones that your child will return to time after time.

Wooden bricks

A set of well-made, different coloured and shaped bricks will give your children pleasure for years. You can buy bricks, but the first basic cubes may come with a push-along trolley that you buy for your toddler.

Wooden bricks are more stable than large plastic cubes. They can be used to build anything from the first tower that your child piles up, and immediately knocks down with a delighted laugh, to the more ambitious building projects of your older children – sets of towers, bridges, walls and then buildings.

Lego and its lookalikes

Your children will also get years of satisfaction from a set of interlocking plastic bricks and other compatible shapes such as Lego, the Duplo range or Stickle Bricks. The best value are those sets to which you can add as your child gets older. Some sets have large size pieces suitable for under threes but which are made to scale so that they will fit with the smaller sizes in sets for older children. A plastic, holed foundation sheet is very useful and is often sold with sets, so that any construction can be fixed firmly at the base and can stay assembled until everyone in the family has admired it. There is no need to feel under pressure to get lots of different kinds of construction sets; your child will find plenty at playgroup or nursery.

Children enjoy putting together simple pull-apart toys in these sets and can progress to making all kinds of constructions. Apart from the sheer pleasure of making something, children are learning to look with care, to experiment with how to fit pieces together and they are learning to plan ahead – to think how to make the construction that they want.

Jigsaws

There is a very wide choice of jigsaws. Toddlers need wooden pieces or jigsaws made of thick card, or the kind of jigsaw with little knobs on the pieces which are easier to handle. Jigsaws suitable for young children have only a few pieces but you can also simplify a jigsaw intended for an older child by making part of it for your young child and leaving easily identifiable shapes for him to do.

Some children are more enthusiastic about jigsaws than others but it is worth making this an enjoyable shared activity with young children. If they become interested in the challenge, completing jigsaws can help children to look carefully for details in the partly completed picture and the remaining pieces. Children are also practising their fine motor skills (see pp. 187–8) as they pick up, hold, turn around and try to fit pieces.

AROUND THE HOME

The great advantage of a home is that your child sees you doing normal adult tasks – everything that keeps a household running. Many of these activities are probably boring to you but they are fresh to your child. Toddlers and children can be just as enthusiastic to help you out in domestic tasks as they are to sit and build a brick tower with you. And they will much rather be your welcomed assistant than wait for what seems like ages until you have finished.

If you let them join in, you will be helping your children's learning as they practise their physical skills, talk with you and actually come to understand more

Making a swag bag

Make up a special swag bag with collections of safe objects that your child can tip out and pore over. Use an old, large handbag or a good-sized cloth bag. You might put in any of the following:
- large squares of material that have different textures
- large empty cotton reels
- cardboard inner tubes from kitchen towels or toilet rolls (toddlers can look through these as well as posting smaller wooden or Duplo bricks through them)
- different sized and coloured boxes or plastic containers and cups
- plastic spoons (strong children's ones, not the disposable kind)
- soft foam or fabric balls
- large wooden curtain rings, not the smaller metal ones
- a set of plastic play keys or a small rattle

Make sure that there are no small objects that could go up the nose or be swallowed, such as beads or small buttons, and nothing that would be unsafe to suck, since toddlers still put objects in their mouths.

You may have to check the bag from time to time since toddlers sometimes gather up objects of value that you may be seeking, like your watch or the remote control. Don't be cross, because it will almost certainly have been kept safe.

about how things work. And, since what they do with you will often reappear, in their own version, in their imaginative play, you are helping them with the raw material for other kinds of play.

Washing and cleaning

Although young children cannot do the washing, and you need to warn them from fiddling with the knobs on washers or dryers, they can give you clothes to put into the machine, and hand you wet clothes to peg out, if you have a line. They can help you sort and fold the clean clothes, and carry a pile to put away.

Young children will not clean up to the same standard as an adult. However, they will be keen to help and it is a very good idea to teach them how to be a helpful member of the household when they are willing. Toddlers and children can use a dustpan and brush, do a bit of dusting or polishing, hand you cutlery or plates that you put in the dishwasher and wash up plastic cups, plates and cutlery that is not sharp.

Young children can also help to wipe up after their painting session or help you to put their toys away. Mobile babies and toddlers enjoy putting smaller objects into bigger ones, especially if there is a clunking sound as a result. Your child can help you put any fitting or stacking toys back together. Young children will help search for the last piece of jigsaw, so long as you do not rush and you show genuine pleasure and satisfaction if they find the missing piece.

Preparing food and cooking

Children can be involved in preparing a meal as well as doing some cooking with you. Even young children can pick out vegetables or fruit for you to peel or cut up. It is good for them to learn the names and shapes of different items as their understanding grows, and you can begin to talk about how they grow and where they come from. They will soon be able to do simple preparations such as peeling a banana, spooning out rice or putting a cake on a plate.

Through cooking, children practise the physical skills of stirring, mixing, cutting and shaping; they learn about hygiene; they begin to understand about measuring; and they observe that some food changes colour and texture, and from solid to liquid as it is heated and cooked.

Using heat

If you show them carefully and supervise them closely, four- and five-year-olds will be able to heat up ingredients on a stove or hob. Never turn away from them, even if you have taught them about heat.

- Using dough, let the children shape what they want. Yeast dough, for buns or pizza bases, is more tolerant of handling than pastry which gets tough.
- Cakes and biscuits, made in different shapes, offer a wide range of possibilities. Creaming butter, or margarine, and sugar is difficult for children, so pre-warm the mixing bowl with boiling water, to help soften butter or margarine or use liquid sugar in the form of honey or syrup.
- If your child has trouble holding a mixing bowl steady, put it on a damp cloth or rubber mat. If your child is too young to use heat, try:
- Decorating plain cakes or biscuits with icing.
- Making fruit salad or ice cream sundae.
- Simple recipes that do not need cooking, like peppermint creams or crispy cereal cakes.

Everything has some play value – even dusting and polishing are fun to preschoolers.

Shopping and other trips

Children obviously enjoy special trips out, puppet shows or the theatre or museums and exhibitions that have displays that they are encouraged to touch. But they can also enjoy local trips, as long as you avoid huge amounts of shopping and chatting with other adults. There are many ways to involve your child in what is going on. Be ready to talk with him about what you see in shops or on the street and spot anything out of the ordinary or of interest – animals, police cars, people that you know.

- Post offices and banks can be interesting if you let your child collect some forms and leaflets. He can use these in his own pretend post office or bank, or put them in his swag bag (see p. 211).
- Make a diversion for shop windows that intrigue your child (this will not necessarily be a toy shop).
- Wherever possible, let children make choices for you in the shops. They can pick out the vegetables in a serve-yourself section, or find the packet or tin that you are seeking. Children who are occupied selecting items that you do want are less likely to make a fuss about sweets and crisps that you don't.

IMAGINATIVE PLAY

Toddlers start to use their imagination in play as soon as they pick up a cup that they know is empty and they pretend to drink from it.

What can you do

Children do not need child versions of everything. In a normal home your child can see some of the actions and responsibilities that are involved in adult life. He does not need a little washing up set if you will let him get up safely at the kitchen sink. But since he cannot play with a real car, provide toy cars or a toy driving wheel and control panel for his play.

Scaled-down domestic equipment

It is worth buying a few plastic saucepans and a tea-set. Your child can use this equipment for cooking on the floor but it will also work well when he is making playdough cakes and playing with sand or water.

Imaginary friends

By the age of three your child will probably be able to play with other children in a pretend sequence. Sometimes part of the play is the involvement of imaginary people. Quite a few children develop and talk about an imaginary friend by name, even blaming this person for wrong-doing. There is usually no need to worry about such a pretence, although you do not have to pretend to see the friend yourself. You would be right to become concerned if play with this imaginary friend was pushing out most other kinds of play for your child, or if your child actually seemed to be frightened by some aspect of the friend. This is something you should talk about to your doctor or health visitor.

You do not have to try to buy a child version of everything in your home. You can, for example, make a believable cooker from an upturned cardboard box with hot rings marked with a thick felt pen. Watch your child and see what interests him before making 'big' purchases.

Pretend child care

Boys and girls equally enjoy playing with cuddly toys and dolls. They enjoy pretend feeding or taking dolls out for a trip, telling them off, taking care of them when they are sick or putting them to bed.

Some children may want a proper doll's cot or a buggy for their birthday or other special occasions. But dolls and teddies can just as easily be put to bed in an box with material cut to size for the bedding.

Dressing-up clothes

A well-stocked dressing-up box can give children a great deal of pleasure and will be used by them for years. There is no need to pay for anything – simply fill a box with adult or older children's cast-offs. You can cut a length off any item that is so long that your children may trip but there is no need to make extensive adjustments.

Miniature size toys

It is worth seeing what kind of setting interests your child most. It might be a garage with cars, a simple house or similar building with furniture and play people or animals, a farm with animals or a castle.

Flexible props

Three- and four-year-olds can create a pretend setting out of props that need cost you nothing at all. Large cardboard boxes are worth holding on to, since they can become a bus or car, a spaceship or a lion's den. Cushions on the floor may become a castle, and a blue blanket can be a swimming pool. A few basic props and any corner of the room can become a hospital or a shop.

The value of pretence

Your child will not lose sight of the real world if you let his imagination soar in his play. On the contrary it is his chance to explore and try out many of the situations that he sees in your home that you would not let him do in reality – boiling water for a cup of tea, changing the baby's nappy or having lengthy conversations on the telephone.

If your child wants to involve you in his play, take it as seriously as he does. You can follow his lead and still add something yourself. For instance, you can accept a cup of tea and perhaps ask for a (pretend) biscuit or you can watch your child as he swims in a pretend pool and ask him if the water is cold today. In this way, your child is able to practise both the

words that he knows and the physical abilities he possesses as he copies what he has seen you do and adds details and variations of his own.

CREATIVE PLAY

Children love to make things and are delighted when you admire what they have done. Try to display what your child has made, if only for a while – a picture pinned to the kitchen board, a completed jigsaw or a brick tower left for someone else to see as well (do not allow older siblings to mock).

When children go to playgroup or nursery they will be introduced to a very wide variety of arts and crafts. There is no need to try to duplicate every activity these groups can offer, but your child will also enjoy doing simple activities at home with you. You don't need to buy expensive materials; all you need is a few basics plus a selection of those things you would otherwise put in the bin.

What you can do

It is sensible to think carefully where to allow your children to do any activity that involves paint (including some markers), glue or playdough. Tips and spills are likely and you will be less fraught if you, often with your child's help, can clear and wipe up

Play for under fives

Make believe is important to children. Putting teddy to bed if he is tired or unwell encourages emotional development.

Most children like 'real' cooking, but a play cooker can also give hours of pleasure – mixing, stirring, tasting and serving out.

Painting is very creative – if a little messy. Put a plastic sheet on the floor and get your child a plastic overall.

relatively easily. You do, however, have a wider role than simply mopping up spills; your presence and help will also usually be welcomed.

Making pictures

From as young as 15 or 16 months toddlers relish creating something of their own on paper or card. Pictures do not have to be of anything in particular, although once he gets to three your child will increasingly tell you that he has drawn a person, a house or something else (see pp. 190–1). Sometimes he will enjoy simply making patterns and experimenting with different colours and textures.

Painting and printing
Children can paint on scrap paper, card and the back of leftover wallpaper cut to a manageable size. Under threes really need thick brushes but four- and five-year-olds are ready for slimmer brushes too. Some thicker paint mixes are designed to be used for finger painting or printing with leaves or cut wedges of a firm vegetable such as a potato.

Drawing
Crayons and chalks are less likely to cause damage than paint but drawing still needs supervision. Under threes need non-toxic wax crayons, preferably thick ones which are easier for them to hold. Three- to five-year-olds will still like the wax crayons but will be ready to try some coloured pencils and thick felt tip pens. (Watch out for the tops – younger children put them up their noses and in their mouths and may choke, and if they are not replaced, pens dry out.) Chalks and a chalkboard can work well, especially if you have a garden – chalk dust tends to spread about.

Pre-cut stencils or ready drawn, black outline pictures to colour in help over-threes to practise their control of a crayon or paintbrush and to choose their colours for pictures that they could not yet draw themselves. This kind of material works well for children, but make sure that they also have a chance to make their own drawings and paintings in their own way.

Sticking
As well as drawing and painting children like the possibilities that sticking can give them. You need to buy non-toxic glue that is suitable for children – look carefully on the label, never use glue that contains solvents, or aerosol glue. Plastic spreaders for glue are a good idea – these are easier to clean than brushes, since the glue will dry and then peel off the spreader. Let your child use blunt ended scissors so he can do some cutting himself.

Children can use thick paper, card or little cardboard boxes and experiment with their own collages. Some children like to start a scrap book, perhaps for particular collectables or pictures.

Creative activities

A sketchpad and some crayons will give your child hours of enjoyment as his skills and ability develop.

Sticky shapes – buy packs of precut shapes or sheets of sticky paper to cut yourself – give hours of fun.

Making your own playdough

Most stores sell modelling doughs in different colours, some of them fluorescent, but you can easily make and colour your own (especially if you have run out of yellow when only yellow will do). Mix together in a large saucepan:

2 cups of plain flour
2 cups of water
1 cup of salt
2 tablespoons of cooking oil
2 teaspoons of cream of tartar
food colouring or powder paint

Cook the mixture gently over a low heat and stir continuously. The mixture needs to be well blended and thicken up. Empty on to a plate and let the dough cool before children use it. The salt in the recipe discourages them from eating the dough and it helps to preserve the mixture. You can drop the cream of tartar if you don't have any but the oil is useful because it makes the mixture more pliable.

This dough will keep for several weeks in a plastic bag in the refrigerator.

It is worth keeping items for collage in a box or bag; these include:

- cut-up shapes of felt or any interesting cloth
- lengths of cotton, embroidery silks or wool
- washed and dried milk bottle tops
- dried pasta shapes
- sticky paper shapes
- dried leaves, flowers or grasses
- cut-out pictures from magazines
- old greetings cards

Modelling dough

There are a number of modelling doughs that you can buy, but you can just as easily make up your own.

Playdough is a versatile material for modelling. You can add a small rolling pin and some cutters, which can be small biscuit or pastry shapes. Children can use the dough for pretend cooking, either with toy saucepans or using the plastic trays that supermarkets have for standing yogurts in. Children can shape up animals or snakes and make pretend food. The dough can

The material from which to construct buildings and mould animals, as well as something to squeeze, roll and prod, modelling dough has enormous play value.

Messy play

It is easy to say that a child should be free to explore sand and water, paint and watch the way in which different foodstuffs hit the floor. But allowing a child to go in for messy exploration if you live in a small flat without a garden is difficult and nobody likes clearing up a lot of mess.

It is important for children to be able to make a mess, however. One of the problems nursery schools find is that children who have never been allowed to 'be dirty' develop a fear of messing up their clothes and never choose any of the activities on offer which might involve the possibility of making a mess. Even when they get to nursery or school, they shy away from such materials as paint, glue and modelling clay.

To cope with messy play:

- Find somewhere else to go and play: mother and baby groups often provide messy activities for children; playschool and nursery will provide facilities; parks often have sand pits and paddling pools.
- Keep messy play for a messy hour each day.
- Define a 'messy corner' by putting down a mat: messy play never strays off the mat.
- Use a groundsheet or a piece of polythene (from builders' yards) to protect carpets.
- Sugar in a saucepan can be run through the fingers like dry sand; rice makes even less mess.
- Playdough can be moulded like wet sand.
- The best place for water play is in the bath.
- If you don't have a table for painting, set up an easel in the messy corner or in the bathroom.
- Put a groundsheet or old shower curtain under the coffee table and let him use that for drawing, gluing and sticking.
- Play outside: put on wellingtons and look for puddles to stamp in and mud to walk through.

be rolled back into a big ball at the end or some models can be left to air dry. (On exposure to air, dough starts to harden, which is not a problem when hot little hands are manipulating it. When your children have finished a playdough session, however, encourage them to roll up all the lumps they have finished with and replace them in the containers or in a plastic bag in the fridge.)

If your four- and five-year-olds take to modelling then it may be worth buying some of the modelling clays that are available in a range of colours. The finished models can be baked in a low oven.

SAND AND WATER

Children like natural materials that they can move around and use in many different ways. You may sensibly keep your under-fives away from soil and compost but there is plenty of scope in both sand and water.

Sand

If you have a garden you may have space for either a fixed sand pit or somewhere to put a container that could hold sand – like an old baby bath. Any sand pit or container in the garden needs a secure cover in order to avoid both a rich array of creepy-crawlies and to deter cats from using it as a public convenience.

Use silver sand, obtainable from garden centres. Builders' sand is cheaper but stains hands and clothes and sometimes contains chemicals which irritate skin.

Children will happily play with sand – either sitting in a sand pit or leaning over a container – using buckets, little spades, scoops (like the ones that often come with washing powder), plastic cups and toy saucepans. They like the feel of soft sand and can experiment with filling and emptying and pouring with dry sand. Sand has to be wetted if children want to turn out shapes that will not collapse.

Take care when moving a container – even a small one – full of sand.

Water

There are lots of ways that children can play with water, both indoors and out.

At the sink

Many of the playthings that your child uses in pretend play, like teasets, containers and toy saucepans, will be suitable for playing with in a bowl of warm water at the kitchen sink. He may also like to wash clothes – dolls' and teddies' clothes or something small like face cloths or his own vests.

Your child needs to be safe in how he sits or stands up to the sink, so use a step-stool or a solid chair with the back pushed against the sink. Make sure that the water is not too hot.

Bath time

All you need here is a range of playthings that will survive in the bath. These may be boats and plastic ducks but they can also be any of the playthings your child like using for water play at the sink. He will be able to explore filling and emptying, floating and sinking, and creating bubbles.

Follow the safety guidelines on p. 169 or get in the bath with your child. Apart from the enjoyment of playing with your children, they often chat to you during a relaxing bathtime.

Paddling pools

If you have a garden then warm weather is the time to get out a paddling pool or to fill up child-sized containers like the old baby bath. Children and paddling pools need constant supervision (follow the advice on pp. 169 and 172).

A washing-up bowl at the sink or on the kitchen table allows your child to play with water, but keeps the mess in a limited area. Move breakables and sharp implements from the drainer.

FUN WITH MUSIC AND SONG

When your children are teenagers, you and they may disagree utterly on what constitutes good music. But you have many years to go before then; certainly, during their babyhood and childhood you can enjoy music with your children.

Singing together

Babies and children are simply appreciative if you sing to them. They do not hold up score cards and will enjoy your efforts so long as you look and sound as if you are enjoying yourself too. If you are self-conscious about your singing, then by all means restrict yourself to indoors but do open up this possibility of a shared time with your children.

Songs for young babies

Babies like soft music produced by the human voice. There is evidence that they can hear songs or other

music before they are born and they are able to recognize the pattern of a familiar song.

Babies like and are reassured by the sound of your familiar voice. If he is distressed he can often be calmed by a cuddle, which gives him your familiar feel and smell, and a soft song or lullaby which adds your voice. Lullabies will not automatically send a wakeful baby to sleep, but they are a good and peaceful way of entertaining him in what are going to be longer and longer wakeful periods of his day. (Of course, babies are not interested in songs if they are hungry; basic needs come first.)

If you do not know or cannot remember any lullabies, sound tapes with songs and lullabies will give you more ideas, but do not put on tapes for your baby instead of singing yourself.

You do not have to restrict yourself to lullabies. Try other songs with your baby that you would enjoy singing and see his reaction. Singing is like talking with your baby. It matters less what you sing than how you sing it – with expression, smiles and pleasure.

Songs for toddlers and young children

Once babies are past the early months they will enjoy and begin to recognize songs that you sing regularly. They may also like particular songs from tapes, records or CDs and once they are able to hold themselves up against the furniture they may perhaps bounce up and down in time to the rhythm. There will come a point when your young child will develop a word to request a song and the request may be repeated many, many times.

By the time your baby is two years or more your singing times will become as much singing with him as singing to him. When he goes to playgroup or nursery a whole new source of songs and rhymes will enter your home. However, if you are looking for ideas for your first child, supplement your memory and ideas from within the family by bought tapes and books which give songs with hand movements.

Listening and dancing to music

As well as singing songs to your children, you can enjoy different kinds of music together. This can be selections from your own choice of music – the more varied the better – in addition to music aimed at children. Young children can get the taste for many

Good songs for children

The best songs for children are those that have features that help them to recognize the pattern easily – such as:

- A relatively simple tune which can be sung with lots of expression.
- A small number of words in total.
- Lines or phrases that are repeated in the song.
- A basic verse to which new ideas are added or slight variations made.
- Sounds or perhaps animal noises that accompany the words.
- Hand movements which are part of the song.

kinds of music. If you listen together you will find that even your toddler will develop clear preferences.

Listening to music can be a quiet time of sitting together on a large chair or sofa that has the space for you and one or more children in comfort. Music can also help make a long car journey far more relaxing.

Your children will also enjoy dancing with you to music and not make harsh judgements about your ability. Either both stand and dance together or take your child in your arms (this, too, can be a way to soothe a fretful baby, if you choose something slow and rhythmically rock him). It will not be until they are well into middle childhood that your children will tell you firmly that you are not to dance in front of them, or more importantly, in front of their friends.

Counting the cost

Music can be a potential source of conflict. Children of three or four, or even younger, want to insert cassette or video tapes or CDs themselves. They have seen you do it, it looks easy and children like to do as much as they can for themselves.

Young children sometimes get muddled and may try to insert a sound cassette into a video recorder. They do not know enough to avoid this kind of mistake, and are showing that they have watched you insert a cassette and are trying to do the same. Under other circumstances you would be pleased with your child's willingness to persevere. So try to keep to one side your knowledge of how much this equipment has cost you and the likely bill for possible repairs.

Think about what is best for your household:

- You may decide to keep young children completely away from an expensive system. Your young child will learn to obey a warning look and simple phrase like 'No, not the CD', so long as your family life is not cluttered with masses of 'Nos' and lots of equipment that is out of bounds.
- Teach your child how to use simple controls. Show him carefully how to put in a tape and what controls to use. Stay by him and be prepared to show him as many times as is necessary for him to understand the buttons and the sequence.

If you have taught your child carefully, by the time he is five or six years old he may be more reliable with the controls of your equipment – sound or video – than adult relatives who do not know your system.

Consider buying your child a portable cassette recorder and his own tapes. Show him how to work the buttons and controls. Teach him that this kind of equipment must be treated with care and should neither be bashed nor used with sand or water.

Making music

Babies start to make rhythmic sounds as soon as they can bang a spoon or their mug on the tray of their highchair. They enjoy making the noise and the way in which it gets your attention. Babies and toddlers like exploring the sounds they can make with objects that can be hit, shaken or squeezed. They also get a thrill out of trying to repeat similar sounds by using toys that are designed to make sounds, like rattles. This is the beginning of making music.

You may not have a musical instrument, but this is not a problem since most young children are quite happy with basic instruments such as:

- drums or simple xylophones – or anything that they can bang in rhythm;
- bells – either little hand bells or toys with bells fitted inside;
- all kinds of shakers – you can make effective shakers from an empty plastic bottle half filled with something like lentils, with the top screwed back tightly, or two empty yogurt cartons filled with lentils or beads and then taped together.

Children enjoy the pattern of sounds that these objects make and the physical movements are not too difficult for little fingers and hands.

LEARNING TO LOVE BOOKS

Looking at books, reading and telling stories can be introduced from the early months of life. These activities help to stimulate your child's imagination, develop listening skills and the patterns of speech. Your child will also learn to associate books with interesting information, an essential step towards learning to read. You can enjoy books with your child from his early months. Babies and young children like simple pictures and the sound of your voice as you talk to them about the picture long before they are able to listen to a lengthy story. The range and quality of books for babies and children has dramatically improved over the past 20 years – although classic stories and nursery rhymes still have a place – so you can find something suitable for all ages and interests.

Books for babies and toddlers

Very young children tend to grasp and scrabble at books partly because they are fascinated by the pictures, and partly because they like to explore the physical texture of any object, so pages tend to get torn too easily, or get chewed or sucked. It makes sense not to leave them in a toy basket or put them in your baby's cot. Show your child how to turn pages with care, but try not to worry about torn pages.

Reading to your toddler

If you spend time looking at books with your baby, before he is two he will show that he has favourites and will clearly want to have book time with you. This can be a special time, when he has your full attention.

By about two years of age young children are able to attend, with pleasure, through books of 10–12 pages with maybe a dozen lines on each page. This kind of absorbed interest does not happen automatically with the second birthday; it will have developed in part through the time you have put in during the previous months. However the pleasure small children derive from stories makes reading time a rewarding, shared experience for both adult and child.

Reading to one or more children is not a complicated technique but it is one that deserves your full attention.

- Make the tale sound interesting by reading with plenty of expression in your voice. Sound as if you are enjoying the story, even if this seems like the hundredth time you have read it.
- Go at a steady pace, not too fast, and leave pauses for you and the children to look at the pictures. Some stories have suitable places for a tense pause, or even an excited 'What's going to happen next?'
- It is best to sit very close to your child so you can both see the book clearly and from the same angle. He could be on your lap. If you are reading to several children make sure they can all see – you may need to be on the sofa or even on the floor to do this.
- You can look together and perhaps point sometimes to a picture. But, if it is a story book, do not take long breaks in the story to talk about a picture or your child may lose concentration.
- When children are able, let them turn the pages.

Learning by repetition

Older babies and toddlers will like you to say the same, or a very similar, sequence of words as you talk your way through a picture book. They enjoy the repetition and may well start to repeat words at the right moment, or even correct you if you make a mistake or, worse still, try to skip a section! If books do not come with a story line, you can always make one up around a set of pictures that your child likes.

Once you have created a story around the pictures your toddler will want the book this way each time, so explain it to others who may be 'reading' it to him.

Choosing books to suit your child

To get to know the kind of book that most interests your child so that you do not spend money on a book that is only opened once, try out books first from your local library and then buy your child's favourites, or contact the Young Book Trust for a list of titles. Children's libraries have a welcoming atmosphere, usually with a book box and reading area for young children to encourage them to feel at home.

Try for a range of stories:
- some with people as well as animals as characters;
- some storylines with repeating phrases, since your young child will recognize and start to join in;
- books with good, clear pictures;
- books that have a range of people, including some that look like your family and who do things that your family does, and others that are different.

Books for under-twos

Do not be afraid to buy books for your baby. While it is true that beautifully illustrated hardback stories can be expensive, these are not the best for a small child in any case. There are plenty of inexpensive books that are suitable for even the youngest of children.

- **Thick board books**
  These stand up to tough handling and page turning. You can buy picture books with drawings or photos. Some board books are designed with an extra interest, for example, holes to look through. Some will stand up like a cardboard frieze.
- **Cloth or wipeable plastic books**
  Your baby may like the feel of cloth books since babies go through a stage of stroking and rubbing soft things. Some plastic books are designed to survive in the bath.

- **Clear and brightly coloured picture books**
  Babies and toddlers often like a shiny surface to books. The best pictures are visually interesting but not too crammed full of detail. Young children are still learning to scan pictures and too much on one page can simply confuse them. You can make up your own picture books by putting drawings, cut out pictures and photos in a small pocket album or a photo cube.
- **Books with a simple storyline**
  There are plenty of books that tell a story by no more than a line or two on each page. Reading this kind of book allows you to pace the story for a young child and to spend as much time on the pictures as the tale. It also enables children to begin to recognize simple words because of their association with a clear picture – 'cat', 'dog', 'car', 'boy', 'girl', 'baby', 'cup'.

Making up a story

Suppose your toddler really likes a set of photos of a young child going swimming. There is no text except for the book title, so you made up your own. Perhaps it will go something like this.

- Picture of little girl in her costume: 'There's Martha now. What's she doing? She's going swimming. Going swimming with Daddy.'
- Picture of girl being lifted into pool by her Daddy: 'In she goes. Daddy's got her safe. Into the water. Will it be cold – brrr?'
- Picture of a girl splashing in the water: 'No, it's not cold. Look at her splashing Daddy. Poor old Daddy. Just like you splash your Daddy.' And so on …

Books for twos to fives

Children do not become ready for a different kind of book by their second or third birthday. It is a steady development. You will also find that older children still want to pore over much-loved baby books.

Your child's attention will be held by longer stories and he will be ready to hear new stories rather than always wanting the old favourites. He will still want you to read to him and to look at picture books together but, if you have introduced him to the enjoyment of books when he was young, he will also like to look at books on his own.

Different kinds of stories

You can meet your child's interests as well as extending them. Try for a range of different books.

- Ones about people like yourselves.
- Stories that are out of your own experience, set in other countries or times.
- Fairy stories or myths retold for children.
- Stories in a series about a character your child likes.

Poetry and rhymes

Some very good poetry is now written for children and you can introduce your under-fives to the feel of poetry through rhymes that you chant or sing. Traditional nursery rhymes are particularly good for this – they originate from a time when stories were passed on through the oral tradition, so they had to

have easily memorable themes and rhythms. Pick some books that also have good or amusing pictures.

Books about topics

You will also see many, well-produced books designed for under-fives that have several easily accessible pictures around a specific theme – perhaps cats, life on a farm, dinosaurs, space or another subject – with some text; these are your child's introduction to reference books.

Libraries are an excellent source of this kind of informative book and your child may well begin to develop special interests in one or two topics and be pleased to look for books in order to find out more.

Novelty books

Technical advances in paper engineering have released some very creative books on to the market. You will see pop-up books ranging in design from the very simple to the extremely complex. Books may have:

- flaps to lift or windows to look through;
- parts to feel or to smell;
- items threaded through the book;
- a story that unfolds through additional illustrations on the page as another item is added to the picture;
- pockets or envelopes which hold something else to look at and for you to read out loud.

You will discover which of these books your child likes but remember that novelty books do not survive fierce handling. You may want to keep such books out of reach, for looking at with adult supervision.

Bilingual families

If your family is bilingual you will be talking to your child in the two languages that he needs to speak and you will want to extend this to books as well.

You can use the children's books that are now published in a range of languages, or try a dual-language version with two languages on the same or opposite pages in the same book.

Your two, or more, family languages may follow a different direction of writing and/or a different alphabet. Be ready to point this out to your child so that he associates the different ways of presenting text in the two languages right from the start.

Stories on tapes and television

Many children's books are now available on cassette or may be read on television in the morning or afternoon children's slots. You can buy cassettes but, of course, you could tape-record yourself reading books.

It is not a good idea for you to get your children to listen to tapes so that you can give up reading to them yourself. But listening to a new story or an old favourite professionally read can be another way of enjoying books. There is every reason to sit down with your child and enjoy a tape with her. You can look at the book at the same time, or simply relax together and let your imagination create the illustrations.

Cassettes of stories can be especially useful to put on the car tape deck for longer journeys. This can be a real boon if your children start to feel sick when they look at books in a moving car.

Story telling

Before books were widely available tales were passed on by word of mouth, by story tellers. This skill is being revived to an extent and a local story teller may visit your child's playgroup or nursery. You may never wish to tell stories to groups of children, but it is a skill worth acquiring for use with your family.

If you have made up a storyline for picture books, you are well on the way to becoming a story teller. If you read a great deal to your child you will know some stories by heart and may remember favourites from your own childhood. It can be useful to tell stories when you are waiting with your children to be called in to an appointment or on a train, coach or plane journey. Again the same story may have to be told in exactly the same way if you repeat it.

Pre-reading skills

Children often learn favourite stories by heart. They start by joining in but move on to knowing a story so well that they can repeat the words to themselves as they turn the pages appropriately. This is not yet reading but it gives an idea of the pattern of reading and they learn that words and pictures go together.

If your child wants to know what words say or starts to recognize and read words, help him. Show him the letters of the alphabet and their sounds. But don't push him into being a preschool reader for the sake of it. The best help you can give is to build the basic skills which put him on the path to reading.

A positive view of books

If you have taken time and given your attention in enjoying books with your child, you will have taught him a genuine love of books and an interest in what you can find out from them. He will also learn to take care of books.

Helping concentration and observation

Your child will have developed his ability to attend well for periods of time, even to settle back with his books if he is interrupted. He will have learned how to look at a book, scanning the pictures, noticing the details and working through page by page.

Understanding about reading

You will have shown your child how people read so he is not puzzled about the process of reading itself. He can understand how the words tell the story, how you are reading the words and how you stop and turn the page when you have read the last one. Point with your finger to show how you move along the line, or hold back his hand on the page and say, 'I've got one more sentence to go. Look, I'm up to this bit.'

As you share books with your children they have been learning the rules that apply in your written language. English is written and read from left to right and from the top of the page to the bottom. This order is not obvious to children, nor is it a universal way of organizing writing. For instance, Arabic is written from right to left, as is Urdu.

Other reading material

Books are not the only source of written material. You may have shown your child handwriting, and the written instructions to the construction toys you put together and on the board games you play. Advertisement hoardings, cereal packets, road signs, shop fronts, the sides of buses or trucks, all use words and provide your child with a different view of writing and reading, which may encourage him to go back to books and match the words he notices in the wider world.

Relaxing with books

If you take time to enjoy all kinds of books with your child you will help his ability to concentrate, his interests and general knowledge and you will provide him with a head start in learning to read. All these are very valuable, but, in a busy life with children, never underestimate the advantage of a relaxed 'sit-down' time with your child. Reading a book at bedtime is an excellent routine to establish as it relaxes your child and prepares him for sleep. When you look at books with your toddler or read a story to your four-year-old, you can relax for ten minutes and there are not many kinds of play with a child where that is possible!

PLAY AND TECHNOLOGY

There are three important areas where you can help and guide your child as he plays with the technology available to him. These are:

- Developing the habit of making a choice about switching on a piece of technology – and switching it off in order to do an alternative activity.

- Finding out what a set of controls will do and how you work it.
- Taking care of equipment like remote controls, keyboards and control panels of appliances or music systems.

Television

There is a positive side to having a television in your home. You and your children can watch excellent programmes designed specifically to inform and entertain children. You can also enjoy together some of the broader interest programmes that will bring into your living room parts of the world or aspects of nature that you may never otherwise get to see.

But in order to enjoy the benefits, it is wise to establish some ground rules about the television set.

Make a choice about switching it on

Once young children know how to work the television you will need to discourage them from putting it on and cruising the channels, with no idea of what they are going to watch. (It is very unwise to put a television in a small child's bedroom for the precise reason that it is even more difficult to keep track of his viewing, see also pp. 293–4.)

You can develop the habit of checking the daily programmes with your child, long before he can do the reading. Make a decision about what he will watch and watch with him sometimes. Offer something else to do with you, if there is nothing of interest on and your child complains, 'But I'm bored!'

Watch programmes with your child

Watching selected programmes with your child has the following advantages:

- You keep each other company: this can be a relaxing time spent sitting together with your child and enjoying something on his terms.
- Some of the children's general interest programmes come up with good suggestions for activities to do with your child at home, so you gain a source of play ideas.
- It provides a chance to talk together. Your child will probably not want you to chat throughout a programme, but, as you watch, you may point things out to each other or comment briefly on what is going on. After you have finished watching

a good programme, talk with your child about what you have watched together. A particularly funny, unusual or interesting programme may be a source of happy reminiscences for some time.

Keep a limit on total hours

Even if your child is watching something good, you do not want him glued to the television for hours at a time. The main problems with television and children come from all the activities that they do not do simply because they are watching so much.

Children need physical activity that uses energy and gives them the opportunity to develop and practise all their skills. If they are sitting slumped or lolling on the floor then they are not running about in lively activity. Nor are they using other physical skills that get practice when they are building, drawing or playing with a bowl of sand or water.

One possibility of sitting around for too long, whether he has been watching television or indeed reading books, is that some children have a burst of wild energy at a really inconvenient time for you. Even more worrying, in the long term, is if children lose the motivation to play in a lively way and slip into a sedentary life style. So think about the balance of active and quiet play in your child's day.

Video

The main difference between television and video is that a video can be played at any time, rewound, sped through and replayed again. You will need to establish limits to how long children watch videos, perhaps confining replays to one a day and making sure that any video within reach is suitable for young children.

Electronic toys

Technology is now applied to toys, but just because a toy uses up-to-date technology, it does not necessarily mean that it will offer the best way for your child to play or the best value financially for you.

It is as well to be wary of expensive electronic 'educational' toys that claim to teach your child all about shapes or numbers. Children learn these concepts through experience and not from a control panel of just half a dozen fixed examples. Your child may enjoy having a toy like this, but it will not take

the place of a helpful and attentive adult and play materials that offer lots of examples of the concept.

Some sound-making control panel toys claim to teach your child his first words. No toy can teach your child to talk. Children learn to communicate with other human beings and they should be learning from the real thing. There is no point in your toddler being able to say 'Mummy', like the voice on the toy, if he has no idea what a 'mummy' is and uses the word to the console, not to the real person.

Other toys claim to teach your child the basics of reading. Again, they cannot take the place of the ideas described on pp. 220–4. They are generally repetitive and of limited interest, and fortunately children get bored with them quickly.

Computers

If none of your children is over five, you may not be facing choices about computer and video games. If games or hand-held systems have entered your home then you will need to keep track of time your children spend playing with them in much the same way as with television and video.

It is useful, indeed essential, for children to develop confidence with computers. You may find that your child's nursery class has a computer and, if you have a personal computer at home, you can introduce your child to what it will do. However, computer literacy will not be learned more effectively in play dominated by electronic toys. Nor should the technological hardware available at home take the place of interested and involved parents who play with their children.

PLAYING WITH OTHER CHILDREN

Children younger than three do not play in a co-operative way, but play alongside others (see pp. 201–2). But that is only half the story. Research into play is often based on observation of pairs or groups of similar-aged children. A group of two- or three-year-olds, with no older children present, may play in parallel rather than together. Children of this age often watch each other and copy what the other one is doing. They may exchange a few words and gestures, but their language and social skills are not sophisticated enough to deal with the give and take in play or with starting and holding on to sequences of play together.

The other half of the story can be seen when there are more children in the family, or the children of two or more families come together. Then the four- and five-year-olds may include the younger ones, once they are mobile and can follow simple instructions, in play. As a result, young children do have a role in pretend play and are tolerated in physical games.

Brothers and sisters do not always get along and older ones will not be pleased if they can never escape from the younger ones. Yet a genuine 'playing together' can develop when siblings are young.

What you can do

There are many things you can do to help children to play together, whether they are your own or other children come to your house.

Adults remain responsible

Adults are the ones who keep everyone safe, especially babies and toddlers. Older children may need to be warned that they cannot treat the baby like a doll or teddy. Even placid babies should not be used as props.

Babies of a few months can be interested in older children, who may be prepared to take part in the kind of repetitive play that babies relish, such as shaking rattles, dropping and fetching and making faces. But older ones cannot be expected always to take younger ones into their play and should never be left with sole responsibility while adults do something else.

Be an available umpire

Children often cannot sort out disagreements beyond one or two attempts and under-fives do not have the same array of strategies for resolving people problems as you do.

If you stay within sight or easy earshot, you can swiftly intervene if tempers seem to be frayed. Do not assume it is always the youngest who are hard done by or the boys who started the hitting.

Child needs and adult needs

Children from different families may not always want to play together for the same length of time as their parents want to socialize. Be sensitive to their needs as well as your own and give the children time apart.

Give children time apart

Even children who get on well together get jaded if they never have a break, or a chance to be alone for a while. Children also get fed up if they always seem to have to share you with another child and never, ever have time just for themselves with you.

Children of different ages will play with different toys and the older ones will be distressed and angry if their painting is destroyed by a crawling brother or if an unsteady sister crashes into their tallest tower before you have seen it. A first child will have become used to playing on the floor and you will need to protect his play area from his naturally curious younger brother or sister. In addition, the older child's little toys, like plastic bricks and crayons, need to be kept away from the baby's or toddler's mouth.

By three or four years children may get breaks in their family day offered by playgroup or nursery. But at home, it helps to give the older child special attention in a quiet time with you when the younger one is having a daytime nap.

Sharing

Life is easier and more enjoyable for everyone if children learn to share. But sharing is one of those areas in which adults expect a great deal more from children than they would from adults.

Parents often say 'Go on, share your toy with your friend' even when the other child is not a close friend, or is a well-known wrecker, or the toy in question is brand new, or all three. Would those same adults hand over something equally precious of their own – a brand new item of clothing, the keys to the family car or a book or CD in the same circumstances?

You can take practical steps to help your children to share, without demanding an unrealistic standard of selflessness.

Know what you are asking

Adults tend to use the single word 'sharing' to cover several slightly different kinds of behaviour. All have their place and can be learned by children if they are not put under unreasonable pressure.

Borrowing and lending

This is the kind of sharing of toys that probably goes on in your own home. The original owner is not in doubt, nor is the fact that the toy should be returned. Borrowers should ask first and be willing to lend in return and those who do not return toys or books in a reasonable state will not be able to borrow again in the near future and may have to make recompense.

Giving

A limited quantity of anything is given. Children learn that it is selfish to have more than your fair share or tuck into something that is not available for all.

Taking turns

Being able to take turns is vital when play materials – the roller for the playdough, the pot of red paint, the swing in the garden, the bikes at playgroup – are limited. Children learn that no one child has the right to hang on to the paint or sit tight on the bike and prevent other children having their go.

Be reasonable

It is fair that your child can put precious possessions to one side when other children visit. A new toy or something that would be devastating if it were broken can stay in the cupboard. A child's toys are not his own if you overrule his wish to keep them safe.

You may have a longer list of toys put to one side if a visitor is known to be careless or a deliberate breaker. But it is not fair for your child to bring out something that he will not then share.

Impose your house rules

As awkward as it may feel sometimes, you have the right to impose your own house rules on child guests. Often children simply assume that fairly wild behaviour is allowed, unless told specifically not to do something. More often than not, once you say, 'Nobody is allowed to throw toys down the stairs in this home', the child will stop.

Learning to follow rules

Four- and five-year-olds devise and impose rules on each other in their play and by this age children are ready for simple games with built-in rules. With you as a teacher and umpire, they will enjoy board and card games.

Suitable board games include those based on pictures. (There may be writing or numbers as well but under-fives need the additional help of illustrations.) Picture dominoes help children to look carefully and to match like with like. You can buy lotto games that depend on matching pictures. Some four- and five-year-olds are ready to match numbers, shapes or even simple words to pictures, but make sure that they have first understood the idea of a board game with pictures. Playing 'Pairs' with illustrated cards helps children to remember and match similar pictures. Snap cards with pictures and card games like Happy Families are possible for four- and five-year-olds who have learned to look carefully.

If you have children older than five, they may be keen on a range of board games that involve counting or following written instructions or illustrations (like snakes and ladders). Younger children may take part in such games so long as you play as their partner.

WHY PLAY COUNTS

Play is a social activity and, although children can be happily absorbed for some time playing on their own, they also want company. If you are willing to get involved in your child's play you will be a real help to him in all the different areas of development in which he is learning so fast. You will miss far too many opportunities if you hold back, feeling that play is not for adults. So don't always expect your child to 'go away and play', or tell him 'play nicely, be quiet I'm talking' or keep saying 'later, later'.

Children do not take a narrow view of play, so you need not either. Play is whatever activity absorbs them. In a sense, the most important aspect to play is that the activity is started, seen through and finished because it is of interest in its own right. There may be an end product but the actual result may be more of a warm glow that comes from having a good time.

Playing with your children need not stop when they go to school. You will enjoy advanced versions of games with your older children and their own play, alone or with friends, will be more complex. The way that you play with your under-fives can build up interests which will develop into hobbies and absorbing leisure activities later on in his life.

Through spending time together, enjoying play and communicating through play activities, you will be creating a close and caring relationship with your child. Not least of all, you will also have fun.

CHAPTER NINE

Help With Your Child

Sooner or later, you are going to have to leave your child, whether for a couple of hours or a full working day. Although handing your baby or small child over to someone else is always difficult, good, reliable child care can both enrich your child's life and make your own life easier.

Sharing the care

Babies and children are social beings. They like and want contact with other people of different genders and ages. And although they need some level of predictability and familiarity in their lives, it is not necessary, or even beneficial, for a baby or young child to be cared for by one person alone.

WHAT BABIES NEED

In the first months of their lives, babies become attached to a few key people. One person may be the most important, or at least the most important for a while. This key person is often the baby's mother but this particularly close attachment tends to come about because in most societies women do most of the child care, and especially the baby care.

Very young babies are still building their knowledge of how to tell one person from another. But older babies and young children show clearly that they are happy with, and would choose the company of, several different people that they know well – father as well as mother, an older brother or sister, a grandparent or other close relative. With a proper chance to settle, they are also able to form a good relationship with a carer who is not a member of the immediate family.

If you are a first-time mother, it is understandable that you might feel concerned that nobody else, even within the family, can take proper care of your baby, because nobody else will do it exactly the way you do. There are great advantages, however, in sharing your baby and allowing other members of the family, especially her father, to become expert. Not only will you be overwhelmed if you cannot get any break at all, but your baby needs to get to know other people in her life and to have this experience in a way that helps her to sort out the familiar from the unfamiliar.

What fathers can do

Fathers can perform every aspect of baby care, except breastfeeding. Mothers are not born knowing what to do with babies. They learn from the experience of having a baby of their own, and from others who are already experienced, often fellow parents or members of the family. It takes time to build a personal relationship with an individual baby, with the result that some mothers find that they get along more easily with one of their children than another.

The point is that 'mothering' does not unfold automatically, so as a father, you do not need to feel that your partner was born to be a better parent. In a family in which you are involved from the outset in her care, your baby will be as happy with you as she is with her mother, and as pleased to see you and conscious of your absence, in the same way too.

Apart from finding out what you need to know about good baby and child care, the most important step for you as a father is to give time to your babies and children so that your experience and confidence grow. If you have not spent much time with your baby, it is easy to think that anything that goes less than smoothly is your fault. But remember, your baby yells at her mother sometimes and is hard to comfort for no obvious reason with her too.

Other contacts

Through becoming attached to a small number of people, your baby will develop a secure base on which to build future relationships. Initially, she will make these relationships, which will not always be peaceful, with her brothers and sisters and through them find her position in the family. Once she has this measure of a social life, supported by you, she can begin to 'broaden her circle' and choose her own friends.

Grandparents can play a very special role in the lives of babies and young children, often developing strong and lasting bonds with their grandchildren.

These developments should be a steady process rather than sudden big changes. In order to develop socially and learn how to relate to different adults and a range of other children, your child has to have the opportunity to make friends. You may give her this through links with other families and later through preschool groups. And, if you have to organize child care to cover for your paid work, a good arrangement can also open up your child's social world.

TAKING A BREAK

From the start, get your baby used to being with other people in the family. This can be for very short periods of time and sometimes you can also be in the same room. Among the possibilities are:

- Stand back and let a grandparent cuddle or sing to your baby, without your hovering close.
- If you are a mother, then let your baby go to her father sooner rather than later. Trust him with her.
- Let a grandparent or aunt or uncle hold and play with your baby while you cook a meal, pop out to the shops or take a much-needed nap.

- If you have close friends who have babies or children of a similar age, spend time together – a social time for the children as well as for you.

If your older babies or young children are happy, you may be able to arrange part of each week in which, for short periods of time, you take turns in having a friend's children and he or she yours. This might allow you to do something you would enjoy just for yourself – a fitness session, a trip to the shops or just a chance to sit and read a book.

There is no reason why swapping arrangements with friends should not work just as well for fathers as for mothers. If you are a father and your baby's prime carer, think about its benefits for both of you.

Time off during the day

However much you love your baby, you will get depressed if you and she scarcely leave the four walls of home. Try to get some variety into your days and include trips out within easy travelling distance. If you know people locally who also have children, get together in each other's houses. Local groups of the National Childbirth Trust are sometimes lively social networks and can put you in touch with other parents with children of a similar age to your own. Consider, too, any drop-in facilities for parents and children. Your local library or GP's surgery may have posters or leaflets, or contact the children's department at your local Social Services. There are several options:

- Parent and child groups at which you stay with your child. These groups may be called drop-ins, one o'clock clubs, toddler groups or parent-and-child clubs. There may be a small fee.
- Some local playgroups or community nurseries may have a special afternoon when local parents are invited to drop in and stay with their children.
- Special parent and baby, or toddler, sessions at local leisure centres or swimming pools.

Groups of this kind can be very enjoyable: you get some adult company and a change of scene and your child gets a different choice of toys and play materials and perhaps some open space. Sessions at leisure centres can ensure that your young child gets to use the facilities in a suitable environment, without older and larger children moving at speed. Your child may start to make friends and you may also find that some of the other parents become your friends.

Group experiences introduce your child to the ground rules of groups of children, including the need to share and take turns. You remain present, so your child can let go of you to an extent, but has the choice of staying by your side and playing with you if she prefers. This experience can mean that playgroup or nursery school, when you do leave your child, may be less of a wrench – although it will not ensure that there are no tears at all later.

If you are a full-time father, it is inevitable that you will be out-numbered at coffee mornings and drop-ins. Take the line that you know exactly what you are doing with your baby or young child – as indeed you do – and you are seeking social contact, not advice. You may meet the suggestion that you have simply stepped in temporarily: ignore it or dispel the misconception as you see fit.

Your agreement with a babysitter

A number of considerations apply to your relationship with any sitter, although some are more crucial if you are using paid sitters. You can reasonably expect a sitter to:

- arrive on time and stay in your house for the whole duration of the sit;
- follow your house rules on habits such as smoking;
- not use alcohol or other recreational drugs while sitting for you;
- arrive in person and not send a deputy, except in case of illness when he or she should let you know in advance;
- not arrive with a friend in tow unless agreed in advance with you;
- focus on your children: he or she should be able to hear the children when they have gone to bed, so there should be no loud music and the television should be low; some sitters arrive with a bag of homework or a book, which is fine so long as it does not come out until the children have gone to bed;
- use your telephone only to call you in an emergency; if you are going to leave other people in charge in your home, get an itemized phone bill;
- not 'nose' about your house.

Getting out in the evening

Children are all different, so you will have to make a decision with each one about when it is feasible to go out in the evening and leave your baby or toddler with a sitter. You may find that your first baby's sleeping pattern is reasonably predictable after only a few months, or that she is happy for a familiar sitter to bottlefeed her if she wakes. Yet your second child may develop an uncanny ability to know when you are going out and either refuse to settle to sleep or wake during the evening and reduce a sitter to a wreck.

If your baby becomes so distressed at your absence that the sitter has to phone you to return, or you arrive home to a desperate child, you may have to take her with you until she is a little older. This, obviously, is probably reasonable if you are going to dinner at a friend's house, but not an option in a cinema or the vast majority of restaurants. It also does not get round the fact that you need time with your partner, without your baby: in a very short time, you can get out of the habit of talking to each other on topics that have nothing to do with children. It is also important to get out if you are a single parent, or if your partner is frequently away on business and just wants to sit in when he or she is at home.

Once you can reasonably organize it, therefore, try to get a reliable baby-sitting arrangement. If you are handing over responsibility, even for short periods of time, you need to pass over any important information about the care of your baby or child and where important equipment is kept. Always leave a number where you can be contacted.

There are several potential choices:
- Sitting arrangements without payment. A relative may be able, and happy, to sit for you.
- Friends with children who also need sitters may be pleased to sit for you and you sit in return, for equivalent amounts of time.
- You may find an organized circle in your area. Such circles usually include at least a dozen or so local families. Each month someone in the circle keeps a record of everyone's name, address, phone number, the children and the sits requested and done. Sitting works on a credit–debit system so if you want a lot of sits or long evening sits, you will have to be prepared to sit to this extent for other families. A circle can work well, and avoids payment, if you are a two-parent family with conventional hours – one of you has to be home with your children while the other is out sitting.
- A paid sitter may suit you better, or be your only option. You may have friends or neighbours with teenagers who would like to earn money by sitting. Meet a potential sitter before you use him or her for the first time to assure yourself that he or she is reliable. Some agencies will provide sitters but you may not know in advance who is coming. If you approach an agency, then find out all the details on fees, any other expectations and how the agency finds and vets its sitters. Try to use an agency that allows you to book a particular person whom you have met, like and trust.

Sitting is a two-way relationship and babysitters can give as many stories of lack of consideration or exploitation as parents can of sitters. It is reasonable for a sitter to expect that the evening is spent sitting, not bathing or feeding the children unless you want him or her there early and agree this in advance. Obviously when your children are older, the sitter cannot expect them to be in bed, but he or she can expect them to go to bed when asked without a big fuss. Sitters should not be expected to do any domestic chores, except perhaps take a message if there is a telephone call and clear up their own cups or snacks.

What a sitter will expect

- that you sort out in advance what the rate is, any increases for time after midnight or at bank holidays, and pay up in full and in cash on your return;
- that you do not cancel arranged sits at very short notice unless you are prepared to pay, because the sitter may well have turned down other families for you;
- that you are home at or close to the time you have promised;
- that if the sitter does not have transport, you either take her or him home or pay for a cab; if your sitter lives close by, walk or watch him or her home.

CHILD CARE

If you want or need to hold down a paid job as well as being a parent, you will have to organize reliable child care. Even if you work from home it is most unlikely that you will be able to fit in your working commitments around caring for your children. Babies and young children need plenty of attention, as well as safe supervision, from a caring adult. They will not be happy to wait while you complete your paid work.

If you are able to pay for a nanny or an au pair to help you in the absorbing task of full-time child care, you are in a minority. The majority of families seeking child care want cover for the time that both parents, or the only parent, are working. The advice here is written from that perspective.

Making the decision

For some families there is no real decision about whether one or both of you continues to hold down a job. Family finances may mean that the income of a single parent, or incomes from both parents, are essential. For some parents anything more than a short break from their profession will have serious consequences on their future career.

Regardless of your initial impulses, however, it is worth thinking about jobs in relation to child care. Talk over the realities with parents who are combining family and careers. Having one or more children is a life change that requires compromises – decide for yourself what these are going to be for your family.

Balance the following important issues:

Income
What do you really need? There comes a point in most families at which basic necessities are covered and your child may prefer your presence to expensive toys or the treats for which your working hours pay. Might part-time working or an ordinary working week, rather than overtime, meet your needs?

Career compromise
What level of compromise are you allowing in your, perfectly reasonable, wish to have the satisfaction of a job or to maintain continuity in your chosen career? Some leeway will be necessary. It is simply not possible to 'have it all' – very involved parenthood and a highly absorbing job – and anyone who claims it is either possible or easy is talking nonsense. A close relationship with children takes time to build and dedication to an ambitious professional career ladder does not leave enough hours in the day, or physical and emotional stamina, to go round. You may have to accept that a refusal to work the elastic hours you managed before your children were born results in a quieter period in your career.

If one or both of you finds that your career suffers in this way, remember that this is certainly not something for which your children can be blamed.

Needs of children
What do your children need and want from you? Many parents who work do succeed in giving their children their full attention when they are all at home together. Family life is organized around providing what children want and family agendas are deliberately child-focused. You will probably find that you wave goodbye to any time dedicated to what you, as an adult, might wish to do, while your children are younger. But do try to get some time alone or with your partner when you can (see pp. 118–20).

Options in child care

A major part of dealing with the feelings and pressures of combining child care and paid work and shifting your focus from job to home and back again, is to make the best child-care arrangements that you can with time to spare. Find out about possible arrangements well before you need care. You may have to get your name on a waiting list for some kinds of care. You can, of course, leave final details until closer to the time that you actually need cover.

Even a good arrangement will not last for ever. Sometimes you and your child will have to deal with change, sometimes with less notice than you would like. The best organized lives and excellent arrangements have an unfortunate tendency to collapse, sometimes with the most inopportune timing.

The law and child care
Although many of the decisions about child care are personal, you are affected by the law of the land. It is against the law in Scotland to leave any child under

12 years of age unattended at home. There is no equivalent law in England and Wales but you can be prosecuted for neglect if a case can be made that by leaving your child or children unattended you are acting irresponsibly or endangering their safety. Factors taken into account are the age of the children, the length of time they are left alone and conditions in the home, including anything hazardous to a child.

In addition, the law does not recognize that it is possible to hand over responsibility to anyone outside the family who is under 16. So if you leave your child with someone under 16, you remain fully responsible for whatever happens in your absence.

Certain kinds of facilities for children must be registered and inspected by the local Social Services under the Children Act of 1989. This law is applied when the children are under eight years of age and the facility is open for more than two hours a day. With few exceptions, this legislation covers childminders, day nurseries (private, workplace or local authority), private nursery schools which take only under fives, playgroups and after-school or holiday schemes.

State-run nursery schools and classes are the responsibility of the Department for Education and Employment. Private nursery schools which have older, school-age children on the premises also fall under the jurisdiction of the DfEE.

The law does not apply to child-care arrangements made within the family with close relatives. But most other arrangements with carers who are not relatives are governed by the same registration and inspection provisions as childminders since carers are judged to be acting as such. These arrangements include nannies who are working for three or more families (but not a nanny employed exclusively by you) and friends who have regular arrangements involving payment. Payment does not, strictly speaking, have to be money. Handing over bags of shopping that you had paid for could be judged as payment in kind.

If you are in any doubt about an arrangement, contact your local Social Services department. Names vary, but look for something like 'day care for under eights' or 'registration and inspection of day care'. Under the Children Act this department has to keep an up-to-date register of child-care services, so it will be a source of the registered childminders in your area, private day nurseries, playgroups and any other schemes for children governed by the Children Act.

Weighing up the issues

When you are trying to decide what kind of child care could suit you, your child and the rest of the family, consider the following factors:

Your child
How old is your child? Babies and toddlers need to be able to relate on a predictable basis to a small number of carers. They will almost certainly become distressed if carers change without warning in a day nursery, or if a nanny or childminder insists on fitting them into a busy social round.

What kind of person or place do you think would suit your child? You may not get your ideal but at least be clear about what you believe would benefit your child.

How many children do you have? Kinds of child care (and the travel involved) which seem manageable with one child may not be the best choice for two or more. The cost of any type of care involving a fee per child may start to rival more expensive forms of care like employing a nanny.

Timing
When will you need care for your child? How many hours of the day do you need and is any of this time during antisocial hours – do you work shifts, evenings or weekends, for example?

Do you work the same days of the week or are you looking for a person or place that could take your child for a different pattern each week?

Do you need child care that will dovetail with your child's preschool playgroup or nursery – taking and pick-ups as well as providing the emergency contact if your child becomes ill or has an accident during playgroup or nursery hours? These provisions will also be important when your child starts primary school.

Location
Where do you want care for your child? Is it easier to have her cared for at, or close to, home or near your or your partner's workplace?

Type of care
What sort of care do you ideally want for your child? Would you rather an individual carer or introduce your child to group care? Does your child have special

needs that may require a particular setting or expertise in the carer? Do you have twins?

Cost

How much are you able to pay for care? Costs of the different types of care vary widely. You will usually pay money, although arrangements between friends may be in terms of favours or hours returned. You pay for child care out of your net income. The cost has not so far been allowed as a deductible expense for income tax purposes. You should not normally pay tax on the value of a place in a nursery provided by your employer, but you will have to pay tax on any cash allowance or voucher given to you by your employer to help toward the costs of child care.

Availability

Being clear about what you would like ideally is a good start, but the reality is that sometimes there are more families seeking child care, and particular kinds of child care, than are available in an area. You will need to weigh your preferences with your constraints to select the best out of what is actually available.

Family and friends

You may be able to get the help you need without looking beyond the confines of your immediate circle of family and friends. It is worth investigating the possibilities before you start trying to find an outsider.

Between two parents

If you are a two-parent family, you and your partner may be able to arrange your working hours so that you are never both at work at the same time. This can be successful if you both have predictable hours and you either work part-time or in staggered shifts. Your child care is free and your children get to spend time with each of you. A potential disadvantage is that you and your partner may not get to see each other much as one of you tends to go out as the other comes in. It also means that the times you spend together as a family may be more limited.

Other family members

A relative may be able to care for your child. This can work well if your relative lives nearby or with you, and the number of hours involved do not seem burdensome. The care is probably free and your child knows her carer already. The relative may enjoy the regular contact. Be honest about what is expected and for how many hours. Family relationships are more likely to stay happy if you discuss changes in arrangements and do not simply assume that your relative will do more hours or change days without warning. Relatives need to be able to end the arrangement when they wish, rather than feeling obliged to continue for ever, although you must have sufficient warning to make other arrangements.

Arrangements with friends

If you are seeking cover for only a few hours, you may be able to develop a barter system with a friend. Your friend takes your child or children for agreed times and you do something in return. You may be both fitting working hours into this arrangement. Some people take on job shares with the understanding that the person who is not working takes responsibility for the children from both families.

The advantage of this kind of arrangement is that your child care is free but, of course, your week is fully committed either to your paid work or to the shared child care. It is an arrangement that can work well if the children get on well together and do not mind being in either of the family homes. Young children do, however, sometimes become irritated or sad at always having to share you.

Think carefully about a friend caring for your child for nothing in return. This may work in an emergency until you have a longer term arrangement, but it is inequitable and may affect your friendship in the longer term. And remember if any form of payment passes between friends for child care, the arrangement may bring you under the requirements of the Children Act of 1989 (see p. 233).

Home-based help

If you want your children cared for at home, and none of the 'within-the-family' arrangements is possible, you will have to look for a nanny or an au pair.

The major advantage of home-based child care is that your children stay in their own home, which may be very important to them. You may also get some housework done for you, if you make that part of the agreement. The success of the arrangement depends

Making time to talk

For care within the family or with friends to work well, both parties involved need to make time for conversation. Although an arrangement of this kind is less formal than if you are employing someone or taking your child to a nursery or childminder, you still need to have reasonable consistency between the different people who are caring for a child.

It can be more difficult talking to a member of your family about how he or she is spending the day with your child, but you need to be as sure with a family member as you are with a nanny or nursery that your child is getting the love, care and stimulation that she needs.

It is also important that you and your child's carer are taking a similar line on such developments as toilet training, mealtimes or handling tantrums. The way Grandma brought up her children may not be exactly the way you want her to help bring up yours!

on whether you, your children and the carer get on well. Although a nanny or au pair may be very competent, you may find a clash of child-care style or temperament. You should also consider how tolerable or stressful you will find having someone living in your home, or at least spending long periods of every day there.

Nannies

Nannies are employed by you to take sole responsibility for your children in your home, for agreed hours and conditions. Some nannies have completed training in child care and, unless you are their first family, they will have some experience to offer. Less experienced or untrained carers used to be called mother's helps, but the dividing line has become blurred. It is still the case that the majority of nannies are female.

Employing a nanny is the most expensive form of home child care since you are paying for the exclusive use of a nanny's time for your family. You can try to reduce this by sharing a nanny with another family, but, if the nanny-share involves three or more

families, then the nanny must register with the local Social Services department, since she, or he, is judged to be working in the same way as a childminder (see p. 240) and must fulfil the same conditions.

Daily or live-in?

A nanny who leaves home to seek work at a distance will almost certainly want accommodation with the job, otherwise your choice will be based on the hours for which you need care. You will almost certainly need a live-in nanny if your working hours are long or erratic, or if you have business trips that take you away overnight. If you are a single parent, or if your partner has similar working conditions, then you will need total cover.

Cost

The wages that you should expect to pay vary according to where you live and are related to whether the local demand for nannies is outstripping the supply. Other families you know, who are currently employing nannies, or an agency specializing in matching families with nannies, should be able to give you an idea of the going rate in your area. If you choose to have a live-in nanny, you may pay less, but you must consider the cost of additional food and unpredictable items such as use of the telephone and, perhaps, the car.

You are the nanny's employer, so you will have to cover net wages, plus income tax and two kinds of national insurance – employee's and employer's. Some nannies used to operate as if they were self-employed, especially if they worked for more than one family, but the Inland Revenue no longer regards this as a grey area: nannies are definitely employees. Contact your local income tax office and ask for the New Employers' department. You will be sent a starter pack for small employers which will contain all the information and the forms that you need. If anything is not clear, contact the local tax office for advice. There is also a freephone line on National Insurance (see Useful Contacts, pp. 390–3).

In 1995, a daily nanny with experience would expect at least £200 a week in her hand (more in some areas, less if she were less experienced); this means that your outlay would be in the region of £330. A live-in nanny might expect around £130–£150, again with you paying tax and N.I.

Choosing a nanny

You can place an advertisement for a nanny in magazines such as *Nursery World* and *The Lady* which also have regular advertisements from people seeking such work and from agencies. An agency will find you someone for a fee. (If you use an agency, pick one by word of mouth and always ask how it vets its nannies, whether it checks their qualifications and so on.)

Always interview a prospective nanny, even if he or she has been found by an agency. Consider having your child with you: she may well have an opinion and you will also have an opportunity to see how the nanny reacts to your child. Do not feel uneasy about asking searching questions of any prospective carer. Do not feel grateful to have found anyone at all. (Mothers can be vulnerable to feeling that child care is a favour, since mothers are more likely than fathers to feel a mixture of emotions about whether they should be working at all.) When you interview a prospective nanny, cover the following areas.

Training and experience

Reliable courses in child care are the NNEB, the more recent NNEB–CACCE diploma, BTEC, NVQ and GNVQ in child care and education. This area is in a state of change so other courses may evolve. Someone holding one of these qualifications will have studied child development up to seven, play and learning and the ups and downs of being with children; she should have had practical experience in different settings. She may not have covered special needs. Always ask what the course involved. (Only private nursery colleges train specifically for nannying.) Ask a nanny to bring certificates to the interview and follow up references, preferably by phone.

Fitting in

You need to gain a reliable sense of how any nanny would relate to your child and to you. If you are going to be at home at the same time as the nanny, it is going to make life easier if you get along.

Your contract with a nanny

A working agreement should cover:
- Normal hours and extra duties, for which a nanny would get additional wages or time off in lieu. Live-in nannies in particular can get caught with being potentially on duty whenever they are in the house.
- Wages and when they are paid. It is the nanny's right to be paid in full and on time.
- Living conditions. A live-in nanny is joining your family and your home. She will, quite reasonably, expect her own room and full board. (A daily nanny should also have her meals as part of her normal day.) However, since a nanny is living in your home it is reasonable for you to set ground rules, when friends can visit, for example, and whether you are willing to have a partner sleep over.
- Notice. An agreed period of notice that either of you has to give in order to end the arrangement may be four weeks once the nanny is settled and you are happy, but make it a shorter period, perhaps a week, within the first month. If at any point you are seriously dissatisfied with a nanny,

pay her the notice period and tell her to go immediately – a disaffected nanny is a potential danger firstly to your child and also, perhaps, to your home.
- Activities and trips. You want your nanny to have initiative but it is preferable to discuss what your child's days will be like. A nanny's responsibility is to organize the day around your child. Trips out should be for your child's interest and enjoyment and any visiting must be focused on your child's enjoyment with other children, not your nanny's with other nannies.
- Consistency. You and your nanny must be consistent in your treatment of such issues as your child's behaviour or eating sweets. Changes like weaning or toilet training should also be joint decisions.
- Housework. Traditionally, nannies will only cook and clean for your child. If, however, there are times of the working day when all the children are out of the house, perhaps at nursery or playgroup, and you want her to do other domestic chores, discuss it with her.

Ask how she would organize a day, given the age of your children. Put a few common ups and downs of life with children to her – arguments over toys, not wanting a nap – and ask her what she would do.

The terms of the job

Make sure that the nanny knows and understands your terms, including wages, hours of work and any other important parts of the working day as you envisage it. Do not leave out any item that is central to the job you want done – such as the ability to drive, that the nanny is a non-smoker, or that you want a certain amount of evening babysitting.

Be clear about whether you want her to take sole charge for all her working hours or whether you, or your partner, will sometimes be in the home and want to spend time with your child.

Give her an opportunity to ask questions; if she looks doubtful or puzzled, ask her about it.

The contract

Organize at least a couple of days when you will be at home with the new nanny. This is your chance to show her the ropes and to discuss details of the arrangement now that she is in your employ. Then, to make misunderstandings less likely, finalize a contract. (You can get examples of contracts from Parents at Work, see Useful Contacts, pp. 390–3.)

Reviewing the arrangement

It is important to get your working relationship as clear as possible from the outset. Make a time to review how things are going after your nanny has been in the job a week or so. Apart from the regular conversations that should be a part of sharing care of children, you may need to have a definite discussion if your nanny is not working in the way that you want or expected. Some give and take is necessary in shared care but it would not, for example, be acceptable to find that a daily nanny took your child back to her own home each day or that a daily or live-in nanny organized trips around her own shopping, friends or leisure interests.

Once your child can talk, she will tell you honestly about what she thinks of a nanny and what they all do each day. Your child's opinion – volunteered or requested – will be an important source of information for you on any care arrangement.

Au pairs

A male or female au pair joins your family from abroad. In exchange for help with child care and some housework, you give the au pair board and lodging and regular payment to help with living costs. Those whose first language is not English may need time off for study. Technically, au pairs are aged between 18 and 27 and from Europe; if you employ anyone outside these limits, he or she is not legally an au pair.

An au pair is likely to be with you only for a year, so this form of child care inevitably involves change, which can be disruptive for children. However, some families find, for various reasons, that they have an equally high turnover of nannies or childminders.

Finding an au pair

To the extent that you have any choice in the person who joins your household as an au pair, you are balancing up the same issues as with nannies.

Decide first whether nationality is important: you may, for example, want an English speaker (someone who is bilingual rather than learning English), especially if your children are still in the early stages of learning to talk. If you are bilingual yourself, it will be an advantage to seek an au pair who shares one, if not both, of your languages and can support you in helping your children to grow up bilingual.

Contact the relevant embassy: you can get a number from Directory Enquiries. The embassy will give you the address of the organization that makes contacts for that country. This organization will also be experienced in the paperwork, such as visas. Alternatively, make contact with local networks abroad: your church or community association may have international links. Agencies (nanny or au pair) will make introductions for a fee, but they are only using the same channels that you can. A good agency may attempt a match between your family and the prospective au pairs, and then send you the details of several young people from whom to choose. An agency that offers this kind of service may be worth the fee to get you started with your first au pair.

Once you have had one happy relationship with an au pair, you may find that this contact leads to another. Your au pair may have a friend at home who would like the place or help you to contact a school or a community group in his or her area at home.

Setting up the arrangement

Since au pairs are essentially young people who want to spend a year in England they will not necessarily be experienced with children. For this reason an au pair is unlikely to be a good choice to care for a baby, if you wish to leave him or her in sole charge. Neither is an au pair likely to be suitable for a child with special needs.

Spend time with the au pair, explaining how you wish him or her to work with your children. And make your expectations clear on most of the issues that apply to nannies (see box on p. 238).

Cost

This varies, but in 1995 you could expect to pay around £40 a week for up to 25 hours' help with housework and child care, no more than five hours of which should be in any one day. You are responsible for his or her board and lodging, although au pairs are not liable to pay tax and National Insurance.

CARE OUTSIDE YOUR HOME

If you are seeking care outside your home, all your options will be registered and inspected by your local authority. The possibilities are individual care from childminders or group care in a day nursery or children's centre. Your local Social Services under-eights department will give you a list of registered minders and groups. It may also produce a booklet explaining the standards that the department expects of anyone who offers child care. (Childminders and nurseries are usually inspected yearly.) This material may give you some guidance on the kind of questions that it is sensible to ask a prospective carer.

The officers of the under-eights department will not make specific recommendations for a minder or a group unless your child has special needs which require additional experience or adapted surroundings.

Childminders

Childminders are people who take other families' children into their own home; sometimes a minder also has a child at home. The majority of registered childminders are women, although there are a few men and couples registered together. All childminders have limits on how many children they can take at any one time, so not all the local minders will have vacancies. Including his or her own children, minders can have only three children under the age of five, only one of whom can be less than 15 months.

There are several potential advantages in taking your child to a childminder. The arrangement is more personal and your child is with a relatively small number of children in a home setting. If your child likes the minder and the other children he or she looks after, this can be a happy form of child care. Your child has 'instant' friends and, for only children, this can be an excellent way of learning what siblings learn naturally: that some toys are for sharing; that babies need looking after; and so on.

The disadvantage is that if your child does not like either the minder or the other children, she does not have the same choice of others to play with that she would find in a group.

Nurseries and day-care centres

Any good nursery or centre will be organized so that children spend much of their time with a small group of children and relating to one, or two, members of staff. Your child should not be trying to make a relationship with many adults or other children. The aim of keeping groups small is also that staff and parents can get to know each other and have opportunities for conversations about the children.

There are many kinds of group care, not all of which will either be available or possible for your family:

Local authority day nurseries

In your area the Social Services department may run its own nurseries, which may be called children's centres or family centres. Although these nurseries may be open for a long day, it is very unlikely that they will offer places solely on the basis that a parent needs day care in order to work. Most local authority nurseries offer a place, which may be part-time, to families who are under stress or to children who need specific help with their development.

Private day nurseries

These are run as businesses, either on an individual basis or as part of a group. A nursery may follow a particular philosophy of care or early education, such

Is it working?

Child care inevitably involves making allowances for differences in style, but these should not be great, nor should your child be unhappy. If an arrangement does not seem to be working, as hard as it can be, you need to look at alternatives.

A good test of whether you should be concerned can be to imagine a friend describing to you what you are currently feeling or have seen going on at your child's minder's or the nursery. What would you advise your friend?

You know how difficult it was to find your child a place to begin with and are almost certainly weighed down with the worry of making alternative arrangements. If you were freed of this anxiety, what would you be saying to a friend? Would it be to think first of the child and take her out of this arrangement? Then do it!

as the Montessori method. Some private groups call themselves day nursery schools. This should mean that there are some qualified teachers on the staff and that an early years curriculum is followed, but check any written material and ask when you visit. If there are school-age children on the premises, a nursery will not be inspected by Social Services, but come under the jurisdiction of the DfEE (see pp. 234–5).

Community nurseries

Community nurseries or centres are usually set up by a children's charity or as a joint enterprise between a children's organization and the local authority. Such nurseries usually offer places to local families.

Workplace nurseries

Some companies or large organizations have established on-site nurseries or made arrangements for places with local private day nurseries. These nurseries help employees who could not accept a job without reliable child care. A place in a workplace nursery will be tied to your job, so bear that in mind if you are not sure about the job in the first place.

After-school and holiday clubs

Once your children are of primary school age, check if your area has schemes for children after school and in school holidays. Some schools offer this facility on site, others have arrangements with clubs that pick up the children from school and take responsibility for them until you pick them up at an agreed time. In some cases you must put your child's name down in advance for a place on a holiday scheme, others operate on an open-access policy. Schemes offer a range of activities and are run in different locations – schools, parks, leisure centres and so on.

Any after-school club or scheme that takes under eights for more than two hours daily must be registered and inspected by the local Social Services department.

Be prepared: in some areas, virtually nothing of this kind of care for over fives exists.

Other groups or centres

State nursery schools or classes, private nursery classes and many playgroups are not set up with the objective of providing child care. They are offering children a preschool experience with the result that unless you work part-time hours that conveniently fit a playgroup or nursery school session or day, these groups will not in themselves offer the child care you need. Even if they do, you will still need cover during the holidays (nurseries and playgroups often take school holidays). Such groups may fit your arrangements if someone else takes your child to and fro and covers the hours that you are at work, plus school holidays.

Deciding on care outside your home

Visit any childminder or group and make your own decision. Try to take your child with you and, if you have more than one potential choice, visit them all. Your priority should be to discover whether the kind and style of child care will suit you and your child. A responsible minder or group leader will be open with you about the general pattern of their days with children and the extent to which they can, or cannot, be flexible to specific requests.

During your visit, and in looking at anything written that is given to you, you need answers to the following kinds of questions:

Cost

How much will your child's place cost? Minders' fees vary around the country; the cost of a place in a nursery depends on the extent to which it is subsidized or has to make a profit. You also need to know what happens about payment if your child does not attend, for instance, if you are on holiday. Since neither a minder nor a group can slot another child temporarily into your child's place, it is likely that you will have to pay something to hold the place, probably half or perhaps even full fees (ask the Social Services department what is normal in your area). In 1995, minders' fees were £55 to £85 per week per child; nurseries anything between £70 and £125 per week (ask what is included in the fees since low fees may mean restricted hours).

You are not a childminder's employer. You pay the agreed fees, but childminders deal with their own tax and National Insurance since they are self-employed.

Notice to end the arrangement

It is unreasonable for either a parent or a minder, or a group for that matter, to give only days' notice. Check what is expected by both a minder and group.

What will your child be offered?

What do childminders do with the children? A minder should organize her day around them; they should not take second place to her domestic routines. A good minder will take account of the ages and interests of the children in her care.

What plans and programmes does a group offer? Although any group worker should also be flexible to the children, you can expect a nursery to have some clear plans for each day and the pattern of a week. Look for a range of activities that includes some quiet play but also physical games and the chance to run around in a safe outdoor space. Are trips regularly offered – to the local park? the market? the library?

What toys are available?

What kinds of toys and equipment are available in the minder's home or laid out in the group? What can you see that is stored away and when does it come out? Are there signs of children's work around: paintings fixed to the wall or on a minder's fridge? Lego models or playdough figures left on display to be admired?

Ideally visit a minder or nursery at a time when other children are present. Do the children there at the moment look happy? What are they doing? How are any adults spending time with them? How does the minder balance up her conversation with you and

attention to other children, including to your own? What kind of indoor and outdoor play space is there? How safe does it look?

How are the children treated?

How does the minder or the group leader react to your questions on common dilemmas? You want a sense of how they deal with the ups and downs of time with children. Does the minder or group worker ask about your child and what she might like or enjoy? How has your child reacted to the minder and her home, or to the nursery or play scheme?

How have you been treated?

Were you welcome? Were you given answers to your questions in an open and friendly way? Minders and groups cannot agree to change their way of working for one parent, but they should be flexible to family preferences. Overall, do you get the impression that you will be able to have a conversation in the future about your child and how everything is going?

Settling in

Settle your child into an arrangement as well as you can. A childminder should be willing to invite you to part of her day or to have your child start with a couple of shorter sessions. A group should be flexible, since its aim is to settle new children calmly.

Some minders and groups have an agreement to go through with each parent. Such agreements or contracts lay out what is expected of you and what you can expect of them. The pattern of rights and responsibilities should be reasonably equitable, not one-sided. Read any agreement carefully before you sign and ask any questions you wish. In order to retain her registration a minder will need your work telephone number so that you can be reached easily if your child has an accident or becomes ill. A group will also need this. When your child starts, you should also cover:

- the name and address of your child's doctor
- any childhood diseases that your child has had and a record of vaccinations
- any individual health conditions that mean that your child needs either special care, adjustments to her diet or the circumstances under which you must be called

Discipline

In December 1994, the Department of Health stated that childminders should not normally smack children, but that parents could give a minder (but not staff in a nursery or other group) written permission to smack 'as a last resort'. Even if you agree with smacking, think carefully about giving such permission which could then be applied under circumstances of which you would not approve.

- personal information: correct pronunciation of her name, or any shortened form by which she is known; whether she has a comfort blanket or her teddy when she goes for a nap; and so on.

Reviewing the arrangement

Once you have made your decision and your arrangement has started, be alert to your child's feelings. If possible, talk with her about her time with her carer. If she is used to communicating with you, she will give you her opinion and tell you about her day, even if she does not yet have large numbers of words. If you talk with your child, you will help her to make the link between her child-care setting and her life at home. You show that you are interested and care very much about what happens while you are apart. You will also pick up on anything that might concern you.

A period of settling in is inevitable but do not carry on with any group or individual who is not offering good care to your child. Try to weigh up whether your child's complaint or unhappiness is a temporary matter – an argument with one of the other children over a toy, for example. Take seriously any continuing concerns and raise them with a minder or the group worker who is responsible for your child.

If your child spends a lot of time with another person – whether that is an individual childminder or nanny, or in a group – you have to accept that she will be influenced by the other people. The effects can be positive in that children are learning that not every adult behaves in exactly the same way and adults all have different interests and skills. Yet it is

Many playgroups follow a nursery-school approach with children working on a specific theme and several activities geared to that theme.

Vouchers for nursery education

Pilot tests are due to run in April 1996, with a view to the introduction in April 1997 of a voucher system for nursery education. It is proposed to give every parent of a four-year-old child a voucher worth £1,100 to spend at an approved (private) establishment offering preschool education. The voucher can be 'topped up' by parents if it does not cover the full cost of fees. The system will benefit those parents who wish to educate their children outside the state system, as well as those who live in areas where state provision is patchy or non existent.

important that all the key adults in a child's life work together in a consistent way on key issues and do not complain about other adults' styles in front of children. Talk with your child's carer if there seem to be differences in your approaches to sweets and crisps consumption, for example, or acceptable table manners.

It is reasonable to expect a carer to acknowledge your family's religious beliefs, or lack of commitment to any faith, and not impose other views on your child. Many groups introduce children to some aspects of a range of world faiths, through festivals and stories, but this is undertaken with respect for all the faiths.

Time with your child

Life can be very demanding if you are a parent who is a full-time homemaker. If you have a paid job on top of your family responsibilities, then you may have a limited amount of time to spend with your child. It is important to use whatever time you do have to give your child your full attention when you are home together. Different patterns work better for different people but the following ideas are a good guide:

- Try to have a space between coming home from work and any home responsibilities and make this time available to your child. You can be guided by your child and what she would like. She may not want to play, but simply to be with you.
- If you are tired, activities that involve sitting down may be best. Look at books together, or watch your child's favourite programme, or video. Just sit and be together.
- On pleasant days and light evenings go for a walk together, or to the local park. You can talk and enjoy the sights without being tempted to start the evening meal or fret over the bills that have arrived.
- If you cook the evening meal, have your kitchen organized so that your child can be with you. Talk together about your respective days. Most working days produce something of interest to a child.
- Don't get into the habit of bringing something home for your children from work or business trips. It is better if, tired as you may be, you give children your time and attention. Presents or sweets are not substitutes for your presence and will soon be expected as a matter of right, with only the absence of anything special being noticed.

When you are short on time, play games and introduce activities that your child does not do with whoever looks after her in your absence. Then, whatever you do will be special, marked by a cuddle that says, 'I'm so pleased to see you.' Children often like homecoming rituals – perhaps she picks up the mail, chooses the vegetables for dinner, or puts fresh milk in the cat's bowl.

PRESCHOOL ACTIVITIES

There are a range of facilities that offer children the opportunity to interact with others before they reach the age at which they start primary school.

State nursery schools and classes

A nursery school is a separate entity from a primary school, while a nursery class is part of a primary school. Both offer a similar curriculum. Places in state nursery schools or classes are free and your local education department will give you information. Alternatively, telephone the nearest schools or classes and talk with the head teacher. Find out the procedure for getting your child's name down well before she is old enough. A state nursery is unlikely to take a child who is less than three years and in some areas children may be close to four. Most offer half-day places (two to three hours), perhaps extended to a whole school day in the last term before your child enters the reception class of the primary school.

Provision varies widely and nursery places may be restricted. Find out what the priorities are in your area: sometimes children with special needs are given priority; local residents may be close to the top of the list; and so on. It is reasonable to want to choose which school or class you would like your child to attend but be realistic. If priority is given to local residents, it is probably not worth applying to a school that is miles away (or be prepared to be turned down).

The emphasis in nurseries is on learning through play. The staff will have a plan for what they offer to the children and a variety of activities within each session. The aim of an early years curriculum is for children to extend their skills and knowledge in all aspects of their development. In the broadest sense they are being prepared for school. Children are not usually taught specifically to read, write and do number work. But the activities that they are offered and the help that the staff provide can be effective in building up the skills that must be in place before a child can read, write or understand numbers.

Private nursery schools

The choice in private education extends to the nursery age group. You pay fees for a private nursery place and the cost varies. Find out the individual details of any nursery school – the age that they will accept children, the size of the school, whether it prepares children for a particular preparatory school, the length of the daily sessions and the school term.

The curriculum followed by private nursery schools varies according to the philosophy of the school and head. Some have a learning through play approach that is similar to state nurseries, some opt for a more formal curriculum with emphasis on literacy and numeracy skills. Others may follow a specific educational philosophy.

Playgroups

The playgroup movement developed as a response to the lack of nursery education. Playgroups are now established as a form of preschool provision and many are affiliated to the Preschool Learning Alliance (PLA). They are now sometimes known as preschools, but not all operate in the same way.

Most charge a fee per session, which is usually low, but bear in mind that over a ten-week term two or three sessions a week can mount up. Groups tend to be run on a sessional basis and some have no facilities for offering anything more than a simple snack. Groups that can offer lunch may have some full day places, with hours rather like a nursery school. There will be some permanent playgroup staff but many groups are dependent on parents' commitment to help in the group on a rota basis. Children usually have to be at least three years old to attend and it is worth finding out in advance what the enrolment procedure is: some playgroups are better than others and you may have to wait for a place.

The playgroup movement has a learning through play approach and some groups offer a daily programme that is very similar to a nursery school curriculum. When the playgroup movement started, a strong part of the philosophy was that parents had a great deal to offer and should be involved in their children's preschool experience. Although this was a novel philosophy in the 1960s, schools have changed tremendously in the subsequent decades and you will probably find less of a contrast today between playgroups and nursery schools.

Choosing a preschool group

Any choice that you make will be shaped by what, exactly, is on offer in your area and then by any vacancies. Since some have long waiting lists, it is sensible to make enquiries at least a year before you would ideally like a place. Talk to other parents with older children, and find out their opinions and information about the ease, or not, of getting your child into a particular group.

Once you have some ideas, visit possible nursery schools or playgroups with your child. If your child's friends are attending, or about to attend a group, she may want to go as well. If you want your child to go to a particular primary school then it would be wise, although not essential, to get her into the nursery class, if there is one (a place in the nursery class does not necessarily guarantee your child a place at the school, so check this too).

Apart from gaining any practical information you need, look and listen, so that you have a feel of the place and people.

Cost

What are the fees, if any? Are parents expected to provide their children with any special clothing, uniform or equipment? Will you have to offer your time on a rota to help out as a condition of a place?

What activities are on offer?

What kind of programme does this group set out to offer and what seems to happen in practice? A plan, or a curriculum layout, can look good on paper but is worthless if staff lack the enthusiasm to bring it alive. Alternatively, a rather general outline can be delivered with energy and lots of attention to each child.

What is the overall feel of the group?

Is it calm without being over-controlled? Do the children – both those on the climbing equipment and those painting quietly – look happy? Do the adults look involved? Is the children's work on display?

What qualifications do the staff have?

State nursery schools and classes have qualified teachers, usually supported by nursery assistants who may have the NNEB certificate. Play-groups should have one adult with the PLA leader qualification. Private nursery

schools should have some trained teachers and some staff with child-care qualifications and experience.

What are the group's aims and policies?

A responsible and effective preschool group will have ideas not only on the programme of activities or early years curriculum, but also on its overall philosophy. Ask the group leader or the member of staff who shows you around to give coherent answers to your questions about how they handle children's behaviour and in what ways they keep in contact with parents. Many produce newsletters to keep you in touch with what they are doing with the children, and give details of forthcoming outings, and so on.

What does your child think?

Children vary in temperament so your child may not actually want to join in any of the activities on offer during your visit. What does she say later? How do the staff react to her? Do they talk to her?

Try to spend a little time with your child when you get home from work. Coming-home routines can be very special times to relax with your child.

Settling in

You can help to prepare your child to join a preschool group and, if you think broadly, you may realize that you have already done a lot of groundwork. If you have already given your child experience of time away from you, this will help but will not always smooth the way completely. Ideally coach your child in the ability to take care of herself. Review what she can already do and where she needs more help. In any preschool group no worker should get irritated at being asked for help. Three- and four-year olds are not yet fully competent.

- Can she manage her own clothes and shoes? If some clothes are harder to do up, perhaps she should not wear them to the group initially.
- Can she manage in the toilet – actually going to the toilet, getting clothes up and down and washing hands afterward?
- Is she confident to ask for help if she needs it, not only for her own care but in her play?
- Is she used to dealing with other children?
  A responsible preschool group will suggest ways in which you can help to ease your child into the group. Perhaps initially they may want you to stay with your child or suggest that she attend a couple of short sessions to begin with. No group should be inflexible about this, since children vary. A young child who knows a group from visiting to drop off an older sibling may well be counting the days until this is her group too. She may wave you goodbye with a flourish within five minutes. Another child may be extremely wary and need careful settling over several weeks. Some children are keen on the idea of playgroup or nursery until they realize that you are going to leave. It may be a very welcoming group but at the moment your child would rather you stayed. Playgroup and nursery staff are experienced in comforting children who are temporarily upset and should give priority to a cuddle for new arrivals.

You may decide, with the agreement of a worker, that after a long attempt to settle your child, you will say an affectionate and firm goodbye and leave, even if your child cries. All parents find this hard but you may decide it is necessary. It is unwise to simply slip out without saying goodbye to your child – this will shake her trust in you.

THE IMPORTANCE OF HOME

Some aspects of group life will not make sense to your child until she has attended a playgroup or nursery. She may need to learn that adults have to share themselves out and that part of group life is waiting for attention and accepting that her idea for a book or a song will not always be the one taken up.

Your child will be coming into contact with other children whose approach to play or conflict may not be your family's way. If the situation sounds out of hand to you, or your child seems distressed, talk to a member of staff. Your child should not be hit or bitten by another child, but remember that some things would happen even if you were there. It is reasonable for you to be told about accidents when you pick your child up, not find scrapes and bruises later.

Changes for you

You may be excited that your child is going to a preschool group, yet also find yourself feeling sad. The preschool experience is a broadening of your child's horizons, more evidence of the changing of your relationship and your place in her life.

If she settles quickly and with few tears, part of you will be relieved. Yet parents usually admit that they want the best of both worlds – a child who seems happy to spend time without you, but misses you while she is doing so and is pleased to see you again. Be pleased for your child and show interest in what she has done, but do not feel that the value of her group means that you are no longer important.

Your child may enjoy playgroup and look back in later years with nostalgia to her time at nursery, but time there does pass: home and family provide her continuity. You are your child's first playmate – the person she will stare at and try to grab, the person whom she will copy and want to make smile. You will get to know your child with a knowledge that will never be equalled by anybody else who passes through her life and that knowledge will help you to support her as she builds one skill upon another and adds today's discoveries to what she worked out yesterday. You will still be her parent, her continuity and the one who is there for her, when nannies, minders or nurseries are a memory. Your aim should be to help make that memory a happy one.

CHAPTER TEN

Healthy Eating

Parents are rightly concerned about the quality and
sometimes quantity of food their young children eat.
Good food habits from the start can help to avoid
problems later on, but most preschool
children go through a fussy
phase of sorts. Try to keep it
all in perspective – by the time
they start school, the majority
of children are happy with a
variety of foods and those that
are not are still almost certainly
contented and healthy.

Feeding your preschool child

For the first year of a child's life, food is an important fuel. Between the ages of 12 months and five years, children are developing very quickly, although the rate at which they grow slows down around 18 months. Once growth begins to slow, appetites may wane; this, combined with fussy eating and food fads, may make it seem as if they are barely eating enough to keep a sparrow alive! You will probably worry that they are not getting the correct balance of nutrients necessary for good health and growth, but this rarely happens. All of the important nutrients are available in a wide variety of foods, so it is highly unlikely that your child will become deficient or malnourished.

EATING FOR HEALTH

Good food habits should be encouraged as early as possible but it is a mistake to apply healthy eating principles too stringently to under-fives. Young children have small stomachs and appetites and need fat and carbohydrate for energy and protein for growth. A diet which is too low in fat or high in fibre makes it difficult for them to eat enough food to meet their requirements. Diets which contain too much fibre can cause loose bowel movements and the fibre may interfere with the absorption of some minerals. Include some high-fibre, low-fat products in your child's diet but being too strict at this age can lead to problems.

What makes a balanced diet?

Offering a variety of foods will help ensure that your child receives a balanced diet. Make sure that an item from each of the four main food groups is offered throughout the day. A recommended number of servings from each group is given below. The word serving refers to an average-sized child's portion, and

you will soon learn how much your child is able or willing to eat at a single meal.

Bread, rice, cereals, pasta, potatoes

Starchy foods (carbohydrates) should make up the bulk of your child's diet. They are low in fat and are usually a good source of other important nutrients such as vitamins and minerals. The wholemeal or wholegrain types such as wholemeal bread or brown rice provide dietary fibre.

Aim for 4–5 servings a day to satisfy appetite

Mealtime suggestions: Breakfast cereal; mashed potatoes with lunch; toast for tea; pasta for supper.

Fruit and vegetables

Fruit and vegetables (fresh, frozen, canned or dried) provide vitamins A, C and from the B group, dietary fibre, plus some carbohydrates and natural fruit sugar.

It is not always easy to persuade children to eat vegetables, although most children will accept at least one type of fruit. Concentrate on those they will eat rather than trying to force them to eat those they dislike. This will just lead to a battle of wills, and in some cases, genuine distress. Children often prefer raw vegetables to cooked, which is not a problem since cooking can destroy some of the vitamins, especially vitamin C. You can disguise some vegetables by adding them to other dishes – parsnip or swede can be puréed with mashed potato, vegetables can be made into soup or incorporated into popular dishes such as spaghetti bolognese or cottage pie. Canned vegetables often contain added sugar, so check the label if this worries you.

Fresh fruit is a very good 'between-meals' snack and if your child has an aversion to green vegetables, give fruit instead. Dried fruit is nutritious, but it is a concentrated form of sugar and can be damaging to teeth, so give as part of a meal rather than as a snack.

Avoiding obesity

Most Western babies are plump. They have fat tummies, chubby cheeks and plump legs. Some are plumper than average and a small percentage are obese. Allowing your baby to put on too much weight predisposes him to obesity, and obesity – whenever it occurs – predisposes to later obesity. This is because most of the fat storage cells in the body are made in the first years of life. They can be filled (and emptied) at any time but even when empty the cells do not disappear. Allowing a baby to put on too much weight encourages the production of extra fat cells which will stay with him for the rest of his life, waiting to be refilled.

Do not:
- add sugar
- force food on a child who clearly does not want to eat
- offer food for 'comfort' – cuddles are better than biscuits
- give your child the message 'eat this to please Mummy' or 'Daddy' or 'Grandma'
- praise him for eating it all up
- use sweets or canned fizzy drinks as rewards, or as substitutes for your time, attention or involvement in his play

Fat children tend to have fat parents. There is a 7 per cent chance of a child being fat if neither parent is fat, 40 per cent if one parent is fat and 80 per cent if both parents are fat. If you come from a family which has many plump members, the best you may be able to do is to keep weight gain within certain limits.

Of course you do not want your child to be obese, but there are major health risks from severe dieting in childhood and at puberty: some children are anorexic before they leave primary school. The best advice is to be careful with your child's diet without being obsessive.

- fry food which could easily be cooked without added fat
- give lots of cereal
- make sweets and crisps 'special' by banning them

Do:
- use raw vegetables or pieces of apple as snacks
- ration sweets/cakes for all the family
- give fruit rather than puddings
- encourage boisterous games
- active things together such as swimming or going to the baby gym

Aim for 4–5 servings a day.
Mealtime suggestions: Banana cut up in breakfast cereal; an apple or orange cut into pieces or segments after lunch; dried fruit added to cake or biscuit recipes at teatime; puréed soft fruit added to plain yogurt for supper.

Meat, poultry, fish, eggs, pulses, nuts, tofu
These are protein foods which provide the building blocks for growth. They provide B vitamins and minerals (iron, zinc and magnesium) and some fat, especially animal products. Pulses (lentils, peas, beans) and nuts are protein-rich but do not give whole nuts to under-fives because of the risk of choking.
Aim for 1–2 servings a day.
Mealtime suggestions: Meat or fish at lunchtime; baked beans or an egg for supper.

Dairy products
Milk, cheese and yogurts provide protein, calcium for teeth and bones, and vitamins B12, A and D. Providing your child has a good appetite, you can introduce semi-skimmed milk after the age of two and skimmed milk from the age of five.
Aim for 3 servings a day
Mealtime suggestions: Milk with cereal for breakfast; a yogurt flavoured with honey after lunch; cheese on toast (Welsh rarebit) for supper.

Fat
Fats are an important source of energy for young children, so do not restrict them too severely. But do include some reduced fat products such as low-fat yogurt in your child's diet. You can use low-fat spreads and cheeses too.

It is worth looking at the amount of fat used in all the family's meals and trying to cut down. There are many foods, such as biscuits, crisps and processed meats, which contain a lot of hidden fat. Check the nutritional value labelling on manufactured foods – even those from the chill cabinet. Too much fat at this stage of life could have long-term health implications. If your child is very energetic, let him fill up on carbohydrates like wholemeal bread, pasta, rice or potatoes – boiled or baked, rather than chips!

Sugar and salt

A high intake of sugar and other refined carbohydrates has been linked with tooth decay (see pp. 128–9). It is not necessary to cut it out completely, but it makes sense to keep intake to a minimum. Remember that glucose, dextrose, fructose, sucrose and maltose syrup are all forms of sugar.

It is not a good idea to add salt to food since salt occurs naturally in a wide variety of foods. As long as your child is eating a varied diet, he will get all the salt he needs without adding any extra to food.

Food additives

In recent years there has been a great deal of controversy about the safety and effects of various food additives (E numbers). All additives permitted in Britain have undergone thorough testing and safety evaluation so that it is not necessary to avoid additives completely, but it does make sense to reduce their intake as much as possible. Since most additives are added to processed foods, and these are the same foods that are often high in fat, salt or sugar (or all three), do not to eat such foods regularly.

Children may develop an allergy to a specific additive or a group of additives, but this is very rare. If you think your child may be allergic to additives discuss the matter with your health visitor.

Vitamins and minerals

From six months of age until he is two, you should give your child the vitamin drops supplied by your baby clinic or health visitor. After the age of two, providing his appetite is good and he is eating a mixed and varied diet, he should be able to get all the vitamins he needs from the food he consumes. If he has a poor appetite it is advisable to continue with the drops until he is five. Never give your child vitamin supplements in addition to those recommended by your health visitor or doctor, since there is a real danger of overdosing.

A few years ago one or two studies suggested that giving children extra vitamins could help improve their IQ. These reports have now been largely discredited by nutritionists. Vitamin supplements should never be seen as a substitute for a healthy diet, but if your child is excessively 'picky' and you feel that he may not be getting all the vitamins and minerals and other essential nutrients he needs, discuss the matter with your health visitor or family doctor before giving any supplements.

Hyperactivity

True hyperactivity is much less rare than many parents suppose. A truly hyperactive child is unable to concentrate on anything for long – even the things he enjoys. Children who are seriously affected should be referred to a clinical psychologist or a paediatrician for diagnosis. If food is thought to be contributing to the problem, an exclusion diet may be recommended. Always seek medical advice before you severely restrict your child's diet. The most common offenders are:

- **Artificial colours (Azo dyes)**
  These include tartrazine (E102), quinoline yellow (E104), yellow (2G E107), sunset yellow (E110), reds (E122–129), patient blue V (E131), indigo carmine (E132), brilliant blue (E133), green S (E142), black PN (E151), brown FK (E154), brown HT (155), pigment rubine (E180).
- **Natural colours**
  Annatto (E160b)
- **Preservatives**
  These include benzoates (E210–213), sulphites (E220–228), nitrates and nitrites (E249–252), antioxidants (E310–321).
- **Flavour enhancers**
  Glutamate (E621–623u)
- **Flour improvers**
  Bleaches (E924–926)

FAMILY MEALTIMES

By the age of one, your child will be able to eat the same food as the rest of the family, suitably chopped up, and his mealtimes can be adjusted to suit those of the rest of the family, especially during the day. If you generally have a meal quite late in the evening, you will probably find your child continues to have an earlier meal for some years.

Allowing your baby or toddler to join family meals is an important stage in his social development. These are a time for communication and sharing and a good opportunity for children to learn social skills. It takes some time for them to develop the manual dexterity to use cutlery so be prepared for disruption and mess, but try not to let this worry you. Bring his high chair close to the table where you can help feed him and clear up any mess quickly. Later on use a fixed booster seat on an ordinary chair, or a high chair without a tray to bring your child level with the table top.

Fussy eaters

As children get older and more independent it is not unusual to start refusing to eat certain foods, often those that were favourite only a short time ago. And they quickly realize that refusing food is a good way of gaining attention. Although it is difficult not to be concerned when your child refuses his dinner, be reassured that food fads are only a passing phase.

Family mealtimes can be relaxing, social occasions.

What you can do

- Don't allow mealtimes to turn into a battle of wills – you will both end up frustrated and unhappy.
- Never bribe or force a child to eat or coerce him into eating. If your child refuses a certain food or meal clear it away without comment, but don't let him fill up on snacks or drinks, other than water, between meals.
- Children often make a fuss about food as a way of gaining attention, so try not to let your child see that you are worried or angry if he does not eat.
- Never use food as a punishment, bribe, reward or threat – this could cause eating problems later.
- Coaxing is likely to make the problem worse and may take away what little appetite he does have.
- If you know your child is going through a picky stage, don't spend large amounts of time (or money) preparing special meals. The more time and trouble you spend preparing the meal the more frustrating it will be for you if he rejects it. Concentrate on food that is simple and quick to prepare – he is rejecting the food, not you.
- Try putting less food on your child's plate. Children often find a big pile of food intimidating. It is much better that your child eats a small amount rather than nothing at all.

- Make sure that your child is not filling up with too much fluid between meals. Do not give drinks, other than water, for an hour before meals, and at mealtimes offer drinks when the food is finished.
- Peer group pressure can influence an older toddler's likes and dislikes. Invite friends who are not picky eaters round for meals. This also helps to take the focus away from food.
- Children often pick up bad eating habits from other members of their family. Discourage older siblings from being fussy, because younger children will often mimic their behaviour, and make sure your own eating habits are setting a good example.

Making food fun

There are some things that your child may never eat, but do not be afraid to make food fun. It takes only minutes to prepare food in a way that a child may accept, and you may be instilling good habits for life.

Food should be interesting and attractive and have a variety of textures, shapes and colours.

- Allow children to get involved in shopping for food, choosing menus and food preparation. Let them help in the kitchen with jobs like sifting flour, beating eggs, rolling out pastry and so on.

An interest in food preparation

Children who are still at the helpful phase of their development may well want to help you in the kitchen. They are also more likely to eat dishes they have prepared for themselves. This does not necessarily have to involve heat, or inordinate amounts of time when you are trying to feed the rest of the family or several of his friends.

Even quite small children enjoy mashing, and as they get older can easily spoon sandwich fillings on to bread, and perhaps decorate their efforts.

Hair, eyes, nose and mouth can all be cut from food and used to make faces.

- When the weather permits, pack up a picnic to take to the park or eat tea in the garden.
- Compromise is often the best policy. Mix the sugar-laden breakfast cereal your children want with something a little healthier; make sandwiches of one slice of white bread and one of wholemeal.
- Make meals a social occasion. If you cannot invite friends round and family members are absent, have a party with the teddies and stuffed animals.
- Make food fun: invent silly names for dishes; make up stories about food or meals.

- Use fruit or vegetables – apples, oranges, bananas, carrots, tomatoes, cucumber – to make faces on food and let your child eat them with his fingers.
- Young children often like small, individual portions, so choose a mini bread roll, cherry tomatoes, mini cheeses, a small box of raisins, and so on.
- Use a sharp knife or pastry cutter to cut out shapes from toast, sandwiches, cheese or vegetables.
- Soups may be more popular than vegetables. Cook lightly in their own stock, then liquidize so the main nutrients are preserved.

Animal-shaped biscuit cutters make fun open, toasted and conventional sandwiches. Top or fill with soft cheese, tuna, taramasalata, egg and any other of your child's favourites. Make cucumber fins, snip chives for whiskers and use pieces of olive and spring onion for eyes.

CHAPTER ELEVEN

Schooldays

Your big girl suddenly looks very vulnerable as she stands in the school playground, but starting school is an exciting experience for young children, one which, regardless of your pangs, it is important to share. The years between five and ten are when children make – and break – friends, and learn about themselves and the world around them. With your support, your child will grow in knowledge and confidence in these important years.

Out into the world

The years between five and ten have a special quality for children and for you, their parents. Children in this age group have grown beyond the physical dependence of infancy, but they still need, and generally like and respect, your support and guidance. In these years, they tend to take to heart the attitudes and orientation to life that they informally absorb from you, the rest of their family, their school and community, although they may challenge or reject these attitudes in adolescence.

Five- to ten-year-olds are largely uncomplicated. They delight in their progress and achievements, and enjoy their friendships and leisure time. Most are happy at school, mastering reading, writing and numeracy, in addition to joining in a wide range of educational and cultural activities which bring the curriculum to life, and broaden their mental horizons.

Options in education

In Britain education is compulsory for all children between the ages of five and 16. More than 90 per cent of children are educated in the country's state-maintained primary and secondary schools. Slightly more than seven per cent attend independent schools. If you are thinking of educating your children in independent schools, contact the Independent Schools Information Service (ISIS) – see Useful Contacts, pp. 390–3 – for information and advice.

Under the provision of the 1944 Education Act, which allows for children to be educated by 'attendance at school or otherwise', a small but growing number of children are now educated outside the school system by their parents or by tutors. For information and advice, contact the self-help group Education Otherwise.

Given a loving and stable environment, their lives at this age can be substantially stress free. The important GCSE public examinations are some years away, and sensible parents ensure that hobbies, sports and leisure interests are pleasurable and enriching, rather than sources of unnecessary anxiety or pressure. Sandwiched between the charms but limitations of infancy, and the traditional anxieties of adolescence, the years between five and ten are a precious time for your children and for you.

OFF TO SCHOOL

In some areas, your four-year-old may be offered a place in a special nursery class attached to the primary school she will attend. Elsewhere it is common for children to start school in the term in which their fifth birthday falls, so that a child with a February birthday may start school in January, one born in May will start after Easter. Policy between schools and areas varies, depending on resources and on the number of children in the age group who must be accommodated. In some cases, there may only be one or two entry dates a year, so it is worth checking in advance what is normal for your area. You are not obliged to send your child to school until she is five and, indeed, there is evidence to suggest that children with summer birthdays, who start school as the youngest in their year (perhaps as soon as a couple of weeks after their fourth birthday), may be at an educational disadvantage. If you feel your child is not ready for school, think about delaying her entry.

Starting school is always a significant step for children and their parents, no matter what type of school you choose and when your child starts. Not only is it the first step on the ladder of compulsory education, but children also have to adapt to a situation in which, instead of being one among a few other people in a family, they are one among many others. They must learn to cope with a large building, peopled mainly by children larger than themselves, and by a smaller number of, initially, unknown adults. And you have to learn to 'share' your child, to accept the influence of others, and to enter into a 'partnership' of rights and responsibilities with the school.

If you have not been inside an infant department since you were a pupil yourself, you will immediately notice that most schools today are more sensitive to the needs of their youngest pupils. The atmosphere is open and welcoming, and there is less sense of mystery as to what actually happens in the classroom. Both state-maintained and independent schools now produce prospectuses, which explain policies and procedures, as well as setting out information about the school's results in national tests, and rates of unauthorized absence, or truancy. The prospectus will give you a 'flavour' of the school by setting out its aims and values, explaining its approach to moral and spiritual education, to sex education, and to how it deals with the needs of its academically able children and those with learning difficulties.

If you are the parent of a reception (a class for children who are not yet five, but who will have their fifth birthday during the academic year) or Year One child (or of older children new to the school) you should receive a booklet or information sheet giving practical information about such matters as uniform and lunchtime arrangements. This may also explain what your child will be doing in the first few weeks, how she will learn to form letters, and the reading and maths scheme(s) used by the school. You and your child should also have the opportunity to look around the school and meet her teacher before she begins to attend regularly.

For most children, the period of adjustment – of 'children' learning to be 'pupils' – is not difficult. The majority of four- and five-year-olds are proud of their new status and adapt to the school routine within weeks, whether you have prepared them well or not. But their path is eased if you have taken some care, in the months leading up to school, to get them used to being in the company of other children and to the sorts of situations they may meet at school. It is sometimes helpful to think of preschool preparation, and settling into school, as having two, complementary, aspects.

The National Curriculum

All state primary schools (except in Scotland) follow the National Curriculum. The subjects studied at primary level are: English, maths, science, technology, history, geography, music, art, physical and religious education. These subjects should take 80 per cent of the school week; the remaining time is for 'non-curricular' activities, which the school is free to choose. Children who have a statement of special educational needs (see pp. 284–7) may follow a curriculum designed in accordance with their needs. Children are divided into year groups (unless the school is very small), and the National Curriculum is divided into 'Key Stages':

Key Stage 1
Year 1 (age 5/6)
Year 2 (age 6/7)
Key Stage 1 tests in reading, writing, handwriting, spelling and maths

Key Stage 2
Year 3 (age 7/8)
Year 4 (age 8/9)
Year 5 (age 9/10)
Year 6 (age 10/11)
Key Stage 2 tests in maths, English and science

Scottish children attend primary school from 5 to 12, and follow a programme of study based on five areas: language, maths, environmental studies, expressive arts and religious (including moral) education. There is a broad consensus over what is taught but responsibility rests with education authorities and individual schools. A system of national testing is used, with tests taken when a teacher considers a child has completed the work at one level and is ready to move to the next.

The social side of school

In any explanation of the sorts of 'educational' activities your child can expect at school – learning to read, write and work with numbers, for example – it is easy to underestimate the demands of the more practical, social side of school life. Some five-year-olds are understandably worried by the noise and bustle of cloakrooms and playgrounds. Others dislike using the toilets on their own, or find the hall or the dining room intimidating. First-born and only children, in particular, are dismayed by the 'uncivilized' behaviour of their classmates. If you have been accustomed to adults who say 'please' and 'thank you', who do not snatch your pencil or skipping rope, or push roughly past you, it comes as a shock to meet children who do.

Encourage mixing

Ensure that your child has had and continues to have opportunities to mix with children of her own age. If your child is your first born, or is an only child, you may have to make a conscious effort to ensure that she mixes, to show great patience if she seems reluctant to do so and be content to let her watch other children playing at first. If you are relaxed and calm, and accept your child's need to make contact in her own way, she will soon adjust. Build her confidence by showing interest in her playmates, toys or activities, and pointing out further play possibilities.

Prepare your child for being left

Obviously, if she has been to nursery or playgroup, or spent time with a childminder, she will have an advantage. If your child has not been left often, she may take longer to adapt. But in most cases, children settle down to school quickly and enjoy the company and stimulation of their teacher and classmates.

Expect setbacks

During this period of adjustment, expect the odd setback: complaints of the 'Ben pushed me over' or 'Laura wouldn't let me play with her' variety are inevitable. Try to play down minor problems – sympathize over the fall or squabble, but find something positive to

Right: Mixing with siblings is a good start, but having contact with children of the same age is an excellent way to introduce the social aspects of going to school.

say ('Did somebody help you up?' or 'Did you find somebody else to play with?'). Show your concern, but keep a sense of proportion: children of this age make and break friends rapidly, and mishaps and accidents are very common.

Practical skills

Encourage your child toward independence in practical skills, such as dressing herself. Simple clothing is best, and shoes with Velcro fastenings preferable to laces or buckles. Girls' hair styles need to be simple. Your child's school may stipulate a uniform with buttons, tie, and lace-up or buckle shoes, but no one can expect a five-year-old to cope with these intricacies alone – it is quite an achievement to get the uniform on in the right order! She will not feel anxious if you encourage her efforts to be independent, and reassure her that teachers and classroom assistants are there to help if she cannot manage.

Most five-year-olds are capable of going to the toilet on their own. Remind her to ask to go before she is desperate, and to remember to flush the toilet and wash her hands afterward. It is quite common for small children to develop an aversion to school toilets, and this may become something of an issue in the first few weeks or even months of school. Children sometimes worry about going on their own, or complain that the doors do not lock, or that there is a mess or a smell. Infant teachers are sensitive to these concerns, and can be relied upon to remind children to use the toilets before and/or after play, and before going on an outing. Teachers will also see that anyone who dislikes going on her own is accompanied.

Finally, try to encourage your child to use her initiative and to be proud of her growing independence. Some five-year-olds become so reliant upon adults for reassurance, approval or guidance that they are unable to get on without it. Teachers are not able to provide every child with constant, individual feedback. So get your child used to having a choice of things to do and, when one activity is finished, to being able to put what she has made away and move on, without fuss, to another.

Preparing to learn

There are many ways in which you can contribute to the ease with which your child copes with the first weeks and months of her formal education.

The importance of reading

A large-scale study at the University of Bristol, of children making the transition from home to school, found that the single most significant way in which parents could help their children's educational progress was by reading to them. If you read for pleasure yourself and have fond memories of childhood stories, this observation will come as no surprise to you: reading to your child is probably as natural an activity as feeding her. Yet surprising numbers of children arrive at school with little or no experience of books. Some are unsure of how to sit and look at a book for themselves, others are unable to sit still as a story is read to them.

For all their use of new technology, schools still depend heavily on books, and on the written word. Education is about acquiring skills and passing on knowledge, but it is also about learning to live a civilized, communal life, in which people show

---

School dinners

Some young children find the school dining room and the whole lunchtime routine daunting. The noise and bustle, allied to what may be unfamiliar food, can be very stressful for a four- or five-year-old.

- Find out in advance what your options are – a school meal, a cafeteria system, a packed lunch, or coming home – and in consultation with your child choose the most appropriate for her.
- Notify the school of any dietary requirements (allergies, for example, or religious restrictions).
- Make sure your child can cope with washing her hands before a meal, using a knife and fork, and sitting at the table until everyone has finished.
- Water may be the only drink on offer so make sure your child is prepared.
- Reassure her that the school meal assistants are there to help with cutting up food and any other problems, and that they are there afterward in the playground. A school meal assistant can become a trusted friend.

concern for others. Children whose parents read to them absorb both pre-reading practical skills, and the beginnings of the ability to empathize with others (see pp. 220–4). These practical skills and personal qualities will help them in the early months of school, and throughout their school careers.

Science and technology

You may be surprised to find that children as young as five and six now study science and technology. For children of this age, these are lively, practical subjects which lay the foundations for later, more abstract learning. They build confidence, and allow opportunities for the practically inclined to shine.

Even if you consider yourself scientifically illiterate, take an interest in the ideas your child is covering at school, and allow time at weekends and in the holidays to follow through and develop her growing understanding. This may mean buying your children (girls as well as boys) construction games such as Lego or Meccano (see pp. 210–11), and actually playing with these sets with them.

As your child gets older, simply asking her to explain or show you what she has been doing at school will increase her confidence. Most children also enjoy visits to museums of science and technology. You can ensure that museum visits are enjoyable and

worth while by advance planning. Try to focus your child's attention by looking forward to one or two aspects of the museum, instead of trying to take everything in. If your child is fascinated by a specific area of science, or has enjoyed working on a topic at school, concentrate on that. Find out in advance what the museum has to offer, and select an area which you think will appeal to her. Read and talk about it before your visit and perhaps suggest some aspect which you could investigate further. Do not expect the under-11s to be able to concentrate for long, and leave some time simply to go off and explore and have fun.

- There are scores of construction and activity sets on the market. Many children enjoy the likes of Technic Lego, chemistry sets and activity kits – from equipment for collecting and identifying insects to the components for constructing a basic radio. Be guided by your child's interests and abilities, as much as by the 'suitable age' indication on the box.
- Many five to tens are naturally curious about the night sky, the stars and planets, and it is wise to be prepared for questions which defeat you ('But Mum, what happened before the Big Bang?').
- There is an enormous range of books on various aspects of National Curriculum-related science and technology, including astronomy, in book shops and libraries. Your library will also carry lists of

Introducing science and technology

Bug kits, wildlife cards and games, seed kits and weather stations introduce elements of science into your child's experience of the world.

Today's children become familiar with computer equipment early – they may use a keyboard at nursery and in the reception class.

local scientific societies which have a junior branch, or encourage the interest of children.

Familiar parts of the primary curriculum

Apart from science and technology, the primary school curriculum includes a great deal that will be familiar to you and your child.

- In the early weeks of school she will probably do art and craft work using a variety of materials (chalks, crayons, paint, clay), singing, listening to music and using simple instruments, and both indoor and outdoor physical education.
- She will gain experience of talking and listening collectively in a class situation, and also of working individually and in small groups. There may be worksheets which involve colouring in, or joining up dots to make a picture, or letters of the alphabet, all of which are designed to help basic literacy. As she becomes more proficient, there will be counting and sorting tasks.
- It is helpful to teachers if children starting school can identify the basic colours and know their names, and have had the opportunity of using paints, felt tips, crayons, pencils and (children's) scissors.

Some children starting school are able to recognize their names on name cards; some may be able to read. There is wide variation in what teachers sometimes call 'reading readiness' or, indeed, reading proficiency, at this stage (see p. 273), and there is no need for concern if your child seems unable to recognize her name, and shows little interest in doing so. In the same way, some children may be able to count aloud, to count objects (the skills are different), to recognize numbers, and to do simple sums. Other children show no interest whatsoever. Again, this is nothing for you to be anxious about. Differences in reading, writing and number skills become far less pronounced as children move up the school.

If your child is able to read or write, or knows her numbers and can manage simple sums when she starts school, it is helpful if you tell the teacher, but do not assume that this means your child can skip the basics and forge ahead of everybody else in the first few weeks. Teachers see children in the context of a class. An individual may be ahead in maths, but lag behind in reading, social skills or confidence. She may refuse to join in singing, or cry when the class has PE.

Such children need time to settle into the day-to-day school routine before being pushed academically.

Remember too that the teacher is professionally concerned with your child. He or she cannot take your word that your child is literate and numerate, but must ensure that all children have covered the same ground, and that they can all walk, academically speaking, before they start to run. The more mature, and the more academically capable among them, will soon begin to work at their own, faster pace.

The time

One of the more difficult concepts to be learned between the ages of five and ten is the way that time is divided into years, months, weeks, days, hours and minutes. Children's understanding of time continues to mature and develop throughout the primary school years, and you will find that they return to it in their maths, geography, history and topic work.

Reception class and Year One children may well begin their day by inserting printed cards or wooden pieces into a calendar. These describe the weather, season, month and day of the week. You can help by talking about these topics out of school, by drawing your child's attention to an activity which you always do on Tuesdays, say, and by pointing out that it is autumn and the leaves are falling, by talking about the months in which members of the family celebrate their birthdays. Most children enjoy reciting the names of the days and the months, or poems and rhymes which help them to understand seasonal patterns.

Working with the school

Children progress more happily and satisfactorily through school if you support the school in what it is trying to do, and if teachers make themselves available to you and listen to your concerns. Like all partnerships, that between home and school demands effort on both sides. As a parent, it is important for you to try to be supportive of the school in your child's presence. If you feel you have cause for concern or wish to complain, gather as much information as you can, and go to the school in a constructive rather than confrontational frame of mind. Follow the school's guidelines if you want to see a member of staff. Some schools allow more or less open access; others prefer you to make an appointment. Ring and check.

Homework

Make sure that your child sets aside time for homework, and that she has a quiet place in which to do it. If you do not pick her up from school, ask whether her after-school carer is prepared to supervise homework (a good carer will be interested herself, or may have children who are doing homework too); alternatively, check whether the after-school club makes any provision for a quiet area in which children can do homework. If your child has to do her homework after you arrive home, make sure you or your partner is available to help and that home-work does not have to be rushed to fit in a meal, bath and other evening activities.

At infant level, your child is likely to bring home a book to read to or with you (see p. 275) or a maths activity. As she moves into the junior department, she may well bring home spellings or tables to learn. Few children (or adults) are able to commit facts to memory without writing something down, and you may find 'read – cover – write – check' a helpful formula. Encourage your child to read the word to be learned, to cover it, to write it out, and, finally, to check the answer. As your child gets older, depending on the school's policy, she may be asked to finish off project work at home, or to continue with some work begun in class. (Children attending independent schools will have regular homework from the start.)

What you can do

Your child will need time to unwind and have something to eat and drink before she tackles homework, so it is a good idea to establish a routine, especially if your child is likely to get homework regularly. Discuss this with her, so that she feels some sense of control (however illusory), and is encouraged to organize her own time.

It is also important to set a time limit, so that some of the evening is left for relaxation, and to agree this with your child. Some children see the sense in good organization, and get on with their work without fuss. Others find it difficult to apply themselves and at the end of the agreed time have not finished their work. If this happens regularly, it can cause tension and is stressful for you and your child: either you give in to pleas for 'just a few more minutes', the work is rushed and your child has no free time left over

before bed; or you explain that she has used up the time set aside for homework, and must speak to the teacher who gave the work and negotiate extra time.

You can help avoid this situation by encouraging enthusiasm and being interested and enthusiastic yourself. Point out aspects of her homework that link with other topics she is covering at school or relate to something you have done together. Help her select library books that are appropriate. If it happens again and again, talk to your child's teacher: is this a common syndrome among her peers? does her teacher have any advice? As the move to secondary school looms, it becomes increasingly important that your child can handle her time and assignments effectively. Try explaining your concerns, but do not nag. Remind your child that she is loved for being herself.

Non-homework activities

Without being too obvious, ensure access to books and quality leisure time, as well as opportunities to play and relax. Encourage hobbies – many require the concentration, attention to detail, problem-solving and co-operative approach you are trying to get her to apply to her schoolwork. You may well find that such measures, along with her increasing maturity and the fresh challenges of secondary school, help to bring about an improvement in her work habits.

Separation anxiety

Despite the best possible preparation for school, your child may become distressed when the moment comes for you to leave her. (Find out in advance what the routine is – in some schools it is usual to take new children to the classroom for the first couple of weeks, in others children line up from the start.) A few cling, cry or scream, resisting all attempts to calm them. In some cases, this form of anxiety does not show itself until well into the term, or it occurs intermittently, or whenever the child moves into a new class.

There are a variety of reasons for this sort of behaviour and, as with adapting to school more generally, it tends to happen more with first-born or only children, or with children whose parents are over-protective. Your child may have a general dread of being left, or there may be a specific cause. Children who are perfectionists by inclination may fail to measure up to their own high standards, and worry that their efforts are not good enough. Others may still be too immature for school (see box below).

Your child will grow through separation anxiety, and is unlikely to suffer lasting ill-effects if you stay patient and calm. Cancel after-school activities, so that you can take her straight home to relax and rest. It is helpful if you or another carer can devote even a few minutes exclusively to her, perhaps setting out a game together or reading a favourite story.

- Try to reassure your child by explaining that although school may seem strange at first, it will soon be interesting and fun. If your child senses that you are as upset as she is, she may become convinced that her fears are justified.
- What works? Does she settle down within a few minutes of your leaving? If the answer is 'yes', then a reassuring hug and a 'Goodbye, see you later' may be appropriate. Is she less distressed if Daddy, or another relative or friend takes her to school? Does it help if the teacher arranges for her to do something first thing in the morning, perhaps feeding the class gerbil or giving out the pencils? While separation anxiety is distressing, it is quite common, and virtually all children grow out of it without any lasting psychological damage.
- Are you pressurizing? Is your child getting too much, intensive contact with one parent, and not enough time with other children? Are you or your partner putting pressure on her to succeed? Is a particular aspect of school causing anxiety? Is your child not getting enough parental attention? While you can make efforts to ease the situation, remedial action takes time and may not help immediately.

There are, in fact, no hard and fast rules. In the past, children were often carried into the classroom, and the door was firmly shut. They were encouraged to submerge their feelings, and parents were left to fret. Some children, no doubt, harboured deep-seated feelings of distress and resentment; others found that, once their parents had gone, they were able to cope. The modern tendency to expect a child to be able to 'discuss' or rationalize, or even articulate her feelings, exerts its own pressure and can prolong the anxiety.

Very occasionally, children do not grow out of separation anxiety, or it may occur suddenly in an older child who has previously been happy at school. These situations obviously merit immediate attention, and you should arrange to see your child's teacher as soon as possible. You can also try the School Phobia Helpline (see Useful Contacts, pp. 390–3).

Too young for school?

Some children, particularly those who are young for their school year (with June, July and August birthdays), do not have the physical or mental stamina, the social competence, or the resilience necessary for school. These children often try hard to do what is required of them in the classroom, and find security in the school routine, but they are upset or bewildered by out-of-the-ordinary events such as sports days, concerts or school plays.

Your child may be tired, irritable or tearful after school. She may resort to comfort blankets or thumb-sucking, or revert to bedwetting, as well as crying when she is left at school in the morning. Such children are often not really ready for school and, in an ideal world, would be withdrawn for a further term at nursery or at home.

If this fits your child, bear in mind that you can keep your child at home until the term following her fifth birthday. Recent research has shown that

'young for their year' children perform less well in tests at seven and that differences may persist until GCSE level. Ignore those who boast that their children have 'outgrown nursery'. If you feel it is right, keep your child at home and encourage social and educational activities (preschool music club, tumble tots, swimming and so on).

If your July or August born child has to start full-time school earlier than you would like, try to choose a school with a good pupil–teacher ratio: at least one trained adult to 13 children. Talk to the reception class teacher(s). Make sure that they are warm and friendly and prepared to be flexible with children whose attention span and fine motor control may be less developed than those of children nine months older. It helps if there is a separate play area for the youngest children that is out of bounds to older ones (although you cannot guarantee that your child will take advantage of it).

MAKING FRIENDS

Friendships become increasingly important to children between the ages of five and ten years, and the nature of their relationships changes considerably as they grow up. Five-year-olds enjoy playing with other children, and they can play co-operatively, but they also tend to be self-centred. You may notice, for example, that your child appears to be playing with other children, but if you look closely you will see that, as at nursery, she is actually playing alongside them. Games at this age may include a considerable element of rivalry and challenge, as children discover who can run the fastest, or hop the

Playground games

Five- to seven-year-olds enjoy variations on 'tig', and fantasy games of 'horses', (still) cowboys and Indians, Robin Hood, or the current television heroes. They like hide and seek, and games of rivalry. You may see small groups of children crouched in dusty corners, making houses for wood lice, or seeing whether worms can 'swim' in puddles. Skipping continues to be popular for girls throughout the five-to-ten age group, and many children love the old, traditional games such as 'In and Out the Dusty Bluebells' or 'The Big Ship Sails through the Alley-Alley-O', if an adult can be persuaded to teach them. You are also likely to hear clapping, ball and skipping rhymes whose rhythms sound familiar, although the words may be updated.

Eight-, nine- and ten-year-olds gradually progress to games which involve more complex rules and skills. Gymnastic, skipping and ball games are all popular, and older children can usually organize themselves to play rounders, cricket or soccer. Many seven- to ten-year-olds like board games, and computer games are popular (although these encourage quick reactions, they are solitary and children should not play every day, or for hours at a time). This is also the age for gangs and secret societies, and seasonal games, such as marbles and conkers, still flourish in some schools.

furthest, or spin in circles the longest. Squabbling over toys or the organization of games (who is 'it' this time) is common, and calls for firm but kind adult supervision and diplomacy.

By the time they reach the age of ten, both girls and boys will probably mix well with a large number of children, but have a small number of special friends. They will squabble less, confide in one another more, and enjoy un-adult-structured co-operative and fantasy play, as well as organized games with fairly complicated sets of rules (soccer, rounders and so on).

You can expect slow but significant progress in social skills over the three years between the ages of five and eight. There are usually peaks and troughs as some aspects of behaviour seem to improve and others to plateau or even to deteriorate. Six-year-olds, for example, can sometimes appear less emotionally stable than they were at four or five. Your child may swing from being friendly and loving with family and friends to being furiously angry, and may react dramatically to such minor frustrations as dropping a ball or losing a book. Quarrels with friends may erupt over the ownership of, or access to, toys, and you may be needed to resolve them. Within a year, however, most children show increased control and stability. With stability comes an improvement in both gross and fine motor movement, so that children are less frustrated by their own 'clumsiness', or failure to master coveted skills.

Encourage a wide circle of friends. Although at this age she may show a strong preference for a particular individual, relationships are often brittle, and sometimes one-sided. Arguments at school may mean that a child with a limited friendship circle has nobody to play with, and cause tears and anxiety. Encouraging a range of friends also allows her to explore different aspects of her personality – with one child she rides her bike and makes dens, with another she watches her favourite television programme and acts it out afterward, with a third she plays house with dolls and cuddly toys. Friendships formed at school are usually pleasurable and important to children and, once they become accustomed to it, the playground becomes 'their' territory.

In the playground, children of the 1990s can enjoy a taste of the freedom that their parents took for granted in the 1960s and '70s, before the volume of traffic and fear of crime against children began to restrict traditional forms of play in streets, parks and

Sleepovers

From seven or eight years upward, children enjoy sleeping over at one another's houses, perhaps watching a suitable video beforehand. If you are the host parent, ask commonsense questions about medicines and allergies, and make sure that you have the visiting child's home telephone number. Children do sometimes become excited or tearful at bedtime, but generally respond to reassurance in the form of stories and cuddles. It is sensible to leave a night light or landing light on, so that possibly disorientated visitors can find their way to the bathroom.

A few young children do not like the idea of staying away from home, especially if they have never stayed overnight with grandparents or other relatives. It is counter-productive to try to shame or force your child into doing so. She may cause problems for the host parents by crying and refusing to settle, and in extreme cases could develop stomach pains, or even vomit. It is not fair to inflict such anxiety on a young child, or its effects on host parents. So long as you are not over-protective, your child will almost certainly outgrow her unwillingness to sleep away from home by the age of eight or nine. It may help to let her play host a few times so that she can get used to the whole idea, before she feels confident to sleep elsewhere.

countryside (see pp. 297–9). At school, although there is always the security of an adult on hand to deal with accidents or antisocial behaviour, children are their own masters.

Take an interest in your child's friends, and enjoy watching them grow along with her. Friendships developed at school usually transfer well to home, although allegiances change over time, and last term's best friend can be dropped or, worse, transformed into this term's enemy. All five-to-tens enjoy having one or more friends to play at home. Some five-year-olds still become anxious at being left. They are shy with other children's parents, or worry that they might be made to eat food they don't like, or are frightened of the family dog, or boisterous older siblings. These sorts of fears are common, and will

pass. You can ease the situation by keeping play sessions short, and either accompanying your child if she is apprehensive, or, vice versa, inviting the visiting friend's parent to stay for coffee. By the time they are six or seven, even the least outgoing children have usually got over their anxiety.

Unless you work school hours, or work at home, it can be difficult to arrange to have other children around after school, but see whether whoever normally collects your child would be willing to pick her up from a friend's house, try to negotiate one afternoon every now and then when you can leave work early, or invite friends to your house at the weekend. Try not to deprive your child of what in many cases can be a burgeoning social scene.

Unsuitable friendships

It is almost inevitable that your child will, at some stage in her life, develop a friendship with a child about whom you have misgivings. Such friendships are often passing phases and seem to fulfil a need – perhaps the other child is confident or popular, and boosts your less outgoing child's own confidence and standing within a friendship group. Perhaps your child from a caring, protective home is excited by the freedom which another child seems to enjoy. It is important to sort out what matters to you. Is there an element of snobbery in your objection to a child's accent? Are you put off by some aspect of their physical appearance – multiply pierced ears, haircut or style of dress, for example? Or, does this child's behaviour give legitimate cause for concern?

Children who are involved in delinquent activities such as shoplifting, vandalism or drugs are a genuine worry. Even though some children do get caught up in what is usually petty criminal behaviour, and the vast majority grow out of it, they and their friends need to know that adults and other children disapprove. Associating with a child who is a known delinquent increases the risk of your own child (especially if she is impressionable) becoming carried along by the group and ending up in trouble herself. The risk is especially high if the children are allowed to go out on their own together, or are left to play unsupervised for long periods of time.

Be wary, too, about a friend who constantly initiates sexual play. It is absolutely normal for children to be curious about their bodies, and to pass through phases where any mention of bottoms or willies sends them into fits of giggles. If, however, you come across play which makes you feel uncomfortable, or sense that something is seriously amiss, try to divert the children's attention, rather than making them feel 'dirty' or ashamed. It is always useful to talk the situation over with your partner or a close friend, and then, quietly, to take appropriate action.

What you can do

Try not to teach your child to shun those who are involved in delinquent or socially unacceptable behaviour: delinquent and poorly adjusted children need friends too (probably more so than other children), but their friendships need to be watched closely but unobtrusively.

Perhaps such friendships might be better if they were confined to school. If they extend to home, make sure that children meet on your home ground, and on your terms. Older children in the five-to-ten

age group deserve truthful (but not frightening) explanations about your concern.

As always, prevention is better than cure. Minimize the opportunities for your child to become involved with troublemakers. Make sure she has plenty of after-school clubs and activities and encourage hobbies that direct her energies and help to develop skills. 'I've got to go to football training' is a more acceptable explanation for your child than 'My mum says I mustn't hang around with you'.

Boys and girls

Even in this so-called post-feminist age, it is more socially acceptable for a girl to be 'going through a tomboy phase', than it is for a boy to appear 'girlie'. There are still many families and communities in which a boy cannot admit to hating sport, or cars, and where an admission that he would actually rather play with girls is a matter for concern. A girl who climbs trees and is desperate to win running races, on the other hand, raises no eyebrows.

Left to their own devices, most fives to sevens will play happily with friends of both sexes. But the need to have the approval of their peers does become stronger toward the top end of this age group, which may mean that a boy of nine or ten will be content to play at a girl's house or if they meet in the park, but may refuse to have anything to do with her at school, and vice versa. This situation may continue until your child reaches adolescence.

What you can do

If your child finds it difficult to mix with children of the same sex and becomes upset by teasing (which unfortunately can be intense toward the top end of the primary school) it can be helpful to discuss ways of coping.

Usually, this amounts to distracting other children's attention. It may be through developing a skill, or having a toy or a piece of clothing or equipment which the others admire. If the problem is serious, you should speak in confidence to your child's teacher who will almost certainly be aware of what is going on. It is reassuring to know that most children are tolerant of one another, if they are encouraged to be so by fair-minded adults. And that, as they grow into adolescence, their tolerance usually increases.

Serious trouble

It is always a shock when children get into trouble with the police. Regardless of your initial reactions, focus first on your child. Be reassured that for most children from caring, supportive families, once is enough – a police caution or court appearance frightens them, and they are unlikely to re-offend.

- Try not to alienate your child by constantly referring to the offence. Although your child must know how seriously you view the matter and accept that you need to discuss what happened, try to look to the future.

- Encourage your child's active involvement in a sport, hobby or community activity, rather than setting draconian limits on her freedom.

- If your child does re-offend and you sense matters are escalating beyond your control, don't try to cope alone. Your child's teacher or head, the school nurse (see box opposite) or your GP (who may be able to refer you to a child psychiatrist) may all be able to offer help. If you prefer an 'outsider', contact Parentline (see Useful Contacts, pp. 390–3).

HOW CHILDREN CHANGE

Between the ages of five and ten years, children change physically. They develop from little people just leaving behind the large-headed, short-limbed proportions of babyhood, to well-grown pre-adolescents, sometimes as tall or as heavy as their mothers, and often larger footed. The changes which they undergo mentally are just as dramatic, although less visible. Boys may lag behind girls intellectually throughout the primary school years, although there are always exceptions. Differences are often especially marked at the infant school stage, where more boys than girls experience difficulties in learning to read and write. Some of these differences are probably biological in origin and may resolve

Physical growth and development

Routine health checks for five to tens vary slightly according to the area of the country in which you live. In most cases, you can expect your child's vision, hearing, height and weight to be checked by the school nurse when she starts school at four or five (see p. 157). If there is any cause for concern, your child will be re-checked at regular intervals, or referred to an appropriate consultant. Vision is usually tested again when children reach Year Three (7–8 years). In Year Six, before children move on to secondary school at 11, their height and weight are re-checked, and their colour vision is assessed.

Although there are regional variations, many areas now operate a 'named school nurse' system. This means that named nurses are attached to particular schools (you should find your school nurse's name and telephone number in the school prospectus), and are available to advise on all aspects of children's health and development – from dietary guidance to how to deal with head lice, or bedwetting.

If your child goes to an independent (sometimes known as 'private') school, you may have to make your own arrangements for health checks. This can be done through the normal channels of health visitor and GP.

themselves as boys grow up, but others are cultural – the 'feminine' environment of the primary school may make it more difficult for some boys to settle into learning – so parents, and especially fathers, can help by taking an interest in boys' work and encouraging their efforts.

Intellectual development

The child's developing brain is thought to be at its most active in the years up to puberty. Between the ages of five and ten, your child steadily moves from being self-centred in the way she thinks, to being able to see situations from another person's point of view. Her ideas of right and wrong, fairness and justice develop (given adult guidance) from simple to more complex models. She understands complex mathematical relationships, and her grasp of ideas becomes steadily less dependent on having experienced a situation for herself. Gradually, she moves toward a more accurate and realistic understanding of the world in which she lives, and becomes increasingly capable of abstract thought and argument.

The education your child receives as she progresses through the primary school is based on current understanding of children's intellectual capacities at various stages of their development. All those involved in designing the National Curriculum have had substantial experience of either working with children or studying their development, and all primary school teachers have studied some developmental psychology. Just as importantly, most teachers also have an intuitive grasp of what children can do, and what is, at any point, beyond them. In most areas of the curriculum, your child will do some work as a class, some in small groups, and some at her own pace.

History and geography

You may notice that the work your child covers in history or geography is much more practical than the work you remember at the same stage (this is especially true if you are an 'older' parent of a young child, and went to primary school in the late 1950s and early 1960s). The rationale behind this emphasis in primary schools is that children of this age are not yet fully mentally equipped to deal with abstractions (although their capacities obviously vary) and so work best, and understand most, when topics begin from their own experience. So history may begin not with the Stone Age, but with project work on the children themselves and their families, gradually working back through the generations. Geography may begin in the same way, with a focus on the local area. In geography and history, and in topic work, your children are likely to go on trips relating to their work.

What you can do

Encourage your child to read (or read to her) some of the children's historical novels or try the 'Fax Pax' series (picture cards with information on the reverse), which are good value for money.

Your child will almost certainly not study history chronologically at school, so you can complement her school work by helping her to see and understand the order in which events happened. If you have the time and energy, making a timeline can be fun. And, of course, visits to sites of historical interest help the subject to come alive.

A world map and a globe are useful, as is a good atlas. Even if you and your child have not travelled widely, it is helpful to pinpoint countries or areas which are in the news. Children are usually fascinated by large-scale maps of their own area, or even by street plans (pinpointing 'their' street and those in which their friends live).

If you are going on a car or rail journey, show her the route on a map, or point out where ferry routes that you might be going to use operate.

Maths

You may be especially struck by differences in the ways you and your child approach another core subject, maths. Your five- to seven-year-old is likely to spend time on matching, sorting and weighing, in addition to number recognition and simple arithmetic. Progress may seem slow to you, but many five-year-olds find it impossible to count more than five or six objects at a time, and often count one object twice and miss another out altogether. This is especially so when the pattern of objects on the page is irregular. As her competence improves over the year, your child will probably be able to manage up to ten objects comfortably. Most six-year-olds can cope with numbers up to 20, and by the time your child is

seven, you can expect her to be starting to work with tens and units (for example, 10 + 12, 16 – 13). From her seventh or eighth year onward, you are likely to notice quite a dramatic development in your child's progress in the subject as she becomes better able to understand relationships between numbers. She will be able to understand that multiplication is repeated addition – in other words, that 7+7+7+7+7+7+7 is another way of saying 7 x 7, and that both make 49, or that 8 x 7 = 56, so 56 ÷ 8 = 7.

Another conceptual hurdle is 'carrying numbers'. In calculations such as 28 + 23, for example, the child

Carrying numbers

Although the method your child uses will be similar to the one you used, she is likely to write the number to be carried *underneath* the sum: you probably squeezed it in.

Your method:

```
      T   U
      2   8
  +   2₁  3
      ‾‾‾‾‾
      5   1
```

Method:

1 8 plus 3 equals 11
2 Put 1 in the units column and carry 1, which is actually 10 into the tens column by putting it 'on the doorstep'
3 Add the 1 to the numbers there
4 The answer is 51

Your child's method:

```
      T   U
      2   8
  +   2   3
      ‾‾‾‾‾
      5   1
      1
```

Method:

1 8 plus 3 equals 11
2 Put 1 in the units column and carry 10 into the tens column
3 Add the carried 10 to the numbers there
4 The answer is 51

must realize that because 8 and 3 make more than 10, it is necessary to 'carry' one group of ten into the tens column. A great deal of effort today goes into ensuring that children understand what they are doing, and there will be practical help in the form of blocks or bricks to reinforce the teacher's explanations. You may be surprised at the way in which your child sets out her calculations, and it is well worth asking either your child (if she seems confident) or the teacher to explain. This is a case where you should not force your own methods on your child, who may become confused.

Practical maths

As your child gets older, you will find that much of her maths work is familiar to you. Your ten-year-old will work with fractions, decimals and percentages, and at problem-solving, for example, but you will notice more emphasis on practical maths than you may have experienced. Your child will learn to construct and read a variety of types of graph, and to work out averages. She may work out problems of time by answering questions about railway timetables, and problems of area and volume in relation to questions about re-decorating a house.

There may also be work on topics which are unfamiliar to you, such as the binary system, sets and Venn diagrams. And, of course, work on weight, length and capacity will all be conducted using metric units of measurement. There is less emphasis in maths teaching today on repeatedly practising the skills of addition, subtraction, multiplication and division, and on mental arithmetic.

Causes for concern?

You may find yourself worrying, especially if your child is either very good at maths, or seems to be struggling. Rest assured that your child is probably getting a broader grounding in maths than you did; today's children seem to understand what they are doing and why, whereas many of their parents simply followed a formula with only a vague idea of its rationale. Perhaps more importantly, your child may appear less anxious about maths than you were.

It is worrying if your child seems unable to perform the sorts of mental calculations necessary when shopping, for example, or seems totally dependent on her calculator. If you are concerned about your child's progress or general competence, approach the school. Children who are good at maths should be allowed to move on at their own, faster, pace and teaching staff are usually willing to offer more challenging materials to those who would benefit from them. Children who are having difficulties in maths may have a general problem with the subject (although this is not common at primary school level), or may simply have become 'stuck' on a particular topic. Quite often, when this is the case, they seem to understand the principle at stake, and can tackle a question with a teacher or parent, but then forget what to do when asked to try on their own. If your child really does not seem able to grasp, for example, fractions or long division, she may be encouraged to move on to another topic and come back to the problem area later. If it is an issue of forgetfulness or 'careless working out', she may be helped by making a note of the formula, and by repeated practice.

Sets and Venn diagrams

Children use sets and Venn diagrams to help them to classify objects, people or numbers; to represent their classification in the form of a diagram; and to answer questions.

For example, the universal set in a question, E, might have as its members or elements the children in Year Five. Set A might be the children in Year Five who own dogs; set B the children in Year Five who own cats. The intersection of sets A and B (A n B) represent the children in Year Five who own both cats and dogs. As a Venn diagram this information would look like:

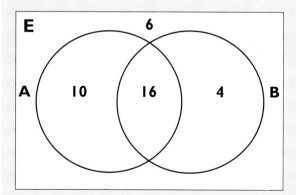

There are 36 children in Year 5.

Helping with maths

Most good bookshops stock a selection of books which you can use at home to help your child with maths. It is better not to buy the particular scheme your child uses at school, as she may become bored. See Problems at school, pp. 280–7.

Language

By the time children reach the age of five, they can usually speak fluently in their mother tongue and, sometimes, in a second language too. The average five-year-old has, without conscious effort, mastered most of the grammatical rules and structures of her mother tongue, and has a vocabulary of between 3,000 and 5,000 words, between two-thirds and three-quarters of the vocabulary she will eventually have as an adult.

Your five-year-old has mastered the rules of sentence formation so that she can produce grammatically well-formed sentences such as 'I rode my bike round and round the garden', and not simply random strings of words ('My rode bike I garden the round and round'). She can use grammatical tenses appropriately – she says 'I am going to Granny's house tomorrow', not 'I went to Granny's house tomorrow'. She also 'knows' complex rules of word ordering, such as to say 'The big brown table', not 'The brown big table'.

Linguistic development is not complete by the age of five: there are many words and expressions which your five-year-old does not understand. She may confuse strong and weak verbs, saying 'We rided our bikes' instead of 'We rode our bikes', 'I growed two centimetres in the summer holidays' instead of 'I grew two centimetres' (applying the rules, without understanding the exceptions). Also, her mastery of the personal pronoun system may be incomplete. Yet in five years, she has performed an incredible feat. (To put it in perspective, think of the problems you had when you tried to learn a foreign language.)

Your child's primary school will aim to extend her vocabulary, to help her become an effective (written and verbal) communicator, and to enable her to use spoken (and written) language appropriately, according to social context or setting.

Dialect and accent

Standard English was originally a regional dialect of English spoken in the south-east. Until the 18th century, it had the same status as any other dialect, but because of the influence of the capital London and the university cities of Oxford and Cambridge, it came to be seen as correct and prestigious.

As late as the 1960s, a head teacher in the West Riding of Yorkshire is reputed to have caned a boy for saying 'I were laikin'' instead of 'I was playing'. This point of view was challenged in the 1960s and '70s, and some teachers began to allow dialect forms of English in both spoken and written work. They argued that, in linguistic terms, dialect English was as rich, rule-governed and grammatically complex as so-called Standard English. In the 1980s, this liberal approach itself came under attack. The trouble was, critics argued, that some children were not learning when it was appropriate to use their local dialect and when it was more appropriate to use grammar and vocabulary which everybody could understand.

Many schools now try to make children effectively bilingual, if they live in an area of the country which still has strong local dialect traditions. So a child in York may not be corrected for saying 'I aren't coming' in the playground, but her teacher will explain that this is not appropriate in a piece of written work, unless, of course, the child is writing a piece of dialogue.

Teaching children to use Standard English and Dialect English appropriately does not mean, as some teachers and parents feared, that a child's pronunciation or accent (the way in which – predominantly – vowels and consonants are produced) will be ridiculed or corrected. It is quite possible to speak Standard English in a Cockney, Yorkshire, Geordie, Liverpool or West Country accent, but it is only fair that you teach your child to recognize that there are situations when the use of non-Standard grammar – 'I ain't' and 'I aren't' – may put her at a disadvantage or lead to misunderstanding.

What you can do

There are many ways in which you can help your child's language development at home, so that home and school complement one another.

Try to encourage your child's spoken language and give her your attention; she needs time to explain what she means. Try not to guess at her meaning – cutting her off and supplying your own definition or summary – but to allow her to try to explain herself.

Answer questions about the meanings of words in terms which she can understand, trying not to be abstract or dismissive. You will actively discourage her by laughing at her, ignoring her, drawing attention to her mistakes, or making her feel 'naughty' if she talks at an inconvenient moment. Obviously, it is not always possible to answer her questions then and there, and there are times when she has to learn to be quiet, but a promise to answer a question later is preferable to a negative or discouraging response.

As she gets older, extend her competence and understanding by building on what she already knows – answer her questions about what words mean by going a little further than is strictly necessary. Give her some examples of the word in question being used in sentences, or in a story. You can also help to extend your child's vocabulary simply by visiting new places, trying new experiences, thinking about issues. This does not mean that you have to spend a lot of money on travel and foreign holidays. Many activities and places of interest are free, sightseeing can be done on the cheap, and occasional trips to the theatre or cinema can be supplemented by thoughtful use of the television. Doing crosswords is an inexpensive and enjoyable way of extending vocabulary.

Learning to read

Most children absorb pre-reading skills at home, by being read to (see pp. 220–3). Once they are at school, the job of teaching them formally begins. There is enormous variation in the speed at which children learn – some can read simple words at between two and three years, others do not reach this stage until they are five or six. Some are reading fluently at six, while others read jerkily, one word at a time, until they are seven or eight. This variation explains why it is difficult to spot children who may have learning difficulties at this early stage.

Do not be afraid to begin to teach your child to read at home if she is developmentally 'ready' to do so. Many schools start their pupils reading on the 'look–say' method, in which they concentrate on learning the overall shape of words rather than 'sounding out' the letter sounds to make words (c–a–t = 'cat', for example). Write such words as 'Mummy', 'Daddy' and your child's name on small cards. If she learns to recognize them, enthusiastically and without difficulty, add the names of some everyday objects – 'door', 'window', 'car' – to the list. This all helps to increase your child's 'sight vocabulary'.

At the same time, start teaching your child the letter sounds from an alphabet frieze. Teach 'a' as in 'apple', 'b' as in 'ball', rather than calling the letters by their 'proper' names – 'Bee', 'Dee' and so on. If you do teach the letters, it is better to do so casually rather than formally, perhaps making it part of the bedtime routine. Encourage your child to choose a letter or letters, look at it, say its sound. Friezes and books designed for young children usually have the lower case versions of the letters prominent, with the upper case letters shown in the background. Concentrate on the lower case, but explain from time to time that the upper case letter you can see in the background is a capital letter and that these are used for the first letter of people's names (use your child's name as an example, especially if she has a name card at school).

It is useful for your child to get to know her own name by sight. Don't worry if she cannot manage this during the first weeks at school, her teacher will probably give her a picture sticker alongside her name so that she recognizes her picture if not her name. Some children's names can be broken down phonically as they learn the letter sounds, so that you can explain that 'B–e–n' go together to make 'Ben', for example. Names such as Alice, Claire or Thomas are too complex for children of this age to 'sound out', so your child will have to learn to recognize the whole word. If you repeat the letter sounds every time you write out her name and those of her friends, she will absorb this information without having to sit down and learn it.

If your five-year-old is not interested in learning the letter sounds, or learns the individual letters but cannot blend them together to make simple words, do not worry. Some children do not initially make the connection between letter sounds and words. An infant teacher can spend 10 minutes explaining that 'This is letter "b". It's the sound that starts off words like "bear" and "boy" and "balloon". Can anyone else think of a word that begins with a "b" sound?', only to have a child answer 'elephant'. If your child is either not interested, or reaches an impasse, forget about it for a few weeks. Try again every so often, until you feel that she is ready to move forward.

Most primary schools use a variety of methods to teach children to read; the major ones are 'look–say', 'phonics' and 'real books'. Each method has its advantages and disadvantages, its adherents and detractors.

Look–say

Look–say is based on the idea that children notice and remember the shape of words, and can learn to recognize words such as 'house' or 'bounce' before they understand the letter sound patterns that go into making them. Schemes such as 'One, Two, Three and Away' use look–say methods. Look–say usually works well for children who have an average to above-average visual memory, but is less effective for those with a below average visual memory, and those who are dyslexic.

If your child is learning to read in this way, she may begin by matching words printed on cards to words in a reading book, and will probably soon develop a reasonable 'sight vocabulary'. She will work through a series of graded readers, with much repetition of known words and gradual introduction of new. In parallel, she will learn simple phonic skills, so that she can decode new words by sounding them out, thus building up 'word attack' skills (the ability to read new words by relating letters to letter sounds).

Phonics

In phonics children learn letter sounds, and then combine these sounds to make words. If you are a 40-something parent, you may have been taught to read (and spell) with a heavy emphasis on phonic skills and many parents intuitively start to teach their children to read using phonics.

Phonics has gradually lost favour as the major tool in teaching children to read, partly because it is associated with repetitive drilling and reading without meaning. Its critics also argued that English is not consistent and logical in spelling and pronunciation,

so words such as 'their', 'house', 'bough', 'bought', and others, cannot be 'sounded out' according to rules. This does not mean that there are no patterns in English spelling; if it did, every single word would have to be item-learned.

In phonics, children learn to read and spell groups of words which follow the same patterns (field, grief, brief, grieve, niece, but seize, ceiling, receive, receipt). In some circles, phonics continues to suffer from an image problem. Yet this is largely unjustified. Children need to learn letter sounds, letter blends and spelling patterns to decode new words, and to spell correctly, and these skills have to be taught.

The 'Letterland' and 'From Alpha to Omega' series are examples of phonic approaches.

Real books

The 'real books' approach to reading is based on the idea that conventional (that is, phonics and look–say) methods fail many children, because they read without meaning, or pleasure. Real-books

Reading games

Matching pictures and whole words helps your child develop a 'sight vocabulary', the basis of look–say reading methods.

advocates say that a child can learn to read without the laborious, repetitive (and often demoralizing) business of pre-readers, word tins, flash cards, or graded schemes.

With real books, children effectively become 'apprentices' to adult readers, who read children's books (not 'reading books') to and with them. In time, the child begins to recite stories, using memory or picture clues. She can follow the sense of a story, and recognize words. She learns, in parallel, to write stories, often with a 'Sentence Maker' set, where printed words on small cards are slotted into spaces, and copied. She begins to recognize words in books which she has encountered in writing, and builds up a stock of known words. Phonic skills are also taught to cope with new words.

Real books was popular in the 1980s and can be effective in the hands of a skilled and enthusiastic teacher. It was, however, at the heart of a prolonged debate about a drop in reading standards in the late 1980s and early '90s, and has lost ground as a result.

The 'combination' method

Most schools use a combination of reading methods. Your child may begin with a pre-reading book, and be asked to match up words printed on small cards to words in the book (look–say). She may bring home a 'real book' for you to read together (see also Homework, p. 264). And she may do some phonic work with her class, or in a small group, at school. As she progresses, she may choose among a selection of reading books of the same standard, switch from one scheme to another, bring home lists of spellings to learn, and so on. (The Oxford Reading Tree scheme is based on a combined approach.) The vast majority of children learn to read without a great deal of difficulty, using a combination of methods.

Your child's school should provide you with information about the methods used in the school, and how you can best support your child. You may be invited to attend a meeting at which all this will be explained, or be given a fact sheet when your child starts school.

Through games children become more familiar with the characters who live in Letterland and the sounds that they make in words, the phonics approach.

Dot-to-dot, linking letters, whole words and images, some phonic skills, and reading real books typifies the Oxford Reading Tree, a combined approach.

Problems with reading

Children's abilities in the various skills needed to master reading differ widely.

Some have excellent visual memories, learning to recognize words quickly and can soon 'read' the books they bring home from school. But they may be less proficient when it comes to phonics. They find it difficult to grasp how sounds combine to make words, and their 'word attack' skills will consequently be less well developed.

Others make little headway with predominantly look–say methods. Whether because they are still immature, or because they have a learning difficulty such as dyslexia, the printed text appears to have little meaning to them (although they may love hearing stories read to them). Such children may, however, have an excellent aural memory, latching on quickly to the fact that 'd–o–g' combines to say 'dog', and they can make rapid progress if the teacher is prepared to put more emphasis on phonic materials for them. If your child falls into this category, paired reading of real books may also help by serving to remind her that reading is enjoyable, and the fact that she can recite a well-loved story can be an enormous confidence booster.

Real books may help to consolidate the skills of children who are progressing well with a look–say

Right: Regardless of the scheme(s) used in your child's school, she will enjoy looking at and reading real children's books, not simply 'reading' books.

scheme. It is the skill of a teacher in assessing just when a particular child needs a change of emphasis, or when she has made a significant step forward that can make the difference in how easily your child learns to read.

Reading for pleasure

Whether your child finds it easy or difficult to learn to read, it is important that you continue to read to her well beyond the age when she can easily read to herself. Her intellectual and moral development can be enhanced by what she reads and what is read to her (see pp. 261–2). Just as importantly, most children and parents enjoy the intimacy of reading a book together. Be guided by your intuitions, and read stories (or extracts from reference books) which you know will appeal to your child. Do not be ashamed to read 'unfashionable' authors such as Enid Blyton if your child likes them: her books got thousands of children 'hooked' on reading, and you can always discuss issues such as sexism in the Secret Seven.

Older children in the five-to-ten age group can understand that some stories 'work' at

different levels: an adventure story may also be about good and evil, for example, while the exploits of a group of animal friends can be concerned with living in a community or managing the environment. Learning to discuss how stories work, and what makes a good story – at however basic a level – is both good preparation for secondary school, and encourages your child's personal development. It may help her in her own efforts at creative writing, although this ability (like skill in other creative arts) does not necessarily come to all who can appreciate it.

A more practical reason to continue reading to your child is that you can expand her literary horizons at a time when they might otherwise become limited. It is common for older primary school children to become lodged in a particular genre or to read only reference books. Some children go on to develop a virtually monogamous relationship with a single, favourite author.

Reading to your child can be a means of introducing a range of styles and genres, as well as social issues. It is also enjoyable to share your childhood favourites with your child, on a par with introducing her to an old and much-loved friend. Re-reading the exploits of your own favourite characters can bring back intensely vivid feelings and memories of childhood which, in itself, can help to develop close relationships within families.

Writing

Like reading, writing comes very much more easily to some children than others. Some children starting school are lacking in fine motor control and need time simply to experiment with paints, felt tips and crayons, and to try activities such as sewing and other handicrafts. Others are ready to begin joining the dots, maze-tracing and the other pattern-making activities which precede learning to form letters.

It is important for children to form letters correctly, and your child's school will probably give you guidelines for use at home. Some schools now teach 'joined-up' writing almost from the start, and this can be very helpful to many children, including those who are dyslexic. Because the action of joined-up letters is more or less continuous, there are fewer opportunities to take the pencil off the page and start new letters the wrong way round.

Your child may use lined or unlined paper, depending on the activity being undertaken, and/or her age. Some teachers feel that lined paper inhibits young children's efforts; others that it helps them to position their letters correctly in relation to one another, by giving them proper reference points. As they become more confident and proficient, it is usually helpful for children to have lines, which do improve the appearance of their work. If your seven- to eight-year-old's handwriting is particularly untidy, with insufficient space between words, poorly formed letters, or frequent reversals of letters, arrange to see her teacher. Handwriting practice at this stage can sort out habits which may be difficult to break later. Certain types of poor handwriting can also be an indication of dyslexia (see pp. 285–7), which is also better tackled sooner rather than later.

Learning right from wrong

The last few years have seen mounting public concern over the behaviour of under-tens who have been involved in vandalism, theft and even murder. None of this (regardless of what the tabloids say) is new: children were involved in delinquency and lawlessness, crime and prostitution in Victorian England. This does not mean, however, that you are wrong to be concerned, or that selfish disregard for others is somehow inevitable. Nor is it the case that because moral issues – which so often involve political and economic factors – are difficult, you and your child should avoid talking about them when you feel she is old enough to do so.

Most people, not just parents, feel that society should move forward rather than regress, in other words that the quality of life should get better, not worse. Civilized communal life, however, depends upon everybody learning to show a basic concern for other people. So how can you make sure that your child learns to respect the rights of others, to show consideration for the weak and vulnerable, and to refrain from lying, stealing, cheating and violence?

Early influences

Children's moral development is closely related to their more general intellectual development. In other words, the older the child, the more sophisticated her understanding of moral issues should be, and the more controlled her behaviour. Psychologists generally agree that moral behaviour is mostly learned, rather than coming naturally to children. First and foremost your child will learn from you and her immediate family, through the attitudes, standards, and practices of your home as much as through explicit discipline or advice.

Below the age of about three, children assume that what goes on in their own home is normal, but as your child sees more of the world outside her home, and becomes better able to understand what is going on around her, the influence of people outside the family becomes steadily more important. So the attitudes and behaviour of nursery and infant school teachers, friends and neighbours (both adult and children), together with factors such as television, videos and reading material, all combine with the influence of the home to affect your developing child.

Very young children are naturally self-absorbed and demanding, and have no real moral sense. Your two-year-old will allow another child to play with her prized toy because you praise her for doing so rather than because she understands that the other child might enjoy doing so. In general, she will be 'good' if being good has pleasant consequences and if 'bad' behaviour is discouraged. This calls for a huge investment of time and energy on your part, which even with the best intentions you may sometimes feel too exhausted or busy to give. This is where the support of grandparents, friends and good-quality child care and pre-school education is invaluable. See also Coping with bad behaviour, pp. 294–5.

Control to self-control

As your child grows beyond infancy, in the years between five and ten, you have the delicate task of moving from controlling her toward a situation in which she increasingly controls herself.

Six- and seven-year-olds often make an effort to please adults in particular situations – your seven-year-old may try to help you with the tidying up, for example. As she develops a more general idea of what being 'good' means, she will try to be helpful, without being asked, in a wider range of situations.

Between the ages of nine and eleven, children develop more of a sense of order and respect for authority. Your child may take on, and take very seriously, a position of responsibility at school, or in

Cubs, Brownies, or other out-of-school organizations. Some children have a very strong sense of duty, of doing something because it is right, at this age. Give your child opportunities to take responsibility, but be aware that at the same time, she needs careful supervision. Those who are over-controlled or organized by adults may have problems negotiating the transition from adult-imposed control to self-control, in consequence only behaving well when there is a controlling adult around. Children who receive too little or wildly inconsistent guidance are also unlikely to behave well when they are on their own, or to develop conscience and self-control.

Generally it is only as children move into their teens that most develop a mature moral sense and become concerned with fairness above the simple application of 'rules', and able to see the shades of grey as well as the black and white of arguments. (Some children may, however, show this sort of maturity, and enjoy discussing moral issues, as young as nine or ten.)

Giving the right sort of moral guidance, and providing the right sort of opportunities for your child to develop a moral sense, is a delicate balancing act. Achieving this balance is particularly difficult since ideas of right and wrong seem to be less clear-cut than a generation ago. High on the list of qualities for achieving a balance, however, must come a loving and stable home environment, where parents are not afraid to impose reasonable limits or to discuss issues with children. It is important at least to try to be consistent (nobody achieves 100 per cent consistency), although not unsympathetically rigid and rule bound. The old maxim 'do as you would be done by' is useful with younger children, who usually respond to questions of the 'how would you like it if someone did that to you?' variety.

Self-worth

Guiding your child toward good manners may sound worthy and outmoded, but simple things, like learning to take turns with toys, holding open doors for elderly people or parents with buggies, offering the plate of cakes to other people first, all encourage her to control immediate, selfish impulses and to think of other people and their feelings. At the same time, she needs to develop a strong sense of self-worth, to know that, whatever her personal qualities, physical appearance, talents and weaknesses, she is loved and wanted simply for being herself.

This does not mean constantly indulging or spoiling your child or giving her an inflated and unrealistic sense of her own abilities and importance. It means helping her to control and channel her natural impulses and self-centred feelings, but at the same time teaching her not to feel ashamed that she has such impulses and feelings. It means helping her toward understanding and being kind to herself as well as to other people. And it means showing her that she matters to the people who love her.

Aiming for consistency

Real, live children do not always respond to discussion, polite requests and repeated reminders. So, like the vast majority of parents, you will sometimes lose your temper over trivial incidents, and let misdemeanours go when you know you should show your disapproval. Although you sometimes fall far short of perfection, it is important to have ideals – to aim for high and consistent standards, and consistent methods of discipline. Your child will develop the feeling that she is significant and interesting, or otherwise, through the little things that you say or do not say, do or do not do. It is important, for example, to praise good behaviour which other people might not notice, and to listen to and show respect for your child's opinions, immature and inconsistent though they may be. You do not have to agree with her. In fact, it is often good to argue, but you can at least listen. Your child will also benefit from feeling that you are interested in her friends, and in her hobbies, and from your acknowledgement of her efforts, even if they are not successful. A child who comes third in a race needs praise for her effort and achievement, not remarks of the 'People only remember the winner' or 'First next time, eh?' variety.

Your child also needs physical affection. This does not always come easily, especially to fathers, but mothers, too, seem to drift out of the habit of hugging, kissing or touching once their children have grown beyond infancy. Mothers can also become critical of their children's – especially daughters' – physiques, which undermines confidence. It is, simply, reassuring and pleasurable to children to feel that they are physically liked, and adds to their general sense of security and self-worth. If occasional hugs and kisses are not natural in your family, perhaps other, small physical kindnesses – an arm around her shoulder, stroking her hair – might feel more appropriate to you.

It is encouraging to remember that even though most parents fail to live up to their parenting ideals, most children turn out to be decent, law-abiding, non-violent adults. It is still a minority of children and young people who transgress to a serious extent. These young people are very often the product of a chaotic home life, where parents have been unable to provide a secure and stable environment, and the outside agencies of school and community have been unable to make up the missing ingredients.

Learning about money

Young children have no idea of the value of money. They do not understand large numbers or the costs involved in running a household. Your child is as likely to ask for a pencil as a pony for her birthday, and to pester you for electronic toys and gadgets that are beyond your means (and those of most other parents, too).

You can help your child's growing understanding of finances by giving her pocket money, and encouraging her to buy things for herself and to save. Talk about the differences between things you really need and luxuries which have to be saved for. Ten- and eleven-year-olds have a better understanding of the relative cost of different toys, clothes and sports gear, but it is generally not until they are in their teens that most children fully understand the need to budget, save and prioritize spending.

Children's so-called pester power can create problems, even for parents who are comfortably off. If you are out of work or on a low income, it can make you feel guilty and distressed. When people had less in the way of possessions, they tended to be better at making the most of free services and cheap entertainment (picnics with other families, making dens or go-carts, ball games). Although many children today do have expensive tastes and seem to have an overwhelming need to be entertained much of the time, they can be taught to enjoy simple pleasures and value the time they spend in activities with you.

If your children have to use their imagination and entertain themselves, they learn to value and enjoy

Birthday parties

Children's birthday parties have become increasingly extravagant affairs in the last few years. In addition to coping with hordes of over-excited children, today's parents can feel obliged to engage 'entertainers', to produce a cake sculpted and iced to professional standards and to send each child home with a bulging party bag. And woe betide you if any of your guests has already seen 'Uncle Charlie's Magic Show' or if your party bags are not up to scratch: today's children can complain long and hard.

Know your limitations. If lack of money, space or your temperament are problems, have the courage to do the party your way.

- Have an old-fashioned party with well-organized games.
- Take a couple of children to the theatre or cinema, or out to tea.
- Swimming parties, when you provide the food afterward, use up surplus energy, but must be properly supervised.
- Some community centres cater for children's parties and the cost may include the hire of equipment, such as a bouncy castle. These can be fun, but restrict the numbers using the castle at any one time, and bring off anyone who is being silly.
- Ten-pin bowling, roller and ice skating are also popular and older children enjoy barbecues.

Finally, you are not obliged to give party bags. Teach your child not to demand them, and not to make disparaging remarks about their contents.

what they have. They also learn that life is unfair sometimes. It is hard for a child to accept that her parents cannot afford a new bike or a computer when a friend at school has one. Tell her you understand that it is hard. And remind her that it is difficult to have it all: Tom may only have a new bike because his mum has a good job that takes her away a lot. But he doesn't have anyone to help with his homework.

As long as you have a consistent attitude to money, your children are more likely to remember later the day you walked along the river with a picnic than that they did not have the latest pair of trainers.

PROBLEMS AT SCHOOL

The chances are that your child will experience problems at school at some point in her life. In most cases, problems are temporary and easily resolved simply by talking to the people involved, but sometimes they are more serious. Standards of pastoral care in today's schools are generally very high, with teachers genuinely concerned for their pupils' happiness and well-being. You should also remember that in many areas schools are now in the position of having to compete with one another for pupils: it is in their own interest to take problems seriously, and to do their utmost to resolve them quickly, efficiently and tactfully.

School phobia

Sometimes children develop a fear or hatred of school and refuse to attend. The form of refusal may be dramatic and alarming: your child may scream and flail; have panic attacks; or display physical symptoms such as vomiting or severe headaches. In some cases, such children have always disliked school, while in others, the problem appears out of the blue. In a sense, there are as many reasons for school phobia as there are children suffering from it, but the main questions to ask are:

Is your child being bullied?

Bullying is a major cause of a sudden refusal to go to school (see pp. 282–3).

Has your child moved to a new class?

Children are quite often unsettled by moving to another class, especially if they were particularly fond of their previous teacher. They may have heard rumours (usually unfounded) of how strict the new teacher is, or of how hard the work is in his or her class, and be genuinely frightened of what awaits them. If this applies to your child, first reassure her that you will sort things out. Depending on how severely worried your child is (for example, if she feels or is sick, or begins to sweat, breathe rapidly, or turns very pale) it may be sensible to keep her off school for a day or so, until you can make an appointment to speak to the teacher in private.

If you have to do this, do not let your child dwell on her problems. Keep her occupied, and try to include some school work in the day's activities. Question her discreetly to make sure that there are no additional problems. Has she been misbehaving at school, for instance? Or has she failed to complete a project or homework assignment?

When you speak to the teacher, try to explain the situation calmly, and be honest without being abrasive. Listen to the teacher's and the head teacher's observations and suggestions, so that, together, you can decide on a course of action. It may be that you need to take your child to speak to the teacher, out of lesson time. On the other hand, your child may be happy that you have seen the teacher, and be prepared to try returning to school as normal.

You may need specialist help if the situation has not resolved itself within two or three weeks, as your child may quickly settle into the new routine.

Is there an undiagnosed learning difficulty or health problem?

If your child suddenly refuses to go to school, or becomes very agitated and upset, it may be that she is experiencing problems with her work because of an undiagnosed learning difficulty. It sometimes happens that problems are caused by a relatively minor deficiency in eyesight or hearing, which can easily be checked by the school nurse and, if necessary, followed up by a visit to the appropriate specialist. In other cases, a child has a more potentially serious problem or an undiagnosed illness which is preventing her from performing as normal. Again, this sort of difficulty can be pinpointed through discussion with your child, and consultation with her teacher, school nurse and GP.

A child of seven, for example, may have managed to get through

Years One and Two without anyone realizing that she had a learning difficulty. As she reaches the age of seven or eight, and more is expected, she can respond by becoming school phobic. The discovery of a learning difficulty in this sort of situation always comes as a shock to parents, who often feel bitter: how could the school have failed to notice that something was wrong? In fact, it is often extremely difficult to

Right: It can be difficult to cope with problems at school, and above all your child needs your reassurance.

pinpoint learning difficulties in young children because of the enormous variation in their abilities at the infant stage (see Spotting learning difficulties, pp. 284–7). Once such problems are identified and the appropriate help is provided, the outlook is hopeful and children who are school phobic for this reason quickly become more confident and settled.

Does she 'fit in'?

It is sometimes difficult for children to pinpoint exactly why they are unhappy at school. You can probably look back on your schooldays and understand any problems you may have had but young children lack the social experience to analyse their situation. Is she being taunted because of her race or religion? Does her accent 'fit'? Are her clothes slightly different from those of her classmates? Is she the only one not allowed to watch television from the moment she gets home from school until bedtime? Has a particularly dominant child taken an irrational dislike to her and encouraged other children to start shunning her?

It may be that no physical bullying occurs, but a sensitive child can feel desperately unhappy, and be unable to put into words what, exactly, is the matter. Some sensitive children respond by becoming school phobic. If you suspect that your child finds herself in a situation of this type, think carefully about the social aspects of her education. Try, gently, to get to the bottom of the problem: Do other children tease or taunt? What sorts of things do they say? If your child cannot or will not explain, back off (although she may be willing to write down, rather than talk about, her experiences, so give her the opportunity to do so). It may be that you and your family are the butt of jokes or taunts. Children are often fiercely loyal to their parents. And if, for some reason, you are at the root of the problem, your child may not feel able to tell you.

If your child will not or cannot enlighten you, arrange to see her teacher. As ever, be frank but do not make unfounded accusations; you want to find out what is wrong, not to alienate the school. After discussion, the school may be able to act, and your child may settle down. If, however, matters do not improve and, after careful investigation, you conclude that your child simply does not 'fit in', it may be sensible to consider moving her.

Bullying

The issue of bullying is now high profile. Although there will probably always be individuals who gain satisfaction and kudos by hurting or intimidating others, schools are now taking a concerted stand against bullying, whether verbal or physical (including any form of intimidation, particularly but not exclusively of a racial nature). If your child becomes involved, whether as victim or perpetrator, you can expect matters to be taken seriously.

Many schools have a 'whole school' policy on bullying. This means that staff members have come together, discussed the issue and formulated a policy so that pupils, parents and staff know exactly where the school stands, and who to approach if bullying is going on. Some primary schools feel confident that their existing supervisory and disciplinary systems are sufficient, and may not have a policy statement on bullying as such, but this does not mean that they are unconcerned and, as in other schools, a complaint about bullying will be treated seriously.

The school prospectus may include the school's policy on bullying, or you may be told what can be expected if bullying is going on if you are invited to a 'new parents' meeting when your child starts school. If you are not informed, ask.

Who becomes a victim?

The popular view is that the children who become victims of bullies are always 'different' in some way – obese, members of a racial minority, hopeless at sport, quiet and studious. But any child can be bullied and bullying is not necessarily physical. It is usually begun by a dominant child whose friends then join in and can quickly gather momentum and become habitual in a group or class. Individual members of the group may not realize that their 'teasing' or 'horseplay' is actually a form of bullying.

If the school acts promptly and sensitively, victims may suffer no long-term damage. If it is allowed to continue, a victim's self-esteem and confidence may be badly damaged and she may carry the scars into adult life.

Help with bullying

Kidscape publishes a 'Stop Bullying' leaflet and operates a Parents' Bullying Line (Monday and Wednesday 9am–5pm). Try also the Anti-Bullying Campaign (see Useful Contacts, pp. 390–3).

Books about bullying include *The Angel of Nitshill Road* by Anne Fine (suitable for ages 7–10), *The Present Takers* by Aidan Chambers (age 9–10 upward) and *Lord of the Flies* by William Golding (age 10–11 upward).

If your child becomes (or you suspect that she has become) a victim of bullying, alert the staff immediately. If your child is below the age of seven or eight, she is likely to feel angry or frightened, and will expect you and her teacher to put matters right. Unless they have been told by parents or older children not to do so, young children do not usually concern themselves about 'sneaking' or 'telling tales'. Beyond this age, children generally do balk at reporting bullying. They may also feel ashamed of being a victim, and worried about confiding in parents or teachers.

This is where strong leadership on the part of staff and good organization within the school are vital. Children should feel confident that bullying will not be tolerated, and the school day should be organized and supervised so that opportunities for bullying are minimized. This means that break times need to be properly supervised (school meals assistants may keep responsibility for 'their' class through lunchtime play), and that areas such as cloakrooms or secluded corners have to be watched, or declared off-limits. Some schools have introduced off-limits quiet areas in the playground where children who do not like the hurly-burly of the playground can sit in peace, which again can help if bullying is going on. Schools in which children are occupied with lunchtime clubs and activities are also less likely to have problems.

Making a complaint

Regardless of the school's declared intolerance of bullying, you may still be unsure when to make a complaint: where, for example, does the normal rough and tumble of school life end, and bullying begin? There are no easy answers, as children vary so much in temperament; one child responds to threats or taunts in kind and makes a fuss, another is meek and mild and goes home to brood.

You have to rely, to some extent, on common sense and intuition. If your child is obviously unhappy, and you are aware of unpleasantness at school, then you must investigate. You can go to the school in confidence, without telling your child, if necessary (a good school will make enquiries and report to you). Good relationships with a couple of other parents may help you to sort out what is going on too.

If your child is a bully

It can be just as devastating to discover that your child is a bully as to find out that she is being bullied. In some cases, a child who bullies others does not perceive herself as a bully, and is unaware of how distressing her behaviour is to her victim(s). It is in her long-term interest to be made aware, and to be encouraged to be more sensitive. A child who bullies has to know that you, other children and adults disapprove, and has to learn other, more socially acceptable ways of channelling her energies and abilities.

- If your child is bullying others, confront the problem, but do not to leave her feeling that by labelling her a bully, you have, in some sense, written her off. She should be left in no doubt that what she has done is wrong, and should be given time to think matters over and explain herself, but she also needs a way forward.
- It may help to talk things over with friends and with the staff at your child's school. Opportunities to try out a new sport or leisure activity may also help to provide a framework and structure for your child. It is usually better to choose interests or activities in which she stands a reasonable chance of success, and which have clear systems of goals and rewards.

If you feel you are making no progress and your child persists in bullying others, you should ask for help (in the form of counselling or psychological assessment) through her school. Sometimes children who bully manage to control their behaviour at school but, once they reach home, sneak off and torment animals or younger brothers and sisters. Again, children who are behaving like this need specialist help.

Spotting learning difficulties

The learning difficulties faced by children born with conditions such as Down's syndrome or cerebral palsy, can be predicted by medical and educational support staff who will also monitor such children, and provide specialist help at the appropriate time in a child's development. In other cases, however, a child appears to fall within the 'normal' range of abilities and development but at some point in her school career you or her teachers may become aware that she is having particular or more general learning difficulties. Although the diagnosis of a learning difficulty can cause distress and anxiety, it is better if a problem is identified early, so that you can seek specialist help.

This is, unfortunately, not always easy. Not only is the range of normal development particularly wide between the ages of five and seven, but children are also adept at coping with their difficulties, and sometimes manage to conceal problems for weeks or even months, until they are revealed by routine medical checks or school tests. A gradual deterioration in hearing or sight, for example, can be masked for quite a long time if your child is sufficiently determined. (Make sure she knows that her sight should not be deteriorating with age: she may have heard a grown-up bemoaning this fact.) Problems with maths can be got round by copying

The independent schools' position

Independent schools are not obliged to provide for special educational needs, although they may do so. This is a point to raise when you go to look around a school, if you know that your child has special needs. If a problem arises during the time that she is a pupil, arrange to see the head teacher. Staff of a good school will be sympathetic to your child's needs (although this may involve a recommendation that you change school), and may be able to arrange a psychological assessment through the LEA, or privately. The Independent Schools Information Service (ISIS) can advise on which school(s) may be most suitable for children with special educational needs.

the work of the other children on her table. Or she might remember the passage in a book and recite it almost verbatim to her teacher. Teachers, and you, need to be vigilant. (Although their value has been questioned by some teachers, the national tests at seven and eleven may help them identify children who are masking learning difficulties.)

There are two broad types of learning difficulty: specific (such as dyslexia) and general (problems with many or most areas of the curriculum). A child with either type of difficulty may experience problems for a whole range of physical or mental reasons. She may, for example, have behavioural problems in relating to other children or to staff, and so make little academic progress. Or, her development may be delayed due to complications at birth, or because she was a premature baby. Often, the reasons are more difficult to pinpoint.

Children who had physical, mental or behavioural problems used to be classed as mentally or physically 'handicapped', 'educationally subnormal', 'severely subnormal', and so on, and were usually educated in 'special schools'. One of the aims of the 1981 Education Act was to integrate as many children as possible within 'normal' schools. Efforts are now made to provide such children with the specialist help, materials and facilities they need, without withdrawing them from ordinary lessons. This is usually to the benefit of the children involved, and helps to promote tolerance and understanding within the school and outside community. In current parlance, children with learning difficulties are therefore thought of not as 'handicapped' or 'retarded', but as having 'special educational needs'. A new code of practice for the identification and assessment of special educational needs came into force in September 1994.

What you can do

- If you suspect that your child is experiencing learning difficulties, speak to her teacher in the first instance (if her teacher has noticed problems, he or she will approach you). You will be given the name of the school's special needs co-ordinator, who will speak to you and your child's class teacher, and see your child. The special needs co-ordinator will then draw up an 'individual education plan' with specific targets, and set a date for a review of your child's progress. That may be all that your child needs.

- If the staff at your child's school feel that it is appropriate to call on specialist advice, a specialist teacher or educational psychologist may be brought in. He or she, in collaboration with the school's special needs co-ordinator, will then draw up a plan for your child.
- If you or her class teacher are still concerned about her lack of progress, the head teacher may ask the LEA to make a 'statutory assessment' of your child. A professional involved with your child (such as your GP) or you yourself can also request a statutory assessment, but always talk to your child's school first.

The special assessment procedure

The LEA will consider all relevant information and tell you whether or not they feel that your child should be assessed. If the LEA decides not to make a statutory assessment, both you and your child's school will be informed in writing why not. Your child's school, possibly with outside specialist help, will then be expected to provide for all her needs.

Once the LEA has decided to proceed with an assessment, you and the school will be informed and the LEA will begin to gather information (your views, those of her teacher(s), relevant medical details and so on) about your child. At this stage, the LEA will also give you details of specialist help in both mainstream and specialist schools in your area. You will be told that you are welcome to bring a 'named person' of your choice along with you to any further meetings or interviews. (A named person is someone you choose who should be able to give you information and advice, as well as moral support, perhaps an as yet uninvolved health or educational professional.)

After statutory assessment, the LEA will decide whether to go ahead with a 'Statement of Special Educational Needs' (often referred to as a 'statement'). This is a document in six parts, which sets out in detail your child's needs and the specialist help she should have. Before the statement is sent out in its final form, you will receive a 'proposed statement', complete except for part four, the section stating which school your child should attend, and other special arrangements for her education. The LEA will also provide details of all the schools – ordinary state schools, special state schools, non-maintained special schools (that is, non-profit-making schools which charge fees), and approved independent schools.

You have the right to express a preference over which school you would like your child to attend at this point, as long as: the school is deemed suitable for your child, your child's presence will not affect the 'efficient education' of existing pupils, and sending your child to that school is agreed to be an efficient use of LEA resources.

If the LEA decides that a statement is not appropriate in your child's case, you may be given a 'note in lieu of a statement', explaining the LEA's decision. You will also receive copies of all the letters and reports made about your child during the assessment period. With your agreement, this information will also be sent to your child's school to help staff draw up an appropriate programme of work for her.

You have various rights of appeal. You can appeal to the Special Educational Needs Tribunal if:
- your request for a statutory assessment is turned down in the first place;
- after assessment, the LEA refuses to make out a statement; or
- you disagree with the description of your child's learning difficulties, the special help to be given, or the type of school or particular school recommended by the LEA.

You can also appeal later, if your child has a statement and the LEA refuses to reassess her or decides to stop maintaining the statement.

Dyslexia

Dyslexia, also referred to as a 'specific learning difficulty', is a neurological condition which impedes the development of the skills needed to read and write. It is the single most common learning difficulty among primary schoolchildren, believed to affect in the region of 10 per cent of the population; its effects range from slight reading or spelling difficulties to complete illiteracy.

An experienced observer can spot indications that a child may be dyslexic at the preschool stage, but it is usually when she is between seven and eight that her difficulties become most evident. This is because many of the features of dyslexia – a tendency to reverse letters or numbers, or to 'mirror write', and

Spotting dyslexia early

Research financed by Humberside County Council has developed a cognitive profiling system (COPS) for identifying dyslexic children as soon as they start school. The system, which runs on a CD-ROM, consists of eight simple skills tests which pinpoint potential problems and suggests the most appropriate teaching methods for individual children. For further details contact Lucid Systems (see Useful Contacts, pp. 390–3).

If your child is dyslexic, you may find *Dyslexia: What Parents Ought to Know* by Vera Quin and Alan Macauslan, informative.

difficulties in learning to read – are also found in other, young children. You should not, therefore, assume that because your five- or even six-year-old writes d instead of b, or ɘ instead of e, or cannot read her school reading book with reasonable fluency, that she is dyslexic.

Remember that in much of continental Europe, children do not begin to learn to read and write until they are six or seven. In this sense, the British system with its enormous emphasis on reading skills, expects a lot of some of its Years One and Two children. At the same time, it is better for a learning difficulty to be diagnosed sooner rather than later.

Indications that your child may be dyslexic, rather than having general learning difficulties or simply being immature include:

- She appears bright and articulate but makes little headway with reading or writing.
- She may repeatedly confuse right and left.
- She may make little progress with 'look–say' reading methods, or with the 'real books' approach (see pp. 274–5).
- She may have a short attention span when reading and writing.
- She may appear to read a word in a reading book, but fail to recognize the same word further down the page.
- By the age of seven, she may have developed a complete antipathy toward reading and/or school work in general.

By the time a dyslexic child is seven, her difficulties are more noticeable because they are set against the increasing competence of other children. A dyslexic child is still struggling with her reading, and may read in a jerky, staccato style, punctuated by long pauses, when other children are beginning to read fluently. A dyslexic child still struggles to form letters, continues to reverse letters or writes from right to left, when other children are becoming faster, neater and generally more proficient. And while a dyslexic child may have been previously unaware of her shortcomings, she now begins to notice them – as do the other children.

There are several routes open to you if you suspect your child is dyslexic.

- Speak to your child's class teacher and arrange to see the school's special educational needs co-ordinator. Depending on your child's age and the severity of her problems, and the school, good quality help may be available within the school, or from visiting specialist teachers. You may consider moving your child to a school with good resources in this area.
- Consult your GP. There are many reasons for dyslexia and some children may be helped through simple medical treatment. If your child had a difficult birth, or has problems with her ears, sight, speech, or with breathing and adenoids, the medical angle may be worth investigating.
- Request an assessment by a specialist psychologist with an organization such as the Dyslexia Institute. An assessment takes about two hours, and will be followed by a consultation between you and the psychologist (your child will be able to go to a play area).
  You will be given immediate, practical advice (where to buy the appropriate books, pencil grips, and so on). The psychologist may also recommend a course of lessons, which are geared specifically to the needs of the individual child, at your local Dyslexia Institute centre. Depending on the nature and extent of your child's dyslexia, you may be able to help her at home. Again the psychologist can offer specific, individual advice. Dyslexic children have a poor visual memory, but some have an excellent ear for sounds and respond well to phonic methods of teaching of reading and spelling (try 'From Alpha to Omega', see p. 274).

Although the discovery that your child is dyslexic can come as a shock, her educational prospects are by no means hopeless. Not only is knowledge and understanding of dyslexia increasing, but modern specialist teaching can also help your child to cope with and overcome her difficulties. You can make sure that she does not miss out because she cannot read to herself by reading to her regularly, and borrowing or buying story cassette tapes.

When she is old enough, it may be helpful if she learns to type and use a word processor. This gets over the problem of indecipherable writing, while erratic spelling can be corrected by using a word processing programme with a 'spell check' function.

General learning difficulties

Some children work at a slower pace than others and have problems across many or most areas of the school curriculum. There may be medical, psychological or sociological reasons for their slower rate of progress and remedial action may call for a multidisciplinary approach (see pp. 284–5).

If your child does seem to be having problems, her teacher will contact you to discuss her progress. It is important to co-operate with the suggestions made by the school, for example, to help with reading and other assignments at home. It is also vital that your child develops a strong sense of her own self-worth (see pp. 278–9).

Is your child gifted?

You or your child's teachers might notice that she has an extraordinary talent, ability or potential. Perhaps she is highly accomplished in one of the performing arts or a sport, or shows outstanding spatial/mechanical ability, or an exceptional level of academic attainment. Sometimes, a child may have a very high IQ, but – for a range of reasons – be underperforming at school.

If your child is gifted, you face the dilemma of reconciling perhaps advanced educational requirements with normal emotional and social needs. This is not easy. In some cases, it may be worth considering moving your child to an independent school, with a high teacher–pupil ratio and the flexibility to allow her to work at a faster pace in certain subject areas.

Alternatively your child may be happier at her local school, with extension activities after school or at weekends. The National Association for Gifted Children (see Useful Contacts, pp. 390–3) provides information on how to tell whether a child is gifted, and on the best ways to give gifted children encouragement and the opportunity to develop their talents as fully as possible. The Association also provides moral support for gifted children and their families, and organizes a range of out-of-school activities for children, and meetings/networks for families.

Finding a private tutor

From time to time, you may worry that your child's teacher is not 'stretching', or expecting enough from, her. In many cases, such worries are ill founded: an investigated child is usually found to be working at a level well above national averages. There are occasions, however, when children do under-perform in relation to others of their age.

If this is the case with your child, speak to her teacher, and discuss your concerns with the head teacher. If matters do not improve, speak to a school governor. (The school should provide you with a list of governors' names and contact numbers each year – practices vary, but usually some retire each year, making space for new ones. Some of the governors will also be parents of children at the school, often making a point of being available in the playground before or after school.) Ask for the matter to be raised at the next Governors' meeting. You are entitled to attend the school's annual parents' meeting, and will receive a copy of the annual report, which sets out details of the school's performance and future plans.

You may feel that your child is progressing reasonably well, but needs more individual help than her teacher is able to give. This may be in relation to a particular subject, or it may be across the board. (Many parents are especially concerned if their child is about to move from a state primary school to an independent secondary school, with entry by competitive exam.) In such cases, your child may well benefit from working with a good private tutor. If she is going to take an entrance exam, make sure that the tutor is experienced in coaching for exams. In all cases, check references and, if possible, select a tutor on personal recommendation. (The Association of Tutors vets its members and will recommend tutors in your area, see Useful Contacts, pp. 390–3.)

OUTSIDE SCHOOL

One of the major differences between your childhood and that of your children is the slow but sure erosion of childhood freedoms. The volume of traffic on the roads, and the fear of violent crime have led to a situation in which you are almost certainly unhappy about allowing your children the liberty you once took for granted (see also pp. 297–9). One result of this shift in attitudes is that children's leisure time has become increasingly planned by adults. Children once learned to run, jump and climb with friends in the local park – now you take them to sports centres and gym clubs. They learn the same skills, probably more safely, but adults are in charge and the skills often have to be mastered, performed, tested and graded.

Right: Children need the freedom to relax with friends, as well as taking part in structured activities.

The case for moderation

The level of children's skills and accomplishments is often astonishing. They perform complicated gymnastic tumbling sequences; they gain medals and certificates for swimming before they leave primary school. But there are real dangers inherent in both over-structuring by adults, and pushing children too hard, too young, and in too many activities.

To begin with, some children noticeably lose the ability to amuse themselves, so that you have to 'lay on' or manufacture all their fun. At the same time,

supposedly pleasurable, leisure-time activities become stressful, with youngsters of slightly better than average ability in, say, music or sport being made to work as though they were young professionals. There is also the very real danger that children of primary-school age who have been shuttled from piano lessons to horse riding to football practice to drama club, develop a 'been there, done that' attitude before they reach their teens.

Obviously you want to see your child performing ably, and it is satisfying to be able to nurture her talents, especially if you feel that you were denied ample opportunities to develop your own gifts when you were a child. But for children to enjoy their out-of-school activities, and to remain happy and well adjusted, moderation is essential. One or two activities per week are enough for most children in the five- to ten-year age group, and some free, un-adult-structured time each day is essential to their well-being.

Providing opportunities

Most five-to-sevens are still at the stage where they find the school day tiring, so, depending on your child's stamina, it is probably better to try to organize activities, especially for younger ones, at the weekends rather than after school. The range of activities open to children is immense. You are probably aware of the popular options, but if your child would like to try some of the more unusual sports/leisure activities, your local sports centre or library should have full details of what is available in your area.

If your child has a special talent (see Is your child gifted?, p. 287), it is important to get the best tuition you can afford, and to get informed guidance from qualified people (get a second, or even a third opinion, so that you can make a balanced judgement). Generally, it is difficult not to notice prodigious or outstanding talent: your child's natural ability, together with her fascination for her subject,

Bedtime

Some parents are prepared to let their children stay up until they are tired and ask to be put to bed or take themselves off. As long as your children do not become overtired and unable to work at school, then that choice is yours.

Most parents, however, have neither the stamina nor the temperament to cope with this sort of flexible arrangement and need to establish a bedtime routine.

- The majority of fives to sevens are tired by the school day. After school they need time to relax, have a meal and complete any work they have been set at school. If your child has begun to play a musical instrument, she may need to practise. By around seven o'clock, most are ready for a bath and story and want to sleep within half an hour or so. Avoid exciting play, stories or television programmes, especially if your child is afraid of the dark, fears monsters under the bed or has nightmares. Leave a light on if she is genuinely frightened.
- Between the ages of seven and eleven, children develop more stamina. They can bath themselves, but they still need attention in the

form of play, stories or opportunities simply to talk to you. Use your discretion over what television programmes you allow your children to watch (and remember that some early evening soaps tackle issues that may worry young children). Most sevens to nines should be in bed around eight or eight thirty during the week; nines to elevens around an hour later. Many children like to read in bed, although you should set a time limit. Some parents are against their children having a cassette player in the bedroom, but a carefully chosen story can soothe a child to sleep and is ideal for a slow or reluctant reader. Whether you allow radio or television in the bedroom is up to you. If you do, set time limits on the type and extent of watching or listening. It is also sensible to observe the nine o'clock watershed for TV programmes.

You can relax weekday bedtime routines at the weekends and during the school holidays. It is good for your children's social development – and enjoyable – when they can stay up later with you, go out in the evening, or socialize when you have friends round.

and dedication to practice or training, combine to produce what is, in fact, a very rare phenomenon.

In some ways, it is more difficult to decide what to do if your child is merely talented, well above average in sport, drama, dance or music, but not in the 'child prodigy' class. There are two main pitfalls.

- You may simply overlook or even deny that she has a talent at all so that her gift remains undeveloped. When she grows up and is earning her own living, she may take private lessons and make rapid progress. But she will not have put in the years of practice needed to become a professional. If her talent is for a sport, her age will be against her.

- You may exaggerate your child's talent, and push her too much so that she faces a childhood of competitions and exams, with little time for anything else. Many children who have been effectively robbed of a normal childhood, end up jaded and burned out in their teens.

This does not mean that you should not encourage your talented child and provide her with as many opportunities as possible. But keep a sense of proportion: talented children also need to play, read, and slump in front of the television, in addition to practising, training and coping with school work.

Dancing

Dancing continues to be a popular pastime, particularly among girls, but boys who want to learn also deserve parental encouragement. Most children begin with ballet and tap, but modern and jazz dance are growing in popularity, and are probably more fun for those who enjoy the expressive rather than the precision side of dancing.

Most teachers of dance go to great lengths to ensure that working for exams is balanced by performing in shows for family and friends. When choosing a school, ask about the teachers' qualifications, check that the floor is wooden (a surface that does not 'give' can harm young backs and legs) and that the

room is heated, and make sure that the children are not forced into working for exams too young.

Many young children, including those of only average ability, love dance and keep up their interest into their teens and beyond. Natural ability is often apparent from a very early age, but you and your would-be performer should remember that the world of professional dance is fiercely competitive, and that performing careers are comparatively short.

Swimming

Five to six years is a good age for children to learn to swim, and most enjoy it. If she has attended preschool swimming sessions and feels confident in and around water so much the better. If your five- or six-year-old has never been to a swimming pool, however, there is no need to worry, although you may have to be patient if she is more frightened of the water than some toddlers. Take your child to the pool a few times as a family before you embark upon a course of lessons so that she becomes familiar with the layout of the changing rooms, can find the toilets, and gets used to the sounds and smells of the pool. Do not try to overcome your child's apprehension by splashing her, or pressurizing her to jump into the water or go down slides.

Most swimming pools organize children's swimming lessons under the auspices of the Amateur Swimming Association (ASA); the ratio of adults to children should be no more than 1:6 for five- to six-year-olds. Boys under the age of about eight are usually allowed to use the women's changing rooms if they are accompanied by their mother. Make sure that the men's changing rooms are supervised if you have an older boy who is using them on his own.

Once your child can swim, it is often more interesting and enjoyable for her if you

Left: Ballet lessons do not have to mean endless exams – both boys and girls like moving to music, and social contact with like-minded peers.

vary the pace and nature of any further courses. Stop formal lessons for a time so that she can consolidate her skills and simply enjoy swimming. Alternatively, try a stroke improvement, water polo or a diving course. It is important to be able to swim and it is satisfying to be able to swim well, but there is no obligation for children to have achieved both goals by the age of ten.

Gymnastics

The years between the ages of five and ten are also good for children who want to try gymnastics. Since the sport became popular in the early 1970s, clubs have flourished, and courses and activities are widely available for both girls and boys. In beginners' and novice classes, children learn basic rolling, balancing, swinging and jumping movements, and begin to work toward the Amateur Gymnastics Association award. Boys' and girls' classes are segregated from the time they begin to work for awards, as the disciplines in men's and women's gymnastics differ. Most children can accomplish what is required in the first award without too many problems, but thereafter the going gets more difficult. Some are willing to persevere for a time, at a slower pace than the naturally talented children, others effectively de-select themselves from the age of eight or nine. Be guided by what your child wants and do not force her to continue if she really does not want to.

Right: Playing an instrument can be very satisfying, but practice is vital.

Music

A large number of children learn to play musical instruments and, as they get over the early stages, enjoy playing in a variety of groups and ensembles.

Most children are ready to begin an instrument at around the age of eight (one of the most common reasons for children giving up on music is because they start too early). By this age, your child should be reading reasonably fluently and have the physical stamina and co-ordination to be able to enjoy lessons. She will also need to understand that she must practise regularly and needs the energy to do so.

The piano

It tends to come naturally to start children with piano lessons, but the piano is not necessarily the most suitable instrument to choose for your child. She will have to learn to read two lines of music, for the right and the left hand; progress is comparatively slow; and the piano tends to be a solitary instrument, so that children miss out on the fun of playing in groups together (although they can, of course, make music on their own, without needing the support of other instrumentalists).

Other instruments

Children who play stringed instruments, such as the violin and 'cello, can begin quite early, depending on the teacher and method you choose, and if your child has enjoyed the recorder (still usually taught at school), she may be ready to start the oboe, flute or clarinet, but remember that it takes time to develop the technique necessary to produce a note.

If your child expresses an interest in playing one of the brass instruments, she may have to wait until she is older. The one exception to this is the cornet, which some young children do take to quite readily. It is a good idea to wait until her second teeth are firmly in place, before allowing her to start playing any instrument that involves blowing.

What you can do

- Whatever instrument your child plays, regular practice is essential. In the early stages, 10 minutes a day may be sufficient (your child's teacher will give guidelines). It is also important that your child likes her teacher.
- Try to resist pushing your child through the grade exams as quickly as possible. It can be stressful for even a musical child to cope with one exam after another, with no space to consolidate what she has learned, develop her musicianship and simply enjoy playing. Compliant pre-teens have a habit of becoming obstreperous teenagers. And parents who push too hard too soon may produce children who, once they find their own voices, say 'no'.

Sports and games

Toward the upper end of the primary school, most children begin to enjoy team games, which often call for high levels of skill and co-ordination. At this age the choice of sports might be limited to netball, soccer or rounders but once your child moves on to secondary school, the range becomes wider. If your primary-school child is interested in rugby football, hockey or cricket, it is worth contacting your local sports centre or clubs to see whether there are training programmes for youngsters. Some children prefer individual sports to team games. In all but the most remote areas of the country, there are generally facilities for those wanting to try these activities. Sports clubs and leisure centres should have details; alternatively, contact the Sports Council for advice.

Tennis

The advent of 'short tennis' and lighter rackets have meant that children as young as five can learn basic tennis skills, and children of ten can become strong

Many sports develop children's team spirit, in addition to physical fitness. Try to encourage without pushing.

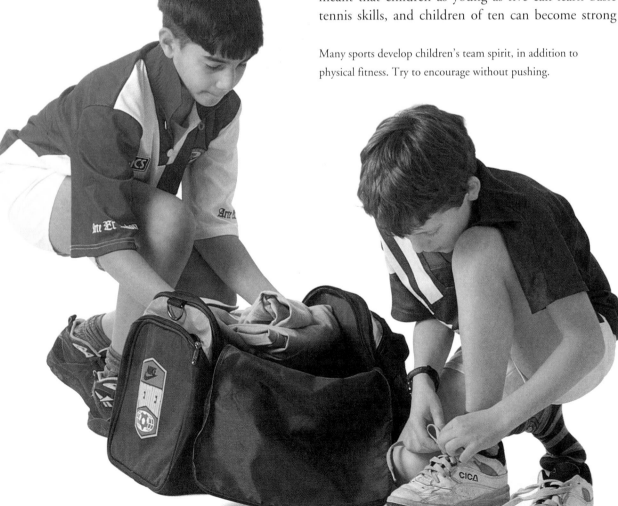

Non-sporting activities

The sedentary lifestyle of many of today's youngsters is causing concern, with fears that 'couch potato' children are laying the foundations of health problems in later life. If your child hates team games, and lacks the co-ordination for dance or gymnastics, there are many other forms of physical activity which help to build strength, stamina and a sense of physical well-being.

Walking in the country on flat or hilly ground, and the challenge of map-reading thrill some children. Some progress to orienteering.

Cycling has become much safer with the opening up of cycle ways and the development of helmets. Bicycles should be in good order with efficient brakes and lights, and your child must wear reflective bands on her clothing. Your child's school or the local road safety officer should be able to give you advice.

Climbing is often introduced on school activity holidays, but some sports centres also have climbing walls, where young children can have a taste of climbing, in safety and under supervision.

Fishing and birdwatching are healthy, outdoor activities which can involve a lot of walking, and which can also build up the confidence of a child who thinks she is no good at anything physical.

Gardening can become a lifelong passion from a young age, with your encouragement.

Horseriding need not be expensive at beginner's level. Ensure that your child wears a properly fitting hard hat – schools allow children to borrow at first – and check that the school she attends is approved by the British Horse Society.

Ice-skating rinks are few and far between, but your child may enjoy roller-skating.

and proficient players. Many sports and community centres have facilities for short tennis, and local tennis clubs may provide lessons and court time for youngsters. Because some children do become good players, the temptation to train hard is strong. But the dangers of over-playing – in the form of physical injury and mental burnout – at a young age are well documented. Keep a sense of perspective.

Television and video

There is no doubt that television and video have a significant influence on most children's (and adults') lives. Although the quality of British children's television is good, and some programmes are exceptional, there is concern about the amount of television some children watch. It is difficult to prove direct, causal links between, say, television or video violence and violent crime. But you may have misgivings, especially when you can see the influence of favourite programmes, and advertising, on your child.

The problem with allowing your child to watch television is not simply that she may watch 'too much' of a possibly negative nature, but also that while she is spending time in front of the television, she is not doing other things, especially activities which involve other people, and/or being outside and moving. As a result, she may over-identify with programmes and characters, and miss out on the range of leisure opportunities which now exists. As she gets older, her school work may also suffer.

Despite a tightening up on issuing adult videos to underage consumers, it is still possible for irresponsible adults to allow children access to sexually explicit and violent videos in the home. This is something to check up on if your child is spending the night at a friend's house. As she gets older, and her friends boast about what they have seen, it is understandable for your child to plead to see films which you may find distasteful or inappropriate. If you firmly believe that a film is unsuitable, say so, explain why, and suggest an alternative.

What you can do

- If you are concerned that your child is watching too much television, cut down gradually rather than banning programmes altogether.
- Arrange activities at some of the times when your child would otherwise slump in front of the screen, so that she does not realize that she is being 'deprived'.
- Try to select programmes in advance, and watch together, so that television viewing comes to be seen as special, rather than an automatic option.
- Encourage your child to listen to the radio (not just the pop stations) as an alternative to watching television.

Videos and video games

The British Board of Film Classification offers a guide to suitability for films released on video. These are:

U   Universal
Uc (Universal, but especially for children)
PG Parental Guidance (may be unsuitable for children, especially young children)
12 Not suitable for under-12s
15 Not suitable for under-15s
18 Not suitable for under-18s.

All video games featuring real people, sex or undue violence must also have a BBFC rating.

The European Leisure Software Publishers Association recommends age guidance for video games, but the scheme is voluntary. ELSPA ratings are: 0–10; 11–14; 15–17; 18+.

- Children under ten should not, by and large, watch adult programmes scheduled after the nine o'clock watershed (though obviously you have to use your own discretion). Their content may be disturbing: this is equally true of documentaries and fiction.
- Think carefully before allowing your child to have a television set in her room.

HOW CHILDREN BEHAVE

Fashions in how to manage children and how to cope with problems in behaviour change: compare the 'children should be seen and not heard' philosophy of the Victorians, with the 'progressive' child-rearing methods of the 1960s, for example. There has been something of a backlash in the 1990s, with the idealism of the 1960s – never say 'no' to a child, but 'negotiate' a course of softer options – now seeming dated and unrealistic. It is important to remember, however, that the philosophies of the '60s came about as a reaction to what had gone before, which was all too often a somewhat stiff and unbending formality.

Thinking about your own childhood and the attitudes and assumptions you may have inherited can help you to lay down your own standards of good parenting (although this is often an unconscious process), and to increase your confidence in your own abilities. It may also help you to combine the best aspects of former approaches to child rearing and discipline with your own ideals.

Most parents set reasonable standards of behaviour through example, through the routine way in which you conduct your day-to-day life. It is important to have standards, and a good idea to explain the reasons for them if your child balks at something you want her to do, or asks for something which you feel is inappropriate. It cuts down on resentment if you explain as clearly as possible your reasons for a decision which goes against your child's wishes. This can be difficult. An eight- or nine-year-old may find it impossible to understand why you do not allow her to watch violent videos, when other children at school do. In such cases, remain firm, but suggest that you hire or go to see another film – in other words, employ the carrot as well as the stick. A ten-year-old who begs to stay up until 11 because 'everyone else does' needs to be told that this is not possible on a weekday night, because she will be too tired for school, but perhaps she could do it on a Saturday.

In the interests of family harmony, try not to be so unbending that you build up a stock of parent-directed anger, which may boil over in adolescence. Be open to negotiation sometimes.

There is no magical recipe for producing a well-behaved child, and all children behave badly on occasion, but trying to be realistic and consistent is a step in the right direction. In practical terms, this means not expecting too much of your child, not making threats or promises which you know you cannot keep, and developing your own ways of dealing with dangerous or antisocial behaviour.

Coping with bad behaviour

When it comes to the 'how to' of dealing with bad behaviour in the five- to ten-year age group, much depends on your values and personality.

- If you object strongly to smacking, and can manage your children without resorting to it, well and good. You may, on the other hand, find that there are occasions – when you have told your child repeatedly not to play with matches/kick her sister/spoil another child's game and she still persists – when a smack shocks her into compliance, albeit temporarily. It is important to remember that virtually all methods of disciplining children – smacking, sending to bedrooms, loss of privileges – are temporary. Most normal children are naughty, or selfish, or thoughtless, or cruel on far more than one occasion, however thoroughly you may have explained, discussed, or withdrawn your approval. This is one of the reasons why bringing up children can be an exhausting, repetitive task, and arguments against smacking really boil down, in the end, to whether or not you find the idea of physically punishing your child to be morally objectionable. Most caring parents would agree that the routine use of smacking – as a first resort and with no explanation – is wrong.

- Even in situations where a child persists in potentially dangerous or antisocial behaviour, it can be as effective to withdraw the child as to lose your temper and smack her. Give her (and yourself) a few minutes to cool off, and then talk. Ask your child for an explanation of her behaviour, and whether she would like someone else to do that to her. Don't be afraid to show your anger and disapproval: she has to learn to control herself. You can then decide on an appropriate form of punishment – tidying up a room, missing a television programme, sweeping the drive – but try to make it immediate and constructive.

- Many child-care experts now warn against simply sending a child to her bedroom – she will have a relaxing time playing or reading – although this can be useful as a way for both of you to 'cool off'. Try, too, not to be overly harsh. You, as well as your child, will probably regret it if, in the heat of the moment, you threaten to cancel a long-awaited outing or treat.

- In general, it is counter-productive to yell and scream at a child, or to humiliate her in front of others. If she is misbehaving to get attention, you are reinforcing the very behaviour you want to discourage. Withdrawal, cooling off and discussion will probably work better. Children may also misbehave on occasions such as birthday parties, when they can become very excited. Again, whether the child is your own or is a guest, it is sensible to take her aside, and give her a chance to cool down. If one or other of your children has boundless energy, or subversive tendencies, and/or leadership qualities, which often lead her, and other children, into trouble, try to channel her energies and talents into socially acceptable – and energy-sapping – activities.

One of the pitfalls of this supposedly child-centred age is that it can be easy to be sentimental about children. You want to believe that they are 'innocent', and incapable of cruelty or malice. Anyone who has been around children for any length of time knows that this is not the case. They are innocent in some respects, and they deserve adult protection and guidance, but they can also (like adults) display a darker side. Apparently angelic children can gang up and be hateful to another child in the privacy of the cloakroom. And straightforward ones from caring homes can, despite all their parents and teachers have taught them, turn on a child who is slightly different and make her life hell.

If you care about real children, and not about a chocolate box vision of how you think they ought to be, you owe it to them to recognize their negative as well as their positive potential. Your children have as much right to your calm and careful supervision and guidance as to your indulgence.

Sibling rivalry

Rivalry between children of the same family is normal and you should expect it (see also p. 203). A seven-year-old can be furious when a toddler disrupts games and breaks toys. And a ten-year-old will lose her temper with a seven-year-old who asks 'silly questions' or interrupts a favourite television programme. Younger children may be jealous of the achievements or greater competence of their older brothers and sisters and the oldest child may resent having to 'mother' the younger ones.

If you do not manage them carefully, these tensions can build into a generalized bitterness and resentment which can continue into adulthood.

What you can do
Some areas of potential conflict can be avoided with a little foresight.

- Help your seven-year-old to set up her games on the table, not on the floor and engage your toddler's attention elsewhere while the game is in progress.

- Avoid making comparisons, or making children feel ashamed of negative feelings toward siblings. Remarks of the 'James was swimming long before he was your age' type are not going to help a reluctant swimmer and will do nothing for your child's relationship with you or her brother.

- Accept that each child has her unique talents and weak spots and that each has to be respected for her efforts as well as her achievements.

- If one child is jealous of another's success in passing a music exam that the other has failed, avoid negative comments of the 'Yes, well, you're not very musical, are you?' type. Instead, praise what she has done: 'You're more sporty really. You did well in the match last week, but your brother finds sport difficult.' In this way you acknowledge that one is better at music than the other but do

not attach undue importance to the fact. And you show your non-musical child that you have noticed – and admire – her talents too.

- Make time for each child to spend with you and arrange to do things with each on his or her own. Older children need to know that you understand how frustrated they feel when a younger brother or sister is annoying. Explain why the youngster may have behaved as he did; suggest ways in which the older child might avoid such situations in future.

- Younger children should not be allowed to spoil older ones' activities. Young children – and especially the 'baby' of the family – can be quite adept at manipulating older siblings, and you, into making allowances for them. Try not to do so.

- Remember that, however hard you try to be fair, there will be times when you make an unjust decision or feel too exhausted or irritated to sort out the rights and wrongs of the latest squabble. Your children will accept that you are not perfect, as long as the general atmosphere in your home is one of understanding, fairness and consideration for others.

Siblings can enjoy playing together, as long as they both get time and space on their own too.

SAFETY

It seems that hardly a week goes by without reports of women masquerading as social workers trying to persuade mothers to hand over their children, or attempted abductions from streets, shops and even gardens. Since the so-called Moors murders of the 1960s, the abduction and murder of children appears to have become commonplace. The climate of anxiety created over the last 30 years has led many parents to place their children under what amounts to a form of voluntary curfew and house arrest. The grim picture of a generation of children which has virtually lost its rights to reasonable freedom is completed by the problem of traffic. The volume of motor vehicles on the country's roads, the speed at which they travel, and the danger caused by thoughtless drivers means that you – understandably – may be afraid to let even quite old children out of your sight.

The combination of these factors has had repercussions on many aspects of children's lives. Because they are escorted everywhere, they lack confidence in crossing roads. They are not used to shopping, for themselves or their families. They do not know how to use libraries, swimming pools and other public facilities alone. Few use public transport on their own or with friends. Around 90 per cent of primary school children took themselves to and from school 20 years ago; the figure is now some 10 per cent.

Paradoxically, making children more safe also makes them very vulnerable. In depending on you and other adults, they are denied opportunities, gradually, to find their feet. And too often, at the age of eleven when most children transfer to secondary school, they are expected to display social and practical skills which they have never had a chance to practise. Importantly, one of the skills in which many under-tens (and older children) are most lacking is the ability to distinguish 'good' from 'bad' strangers, and safe from potentially dangerous situations. So they refuse to talk to adults who innocently pass the time of day, but will be quite open with a sinister-looking individual because 'he told me his name'.

Journalists and commentators who urge parents to let go of the reins, on the grounds that the risks are more imaginary than real are missing the point. You almost certainly do not think in that way: it is no consolation to you if your child is assaulted or knocked down to know that the chances of it happening were so many millions to one. The question is, instead, one of avoidable and unavoidable risk and of how you can keep your child safe, while making her independent and 'streetwise'.

On the roads

Initially, drill the physical aspects of safety into your child. Show her safe places to cross roads (Green Man crossings, places with a crossing patrol, away from junctions and parked vehicles, see p. 376). If she has to cross near a junction, make sure that she understands that she must look for traffic from all directions. Explain how one-way systems work, and how this affects the direction from which traffic comes. Teach her not to run blindly across entrances and drives, or in car parks, where vehicles may be manoeuvring.

- Children of five should not be allowed to cross roads on their own, but should gradually be encouraged to take more responsibility.
- Below the age of about seven or eight, it is difficult to estimate the speed of traffic.
- By the age of eleven, they should be able to get themselves out and about to some extent.
- From nine or ten upward (younger if she is accompanied by a responsible older child), encourage her to be independent by splitting up in town, and arranging to meet in half an hour (choose your locations carefully, bearing in mind roads she may have to cross).

The extent to which you can allow your child out on her own, and at what age, depends on your area and your child's maturity, but try to make sure that she is confident and competent by the time she goes to secondary school. In the last year of primary school, try allowing her to walk to school with other children if you live close enough. If you live a bus ride or car journey away, park at some distance from the school and let her walk. Ensure that she knows a safe route and, preferably, walks with other children.

Public transport

If your child has rarely or never used public transport, teach her to do so. Once she is at secondary school, she will probably want to get a bus into the town centre to shop with friends, and she will need to feel confident and relaxed about doing so. Do a few journeys together so that you can show your child where the bus stops are in relation to home and your destination, and point out how to distinguish buses by their numbers (many children do not know even these basics), and which service(s) follow the route she needs. Explain how to buy a ticket and the importance of having change. Get a timetable and show her how to use it, and explain what to do if the bus fails to turn up. If she is using buses without you or another adult, she should travel in a group of two or more.

It is also useful for children to know how to use trains, and to find their way around railway stations and timetables although there are attendant risks in this. Stations and carriages can be virtually empty at some times of the day, providing opportunities for criminal activity, from theft to assault. If your child is going to travel by train on her own, choose routes and times carefully, and make sure she knows how to get help if necessary.

Using the telephone

Teach your child how to use a public telephone, with both a card and money. She should know her own telephone number, and how to contact the emergency services. Most children like answering the telephone at home, and should learn how to take messages and make a note of callers' numbers. It is useful if you can make out a list of the numbers of friends and relatives, and people such as your family doctor, and keep it in a set place. Children become confident in using the telephone by being allowed to make calls to grandparents or friends, and can be taught to make social arrangements through, for example, booking a music lesson themselves, or inviting a friend round. As soon as she can read well enough, teach your child how to use the telephone directory, and Yellow Pages.

Strangers – and people closer to home

Your child will receive advice about how to deal with strangers at school, from both her teachers and through talks by visiting police officers. She will be taught never to go anywhere with a stranger, however convincing the reason he or she gives, and to scream, shout, and generally attract attention if a stranger should ever attempt to abduct her. You should reinforce this advice, without frightening your child and making her paranoid about all strangers.

It is less easy to help children distinguish between potentially dangerous situations involving strangers, and innocent, everyday interaction. It is also difficult to explain that the sorts of dangers associated with strangers – in particular, the danger of sexual assault – may also apply to adults whom they actually know. Children do not usually have the protection of intuitions, gained through experience (not necessarily direct), which alert adults to the fact that an individual may be 'suspect'. They have to be guided, sensitively, toward arming themselves in this way.

What you can do

You can help, firstly, by preventing her from being in situations where she may be at risk – select nannies, babysitters, or private tutors carefully, checking references. Also teach your child that her body is 'hers' and that it is not normal for an adult to want to touch her sexual organs. She should understand that if anybody does approach her in this way, she does not have to 'do as she is told' or 'keep a secret', and that she must tell you or a teacher.

As they grow older, children do need to be told of the danger posed by paedophiles. You may prefer not to, on the grounds that it undermines your child's confidence and destroys her innocence. But a child who is unaware of potential risk is vulnerable to it. People who assault children may appear perfectly normal (they are not always pathetic characters in macs who hang around public toilets). Girls are also vulnerable to apparently normal, heterosexual men and, as they approach puberty, need to be forewarned.

The alternative to informing your child about these issues is to keep her away from all situations in which she may be at risk. But at-risk situations can, theoretically, include sports coaching sessions, individual music/dancing/drama lessons, and even visits to friends' houses, where men so inclined can find opportunities to assault unsuspecting children. Youngsters toward the top end of the five-to-ten age group can be taught to avoid potentially risky situations, so preparing them for the greater independence of life as an adolescent.

Home alone

There is no set age at which it is acceptable to leave your child in the house on her own. You may feel your child is mature and sensible enough to cope for a short time from the age of nine or ten, but there are always risks. What would happen if there was an accident? (Most accidents, after all, happen in the home.) What would happen if you were delayed? How would an older child cope with a younger one who was being silly, or became ill?

The NSPCC recommends that babies and young children should never be left alone, that children under 13 are not mature enough to cope with emergencies, and that nobody under 16 should be left alone overnight. If you do have to leave your child alone, leave clear instructions on what to do if there is a problem: leave a list of people she could telephone in an emergency, and remember to put obvious dangers, such as matches, medicines or knives out of reach.

LEARNING ABOUT SEX

Most children learn about the physical, mechanical aspects of sex and sexual development quite readily. They can understand how babies are conceived and born, and know the differences between the sexual organs of adult men and women. Answer your child's questions truthfully, and pitch your answers at a level which she can understand. Even in an atmosphere of openness, young children can be taught that sexual matters are private, and might embarrass some people, so that they do not offend elderly relatives or friends, or less liberal parents. Both boys and girls can be helped to look forward to being parents themselves.

The issue of sexuality is more complex, as is sex education. You may find this difficult, but your children will be better prepared for adolescence, secondary school, and, ultimately, adult life if you go beyond explaining the bare, physiological details. Many primary school children can tell you all about what goes on sexually between adults, about AIDS, about homosexuality, and all kinds of sexual variations. Yet they may hold misconceptions, be puzzled, and are often mystified by why adults have sex if they do not want any more babies. Most under

tens find it difficult to understand sexual drive and desire, and totally mechanical explanations of 'the facts of life' leave them unprepared for their own awakening sexuality, and that of others around them.

At the same time, children may be bombarded with sexually explicit material. If your child is mixing with families who are active members of a religious faith, a 'sex is naughty but nice' attitude can be grossly offensive. Your child must also be told that large numbers of women (maybe you and her friends' mothers) are offended, or made uneasy, by the 'Page Three' mentality which, the argument goes, makes for a climate which encourages sexually motivated crime against women. Whatever your views, the likelihood is that your child is aware of, and is perhaps fascinated by, this sort of material. If you forbid all access, or try to pretend that sexuality does not exist, it can take on the lure of forbidden fruit. This is especially so when children are on the verge of adolescence.

What you can do

If you find this aspect of sex education a problem, it pays to be honest with your child. Explain that you find this a bit embarrassing or difficult to explain, but that you will do your best. Have a look in your local library or bookshops for books which explain facts and feelings. You will find a large variety, some of which may seem glib, but in the end, you should be able to find something which strikes the right note for you. This is important, as you must feel comfortable.

Your child may ask questions which you are able to cope with and which enable you to introduce further, related topics. On the other hand, she may sense your unease, and keep quiet. In this case, introduce the topic by saying that you have brought home a book which you think she may find helpful. Say that it talks about growing up, and pick out a few bits which seem to match your child's stage of development. Suggest that she has a look at it, and that afterward you can talk over anything which she finds puzzling.

You will probably find that your child disappears for an hour or two, and that you will be asked a number of questions over the next few weeks. But she will probably also feel flattered that you think she is mature enough to think about sexuality, and she may also seem more settled about sexual matters – the reality is less colourful than her confused imaginings.

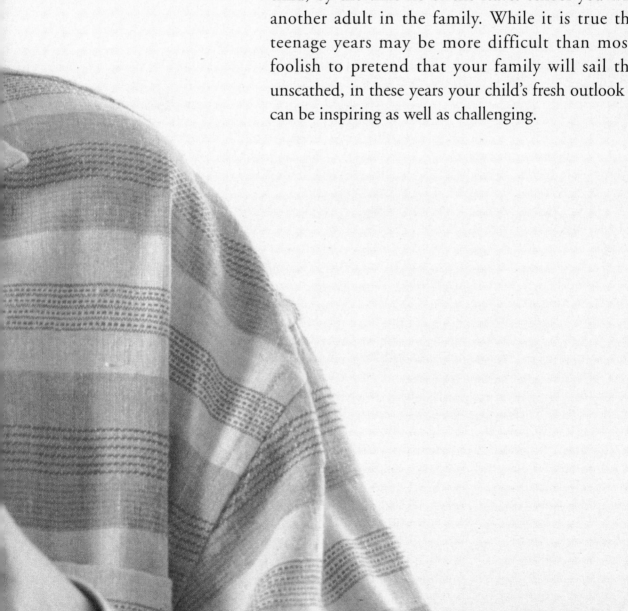

CHAPTER TWELVE

The Teenage Years

At the age of 11 or 12, your son or daughter is still a child; by the time he or she leaves school you will have another adult in the family. While it is true that the teenage years may be more difficult than most, and foolish to pretend that your family will sail through unscathed, in these years your child's fresh outlook on life can be inspiring as well as challenging.

Up and away

When your children reach adolescence and start to become independent, your parenting skills are likely to be put to their greatest test, so it is wise to be prepared – parents who believe that their child will never present them with problems in adolescence might be in for a nasty shock, while those who are prepared may be pleasantly surprised. There are very few families who manage to survive the teenage years without a few ups and downs, but as long as you realize that most difficult behaviour is perfectly normal and in fact happens in most families regardless of culture all over the world, you and your teenagers will survive and they will emerge as happy, well-balanced adults.

Of course, the 'horrors' of the teenage years are often over-estimated. Some children manage to slide gracefully into adulthood with very little difficulty. Others behave in a manner so extreme that it puts enormous stress on the family and can lead to the breakdown of the parent–child relationship. The majority are somewhere in the middle. Sometimes your adolescent will be charming, funny, wonderful to be with. At other times your beloved son or daughter becomes a moody, insolent individual you barely recognize as your own.

Adolescence is broadly defined as being between the ages of 10 and 19, but parental patience is most sorely tried during middle adolescence – the post-puberty period when your child is trying to carve out his own identity.

During the years of puberty – on average between 12 and 14 years – rapid physical changes take place but your son or daughter is to all extents and purposes still a child, with a childish way of coping with life. It is middle adolescence – the 15 to 17 age range – when the young person is neither child nor adult and is consequently most unpredictable, swinging between the two.

WHAT HAPPENS AT PUBERTY

The physical changes that indicate a child is becoming an adult are apparent in girls earlier than in boys. Both average the same height and weight until about 11 years when the girl suddenly spurts ahead. This difference is maintained for about two years until the average boy has his growth spurt, overtakes the girls and maintains the additional height and weight for the rest of his life.

Puberty in girls

Signs of approaching womanhood are brought about by the ovaries which begin to produce increasing amounts of the female sex hormone oestrogen.

Breast development
The first visible sign that your daughter is approaching puberty is normally the appearance of a small mound behind the nipple which indicates that her breasts are beginning to develop. The average age for the beginning of breast development is 11 but a small percentage of girls show signs of budding breasts as young as nine years old.

Your daughter's breasts will not develop at the same rate; one breast may begin to appear up to a year before the other, and the difference may persist for a long time. She will probably find it more comfortable to wear a bra once there is significant breast development, especially if she plays a lot of sport. Many young girls find they get sufficient support and comfort from wearing stretchy vest tops but if you are investing in a bra it is worthwhile getting one properly fitted. At this stage your daughter may prefer to go to a lingerie specialist or discreet lingerie department in a large store rather than a chain store, which can seem very public.

Body hair

In some young girls, the growth of pubic hair may precede the first signs of breast development. Hair begins to appear in the genital area on average between 11 and 12; underarm and leg hair also grows and thickens about the same time. Try to discourage your daughter from shaving underarm and leg hair while it is sparse, but she may, despite your advice, bow to peer and media pressure and begin shaving or using depilatory creams. Deodorants are marginally more effective if the underarm area has been shaved although thorough washing with soap and water is the best way to avoid a build up of perspiration which causes odour.

Internal changes

Your daughter is also undergoing rapid changes internally. The female sex organs are very small until puberty when they grow significantly. In a young child the uterus is some 2 g (⅔ oz) – or the size of a pea – but it will weigh about 80 g (35oz) in maturity.

When you sort the washing, you will begin to notice signs of mucous secretions on your daughter's underwear. This is something which usually becomes obvious about two years before the onset of her periods and is nothing to worry about unless it causes soreness or irritation or is of an unusual colour or consistency. On the other hand, any liquid discharge from your daughter's nipples, something which normally only occurs during pregnancy, after birth or after an abortion, should be referred to the doctor.

Onset of menstrual periods

The average age for the first period is currently 12 years and 8 months. Only 10 per cent of girls begin before the age of 12, and 10 per cent after the age of 15. Periods do not normally start until around 17 per cent of body weight is laid down in fat so thin girls tend to start later. An early start or a delay in the onset of menstruation often runs in families, so your daughter's menstrual pattern may well follow your own and her grandmother's.

Few girls are regular from the beginning; it takes two years or so for the cycle to become established.

The length of each period varies at the beginning as does the amount of blood lost. Once a pattern has been established, emotional upsets, intensive exercise or excessive weight loss can make girls miss a period.

Discuss the onset of menstruation with your daughter in good time, particularly if she shows early signs of development. Younger girls can find menstruation difficult – even frightening – to deal with, particularly if they are still at a primary school which may not be geared up to their needs. It is a good idea to discuss what the school provides and how it can help with one of the female teachers or with the school nurse, so that there is someone your daughter knows she can go to for help if she starts her first period at school. If she is going on a school trip, provide her with some sanitary towels, just in case.

If she is the first girl in her crowd to start her periods she may feel embarrassed and a bit odd, until her peers catch up with her. Then she can allow herself some satisfaction that she has known what it was all about for ages. Girls enjoy sharing their secret with other girls and the one who is a late starter is likely to feel excluded so that there is only relief and excitement when her first period arrives because she is at last one of the gang again.

Ovulation

It is very unusual for ovulation to occur before the onset of periods so your daughter will probably ovulate for the first time between three and 12 months after she starts. It will only happen regularly when her menstrual cycle is well established.

Pads or tampons

Your daughter should be allowed to make her own decision about what kind of sanitary protection she uses, with sensible advice from you, the school nurse or another adult she trusts. She may want to use tampons from the beginning, and they are perfectly safe to be used by young girls as long as they follow a few simple rules on changing frequently and using the right absorbency.

Some girls do prefer to start off with pads and it is worth the extra cost to buy those which are very slim and also very effective. This type also come with wrappers that allow for easy re-wrapping when they have been used, which makes pads a lot less irksome and uncomfortable than of old. If you are buying

Safety with tampons

- Change at least every six hours
- Do not use a tampon at night – use a pad instead
- Wash your hands before as well as after inserting a tampon
- Check that you have removed a used tampon before inserting a fresh one

tampons for her, choose those which are unbleached or non-chlorine bleached and buy a couple of absorbencies so that she does not use a large tampon for a light bleed; this can cause severe dryness and irritation and may trigger infection. A regular tampon with a pad for extra protection for the heaviest part of her period may be better than super tampons at first. If she is keen to use a tampon but finds it difficult to insert – most girls do at the beginning – a lubricant such as KY Jelly smeared on the end of the tampon can help.

Secondary schools should provide facilities for disposal of pads and so on. Tampons are most convenient for managing menstruation at school as they are small and easily disposed of, and also more discreet for PE and games. If your daughter prefers pads, provide the individually wrapped, self-stick ones and small plastic bags for disposal.

Painful periods

Many adolescent girls experience some kind of discomfort or pain at period time. However, the pain only occurs when ovulation has taken place so this problem should not occur in the early months. Cramps usually occur just before and just after a period starts and are usually only severe on the first day or two. Painkillers and a hot-water bottle to hug will help. For the over-12s, ibuprofen or aspirin, which act directly on the prostaglandins that cause the pain are best, but check with your GP if your daughter has asthma, which these drugs may aggravate. Make sure she has painkillers to take if she needs them at school, although try to monitor how many she has in any one day. If your daughter is very health conscious she may prefer one of the homeopathic remedies available from health shops and many chemists.

If the pain is so severe that it means her taking time off school or is accompanied by nausea, severe headaches or fainting fits, take your daughter along to the GP (see also Your Child's Health, p. 350).

Attitudes to menstruation

Discourage your daughter from using vaginal deodorants or wipes when she starts her periods – they are totally unnecessary and can cause irritation to sensitive skin. If she says she needs them, perhaps she feels that menstruation is in some way dirty, or maybe she is just feeling very unsure of herself. The best thing you can do is to quietly reassure her by talking frankly and positively, but discreetly, about the whole issue, making sure that she realizes it is nothing to be ashamed of, and encouraging her to shower or bath whenever she feels the need.

Puberty in boys

Most boys are less well informed than girls about sexual development and are also less inclined to discuss changes to their bodies with either their parents or their friends. This means that boys often conceal their anxieties and agonize in secret about whether they are normal or not. It is as important for your son to be as prepared for puberty and understand what is about to happen as it is for your daughter.

The testicles

Your son needs to know that although the testicles are present in the unborn child and descend shortly afterward, it is not until puberty that their function begins. The first sign that puberty is imminent in boys is the growth of the testes, leading to an increase in the production of the male sex hormones. In a small boy the testes are 1–2 ml in volume and they grow to 4–5 ml in the young adolescent.

The testes do not normally lie at the same level in the scrotum and one might hang lower than the other. Once the testes begin to grow, the scrotum around them also enlarges and the skin there thickens and becomes much more wrinkled. The penis also begins to grow in length and width and the glans of the penis becomes more obvious.

The ultimate adult size of male sexual organs is very variable and your son will need to know that the size of the flaccid penis bears no relation to its size when erect, despite all the boasting which goes on in the school cloakroom. A small penis does not mean that he will make an unsatisfactory lover and it is a good thing to get this old wives' tale out of the way before any fears have time to take hold. A discussion of size is also an opportunity to talk about how sensitivity and mutual affection in lovemaking are far more important than physical endowments.

Body hair

Pubic hair will begin to appear once the growth of the testicles becomes obvious (between about 11 and a half and 12 and a half) but facial hair will make an appearance much later. The age at which boys need to shave or are able to grow a beard varies considerably. Most boys begin shaving earlier than they really need to and with great relish. There is no

harm in this except for the fact that it can often coincide with outbursts of acne when the skin would be much better left alone. Whether your son chooses to use an electric razor, or wet shave with plastic disposables or a standard razor, is up to him and he may follow his father's example or that of elder brothers. Many dark-haired men find that wet shaving is more efficient but it is really down to personal preference.

If he has acne he may prefer disposables but, if not, it is worth spending more initially so that he has a substantial razor which will last. Try to ensure he is scrupulous about keeping his razor for his own use only and that he cleans it properly. Most boys really enjoy being bought aftershave and other toiletries, especially when it is such an obvious sign of their developing masculinity.

Changes at puberty

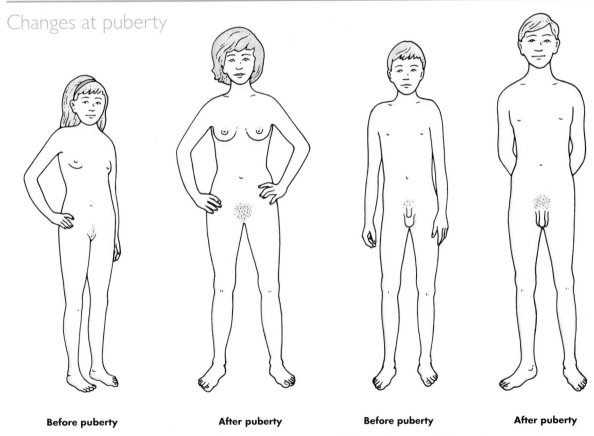

Before puberty   **After puberty**

Before puberty   **After puberty**

In girls, the most visible changes at puberty are the development of the breasts, the growth of pubic hair and the widening of the hips. Breasts bud outward from the nipples (which also become larger and more prominent), then become more rounded; pubic hair tends to grow along the middle of the pubic area first, then fill out toward the top of the legs.

In boys, the most obvious changes include the broadening of the shoulders and the enlargement of the testes, scrotum and penis, in addition to the growth of facial and pubic hair.

The penis takes about two years to reach its mature size, during which time the amount of pubic hair also increases up toward the navel and outward.

Vocal changes

Another distinctive feature of the growing boy is his deeper voice. Some pubescent boys suffer severe embarrassment while their voice is breaking – never quite knowing whether what they say will come out high pitched or surprisingly deep. For others the voice just gradually deepens over a few months.

Spontaneous erections

It is also about this time that erections become more frequent. Spontaneous erections usually occur in response to sexual stimulation – however slight – but may happen without any stimulation at all. This, again, can cause embarrassment but he should be reassured that it is normal and that erections become less frequent and more appropriate to the sexual situation as he gets older.

Once his testes are producing sperm he may be awoken in the night by orgasm and ejaculation and must understand that these are common and out of his control. They occur when there is a build up of sperm so he is less likely to ejaculate involuntarily in this way if he is masturbating regularly to get rid of it.

Wet dreams require the same approach as you would use with a young girl and menstruation – privacy, and a discreet way of coping with stained pyjamas and bedlinen. Above all else never tease. It helps if he can have a man-to-man chat with his father or another male close to him who can explain that they went through exactly the same experiences.

Other physical changes

More than a third of boys at the stage of mid and late puberty have some breast tissue, which can be the result of obesity. Monitor his diet without being too restrictive and encourage him to exercise (see pp. 312–13). Sometimes breast development becomes obvious but they usually regress, even when they have been quite large, when full maturity is reached.

The shape of the face too can change quite markedly, something particularly noticeable in boys. The greatest increase is in the size of the lower jaw which grows in length by about a quarter in puberty and projects further compared with the rest of the face. The upper jaw also grows forward at this time so that, in profile, the face looks much straighter and longer than in a younger child with a more projecting nose. The muscles of the face also grow considerably.

Children in their mid teens – particularly boys – often look lanky and awkward because different parts of the body grow in phases and at a different rate throughout these years. So your son will, for a time, have what appear to be enormous hands and feet and long limbs in comparison with the rest of his body. By his late teens his trunk will have expanded and he will become beautifully in proportion once again.

Attitudes to puberty

There is a wide disparity in the ages at which boys reach sexual maturity. Late maturing boys may feel at a disadvantage because they are less strong and manly than their peers and suffer a lack of self-esteem for a time. A boy who is physically undeveloped compared with others of his age may demonstrate very childish behaviour to gain the attention he feels he will otherwise lose out on. Meanwhile, the early maturer is likely to revel in his precocious development and because of his size will often be treated in a more adult way by both parents and teachers. It can be difficult to scold a 14-year-old who is taller than you!

BECOMING INDEPENDENT

As teenagers struggle toward independence, there will invariably be times when they are unbearable to live with. It is difficult to accept that your child no longer regards his home as the centre of his universe. In fact, he may appear actively to dislike it – and you – and will try to escape as often as possible. The household routine can be seriously disrupted and regular mealtimes abandoned. He will resent participating in family activities, and may be nasty to younger brothers and sisters. How far you are prepared to put up with such behaviour depends on your own temperament and how tightly run your household has been up until now. Such behaviour is easier to bear if you remember that it often conceals fear of the future and regret about the inevitability of leaving the security of childhood behind.

Parents tend to fall into three groups. There are autocrats who believe that they know what is best for their child and will brook no argument. There are the democrats who believe that their teenage child should be allowed to participate in decision-making but not necessarily to have the final word. And then there are the permissive parents who relinquish all control and give their teenager carte blanche to go ahead and do whatever he wants. In general, adolescents with democratic parents tend to be the most self-confident and happy because they have the opportunities to make their own decisions but under parental supervision. If they are always told what to do and what to think, it is difficult for them to grow into the independent people they must become one day. Laying down hard and fast rules about everything is not wise – leave some areas in which negotiation is a possibility.

At the other extreme, permissiveness can also be counterproductive. You may believe you are right to allow your child free rein but in fact adolescents usually need a few rules against which to rebel and boundaries can provide security. And if you allow your child to do exactly what he likes, he may end up feeling that it's because you don't care about him. Achieving the right balance is not easy and you may sometimes fail to live up to your own standards. There will be times when you are feeling too tired or upset to cope with yet another adolescent tantrum in a calm and reasoned way and there will be occasions when it is permissible to tell him exactly what you think of his behaviour. That's one way of letting your child know that you have needs, too.

The parental role

For most of the time the parental role or stance is so ingrained and natural that you are perhaps not aware what 'type' of parent you are. You will find that you slip out of your chosen role occasionally, especially when your child is putting you under pressure. If you are usually democratic, you may veer toward being autocratic, or if you cannot face another row, you will give up and allow your child to make his own decision.

It will probably seem obvious to you that in choosing the first option in the box (right) each time you are adopting the role of the autocratic parent. Perhaps you feel this works for you but you should consider if you really know and understand your child's feelings. The children of disciplinarians may break away from their families altogether later on in life in order to find the independence they were not allowed as adolescents. The second statements indicate democratic parents who are prepared to accept that their child is an individual. This may not

What sort of parent are you?

Think about the statements below and tick the response which comes closest to your own.

Your child tells you he has been invited to a party.
- You reply that you will be picking him up at 9 o'clock.
- You negotiate a time when you will expect him home. You also make a note of the address where the party is to be held and consider checking with the parents.
- You ask him if he will be coming home that night so that you know whether or not you should lock the door.

You have found a set of pornographic magazines in your child's room.
- You immediately confront him with them and insist that he burn them.
- You say nothing directly about it but try to initiate a general discussion about pornography and attitudes to women at a later date.
- You tell him there is no need to hide anything from you and flick through the magazines yourself.

He says he no longer wants to go with you on your weekly visit to his grandmother.
- You put your foot down and insist he toes the line.
- You let him stay at home on alternate weeks.
- You say fair enough and tell your mother he doesn't wish to visit her.

seem like the easiest route at times but it is generally thought that the children of such parents find the whole business of growing up much easier.

The third statements depict the permissive approach which in the short term avoids the conflict that many parents suffer, but in the long term means your child could end up thinking that you simply do not care enough. The permissive parent often tries to behave more like a friend than a mother or father, and is surprised when the child does not respond accordingly. Indeed, your child may find this excruciatingly embarrassing. It is parents he needs at this stage: he can make his own friends outside the home.

PSYCHOLOGICAL AND EMOTIONAL CHANGES

It is easy to sympathize and empathize with the shyness and embarrassment involved in your adolescent's physical development. You will probably find it much harder to be tolerant and loving when the psychological and emotional changes he is grappling with make him totally unreasonable. It helps to remember that as he cannot help growing taller and ganglier neither can he control the mixed emotions which lead him to behave as a child one moment – slamming doors, sulking – and expect adult privileges the next. At the times when he is most defiant and uncooperative, he is probably feeling at his most uncertain and confused. He knows he is still dependent upon you and yet aware that he must become self-reliant and assert his independence. It may reassure you to know that the child who is ultimately most likely to need help in growing up is the one who remains compliant to his parents in his early and mid teens and shows no signs of wanting to break free.

As long as you are aware that some difficult behaviour is normal then you will find it easier to deal with and to tolerate his outbursts. Normal behaviour is defined as that which the majority of his peer group will be exhibiting at around the same time. Rebellious and unreasonable behaviour which persists beyond the expected time might be a reason for concern, but for this age group some rebellion or questioning of the parental standpoint is appropriate. It is worth bearing in mind that at school or college he will be being encouraged to question and experiment in his school work as part of the learning process.

However, this does not mean that you have to be prepared to put up with anything or everything he cares to throw at you. The adolescent whose parents wait on tenterhooks for the next outburst and appear to be cowed by his moods, is likely to develop an over-rated sense of his own importance and will get a nasty shock when people in the world beyond do not react in the same way as you do. You have to decide how far you are prepared to let your teenager disrupt the normal household routine, and you must both then be consistent. There is nothing that a self-centred teenager likes better than his parents feuding over him.

Areas of conflict

Life with a young person in his mid-teens is often a battlefield while he tests out his newly developed intellectual skills. He now has the ability to be much more analytical and to see that there is more than one side to every issue, which will lead him to question your values and beliefs and invariably take the opposite stance. Having your views on religion or politics constantly challenged and criticized can be trying but try to respect his right to have his own opinions, however tedious and simplistic they may seem. At least he is talking to you!

Staying in bed

One common source of warfare between parents and their adolescent is the amount of time he spends in bed. It is a shock when your lively child who was always up with the lark converts to a sloth who needs call after call to get him up for school and insists on sleeping late whenever he can. You may even be worried that it's a sign that he is ill, but that is unlikely. Nearly all adolescents suffer from periods of excessive sleepiness, caused by the hormonal and physical changes taking place and which do tend to alter sleep patterns. This may be something you choose not to make an issue about, even if it does mean he always misses breakfast with the family and may well end up eating his cornflakes at three o'clock in the afternoon.

Adolescents are also likely to take an afternoon nap whenever possible. As long as this sleepiness is not sufficiently serious to affect his performance at school it really is nothing to worry about, however exasperating it can be to find a child sprawled on the settee and gently snoring in the middle of the day. Even if he is not actually asleep, he will appear to have regular bouts of lethargy, when he sits around yawning and doing nothing very much. This might, of course be a sign of depression or possibly the effects of drugs and may need investigation (see pp. 306, 318–20 and 348). But if he is able to spring to life the moment the telephone rings for him or a friend calls round, there is very little to worry about.

A very small number of adolescents complain about insomnia but this can usually be attributed to eating a heavy meal late at night or drinking too much coffee.

Untidiness

Another characteristic of adolescents which often leaves parents tearing their hair out is their chronic untidiness. However good he was as a younger child about putting his toys away and hanging up his clothes, all these good habits may just disappear. His school books and sports equipment will be strewn about the house, coats dropped in the hall, shoes left lying in the middle of the living room and wet towels will litter the bathroom floor. If he makes himself a late-night meal – and adolescents do have an infuriating tendency to become ravenous just as the rest of the family is going to bed – you are likely to find the kitchen a mess in the morning and he will never do the washing up (nor even load the dishwasher) without being asked.

There is no reason why you should allow your home to become your adolescent's personal pigsty and you should insist that he collects his belongings up and takes them to his bedroom. Chances are he will merely dump the stuff on his bedroom floor along with the rest of the things he hasn't put away, but insisting that your offspring keeps his room tidy, too, may be pushing things a bit far. The floor may be littered with clothes, magazines, books and unwashed coffee cups through which you will have to battle sometimes to change the bedlinen – don't expect him ever to notice that the sheets need changing – but if he has chosen to live in that kind of mess, let him do so. Like so many other situations at this stage of your child's life, this is best resolved by compromise and toleration. And one day you may be pleasantly surprised to hear the sound of the vacuum cleaner coming from his room.

One tried and tested solution to the problem of disgusting bedrooms is to give him the go ahead to decorate and furnish his domain himself to encourage some pride in it. Don't be alarmed if he decides to paint the whole room black. It's amazing how many teenagers – both boys and girls – opt for this kind of decor, and it's much more likely to be a sign of minor rebellion than a symptom of deep depression.

If he still persists in leaving his things all around the house, position a large box at the foot of the stairs, or in another prominent position, and put everything of his you find in there. You can direct him to this each time he complains that something has been mislaid.

Staying out late

The time your teenager comes home at night is another area of possible conflict or compromise. You might, for instance, relax your 11pm or midnight curfew for a special occasion, on the basis that he can get up to mischief just as easily before midnight as he can afterward. There is also the matter of safety, but you can help to alleviate your own worries here by making sure you know where your child is going, who with, and that he has money and a telephone number for a reputable late-night taxi service for use in an emergency.

The argument that parents frequently put up against allowing their child to stay out late is that they have to wait up or don't like to go to bed leaving the house unlocked. However, young people need the independence to be allowed to come and go as they please to a certain extent. A 16-year-old should be capable of entering the house quietly and locking the door behind him. Of course, it is unlikely that you will fall asleep the first few times you go to bed before your child arrives home safely, but young people respond to having a certain amount of trust placed in them and will, hopefully, behave in an appropriate adult manner.

It can be more difficult if you have a child who appears to have no sense of time whatsoever and persistently ignores your deadlines or constantly telephones in the small hours to tell you he has missed the last bus home and expects you to go and collect him. If all else fails you might try playing him at his own game. On a night when you know he is going to be at home make your own arrangements to go out and stay out long beyond the expected time. Chances are that a worried, ashen-faced adolescent will greet you at the front door demanding to know where you have been all this time as he has been worried sick about you. At least then he will have an understanding of how you feel.

If you know approximately where your child is, the occasional late night need not to be worrying as long as you know how he intends getting home. Make sure that you have the telephone numbers of his friends so that you can ring other parents if you become really alarmed. This is as important with boys as with girls. In fact, a good relationship with the parents of your teenager's friends can be enormously supportive during these anxiety-ridden years.

COPING ON YOUR OWN

One in five children in Britain experiences a family breakdown before the age of 16. Although older children tend to cope better with the trauma, mainly because they are likely to have more social support outside the family, parents who are splitting up owe their teenager an explanation of why the break is taking place and what their plans are as far as he is concerned.

In a family where there has been tension, older children often benefit from the relaxed atmosphere at home after a separation or divorce and their performance at school may improve. The child in a single-parent family often feels more grown up and mature than his friends who live with both parents.

On the negative side as a single parent you may rely too heavily on your adolescent for company and support, as a substitute for the partner who is no longer around, and your child may feel guilty about leaving you alone when he goes out with friends. There may also be financial problems – teenage children cost considerably more than children still of primary school age – they need adult-sized clothes, and there is more peer pressure on what they wear. Take this into account in working out maintenance arrangements – if your child is living with you, you may need to take legal advice. It can help to encourage an older teenager to get a Saturday job so that he has his own money.

This can be a difficult time if you are the parent apart from your child. You may find the physical changes alarming, especially if you are not in frequent contact, making it much more difficult to relate to your child. The time you spend together may have to be reorganized and rethought given that a teenager will no longer be happy with a trip to the park or a zoo. In fact, a young person may resent spending time with his separated parent, particularly at weekends when social activities with his own friends tend to be concentrated. The father/daughter relationship can become particularly difficult as some girls become shy of spending time alone with their fathers, especially if it involves overnight stays at his home.

Do not abandon the relationship, even if contact is mainly by letter or telephone. Your child may appear ungrateful for the efforts made on his behalf, but he needs both parents in the background at this time.

DEPRESSION

Although the majority of teenagers seem happy and confident, from time to time there will be feelings of gloom and self-dislike. Research has shown that many adolescents have at some point longed to hide themselves away from everyone and everything. It is also true that 1 in 5 has at some time felt that life was not worth living. These common feelings, while painful at the time, need not concern you if they appear transitory. But even you, as his parent, may not always be aware of the depth of your child's feelings. It is important to recognize when depression has gone beyond the usual teenage angst, because between 10 and 15 per cent of teenagers do experience significant psychological problems and serious mental illnesses like schizophrenia usually begin to manifest themselves during adolescence.

The rate of suicide rises sharply during the teens and ranks among the most common causes of death in older adolescents, with young men being at the greatest risk. This is why threats of suicide should always be taken seriously and your doctor informed.

Two main symptoms of severe depression are loss of appetite and loss of interest in his surroundings. He may also appear excessively tired all the time and complain of vague aches and pains.

TEENAGE HEALTH GUIDE

Being healthy helps teenagers to cope with the physical and mental demands of growing up. But the teenage years coincide with the period when you have less control over what they are doing to their bodies. And, peer pressure may turn even a previously committed sports enthusiast into a couch potato.

Maintaining a good diet

By the time children reach adolescence, the influence you have over their dietary choices and eating habits is ever more limited. Almost all teenagers opt out from some family meals and want to choose their own foods for a greater or lesser proportion of the time and to lay down the law over this is not conducive to a return to harmonious family mealtimes. As with babies and toddlers, keep all matters relating to eating

Checklist for signs of depression

- Looking perpetually miserable and unhappy. Rarely smiling.
- A marked change in sleeping and eating patterns, usually with a loss of appetite although binge eating is also a sign of emotional disturbance.
- Apparent feelings of hopelessness and self hate.
- Refusal or reluctance to see people who were previously close friends or to take part in any social activities.
- Difficulty in concentrating on any task at all.
- Apparently finds everything an effort.
- Irritability and aggression.
- A sudden deterioration in school work.
- Taking risks with alcohol, drugs etc.
- Regular complaints about non-specific aches and pains.

and food choice low key. If you make an effort to maintain healthy eating habits yourself and keep the refrigerator and freezer stocked with nutritious food, your children will be less likely to become 'addicted' to junk food. Turning vegan overnight or fasting for the odd day to support a third world charity is simply another way of asserting independence and taking a healthy interest in the world, and their increasing involvement in it. If you and the rest of the family do not wish to become vegetarians there are still ways, which will not take up too much extra time, of combining meal ingredients to suit everyone. If your teenager wants to take responsibility for preparing some of the family's meals, then so much the better.

Stimulate any interest in food by discussing recipes and eating out, as a family if possible. It's vital to avoid the concept of food as a foe and hunger as something to fight against. Avoid hamburger chains – your children will sample plenty with their peers.

Influencing nutrition

It is important to somehow ensure a varied and nutritious diet at a time when your child may be subject to growth spurts and need all the solid fuel he can get. Girls who decide to become vegetarian at

this age should be watched carefully; if the decision coincides with the onset of menstruation there is a possibility of that your daughter may develop iron deficiency and need iron supplements.

Variety is the key to a good diet, with fresh fruit and vegetables and plenty of high-fibre and starchy foods like potatoes, bread, chapattis, naan, pasta and rice, taking precedence over foods high in fats and sugars, but it is equally important to avoid lecturing on the subject. It is as difficult for a teenager to imagine becoming ill or not enjoying good health through a lack of milk or cabbage as it is for him to imagine dying of old age or indeed wanting to live beyond 35. Fortunately, schools do a lot more these days in terms of health education and you could also look out for some of the nutrition information leaflets available from supermarkets and doctor's surgeries.

Drinks and thirst

One, often overlooked, aspect of diet and nutrition is drinks. Many children survive a whole school day with just a small carton of juice and maybe a quick slurp at a water fountain or resort to buying fizzy drinks on their way home, but medical experts are starting to stress the importance of drinking considerably more water than we usually do. The problem is that most children don't consider drinking water unless they feel uncomfortably thirsty, when they really need to sip water throughout the day in order to be sure of flushing out toxins and keeping everything running smoothly. Small bottles of mineral water have an acceptable image and will fit into a school bag easily. Home-made ice lollies, using unsweetened juice and mineral water will also help. Try to keep a jug of fresh water in a prominent place to encourage the urge to drink.

Overweight

If your child is overweight you should try to do something about it, but again, help should be subtle and non-judgemental. Firstly you need silently to decide whether your child is genuinely overweight or simply enduring the clumsy, podgy stage induced by 'growth spurts'. Is your assessment of his weight influenced by an unreal attitude to body image that you may be harbouring yourself? If you instil unnecessary notions about thinness now, you may saddle your child with an eating problem for life, so you need to tread very carefully.

If your child really is verging on the obese then it is often the case that the whole family is overweight and everyone's diet needs to be assessed and modified. There is an 80 per cent chance that the children of obese parents will be obese but this is more likely to be down to learned eating habits rather than genetic characteristics. If this is not true in your family, observe how much exercise your child takes and how much snacking goes on simply out of boredom. It may be his leisure habits which need changing more than anything else. If you can see clearly that too many fatty, high sugar foods are being consumed then you need to try to make gradual changes without becoming too despondent when binges take place due to adolescent depression or disappointments.

If your child is openly concerned himself about his weight then it will make matters easier but if he doesn't talk about it then you can still influence things by what you keep in the refrigerator and serve at mealtimes. Some weight problems start simply when the child suddenly decides not to eat breakfast. This may even happen as part of an effort to lose weight but it always has the reverse effect because the body cannot function properly throughout the day without a good 'kick start' first thing and it then craves a quick 'fix' in the form of a sugary, temporarily filling snack. If cereals and toast do nothing to tempt in the mornings perhaps flavoured milk shakes with plenty of fruit blended in will be more acceptable. They take the same time to prepare as toast and cereal.

You cannot rely on what your child will eat at lunch times to provide the right nutritional balance, even if you pack him a lunch yourself, because so much food swapping and throwing away goes on. The evening meal should do most to sustain and aid healthy growth. What often happens is that, having survived all day on a small snack teenagers are too ravenous when they return home to wait for dinner time. If you are out at work when your child comes home the problem is magnified. But providing something filling like muffins, chunks of bread and fruit, or a bowl of soup is better than leaving him to empty the biscuit tin and then refuse dinner later.

Eating disorders

All adolescents feel a continual need for privacy and independence and this is as it should be, but it does make it difficult to know what is going on with regard to diet. Eating problems usually involve girls, although some boys are also affected, and the problem has been noted in children as young as nine. If your daughter has apparently lost her appetite and is losing weight, is depressed, no longer has periods, lies about what she has eaten, and is obsessively preoccupied with body image, there is cause for concern as these are the classic symptoms of anorexia. Adolescents develop eating disorders for a variety of reasons and the problem is complex and aggravated by a society which places so much emphasis on being the fashionable shape and uses the media to confirm the message. For many girls also there is an underlying fear of maturity – anorexia often accompanies the onset of puberty.

It is important not to panic if your child looks like becoming, or already is, a victim of this condition, but it is important to seek professional help swiftly. As well as denying herself the food she needs (anorexia), your child could also be bingeing on food and then forcing herself to vomit (bulimia), or be using laxatives excessively. All this may be going on without your knowledge and to the long term detriment of her health. If you fear this is so talk to your GP about it (see also Your Child's Health, pp. 350–1).

Exercise

Making sensible exercise a part of your family life from as early as possible is the best way to avoid the 'couch potato' syndrome and to help your child maintain his sense of worth and equilibrium throughout the often turbulent teenage years. An interest in sports and games, swimming and non-competitive exercise classes, or long walks to different locations, is an excellent way of saving your child from some of the black moods which may often threaten to engulf him and can be a marvellous tonic during times of hard study or emotional turmoil. If you can manage to enjoy some activities regularly, with the whole family joining in, then you are almost certain to enjoy the kind of conversation with your children which follows naturally from the shared experience of a hard game of badminton, or a long swim. A few hours out of the house together, with a refusal to discuss difficult topics, can sometimes be almost as good as a holiday, and taking the kind of exercise which makes you breathless, raises the level of endorphins in the body. Endorphins are caused by chemical compounds released from the brain and they are frequently dubbed 'happiness hormones' because it is thought they help to bring about the sense of well-being which follows exercise.

If you can't persuade your teenager to join in family activities or there comes a point where he refuses to join in any more, encourage him to join a group or sporting club for young people. This is difficult to achieve once adolescence has been reached if he hasn't shown previous interest – think ahead and get him interested while he is at primary school.

While it is desirable to encourage all kinds of sports and different routes to fitness, you should watch out for any particular activity being obsessively pursued. If a child shows great promise in a particular sport it is tempting for sports teachers and coaches, and parents too, to push harder and, if the child starts to achieve some level of success, for him to become sucked into a punishing routine. Remember that adolescents are still growing and developing and it is vital that their health is not undermined by over-disciplined fitness regimes which could set them up for arthritis and other muscle and bone complaints later on in life, as well as depriving them of the wider social circle which they need. If your child is complaining of a specific ache in his joints or muscles which you have put down to 'growing pains', try to ascertain whether it is his chosen sports activity which is causing the discomfort. Try to persuade him to stop training for ten days or so to see if there is any improvement. If not, take him to the family doctor.

Spots and other problems

However healthy your adolescent's diet and lifestyle there is still a 70 per cent chance that he will get acne at some point. There is no firm evidence to suggest that acne is connected to eating too many fatty and/or sugary foods, although everyone seems intent on promoting this idea, perhaps because it fits in with some underlying puritan notion of punishment – eat the cake and suffer the spots afterward.

If and when your child gets acne, your sympathy and understanding are vital. Many adolescents only experience one or two occasional spots, on the face and/or back; others suffer unsightly outbreaks. You may find it difficult to console a child who is very concerned about what, to you, seems trivial and hardly noticeable. It helps if you can appreciate just how body-conscious and concerned over their appearance most adolescents are. Never, ever, resort to name-calling with regard to their spots or general appearance, even in jest or when they are using insulting phrases themselves; and never allow any of your family or friends to speak in this way.

For adolescents to develop acne, when it is so important to them to appear attractive to the opposite sex and to their friends, often seems like a dreadful failing on the part of nature, but in fact it is triggered by the male hormone testosterone (which is why more boys than girls are affected by serious acne). The production of this hormone, which is found in both sexes, combined with the increase in the size of the sebaceous glands and rate of sebum secretion, result in greasy skin and acne.

Acne is formed when a hair follicle becomes blocked by a blackhead. The contents of the follicle then leak out on to the surrounding skin and cause inflammation. Blackheads, contrary to popular belief, are not particles of dirt in an open pore, they are the tip of a blocked pore which is coloured with melanin, the same substance which gives you a suntan.

Treating acne

There is a great deal of false association between spots and dirt, or a lack of cleanliness, and this aspect is often powerfully asserted in advertising which is aimed at vulnerable adolescents and designed to sell medicated washing creams, soaps and the like. While a medicated soap can be helpful for greasy skin, it is not a good idea to encourage the sufferer to try one product, then another, spending more and more money in an attempt to be rid of his spots. Similarly, it is not a case of washing away the grease and the spots, because constant overuse of medicated products will make for sore skin and more risk of infection. It would be useful, if the acne is a mild to moderate case, to discuss with your child what product he thinks is likely to be best, make sure yourself it is not too strong or abrasive and then encourage him to continue its use rather than swap from brand to brand. It is frustrating when a product does not work wonders and it can be irritating to be told that acne has to take its own course and will go away eventually. Tactful discussions and patient listening is the best course to follow.

If your child wishes to keep a face towel and flannel to himself you can treat it as an opportunity to buy a whole new set he will like, but don't insist he suddenly restricts himself to certain towels because acne is not catching. The advent of spots is not a valid reason, either, to lecture on improved diet or the need for more sleep and spending less time out at night, because there is no correlation between lack of sleep, diet and acne. Stress may make acne worse but it is not the cause of it in the first place.

Many acne sufferers spend a great deal of time trying to remove the spots themselves through picking and squeezing and this can be particularly galling to parents and the rest of the family, when the results usually make the sufferer's face look sore and unsightly. But it would not be accurate to say that it will cause scarring, unless carried to extremes. Try to gently discourage the habit because it does not do any good and can mean it will take longer for the skin to clear. Girls often resort to make-up to camouflage a spotty skin; this can work if the foundation or con-cealer stick is not too heavy and is medicated, but it is important not to clog the skin even further with greasy products. Boys should go gently with shaving and stop altogether if the spots are very bad.

Acne can take months or even years to clear up so it is best not to put too much emphasis on time in your discussions because you could make your adolescent very gloomy. If his acne is already a cause for genuine depression or is severe, a visit to your GP is sensible, for medication to relieve the condition.

Keeping clean

The arrival of spots often heralds increased standards of cleanliness and personal hygiene in your ado-lescent son or daughter. While constant showering and bathing is irritating for the rest of the family, especially when they wish to use the bathroom, and can be expensive in terms of how much deodorant and soap is used, this is not a fad to be worried about unless it is accompanied by extreme anxiety. It

usually lasts only a few months and is preferable to dealing with children who refuse to wash or change their clothes for weeks on end. Refusing to wash is often used as a form of protest against parents. If hygiene becomes truly obsessional and begins to prevent a young person from leading a normal life, seek professional help.

Hair

Greasy hair nearly always seems to be part and parcel of adolescence and, as with acne, there is no harm in buying a product designed to help, providing you do not have to pay for an enormous collection, all of which are basically the same. A greasy fringe or hair which has been heavily conditioned or styled with gel may aggravate (but not cause) facial spots. Suggest an alternative style, though your child may not agree because the fringe can cover spots too. There is no harm in washing hair every day providing the shampoo is a mild one.

At an age when hair is at its best in terms of texture, colour and thickness, many adolescents want to dye it. Frequent and drastic colour treatments can alter the condition of the hair and take away its strength and elasticity for years to come. And evidence suggests that certain hair dye products are carcinogenic when used over a long period of time. As with other risks it is unlikely that your adolescent will feel concerned if she (or he) has already decided that what she most desires is green or purple hair. Apart from suggesting semi-permanent colourings or henna, console yourself that these enthusiasms are usually short-lived.

Teeth

One in three children needs orthodontic treatment and although children are entitled to free treatment on the NHS, it has to be for health, not cosmetic, reasons. You may find, even if you have managed to keep your child on an NHS dentist's list, that you have to contribute toward the cost. The dentist may have told you as soon as your child's second teeth came through to expect that he would need orthodontic work later, but most braces cannot be fitted until the teeth and mouth have grown sufficiently, often around 12 years old.

The success rate, when braces are worn properly and consistently, is excellent, and most adolescents do get used to the idea quickly, although many take to speaking with their hand across their mouth to cover embarrassment. He will relax and adapt to wearing his brace more readily if you try not to mention it and friends and family are asked not to draw attention to it.

Remind your teenager that during adolescence many people find that they need fillings. This is because parents are no longer overseeing regular teeth brushing and that, combined with coming home late, hurrying out of the house in the morning, and having a freer rein to eat sweets and have sugar-filled drinks at intervals during the day, frequently leads to problems in what were up to now teeth free of fillings.

Eyes

It is unlikely that your teenager will damage his eyes by peering through a fringe, watching too much TV or going short of sleep. If your child does complain of headaches, and playing on his computer in a dim room is not to blame, make an appointment with an optician. It is important to choose someone that you and your child have confidence in. Eye tests are free until your child is 16 (19 if in full-time education).

A prescription for spectacles can seem like yet another catastrophe to an adolescent. Glasses have, at best, a shaky image and only sunglasses have complete credibility. Contact lenses might seem the best solution but your child must be guided by

the optician who may feel he is too young. A regular, thorough hygiene system is necessary for lenses and your child must remember to take them out at night.

General 'hypochondria'

Complaining about his aches and pains is another way of expressing insecurity and being unsure about letting go of you and moving toward independence. This can also be a way of getting attention – if school work is stressful, imagined illnesses are more likely to elicit sympathy and concern than moaning about homework might. Be quietly sympathetic without displaying signs of panic or, worse still, derision. Be aware of physical symptoms, and if you think there really is an underlying medical problem, call or visit the doctor.

Some teenagers get through these years with good skin, clear eyes and shiny hair, but rare is the adolescent who suffers no problems.

SMOKING

Smoking is something you can and should openly condemn, for obvious health reasons. But it is important to differentiate between condemning the habit and the child. Many children start smoking (and one in five 15-year-old girls is a regular smoker) in an attempt to boost low self-esteem, so frequent and sustained attempts to boost your child's confidence are a more positive route to encouraging him to stop smoking or deterring him from starting in the first place, than trying to frighten or bully him out of it. It is a sobering thought that at least 300 out of every 1,000 adolescents who continue to smoke will die from a smoking-related disease, but thanks to school lessons and public health promotions your child is probably better informed than you are about the risks and the awful statistics accompanying them.

Ideally, you should start your 'anti-smoking' campaign as soon as your child is old enough to understand what you are trying to convey – primary schools will almost certainly help here – because once children reach adolescence the pressure to smoke can be very heavy. Example is an important element here, as elsewhere in behaviour patterns. If you or others in the family smoke then you need to stop as soon as possible for everyone's sake. Enlisting your adolescent's support in helping you break the habit will also help him to stop or prevent him from starting. If older siblings or other family members or frequent visitors smoke, then you have to ban smoking from the house and try to win them over so that they will not influence your adolescent.

Strategies to deter smoking

The recent evidence concerning the dire effects of passive smoking is beginning to have some effect on what teenagers think about their friends who smoke, but if your child is anxious to be part of a certain social 'set' or finds it difficult to mix in then peer pressure could be a problem here.

Effect on relationships

In surveys carried out in the United States a huge percentage of boys and girls stated that they did not want to date anyone who smoked. It may be worth suggesting your teenager thinks about that, although obviously that is not going to have much effect if your teenager is already going out with a smoker.

An increasing number of social venues now ban smoking, which – depending on his habits – may go some way to persuading him to stop.

Career prospects

If your child has set his sights on a certain career then it may be that smoking would hamper his chances and it is worth finding out and pointing that out to him. An ever-increasing number of workplaces now ban smoking.

Sport

Any strenuous sport at professional or amateur level becomes more difficult for a regular smoker to pursue successfully. You can convey this point, if your child is already a regular smoker, by organizing a swimming session or game of badminton: he is likely to notice the difference in his own aerobic fitness without your spelling it out. If he is playing a sport for the school, his teachers are almost sure to take the effects of his smoking into account when selecting teams and so on.

Confrontation

Some parents allow their children to smoke in the house because they feel that otherwise they would be forcing them to act deceitfully, but many professionals feel that smoking is the gateway to drinking and drug-taking for adolescents and this is probably one of the rare issues which needs confronting head-on. This does not automatically mean you need to fight about it but you do have to decide what you are going to say and do before you discuss it in order to ensure that things stay calm.

Financial constraints

Smoking is an expensive habit. Some parents use a reward system to keep their children from smoking but, again, there is the element of risk here of driving your child toward telling lies. If he is not concerned for his own health or for the environmental damage he is causing, perhaps you can make your opposition clear by refusing to subsidize his habit and making him realize that every penny spent on cigarettes means that much less to spend on clothes, going out, computer games and anything else he wants.

ALCOHOL

Many people see alcohol as the acceptable face of substance abuse; to others wine is an extension of food. Whatever your views you need to convey the correct message to your adolescent. It helps to remember that almost all adolescents experiment at some point with alcohol but very few of them turn into alcoholics. That said, it is illegal to buy alcohol under the age of 18 (although it is not illegal to drink it) and as a parent you should be seen to uphold the law in your children's eyes.

As with smoking, many experts believe that for some adolescents drinking can lead to drug taking and it is a fact that almost all hard drug users began with alcohol and cigarettes, although the vast majority of people who drink or smoke do not progress to illicit drugs. As with most things, to take draconian measures like preventing your child from going out in case he becomes involved in heavy drinking sessions, cannot succeed in the end and may lead to more serious misdemeanours. However, it does not serve any real purpose, either, to relate at length your own drunken binges and over-indulgences of earlier years (if indeed you had any), because teenagers have a habit of clinging on to this type of information as an affirmation of their own behaviour when they may be wavering over the decision of whether to drink or not.

Because alcohol itself is a drug, it is necessary to ask why children want to drink. As with smoking there may be peer pressure or stress at school, the child may be suffering an acute lack of confidence or he may be following the example of older members in the family. If your child is using any of the above reasons to drink then you can help him in the first instance by giving him a valid reason for deciding not to drink. It is important that the child sees the decision as his for it to become a firm commitment on his part and it is obviously vital that you support his decision in every way you can without constantly reminding him every time he leaves the house that he is not to imbibe. You also need to try and do something about what he perceives to be the cause of his need to drink, but firstly and simply it may be that he just needs you to say 'No, you are too young'. If he is under 18 he can then use this as his reason for his decision to abstain. Teenagers don't have to drink. This may sound highly simple but many parents so take for granted the use and abuse of alcohol that it doesn't even occur to them that in this case they can simply say 'No' and take some of the choice away from their child.

Keeping it under control

- Convey to your child that if he dislikes the taste and the after-effects then that is another valid reason for deciding not to drink.
- Make it clear that if he buys alcohol himself under the age of 18 he is breaking the law and must face the consequences.
- Never drink excessively or drink and drive yourself.
- Let your child see that the way to treat alcohol is to have one or two glasses of wine with a meal, or socially, without anyone feeling obliged to drain the bottle. Experts on preventing alcoholism say that it is better to offer a glass of wine to older teenagers – perhaps watered as a 'spritzer' – than ban alcohol. This is not the same as introducing your child to lots of different drinks with the idea that it is better if he 'learns to drink' at home, or even that it would be amusing to see your child get 'tipsy'. This conveys completely the wrong message.
- Limit the time he spends at parties or gatherings of friends, or the number of times per month he goes out, if you suspect unacceptable levels of drinking are going on. It is far preferable in the long run however that he reaches his own decision not to over-indulge with your help and support.

Spotting a drink problem

Your child may be secretly drinking if:
- he is unusually moody and/or suffers violent mood swings;
- he acts aggressively;
- he is uninterested in his studies and hobbies or pursuits;
- he has lost his appetite;
- he is eating at unusual times.

Get professional help at once. Note that some of these symptoms may also indicate drug-taking or depression.

ILLEGAL DRUGS AND SOLVENT ABUSE

While finding an empty lager can under your son's bed or a crumpled packet of cigarettes in your daughter's drawer will fill you with concern, discovering that your child is smoking cannabis or is involved with solvent abuse is likely to send you into paroxysms of anxiety. In your heart you probably feel that some experimentation with cigarettes and alcohol is inevitable. Those things are socially acceptable, albeit neither desirable nor legal for the young teenager. However, it is very different when you are confronted with evidence that your child is experimenting with some kind of illegal substance. Accept your emotions – you have a right to feel upset – but try to remain as calm as possible in order to keep a sense of proportion.

Certainly, the parents of today's teenagers have every reason to be concerned about drug-taking. Many studies have shown that drugs of all kinds are available and that children are using them, often while they are still at school. Latest research has shown that around 40 per cent of schoolchildren aged 14 and 15 years have tried a drug of some kind, boys being more likely to have done so than girls. If you discover that your child has been indulging, your immediate reaction will be to ask yourself what you can do to prevent his ever doing it again. But draconian punishments like grounding him for an indefinite period are unlikely to be effective and will only serve to provoke hostility between you. Keep the lines of communication open so that you can discuss your genuine concerns rationally.

What and why

First, it is important to remember that while we tend to talk about drugs in a very general way there are so many different types and their effects and hazards vary enormously. Although the figures sound high one needs to ask what kind of drugs those schoolchildren in the surveys were experimenting with. Less than 1 per cent of the population has ever taken heroin and a tiny proportion had injected, so the horrors of heroin, crack, cocaine may be misplaced. The most mild and popular illicit drug is cannabis which one study found around 10 per cent of all people in this country have used in their lifetime. The reasons why children try drugs are as variable as the substances themselves. Those who are living in deprived conditions or feel estranged from their parents are more likely to indulge, although over the population as a whole, middle-class and professional people are more likely to use illicit drugs.

Some parents of teenagers will themselves have puffed on a joint in their youth, and perhaps for them the prospect of their child trying one may not be as terrifying as for parents without that experience. However it is undeniable that illegal drug use is a growing problem and the difficulty for parents is to find a balance between over-reacting and resolving never to let your child out of your sight again, and assuming that drug taking is a normal part of growing up. It is important to know what drugs are being made available to your child and what signs to look for to indicate that he may be using them.

Cannabis

This is the most commonly used of the illegal drugs and is usually smoked in the form of 'resin' or 'hash', a brown solid crumbled and mixed with tobacco. A quarter of an ounce of cannabis resin costs £15–£25 and makes about 20 cannabis cigarettes. Some people feel little effect, others achieve a sense of well-being. Sometimes there may be mild hallucinations. The main danger is that in a euphoric state users may be careless of their own safety in crossing the road or riding a bike. Whether or nor cannabis leads to the use of hard drugs is an on-going debate but at present there is no hard evidence that this is so.

SIGNS OF USE Uncontrolled giggling, lack of co-ordination, dilated pupils. Persistent users may show symptoms of paranoia. Packets of cigarette papers in your child's bedroom are likely to be an indication that he is rolling joints.

RISKS A frequent user may become psychologically dependent and, of course, there is the same risk of lung damage as with smoking tobacco.

Stimulants

These stimulate the nervous system and enable users to stay awake and alert for long periods. Amphetamine is the most common (available as Purple Hearts to the sixties generation). Now it is mainly found as white powder which is usually sniffed but can be injected.

SIGNS OF USE Hyperactivity, swift changes of mood, aggression, lack of appetite, insomnia, exhaustion, anxiety.

RISKS Psychological dependence, dehydration, exhaustion from overactivity, heart and blood pressure problems, reduced immunity, panic and paranoia.

Ecstasy

This is usually available as white, brown, pink or yellow tablets. It starts to take effect after about 20 minutes and it can last several hours. It is supposed to have a calming effect and give heightened perceptions of colour and sound. Teenagers are encouraged to use it at parties and raves because it is reputed to make people feel calm and warm and friendly toward each other, but also provides the stimulation required for an all-night dancing session. However, as the effect wears off it can leave the user feeling pretty miserable.

SIGNS OF USE Impaired co-ordination which makes the user accident prone, sleeplessness, excessive thirst, raised temperature, jaw clenching. Some girls who have used the drug on a regular basis have found that their periods are heavier.

RISKS High doses cause anxiety and confusion, depression, lack of energy and insomnia. Immediately after a dance session at which Ecstasy has been taken, heat exhaustion can be a serious problem – a young person's temperature may be raised and he may be severely dehydrated. Call the doctor at once if your child returns from an all-night party or club in this state. Once again, with prolonged use there is the possibility that users will become psychologically dependent. Regular use can make the user suffer temporary paranoia and insomnia. Some young people have died after taking Ecstasy from excessively high temperatures or from taking adulterated tablets. There is a particular risk in combining Ecstasy with hard drugs.

LSD (Acid)

This is manufactured illegally; minute quantities are impregnated into small squares of blotting paper which are dissolved on the tongue.

SIGNS OF USE Very obvious. Users can feel confused and disorientated, particularly after they have tried it for the first time and may believe they are going insane. It can be a very alarming experience for

parents if a child does return home apparently 'out of his mind'. If he refuses or is unable to calm down after several hours he will need to see a doctor.

RISKS The effect on the mind of this hallucinogen can be very frightening. A bad 'trip' means that the young person is plunged into some kind of living nightmare which can come back to haunt him for many months afterward. The main danger of any hallucinogenic drug is that it may be damaging to someone who is suffering a mental illness or may act as the trigger in someone whose condition was undiagnosed.

Solvent abuse

Younger children are more likely to experiment with solvent sniffing mainly because the wherewithal is more accessible – there are, after all, over 30 'sniffable' products in the average home. Aerosols and refills for cigarette lighters are more commonly used than glue. They are especially dangerous, so do talk to your child if you find a surprising number of containers in the rubbish bin or in his bedroom. The peak age for sniffing is around 13 or 14 and there are over 100 deaths each year from solvent sniffing. Most of those who try it do not do so again, but all children from all classes and areas appear to be at risk.

SIGNS OF USE Similar effects to being drunk and children may be surprised at their first attempt how quickly they become intoxicated. Other indications are a rash around the nose and mouth, stomach cramps, uncoordinated movements and slurred speech. They may also go off their food and complain of frequent headaches or suffer from a sore throat and runny nose.

RISKS There is a serious risk of loss of consciousness, suffocation or heart failure. In the long term there is the possibility of damage to the lungs, heart, kidneys, liver and central nervous system.

Reacting to teenage drug-taking

Remember that your child is not an addict simply because he has taken a drug; your over-reaction could make matters worse. For some children trying just once is enough, but dramatizing the risks will probably not succeed in convincing him to stay away from them for good. Teenagers, after all, enjoy risk-taking and it is the adolescent who feels closer to his peer group than to his parents who will be prepared to take the most risks in order to impress them and sustain friendships.

Remember that drug-taking can be a very enjoyable experience, particularly if it does blot out unpleasant aspects of life. Some young people argue that taking drugs is beneficial in heightening their awareness of the beauty of the world, offering them something akin to a religious experience.

In general most parents are not well informed about drugs and there is a lot of misinformation around. One thing to remember is that the effects differ from person to person and on each occasion. For instance, the experience of taking LSD might be completely different whether someone took it with friends, with strangers or was alone.

Having some clear information will help you understand the subject and convince your child that you have done your research and do know what you are talking about, otherwise he will assume he has an advantage over you. You should always emphasize that one of the main dangers with drugs is that people often do not necessarily get what they pay for. Substances have been mixed with things like sugar, laxatives, talc or even cheaper or more lethal drugs.

Many young people have been duped into handing over money and have ended up looking foolish as a result. This might be a greater deterrent than the risks to their health. Emphasizing the physical and psychological dangers may not necessarily put your child off drugs. After all, one marked characteristic of adolescence is recklessness – a disregard for personal safety.

Schools and drugs

No parent can afford to be complacent about the drugs risk. They are easily available to young people these days, even in the school playground. If you have evidence that this is happening at your child's school you should report it to the head teacher immediately so that the practice can be stamped out with the support of staff and other parents.

Many schools offer an evening lecture or series of talks on drugs awareness for parents and if your child's school is doing this you should go along; if not, then it is well worth suggesting to the head teacher that something similar might be organized.

A realistic attitude

The fact is you can't lock your child up for 24 hours a day and it is almost inevitable that he will at some time in his early teens come into contact with someone able and willing to give him or sell him some kind of drug. Indeed research shows that most teenagers obtain their first drug from a friend. Berating a child about drug-taking is unlikely to be very effective if you smoke or drink yourself or even find paracetamol indispensable.

If you have experimented with illegal drugs yourself it is probably best to be honest about it in the hope that they will lose some of their attraction once your child knows that you have already 'been there'. But in this case you will need to tread very carefully so that your past does not become another excuse for him to go ahead and take more drugs.

All the evidence shows that the majority of teenagers who do become psychologically dependent and persistent drug users are those who are coping with serious problems in their lives and for many their family relationships have broken down. The safety net for most is a loving, supportive family who will help them through difficulties with friends or school so that they do not need to resort to drugs as a way out of their feelings of loneliness and isolation.

Drugs and the law

- Make sure your child knows that, as he is over the age of ten, he can be charged under the Misuse of Drugs Act if he is caught possessing, giving away or selling illegal drugs. These drugs include cannabis, heroin, amphetamine, Ecstasy, cocaine, crack and LSD. There are severe penalties for drug pushing but most young people under the age of 17 who are found 'in possession' are usually treated leniently for a first offence and are let off with a fine. He will also probably be referred to a social worker.
- Even if your child is not using drugs himself, one of his friends may be and if he is bringing them into your house, you are committing an offence by allowing someone on your premises to produce or supply illegal drugs.

YOUR CHILD'S SECONDARY EDUCATION

It is unfortunate that the upheaval of adolescence occurs at the same time as academic demands increase and teenagers have to prepare for their major public exams. Sometimes difficult behaviour at home is balanced by a well-ordered and diligent performance at school – so much so that on parents' evenings you may find yourself amazed at the contrast between the child you live with and the one the teachers are describing. Of course, it may work the other way round. In a very strict family it is more likely that the child will rebel at school and this can be much more damaging to his long-term prospects. If your child is to have a difficult adolescence it is best if his rebellion is against the people he is closest to and whom he knows will ultimately support him however he behaves, rather than against the school where bad behaviour will not be tolerated.

The great eleven plus dilemma

Finding a secondary school for your child can be an agonizing process. It is crucial that the school you choose provides the kind of environment in which he will develop successfully academically, socially and emotionally during these important years of transition from childhood to young adulthood.

State schools fall into the following categories:
- County: maintained by the local education authority
- Voluntary aided: also maintained by the LEA, but usually church schools
- Grant-maintained schools: these schools are managed by the governors and are directly funded by the Funding Agency for Schools.
- City Technology Colleges: these are mainly in urban areas and are established through a partnership between government and business. As the name suggests, they place special emphasis on technology and science.
- Language schools: these are an expansion of the specialist schools programme begun with CTCs and will place special emphasis on teaching modern foreign languages.

You may not, of course, have the full range in your area and your choice will necessarily be limited by your own attitudes and beliefs. You may be convinced that a single sex school is the only possible place for your child. If you are a practising Roman Catholic you may only consider a school of that denomination. (Many parents are attracted to church schools even if they are not of the faith themselves, believing that such schools offer a more disciplined and principled education, which may or may not be the case.)

Other considerations – such as the time and cost involved in travelling to attend a particular school – may also limit your choice. You may be tempted to dismiss some schools out of hand on the basis of a 'bad' reputation. It is impossible not to be influenced by unfavourable comments of other parents about a particular school, but do remember that when they talk about a 'bad' school they may be making judgements which would not necessarily be your own. And they may be out of date – a change of head, for example, can make a huge difference. It is important to research the school yourself and not rely on hearsay. Only you can decide whether the values the school promotes are in line with your own thinking. You can do this in several ways:
- Collect the prospectuses of all the schools you are considering.
- Study each school's performance tables. Published annually, these provide information about truancy rates as well as public examination results.
- Ask the advice of your child's primary school staff. State primary schools 'feed' particular secondary schools, usually geographically close.
- Visit each school yourself and talk to the head teacher, staff and pupils. Schools are in the business of selling themselves to parents and will offer you a warm welcome. If your child has special educational needs it is even more important to discuss them to ensure that the school you choose will cater for those.
- Make sure you attend the open evenings especially arranged for prospective parents. Check whether your child will have an opportunity to visit in his last term at primary school.
- Consult your child and take his wishes into account. If all his friends are going to the same secondary school, he may well fare better if you choose to let him go there too, particularly if he is not especially outgoing.

How to apply

You need to apply for a place at a state secondary school during the first term of your child's last year at primary school so by that time ensure you have compiled a list of possibles. (In Scotland and some parts of England, children transfer at 12 not 11 years of age.) Remember, you can apply to more than one school (ask what the policy is on not putting a 'feeder' school top of your list) and you can apply to schools outside the authority in which you live. Before you apply you need to be aware of the admission policies. The local education authority or the school will publish guidance on these policies each year and you should be able to obtain copies either from your child's primary school or direct from the LEA.

Admissions criteria, while based on guidance from the DfEE, vary from school to school but children are likely to be given priority for the following reasons:

- they have brothers or sisters who attend or have attended the school
- they live nearest to the school
- they live within a clearly defined catchment area
- they attend a 'feeder' primary school
- they have a particular aptitude in a subject such as music, art or sport (this only applies to a small number of non-selective schools).

The right to appeal

If your application in unsuccessful in the first place, don't panic. You have the right to appeal against the school's decision, although your chances of success depend on your child meeting all or most of the school's criteria for admission. In fact over 40 per cent of appeals are successful.

If an appeal fails and you think there was maladministration in your case, you have two further courses of action. You can refer to the local Ombudsman – the address and telephone number should be in the phone book under Commission for Local Administration or Ombudsman – Local. Alternatively, you can complain directly to the Secretary of State if you believe that the admissions authority has acted 'unreasonably' or 'illegally'.

Opting for an independent school

While many parents are happy to use a state primary school they sometimes choose to switch to an independent school at secondary level (this may be at 13 for boys). An independent school is one which receives no direct income from either local or central government but is funded entirely or mainly by the fees paid by parents. There are about 2,500 day and boarding independent schools in Britain. The Government currently runs the assisted places scheme to help children of 11 years and above who are considered academically able but whose parents cannot afford the fees to take up a place at an independent school. Such grants only cover tuition fees, not the cost of boarding. Children are usually selected by a school involved in the scheme on the basis of an entrance exam and an interview. A list of schools participating in the scheme can be obtained from the DfEE (see Useful Contacts, pp. 390–3); ISIS (see Useful Contacts) can provide advice and information on all aspects of independent education.

Testing times

If your child is being educated in the state system in England or Wales, his first significant examinations at his secondary school will be the Key Stage 3 national curriculum tests in English, mathematics and science which all 14-year-olds are required to sit.

At 14 plus he will embark on a two-year GCSE course or the Standard grade of the Scottish Certificate of Education. English, mathematics and a science subject are compulsory. Optional subjects are limited by what the school timetable can cope with, but from September 1996 when short courses are planned for introduction, most pupils will take short courses in design and technology, plus a foreign language, and religious, physical and sex education. On average pupils take between eight and 12 subjects and teachers should be consulted if there is a problem with selection, in order to provide a good foundation for further education. If your child is hoping for a university place, he should aim to get grade A to C in the core subjects and at least two others of his choice.

Also designed for children of 14 years plus is the General National Vocational Qualification (GNVQ) Part One, which was introduced in September 1995 as a pilot scheme. This is a vocational qualification in its own right and is the equivalent of two GCSEs. Assessment is through a portfolio of evidence and externally arranged tests. Some pupils in Scotland may take certificated short courses provided by the Scottish Education Board, as well as courses in a wide range of vocationally relevant subjects offered as part of the National Certificate of the Scottish Vocational Education Council (SCOTVEC).

When your child won't work

Many young people are eager to leave school at the earliest possible moment, indifferent to the need to get an education. For them school is boring, merely a way of killing time until they can get out into the world. This is much more likely to be true for the less academic child. When so much importance is based on the passing of examinations, those who aren't so good at that are likely to have their particular gifts and potential ignored or denigrated.

It is natural for parents to believe that their child is intelligent and gifted, and to think that if he is under-achieving, it must be his fault because he is not working hard enough or the school itself is failing him. But though it is difficult for parents to accept that their child might not make it to higher education, it is even more difficult for the child whose parents are pushing him beyond his potential. If yours is a non-academic child try to concentrate on other qualities you admire in him. The child who feels that he is constantly failing to live up to your expectations will suffer from low self-esteem or will, far worse, build up so much resentment toward you that your relationship will be in danger of breaking down.

It can sometimes be difficult to decide whether your teenager is working to the best of his ability or whether he has simply decided mentally if not physically to drop out of school. At around 14 or 15 the received wisdom is that girls show more resistance to school than their brothers, mainly because they feel too mature to be there. They try to wear forbidden make-up or jewellery or make subtle alterations to the school uniform to make a statement about how much they resent having to spend their days in an environment geared to children. Their most animated times are reserved for chats in the cloakrooms and changing rooms. They may respond in class with sullen silence.

But the reality may be subtly different. Once they reach puberty some girls under-achieve in school because boys can make themselves more dominant in a classroom, and peer pressure sometimes denigrates the 'clever' girl. However, evidence is now showing that girls are achieving consistently better examination results at 16 across all the subjects, including maths and science, and that it is boys who are under-achieving – something which schools and parents are having to take note of.

Alienation from school

You need to take action if your child is becoming seriously alienated from school. Sometimes the root of the problem might be one particular teacher with whom your child does not get on or he may be the victim of bullying (see pp. 282–3). It is essential that you work with the school in order to get your child back on the right track. Some schools have their own counsellors but most delegate overall responsibility to one or more of the senior teachers. Whatever the system in your child's school, there should be one member of staff who knows him well and with whom you can discuss his progress freely and honestly. When problems are severe the school may suggest that your child sees an educational psychologist or you may ask for your child to be referred yourself.

Truancy

Children often say they hate school but if they go every day and are making satisfactory, if not brilliant, progress there seems little reason for concern. However, truancy is always a risk at this age and your child needs to know that this is unacceptable. Apart from the effects on his school performance, children who are spending their days out of the control of either school, parents or other carers are at great personal risk.

There is no legal penalty for truancy although in law it is a local education authority's responsibility to ensure that children receive a full-time education. It is also a legal obligation for parents to make sure their children attend school during the years of compulsory schooling – from 5 to 16 inclusive. It is important that you and your teenager realize that parents of persistent truants can be fined. If this is a big problem for you and your child and you have managed to

Exclusion

If your child is permanently excluded from his school you do have the right to appeal against the decision. This will involve your meeting with the head teacher and other members of staff and representatives of the board of governors and making the case for your child being allowed to return.

There are three types of exclusion:

- fixed exclusion – the pupil is given a definite date to return to the same school
- indefinite exclusion – the pupil remains out of school pending further investigation (although this cannot be more than 15 days in any one term)
- permanent exclusion – or expulsion as it used to be known – when the pupil cannot return to the original school and the LEA becomes responsible for finding an alternative school.

define that 'going to school itself' is the difficulty – rather than the desire to be educated at all or the ability to learn – try contacting an education support groups (see Useful Contacts, pp. 390–3).

Avoiding stress

Some parents find that their adolescent child is keen to study and wants to work hard but becomes stressed by the pressures of homework and handing in coursework and assignments on time. You can help by pointing out that it is not the work itself which is the problem but the organization and time management involved, and then work to solve this together without too many difficulties.

If you approach this issue in a matter-of-fact, calm way you will help your child to gain confidence and take away the unnecessary burden of feeling that he is unable to cope with the work load and does not know how to begin to tackle it. Avoid commenting directly to your child about the school's demands on him and restrict your assistance to practical help only. However if you do think the demands unreasonable make an appointment with your child's form tutor or head of department at the school to discuss it.

Sit down together with a calendar or diary and ask him to make a list of the work which has to be done, whether homework or coursework assignments, when it has to be handed in and to whom. In another column ask him to estimate what research needs doing before the work can be written up, and how long he thinks each stage will take. When all this is done in detail you then need to decide together on a realistic amount of time which could be allocated each evening to completing the work. Point out that he cannot concentrate solely on the most urgent assignment, ignoring the rest of his work, or he will always be preparing everything in a hurry and at the last minute.

If you can help him overcome any panic he may feel at the prospect of the term's work stretching ahead, then he will be free to think and write clearly. If he has no outings planned for the weekends then perhaps you could suggest something which you know he would particularly enjoy so that there is always something to look forward to apart from studying. You can, of course, help plan a revision timetable for examinations in exactly the same way as a term's work.

It may be that you only need to be involved in the actual planning of his work for two or three weeks to help your child get into the habit, but if you keep an eye on his moods and on the time he is spending each evening on homework then you will be preventing a build-up of stress. It's a good idea to remain involved in a fairly low-key way for as long as you feel he needs you to, but it is important to remember that the aim is not to ensure he does three hours every night or gets an A mark for every piece of work – your aim is to relieve him from unnecessary stress and wasted time and help him to plan his workload more efficiently. Making sure that their children have a quiet room in which to work, away from other siblings and noise, is something so obvious that many parents overlook it. If you don't have the space in your home, find out if the school provides a homework club for families in this situation.

Encourage your child to study without the distractions of TV and/or background music. Many children insist that they are not bothered by them or even that this kind of noise helps them concentrate but that may not be the case – it is always worth suggesting he try to do without them.

Extra tutoring

If you decide that your teenager would benefit from extra tutoring – and some children find sessions of one-to-one teaching very helpful, even pleasurable – make sure that the school knows what you are doing. Conflicting teaching methods are not going to help the child who is already having difficulties.

Academic choices at 16

At 16, the teenager who has already made a career choice usually presents less of a headache for his parents, unless you believe his aspirations to be totally unrealistic. However, most people of this age haven't a clue about their future nor any strongly identifiable skills or strengths. If your child falls into the latter category he needs to be fully aware of all the options open to him. While advice from you and his teachers will not come amiss, he needs to play the most active part in the decision-making process. He may decide he wishes to move smoothly on to the sixth form of his present school to begin an A level course or to resit or take further GCSEs. (Scottish pupils take SCE Higher grades and in the sixth year the Certificate of Sixth Year Studies.) Some sixth forms in England and Wales offer Advanced Supplementary course (ASs). One AS is equivalent to half an A level.

If your child's school does not have a sixth form then he will have to look at what sixth-form colleges and colleges of further education have to offer him. The range of subjects is likely to be wider than at a school; while many of the students will be following A levels or GCSE courses, there should also be the possibility of taking job-related qualifications like General National Vocational Qualifications or those offered by BTEC, City and Guilds or the Royal Society of Arts (RSA).

Coping with exam stress

Exams are the time when any stress your child may be under academically or socially can become highly intense and where your help might be most needed. Moodiness and bursting into tears for no apparent reason are sure signs of strain. He may, of course, spurn all offers of help, but it is always worth trying. There are several ways in which you can give practical support:

Be understanding
Do not complain about such things as untidy bedrooms and try not to get upset about bad-tempered outbursts.

Persuade him to take time off
Studying without a break can be counterproductive so try to persuade him to take time off. Exercise can be an excellent way of letting off steam; a visit to the cinema may distract him and clear his head.

If your child takes too much time off, strike a bargain such as agreeing to drive him somewhere at the weekend if he stays in during the week.

Encourage positive thinking
Ban thought of failure. Boost his confidence by reminding him of past successes. He must believe he is able to tackle a problem.

Discuss ways to revise
People have different study methods, but it may help to explore the options with your teenager. One method is to combine reading with self testing – the read–cover–remember–check method familiar from primary school. Alternatively, try mind-mapping, jotting down ideas around a central image.

Make sure that your teenager knows what is expected of him in the exam. It is a good idea to look at past papers and be certain he understands the difference between discuss, define and demonstrate, for example. If he is one of those people who cannot do anything in a given time, stress how important this will be in a public exam. If you have already been helping him with planning his workload this may be less of a problem now.

Give help on the day
Being late or leaving something behind can create panic. Make sure that everything he needs is ready the night before; check where and when the exam is taking place and ask how he will get there and with whom; and provide money, phonecard and a contact number in case of emergency.

FRIENDSHIPS

Children are always affected by their friends and the importance of friendships and the influence they have increases considerably during adolescence. Because of the emphasis adolescents place on friendships, and the extent to which their behaviour can be dictated by those they mix with, it is right for you to be aware of and concerned about the friends your children choose. Most parents of adolescents can testify to the incredible difference that friends make to the way in which their children speak and behave, which is why it is vital, here perhaps more than anywhere, to keep your concerns 'low profile'.

It is sensible to get to know your children's friends and be conscious of where they go and what they get up to, rather than on the one hand, giving them a complete free rein or on the other, forbidding everyone who does not conform to strict standards of behaviour to come into your house. It is also worthwhile, though difficult at times, to ensure that your child still joins in with family outings and get-togethers. If your child turns his back on his family completely in favour of his friends, it will make it a lot more difficult for him to ask for help and advice from you if he needs it. The majority of parents worry far more over their child's choice of friends than over the fact that he may not have any at all. It might help to recall some of the friends you chose when you were the same age and whether your parents may have disapproved.

When making friends is difficult

Around 1 in 5 children has difficulty in establishing and keeping friendships; this often starts early and carries on throughout the teenage years. If your adolescent is one of these he will probably be feeling unhappy, isolated and rejected because of it, and no amount of love and reassurance from the family can entirely compensate. Try to look at your child from an outsider's point of view, an outsider who is around the same age as your child, and try to be objective:

- Is your child insensitive to the needs of others?
- Does he find it difficult to listen quietly to other people's opinions?
- Is he prone to gossiping and disloyalty?
- Is your child's self-esteem so low that he conveys negative thoughts about himself to his peers?

If you discover these or other reasons why he is isolated, you can begin to tackle them in a calm and gentle way by building on his self-confidence, carefully pointing out the need to listen to and understand the feelings of others.

Quite a few parents engage in 'social engineering': arranging outings, providing expensive treats, approaching the parents of children they view as desirable companions for their child. This may work on a superficial basis for younger children but it is disastrous where adolescents are concerned and may have the opposite effect to the one you want. It is hard to watch your child suffer and a parent's instinct is to become involved but establishing and keeping friendships is one area where you have to take a back seat.

Style and fashion

If you have problems with the way your adolescent chooses to dress, or his or her hairstyle or make-up, it is useful to take stock of your own attitude toward dress, make-up, jewellery and the like. It may seem like a waste of energy, when there are so many important issues to deal with, to become heated over how your child and his friends dress. If the clothing your child wears is offensive in a more obvious way because it is unwashed and smelly then you obviously have the right to insist that he cleans up his act. If it is your child's friends who are offending in this way you are best just giving them a wide berth. This type of behaviour is usually just another way of rebelling and is a temporary phase.

Peer groups obviously hold sway in your child's choice of clothes and help to give him a sense of belonging which is important. If tattoos and body piercing are part of the image you may feel alarmed. Remind your child that once a part of the body has been pierced and the hole made has healed, it will not close again. It is also illegal for anyone under the age of 18 to be tattooed and a tattooist requires proof that your teenager is over that age before going ahead. A sensible alternative for a teenager wanting a tattoo is to suggest he tries one of the convincing transfers now available, which allow wide scope in the choice of design. They fade quickly so will not incur the wrath of your child's school.

Making room for friends

If your child's friends upset you for reasons other than the way they dress, you need to ask yourself if you are simply reluctant to move over and allow other people into your child's life. Most of the phases your adolescent is going through are also momentous stages for you which take your child further and further away from childhood and your protection

Good friendships can ease many of the traumas of adolescence and are important for your teenager's confidence and self-esteem.

and closer to adulthood and independence from you. Are you, in fact, jealous of the surly and seemingly uncommunicative friends your child brings to the house and enjoys spending his time with?

You need to be honest with yourself in order to avoid becoming locked in permanent battle with your child over his friends. Also, if you have always placed a great deal of emphasis on keeping the house tidy and quiet then this may be the trigger for your child's choice of excessively unruly and disorderly friends.

If your concerns over your child's friends are more serious, for example, you know for certain that they are engaged in illegal activities, or if your daughter is

going out with a much older man, for example, try to voice your fears to your child without becoming judgemental or using any threats. Your chief concern is your child, not his friend and his activities. Make an effort to get to know your child's friends and allow them to spend time in your home.

'Hanging around'

Teenagers, especially boys, tend to do a lot of hanging around street corners, with the intention, many adults presume, of causing trouble. This aimlessness may be an indication that there is nothing else for them to do. Even if there is a youth club or something similar, your child may be reluctant to use what may be associated with adult-made rules and institutional buildings. Make it clear that he is welcome to bring his friends into the house to watch a video. You may resent your living room being taken over in this way but at least you know where your child is and it is preferable to his spending hours on a street corner.

You may find your house becomes a popular venue if your child has his own computer and a good supply of games, but interacting with a screen rather than with the other people around is unlikely to develop social skills. Some children do become obsessed with their computers to the exclusion of all else. If this seems to be happening to your child, be firm about limiting the amount of time he spends in front of it.

HOW TO HANDLE SEX

Research shows that a majority of parents prefer sex education to be given in schools rather than taking on the responsibility themselves. In fact sex education is now a compulsory part of the school curriculum, and if for any reason you do not want your child to take part in these lessons you as parents have to make a formal request to the school for your child to be withdrawn. Parental reluctance to undertake sex education is borne out by a survey in which teenagers were asked where or from whom they received most of their information about sex: 63 per cent said that their school was the main source of information, only 15 per cent said their mothers and a paltry 2 per cent mentioned fathers. The next most

common source of information – or perhaps mis-information – was friends of the same age and sex.

What is taught at school obviously varies a great deal, and the emotional side of the subject cannot be dealt with in the classroom as naturally and intimately as it can by loving parents, however sensitive the staff. But if you have waited until your child's adolescent years to discuss sex with him, then his ideas will already have been formed by his peers, the media and what was taught at school.

Discussing sex

While it is not a good idea to force such discussions on your child, most children signal at varying times that they want to know about a certain aspect of sexual relations or the act itself. Adolescents are sufficiently sensitive to choose a quiet moment to initiate some talk on sex. If you are not comfortable with frank discussion on this subject then this will convey itself to your child and he will probably not look to you for information or advice again. This is a shame because sane and open guidance from parents probably gives your child the best chance of forming a mature attitude toward sex and sexual relationships.

Your child will have strong feelings and urges he can barely recognize. His ideas concerning the opposite sex and how he would like to proceed with them will often be in a turmoil, along with his concerns about his own physical developments. If you have not already talked through the actual facts of sexual intercourse, do so now, providing your child wishes it, giving any extra information that he asks for or that comes naturally into the conversation. Parents often feel awkward talking about masturbation, but to deliberately ignore what is for most people their first sexual activity is to imply that it is not completely normal. If you are concerned or embarrassed that your child may ask you personal questions on the subject, think through your responses in advance.

Most adolescents are aware of the confusing messages about sex which are relayed through news about rape, pornography, paedophilia and so on. To avoid them may force your child to gain less accurate information and opinions from elsewhere. If you avoid your child's quest for knowledge concerning sex, it may be because you do not wish to confront his sexual maturity and acknowledge the end of his childhood.

Fathers and daughters

Many fathers who have held a liberal stance during their daughter's childhood find that they suddenly feel possessive toward them and see all boyfriends as threats. These feelings are natural providing they are acknowledged and not allowed to fester and stand in the way of the child's development and maturity. With boys, mothers often find that their son's behaviour swings between aggression and tenderness toward them, as the boy tries to understand all the conflicting emotions which he experiences.

Daughters may flirt with fathers, which may be irritating for the mother. All this behaviour is like a safe rehearsal for independent life and is best treated lightly but without ridicule.

Dating

Once your adolescent begins taking relationships with the opposite sex seriously and going out with a girlfriend or boyfriend, you have to walk the tight-rope between respecting privacy and ensuring that whatever they do together is safe for both partners. Sexual intercourse under the age of 16 is illegal and it is unlikely that both partners are mature enough to deal with the complexities of a full sexual and emotional relationship before that age.

The more information you have given your child on sex, contraception, venereal disease and AIDS, the less likely he is to behave irresponsibly. It helps if he is surrounded by warm, stable, affectionate relationships at home.

Teenage pregnancy

If your daughter becomes pregnant while still a teenager, she needs all your support and love, especially if she is under 16. Endless recriminations over what has happened are energy sapping and can cause lasting damage to relationships. The issues of abortion, adoption and so on are moral dilemmas which only the child and parents can decide upon and the right decision for the individual involved can only be reached through sensitive and sympathetic talk. It may be extremely difficult in this situation to think clearly about the way ahead and contacting an advisory service or support group could prove useful. If your daughter with your help decides to proceed with the pregnancy, decisions have to be made about who is going to look after the baby, and you need to ascertain whether there are support systems within the local education authority to allow your daughter to continue her education.

If your son fathers a child with an underage partner and he is also underage, take your lead from the girl's parents according to the relationship which exists between your son and his partner. If the girl's parents wish you to be a part of any discussions and plans, be as supportive as you can.

Contraception and the law

While the age of consent for sexual intercourse is 16 for heterosexual relationships, family planning advice and contraceptives can be made available for those under that age in confidence and without parental consent. Doctors are advised by the Department of Health that they should not 'undermine parental responsibility and family stability'. They are also urged to try and persuade young patients to tell their parents about the advice or treatment they are receiving or to allow them to do it for them.

Doctors giving advice on contraception should be satisfied:

- that the young person understands the advice and has sufficient maturity to understand what is involved in terms of the moral, social and emotional implications of beginning a sexual relationship;
- that the doctor could not persuade the young person to inform his or her parents nor allow him/her to inform them that contraceptive advice has been sought;
- that the young person would be very likely to begin, or to continue having, sexual intercourse with or without contraceptive treatment;
- that without contraceptive advice or treatment, the young person's physical, or mental health would be likely to suffer;
- that the young person's best interest required her/him to be given contraceptive advice, treatment or both without parental consent.

The homosexual adolescent

This is a particularly difficult time for a teenager who may be struggling with homosexuality. Your child will have gathered from your attitude to gay people whether this is something he or she can discuss with you or whether you will be so repelled that the subject cannot possibly be broached, indeed that you might even turn your child out of the house.

Most people are neither completely heterosexual nor completely homosexual but somewhere in between and most children go through a period of being attracted to their own sex. But many gay people say that they realized from an early age that they were different in some way. Later, comes the realization that the difference has to do with their attraction to people of the same sex. But the playground rules are to despise anyone who is a 'sissy' or a 'dyke', so the child who is homosexual can never act spontaneously for fear that someone will discover how he really feels.

Loving parents not only have to deal with the shock of discovering their child's proclivities but also with the heart-wrenching knowledge that their young child has secretly grappled with such feelings for so long.

You must accept that if your son is homosexual there is no point in your insisting that he dates girls by way of a 'cure'. In fact, he may do this himself; some people who are predominantly homosexual can change their behaviour by behaving heterosexually but no one can change his or her basic orientation. There is no evidence that homosexuality is an illness, that it is caused by family experiences or that it can be eliminated or changed. However open-minded you are, you are likely to feel a pang when your child tells you that he is gay. Homosexuality continues to be associated with loneliness, and there may also be the natural regret that you may not have grandchildren.

The homosexual adolescent is in the greatest need of family support. He is at much more risk of serious social and emotional problems than his heterosexual peers, not because of his sexuality but as a direct result of the hatred and prejudice which still abounds in our society. Although the age of consent for homosexuals was recently lowered from 21 to 18, indicating a slightly more liberal approach, the fact that it was not reduced to 16 in line with the law for heterosexuals means that society still views homosexuality as some kind of threat to young people.

Counselling may help if you find it difficult to come to terms with your child's homosexuality, as will contact with a support group for parents in the same situation.

First love

It is difficult to recall in later years just how obsessional, powerful and all-encompassing adolescent love can be. In many ways this is the most worrying aspect of sexual maturity because it can so easily blot out everything else in the adolescent's life. Study, family, friends, all are dismissed or cannot be concentrated upon for any length of time and it is pointless to remonstrate about the need to carry on with life as normal, because the emotion is so overwhelming that your child finds it difficult to resist. Sometimes, particularly in early adolescence, adoration is focused on a rock star or TV personality and this can occupy a good many waking hours for the smitten child; alternatively the object of adoration or 'crush' may be someone closer to home but equally unattainable – a member of the sixth form, a teacher at school or a sports coach. However when the real thing comes along it is far more intense and can cause a lot of dissent within the family, especially if the chosen one is less than ideal in parents' eyes.

If this intense relationship is interfering with your child's study, it is worthwhile negotiating so that work, at least, still continues, ensuring that your child sticks to his part of the bargain. If you can be seen to be reasonable about the amount of time you allow your child to see his loved one then you are less likely to push them together even more intensely. It is pointless and non-productive to regale your child with amusing stories of the first time you fell in love, because your child will find it almost impossible to imagine that anyone else could have felt so intensely. The worse sin of all is to ridicule him. Falling in love is a valuable part of your adolescent's development and whether or not you know better is of no consequence. If you have established an acceptable combination of study and times when he can go out, then the only other thing you need to do is listen, both to his elation and to his depression if the affair comes to an end; having kept your promise to yourself that you would not dole out any worldly wise and knowing remarks at the end of it all.

MONEY MATTERS

Polls have revealed that even when people have been made redundant or have taken pay cuts they do not penalize their children. Adolescents often find pocket money a childish and inadequate concept and you may prefer to think in terms of a weekly allowance which could include money for fares, lunches, stationery, plus an amount for outings and treats. Some parents find that as long as they stick to the agreed amount, this is a better system than constantly doling out small sums. Hopefully, it also teaches your child to take on the responsibility of handling his own budget. Other parents worry that a regular allowance will not be spent on a decent lunch and pens and paper for school work but will be constantly frittered away.

Obviously, it is quite likely when your child has control over a larger sum of money than he is used to he may make silly mistakes to begin with, but the arguments are unlikely to be any greater than those about the amount of pocket money you provide. You need to take into account your child's feelings – if he is very keen to have more control over his life then welcome the fact that he is willing to take on extra responsibility and try not to condemn his mistakes when things do not work out perfectly; after all a great percentage of the adult population in this country live with a bank overdraft!

Try to allow as much choice in the system as possible, while keeping a grip on the things which really matter to you. For example, you could go on providing school uniform but allow him enough in his allowance to buy all his weekend clothes, sportswear and trainers. If he suddenly starts frequenting secondhand shops to save on his allowance, then admire him for his initiative. You could stop making him packed lunches, if that is what he says he wants, and give him enough to buy a snack, but insist he has a meal with the family each evening, so that you know he is properly nourished.

Alternatively, provide lunch money, but if he makes his own packed lunch and saves the money he may well be eating better, as you can keep an eye on what goes into the lunchbox. How far you go with personal allowances is up to you and your child but once you have got over the shock of not making all his choices for him, it can be a relief to relinquish some control.

Jobs for the boys – and girls

Work can be a contentious issue. Some parents believe that part-time or Saturday jobs provide useful experience for their children, preparing them for full-time employment, and are keen that they should not rely solely on handouts for all their needs. Others forbid their children to work because they want them to study and feel that at weekends they should have time off. It is a shame if adolescents do not discover the independence that earning a little money can bring, but it is important to safeguard them from becoming so exhausted that they cannot study or enjoy school, and from being exploited.

If your child is confident that he can cope, and fairly paid work is available, allow him to combine the two for as long as he is happy. If your child does not want to work or you would rather he waits until he is 16, come to an arrangement whereby he 'earns' some money from you in return for regular chores. This encourages a sense of responsibility without pressure.

Legally, 13- to 15-year-olds are only allowed to work for four hours a day and they must not work before 7am or after 7pm. Bear this in mind if your child is considering taking on a paper round. Casual work is governed by local by-laws which can vary, so contact your council offices for information.

AFTERTHOUGHTS

Although the problems faced by parents of babies, toddlers and young children seem quite distinct from those we deal with in our adult life, the behaviour and development of adolescents often comes very close to that experienced by adults. Perhaps it is this similarity that can make caring for an adolescent seem different sometimes – children are no longer children but we cannot communicate with them as we would with other adults, or expect as much from them. But just as most parents view their children's babyhood and preschool years as special times, try to hold on to your children's adolescence as the final part of their journey into full maturity. If you can cope with the practical problems and weather emotional storms with tolerance and understanding, you have done a good job and can look forward to sharing your child's adulthood.

CHAPTER THIRTEEN

Your Child's Health

Every parent should have knowledge of emergency first aid procedures: acting promptly if your child stops breathing, for example, can save her life. And, while most babies and children are fit and healthy for the overwhelming majority of their young lives, some are less fortunate. This chapter describes how to spot and treat some of the most common child health problems, and details what to do in a – hopefully rare – emergency.

A-Z of illnesses and treatments

NOTE: Where medical and common names of an illness differ, most illnesses included here are listed under their medical name. Where appropriate, common names are included, cross-referenced to the medical name, so that for example, the entry for Glue ear will direct you to Otitis media. Similarly, where conditions are discussed fully in the body of the book, you will be directed to the relevant page(s).

ABDOMINAL PAIN

This common complaint in children may have a variety of causes. It is a symptom, not an illness in itself, and children sometimes find it difficult to locate the pain. Babies cannot tell you where their pain is, so tend to cry, become irritable, refuse feeds and so on. Often they draw their legs up and appear to be suffering from tummy pain – though it is always difficult to be sure exactly where the pain is. Toddlers and older children can usually tell you that their tummy hurts, but this may not mean that the cause is actually in the abdomen.

Tonsillitis (see p. 373) and middle ear infections (see p. 364), for example, may cause abdominal pain in young children. If your child complains of 'a bit of a tummy ache', paracetamol may help, but it is not sensible to give it to a child with severe abdominal pain and vomiting – this needs the attention of a doctor. Other causes of abdominal pain include appendicitis (see p. 338), intussusception (see p. 358) and urinary tract infections (see p. 374).

Some causes of recurrent abdominal pain remain unexplained, even after examination and investigation. This sort of abdominal pain may occur regularly at times of stress such as going back to school after the weekend. It tends not to occur when your child is playing happily. The pain is usually in the centre of the abdomen and is not accompanied by fever or vomiting. It is important not to ignore the cause of this pain just because it does not have a physical basis. A child may be unhappy and distressed and unable to express his feelings in any other way. There may be problems at home or at school, such as bullying. On top of all this, a child who has this sort of abdominal pain fairly regularly may also get a real appendicitis and the symptoms may be played down or ignored because of the previous history.

DIAGNOSIS A child with abdominal pain obviously needs to be examined fully. Severe abdominal pain should receive medical attention promptly, especially if your child looks very pale, is being sick or blood is being passed through the rectum. Your doctor will first look to see whether your child is very unwell and in great pain and distress or whether he can be easily distracted from the pain. A temperature, any vomiting or diarrhoea and any blood in the urine or faeces are also relevant. The abdomen is gently pressed to see where the pain is greatest and whether puffing the tummy out or sucking it right in flat makes the pain any worse. Urine is often examined and sometimes an examination of the back passage is necessary as well. The ears and throat are usually examined and the temperature taken. Finally, tests at the hospital such as an ultrasound examination or X-rays may be necessary to confirm the diagnosis.

TREATMENT The pain is treated by finding and sorting out the underlying cause, rather than by pain-killing drugs. Urinary infections are treated with antibiotics and usually referred to a paediatrician for further tests; ear and throat infections are also treated with antibiotics. Appendicitis and intussusception require admission to hospital and possible surgery. If your child is suffering from the cramp-like pains associated with gastro-enteritis (see p. 353), it helps to give her a warm bath and a wrapped hot-water bottle for her tummy.

ABSCESS

This is a localized collection of pus caused by bacterial infection. A superficial abscess is usually called a boil or carbuncle and causes skin swelling and redness. A deep abscess may be painful if it is at the root of a tooth, for example, but may not cause much pain in some circumstances – such as those in the lung or liver (although they may cause other symptoms). Most abscesses occur in the deeper tissues such as the subcutaneous fat and muscle tissue, below the skin.

SYMPTOMS A dental abscess tends to be noticed early on as it causes toothache as well as pain and swelling in the jaw. An abscess in the lung or around the kidney may cause little pain and no noticeable swelling, but the child would probably be tired and generally unwell with a mild fever and no appetite. There may be other symptoms such as cough or back pain depending on the site of the abscess.

TREATMENT The problem in large abscesses is that the pus is gathered together in a large mass and needs to be released surgically before antibiotics can do their job. Thus, surgical drainage may be necessary in hospital though dental abscesses usually clear up with antibiotics and dental treatment.

ACNE

▲ See Spots and other problems, pp. 313–14.

ADENOIDECTOMY

The adenoids are clumps of lymphatic tissue situated right at the back of the nose, in the area behind the nose which connects with the throat. They are part of the body's defence system against infection. The adenoids enlarge with repeated colds and coughs, and may obstruct breathing, causing the child to snore. Enlarged adenoids may also block the entrance to the Eustachian tubes, preventing free drainage of fluid from the middle ear, increasing the likelihood of infection of the middle ear (see otitis media, p. 364). Children with enlarged adenoids often breathe through the mouth, so tend to look a bit vacant. They may also snore loudly and may even find breathing at night so difficult that they can't sleep and are very restless.

TREATMENT Enlarged adenoids can only be seen using special ENT (ear, nose and throat) mirrors, but they do show up on an X-ray. If enlarged, they may be removed surgically, often at the same time as the tonsils, under a general anaesthetic (see tonsillitis, p. 373). The child is usually admitted to hospital for a couple of days. Opinions differ on whether adenoids should be removed surgically (an adenoidectomy); if your child has persistent problems with ear infections which don't respond to decongestants, an operation might be recommended. However children who do not have the operation usually grow out of the problem as both tonsils and adenoids shrink in later childhood as the face grows and the nasal passages get bigger.

AIDS

Acquired Immune Deficiency Syndrome (AIDS) is a serious viral illness caused by infection with the human immuno-deficiency virus – HIV. As the name suggests, normal immunity to infection is severely suppressed, leaving the sufferer open to various fungal, viral and bacterial infections.

Children may contract HIV in two main ways. First they

Children and medication

Medicines can make children 'better' in a couple of hours and there is no doubt of their effectiveness in treating or soothing many minor problems. There are, however, a few basic, commonsense guidelines to follow when dispensing medicines to children.

- Do not give a baby under four months anything, unless on the advice of your GP or health visitor.
- Do not give a child under 12 aspirin or codeine or any product containing either of these substances.
- Use the spoon provided with any medicine, measure carefully and wash the spoon thoroughly between doses.
- Never exceed the stated dose.
- When buying over the counter preparations, consult the pharmacist, describe symptoms as clearly and fully as possible and give him or her your child's age. If in any doubt, consult your GP or health visitor.
- Carers need your permission before they administer anything (even a spoonful of Calpol) to your child. If your child is unwell or simply 'off colour', make sure you can be contacted to give such permission, should it be necessary.
- If your child has an inhaler for use in asthma attacks, your GP may be willing to give her an extra one which can be kept at school. You must give the school written permission to administer this medication to your child.

may have been given an infected blood transfusion or blood product – this is now unlikely in the UK as all blood and blood products are screened for the virus. Second, a baby may be infected during pregnancy if the mother is HIV positive. (Not all babies born to HIV positive women are necessarily affected.) It is often six months or so before it is known whether the baby is affected or not, because an initial positive result is due to the maternal antibodies in the baby's blood – which disappear after several months. HIV may also be passed on in breast milk from an HIV positive mother to her baby.

TREATMENT Affected babies may show no signs of illness for several years. Then they may develop diarrhoea, anaemia, chest infections or thrush. As yet there is no cure for AIDS and no preventive vaccination. The infections are each treated individually and the patient supported physically and emotionally so that he or she can lead as normal a life as possible. Parents are understandably worried about AIDS and its transmission. So far there is no evidence that HIV can be transmitted through normal social contacts. It is a blood-borne infection and is spread by infected blood products, dirty needles used by addicts and sexual intercourse. It is not wise to share a toothbrush or razor with a sufferer; but there is no reason not to go swimming, or have a meal together and so on.

ALCOHOL

▲ See Chapter 1, p. 10 and Chapter 12, p. 317.

ALLERGY

This is a term used to describe a reaction of the immune system to something outside the body which causes the release of histamine – hence treatment with 'anti-histamines'. Most abnormal reactions are in response to substances such as pollen or the house dust mite. The allergic reaction can cause many separate conditions, including asthma (see p. 339), hay fever (see p. 354), and eczema (see p. 350). See also Chapter 6, pp. 160–1.

ALOPECIA

Alopecia is loss of hair, usually from the scalp. In its most common form, alopecia areata, the hair loss occurs in a patch or patches on the scalp. The skin appears normal and hairs are visible around the edge of the patches. The cause of this type of alopecia is unknown and there is no over-the-counter or prescriptive treatment – generally the hair grows back after several months, but the condition may recur. After persistent bouts, your child may be referred to a dermatologist. A cause of circular patches of loss may be ringworm infection of the scalp which needs treatment with anti-fungal creams.

Traction alopecia occurs at the temples and along the hairline when hair is pulled too tightly into plaits or ponytails. Some children may also pull out clumps of hair when disturbed or upset. Sometimes a child will twist a bundle of hair out of habit, also causing it to fall out or break off. The source of the distress needs to be addressed in these cases. Drugs used in the treatment of childhood cancers may cause all the hair on the head to fall out. This can be depressing for the child who already has to contend with the illness and other aspects of treatment. The hair grows back, but in the interim hats or a wig may make life more bearable.

AMENORRHOEA

Amenorrhoea means the absence of menstrual periods. When a young woman reaches the age of 18 and has not yet started her periods she is said to have 'primary amenorrhoea'. There are several possible causes. The most likely cause is family history – doctors often find that all the female members of that family start their periods later than usual. The menarche, the time at which the first period starts, can vary enormously. In some girls it is as early as eight years and in others doesn't occur until fifteen or sixteen. The average age is between 12 and 13 – if your daughter shows no signs at all of sexual development by the age of 15 go to your doctor for advice (see also Chapter 12, pp. 302–4). A possibility is Turner's Syndrome in which the baby is female, but only has one X chromosome (XO) instead of (XX).

If a girl or woman has begun menstruating normally but this ceases at some point, and she is not pregnant, the condition is known as secondary amenorrhoea. Secondary amenorrhoea can occur if girls exercise excessively or lose a considerable amount of weight – it is closely associated with anorexia nervosa. The exact weight at which this happens varies from girl to girl.

ANAEMIA

Anaemia is a blood disorder in which the level of haemoglobin, the oxygen-carrying component of the blood, is low. There are several different types of anaemia, some more common than others. Iron-deficiency anaemia is the most common form in children and babies, though the majority of children who appear pale are not actually anaemic. The only real way to diagnose anaemia is by testing the child's blood.

Iron deficiency may occur because cow's milk does not contain a great deal of iron, so the baby or young child who is fed little else may become deficient in iron and therefore anaemic. Breast milk does not contain a great deal of iron either, though formula milks usually have iron added to them. However, relatively little iron is absorbed from the total amount present in foodstuffs. Iron from animal sources is better absorbed than that from vegetable sources, but many young children do not like red meat very much, so there may be a problem. You can increase absorption of iron by drinking orange juice, or any other juice high in vitamin C, with a meal. Avoid tea, which impairs absorption.

Iron deficiency is uncommon in babies during the first six months of life unless they were born very prematurely and did not have enough time to build up stores before birth. Premature babies are usually given iron supplements after birth. Older children on a good mixed diet are unlikely to have iron-deficiency anaemia unless they have some other problem such as malabsorption (see p. 361) or a chronic disorder such as rheumatoid arthritis. Rarely, blood loss from recurrent nose bleeds or parasitic infection with hookworm in the gut may cause anaemia. Other forms of anaemia include sickle cell disease (see p. 368) and thalassaemia (p. 372). See also p. 311.

SYMPTOMS The anaemic child may or may not appear pale. He may be short of breath on exertion and have little energy, depending on the severity of the anaemia. Generally speaking, it is unusual to have to perform blood tests on the majority of fit young children who experience the usual run-of-the-mill illnesses. But sometimes the anaemia is found when the child has a blood test for some other reason.

TREATMENT Treatment is by adjusting the diet and by providing supplements – tablets or drops – in the short term.

ANAL FISSURE

This is a small tear which may cause rectal bleeding. It may be caused by a child passing a very hard stool when constipated. This causes bleeding and a small quantity of bright red blood may be noticed around the stool, in the nappy or on the lavatory paper. There will be pain on defecation and the child may avoid going to the toilet or become distressed when placed on the potty, so don't force her (see Constipation, p. 346).

TREATMENT The aim is to soften the stool by using a mild laxative and including more fibre in the diet so that defecation no longer causes distress. Your doctor could also prescribe an anaesthetic gel to use. The fissure then heals by itself (see also Rectal bleeding, p. 366).

ANENCEPHALY

This is a severe congenital malformation in which the upper part of the baby's brain and skull does not form properly during pregnancy. The baby cannot live without its brain and will usually die at, or shortly after, birth. However parents generally know beforehand because it can be detected in the early stages of pregnancy (see Chapter 1, pp. 23–4).

ANGIO-OEDEMA

Also known as angio-neurotic oedema, this occurs when the tissues beneath the skin and, to a lesser extent the skin itself, swells up. It often affects the lips, tongue and eyes where it may look most alarming, but can affect any area. The swelling itself may feel sore, but the skin does not itch. It usually goes away within 72 hours, but may recur. Almost half of the cases are associated with urticaria (nettlerash or hive, see p. 60) and it is considered a deeper form of this skin condition.

TREATMENT Treatment is with anti-histamine drugs and by trying to avoid contact with known triggers. If the swelling is severe and affects the tongue and throat, emergency treatment in hospital may be necessary to keep the airway clear. Patients suffering from severe recurrent angio-oedema may be advised to carry an adrenaline injection with them for use in an emergency. There is also a special inhaler available for use with angio-oedema.

ANIMALS AND DISEASE

Animals can enrich a child's life enormously. Owning a pet and learning how to care for it can be a wonderful experience in childhood. Pets also grow old and die, through which a child may learn about sadness and loss. Dogs, in particular, can be great companions and can promote both relaxation (curled up at your feet) and exercise (they have to be walked every day regardless of the weather).

But animals can also bite and scratch and can transmit disease to humans, though this is probably a fairly rare occurrence when the number of animals kept as pets and the number of zoonoses (diseases caused by animals) is considered. Apart from animal bites and scratches, the biggest worry to parents is usually caused by dog and cat excrement.

TOXOPLASMOSIS This infection may be acquired by handling cat faeces or from eating undercooked meat. It may cause a very mild infection with few symptoms, which is hardly noticed by the sufferer. It may also cause an illness with symptoms similar to glandular fever – sore throat, tiredness and enlarged glands. Under normal circumstances, the infection is of little significance.

Toxoplasmosis in pregnant women can cause a variety of problems of differing severity. At one end of the spectrum the baby may be unaffected; at the other extreme, miscarriage or stillbirth may occur. The affected baby may have meningitis or encephalitis which may result in learning disability later in life. Hydrocephalus and eye disorders are also a possibility. The baby may be born jaundiced due to liver problems and may be found to be anaemic. See p. 11.

TOXOCARA CANIS A greater problem may arise with dog excrement and the possibility of catching toxocara (a form of roundworm which affects both dogs and cats) from it. Toxocara eggs may be voided in dogs' excrement which may contaminate parks and pavements. Children falling over may occasionally get these eggs on their fingers and unknowingly swallow them if they happen to suck their fingers or eat some food before washing their hands. Once in the gut, the eggs hatch and the larvae may migrate to the eye causing blindness or to the lungs causing wheezing and fever. The responsibility lies with dog owners who need to clean up dog excrement at all times. Puppies and dogs should also be wormed regularly.

OTHER PROBLEMS Another disease which may be caught from animals is psittacosis from birds, though this is rare. Cat and dog fleas can bite humans and cause severe itching and inflammation. Asthmatic children can also be allergic to cat and dog fur and start wheezing badly when they come into contact with these animals.

DOG BITES AND SCRATCHES Dog bites can be nasty because the teeth may penetrate the skin and underlying tissues deeply. Their teeth are not usually very clean and may contaminate the wound with bacteria. The bite itself is extremely painful and there is often considerable bruising of the surrounding tissues. The wound should be washed immediately in dilute antiseptic solution. Stitching is rarely necessary as the puncture marks are usually very small. If the wound is a deep one, antibiotics may be prescribed and it is important that tetanus immunization is up to date (see Immunizations, pp. 157–8). In Britain, rabies is not a problem as all dogs from abroad are currently quarantined. In other parts of the world anti-rabies injections may be necessary.

Dogs do not usually bite humans unless there is a specific problem and the majority of dogs are well behaved with children. Some breeds are known to be rather irritable and to dislike small children, so it is sensible to seek advice before you buy a dog as a pet and to buy from a reputable breeder. Dogs who have been mistreated in the past may find it difficult to settle in a family with small children. If you intend to get a dog from a refuge or dogs' home it is important to ask the staff about the dog's temperament and behaviour with children. Children should not interfere with dogs while they are eating or try to remove bones or toys from their territory. And a previously good-natured dog who becomes snappy and irritable may be in pain, so should see the vet.

CAT SCRATCHES These can usually be treated by washing in a dilute antiseptic solution and using an antiseptic cream. Rarely an illness called cat scratch fever may develop. This is a viral illness which causes a mild fever, headache and swollen glands. There is no specific treatment other than rest and paracetamol for the discomfort and fever.

APPENDICITIS

The appendix is a small, worm-like, useless organ attached to the caecum, part of the bowel. It is situated at the bottom right-hand corner of the abdomen. Appendicitis occurs when the appendix becomes inflamed and may burst if it is not removed surgically. An acute appendicitis usually causes pain in the right hand side of the lower abdomen, just above the groin, though it often starts more centrally. In children, the pain may be more widespread and less well localized. Children also tend to vomit, be off their food and have a raised temperature as well. The possibility that the child might have an appendicitis is often uppermost in parents' minds when their child has tummy pain.

SYMPTOMS Abdominal pain is fairly common in children (see p. 334) and relatively few cases turn out to be an acute appendicitis. The condition is rare under the age of two and in the elderly and on average a family doctor sees one child a year with an acute appendicitis. Call the doctor if your child is in severe pain and appears to be in shock, if the pain is persistent, or if it is becoming worse.

DIAGNOSIS The family doctor usually takes a careful history from the parents and asks the child questions about where the pain started and what it is like. He or she will examine the child, taking the temperature and pulse and carefully feeling the whole abdomen. The pain of an acute appendicitis is made worse by coughing or palpating the tender area. The pain can actually get worse if the doctor's hand is rapidly withdrawn. This phenomenon, known as rebound tenderness, clearly demonstrates that the peritoneum, the inner lining of the abdomen, is inflamed.

TREATMENT If an acute appendicitis is suspected the child is seen in hospital by either the paediatricians or surgeons. If the doctor agrees with the diagnosis the surgeon operates to remove the inflamed appendix before it perforates. If diagnosis is delayed, the appendix may perforate and cause peritonitis. Sometimes the pus from a perforated appendix forms a walled-off abscess, which has to be drained later .

ARTHRITIS

Osteoarthritis does not occur in childhood, but juvenile rheumatoid arthritis does occur and may affect younger and older children in different ways.

In the younger child the disease is more generalized and often causes a fever and rashes as well as enlarged glands and spleen. The joints may be swollen and painful or there may be little in the way of joint involvement. This type of juvenile rheumatoid arthritis is known as Still's Disease.

In later childhood, the arthritis may cause less generalized illness, affecting the joints in a similar way to the adult disease. It is sometimes difficult to make the diagnosis as the characteristic blood test for rheumatoid arthritis is often negative, so other diagnoses such as septic arthritis have to be considered and excluded. The disease tends to come and go with exacerbations and remissions.

TREATMENT This is usually carried out in specialist centres where a great deal of experience has accumulated. Painkillers, anti-inflammatory drugs, bed rest, exercise and physiotherapy are all necessary at various stages of the disease. The aim of all available treatments is to allow the child to live as normal and pain-free a life as possible and to prevent joint deformity whenever possible.

ASTHMA

This is a chest condition in which the airways become narrowed and a wheezing noise is produced when breathing. Younger children may develop a persistent cough. Asthma is common – about 1 in 7 children has some evidence of asthma, though less than one per cent are severely affected. It is not known if this increase is due to improved diagnosis of the condition or whether pollution is to blame. It is true that children who used to be labelled wheezy are now called asthmatic.

SYMPTOMS In an asthmatic attack, the bronchial muscle around the airways constricts, narrowing the diameter of the tubes and causing obstruction to the flow of air out of the lungs. This reaction can be triggered by a variety of stimuli from exercise to cat fur. Some children only wheeze when they have a cold while in others the only symptom is a cough at night. Attacks also vary in severity from child to child and from one attack to another.

TREATMENT At its worst, asthma is a serious illness requiring frequent admissions to hospital and affecting growth. Fortunately there are effective treatments but these need to be understood and administered by parents, some of whom are worried about side effects and are therefore reluctant to use the prescribed drugs. The mainstay of treatment is inhaled drugs which act directly on the airways. 'Preventer' inhalers contain steroids or sodium cromoglycate drugs; 'reliever' inhalers are used as well during an attack. Parents and children over six are taught how to measure their breathing using a peak flow meter and to adjust the medication as necessary. In this way, most attacks of asthma can be treated early and admission to hospital avoided. There is no evidence that inhaled steroids used in the normal recommended doses stunt growth in children. Indeed, severe uncontrolled asthma is more likely to lead to poor growth and certainly causes educational difficulties as so many days are lost from school. See also box on p. 335.

In spite of all the treatments available, some children still develop severe attacks of asthma and need admission to hospital. It is important to seek medical advice early on in an attack, especially if the child is getting steadily worse and not responding to the usual measures.

ATTENTION DEFICIT DISORDER

This is a difficult area, in which precise medical diagnosis is not possible. The condition is also known as hyperactivity. Many parents perceive their children as hyperactive when, in fact, they are just full of energy and on the go all day, needing little sleep. The problem is that the parents cannot keep up and feel worn out. In some children, there may be problems associated with inconsistent parenting which is excused by calling the child hyperactive and therefore difficult to handle.

On the other hand, some parents report that their children are difficult to handle and rush around the whole time, finding it difficult to concentrate on one task for long and easily becoming distracted. This behaviour may be linked to the child eating certain foods, drinks or medicines and the parents sometimes find adopting an additive-free diet under medical supervision helps. It may also be associated with neurological disorders such as epilepsy. Medication – surprisingly, with amphetamines – can help, but as it can cause depression and restrict growth it is controversial. It is usually prescribed by specialists.

AUTISM

Children with autism do not develop 'normal relationships'; in fact they tend to avoid social contact and may prefer to play with things rather than people. Speech is often absent or delayed and the child prefers to play alone and avoids eye-to-eye contact. Such children need special care to help them learn and adjust to living in a more social way. Parents also need help to cope with their children who seem to live in a world of their own. (See Useful Contacts, pp. 390–3.)

BACK PAIN

Back pain is not common in childhood, though it may be seen in adolescence. Children may complain after unaccustomed exercise, but are not usually beset by the frequent backaches which afflict adults, perhaps because a good deal of backache is due to osteoarthritis of the spine, a condition of wear and tear. When a child does complain of a consistent pain in the back, the symptom should be taken seriously and medical advice sought. The family doctor will usually take a history and do an examination, including testing the urine to see whether a urinary tract infection is the cause of the pain. He or she may well request X-rays of the spine and refer the child to a paediatrician or orthopaedic surgeon if necessary.

In a teenager, backache may be a symptom of a slipped disc or scoliosis (see p. 368). Conditions such as osteomyelitis and osteochondritis (see p. 364) are also considered.

BATTERED BABIES

▲ See Non-accidental injury, p.363.

BED WETTING

▲ See Nocturnal enuresis, p. 363

BEHAVIOURAL PROBLEMS

There are a range of behavioural disorders, each guaranteed to make parents worry. Underlying them all is the near certainty that the child is suffering more than the parent but unable to express his or her distress in any other way. Children's feelings are sometimes ignored – perhaps when something unpleasant happens like the death of a grandparent or parental separation. This may be because the parents themselves are finding it hard to cope with their own feelings, or because they are unaware that even very young children have real lasting feelings.

It is often said that 'children are adaptable' and that 'they will cope' – almost as though this excuses ignoring their feelings. Children do cope, by and large, but often at great expense. They too suffer from anxiety, grief and depression and it may well be worse for them because they do not know why they feel so bad and that these feelings will not last for ever.

Instead of talking about their feelings, children may begin to bite their nails or refuse to go to school. They may begin to wet the bed having been dry at night for many years. Other symptoms of distress include sleeping poorly and having bad dreams, developing habit spasms or tics or taking it out on someone else by bullying or disruptive behaviour at school.

Whatever the particular problem, it is a cry for help and needs to be tackled. The first port of call is usually the family doctor who knows what services are available locally. If the behavioural problems mainly occur at school, your child's class or head teacher may suggest a meeting to discuss it, with the help of an educational welfare officer or educational psychologist. Either way, the family doctor should also be involved. He or she may decide to refer the child and family to a child guidance clinic or child psychologist.

All the people working in the area of child mental health are highly skilled and adept at finding out what is bothering your child. Young children may not be able to put their feelings into words, but can show how they are feeling through play.

Once the cause of the distress is identified, steps can be taken to talk about the problem and tackle the behaviour it has caused. For example, a child might be much more distressed by the death of a grandparent than is apparent, especially if he or she died suddenly and there was no time to warn the child that this might happen. That child may worry that you too are going to leave him suddenly, just like his grandfather. This, in turn, may give rise to clinging behaviour, not wanting to be left alone and refusing to go to nursery.

By finding out the source of the problem and tackling it at that level with careful explanation and reassurance that you are not going to die suddenly as well, the child can learn to understand his fear and cope with it. Not all problems are as obvious, and several trips to the specialist may be necessary.

It is sometimes difficult to know how to handle particular behavioural problems, especially as your child usually chooses the very thing that drives you mad. Common behavioural problems are listed here with explanations and hints.

BREATH-HOLDING ATTACKS   These are particularly scary for parents and are really quite powerful statements made by very young children. They are thought to result from the frustration felt by a very determined toddler.

The child tends to take a large breath as though she is going to cry, but then holds her breath instead. She may go a funny bluish colour and her eyes may appear to roll upward. The child may even have a convulsion if the attack is prolonged and lose consciousness, when he will start breathing normally again. In spite of their appearance, these episodes are not life threatening, and the child will take another breath and not die. The problem is that they attract a lot of attention and parents may try to encourage their child to take another breath by pleading, slapping or shaking. Parents may even try throwing cold water over the child. None of these manoeuvres works. The most sensible advice is not to panic and to try to behave normally, not making a big thing about it. At the same time the cause of the behaviour needs to be addressed.

▲ BULLYING   See Chapter 10, pp. 282–3.

PICA   Occasionally a child eats earth, coal, paper, or parts of their toys. This is called pica and is only really of any concern in that he may develop lead poisoning if the material contains lead paint. Nowadays, reputable manufacturers do not use lead paint. In older houses, however, some of the paint on the window sills, for example, may contain lead.

It used to be thought that children with pica had an iron-deficiency anaemia – the lack of iron stimulating their odd tastes. This has now been discounted. Pica is more common in children with learning difficulties or who are emotionally deprived. There is often a history of pica in the mother as well, and it may also be associated with head banging.

LYING   Very young children have no concept of truth or untruth, nor of right or wrong – they learn primarily from their parents as they grow older. It is not really appropriate to talk about lying in relation to toddlers, or indeed stealing, because very young children also have no concept of what is or isn't theirs. If they like a toy they are playing with at nursery they may well put it in their pocket to bring home.

The concept of ownership dawns gradually. A five-year-old is aware which toy belongs to which friend and is often vociferous in his complaints if one of his friends takes one of his toys. So, when older children lie and steal there is an obvious problem that needs to be sorted out. But it is difficult for a child when his peers have things that he doesn't. Learning to do without some material things under some circumstances is all part of growing up – but it is sometimes a harsh lesson to learn.

Teenage children need some degree of freedom, especially the freedom to think their own thoughts without being pestered all the time. If they are too pressurized to reveal all, they will lie to protect their privacy. Give and take and a fair degree of trust are needed on both sides; when these boundaries are exceeded and a more serious problem develops, professional help is needed.

NAIL BITING Some anxious children bite their nails. Generally, they will stop when they decide to and no amount of bribery or chastisement will stop them. Nasty tasting paints can act as a deterrent, but it is more sensible to investigate the root of the problem and to find out what is causing such distress. Occasionally, painting a young girl's nails with a pretty varnish makes her feel so proud of her nails that she stops biting them (but check that this is acceptable at school).

THUMB SUCKING Lots of young babies suck their thumb or fingers. It is a normal part of their emotional development, the so-called 'oral phase'. It is pleasurable and gives them comfort. If they didn't suck their thumbs they would probably want a dummy instead. It is not really a problem unless it continues above the age of six, when it may cause the teeth to stick out and may also signify an emotional problem.

HEAD BANGING This is often a difficult and distressing problem. It may start as a pleasurable experience for the child, often associated with a rocking movement and sometimes with masturbation. The behaviour continues and becomes more exaggerated and can cause a good deal of noise.

Head banging tends to begin during the first year and usually stops by the age of four. It generally occurs at bedtime and is a behaviour which is also seen in children with learning problems. It is a compulsive, ritualistic behaviour which, in small doses, is probably fairly normal and physically harmless. But a child who continues to bang his head so severely that he hurts and marks himself is more disturbed and needs expert help.

There has also been some worry that children who banged their heads are more likely to develop cataracts as teenagers and young adults. For this reason, children who persist in banging their heads should have their eyes examined.

TICS Habit spasms, or tics, are repetitive movements performed by an anxious child. They often involve the face and may include blinking, grimacing or shoulder shrugging. The cause of the anxiety needs to be addressed and the tic ignored as much as possible. If parents attempt to stop it by constantly pointing it out and reminding the child, they are likely to make things worse by increasing tension within the family and within the already anxious child. The child needs reassurance and acceptance, to know that he is loved, tic and all. As he grows more confident the tic will eventually disappear.

BIRTH MARKS

The majority of birthmarks are abnormalities of the small blood vessels and are called haemangiomas. There are three main types.

STORK MARK The most common is the stork mark, occurring in up to 50 per cent of babies. Stork marks are small pinkish patches between the eyebrows and at the nape of the neck. They are malformations of the capillaries and tend to become redder as the baby cries. Generally these marks fade during the first couple of years of life and do not require any treatment.

STRAWBERRY NAEVUS A more obvious, and therefore more distressing, type of birthmark is the strawberry naevus. This is a bright red slightly raised area which may not be noticeable at birth or for the first few weeks of life. It tends to enlarge during the first few months of life, but then becomes paler and flatter over the next few years. The majority have disappeared by about the age of six either without leaving scars, or with a mild puckering of the skin. Large ugly naevi or those which show no signs of going away may be treated surgically, though this tends to leave a worse scar.

PORTWINE STAIN This is present at birth and permanent. It is formed by dilated capillaries and appears as a purplish red, flat discoloration, often on the face. As the child gets older he may need to camouflage the mark with cosmetics. Plastic surgery can help in some cases; some marks respond to laser treatment.

Portwine stains are 'cavernous haemangiomas' – that is to say the malformation is of larger blood vessels. Very rarely, this type of birthmark is associated with other more serious vascular malformations in the brain.

MOLES Another group of marks are the pigmented spots called moles. Moles tend to appear in the toddler, though occasionally they are present at birth. They occur all over the body and are usually small and brownish. Malignant change is rare in children, but if any mole changes in colour or size or starts bleeding or itching, show it to your doctor.

MONGOLIAN BLUE SPOTS Some babies are born with large bluish-black patches on their backs or buttocks which may be mistaken for bruising and misinterpreted as non-accidental injury (see p. 363). These are Mongolian blue spots and occur mainly in Afro-Caribbean and Asian babies. They are of no significance and fade during the first five years of life.

BLINDNESS

Babies can see as soon as they are born. Straight after birth, the newborn baby will blink in response to the bright lights in the delivery room and may sneeze as well. A baby can see objects held about 20 cm (8 in) in front of his face – just right for examining his mother's face as she feeds and cuddles him. Babies can see in three dimensions, but their colour vision probably does not develop until a few months later.

Generally speaking, parents know when their baby sees them and responds. The mother who feels her baby cannot see or that something is wrong with her baby's eyes should be taken very seriously. Blindness at birth may be due to infection with rubella in the womb, which can cause cataracts. Cataracts in newborn babies may also be caused by other intrauterine factors including toxaemia and nutritional deficiency. An untreated squint may also lead to blindness in the affected eye, so it is essential that babies are referred for proper orthoptic treatment of their squints (see p. 370).

In developing countries, measles may be associated with a severe conjunctivitis leading to corneal ulceration, eye infection and eventual blindness. Other major causes of blindness include vitamin A deficiency and untreated childhood glaucoma. This may be difficult to diagnose particularly if it is present at birth. One further rare cause of blindness in children is infection with toxocara. (See Animals and disease, pp. 337–8.)

BLOOD PRESSURE

High blood pressure (hypertension) is usually the result of a specific illness or condition when it occurs in children. Normal blood pressure in young children is slightly lower than in teenagers and young adults. It must also be measured with a proper paediatric cuff, which is smaller than the adult sized cuff. The majority of children go through their childhood without ever having their blood pressure measured, unless there is a specific reason for doing so.

There are several disorders which cause hypertension in children, one of which is acute glomerulonephritis (see p. 353). Another disorder which can cause high blood pressure in children if left untreated is adrenal hyperplasia. Phaeochromocytoma is a rare adrenal tumour which produces too much adrenaline and causes high blood pressure in both children and adults, as does Cushing's syndrome, which occurs when there is a small tumour of the pituitary gland. This produces excessive amounts of the hormone which stimulates the adrenal gland and results in high blood pressure and a characteristic moon-faced appearance. High blood pressure in childhood is therefore usually part of an underlying kidney or adrenal disorder and is treated by removing the tumour or treating the kidney disease.

BONE DISORDERS

▲ See Osteochondritis juvenilis, p. 364.

BOILS

Boils are superficial skin infections where the skin becomes red and hot and the surrounding area swells and may feel very painful. Pus may be visible at the centre of the boil – which may later burst to release it, solving the problem and relieving the pain. Boils which show no sign of coming to a head and discharging by themselves may need to be treated with antibiotics. It is also a good idea to test the urine for sugar as recurrent boils may be the first sign of diabetes (see p. 348).

BRONCHIOLITIS

This chest infection affects babies and very young children. It is usually caused by the respiratory syncytial virus (RSV) and tends to occur in the winter months. Other family members may have a cold, but the baby reacts differently and over a couple of days becomes quite unwell and distressed with a fast respiratory rate, cough and breathlessness. He will often be too breathless to feed and may in addition be a bit wheezy.

TREATMENT Babies who are very unwell often need admission to hospital, especially if they begin to look blue. There, they may be given oxygen, and fed and given fluids through a tube in the nose. Although this condition is caused by viral infection, it is sometimes difficult to be sure of the diagnosis before tests are done, so most babies are given antibiotics as well in case it is a bacterial chest infection. The baby usually stays in for a few days and is then well enough to go home. Less ill babies may be looked after at home, providing that they are assessed regularly and admitted at once if there is any deterioration in their condition. A fair proportion of babies who have had severe bronchiolitis go on to suffer from asthma (see p. 339).

BRONCHITIS

Bronchitis is a chest infection which is usually caused by bacterial infection and often follows a cold. It can also follow attacks of measles or whooping cough. The infection causes inflammation of the larger airways (the trachea and bronchi) which results in a cough, wheezing, shortness of breath and the production of discoloured phlegm.

TREATMENT Acute bronchitis can affect people of all ages, including babies. Bronchitis in children and young non-smokers usually responds to antibiotics and clears up in a week or so.

BRUISING

A bruise is the well-known result of bumping into a hard object. Shortly after the collision, a tender reddish discoloration develops in the skin which later turns dark bluish purple. The skin and tissues below it have been damaged and blood has seeped into the skin. After a few days the bruise turns brownish yellow and begins to fade and then disappears.

Toddlers and young children are always falling over and their lower legs are often a mass of bruises. Treatment is rarely necessary though some people believe in using tincture of arnica to promote healing. Some people bruise more easily than others and may need investigating to see if they have a bleeding or clotting disorder. Occasionally, excessive bruising or bruising in an obscure pattern or place is a sign of non-accidental injury (see p. 363).

BURNS

▲ See Emergencies and first aid, p. 383.

CANCER

Cancer is a rare condition in children. Several types are specific to childhood, while others are similar to the adult condition. As so many types of cancer are now treatable, the word need no longer bring dread and gloom. Nevertheless it still does, because however treatable the tumour, the child still has to go through the lengthy period of diagnosis and treatment with the inevitable disruption and discomfort so caused. A parent's worst fear is that his or her child may have some form of cancer, and it is this fear that is often behind the obvious reason for the visit to the family doctor.

Approximately 50 per cent of all childhood cancers are leukaemias (see p. 360) or lymphomas (cancers of the lymphatic system). The remainder consist of tumours of the brain, eye, kidney and adrenal gland as well as the tumours which affect the connective tissues – muscle and bone cancers. Cancer can affect any organ in the body, and though all cancers are different, they share several characteristics. The normal tissue is invaded by malignant cells which then reproduce rapidly, usually at the expense of the normal tissue. A range of treatments is used: surgery, radiotherapy, chemotherapy or a combination of therapies. Cancers are now diagnosed earlier and treated more effectively than ever before. In addition to this, the technique of bone marrow transplantation and the enormous European register of potential donors for sufferers of this disease offer the chance of a cure in the treatment of certain cancers.

TREATMENT Childhood cancers should ideally be treated at specialist children's hospitals where every facility is available and staff are used to dealing with children. Permanent intravenous lines can now be inserted so that blood can be taken and chemotherapy given without having to prick the skin. It is also amazing how children accept tests and treatment when everything is explained clearly and honestly to them.

CANDIDA ALBICANS

▲ See Thrush, p. 166.

CATARRH

Catarrh is a common problem, caused by an increased production of mucus in the nasal passages, which runs down the back of the nose, tending to cause a dry sore throat every morning and a bunged-up feeling. The cause of this problem is unknown, though it may be related to allergy and smoking.

TREATMENT Treatment is somewhat difficult as the powerful anti-histamine drugs which tend to ease the symptoms only work in the short term and may be sedative. Some children also react badly to some of the decongestant preparations and become over-active and irritable. Some decongestants are available over the counter, and pharmacists are trained to advise on the treatments available and what is appropriate.

CEREBRAL PALSY

A baby with cerebral palsy has some degree of brain damage which affects her physical development. The injury to the brain may occur when the baby is still in the womb, and can include rubella infection or irradiation. The damage may also occur at birth if the baby becomes hypoxic (lacking in oxygen). Injuries around the time of delivery may cause cerebral palsy, as may severe infections of the central nervous system in infancy. This condition occurs in approximately 1 in 300 live births.

DIAGNOSIS Spasticity is a medical term used to describe the increased muscle tone found on examination. It may affect all four limbs, in which case it is called spastic quadriplegia, or two limbs only. If both legs are affected the child has a spastic paraplegia; if an arm and a leg on the same side are involved the child has a spastic hemiplegia. Some children with cerebral palsy do not suffer from spasticity but may make involuntary movements most of the time. Yet others may have ataxia (poor balance) and co-ordination, or even a mixture of all three types. The baby with cerebral palsy may appear to be floppy and, by the age of six months, will have delayed motor development. The child may be of normal intelligence irrespective of the degree of physical handicap. However, many children with cerebral palsy have learning difficulties too.

TREATMENT Over the years, a considerable amount of progress has been made in caring for children with cerebral palsy. Special centres now exist which combine physiotherapy and innovative ways of teaching affected children.

CHALAZION

This is a painless swelling of one or other eyelid caused by the blockage of the sebaceous glands at the root of an eyelash. The swelling usually disappears by itself. If the chalazion shows no sign of going or becomes so large that it is uncomfortable, it may be removed under local anaesthetic.

CHICKEN POX

This is a common childhood infection caused by the varicella virus. It is spread by droplets coughed from the upper respiratory tract of an affected person. It cannot be caught by simply touching the rash, though if you are close enough to touch the chicken pox you are probably close enough to catch it in the airborne spread. It can, however, be caught from someone who is suffering from shingles.

SYMPTOMS The incubation period can vary between 10 days and three weeks. There is also a period of one to two days before the rash develops during which the child feels generally unwell and may have a slightly raised temperature. It is during this phase that children are most infectious.

Initially, the rash consists of small pinkish spots, which subsequently become raised and blister. Eventually the blisters burst and a scab develops. The spots generally occur on the trunk and face, with relatively few on the limbs. They may also affect the scalp, the inside of the mouth and the vagina in girls. The spots 'crop' – new spots appear every day for about four days, so that at any one time there are pinkish spots, blisters and scabs on the same child. The child is infectious for about eight days or so, until all the spots have crusted over.

TREATMENT Chicken pox is generally a mild disease and the main problem is usually the itching. This may be treated with calamine lotion applied to the rash and an anti-histamine preparation taken by mouth if necessary. Occasionally the rash becomes infected and antibiotics are needed. Other, less common complications include otitis media (see p. 364) pneumonia and meningitis or encephalitis (see p. 351).

COMPLICATIONS Chicken pox is a more serious problem for immuno-compromised children, that is those whose immune system does not act or react as it should. This may be because of underlying disease, such as HIV/AIDS or immune deficiency states, or be drug-induced, through chemotherapy or steroids. These children should avoid contact with chicken pox if possible; and need to see their doctor for advice if they have already been in contact with someone who develops it. At present there is no vaccine although there are trials taking place. Immuno-compromised children can be treated with hyper-immune globulin or the anti-herpes drug acyclovir.

Chicken pox is the result of the first or primary infection with the varicella virus. Following the infection, the virus lies dormant in part of the spinal cord until it is reactivated and produces shingles. (See also Herpes zoster, p. 357.)

CHILBLAINS

These are small, painful, red areas, usually found on the toes in winter, and probably due to the effect of the cold weather on the peripheral circulation which constricts the blood vessels going to the skin. There is no effective treatment. They are best prevented by wearing gloves and warm socks and boots when it is cold outside, and bedsocks at night.

CHOKING

▲ See Emergencies and first aid, pp. 384.

CIRCUMCISION

Circumcision is the removal of the greater part of the foreskin, often for religious reasons, rarely for medical ones. It is probably the most frequently performed 'operation' in the world. The only medical reasons for circumcision are recurrent balanitis (infection of the foreskin) and excessive tightness of the foreskin which may balloon out when the child tries to pass urine. The foreskin does not retract at all at birth, though by the age of three or so, most boys can retract the foreskin.

CLEFT LIP AND PALATE

This is a congenital abnormality in which the two halves of the developing palate and lip fail to meet and fuse in the midline. In mild cases, only the lip is involved; this may not interfere with feeding and can be repaired surgically with excellent cosmetic results. A cleft palate deformity is more serious as it may interfere with the baby's ability to feed. Affected babies may be able to suckle at the breast or use a special teat on a bottle, depending on the size of the defect. Some babies are fitted with a prosthesis to overcome the initial problem and encourage proper development of the maxilla, the upper part of the jaw. (The lower part is the mandible.) At the appropriate time, the defect is repaired surgically.

Speech therapists play a prime role in the management of this condition which includes helping with feeding problems in the early days, as well as subsequent development of speech.

CLUB FOOT

▲ See Talipes, p.371.

CLUMSINESS

Some degree of clumsiness is, of course, normal in the young child who is developing new motor skills and constantly trying them out. The baby who is beginning to walk frequently falls back on to his bottom – which is conveniently near the floor. The young child who is developing his manual dexterity will build a tower of bricks and topple it when he tries to put the last brick on the top. The older child may trip and stumble a bit when he is tired after a long day at school. These are examples of 'normal clumsiness' which disappears as the child grows and movements are refined.

The abnormally clumsy child is different, though the division between what is normal and abnormal is somewhat arbitrary. It has been estimated that about five per cent of children fit this category. They tend to fall more frequently and may find writing physically awkward. They may look ungainly in the way they walk and tend to bump into things or knock things. They are poor at balancing and hopping and are not good at throwing and catching, so they may try to avoid games and get into trouble for being 'careless'.

TREATMENT Clumsy children may be dyspraxic, that is, have some mild disorder of the area of the brain which controls movement. They can be helped by physiotherapy and occupational therapy and by minimizing their limitations and encouraging their skills in other directions, so that their self-esteem does not suffer.

COELIAC DISEASE

This is a condition in which part of the bowel is allergic to gluten which is found in wheat, rye and other cereals. This sensitivity causes changes in the bowel which lead to poor absorption of food with consequent diarrhoea, failure to thrive and put on weight and anaemia.

SYMPTOMS The baby may be rather miserable and have a poor appetite. There may be abdominal distension with thin, wasted limbs. The stools may smell offensive and be difficult to flush away. Coeliac disease is not apparent in the first few months when the baby is fed entirely on milk. Symptoms appear when cereals containing gluten are introduced.

DIAGNOSIS The diagnosis may be suspected from the history and obvious failure to thrive. It is confirmed by taking a small biopsy of the jejunum (the affected part of the gut) and noticing the characteristic changes in its appearance.

TREATMENT All gluten has to be excluded from the baby's diet. Gluten-free breads and biscuits are available on prescription, and the listing of ingredients on packaging means that gluten can be avoided. Some children with coeliac disease may be able to return to a normal diet when they are older, but the gluten-free diet is usually recommended until they are fully grown.

COLDS

Colds are the commonest type of upper respiratory tract infection. They are caused by viruses, which spread among family members and close contacts by tiny droplets coughed into the air. The child with a cold typically has a runny nose and sneezes, feels tired and out of sorts but is not particularly unwell. The whole episode usually lasts for three days or so.

Children with colds also cough, especially when they lie down to go to sleep at night. Generally, children cough because they cannot blow their noses, so the nasal discharge trickles down the back of their naso-pharynx when they lie down and makes them cough. This sort of cough does not mean that the child has a chest infection; most doctors listen to the child's chest and, on finding it clear, do not prescribe antibiotics for the common cold unless a secondary infection has set in.

Young babies with colds may find it difficult to feed since they are breathing through their mouths and are reluctant to take the breast or bottle. The nasal obstruction can be helped by giving nose drops with a mild decongestant in them. The upper respiratory tract infection that is a cold may spread to other parts of the respiratory tract and cause bronchitis, for example → or to the ears via the Eustachian tubes. Antibiotics cannot help cure a cold, but are effective against bacteria, and may be prescribed to treat secondary infections. For this reason, babies and children who do not seem to be recovering as expected, or those babies who are irritable and not feeding well, should be taken to the doctor.

COLD SORES

▲ See Herpes infections, p. 356.

COLIC

▲ See Chapter 5, p. 104 and Chapter 6, p. 162.

CONCUSSION

This is the result of a hard blow on the head which does not cause serious damage, but still leaves the person feeling peculiar for several days. Symptoms may include headache, feeling not quite 'with it' and being under par. Rest and reassurance are usually all that are needed – after a couple of days off school, the child normally feels fully fit again. See also Unconsciousness, p. 389.

CONGENITAL DISLOCATION OF THE HIP

▲ See Hip problems, p. 356.

CONGENITAL HEART DISEASE

▲ See Heart disease, p. 355.

CONGENITAL HYPOTHYROIDISM

▲ See Hypothyroidism, p. 357.

CONJUNCTIVITIS

Conjunctivitis is inflammation of the conjunctiva, the colourless membrane covering the front of the eye.

SYMPTOMS Typically, the eye is bright red and there may be a yellowish discharge visible along the lashes. The eye feels sore and gritty: vision is not affected.

TREATMENT The inflammation is most commonly caused by bacterial infection and is treated with anti-bacterial drops or ointment prescribed by your doctor. The discharge should be removed by cleaning each eye separately with a clean cotton-wool ball soaked in boiled, cooled water.

Conjunctivitis may be caused by viral infection and may be part and parcel of viral illnesses like measles. It may also be caused by an organism called chlamydia, especially in newborns when it is acquired from the birth canal. Conjunctivitis is highly infectious and care must be taken to avoid its spread. Family members should have separate flannels and towels. Hay fever sufferers may also get an allergic conjunctivitis in which the eye is red and weepy. The discharge is not purulent or infected in this case, but watery. This type of conjunctivitis is treated with anti-histamine medicines or special eye drops.

CONSTIPATION

This is an extremely common problem, and one which causes great parental concern, partly because many have the mistaken idea that it is healthy and, indeed necessary, to have the bowels open every day. The bowel moves at its own rate, which is dependent on a number of factors, and may well be different in different people, even within the same family. The size and consistency of the motion are the important factors in constipation, rather than timing. A child passing a soft, well-formed stool every three days or so is not constipated.

DIAGNOSIS A child who passes small hard pellets like rabbit droppings, and has to strain to do so, almost certainly is constipated – regardless of the frequency with which the bowels are opened. A young child who is really constipated may be frightened to open his bowels because it is painful. This, in turn, may set up a cycle of stool withholding which further complicates the problem. Passage of a hard stool may cause a small anal tear or fissure (see p. 337) which reinforces the whole idea that defecation is painful and best avoided.

TREATMENT Real childhood constipation needs to be treated promptly and effectively. The amount of fluid and fibre in the diet may be increased and the stool softened with a mild laxative. However, too much fibre can leave a child feeling full and unwilling to eat more, while still being short of calories. Small babies often respond to some freshly squeezed orange juice with added boiled water, see p. 160.

CONVULSIONS

These involuntary muscular contractions are caused by abnormal electrical activity in the brain, which may occur for a variety of reasons. In the newborn baby, the fit may be due to low levels of sugar or calcium in the blood. These can be measured and corrected during the early days by the staff in the special-care unit.

Another possible cause is meningitis (see p. 361), which can be diagnosed by looking at a sample of fluid from around the spinal cord and treated with the appropriate antibiotic. Damage caused to the brain, possibly during a difficult delivery is another possible cause of fits in small babies. The most likely cause of a fit in the older baby and toddler up to three years of age, is a febrile convulsion which is associated with a raised temperature. The young child becomes feverish because of a viral illness, for example. If the temperature is not reduced by tepid sponging and giving paracetamol, certain susceptible children may convulse and lose consciousness. Some 2.5 per cent of preschool children may have this type of fit – there is often a history of fits in the family – but, the most likely cause of a fit in a child of school age is epilepsy (see p. 351).

A febrile convulsion usually only lasts a few minutes – it may rarely last as long as 20 minutes. Up to half of children who had their first febrile convulsion under the age of one may have a further fit associated with an illness and fever, though only 15 per cent of children who were three at the time of their fit had a further febrile convulsion. This emphasizes the fact that the majority of children who have a febrile convulsion do not suffer from epilepsy and are unlikely to have a fit in later life. If a child has already had one febrile convulsion, act quickly to give paracetamol and reduce the temperature by undressing the child to try to avoid further fits (see also Emergencies and first aid, p. 384) .

A young child who has more frequent or prolonged fits may need treatment with anti-convulsant drugs – diazepam, a muscle-relaxing drug, may be given rectally if the fit lasts for 10 minutes or so, while other drugs may be given long term or during the course of a feverish illness. Many children are admitted to hospital after their first fit, particularly if they are under one year old, to exclude any other illnesses.

COT DEATH

▲ See Sudden Infant Death Syndrome, p. 371.

COUGHS

Children cough a lot, especially at night. They may cough because they have a cold, and mucus is trickling down the back of their throat. A nocturnal cough may also be a sign of asthma. Generally speaking, if the coughing child is well, has no raised temperature and is not producing any purulent (green or yellow) phlegm, she is unlikely to be seriously ill. But there are always exceptions and if you are worried seek medical advice, especially if your child is feverish and unwell and has difficulty in breathing. A cough may also be the sign of a more serious chest infection such as pneumonia or TB.

Your GP will examine your child and listen to her chest with a stethoscope. If there is any abnormal sound he or she may request a chest X-ray and prescribe antibiotics. A persistent cough at night may be the first sign of asthma in a child, who may be allergic to dust mites in the bedclothes (see p. 339).

CRETINISM

▲ See Hypothyroidism, p. 357.

CROUP

Croup is the common name for acute laryngo-tracheo bronchitis, which may affect children under the age of four years. It is usually caused by a viral infection of the larynx.

SYMPTOMS The hoarse barking cough and the whooping sound on breathing in are both typical of the illness and frightening for parents. The child has usually been unwell with an upper respiratory tract infection for a couple of days when the croup begins, often at night. Both child and parents are distressed by the time the doctor is contacted, and the child's symptoms worse because he is breathing rapidly.

TREATMENT Often, examination and reassurance are all that is needed. Taking the child into a steamy bathroom, or

boiling the kettle to fill a room with steam are often helpful, though take care to avoid scalding. Children who are having obvious difficulty in breathing, or those in whom there is any doubt about the diagnosis, need to be admitted to hospital for observation and treatment if necessary.

CRYPTORCHIDISM

▲ See Undescended testicles, p. 372.

CYSTIC FIBROSIS

Cystic fibrosis is an inherited disorder which occurs in about one per 2,500 live births. It affects many systems, but the main problems are encountered in the lungs and the gut. The child with cystic fibrosis produces extremely tacky mucus, which is difficult to cough up. This results in recurrent chest infections. The pancreas is also affected: it does not function properly, so food is poorly absorbed.

DIAGNOSIS The diagnosis is usually made when a young child fails to thrive and put on weight and has recurrent chest infections as well. The child may also pass offensive loose motions, due to poor absorption of dietary fat. The diagnosis is confirmed by a sweat test which shows abnormally high levels of sodium and chloride in the sweat.

TREATMENT Children with cystic fibrosis require intensive chest physiotherapy with postural drainage, prompt treatment of any chest infections and a high-calorie diet with extra vitamins. The pancreatic malfunction can be treated by giving synthetic enzymes before food. With active treatment, increasing numbers of cystic fibrosis sufferers are living longer, including well into adulthood. Developments in gene therapy also offer new hope to sufferers and their families.

The disorder can be predicted antenatally from the family history and confirmed, if necessary, by DNA testing. Advice can therefore be given by a genetic counsellor. The condition is transmitted by a specific gene which is carried in 1 in 25 people of European descent, who have no symptoms themselves. If both parents carry the gene, there is a 1 in 4 chance at each pregnancy of the child being born with cystic fibrosis.

DEAFNESS

Deafness, the inability to hear sounds, may be due to a number of causes. Two main types of deafness exist: nerve deafness, in which the auditory nerve is damaged, and conductive deafness, in which sound waves are not transmitted properly.

The commonest cause of deafness in children is probably that due to glue ear. This is a condition in which the middle ear becomes filled with thick sticky fluid, so that the bones of the middle ear are unable to move properly to transmit the sound waves (see Otitis media, p. 364). Infection with viruses in the womb such as rubella and cytomegalovirus are common causes of congenital nerve deafness.

Deaf children may be thought to be slow learners or unco-operative in class and their learning will suffer unless the deafness is diagnosed and treated promptly. Parents who feel that their children cannot hear them, are slow to speak or have the television volume too loud should follow their instincts and ask to have their child's hearing tested. Glue ear can be treated with grommets if necessary, although medical opinion varies on this issue, and hearing aids fitted to alleviate other forms of deafness. Depending on the type and level of deafness children will be taught to communicate with signing, to lip-read and have special help with speech as appropriate.

DEPRESSION

It is becoming clear that many more children suffer from depression than was previously thought, though they are unlikely to be able to label it as such.

SYMPTOMS In children, signs of depression can be varied and may include loss of appetite and lack of energy. Sleep may be a problem, with the child waking often and sometimes complaining of bad dreams. Socially, a depressed child may be withdrawn and uncommunicative, tearful and anxious or even aggressive and rather destructive. At school, performance may be poor and concentration lacking; there may even be frank refusal to go to school.

Some children complain of mainly physical symptoms such as headache or abdominal pain and may be taken to the doctor and examined many times before the diagnosis of depression is made. There may be no obvious cause for the depression, or it may be associated with a recent bereavement – possibly of a beloved grandparent or pet; or the loss of a special friend. Depression in children may also be the result of parental marital problems or divorce with the child feeling both sad at the outcome and helpless to do anything about it.

Depression in adolescents is on the increase, as is the suicide rate among this age group, particularly among boys. On top of this sad fact it has been estimated that some 50 per cent of suicide attempters from this age group make a further attempt (see Chapter 12, pp. 310–11).

TREATMENT Depression in children and young adults is treated with a multidisciplinary approach. Counselling and psychotherapy are usually tried first, with drug therapy kept in reserve. Some children need to be admitted to specialized child and adolescent units for in-patient treatment (see also Behavioural problems, p. 339).

DIABETES

Diabetes mellitus is caused by the absence or inactivity of the hormone insulin, secreted by the pancreas. Without insulin, the level of sugar in the blood rises too high and the insulin-dependent diabetic will eventually go into a coma, known as hypoglycaemia. There is another type of diabetes mellitus which is called late-onset or non-insulin dependent diabetes. This type of diabetes generally occurs in older people and can be controlled by diet and drugs.

Insulin-dependent diabetes occurs in about one or two per 1,000 children, while the late-onset type is considerably more common, affecting up to four per cent of older people.

SYMPTOMS The condition usually starts fairly suddenly in children, with the child feeling unwell for a couple of weeks only and complaining of thirst and passing too much urine. He may have begun to wet the bed having been dry at nights. Young girls may have vulval thrush and both boys and girls may have started to lose weight and be excessively tired.

TREATMENT This involves measuring the amount of sugar in the blood regularly, and giving insulin injections twice or even three times a day. The aim is to keep the blood sugar within the normal range while allowing the child to lead a normal life and eat a healthy diet. Extra carbohydrate may need to be given before or after sports and school teachers need to know how to treat an attack of hypoglycaemia. Generally speaking, children adapt well to managing their own disease and are happy to prick their fingers to measure their blood sugar level and give their own insulin injections. Disposable syringes for insulin and new pen-like devices in which the dose of insulin can be dialled up, make life simpler.

DIARRHOEA

Diarrhoea is the passage of copious watery stools. There are several possible causes of which viral infection is probably the most common in young children. Bacterial infections and drug therapy are other possible causes of diarrhoea.

TREATMENT The mainstay of treatment is to replace the fluid loss, by giving electrolyte solutions (of sugar, salt and minerals) by mouth. This is known as oral rehydration therapy (ORT). Breastfed babies may need extra fluids as well as milk.

There is no point in giving children drugs to stop the diarrhoea as the fluid loss continues inside, even though there are fewer watery motions. It is safer to let the diarrhoea pass through and replace fluid as necessary. Anti-diarrhoeals such as kaolin solidify the stool but do nothing to improve fluid absorption in the gut. Fluid re-absorption is the important part of the treatment, not 'stopping' the diarrhoea.

DIPHTHERIA

▲ See Chapter 6, pp. 157–8.

DISLOCATION

When a joint is damaged, the two surfaces which move over each other may be disrupted so that they are no longer in the correct position, and the joint cannot move properly. This is a dislocation. It may affect several types of joint and, depending on the type of injury, may also be associated with a fracture.

Dislocated elbow and shoulder joints are the most common in childhood, often sustained when a small child is grabbed by an arm to prevent her dashing across a road, for example. These joints may also be injured when a small child is picked up by the hand and swung around in play.

TREATMENT   Dislocated joints can be put back into place fairly easily in casualty, although they are painful and distressing for the child. Usually the child hugs the joint close and refuses to move it, thus raising suspicion that something has happened to the joint. The child should be kept warm, calm and reassured. An arm may be placed in a sling made from a headscarf, and the child taken to casualty for examination and X-ray. (See also Broken bones, p. 382.)

DOWN'S SYNDROME

This congenital disorder is caused by a chromosomal abnormality. Instead of the usual two, there are three chromosomes at position 21, which accounts for the condition's other name – Trisomy 21.

The risk of having a baby with Down's syndrome increases in older mothers. Fortunately, there are now good methods of diagnosing this disorder antenatally, so that the parents may consider terminating the pregnancy if that is what they wish to do. Recognition of the higher risk to older mothers has resulted in extensive screening, with the result that now more Down's syndrome babies are born to younger women, whose statistical risk overall is in fact much lower.

Currently there are several ways of screening older women but what you are offered depends on where you live as different health regions and districts offer different techniques. A series of tests may be performed on the mother's blood and the results analysed to predict her risk of an affected baby. If, on screening, she is found to have a high risk, the mother will be offered amniocentesis. In this test a sample of the amniotic fluid which surrounds the developing foetus is examined and cultured. The results indicate whether or not the baby has Down's syndrome. The trouble with this test is that it takes several weeks to get the results so that the pregnancy is already

fairly advanced when they become available. Some hospitals offer early amniocentesis or chorionic villus sampling instead, so that the result is obtained earlier in the pregnancy. More recently it has been found that a foetus with Down's syndrome has several characteristic abnormalities detectable by ultrasound examination. Given an experienced operator, this method is likely to become a very accurate way of predicting affected babies, regardless of the age of the mother.

However, parents who would not consider termination of pregnancy, usually choose not to have the tests outlined. Most parents find their lives enriched by having a child with Down's syndrome, even though these children may also have problems with their physical health and have learning disabilities; there may also be heart and duodenal problems which require surgery.

It used to be thought that all children with this condition were mentally retarded. This may have been because nobody bothered to try and teach them anything. But the degree of learning disability is variable and some children with Down's syndrome have had considerable academic success.

DYSLEXIA

▲ See Chapter 10, pp. 385–6.

DYSMENORRHOEA

This describes painful periods. Once menstruation has started, the first few periods are not usually painful because they are 'anovulatory' – an egg is not produced. After the first few months, the periods may become more painful, even causing young girls to faint and miss school. The pain is in the lower abdomen and back and is crampy in character. It is sometimes relieved by having a hot bath or placing a hot water bottle on the pelvis, as well as taking painkillers. The family doctor may prescribe a drug (anti-prostaglandins) to take when the pain is severe. If these fail to have an effect and your daughter is still in agony, your doctor may suggest the oral contraceptive pill as a last resort until the problem is alleviated. This works by stopping ovulation, and periods while on the pill are generally lighter and less painful (see also Chapter 12, p. 304).

EARACHE

This is common in children and may mean an infection of the middle ear (see Otitis media, p. 364) or a problem in the Eustachian tube associated with a cold. If your child is unwell and has a high temperature or other symptoms, such as vomiting or being off her food, she probably needs to see the doctor. But earache in a well child can be managed, initially, by giving paracetamol and applying warmth – a covered hot-water bottle which the child can place under the ear.

If the symptoms do not resolve with this treatment then it is as well to see the doctor. It is not a good idea to fill the ear with warm olive oil. In fact you should not put anything at all into the ear unless instructed to use eardrops by the doctor.

EATING DISORDERS

These problems are centred around food, weight gain, self-esteem and, above all, control. The term covers three distinct disorders: anorexia nervosa, bulimia, and obesity. Treatment is often at specialist centres which see and treat the whole family.

ANOREXIA NERVOSA This is the best-known eating disorder. It usually affects teenage girls, though younger children and boys can also suffer. Anorexia nervosa is not a new condition but it is becoming more common and is estimated to affect at least one per cent of secondary schoolgirls.

The clinical diagnosis is made when a young person has a body weight which is less than 85 per cent of that predicted for age and height, together with the loss of three consecutive periods in girls. There is also a fear of having a normal body weight and an accompanying distorted body image, so that the anorexic girl sees herself as much fatter than she actually is. She may have been overweight as a child and is often a high achiever academically. While unwell and obsessed with food, she manages to avoid 'growing up' and confronting certain issues including her emerging sexuality, which is reflected in the disappearance of her periods. The anorexic girl goes to great lengths to avoid putting on weight, including limiting what she eats, excessive exercise to lose weight and some degree of vomiting and purging to lose the food eaten.

Anorexia is a serious illness with an appreciable death rate if left untreated. Treatment is now usually carried out in specialized units where there is a wealth of expertise. The girl is admitted and attempts made to restore her to a healthy weight in the first instance. Once some of the effects of starvation are corrected, the patient's mental state improves and she stops being quite so obsessed with food and becomes more relaxed and ready to accept psychotherapeutic help. Therapy may be continued as an out-patient.

BULIMIA Bulimia is an eating disorder in which episodes of binge eating predominate. These are sessions in which large amounts of food are eaten rapidly and are usually followed by guilt, depression, vomiting and purging. Huge amounts may be eaten – up to 15,000 kcal at one session and over 40,000 kcal in a day have been recorded. Many bulimics maintain their body weight and do not stop menstruating. Some, however, resemble anorexics and may have been anorexic in the past. These bulimics have a low body weight and need to regain their normal body weight before embarking on psycho-therapeutic treatment. A third group of bulimics tends to display more impulsive behaviour, including overdosing with drugs and slashing their arms and thighs.

Bulimia is estimated to be about ten times more common than anorexia, affecting about two per cent of women between the ages of 15 and 45 years. Bulimia is more difficult to spot than anorexia as the person tends to be of normal weight, menstruate regularly and eat normally in public. They may, however, have problems with their teeth from all the vomiting and may also have marks on their fingers from sticking them down their throats to induce vomiting. Bulimia is also best treated in a specialized unit by experienced psychologists using appropriate psychotherapy.

OBESITY Psychological problems may be both the cause of and the result of obesity. The unhappy or insecure child may eat to comfort himself or to attempt to gain approval. The resulting fat child may perform poorly at sport and be made fun of at school – both of which may increase his unhappiness.

Less is known about the causes and effects of obesity than other eating disorders. It is probable that mild obesity (less than 25 per cent extra body weight) is not a great risk to physical survival. The very fat baby tends to suffer from more chest infections than his thinner contemporaries, but usually goes on to lose the excess weight when he starts moving around. Toddlers may refuse to eat certain foods and the meal table can turn into a battleground. After the age of four, an obese child is likely to remain fat and may be at a disadvantage in a society which overvalues slimness. Fat children may be the product of fat parents, because they are being fed too much and expected to eat to please their parents. It is therefore a family problem and needs to be treated as such.

The main difficulty is in knowing what to do about an obese child, or whether anything can be done at all. There are many factors about eating and the feeling of fullness in particular, that are poorly understood. Children are thought to fall into one of two groups – most are unrestrained eaters who eat as much as they want, may be fat or thin and may lose their appetite and some weight when unhappy. The other group are the restrained eaters who are usually lean but who may eat excessively when unhappy. Try to prevent obesity by providing a balanced, healthy diet including lots of fresh fruit and vegetables, and regular mealtimes – avoid snacks between meals and too many cakes, biscuits, confectionery and crisps. If you are anxious about your child's weight discuss it with your family doctor who will give advice on eating and may refer you and your child to a dietician for specialist advice.

ECZEMA

In this common condition the outer layer of the skin becomes inflamed, making it feel itchy and rough. Eczema is now thought to be caused by a defect in fatty acid metabolism –

some types are caused by allergies, others not. There is often a history of allergy and asthma in both family and child.

TREATMENT Eczema usually starts during the first year of life and children often grow out of it as they get older. In the meantime it can be treated with emollient creams and steroid ointments from your doctor. Some babies and young children are affected by more severe and extensive eczema which weeps and crusts and often becomes infected. The itching and discomfort can both keep them awake at nights and require intensive treatment with emollient creams, baths and stronger steroids to suppress the inflammation. Antibiotics are also necessary, both on the skin and by mouth when the eczema becomes infected. Fortunately the skin usually improves as the child grows older.

ENCEPHALITIS

This is inflammation of the brain, which is a relatively rare disease. It is often combined with inflammation of the spinal cord, when it is called encephalomyelitis, or of the meninges (the lining that surrounds the brain and spinal cord), when it is called meningoencephalitis. It is usually caused by viral infection and may occasionally follow measles infection, with serious results. Other causes of encephalitis include rubella, chicken pox, mumps, herpes virus and poliomyelitis, and also malaria if it is not diagnosed and treated. It is one of the main reasons for immunizing children against as many of these common diseases as possible. Fortunately, the majority of cases of encephalitis are mild and recover completely, though once in a while permanent brain damage results.

SYMPTOMS Symptoms of encephalitis include drowsiness and fits; there may be headache and irritability if the meninges are involved as well.

TREATMENT The disease is treated in hospital with drugs to control the symptoms. There are usually no specific drugs to treat the cause, except in the case of herpes virus infection where there are now specific anti-viral drugs available.

ENCOPRESIS

Encopresis is the medical term for faecal soiling, the voluntary or involuntary passage of faeces into the underwear. A child must be 'continent of faeces' – potty trained – before encopresis can be considered a problem. A child usually has control of his bowels by three years of age.

Encopresis is a separate problem from constipation which may itself result in impaction of faeces and leakage, causing soiling. Children with constipation may fear pain on passing a hard stool so tend to put it off, leading to unintentional faecal

soiling. But some children with encopresis have been found to have an abnormality of the mechanism of defecation. Because of this, it may be that many children with encopresis simply don't have enough time to get to the lavatory.

Encopresis is also associated with emotional or behavioural problems, though this may also be an effect of having to live with the problem of encopresis and its effect on a child's self-esteem. Very occasionally, encopresis is the first sign that a child is being sexually abused.

TREATMENT The soiling needs to be investigated to see whether it is due to constipation, a bowel abnormality or emotional problems. Constipation is treated by regulating the bowel so that impaction and overflow do not occur. Encopresis due to bowel problems needs to be investigated by a paediatrician specializing in this problem. Some degree of bowel training to avoid faecal overload may be appropriate.

Emotional problems need to be identified and referred to a specialist agency – possibly child guidance, where the child will see a child psychotherapist or psychologist. Family therapy may also be needed.

ENLARGED GLANDS

Lymph nodes or glands often enlarge in response to infection. One of the most common examples of this is the large glands felt under the angle of the jaw, in the neck, when a child has tonsillitis. There may be widespread enlargement of glands in glandular fever (infectious mononucleosis – see p. 357), and small glands may also be felt at the back of the head above the nape of the neck in rubella (see p. 158). These glands usually return to their normal size a few weeks after the infection. If an enlarged gland persists, it may need to be investigated further as it may be a sign of a more serious disease such as tuberculosis or even leukaemia (see pp. 373 and 360).

EPILEPSY

This is a condition in which there is abnormal electrical activity in the brain, causing seizures (fits). Anyone can be provoked into having an epileptic fit under the right (or wrong) circumstances, but some children's brains are more easily irritated than others. Epilepsy may run in families or be caused by damage to the brain. It is not in itself a mental handicap; most people with epilepsy have a normal IQ, and prejudice associated with epilepsy needs to be strongly opposed. However, children with petit mal may do poorly at school prior to diagnosis because of their frequent 'absences'.

TONIC-CLONIC SEIZURE (GRAND MAL) This is the classical type of fit in which the person falls to the floor and convulses. The fit may be preceded by an odd feeling or aura, and is usually followed by a period of sleep. This type of epilepsy can be controlled by regular anti-convulsant medication. Even so, it is probably not a good idea for children with epilepsy to climb rocks, hang-glide or ride their bicycles in traffic, just in case they have a fit while doing so, with potentially fatal results. Swimming and bathtime both need to be monitored closely by an adult. Some epileptic children are particularly sensitive to flickering lights and these may precipitate an attack. They may need to take care when they use a VDU (computer screen) or go to a disco with a light show.

ABSENCES (PETIT MAL) This is the type of epilepsy in which major fits do not occur. Instead, the child has short periods of lack of awareness or 'absences' in which he may blink a lot and does not know what is going on. The child does not fall down, nor convulse. The diagnosis may only be made when the teacher complains that he is not paying attention in class. This type of epilepsy is also treated with anti-convulsant drugs; these may differ from those used to treat tonic-clonic epilepsy.

POST TRAUMATIC EPILEPSY This is the name given to the fits which sometimes occur after a severe head injury. These are usually of the tonic-clonic type and controlled by medication. (See also Convulsions, p. 347.)

TREATMENT Every child with epilepsy should see a specialist – usually a paediatrician or a neurologist. Although drugs may cause some side effects, it is important to take them to prevent breakthrough seizures. About one-third of children outgrow epilepsy, particularly those in which there is no known cause.

ERYTHEMA INFECTIOSUM

This is a viral illness also known as 'fifth disease' or 'slapped cheek syndrome' because the child may have a bright red rash on one side of the face which looks as though it was made by a hand slapping the face. The rash is variable, and may reappear when the skin is exposed to sunlight. The child does not feel unwell, but a small proportion of children and many adult women who catch the infection experience joint pains. There is no specific treatment other than rest and paracetamol for the discomfort. If you are pregnant and come into contact with the virus, ask your doctor for advice.

FAECAL INCONTINENCE

Most children have learned to control their bowels by the age of three years, although a few may have problems until the age of seven years. Faecal soiling is usually due to one of two problems: either constipation with involuntary overflow of faeces or encopresis (see p. 351). Older children may sometimes resort to faecal soiling when a new baby is born.

This behaviour stops as soon as the older child gets used to the new set up, realizes he is still very much loved and valued and feels secure again. Try not to scold a child manifesting this sort of behaviour: this will simply reinforce his feelings of rejection.

FAINTING

▲ See Emergencies and first aid, p. 387.

FEBRILE CONVULSIONS

▲ See Convulsions, p. 347.

FEVER

The normal body temperature is 37°C (98.4°F) or slightly less. A persistently raised temperature is usually indicative of some sort of infection and may require treatment. The commonest cause of a mild fever is probably a viral upper respiratory tract infection and can be treated with paracetamol. In young children, under the age of three, the only real cause for concern is that they might possibly have a febrile convulsion (see p. 346) if the temperature is not lowered. About four per cent of preschool children have a febrile convulsion – most do not go on to suffer from epilepsy.

A prolonged fever is more of a problem and may need investigating. A child with a prolonged fever is likely to be off his food and unwell in other ways, so needs medical attention.

TREATMENT A feverish child should be given plenty of fluids and not overwrapped in blankets; make sure the room is not overheated. Paracetamol mixture will help bring down the temperature. If the temperature does not lower, remove all clothes and sponge the skin with tepid – not cold – water.

If the fever persists, does not respond to paracetamol, and if your child is clearly unwell, seek medical advice. The doctor will note the timing of the fever and other symptoms, including recent foreign travel, examine the child and may send off a urine specimen for examination. He may also request a chest X-ray, throat swab and blood tests if necessary.

FLAT FEET

▲ See Pes planus, p. 365.

FOREIGN BODIES

▲ See Emergencies and first aid, pp. 387–8.

FRACTURES

▲ See Broken bones, pp. 382–3.

FUNGAL INFECTIONS

Thrush is the most common fungal infection in babies (see pp. 164 and 166). More severe, internal fungal infection is rare unless the baby or child is immuno-supressed – having treatment for a childhood cancer, or suffering from AIDS.

In later childhood and adolescence, fungal foot infections may be a problem. They respond to anti-fungal creams in most cases. Seborrhoeic dermatitis of the scalp is now thought to be caused by a fungal scalp infection and responds well to anti-fungal shampoos.

GASTROENTERITIS

Most gastroenteritis in childhood is caused by viral infection, usually one of the rotavirus family. Infections often occur in winter and affect babies and toddlers, causing their parents great anxiety. About 10 per cent of children under the age of two have gastroenteritis in a year. Symptoms include diarrhoea and vomiting – and there may be some abdominal pain as well, though this is always difficult to judge in small children. The virus damages the cells on the surface of the gut, preventing them from absorbing fluid normally. This gives rise to diarrhoea, and, unless adequate fluids are given, to dehydration.

Bacterial causes of gastroenteritis, such as shigella or salmonella, are passed from person to person by the faecal–oral route – contamination of fingers, food, utensils and so on with faeces. To avoid this, pay scrupulous attention to hygiene, in particular to hand-washing after using the lavatory and keep flush handles and taps clean – we all turn off taps after we have washed our hands, having turned them on when hands were dirty.

TREATMENT Drugs to prevent the diarrhoea are of little use in children as the poor absorption continues inside and dehydration may result even though the child no longer passes so many watery stools. The problem can be corrected by giving a special solution of salts and sugar as oral rehydration therapy. Given properly, this ensures adequate rehydration while the cells in the gut regenerate – which may take a week or so. Normal feeding should be continued throughout – it is now thought unnecessary to starve the child.

Occasionally, when feeding has been discontinued, young babies get diarrhoea again when they are started back on formula; these babies may need their feeds to be more diluted initially. Breastfeeding should continue throughout an attack of gastroenteritis, supplemented by oral rehydration therapy.

GENETIC COUNSELLING

The risk of passing on certain inherited diseases can be calculated in some cases and parents advised of their chances of having another affected baby. This is genetic counselling and can help prospective parents decide what to do. It is appropriate when there is a family history of certain disorders including thalassaemia, cystic fibrosis and sickle cell disease, or parents have already given birth to a baby with Down's syndrome. See also Haemophilia (p.355).

GERMAN MEASLES

▲ See Rubella, p. 158.

GLANDULAR FEVER

▲ See Infectious mononucleosis, p. 357.

GLOMERULONEPHRITIS

This is a type of kidney infection in which the filtering unit is affected. It may be caused by streptococcal infection, and may follow tonsillitis. Viruses and other bacteria may also cause glomerulonephritis; in some cases the cause remains obscure.

SYMPTOMS The child becomes unwell with pain in the stomach and at the back of the waist; she may also have a fever and headache and no appetite. There is facial puffiness, due to oedema (build up of fluid), plus breathlessness due to fluid in the lungs. Less urine is passed; it may contain blood and protein.

TREATMENT This involves hospital admission to confirm the diagnosis, bed rest and fluid restriction, with additional salt restriction and diuretics if the oedema is severe. Streptococcal infection is treated with antibiotics, often for several months. After a few days, the child begins to feel better and begins to pass more urine, though there is still blood in it. The majority of children recover completely; the prognosis is worse in adults.

GLUE EAR

▲ See Otitis media, p. 364.

GROWING PAINS

These vague pains, usually in the legs, are not meant to exist in medicine in that physical growing is thought to be painless. The problem in calling something a growing pain is that, rarely, some disease process may be going on which will be missed. Persistent pain should be taken seriously; if your child is affected, take him to the family doctor for examination.

GROWTH HORMONE DEFICIENCY

This is a disorder of pituitary function in which insufficient growth hormone is secreted, resulting in short stature. The diagnosis is made by measuring the concentration of growth hormone. It used to be treated by injections of human growth hormone, but the growth hormone now used in the UK is genetically engineered – therefore it is free of the risk of transmitting the slow viral infection Creutzfeldt–Jacob disease.

If your child is markedly smaller than his classmates, consult your doctor or health visitor for advice. Height predictions are made for certain ages – and if a child is deviating widely from these predictions, he may need investigation. Parental height is also relevant – a child with a short mother or father is never likely to be particularly tall.

HAEMATOMA

This is a subcutaneous collection of blood, rather like a large bruise. A haematoma may cause some pain, simply by being there, or it may become infected, particularly if it forms after an operation. Generally, however, it is reabsorbed and disappears over a few weeks if left alone.

HAEMATURIA

This is the passage of blood in the urine. In children, haematuria may be a sign of a urinary tract infection (see p. 372) or other kidney problem, such as a kidney stone (see p. 359). All cases of haematuria in children should be investigated. This will probably involve sending urine specimens for examination and culture to see if there is an infection, as well as referral to a specialist who will often request a renal ultrasound or IVP – an X-ray in which dye is injected into a vein and pictures taken of the dye passing through the kidneys and renal tract.

Occasionally, children who eat beetroot may pass red urine which looks as though it contains blood. The only way to be really sure is to have the red urine analysed for blood cells.

HAEMOGLOBINOPATHY

This is a blood disorder in which there is some abnormality of the haemoglobin, the oxygen-carrying component of the red blood cells.

There are several different haemoglobinopathies, of which sickle cell anaemia (see p. 358) and thalassaemia (see p. 372) are the most common.

HAEMOLYTIC DISEASE OF THE NEWBORN

▲ See pp. 38 and 59.

HAEMOPHILIA

This is an inherited disorder in which the blood does not clot normally, due to a deficiency of Factor 8. This results in excessive bleeding after even the slightest injury.

The gene for haemophilia is carried on the X chromosome, so that it is a disorder carried by a woman who does not suffer from it clinically but can pass it on to her sons. Half her sons will be affected; half her daughters will be carriers. A haemophiliac man cannot pass the disorder on to his sons, but all his daughters will be carriers. Haemophilia used to be a more disabling disorder, as repeated bleeding into the joints caused pain and deformity. Now, haemophiliacs can receive transfusions of Factor 8 to correct the deficiency, especially prior to surgery and dental extractions. This disorder can also be predicted antenatally from the family history and the sex of the unborn child identified by amniocentesis, so that parents can decide whether to risk having an affected boy baby.

HAIR LOSS

▲ See Alopecia, p. 336.

HAY FEVER

This is a seasonal allergy to various pollens and fungal spores which usually causes a runny nose and watery eyes. In severe cases there may be wheezing and shortness of breath. This form of hay fever is sometimes called pollen asthma.

TREATMENT Treatment is much improved today, and though it may be necessary to stay indoors at the height of the pollen season, there is much that can be done to control symptoms. The rhinitis or runny nose is treated with steroid or anti-allergy nasal sprays and anti-allergy eye drops are used if watery eyes are a major problem. Oral anti-histamine preparations may also be used, either as medicine or tablets. Modern drugs do not cause much drowsiness. Any associated asthma is treated in the usual way (see pp. 160–1 and p. 338).

HEADACHE

A headache is an uncommon complaint in the very young child, but tends to occur more frequently as the child grows older. There is often a simple explanation – the child may have suffered a recent head injury, for example. Conditions in which the child is generally unwell may cause a headache as part of the spectrum of the illness, and it is not uncommon for children to complain of headache when they have tonsillitis or 'flu. More serious conditions such as meningitis also cause a severe headache (see Meningitis, p. 361).

Headache as an isolated symptom is less common and may be due to poor vision; an eye test is a good idea when there is little else in the history to go on. Migraine may also begin in childhood (see p. 362). In this case there may be a family history of migraine and other associated symptoms. Recurrent headaches in the absence of other symptoms and explanation may be due to family stress or problems at school. A child whose mother often has a headache when under pressure or feeling anxious may well adopt the same behaviour.

The child with persistent headaches needs to see the family doctor who will ask about any problems, as well as examining him and taking his blood pressure. Occasionally, referral to a specialist for investigation is indicated, but in the majority of cases no serious cause for the headaches is found and the child may simply be given paracetamol for the pain.

HEAD BANGING

▲ See Behavioural problems, pp. 339–40.

HEAD INJURIES

▲ See Emergencies and first aid, p. 388.

HEAD LICE

Head lice are common in schools and nurseries as they spread from head to head and are becoming increasingly resistant to the lotions used to eradicate them. Head lice live for about a month, during which a female may lay up to 300 eggs which she cements on to the hair shaft, near the root. The eggs are difficult to see and not dislodged by ordinary combing or brushing. They hatch after about a week, leaving the empty whitish casing, the nit, attached to the hair. Lice are tiny grey-ish brown parasites which live by sucking blood from the scalp.

SYMPTOMS The only symptom of lice infestation is an itchy scalp which can be extremely irritating. Parents may notice their children scratching their heads. Occasionally parents may notice the nits clinging to the hair; those who have exper-ienced head lice once learn to look for the signs regularly.

Lice will infest anyone given the chance. They cannot jump or fly – they crawl when heads are close – nor can they be spread by towels, bedding or hair brushes or combs.

TREATMENT Head lice are treated with special chemical rinses or shampoos. It is important to ask your health visitor's or pharmacist's advice as to which product to use as different products are used in rotation to discourage the development of resistance. Regular and thorough daily hair-combing is also a useful deterrent as it helps to break the legs of the lice and prevent them from gripping the hair.

HEARING PROBLEMS

In babies, deafness is usually due to the effects of infection in the womb, birth injury or an inherited disorder; in older children the most common cause of hearing difficulty is glue ear (see Otitis media, p. 364). Babies should be able to hear from birth, though it may be difficult to tell if a baby is deaf at first as he may turn to look at a face, rather than turning toward a sound. Hearing is checked on several occasions throughout the first year and for the first few years (see pp. 154–7).

See also Deafness, p. 347.

HEART DISEASE

The term congenital heart disease is used to describe a collection of disorders affecting the developing foetal heart. Some lead inevitably to the death of the baby at or just after birth, but many are amenable to surgery. Congenital heart defects include septal defects, holes in the muscular wall separating the chambers of the heart, as well as problems with the great vessels arising from the heart. Sometimes the defect is an isolated one; at other times it is associated with other heart defects or problems elsewhere in the body. Corrective surgery is usually performed by paediatric-cardiac surgeons in specialized centres, with good intensive care facilities. The simpler defects are most easily repaired – with excellent success rates. More complicated abnormalities are more difficult to sort out and some operations need to be done in stages.

The cause of most heart defects is unknown. A few may be due to intrauterine viral infection with rubella, or associated with specific chromosomal abnormalities such as Down's syndrome.

HEART MURMURS

These sounds, heard through a stethoscope, are caused by the flow of blood through the heart valves. Usually, there are no audible murmurs in childhood, though a child may have one during the course of a feverish illness which disappears afterward.

Occasionally a very soft short murmur is heard in a child who is fit and well. Unless there is any other abnormality, this murmur is usually harmless, though a specialist opinion may be sought to confirm this. Louder, harsher heart murmurs occur when there is a problem with one of the heart valves or a cardiac abnormality (see Heart disease, above). If the child is also short of breath, is failing to thrive or has any other symptoms, referral to a specialist for further tests is necessary. These can usually be done as an out-patient and involve X-rays and ultrasound examination.

HEPATITIS

Children may catch all main types of hepatitis, sometimes known as jaundice because of the characteristic yellowing of the skin that can be caused by poor liver function. However jaundice is too general a term because the yellowing is a symptom of several different conditions.

HEPATITIS A Hepatitis A is also known as infectious hepatitis. It is spread by infected faeces, so is commonly transmitted in food or on eating utensils prepared by an infected person who has not washed her hands properly after using the lavatory. It is usually a mild disease in children with little or no jaundice. The child may feel unwell with abdominal pain and no appetite between two to six weeks after the initial infecting dose. Some children do become yellow, or jaundiced, and pass pale stools and dark urine.

HEPATITIS B Children and adolescents may also suffer from hepatitis B, serum hepatitis. This is spread by contaminated blood and blood products and is rare in the UK where transfusions and blood products are now screened. Infection may also occur through sexual intercourse, drug addicts sharing needles with a carrier, or through insufficient sterilization of the needles used in tattooing.

Hepatitis B is usually more severe and more prolonged than hepatitis A, and a proportion of sufferers will go on to carry the virus. A mother who carries the virus or develops hepatitis B during pregnancy may pass the infection on to her unborn child. This is usually treated by immunizing the baby at birth.

HERNIA

An abdominal hernia occurs when part of the gut protrudes through the muscle layers of the abdominal wall, causing a visible swelling.

▲ UMBILICAL HERNIA See pp. 60 and 167.

HIATUS HERNIA A hiatus hernia is caused when a part of the stomach protrudes through the diaphragm, alongside the oesophagus (gullet). It is one of the causes of persistent vomiting in childhood as some of the stomach contents tend to flow back up the oesophagus. This condition can sometimes be managed by feeding the baby in an upright position, but in severe cases it will require surgery.

INGUINAL HERNIA This appears as a bulge on one side of the groin. It usually requires repair under general anaesthetic.

HERPES INFECTIONS

HERPES SIMPLEX Herpes simplex is the medical name for a cold sore. These are common in childhood and rarely require treatment, although an anti-herpes cream is available over the counter at chemists. Cold sores tend to be recurrent.

However, herpes simplex infection may be more severe in some children and cause a painful mouth infection with numerous small shallow ulcers inside the mouth and on the gums. The child feels unwell, may have a temperature and is reluctant to eat. Herpes simplex may also cause a more widespread, serious infection in a child whose immune system is suppressed, or occasionally in those with severe eczema. Severe infections can be treated with anti-viral drugs if necessary.

HERPES ZOSTER Herpes zoster, or shingles, may follow reactivation of the varicella-zoster virus which lies dormant in the spinal nerves after a bout of chicken pox. Consequently, shingles is more common in adults but may affect children or teenagers who have had chicken pox at an early age. There is normally a defined area of blisters which follows the course of the nerve on one or other side of the chest, neck, face or buttocks. Herpes zoster tends to be less severe in children than in adults but speedy diagnosis and treatment are still important.

HIP PROBLEMS

Young children may complain of a pain in the hip or knee and refuse to bear weight on that side, walking with a limp. This condition is called 'irritable hip' and tends to affect young boys of five or six. The child is not generally unwell, and there is little to find when he is examined by the family doctor. Irritable hip is thought to be due to inflammation of the joint, possibly caused by a virus or minor injury. It will generally settle with no treatment other than rest and paracetamol but the child may be referred to hospital for an X-ray and specialist opinion to make sure that the hip is not septic or damaged.

Perthes' disease, a disorder of the head of the femur (thigh bone), causes pain and, if untreated, may cause permanent damage and disability.

CONGENITAL DISLOCATION OF THE HIP This is a condition in which the newborn baby's hip joint does not fit snugly into its socket. If this remains undetected and untreated, the affected hip does not develop properly and the child will have difficulty in walking properly. The condition is more common in girls than boys, in breech babies and those born full-term rather than premature babies. It also tends to be more common in the left hip than the right.

DIAGNOSIS Every newborn baby is examined at birth to check for this condition (see p. 60). Almost two per cent of babies are found to have some degree of hip instability at birth, though the majority of these do not require treatment as the condition corrects itself. If the condition is not detected on examination of the newborn baby or at the six-week check, parents may notice later that their baby does not like sitting astride their knees, crawls using one leg only and doesn't like having her nappy changed. Once walking, the child may walk with a limp or a pronounced waddling gate. Draw this to the attention of your doctor or health visitor if you are worried.

TREATMENT Babies with 'clicky' hips are placed in double terry nappies. The bulk of towelling between the legs keeps the hips in the correct position.

Babies with true congenital hip dislocation may need to wear splints – to which they adapt very easily. The leg is splinted in a frog's leg position, that is, with the thigh fixed at right angles to the hip, and the knee bent. Parents are taught how to care for their babies by paediatric nursing staff. The splint often has to stay on for several months.

HYDROCEPHALUS

This is a condition which may be present from birth, in which the cerebrospinal fluid cannot circulate properly. It is unable to drain away and accumulates within the skull, often causing the head to enlarge. Hydrocephalus may be associated with other neurological defects such as spina bifida.

TREATMENT This involves draining the fluid, hopefully before permanent damage has occurred, by inserting a long narrow tube between brain and heart.

HYPERACTIVITY

 See Attention deficit disorder, p. 339.

HYPOPITUITARISM

Hypopituitarism means under-activity of the pituitary gland, due to a tumour, haemorrhage, infection or an unknown cause, possibly relating to lack of oxygen at birth. The under-activity may affect all the hormones produced by the gland, or specific hormones only, and symptoms vary according to which hormone is deficient. See Congenital hypothyroidism, p. 346.

HYPOSPADIAS

This is a condition affecting some boy babies, in which the urethra, the tube which carries urine from the bladder to the outside, does not emerge at the end of the penis, but on the underside of the penis; there may also be multiple openings so that urine is passed through several at once. It occurs when the two urethral folds fail to fuse properly before birth and can be corrected surgically, before boys start school. Boys with this problem should not be circumcised as the foreskin may be needed for the reconstructive surgery.

HYPOTHYROIDISM

Congenital hypothyroidism is a condition in which the baby is born without a thyroid gland, so does not produce any of the thyroid hormones which are essential to normal mental and physical development.

DIAGNOSIS At birth, these babies look normal as they have had the benefit of maternal thyroid hormones via the placenta. But within a short period, the baby becomes sluggish, reluctant to feed and jaundiced. Constipation, a hoarse cry and a rather coarse facial appearance with thick lips and a protruding tongue are also characteristic. Both mental and physical development are retarded until the condition is diagnosed.

Children with hypothyroidism used to be called cretins. Now the condition is usually diagnosed and treated rapidly so that children grow up with normal mental function and the term has fallen into disuse.

TREATMENT Thyroid replacement therapy with thyroxine is necessary throughout life, and needs to be monitored and adjusted regularly. With early diagnosis and close supervision, excellent physical and mental development may be achieved.

IMPETIGO

This is a skin disease caused by infection with staphylococcal bacteria. It is usually seen on the face around the mouth and is introduced through tiny cuts or scratches in the skin. As it spreads easily, adjacent areas are often involved as well. The lesions begin as small red spots which then break down and produce fluid which dries into the characteristic yellow scabs.

TREATMENT Impetigo is treated with antibiotics, on the skin and by mouth if the infection is severe. As it is so contagious, children should not attend school until it has cleared up.

INFECTIOUS MONONUCLEOSIS

This viral infection is commonly known as glandular fever, so called because there is usually a mild fever and enlarged glands in the neck and sometimes elsewhere. Glandular fever often affects adolescents and young adults, though there is evidence that younger children may get a very mild form which is not usually apparent or may be diagnosed as some other viral illness.

In spite of its medical name, glandular fever is not particularly infectious. The virus is present in saliva, which may be the way in which it is transmitted. Indeed, it used to be called the 'kissing disease'.

SYMPTOMS Symptoms are variable and may range from a mild viral illness where tiredness and malaise are the main features, to a much more marked disease in which there is a fever, a very sore throat, a reddish rash and enlarged glands, usually in the neck – making it very difficult to distinguish from tonsillitis. There may also be mild jaundice due to viral hepatitis, an enlarged spleen and sometimes symptoms similar to a viral meningitis with headache and neck stiffness.

DIAGNOSIS The diagnosis is made by taking a history, examining the child and doing a blood test to look for particular antibodies. However, several viral illnesses give a similar clinical picture, so the blood test for glandular fever may well be negative. In some ways it is more helpful to look at glandular fever as a syndrome, not just as a specific infection.

TREATMENT There is no particular drug treatment available at present. Plenty of rest, a light diet with lots of fluids and pain-killing drugs for the headache and discomfort may be necessary. The symptoms tend to last for a long time and the illness may take several weeks, even months to get over, though eventually recovery is usually complete.

INFLUENZA

This is a common viral illness which may be a serious problem in the immuno-suppressed, but is much milder in fit children.

SYMPTOMS The headache, fever, sore throat and severe joint and backache of 'flu are probably familiar to most people. Children are not routinely immunized against 'flu every year unless they have special medical problems such as asthma or diabetes, or if they live in homes or institutions.

TREATMENT Children with 'flu should rest, drink plenty of fluids and take paracetamol for discomfort and to lower the temperature. After a few days, the temperature usually drops, but the cough may continue and your child may still feel unwell. Occasionally, influenza is followed by a much more serious chest infection which requires antibiotics and may need admission to hospital.

INSECT BITES

▲ See Bee stings and Wasp stings, p. 382.

INTESTINAL OBSTRUCTION

This is a collection of disorders in which there is a blockage somewhere between the mouth and anus so that food cannot pass through the digestive system. The blockage may be present from birth if it is due to a malformation, or occur at any age thereafter. It may be complete, with severe and continuous symptoms, or partial so symptoms may be variable and inter-mittent. The major signs of obstruction are vomiting, abdominal distension and pain and little or no bowel movement.

OESOPHAGEAL ATRESIA This complete intestinal obstruction is apparent from birth. The oesophagus (gullet) does not pass down to meet the stomach as it should; instead it may connect into the windpipe so that the lower part of the gut fills with air while milk is regurgitated back from a blind-ended pouch. This condition obviously needs urgent diagnosis and surgical correction. It is suspected when there has been an excess of amniotic fluid around the baby at birth and may now even be diagnosed before birth by careful ultrasound examination.

DUODENAL AND RECTAL ATRESIA Both these conditions result from congenital abnormalities. If the obstruction is high, the baby will vomit almost at once. If lower down, vomiting occurs later and there will be more abdominal distension as food collects in the stomach and intestine and has nowhere to go.

TREATMENT As intestinal obstruction is due to mechanical blockage, surgery is usually carried out as soon as the diagnosis is made. In the newborn baby who may have several congenital malformations, this can be extensive and difficult. After the operation the baby will need to be nursed in a special care unit until he can feed normally without vomiting and can produce normal motions. In older children the surgery is easier, simply because they are larger and there is no under-lying gut abnormality.

INTUSSUSCEPTION

This is a form of intestinal obstruction which occurs in babies between 3 and 18 months. A portion of the gut telescopes back on itself, for reasons which are not fully known, though viral bowel infections and a change to a mixed diet may play a part.

SYMPTOMS The baby screams periodically, but is quiet and pale between attacks. He may pass a loose motion containing blood.

DIAGNOSIS The baby will be very unwell and it may be possible to feel a sausage-shaped lump in his abdomen. Blood and mucus may be found during rectal examination. A barium enema, in which a substance which shows up on X-ray is inserted into the rectum, may be needed to show where the twisting occurs.

TREATMENT If the baby is very unwell, time must be spent in correcting fluid and electrolyte balance before surgery. Then, the gut is gently freed, and any gangrenous parts removed.

IRON DEFICIENCY

This is a common cause of anaemia (see p. 336) in young children whose main source of nourishment may still be milk. Both cow's milk and breast milk are low in iron, though that in breast milk is better absorbed. To rectify this, formula milks are fortified with iron. Iron from animal sources is better absorbed than iron of vegetable origin (though this can be improved by taking vitamin C, at the same time), so babies and children from vegetarian families are at risk of iron deficiency. Premature babies are also more likely to be iron deficient as there has not been enough time for them to accumulate full iron stores. Other causes of iron deficiency include persistent gastrointestinal bleeding from any cause, malabsorption (see p. 361) and heavy periods in older girls.

TREATMENT Iron supplements are given by mouth and the child or young person's diet is improved, both under medical supervision. Iron overdosage is very serious in young children, so pills containing iron and vitamins should be kept in a safe place.

JAUNDICE

This yellow discoloration of the skin and eyes occurs when bile pigments accumulate in the blood. These pigments are produced when red blood cells break down and they build up under several sets of circumstances:
- Where an excess of red cells is broken down, the immature liver may be unable to cope with getting rid of them, so they build up in the blood and the baby appears yellow. This is the case in haemolytic disease of the newborn (see pp. 38 and 59).
- Sometimes there is a physical blockage which impairs the circulation and excretion of bile. When this happens the level of bile pigments in the blood rises and the child again appears yellow or jaundiced. This almost always needs to be sorted out by surgery.
- If the liver is inflamed and cannot cope, the child again goes yellow. This happens in viral hepatitis (see p. 356).

JAUNDICE IN BABIES Jaundice is very common in newborn babies, particularly those who are premature. Called physiological jaundice, this usually fades after the first few days; it rarely requires treatment, although severe cases may require light treatment. See also p. 59.

Some breastfed babies suffer from persistent jaundice which may be alarming, but is not harmful. In cases where the baby is particularly yellow or the jaundice is prolonged, investigation is necessary.

JOINT SWELLING

Joints may swell when they are infected or injured in some way. They may also swell in rheumatoid arthritis (see p. 338) and in other conditions such as sickle cell disease (see p. 368) and haemophilia (see p. 354). See also Dislocation (p. 349) and Osteochondritis (p. 364).

KERNICTERUS

This is a serious condition which can occur in haemolytic disease of the newborn (see p. 355 and jaundice, opposite) when there are high levels of bilirubin, one of the bile pigments circulating in the blood. The newborn baby's liver is not mature enough to cope with the increased workload, and there is a danger that bilirubin will be deposited in parts of the brain, causing permanent damage. This situation is prevented by keeping a close eye on the level of bilirubin in the blood and carrying out a special blood transfusion if necessary.

KIDNEY PROBLEMS

INFECTION The growing kidney may be damaged by untreated infection, so that it appears shrunken and scarred in adult life, causing more serious problems. It is therefore very important to diagnose and treat kidney infections promptly and thoroughly. Any child who passes blood in the urine, has an unexplained fever and abdominal pain or complains of difficulty and pain on passing urine, needs a sample of urine examined for signs of infection at a laboratory. If any abnormality is found, the child is usually referred to a paediatrician for further investigation of the urinary tract. The initial test is often an ultrasound, which is painless. Thereafter, other types of kidney tests (X-rays or scans) may be necessary. See also Glomerulonephritis (p. 352) and Haematuria (p. 354).

TREATMENT Urinary tract infections are treated with antibiotics. In some cases, long-term antibiotic therapy is needed to prevent re-infection.

RENAL STONES Some children develop renal (kidney) stones which can trigger recurrent urinary tract infections as well as causing pain and bleeding inside the urinary tract.

TREATMENT Renal stones need to be removed either by an operation or by the newer technique of lithotripsy, in which the stone is shattered by sound waves so that it can be passed out in the urine.

TUMOURS Wilm's tumour or nephroblastoma is a kidney tumour which begins before birth, but does not usually make its presence felt until infancy or early childhood. The child may pass blood in the urine but this will only be detected under a microscope. The tumour usually causes a swelling on one or other side of the abdomen. The diagnosis is made by ultrasound and kidney X-ray.

TREATMENT The tumour is removed surgically and the child given chemotherapy, radiotherapy or both.

LACTOSE INTOLERANCE

Lactose intolerance is a reaction to milk and milk products. It is usually temporary and may occur after gastroenteritis. It is caused by a deficiency of the enzyme which acts on lactose (milk sugar) caused by the gastroenteritis. There are also inherited disorders in which there is a permanent deficiency of lactase – the enzyme normally present in the cells of the small intestine which breaks down lactose – so that these children are not able to tolerate quantities of lactose. Some butter and cheese may be all right.

TREATMENT Current advice is not to interrupt usual feeding, but to give electrolyte solution in addition. With this treatment, lactose intolerance does not seem to be such a problem and regrading of milk feeds is not necessary.

LARYNGITIS

This is infection of the larynx, the voice box. As with all upper respiratory tract infections, it may be caused by both viruses and bacteria. In children, the infection may also involve the trachea and lower respiratory tract as well. In this case it is called laryngo-tracheo-bronchitis or croup (see p. 347).

SYMPTOMS The main symptom of laryngitis is a hoarse voice, though children may also feel unwell and have a mild fever. The child with croup tends to have a barking, croupy cough and may make an odd wheezy sound when breathing in.

TREATMENT The voice should be rested. Steam inhalations may be soothing. Any bacterial infection is treated with antibiotics. Young children who are obviously unwell and having difficulty in breathing may need hospital admission.

LEARNING DISABILITY

This is a general term which encompasses a range of disorders in which the affected child has a lower intelligence level than expected for his or her age. In general terms, children with very severe learning disability tend to need total care and have poor language development, while those who are less severely affected require much less supervision. Further along the range of disability, children with an IQ of around 50 can learn

to care for themselves appropriately and may be able to work in a sheltered workshop later on. Children with an IQ between 50 and 75 can learn to read and write and can usually lead independent lives, working in less demanding jobs.

CAUSES Infection before birth, genetic disorders, maternal rubella and birth injury may all cause learning disability – although in many cases no identifiable cause is found. Other causes may include phenylketonuria, untreated congenital hypothyroidism (see p. 357), and untreated hydrocephalus (see p. 357).

TREATMENT Some of the causes of learning disability are untreatable, though hypothyroidism, phenylketonuria and hydrocephalus can all be treated if diagnosed at an early stage.

Children with learning disability can be taught and looked after in a stimulating environment, by specialist teachers, and increasingly in mainstream schools, often with good results. Other specialists may need to be involved if there is associated physical handicap, blindness or deafness as well.

LEUKAEMIA

This is the most common cancer in childhood, affecting the blood and blood-forming tissues. There are four main types of leukaemia and it is the acute lymphoblastic type which is most often seen in childhood, accounting for 85 per cent of all childhood leukaemias. There is no single known cause of leukaemia, though studies have shown that certain factors may be implicated. These may include viral infections and radiation, although this is not a simple cause and effect situation.

SYMPTOMS The child may be off colour and tired. He may appear pale, be off his food and bruise easily when knocked. On examination an enlarged gland may be felt in the neck, or an enlarged liver or spleen felt in the abdomen, though these signs can occur during the course of other illnesses. The diagnosis is made by looking at the blood picture which will show immature blood cells circulating in the peripheral blood when they would normally only be seen in the bone marrow. A sample of bone marrow is taken to confirm the diagnosis.

TREATMENT The initial treatment is usually undertaken at a specialist hospital. Various combinations of radiotherapy, steroids and chemotherapy are used; the child will need numerous infusions of drugs, and possibly blood transfusions if he becomes too anaemic. Nowadays, special intravenous catheters can be implanted underneath the skin, and anaesthetic creams can be used on the skin surface so that giving drugs directly into tiny veins is not too traumatic. Remission rates for acute lymphoblastic leukaemia are improving all the time. At least 90 per cent go into remission and at least half of them are still in complete remission five years after the initial diagnosis. In certain difficult cases, bone marrow transplantation may offer the best chance of a cure.

LISP

▲ See Speech disorders, p. 369.

LIVER DISORDERS

The liver can become inflamed, resulting in hepatitis (see p. 356). This inflammation can occur for a variety of reasons, though viral infections are probably the most common cause. The liver may be the prime site of the infection as in viral hepatitis, or may be enlarged as a part of a more generalized infection such as infectious mononucleosis (see p. 357). There are a number of congenital disorders which affect the liver. In Gilbert's syndrome, the liver lacks one of the enzymes necessary to metabolize bilirubin. The result is that bilirubin accumulates and the person appears slightly jaundiced or has abnormal liver function tests, but is otherwise well. This condition is usually first diagnosed in adolescence.

In biliary atresia, part of the bile duct system is missing, and the baby is jaundiced at birth; some cases can be corrected surgically. The liver is also affected in cystic fibrosis (see p. 347). See also Kernicterus, p. 359.

LYING

▲ See Behavioural problems, p. 340.

MALABSORPTION

This is a condition in which nutrients, usually fats, are not absorbed properly. The two main conditions which give rise to malabsorption are coeliac disease and cystic fibrosis. A further cause of malabsorption is tropical sprue, thought to be caused by an infection which damages the gut.

SYMPTOMS Fatty diarrhoea occurs, and the child passes a bulky, pale, offensive stool which is difficult to flush away. There is poor weight gain generally and failure to thrive.

TREATMENT Tropical sprue is treated with tetracycline and folic acid supplements. See also pp. 345 and 348.

MALNUTRITION

This is the state of poor nourishment and failure to thrive and grow normally caused by insufficient intake of the right food.

Malnutrition is rare in the western world. There are occasional cases in the UK, sometimes caused by parents inflicting faddy diets on children, sometimes in families on very low incomes. Children presented with a very high fibre diet may be short of both iron and calories; strict vegans may lack vitamin B12.

ME SYNDROME

▲ See Myalgic encephalomyelitis, p. 363.

MEASLES

▲ See Chapter 6, p. 158.

MECKEL'S DIVERTICULUM

This is a small appendage attached to the ileum, part of the bowel. Most of the time it causes no problems, but it can become inflamed and even perforate, like an acute appendicitis. It may also contain some gastric tissue which may ulcerate and bleed and it is a possible cause of gastro-intestinal bleeding in childhood. If necessary it can be removed surgically.

MENINGITIS

In meningitis, the meninges – the layers of fibrous tissue which surround the brain and spinal cord – are inflamed either by viral or bacterial infection. Viral infection is more common and usually less severe; bacterial infection occurs less frequently but is a much more serious condition.

SYMPTOMS The symptoms of meningitis vary with the age of the child affected. In older children and adults, there is usually neck stiffness, vomiting, headache and intolerance of bright lights. A baby with meningitis is more likely to be very irritable and to have a bulging anterior fontanelle, the soft area at the top of the skull before the skull bones have fully joined.

DIAGNOSIS Any child with suspected meningitis is usually admitted to hospital for a lumbar puncture to confirm the diagnosis. This is a test in which a needle is passed through the skin and deeper tissues at the lumbar region of the lower back, through the meninges and into the space around the spinal cord, so that a sample of spinal fluid may be collected. (In babies a needle is passed through the anterior fontanelle.) The spinal fluid is examined under the microscope and cultured to identify the germ responsible for causing the infection.

Most forms of meningitis are serious but treatable in hospital. But one type – meningococcal meningitis – is life-threatening, and develops very rapidly.

TREATMENT Bacterial meningitis is treated with antibiotics, often by intravenous infusion if the child is very unwell. Some types of viral meningitis, for example those caused by the herpes simplex virus, can be treated with specific anti-viral drugs. Other types of viral meningitis are treated with rest and painkilling drugs for the severe headache and discomfort.

PREVENTION Two types of vaccine are available which may prevent certain types of meningitis. Vaccination against haemophilus influenza type B (HIB) is given routinely to young children; vaccination against the meningococcus can be given to people at risk of infection and may be given more routinely in future. Close family and friends, including school contacts, of children with meningococcal meningitis are also treated with antibiotics to eradicate further infection.

MENSTRUAL PAIN

▲ See Dysmenorrhoea, p.349.

MICROCEPHALUS

Another possible cause of learning disability (see p. 360), microcephalus may be the result of congenital rubella syndrome (see p.158), infection in the womb from cytomegalovirus or toxoplasma infection (see p. 337). The brain is not fully developed at birth, the skull does not develop the usual full shape and the fontanelles close early. Other abnormalities may be associated with this problem, particularly in the case of congenital rubella syndrome, in which the baby may also be deaf, have heart defects and eye problems.

MIDDLE EAR INFECTION

▲ See Otitis media, p.364.

MIGRAINE

This severe headache can last as little as four hours or as long as three days if not successfully treated. There is often a family history of migraine, and attacks may be precipitated by several factors, including stress, foods, lack of sleep and bright lights.

SYMPTOMS There is a severe throbbing headache, often one-sided, which is made worse by movement. There is often nausea and sometimes vomiting and intolerance of bright lights and loud noise. The headache in children tends to be of shorter duration than in adults but there is often nausea and sometimes abdominal pain. When the abdominal pain occurs without the headache it has been called abdominal migraine.

This may be a specific form of migraine in children and is not usually seen after the age of 12 years.

TREATMENT Lying down to rest in a darkened room and pain-killing drugs containing paracetamol are sometimes sufficient, if the attack is treated early enough. Many of the specific drugs used to treat migraine are not suitable for use in childhood, since tablets containing codeine are not usually recommended under the age of 12 years (see box on p. 335). Drugs to treat the nausea are often given with the analgesic and are available on prescription. Avoiding known precipitating factors may also be helpful in preventing an attack. There are a few specialized migraine clinics in the UK to which your doctor may refer your child, otherwise she may be referred to a paediatrician to help a persistent problem.

MOLLUSCUM CONTAGIOSUM

These are small raised, round spots with a central depression – looking a bit like tiny smooth warts – which appear on the skin, usually on children between the ages of six and ten years. They are caused by a virus, and, in the healthy child, have no significance other than that they are unsightly. They tend to spread to other children in the family and there may be several at different sites on the body.

TREATMENT There is no treatment. The spots may disappear more quickly if they have been scratched or pierced with a sharp orange stick, but they are generally best left alone.

MOUTH ULCERS

Small, shallow, painful ulcers occur inside the mouth and lips, sometimes during the course of a feverish illness. In the majority of cases, the cause is unknown and they clear up spontaneously – though they may require ointment to help them heal. When they occur in a feverish child they may be caused by the herpes virus, a condition called herpes gingivo-stomatitis. As drinking and eating are painful, it is important to make sure the child has adequate fluids – often as ice lollies.

MUMPS

▲ See Chapter 6, p. 158.

MUSCULAR DYSTROPHY

Muscular dystrophy, a wasting disease, progressively affects certain muscle groups. The most common type, the Duchenne, affects boys and is inherited, carried by the mother and passed to her sons in the same way as haemophilia (see p. 354).

SYMPTOMS Duchenne muscular dystrophy predominantly affects the legs and shows itself as a waddling gait and difficulty in climbing stairs in a boy toddler. By about the age of ten, the boy is unable to walk at all and has to use a wheelchair.

TREATMENT There is no specific cure, so treatment is aimed at preserving mobility and independence. Physiotherapy, hydrotherapy and suitable aids around the home make life easier for both the sufferer and her carers. Antenatal screening and genetic counselling are available to affected families.

MYALGIC ENCEPHALOMYELITIS (ME)

Post-viral fatigue syndrome is now more commonly known as ME. Post-viral fatigue has been associated with glandular fever for many years, but ME appears to be more common, with excessive tiredness and weakness after a relatively minor viral illness. People who are affected do not recover their usual energy and zest for living, but find difficulty in getting out of bed and getting through the day at all. Symptoms tend to be variable, and some days are better than others.

DIAGNOSIS There are no tests for the condition. It is vital to ensure that the symptoms are not due to other problems such as anaemia, thyroid underactivity or neurological disease.

TREATMENT There are several different schools of thought about what is helpful. A low sugar diet and eradication of any intestinal candida (fungal infection) is recommended by some, while others feel that anti-depressants are the best treatment.

PROGNOSIS ME syndrome is debilitating. Teenagers and young adults may lose time from school or work and become progressively less fit and more depressed as the condition continues. Some sufferers have symptoms for years and have to change their lifestyles completely; others recover over several months.

NEPHROBLASTOMA

▲ See Kidney problems, p. 359.

NITS

▲ See Head lice, p. 355.

NOCTURNAL ENURESIS

Bed wetting is a common problem affecting some 10 to 15 per cent of five-year-olds and five per cent of ten-year-olds at least once a month. It is distressing for both child and parents and may restrict the child's activities and social life as he may be too embarrassed to stay the night with friends. There is no simple solution. The majority of children learn to control their bladders at night by the age of five years or so; the rate at which they do so depends on their neurological development in that region. In some families there is a long history of late bladder control. In a minority of cases the child may be emotionally disturbed or under stress.

TREATMENT Behavioural modification with star charts and rewards for dry nights can be used, as can bell and buzzer alarms which sound when the child wets the bed. The drug imipramine, which works by relaxing the bladder muscle, has been used with some success, but should not be used in children under the age of six. Desmopressin can be taken as a nasal spray and works by cutting down the amount of urine produced overnight. Treatment is usually for three months.

NON-ACCIDENTAL INJURY

Not all injuries in childhood are accidental – some are inflicted by adults, who may be under a great deal of stress at the time and may regret their behaviour afterward. Alcohol abuse, unemployment, overcrowding and poor housing, together with relationship problems, may all result in adults taking out their frustrations on defenceless children.

Whatever the reason, physical violence against children can never be justified or condoned. Children are so much smaller and weaker that serious physical injury – even death – may be the result, and the emotional trauma is likely to stay with them for ever. It also teaches them that 'might is right' and rarely, if ever, solves a problem.

Doctors, nurses and teachers are trained to be aware of the problem and may be suspicious of injuries which do not fit the description given. Specialist multi-disciplinary child protection teams exist to investigate allegations and protect the child at risk, and to prosecute the adult if necessary. Children may be placed on an 'at risk' register so that they receive specialist social work support. Work can also be done with the parents who are often at their wits' end and do not know how to cope with their child's difficult behaviour.

It is not a simple problem and there are no absolute rules. Every parent has experienced the feeling of being ready to clobber their child; the difference is that most parents manage to restrain themselves while some (often those who have been physically abused themselves) cannot. When this happens the child needs protecting and the whole family needs help.

OBESITY

▲ See Eating disorders, p. 350.

OESOPHAGEAL ATRESIA

▲ See Intestinal obstruction, p. 358.

OSTEOCHONDRITIS JUVENILIS

This condition affects the growing ends of bones (the epiphyses), and is caused by disruption to the blood supply to that area. Several different bones are often affected and each condition is named after the doctor who first described it.

PERTHES' DISEASE   This affects the head of the femur (thigh bone). It affects boys more than girls and usually shows itself as a limp. There may be pain in the hip, and knee as well. The diagnosis is made from X-rays. Treatment consists of resting the leg, initially with bed rest and traction, until the pain and tenderness have gone. Osteoarthritis tends to develop in the hip in adulthood, and a hip replacement may be necessary.

OSGOOD-SCLATTER'S DISEASE   This attacks the tibial tubercle, the area just below the kneecap. It usually affects adolescent boys and causes pain, tenderness and sometimes swelling. The teenager may need to avoid exercise when in pain; in severe cases a plaster cast may be necessary for a limited period.

SCHEUERMANN'S DISEASE   This affects the spine. It tends to occur at puberty and causes backache and a poor, slouched posture. It is usually treated with physiotherapy and exercises.

OSTEOMYELITIS

This is a potentially serious condition in which a bone becomes infected. For some reason as yet unknown, osteomyelitis is more common in children than adults and in boys rather than girls. The bones usually affected are those in the legs, though how the infection gets into the bone is uncertain.

SYMPTOMS   The older boy may be unwell with a fever and a painful leg, while the younger child may simply refuse to put his foot on the ground and bear any weight on it. There may be an area of redness and tenderness over the site of the infection.

TREATMENT   Antibiotics, given intravenously at first, are used to treat osteomyelitis. High doses of the drugs are given for a prolonged period to ensure that all the infection is eradicated.

OTITIS EXTERNA

This is inflammation of the external auditory canal – the outer passageway into the ear. The canal becomes sore and may fill with thick secretion, making it difficult to examine the ear drum. It is not common in young children, occurring mainly in adults and teenagers. Milder forms are treated with ear drops which contain antibiotics and steroids to treat the inflammation. Severe infections often need antibiotics by mouth too.

OTITIS MEDIA

This is common in babies and young children. The middle ear becomes infected, usually after an upper respiratory tract infection. Germs, often bacteria, are thought to travel from the nasopharynx, up the Eustachian tube to the middle ear.

SYMPTOMS   Very young children are often grizzly and unwell with a raised temperature. They may be off their food, vomit or keep touching the affected ear. Abdominal pain may also be a symptom. Older children will explain that they have an earache and are also likely to be hot and unwell.

TREATMENT   There is a great deal of discussion about the use of antibiotics in this condition. Some authorities claim that the majority of cases will clear up after a few days of treatment with paracetamol and decongestant nose drops; other doctors, and parents of children with recurrent otitis media, tend to prefer to treat with a short course of antibiotics because they have seen the misery and distress the condition causes and the rapid improvement brought about by antibiotics.

COMPLICATIONS   Repeated episodes of otitis media may lead to 'serous otitis media', or glue ear. In this condition, the middle ear becomes filled with thick fluid, making it difficult for the bones of the middle ear to vibrate as they should. The transmission of sound waves is impeded and the child cannot hear very well with that ear. If both ears are affected he may find it very difficult to hear correctly. In some cases this may lead to a delay in talking, or poor performance at school.

Glue ear is often outgrown, but if it persists and causes demonstrable hearing loss, it can be treated by inserting grommets, tiny tubes, into the ear drum. These allow the thick fluid to drain away and improve hearing. Grommets usually fall out by themselves, but occasionally they have to be re-inserted if they fall out before the ear is clear.

PARASITIC INFECTIONS

There are a number of common parasitic infections in the UK, none of which, fortunately, is particularly serious. A parasite is an organism which lives on a host (in this case humans). It is in the parasite's own interest not to kill off the host, its meal ticket. Head lice (see p. 355) and scabies (see p. 368) are both parasites which live on the surface of the skin. Inside the gut, threadworms, roundworms and tapeworms (see p. 371) are all parasites, though under normal conditions they are not harmful.

PARONYCHIA

This is infection around the fingernail, which is often precipitated by picking at or chewing the nails. The skin at the side of the nail becomes damaged and germs can then enter the tissues.

SYMPTOMS The base of the nail may be swollen, red and painful or there may be a localized collection of pus which is often called a whitlow.

TREATMENT Some whitlows can be lanced painlessly, which usually brings immediate relief. Others require a poultice, before they are ready to discharge their pus. If it spreads, paronychia is treated with a course of antibiotics to eradicate the infection.

PERTHES' DISEASE

▲ See Osteochondritis juvenilis, p. 364.

PERTUSSIS

▲ See Chapter 6, pp. 157–8.

PES PLANUS

These are flat feet. Parents often worry that their young child has flat feet because the arch under the foot does not develop fully until the age of six years or so. In young children, there is usually maximum wear on the outer edge of the heel of the shoe. If your child's shoes show maximum wear on the inner edge of the heel, this may be a sign that she has flat feet.

TREATMENT Physiotherapy, both for expert assessment of the problem and in order to teach the child series of exercises to encourage foot mobility and shape, is the first option. In some cases, shoes need to be modified, but orthopaedic surgery is rarely necessary.

PETIT MAL

▲ See Epilepsy, p.351.

PICA

▲ See Behavioural problems, p. 340.

PNEUMONIA

This is a serious illness in which the lung tissue becomes infected causing respiratory problems. Pneumonia may be caused by both bacteria and viruses, the infection usually travelling down from the upper respiratory tract.

SYMPTOMS These vary from a persistent cough in a child who is otherwise not unwell to severe breathlessness and high fever requiring admission to hospital. There has often been a preceding upper respiratory tract infection or infectious illness such as measles or chicken pox. Instead of making a full recovery, the child continues to feel unwell and tired, has a cough and may be short of breath and breathing very fast. Although there may be a few abnormal signs to be heard in the chest, the definitive diagnosis is made by chest X-ray.

TREATMENT A very sick child obviously needs admission to hospital for treatment with antibiotics and oxygen if necessary. Chest physiotherapy may be needed to help them cough up any loose secretions. The child who is reasonably well may be treated at home with the appropriate antibiotic, but must be observed closely and reassessed if he deteriorates. Pneumonia caused by viruses theoretically should not require treatment with antibiotics as they are ineffective against viruses. The problem is that it is often difficult to be sure of the identity of the germ causing the pneumonia since children usually swallow any sputum they produce, so examination of sputum is not feasible. As a result, antibiotics are usually given.

PREVENTION Immunization against whooping cough, measles and haemophilus influenza type B are all available (see pp. 157–9). Vaccination against the pneumococcus, one source of bacterial pneumonia, is available to certain susceptible people and may become more widely available in the future. However there is unlikely ever to be a vaccine to eliminate all types of pneumonia.

POISONING

▲ See Emergencies and first aid, p. 389.

POLIOMYELITIS

▲ See Chapter 6, p. 158.

PYELONEPHRITIS

▲ See Urinary tract infection, p. 374.

PYLORIC STENOSIS

This condition can cause vomiting in young babies. Typically it seems to affect first-born, male children, though why it occurs is unknown.

SYMPTOMS After a few weeks, a previously healthy baby begins to vomit. At first the vomiting is neither frequent nor spectacular, but after a while it becomes more frequent and projectile, often travelling some distance. The baby stops gaining weight and begins to lose weight in spite of a good appetite. A lump may be felt in the abdomen on careful examination after a feed. This is the overdeveloped circular muscle – the pylorus – at the end of the stomach.

TREATMENT This is a simple surgical procedure (called Ramstedt's operation) in which the thickened pyloric muscle is divided so that it no longer obstructs the passage of food.

QUINSY

This is a very severe form of tonsillitis in which an abscess forms in one or both tonsils. Anyone with quinsy will be very unwell with a high fever and is unable to swallow.

TREATMENT Antibiotics are given intravenously and the pus drained surgically, under anaesthetic, by piercing the abscess.

RASHES

Rashes are common; the main worry is usually whether they are part of an infectious illness or not. They may be widespread or localized, itchy or not. A widespread, itchy rash which looks like nettle rash is usually an allergic rash and will probably settle with antihistamine medicines, though you should record it and try to identify its cause. A florid, blotchy red rash in a sick child may be measles (see p. 158). A less marked pinkish rash in a child who is not particularly unwell is more likely to be due to rubella (see p. 158). Sometimes it is difficult to be sure of the cause – particularly in children who have been immunized against measles and rubella, in whom these infections will be very mild if caught at all.

If your child is unwell and has a rash, he obviously needs to see a doctor for diagnosis and treatment. It is probably safer to keep a child with a rash away from school until some sort of diagnosis has been made, though he is likely to have caught the germ from school in the first place. See also Eczema, p. 351.

RECTAL BLEEDING

This is not common in children who are too young to suffer from piles (haemorrhoids) or gastric ulcers which cause this problem in adults. A possible cause is an anal fissure (see p. 337) which might produce red blood on the paper or in the nappy. More profuse rectal bleeding may be produced by an ulcer at the base of a Meckel's diverticulum (see p. 361). Occasionally, rectal bleeding will occur when a child swallows a sharp object – though this would have to show up on an abdominal X-ray to confirm the diagnosis.

Other rare causes of rectal bleeding include intussusception (see p. 358) and onset of bowel disorders such as Crohn's disease or ulcerative colitis, not primarily diseases of childhood. Sometimes there is some blood and mucus in the loose motions passed in gastroenteritis; once the gastro-enteritis clears up, there is no further problem.

TREATMENT Rectal bleeding in a young child (in the absence of an obvious anal fissure) usually warrants further investigation. Treatment is aimed at the underlying problem, whatever that might be.

RECTAL PROLAPSE

This is a condition in which the inner part of the rectum protrudes outside the anus. It is one of the features of cystic fibrosis (see p. 347). Occasionally rectal prolapse occurs when a young child has been straining at the stool for a long time. It may be alarming for both parent and child but is not serious.

TREATMENT The prolapsed part of the rectum can usually be gently replaced inside the anal margin. Try to prevent constipation so that the child does not have to strain.

RESPIRATORY DISTRESS SYNDROME

This condition often affects pre-term babies. It is due to a deficiency of surfactant, a substance which is present in the lungs of full-term babies. Without it, pre-term babies often have difficulty in breathing and need to be ventilated.

TREATMENT Pre-term babies are given surfactant at birth via a tube directly into the lungs where it is needed. When successful, this decreases the baby's need for oxygen and the improvement in lung function can be demonstrated by chest X-ray.

REYE'S SYNDROME

This is a recently described condition, the exact cause of which is not known. It seems to be associated with the use of aspirin which should not be given to children under 12.

SYMPTOMS A child who appears to be recovering normally from a cough or cold or a viral illness such as chicken pox, suddenly becomes very unwell, with vomiting, fever and convulsions. The condition may lead to liver failure and requires urgent admission to hospital for intensive care.

RHEUMATIC FEVER

This disease is now rare in the UK. It affects children between about five and fifteen years, particularly those living in poor conditions. It usually follows an episode of tonsillitis and is thought to be due to an immune reaction to the beta haemolytic streptococcus, which causes tonsillitis.

SYMPTOMS The child does not feel well, has a fever and has pain in the joints – typically the knees, ankles and elbows. There may be one of several types of skin rash and small lumps called rheumatic nodules over the shins, the back of the hands and the spine. The pulse rate is fast and there is a typical heart murmur. Involuntary movements of the limbs called Sydenham's chorea or St Vitus dance may also be present.

DIAGNOSIS This is made from the history, examination and a series of blood tests.

TREATMENT The mainstay of treatment is bed rest and painkillers for discomfort. Penicillin is also given to eradicate any residual infection.

COMPLICATIONS The most serious consequence of rheumatic fever is the permanent damage to one of the heart valves which may necessitate surgery and valve replacement in the long term. People with a history of rheumatic fever with damage to a heart valve are usually given preventive antibiotics before any dental or surgical procedure.

RICKETS

This disease is due to deficiency of vitamin D, necessary for proper calcium absorption and for normal bone growth. The deficiency may be due to poor diet (vitamin D is found in fatty fish and fish liver oils) or by lack of exposure to sunlight (vitamin D is also formed in the skin by the action of sunlight). Another type of rickets is found in children with kidney failure in which vitamin D metabolism is abnormal. Other causes of rickets include malabsorption and some rare congenital disorders of vitamin D metabolism.

SYMPTOMS The long bones of the legs become bowed whilst the bones at the wrist appear thickened. The diagnosis is made by X-rays which show the characteristic bone changes.

TREATMENT Children can recover from nutritional rickets if treatment is given early enough. It is treated by giving vitamin D supplements as necessary and advising on a good diet.

Children with little exposure to sunlight are advised to wear shorts and short sleeves and play out in the sun when possible.

PREVENTION Most baby milks and cereals are fortified with vitamin D to ensure an adequate intake. Some breastfed and pre-term babies may require vitamin D supplements as there is little vitamin D in breast milk.

RINGWORM

▲ See Tinea, p. 372.

ROSEOLA INFANTUM

This is an infectious disease of young children (usually aged between six months and two years) which is thought to be caused by a virus.

SYMPTOMS The child usually has a high fever and may have a febrile convulsion (see p. 346). There seems to be no obvious cause for the fever at this stage, but after a few days a rash appears over the trunk as the temperature subsides and the child begins to feel better. The rash only lasts for a day or so. The problem is that many of these children are given penicillin in the early stages of the illness and may mistakenly be thought to be allergic to penicillin when they get the rash, which is part of the illness rather than a reaction to the antibiotic.

TREATMENT The fever should be treated in the normal way with paracetamol and tepid sponging if necessary.

ROUNDWORM

Minor infestation of this parasite usually causes no symptoms other than great consternation when a worm, not dissimilar to an earthworm, is passed with the motion.

TREATMENT Piperazine or mebendazole preparations are taken by mouth to treat the infestation.

RUBELLA

▲ See Chapter 6, p. 158.

SALMONELLA

This bacterial infection of the gut can cause severe gastroenteritis. It can be found in poorly cooked meat, poultry and eggs, and is excreted by an infected person or carrier. High standards of food hygiene are therefore needed to prevent this.

TREATMENT Salmonella infections can be treated with some of the newer antibiotics, particularly in small babies and those who are frail or extremely unwell. Treatment is not necessary in all cases as the infection is generally self-limiting, that is to say it goes away in time without medical intervention.

SCABIES

This is a skin disease caused by a mite which lays its eggs in small burrows under the skin.

SYMPTOMS Scabies causes intense itching, usually worse at night. Tiny lumps which have been made raw by a great deal of scratching may be seen between the fingers and on the inside of the wrists. Often other family members are affected as well.

TREATMENT Special lotions need to be applied to the whole body, from the neck downward. Clothing and bedding needs to be washed and aired well. The itching may continue for several days, even after successful treatment.

SCARLET FEVER

This is the name for a streptococcal infection which causes a sore throat, reddish rash all over the body and a tongue which is said to resemble a strawberry. There is often a paler area around the mouth as well.

TREATMENT Like others, this used to be a serious illness, but nowadays penicillin is usually prescribed, which successfully controls the infection.

SCHIZOPHRENIA

Schizophrenia is a mental illness which usually affects adults, though early symptoms may occur in the late teens. Indeed, recent research has looked at childhood behaviour and facial expressions of young children who subsequently went on to develop schizophrenia in later life (by looking at old videos) and has commented on certain characteristics which will probably form the basis of further studies. As yet, however, there are no hard and fast signs to look for in early childhood and no obvious ways of preventing its onset.

In the teenager, the previously 'well' child may start to become withdrawn and difficult to talk to. He may stay in his room all day and not wish to join in any family activities. Performance at school may be affected. More florid symptoms, such as hearing voices or having delusions, may occur.

TREATMENT Expert psychiatric opinion is essential. If a diagnosis of schizophrenia is made, the young person may be started on drugs to treat the psychosis. These can be taken by mouth but are often given by intramuscular injection every few weeks. They tend to cause some degree of rigidity and tremor, and other drugs are needed to treat these side effects.

SCOLIOSIS

This is the medical term for a curved spine, often caused by having legs of differing lengths. The spine curves in an attempt to compensate for this problem.

SYMPTOMS Spinal scoliosis may cause back pain in adolescence but will often cause no symptoms and only be picked up at a school medical examination.

TREATMENT Severe scoliosis in adolescence needs expert advice and treatment from an orthopaedic surgeon, as the curvature may progress rapidly at this time. Physiotherapy, spinal braces and even surgery may all be necessary to attempt to correct the curvature and minimize future problems.

SEBORRHOEIC DERMATITIS

This skin problem is a fungal infection which causes cradle cap and dandruff when it affects the scalp. It may occur on the face and cause sore, reddish scaly patches which affect the greasy areas of skin, on the forehead and beside the nose.

TREATMENT The rash is treated with anti-fungal shampoos and creams. Hydrocortisone creams may also be necessary to treat the inflammation.

SEROUS OTITIS MEDIA

▲ See Otitis media, p. 364.

SHINGLES

▲ See Herpes infections, p. 356.

SICKLE CELL DISEASE

This is an inherited disorder which affects the red blood cells; it is relatively common in people of Afro-Caribbean descent. The haemoglobin in sickle cell disease is slightly different from normal adult haemoglobin and behaves differently under some conditions, changing the shape of the red cell into a characteristic sickle shape. The sickled red cell is more likely to break up; this in turn can lead to anaemia. See also Thalassaemia, p. 372.

SYMPTOMS Symptoms depend on whether the disorder is inherited in a major way when a large proportion of the haemoglobin is affected; or whether it is inherited in a minor way, known as sickle cell trait. Under normal circumstances, people with sickle cell trait have no symptoms, though they may show some indication when their blood is examined under the microscope. Occasionally problems arise during operations under general anaesthetic, so it is important to be aware of the diagnosis and to tell the anaesthetist. For this reason, most black people have a routine sickle test before any surgery. Children who suffer from sickle cell disease are likely to have had problems from birth, which may lead to anaemia. In addition they may suffer from bone and joint pain due to small clots which block the blood vessels supplying these areas. Abdominal pain is a common problem for the same reason; clots may occur in the brain causing minor strokes.

TREATMENT Treatment has improved enormously over the years with a corresponding increase in survival. Infections need prompt treatment with antibiotics, while sickle cell crises need treatment in hospital with intravenous fluids and strong analgesic drugs for the pain. Folic acid supplements are given routinely and children are routinely immunized against pneumococcal infection which is a particular danger in this condition (see Pneumonia, p. 365).

SINUSITIS

This is inflammation of the sinuses – spaces in the facial bones, two under the eyes, on either side of the nose and two more above the eyes in the centre of the forehead.

SYMPTOMS There is usually facial pain, tenderness and headache which occur after a cold or 'flu. There may be a fever and the sufferer may feel quite unwell.

TREATMENT Antibiotics and decongestants are prescribed. Steam inhalations and postural drainage may also be helpful. Occasionally, the sinuses may need draining in hospital.

SKIN PROBLEMS

▲ See Erythema infectiosum (p. 352), Rashes (p. 366), Eczema (p. 351) and Warts (p. 375).

SLIPPED FEMORAL EPIPHYSIS

In this condition, the head of the thigh bone (femur) becomes displaced. It tends to affect overweight adolescents, and more boys than girls.

SYMPTOMS Occasionally there is a sudden displacement which occurs after a twisting injury. This causes considerable pain and the teenager is unable to move his leg. More commonly the displacement occurs gradually and the symptoms are pain in the hip or knee and a limp. The diagnosis is confirmed by X-ray.

TREATMENT The femoral head needs to be pinned back into an acceptable position so that normal bone growth and development can continue. This involves an orthopaedic operation and a stay in hospital.

SOILING

▲ See Encopresis, p. 351.

SORE THROAT

The majority of sore throats are probably caused by viral infection and will clear up on their own after a few days' discomfort. In some cases, bacteria – particularly the streptococcus – may be responsible. Unfortunately, there is no way of telling which is which just by examining the throat, as both types will look a bit red. A throat swab can be taken and sent to the laboratory to see if they can culture any bacteria, but this takes several days and is probably not justified in the case of every sore throat. For this reason, most doctors follow their instincts. If your child is generally well and has no associated illness your doctor may just suggest paracetamol to relieve the pain. If the child is unwell (feverish and distressed), antibiotics may be given (see also Tonsillitis, p. 373).

SPASTICITY

▲ See Cerebral palsy, p. 343.

SPEECH DISORDERS

There are several different types of speech disorder, often with different causes. This is because speech has several components to it, including the thought processes in the brain in which the correct word is found, and the physical process of enunciation, the making of verbal speaking sounds.

Damage to the speech-producing areas in the brain, possibly at or before birth can have a profound effect on a child's ability to speak right from the start. Another problem which affects the ability to speak clearly is deafness. The child who is profoundly deaf and cannot hear normal speech will find it very difficult to produce the right sort of sound without proper help. A cleft palate will affect speech as the hard palate is involved in sound-making, though this problem is minimalized by reconstructive surgery.

Lisping and stammering are normal in the toddler as he acquires a vocabulary. When these problems continue into later childhood there may be physical or emotional reasons for them and a specialist opinion should be sought from a speech therapist. Stammering is more common in boys than girls and in children from large families – where parents may not have the time to devote to each individual child's speech.

Elective mutism is a condition in which the child can speak but chooses not to communicate. She may not speak at all or may only speak when and to whom she wishes. This sort of mutism may be caused by severe psychological trauma and requires expert psychological help.

TREATMENT It is important to exclude deafness as a cause of delayed or abnormal speech; after this, referral to a speech therapist for diagnosis and treatment is usually indicated.

Parents need to spend time speaking clearly to their children and listening carefully to the answers. Twins often get only half the verbal stimulation of a single child since parents are busy doing two lots of washing, cooking, ironing and so on. Another adult can often provide the extra stimulation or, better still, do some of the housework so that parents can spend more time talking to their two babies.

SPINA BIFIDA

This is a congenital abnormality in which some of the vertebrae do not fuse properly in the midline, remaining open at the top part, or spinous process. The abnormality may be very minor and only be discovered on routine X-ray (often in adulthood) for some other reason. In most cases, spina bifida can now be detected by ultrasound before birth.

Typically it is the fifth lumbar or first sacral vertebra which is affected. In these cases the condition is called spina bifida occulta and it is of no significance, requiring no treatment. An affected child will have no associated problems and no learning difficulties. More serious problems may occur when the defect is larger or more extensive. In severe cases, the spinal cord is not enclosed at all and lies just below the skin. There may be associated hydrocephalus (see p. 357). When the spinal cord is involved and not protected, nervous control to the areas supplied may be jeopardized. This can result in paraplegia, loss of sensation in the legs and incontinence of both urine and faeces.

TREATMENT The defective part of the spine needs to be closed as soon after birth as possible by skilled surgeons to preserve nerve function. Problems with paralysis and incontinence can also be tackled, but there is often residual disability in severe cases.

SQUINT

▲ See Strabismus, below.

STILL'S DISEASE

▲ See Arthritis, p. 338.

STINGS

▲ See Bee stings and Wasp stings, p. 382.

STORK MARKS

▲ See Birth marks, p. 341.

STRABISMUS

Squints, or strabismus, may be convergent – the affected eye deviates inward – or divergent – the affected eye deviates outward. They are caused by weakness of one or other of the extrinsic muscles of the eye which are responsible for moving the eyes and keeping them in line. Some babies appear to have a squint because of the shape of the skin folds at the side of the nose between the eyes. Young babies tend to squint a little when tired. Long-sighted children have to converge their eyes to such an extent that a squint is produced.

Where there is a concern that a baby may have a squint, the eyes can be examined and a referral to an orthoptist made. It is important to make the diagnosis at an early stage and to initiate the appropriate treatment as untreated squints will affect the development of normal binocular vision.

TREATMENT This may involve covering the good eye with a patch, to exercise the so called 'lazy' eye. An operation to shorten the appropriate eye muscle may also be necessary in some cases and may need to be repeated over the years. Squints caused by long-sightedness are corrected with glasses.

STRAWBERRY NAEVUS

▲ See Birth marks, p. 341.

STYE

This uncomfortable swelling along the edge of the eyelid results from blockage and infection of the eyelash hair follicle.

Initially there is a reddish lump which soon becomes filled with pus, so appears to have a creamy coloured head.

TREATMENT Bathing the affected eye with cottonwool soaked in warm water may be all that is necessary. The stye will either settle on its own or burst – either way the problem is solved. In some cases antibiotic ointment may be prescribed to speed healing and prevent the infection spreading to adjacent lashes.

SUDDEN INFANT DEATH SYNDROME

This syndrome is commonly known as 'cot death', and is the situation when a baby is found dead in his cot for no apparent reason. No obvious cause is found at post mortem examination either, so parents are left not knowing exactly what happened to their child. Not surprisingly, it has attracted a great deal of study and research in many countries and, recently, certain facts have begun to emerge. Cot death affects 1 in 600 live births, with 90 per cent of cot deaths occurring before eight months of age.

SLEEPING POSITION The risk of cot death has been found to be higher in those babies placed to sleep on their tummies. Parents are now advised to place their babies in their cots on their backs, unless there are specific medical reasons for not doing so. The 'Back to sleep' campaign halved the incidence of cot death in Britain in less than a year.

PARENTAL SMOKING Studies have shown a significant relationship between parental smoking and the risk of cot death. Further studies are needed to look at the separate issues of passive smoking and smoking in pregnancy. Infants should not be exposed to cigarette smoke – their parents' or others' – either before or after birth.

TEMPERATURE Two studies have shown that infants who died of cot death had been at greater risk of overheating than other infants. This may have been because they were overwrapped in clothes and bedding, that the room was too warm or that the baby himself had a slightly raised temperature. Room temperature in the nursery should be 16–20°C (61–68°F). Infants need only a little more bedding than adults, and duvets are not recommended for use with children under one year old. Extra heating from hot water bottles or electric blankets is not necessary.

BREASTFEEDING There is no conclusive evidence that breastfeeding alters the risk of cot death.

MATTRESSES Some recent research claimed to show links between cot death and the chemical antimony, which is widely used to make mattresses flameproof or fire resistant.

This caused a great deal of distress to parents of newborn babies and has since been completely disproven.

HELP AND PREVENTION Every health district has, or should have, a designated paediatrician who has a special interest in cot death. He or she is available to see and talk to parents whose baby has recently died of this syndrome.

There is a programme devised by the Foundation for Sudden Infant Death (see Useful Contacts, pp. 390–3) called CONI – care of the next infant. It aims to offer practical help and support to the health visitors and other professionals caring for the new baby in a family previously affected by cot death. Through loans of equipment such as apnoea monitors and room thermometers the new baby can be monitored by parents and some of their anxieties assuaged.

SWELLING

▲ See Angio-oedema, p. 337.

TALIPES

This is the medical term for club foot, a fairly common abnormality that is present at birth. Talipes equino-varus causes the forefoot to be pushed upward and inward so that the sole of the foot cannot be placed on the ground.

Talipes often affects both feet, though one foot may be worse than the other. Boys are affected more often than girls, and the condition may be seen in other family members. There is a milder form which is correctable with physiotherapy and may well be due to the somewhat squashed position the foetus adopted in the womb. There is also a more severe form which is much more difficult to correct and may well be associated with other congenital abnormalities such as spina bifida.

TREATMENT Initially parents are taught how to mould the foot into the correct position. Repeated stretching and exercising in this way are often all that is necessary to correct the deformity, particularly in mild cases. Alternatively, the foot may need to be strapped or placed in a cast to correct the position. More serious problems, however, may require orthopaedic surgery.

TAPEWORMS

These are not common parasites in the human, particularly in the UK, but may be caught through eating undercooked meat. They usually cause no symptoms but may be diagnosed when a segment is passed out in the faeces. A tapeworm segment is flat, pale and rectangular in shape.

TREATMENT A tapeworm is eradicated by taking prescription drugs which allow the worm to be expelled in the faeces.

TEMPERATURE

▲ See Fever, p. 352.

TESTICULAR PROBLEMS

UNDESCENDED TESTICLES Sometimes the testicles fail to descend from the abdomen to the scrotum. This affects up to 4 per cent of boys born at full term and 25 per cent of pre-term boy babies, so it is a common problem. The testes are retractable in a young child, so at examination it may be difficult to decide whether the testicle has failed to descend properly, or whether the doctor's cold hands have caused it to retract back inside the baby.

TREATMENT No treatment is required for testicles that retract but come down again, but undescended testicles need to be diagnosed and treated; if they remain inside the abdomen they may not be able to produce enough sperm and may become malignant in the future. An operation locates the testicles and brings them down to the scrotum where they are fixed.

TESTICULAR TORSION This twisting of the spermatic cord may occur in adolescent boys. It causes considerable abdominal pain, and the scrotum may be swollen and tender. The testis needs to be untwisted surgically as a matter of urgency, before the blood supply is jeopardized.

HYDROCELE This is a collection of fluid in one of the layers surrounding the testicle which shows up as a swelling in the scrotum. It may be associated with an inguinal hernia. The hydrocele usually resolves without treatment during the first year of life. If it does not and is present after this time, it may require surgery.

THALASSAEMIA

Like sickle cell disease (see p. 369), thalassaemia is an inherited disorder in which the haemoglobin – the oxygen-carrying part of the blood – is slightly abnormal. It may be inherited in either a major or minor way. It affects people of Mediterranean origin and the name comes from the Greek word for sea. Cypriots form the largest affected group, although Pakistanis, Indians and Chinese may all suffer from beta-thalassaemia (so-called because it affects the 'beta chain' of the haemoglobin molecule). It has been estimated that there are five million carriers of beta-thalassaemia in Europe and 5,000 babies are born with thalassaemia major every year.

SYMPTOMS People with thalassaemia minor are likely to have no symptoms, but a low haemoglobin level shows up in a blood test. Children with beta-thalassaemia may fail to thrive and gain weight, have unexplained fever and diarrhoea, look pale and have a distended abdomen. They usually need repeated blood transfusions which may cause iron overload. This problem is treated with drugs to avoid diabetes and heart problems. In some cases bone marrow transplantation has been used successfully in the treatment of thalassaemia major.

THREADWORMS

These are the worms most often encountered in childhood infestations. They appear as small white threads in faeces or around the anus. They cause itching which is usually worse at night but are a rare cause of abdominal pain in childhood.

TREATMENT They are treated with piperazine or mebendazole, available over the counter. If reinfestation occurs, the whole family may need to be treated.

THRUSH

▲ See p. 166.

TINEA

This fungus of the ringworm family may affect various parts of the body.

TINEA CAPITIS This is the classic ringworm of the scalp, which may cause an oval area of baldness. It is considerably more difficult to eradicate than any of the other forms of tinea and requires anti-fungal tablets to be taken by mouth, often for as long as several weeks.

TINEA CORPORIS Ringworm of the body appears as a round raised ring of tiny spots which may also appear scaly. It may spread from one area of the body to another and is treated with anti-fungal creams.

TINEA CRURIS This is a fungal skin infection of the groin which is sometimes called Dhobie's itch. It may affect adolescents and is treated with anti-fungal creams.

TINEA PEDIS This is better known as athlete's foot, which causes soreness and itchy peeling skin between the toes. It is treated with anti-fungal creams. It is also important to prevent recurrent problems, to keep the skin between the toes clean and dry and to wear socks made of natural fibres to allow the sweat produced by feet to evaporate.

TINEA VERSICOLOR This fungal infection of the skin often occurs on the chest or back. It characteristically causes lighter patches in people with dark skin and darker patches in those with light skin. It may take several weeks of treatment with anti-fungal cream to clear up.

TONSILLITIS

This is infection of the tonsils, the two lumps of lymphoid tissue which are situated in the throat at the base of the tongue. The infection may be caused by bacteria (usually the streptococcus), but it may also be caused by viruses. The only way to ascertain the infecting organism is to take a throat swab and have it cultured in the laboratory to see if streptococci grow.

SYMPTOMS The throat feels very sore and there may be difficulty in swallowing. There may also be a fever and generalized aching in the back and limbs, and some children may vomit.

TREATMENT The majority of sore throats will probably get better without treatment, given time. Nevertheless, most doctors these days would treat a child who is obviously unwell with a very red throat and whitish patches visible on the tonsils with an antibiotic, usually penicillin. The main reason for this is to eradicate any streptococcal infection as this bacteria can cause acute glomerulonephritis (see p. 353) and rheumatic fever (see p. 367), though both these diseases are very rare in the UK nowadays because of improved nutrition and living standards.

Paracetamol should also be given for the fever and discomfort and the child should be encouraged to rest and drink plenty of fluids.

Recurrent tonsillitis can cause the child to miss a good deal of schooling and this is the main reason for removing the tonsils. The operation is called a tonsillectomy and the adenoids may be removed at the same time if necessary. Although it may not be performed as often as it was 40 years ago, it is still one of the most common operations performed on children. The child usually spends a few days in hospital, and the operation is performed under general anaesthetic.

COMPLICATIONS Peritonsillar abscesses may form which need to be drained and the person treated with intravenous antibiotics (see Quinsy, p. 366).

TORTICOLLIS

This is wry neck, a condition in which the muscles of the neck go into spasm so that the neck cannot be moved. The head is held to one side and the neck feels tender and painful. The condition usually resolves with warmth and painkillers although muscle-relaxing drugs may also be helpful.

Wry neck in newborn babies may be due to a large lump in the sternomastoid muscle – the large muscle in the neck. This lump generally disappears in the course of the first few weeks without specific treatment.

TOXOCARA

▲ See Animals and disease, p. 337.

TOXOPLASMOSIS

▲ See Animals and disease, p. 337.

TUBERCULOSIS

This infection is caused by a bacterium which can affect almost any part of the body and appear in any number of guises. It was much more prevalent fifty to a hundred years ago when it was a major cause of death. Vaccination against TB using BCG (see pp. 158–9) has played an important part in controlling the disease, though improvements in housing, nutrition and the general standard of living have probably been just as important.

However, over the last few years, there has been an increase in the number of cases of TB. Whether this is due to disease imported into this country from the third world or reflects the poor standards of health and housing suffered by people living in inner cities, is not yet clear. Although not as high up a list of possible diagnoses as it was in the last century, the prudent doctor still considers TB a possibility in some cases and a probability in others.

SYMPTOMS The symptoms depend on the organ affected. Pulmonary tuberculosis is probably the most common form of the disease in this country. The sufferer may have a cough and have coughed up blood, suffered night sweats and weight loss. Other chest problems may occur, especially in those who are suffering from immune deficiency states such as AIDS. Among these is a pleural effusion, which is a collection of fluid between the two layers of the pleura, which cover the lungs and line the chest wall. A good deal of fluid may accumulate, compressing the lung and causing difficulty in breathing. It may have to be drained to allow the lung to re-expand fully.

In childhood, TB may appear as a prolonged chest infection, unexplained fever or persistent enlarged glands, particularly in the neck. The diagnosis is made by doing a skin test called a Mantoux test which will be positive in the affected child. Some children catch TB and become immune without ever developing signs of the disease. This is only discovered when they are tested.

TREATMENT This is with a prolonged course of anti-TB drugs, usually for a year. Children who are contacts of elderly relatives with TB may also need a short course of treatment.

ULCERATIVE COLITIS

This inflammatory bowel disease is not a common problem in childhood but may, nevertheless, begin in childhood and continue throughout life.

SYMPTOMS Ulcerative colitis may show itself with chronic diarrhoea or recurrent bouts of diarrhoea which may contain blood. The child may lose weight, feel generally 'under par', and may well be anaemic.

DIAGNOSIS The diagnosis is made by examining the bowel with a flexible instrument called a colonoscope and examining a small piece of tissue. Blood tests and bowel X-rays will also give valuable information about the disease.

TREATMENT This is with anti-inflammatory drugs, including steroids, which need to be taken long term, even though the disease may go through periods of remission and activity. Surgery to remove part of the bowel may be necessary in some severe cases.

UMBILICAL HERNIA

▲ See p. 60.

UPPER RESPIRATORY TRACT INFECTION

This is a general term for coughs, colds and other infections of the naso-pharynx, larynx and trachea. The majority of URTIs are caused by viruses. The infection may be mild and clear up in a couple of days, or may spread down the respiratory tract to cause bronchitis (see p. 342) or pneumonia (see p. 365). Infection may also spread up the Eustachian tube to cause otitis media (see p. 364).

TREATMENT Children catch colds from their family at home and their friends at school. No sooner have they recovered from one episode than they have a runny nose again. They are also not particularly good at blowing their noses so tend to sniff a lot. When mucus drips down from the post-nasal space it makes the child cough, though this does not mean that she

has a chest infection, nor that she needs antibiotics. The majority of coughs and colds clear up by themselves and paracetamol can be given to relieve symptoms. If, however, your child is clearly unwell and there are signs that an ear or chest infection may have developed then she should be examined by the doctor and may indeed need antibiotics.

URINARY TRACT INFECTION

This is a general term used to describe the situation in which there are signs and symptoms of a urinary infection. It is often impossible to know the actual site of infection in children as the symptoms are rather general.(For this reason pyelonephritis, inflammation of the kidney, may also be considered a UTI.) Urinary tract infection is a relatively common problem in young children and tends to affect girls more than boys. It has been estimated that up to 5 per cent of girls and up to 2 per cent of boys will have a UTI in childhood and that unless they are adequately investigated and treated, the majority of them will have further infections.

SYMPTOMS A young child may be feverish and unwell with generalized abdominal pain, or she may wet herself during the day or at night when she would not normally do so. Sometimes she will be reluctant to pass urine, arousing suspicion that to do so hurts her. Occasionally blood is passed in the urine though this may not be visible to the naked eye.

DIAGNOSIS The diagnosis is made by examining a specimen of urine and identifying the bacteria responsible for the infection. Further tests may include ultrasound scanning of the kidneys and scans and X-rays of the urinary tract.

TREATMENT About half of all children who have a proven UTI will be found to have some abnormality of the urinary tract. In some, urine reflows back up the ureter when the child passes urine, and this may lead to kidney damage. Some of the abnormalities may be corrected surgically, while the more straightforward infections need antibiotics. The urine may need to be tested frequently, and children may be placed on long-term antibiotic therapy to prevent infection.

VAGINAL BLEEDING

The most obvious cause of vaginal bleeding is, of course, the menarche, when periods start. The time at which this occurs is highly variable, but it can be as early as eight years old or as late as 16 (see pp. 303–4).

In the newborn baby, vaginal bleeding may occur because girl babies may become used to the high circulating oestrogen levels during pregnancy and bleed when it is withdrawn after the birth.

Vaginal bleeding in young children needs investigation as it may be due to a foreign body in the vagina. Little girls have been known to insert things there, perhaps because they have seen their mother using a tampon. Rarely, such bleeding is the first sign of a tumour of the genital tract. It may also be a sign of sexual abuse, where tissues have been damaged and bleed.

VAGINAL DISCHARGE

This is not uncommon in childhood. The discharge may be whitish or purulent and smell offensive. The vulva may be sore and red and feel itchy. This is called vulvitis and is associated with the vaginal discharge. The discharge and vulval inflammation is usually caused by infection which may be due to candida, a fungus. It may also be due to a streptococcal infection, possibly transmitted to the genital area by a young girl scratching herself at night. A swab can be taken to identify the cause of the infection which is treated with anti-fungal creams or oral antibiotics.

In the adolescent girl, a clear mucousy vaginal discharge may occur normally midway through the menstrual cycle at the time of ovulation. But if she is sexually active, an offensive, smelly discharge may be the first sign of a sexually transmitted disease; she should be encouraged to have further tests.

VERRUCA

This is a plantar wart caused by a virus, and occurs on the sole of the foot. Verrucae may be a bit painful, but are generally not serious, yet a great deal of unnecessary fuss is made about them. Children are excluded from swimming.

TREATMENT Most over-the-counter treatments contain salicylic acid and work by attacking the hard skin around the verruca so that it can be scraped out easily. They have to be applied with care to avoid damaging the surrounding skin. Verrucae that do not respond to this treatment may need to be treated with liquid nitrogen at a special wart clinic.

VIRAL INFECTIONS

Viruses are tiny organisms which are capable of causing a wide spectrum of disease from simple colds to meningitis. Many common childhood illnesses are caused by viral infection including mumps, rubella and measles. Viruses are probably responsible for the majority of upper respiratory tract infections and for the annual winter epidemics of influenza.

TREATMENT A large proportion of viral illnesses do not require specific treatment – the body's own immunity will overcome the infection given time. They may, however, cause fever, malaise and tiredness and these symptoms can be treated with paracetamol, rest and a good diet with plenty of fluids. Antibiotics do not kill viruses, but they are sometimes prescribed because the cause of the infection is unknown and it is safer to treat for a possible bacterial infection, or when a viral illness has gone on for a while and has become complicated by bacterial infection. Some specific viral infections such as those caused by the herpes virus, can be treated with specific anti-viral drugs and it is possible that more drugs will be developed in the future.

PREVENTION While it is not possible to prevent the common cold, other diseases like polio have been eradicated in the UK through immunization. Immunization against mumps, measles and rubella is now recommended in infancy, and in some countries these diseases have almost disappeared. Vaccination against hepatitis A and B is available to protect travellers.

VOMITING

Vomiting is a common symptom in childhood and may be a symptom of several different disorders.

INFECTION Vomiting is often a major feature of gastroenteritis which may be caused by either viral or bacterial infection. Vomiting is also a feature of other infections which do not primarily affect the gastrointestinal tract. It may be seen in ear infections, tonsillitis and meningitis, for example.

OBSTRUCTION Vomiting usually occurs when there is an obstruction in the gut – if the obstruction is high up, vomiting is an early feature while if it is lower down vomiting may not occur until late in the illness.

TREATMENT Children are rarely given drugs to stop vomiting. Efforts are made to prevent dehydration and restore electrolyte balance, while the cause of the vomiting is investigated.

WARTS

These are skin lesions caused by a virus. They may occur all over the body and can be flat or raised. The flat warts on the soles of the feet are called verrucae (see opposite). Warts may also occur around the genital area. Wart virus infection of the cervix has been implicated as a risk factor for cervical cancer.

TREATMENT Various remedies are available, but they must be used with care as they can damage healthy skin. Troublesome warts usually need to be removed using liquid nitrogen.

WHOOPING COUGH

▲ See Pertussis, p. 157.

Emergencies and first aid

Today, the emphasis of 'first aid' is showing how to assess a person who is injured or taken ill to provide the right, sometimes life-saving, care immediately. Having said that, most people survive most minor injuries and there is often little to be done on the spot other than reassurance and, if necessary, prompt transport to the nearest casualty department for treatment or more qualified assessment.

Occasionally a situation arises in which a life can be saved if the correct diagnosis is made and immediate treatment – often cardio-pulmonary resuscitation – given. The best way to learn these skills is to attend a recognized course run by either the British Red Cross, St. John Ambulance Brigade or the St Andrew's Ambulance Association – all of whom award a First Aid Certificate, valid for three years.

There is no doubt that many accidents, particularly those involving babies and small children, can be avoided. Read the advice on pp. 168–72 and try to be aware of the dangers that household equipment and your habits pose for your child.

The Green Cross Code

Children are taught the Green Cross Code at school, but it is important that you are aware of it, and use it too. Reinforce it with your child each time you are out together. The Code is:
1 First find a safe place to cross, then stop.
2 Stand on the pavement near the kerb.
3 Look all round for traffic and listen.
4 If traffic is coming, let it pass. Look all round again.
5 When there is no traffic near, walk straight across the road.
6 Keep looking and listening for traffic while you cross.

ROAD SAFETY

Road traffic accidents involving pedestrians have risen in recent years, so it is important to do your best to teach your child to avoid them, and also to avoid injury if your child is in the car with you when an accident happens.

- Never push a pushchair off the kerb in front of you while you are waiting to cross the road.
- Teach your child to treat roads with caution; learn crossing drill as soon as possible (see box), by example as well as directly. You cannot expect your child always to use the crossing if you do not regularly do this yourself!
- Make sure you have a safe baby seat, properly fitted in your car (check this with one of the motoring organizations), and full safety belts (not just lap belts). Don't encourage your children to sit in the front passenger seat.
- If your child rides a horse or a bicycle make sure he always wears a proper safety helmet.

LOOKING AFTER YOURSELF

If you find yourself at the scene of an accident or some other incident requiring first aid, it is important to remember to keep yourself safe and to prevent further casualties at the scene, as well as assessing those who are directly involved and providing first aid. If an injury or accident necessitates professional help (see box opposite), it should be summoned as quickly as possible as there is often a limit to how much treatment can be given outside hospital without the appropriate equipment. Try to keep calm (this is often difficult, especially when the casualty is your own child); talk to your child and explain what you are going to do and that help is on the way. This is an essential part of first aid and is of great comfort to the casualty.

Emergencies which need immediate attention

It is always difficult to know when to call the doctor or go to hospital, and what can safely be dealt with at home. Some conditions, however, obviously require urgent medical attention – usually in a hospital casualty department rather than at the doctor's surgery, although some rural practices do provide a minor injuries service which is useful if the hospital is a long way away. The following list is not exclusive and is intended as a guide rather than concrete advice as to what to do. It is always better to be safe than sorry and to seek medical help early on, particularly in the case of a sick child.

- Asthma – an attack which is not responding to the usual treatment
- Bleeding – severe bleeding that won't stop
- Bites – from a dog or poisonous snake
- Burns – any burn in a child requires dressing; some may also require intravenous drips, pain relief and specialist treatment
- Cardiac arrest (heart attack) – from whatever cause
- Choking – Absence of breathing or difficulty in breathing for whatever reason, or if your child is turning blue in colour
- Drowning
- Electrocution
- Eye injuries – especially penetrating injuries and splashes from chemicals
- Fits – A first fit in a child, a prolonged febrile convulsion or fits in an epileptic child, which are not responding to the usual treatment
- Fractures – these need to be X-rayed and set properly
- Poisoning – or deliberate or accidental overdose of medicine
- Unconsciousness – whatever the cause

ESSENTIAL EMERGENCY PROCEDURES

Cardio-Pulmonary Resuscitation

CPR, for short, this is probably the most important procedure to learn. To be absolutely sure it is best to learn with qualified instructors at a proper first aid course, because you need practice to get it right. However, what is set out here can be used as a guide or reminder. Cardio-pulmonary resuscitation involves combining artificial ventilation, which aims to inflate the casualty's lungs, and chest compression (sometimes referred to as 'heart massage') to get the heart beating again. It may be needed in a number of situations when an injured person has stopped breathing and has no pulse.

The first step is to assess the state of the casualty, to make sure that he really has stopped breathing and is not just deeply asleep (as could happen, for instance, after a convulsion, see p. 384). To do this shake the child gently and talk to him loudly to try and wake him up. Then SHOUT FOR HELP.

The next step is to follow a simple 'ABC' procedure – Airway, Breathing, Circulation – as follows:

- AIRWAY Lay the child on her back and loosen any tight clothing around the neck. Her mouth should be checked for foreign bodies which might be obstructing her breathing by sweeping the inside of the mouth with a finger. With small children and babies it is important to take care not to push any object further back. Remove anything you do find in the mouth which can be dislodged easily. If the child is still not breathing, open the airway by extending the neck – this is done by tilting the head back and raising the lower jaw by placing two fingers under the chin to lift it upward (right).

- BREATHING Look at her chest to see if she is breathing or not. It may be necessary to listen carefully and to try and feel her breath on your face or the back of your hand.

open airway

- CIRCULATION Check her pulse to see if her heart has stopped beating as well. In young people and adults, this is usually done by feeling the large carotid pulse in the neck – this is located roughly midway between the angle of the jaw and the Adam's apple, on each side. In a child it may be easier to try to feel the brachial pulse in the upper arm; do this by placing your middle and index fingers across the inner, soft, part of the upper arm and pressing down gently toward the bone (see illustration below).

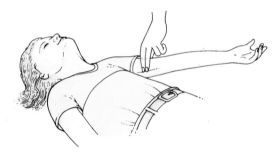

If the child is breathing normally and has a good pulse, she should be placed in the RECOVERY POSITION (see box opposite) and monitored carefully until further help arrives.

If she has a pulse but is not breathing then artificial ventilation should be started. There is enough oxygen in the air you breathe out to keep a casualty alive.

Artificial ventilation

There are different techniques for this (which is also known as artificial respiration) depending on the age of the casualty.

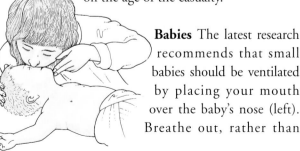

Babies The latest research recommends that small babies should be ventilated by placing your mouth over the baby's nose (left). Breathe out, rather than

blow into it, until you see the chest rise, then stop and allow the chest to fall. Repeat this procedure at a rate of one breath every three seconds, ie 20 per minute, checking every ten breaths that her pulse is still present.

If you cannot see the chest rise, check that her head is tilted back in the correct position (see above) and that you have a good seal round the nose.

Note: This technique replaces that of exhaling into both mouth and nose formerly recommended – it has been found that parents, especially mothers, are unable to cover both nose and mouth properly. Babies breathe through their noses so it is better simply to concentrate on the nose alone.

Children and adults Pinch the casualty's nostrils and blow more strongly into the mouth only, until you see the chest rise. In an adult the rate is slower at ten breaths per minute. If you cannot see the chest rise, check that the head is tilted back as above, and that you have a good seal round the mouth.

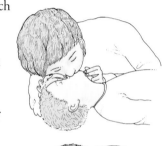

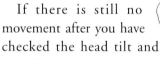

If there is still no movement after you have checked the head tilt and mouth seal, there may be an obstruction in the airways which needs to be removed (see Choking and breathing difficulties, p. 384, for instruction on how to remove a foreign body from the airways). If the child is not breathing and you cannot feel any pulse, you will need to start chest compression as well as artificial ventilation.

Chest compression

As with artificial ventilation, different techniques are needed, depending on the age of the child or young person. Chest compression works by squeezing blood out of the heart and into the circulatory system. It is important to release the pressure entirely between each compression (without removing your hands from the chest wall), so that blood can be sucked back into the heart before being forced out again with the next compression.

Babies Place the tips of two fingers in the centre of the chest, one finger breadth below the level of the nipples. The chest should be compressed 2 cm (¾ in) 100 times a minute. Don't press a baby's chest too hard – this can cause internal injury.

Toddlers and young children Find a point on the child's chest near the end of the breastbone by placing your middle finger at the lower end of the breastbone where the lower ribs meet in the middle. Place your index finger above it on the breastbone

itself. Slide the heel of your other hand down the chest wall until it reaches your index finger. The chest wall should be depressed by about 2.5–3.5 cm (1–1½ in) for this age group (below left).

Older children and adults You need to find the same site near the end of the breastbone and, using the heel of one hand with the other hand on top of it, compress the chest wall by about 4–5 cm (1½–2 in) at a rate of about 80 compressions per minute.

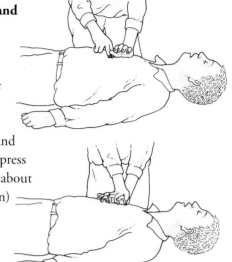

The recovery position

This is the safest position in which to place an unconscious child of any age who is breathing spontaneously and has a good pulse. Place the child on her side, with her head turned to one side and her neck extended so that her airway is not obstructed. Then roll her over toward you very gently, as follows:

- Bend the arm nearest to you at the elbow and lay the arm out at right angles to her body with the palm uppermost.
- Next, bend her other arm up and across so that her hand is on her cheek that is nearest to you.
- Take the leg furthest from you and, bending the knee almost at right angles, bring it up and over her body so that she is turned toward you, on to her side.
- Keep her lower leg straight and her upper leg bent at the knee so that she cannot roll over in either direction.
- Make sure her neck is extended and she can breathe easily.
- Go and phone for help if you have not already done so.

Note: It is very important to follow these instructions exactly to avoid making any unseen injury worse. If you suspect a head or neck injury, make sure you move the head, neck and shoulders very carefully, keeping them straight and level, to prevent any damage to the spinal cord.

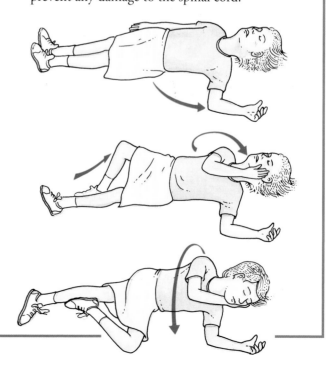

Combining chest compression with artificial ventilation

When you need to combine chest compression with artificial ventilation in children, you should stop after every five compressions to give one breath, then continue with five more compressions, then one breath, and so on, until help arrives.

In adults, the ratio is 15 compressions to two breaths if you are on your own, or one breath to every five compressions if there are two people who are able to share the CPR.

When the child recovers and starts to breathe spontaneously, looks a better colour than before and has a good pulse, stop the above steps, place her in the recovery position and monitor her closely by taking her pulse and watching her breathing and colour until help arrives.

Sending for help

If there are other people about, send one to telephone for help immediately. If you are on your own, attempt the above procedure for a minute, then carry the child to a phone, call for help and resume resuscitation. Carry on resuscitation until the child recovers, professional help arrives or until you simply cannot carry on any longer because you are exhausted. If you follow the ABC outlined above, you will have done your best, whatever the outcome.

A–Z OF EMERGENCIES

Anaphylaxis – severe allergic or hypersensitive reaction

Occasionally someone may suffer a severe and very sudden hypersensitivity reaction – possibly in response to an insect sting, injection, particular food or drug. This condition is known as anaphylaxis or anaphylactic shock.

SYMPTOMS These may include swelling (angio-oedema) of the face, tongue and back of the throat which causes considerable difficulty in breathing and can develop rapidly. The blood pressure may also drop because the smallest blood vessels near the skin – the peripheral blood vessels – expand or widen (dilate), and there is an increase in heart rate to try to compensate for the low blood pressure.

TREATMENT Emergency treatment with adrenaline is required so you should get help as soon as possible by calling a doctor, ambulance or taking the sufferer immediately to the nearest hospital accident and emergency department. Adrenaline reverses the increase in size of the blood vessels and reduces the swelling obstructing breathing. It can be given by injection or inhalation from a special aerosol. People likely to have this sort of allergic reaction are advised to carry the drug so that they can administer it at the first sign of any problem. Failing this, it may be necessary to use cardio-pulmonary resuscitation (see pp. 377–8) until medical help arrives and adrenaline can be given.

Asthma

An attack of asthma which is not responding to the usual treatment needs urgent treatment with steroids, bronchodilator drugs to help breathing and oxygen if necessary. If treatment is started early on, you can do much of this at home, perhaps by giving steroids by mouth and/or bronchodilator drugs by aerosol or nebulizer.

If you have an asthmatic child you will be taught how to monitor his condition and told what steps to take if it deteriorates. Nevertheless, deaths from asthma still occur and it is important to seek further medical advice as soon as possible, particularly if your child is having difficulty in breathing, getting very tired with the effort or looking rather grey or blue. Under these circumstances urgent admission to hospital is essential.

Bites and stings

There are few poisonous creatures in the UK, but a child may be bitten while abroad on holiday or by some exotic creature kept as a pet, so local informed advice should always be sought. Stings by bees or wasps may in rare cases result in a severe reaction –

The first aid box

Most homes have some sort of first aid kit, and parents often wonder what, exactly, are the most useful items to keep in it. Traditionally, a kit from a chemists' shop contains blunt scissors, minute bandages, a few plasters and lots of safety pins – not much use for anything other than a cut or graze. Sterile dressings and proper bandages are now widely available and can form the basis of a more sensible first aid box for home use. (You do not at present have to carry a first aid kit in the car in Britain, but you do in several countries – check requirements before you travel.) The following list of contents can be added to and should be checked occasionally to see that things have not been used up or need replacing because they are out of date:

Antiseptic liquid to be diluted and used to cleanse cuts before dressing is a good idea. Antiseptic wipes are also available for convenience.
Bandages Stretchy crepe bandages are best if a firm pressure is to be applied Tubular finger bandages are also very useful to keep at home.

Paracetamol for pain. Paracetamol is the only painkiller suitable for children under 12 (see also box on p. 335). Buy it in liquid form for babies and younger children, in soluble tablet form or stronger liquid form for older children. Keep it locked in the medicine cabinet or other safe place.
Plasters are useful for small cuts and abrasions. (They are loved by all children and instantly make them feel better.)
Scissors Sharp scissors are needed to cut dressings, bandages and tape.
Special skin closures (Steristrips) can be bought at the chemist's; though expensive, these are ideal for keeping the edges of small deep cuts close together so that healing takes place while reducing the risk of scar formation.
Sterile dressings to place over cuts or burns are always useful. Non-adhesive ones can be bought at the chemist.
Tape Adhesive tape holds dressings in place.
Tweezers may be useful for removing bee stings and splinters.

anaphylactic shock (see above) – and require urgent treatment. Normally, however, the reaction to a sting is localized, the pain caused does not last long and needs only minor treatment, hugs and reassurance.

DOG BITES These are probably the most common hazard and can be extremely painful and frightening. The first job is to get your child away from the dog as quickly as possible; this may require considerable effort and courage. Once the child is safe, the wound should be washed under clean running water and a dilute antiseptic solution applied. If the wound is gaping, bring the edges together as best you can, put on a dressing and bandage and take your child to the nearest casualty for possible stitching and an antibiotic injection.

Tetanus vaccine is part of the routine vaccinations for all infants and is again given at the preschool booster and before leaving school between 15 and 19 years. Your child will therefore be protected against tetanus and will not need an injection unless he has not had his routine injections.

If the dog bite occurs abroad, particularly outside Europe, treatment for rabies may be necessary. This involves a series of injections and close observation. Vaccination against rabies is also available for those travelling to infected areas.

SNAKE BITES The adder is the only poisonous snake native to Great Britain and it is rare to come across one, even in the country. They do sometimes come out to enjoy the sunshine, and it is worth taking extra care if walking across moorland: a female protecting her young may bite rather than retreat.

It is very important to comfort and reassure a child who has been bitten by a snake as he will naturally be frightened. Wash the wound with clean water and take your child to casualty immediately. It is helpful to be able to describe the snake to the doctor so that the right antidote to the venom can be given if appropriate. (The treatment often seen in Westerns in which the bite is lanced and the venom sucked out is not recommended – not is it necessary to apply a tourniquet above the bite.)

BEE STINGS: These can be very painful and frightening, especially for a young child. The sting is left in the skin by the insect and needs to be removed by pulling it out with tweezers. Some people advise bathing the area with a weak solution of bicarbonate of soda and this probably does no harm. Both bee and wasp stings can induce anaphylactic shock – so keep an eye out for any rapid deterioration in your child's conditions (see p. 380).

WASP STINGS: These are also nasty incidents; although the wasp does not leave its sting behind, some people find them more painful than bee stings. The area may be bathed with a weak solution of vinegar, but will also be fine if left alone. Painkilling sprays, specially designed for stings of this sort, bring immediate but temporary relief. One per cent hydrocortisone cream, available from pharmacies, can also help troublesome bites and stings.

Bleeding

Bleeding from small wounds often looks much worse than it actually is, so keep calm and assess the situation:
- Does the child look pale and shocked?
- Where is the cut and how did it happen?
- Is the wound clean or contaminated with dirt or glass?

TREATMENT Clean the wound first by holding it under running water and then put on a clean dressing. To control the bleeding, raise the part of the body where the wound is situated if possible, and apply direct pressure to it, over the dressing. If there is a fair amount of bleeding it is often sensible to use a large pad, such as a clean teatowel or even a sanitary towel, over the original dressing. If the bleeding stops, the wound can be inspected and an adhesive dressing or wound closures applied. If, however, the wound continues to bleed, or if you suspect that it is contaminated with dirt or glass, take your child to casualty for the appropriate treatment. Do not try to apply a tourniquet of any sort – if bleeding continues apply an extra pad over the top without removing the existing one. If your child's vaccination schedule is up to date, a tetanus vaccination will not be necessary (see pp. 157–8).

Broken bones and fractures

Broken bones are common, especially in children who climb trees or climbing frames, ride bicycles or horses, and occasionally fall off. Generally speaking, although painful and distressing for both parent and child, they are not life-threatening emergencies. The exception to this is of course a fractured skull.

Bones may break or fracture in several different ways.
- Simple fracture: A simple fracture is, as the name suggests, a clean break in a bone.
- Comminuted fracture: This is a more complicated type of fracture where the bone is broken into several different pieces.
- Greenstick fracture: Children's bones are less brittle than adults because they are still growing, and they can sustain 'greenstick fractures'. These are injuries in which the bone bends and cracks, rather than having the complete break of a simple fracture.

The fractured bone may also pierce the skin, or an internal organ, causing more extensive damage.

DIAGNOSIS You may suspect a broken bone if your child has had a fall or has tripped awkwardly, and then is reluctant to use that part of the body (schools should notify you of falls that happen there). There may be some redness and swelling visible at the site. although visible bruising usually develops later.

TREATMENT Reassure your child, and splint or support the site of the injury in such a way as to prevent further movement and pain. Depending on the injury, this may be done in the following ways.
- The arm: A fractured arm can be splinted by bandaging it to the body. If this is not possible, you can give some relief by pinning the sleeve of a jacket or coat in such a way as to support the injured arm.
- The leg: A fractured leg can be supported by bandaging it to the sound leg which will then act as a splint.
- If the skin has been broken: If the fractured bone has pierced the skin, apply a large, clean dressing to the area and raise the limb to reduce any bleeding. It may be necessary to apply pressure to control any bleeding without actually pressing on the bone itself.

Then take your child to hospital at once – on a stretcher if necessary – for X-rays and treatment. In hospital the fracture will be placed in the correct position, and a plaster cast applied to keep it in this position until the bone heals. If there is considerable soft tissue swelling around the injury, a half plaster or back slab is usually applied in the first instance and a complete cast fitted when the swelling has subsided.

- Other bones: There is no specific treatment for fractured ribs, other than pain relief, while fractures of the collar bone and humerus in the upper arm are usually treated with a special collar and cuff. Occasionally severe complicated fractures require internal fixation with metal screws and plates, and this would need a stay in hospital.

Burns

All burns are painful and, in children, even fairly small burns may cause problems. Burns can be caused by flames, hot objects such as irons, hot liquids and steam, chemicals and sunburn. Large or small areas may be affected and the burn may penetrate the skin to different depths causing superficial, partial thickness or full thickness injury to the skin. All these factors are relevant to subsequent treatment but do not affect the emergency treatment outlined below.

TREATMENT The emergency treatment of all burns is essentially the same – to minimize the amount of heat-induced damage to the skin and deeper tissues.

- The most effective way is to keep the burned area immersed in cool water for at least 10 minutes. With a small child the easiest way to do this is to put her in the kitchen sink or bath.
- For more extensive burns in an older child or adult whom you cannot move, you will need to pour water directly on to the burn.
- Clothing may be removed carefully, as long as it is not sticking to the burn. In particular, remove belts and jewellery wherever possible as the surrounding area may swell considerably.
- Then cover the burned area lightly with a clean dressing – a clean teatowel or large cotton handkerchief is quite suitable for this. Avoid using cottonwool, kitchen roll or lint as a dressing, as they all have fibres which might embed in the wound. Do not put anything else on the burn.

- Leave blisters to burst naturally – if you attempt to burst them, you may introduce infection.
- If the burn is deep or extensive take your child to hospital for further assessment and treatment as soon as possible.

If the burn is extensive the victim may be badly shocked and require resuscitation (see CPR, pp. 377–8), while burns to the face may cause difficulty in breathing. These severe burns need immediate pain relief, intravenous fluids and ventilation if necessary, usually at the nearest casualty department. The victim then needs to be transferred to a specialist burns unit for assessment and treatment which may involve extensive plastic surgery at a later stage.

Dealing with different causes of burns

FIRE Put the flames out by rolling the child in a rug, blanket or large coat, then immerse the burn in cool water.

CHEMICAL BURNS Immerse these in water in the same way. Care must be taken to remove contaminated clothing and to avoid getting any of the chemical on your own skin.

SUNBURN Sunburn is a radiation burn which causes reddening of the skin followed by blister formation when severe. The best way to deal with sunburn is to

Sunburn protection checklist

- Avoid sunburn.
- Keep babies out the sun altogether.
- Protect children – there is evidence that severe sunburn as a child increases the risk of skin cancer later.
- Limit exposure to sun – seek natural shade from trees etc.
- Avoid direct sun between 11am and 3pm.
- Wear a broad brimmed hat and cool loose clothing.
- Use a sunscreen with SPF of 15+ with additional UVA protection.
- Don't spend extra time in the sun because you are using a sunscreen – there is no such thing as a safe tan.
- Avoid using sun beds.

prevent it. Keep your child out of the fierce midday sun, apply high protection factor sunscreens frequently, make him wear a hat to protect the head and drink plenty of fluids.

However, if your child does get burned, take him out of the sun – preferably indoors, and give him plenty to drink. He may require paracetamol for the discomfort and a cool bath to reduce his temperature. If there is no blistering or peeling skin, calamine lotion or a product containing a mild local anaesthetic will soothe mild sunburn.

Choking and breathing difficulties

Little children put lots of different things in their mouths and occasionally something 'goes down the wrong way', lodges in the windpipe and obstructs normal breathing. The child may try to gasp for air, then go pale and eventually greyish blue in colour.

The foreign body needs to be expelled quickly and the first aid outlined below aims to do this. The obstruction is usually too far back to be able to reach it and pull it out with a finger. Indeed, trying to do this may push it further down the airways and make matters worse. The way to expel an object lodged in the windpipe is slightly different, depending on the age of the victim:

BABIES Hold your baby along the length of your forearm so that his legs are either side of your arm and your hand is around the top of his ribcage at the front – his head should be slightly lower than his body (see illustration). Slap him fairly forcefully four

times between the shoulderblades. Check to see if anything has come up and remove it carefully from the mouth if necessary. If the baby still does not breathe begin artificial ventilation (see CPR, pp. 377–8).

CHILDREN Place your child across your lap, again with his head lower than his body. Slap him four times between the shoulderblades and see if anything is dislodged. If this does not work artificial ventilation should be started and the back slaps repeated until such time as professional help arrives or the foreign body is expelled.

OLDER CHILDREN AND ADULTS Bend the person forward at the waist and slap him hard between the shoulderblades four times. If this fails to dislodge the object, use abdominal thrusts (see box and illustration opposite).

Convulsions

Fits can occur for a variety of reasons. Your child may suffer from epilepsy, in which case you will probably be well prepared and know what to do, unless it is the first time. Fits may also occur after a head injury or serious infection involving the brain. They may also occur when a young child, usually under the age of three, has a high temperature. These fits are called febrile convulsions and are relatively common. They do not indicate that the child is going to grow up suffering from epilepsy (see also p. 351).

FEBRILE CONVULSIONS These are best avoided by keeping a feverish child cool by removing clothing, tepid sponging and the use of paracetamol. If, in spite of these measures, a fit does occur, your baby may arch his back and his eyes may roll upward. The muscles of the arms and legs may twitch and he may hold his breath and look a dusky colour. Occasionally a little frothy spit may dribble from the mouth. This type of fit is frightening for parents but is usually very brief and is over almost before you can do anything about it. However, your child should be placed on his side in the recovery position (see p. 379) to protect against inhalation of vomit. Your child will probably go into a deep sleep after the fit. Make sure he is covered but not too hot, and open the window to

Abdominal thrust

This manoeuvre is designed to expel air forcibly from the chest. Do not use on children less than a year old.

- Stand behind the casualty with your hands around his waist.
- Clasp your hands together and bring them toward you in an upward and inward motion into the area just below the ribs (below).

- Repeat the manoeuvre four times, alternating with back slaps, five of each.
- If the casualty becomes unconscious, lie him flat on his back and continue the abdominal thrusts in this position.
- Sit astride the casualty and use the heels of both hands, one on top of the other, in an upward and inward direction just below the ribcage (below).

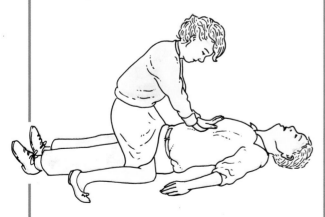

- If normal breathing fails to resume, begin artificial ventilation (see CPR, pp. 377–8).

keep the air cool. Call your doctor for advice as soon as the fit has passed.

A more prolonged febrile convulsion requires treatment with rectal diazepam and paracetamol either at your doctor's surgery or the local hospital. The child is often admitted for a period of observation and investigation afterward. Occasionally, infants who are prone to these type of convulsions are placed on long term anti-convulsant drugs to try to prevent recurrences.

Diabetic emergencies

When a person who is known to be diabetic is found unconscious, it is often difficult to tell whether this is because he has a very low or very high blood sugar level. This type of diabetic emergency usually only occurs in those taking insulin – and it is generally safer to assume that it is due to a low blood sugar level (hypoglycaemia) than a high blood sugar level (hyperglycaemia). This is because prolonged hypoglycaemia can cause permanent damage and should be corrected as soon as possible, while the effects of hyperglycaemia constitute a less serious emergency.

DIAGNOSIS   Clues can sometimes be found in the person's background, if there is anyone around to give it. (If the victim is your own child you of course will know which it is and your doctor will have briefed you on what to do in an emergency.) Hypoglycaemia tends to come on rapidly and may be associated with giving too much insulin or taking too much exercise, while hyperglycaemia tends to develop more slowly and may be associated with another illness from which the person may be suffering at the same time, or with missing an insulin injection. Sometimes the blood sugar level can be measured with the patient's own equipment, and this is the ideal thing for parents of a diabetic child to do.

TREATMENT   Hypoglycaemia is treated with sugar – in the form of a drink if the child is conscious enough to be able to swallow or as a gel which can be squeezed into the side of the mouth and massaged into the cheek. Glucose can also be given intravenously – though this is not usually done by first-aiders. An injection of the hormone glucagon can be given by almost anyone in an emergency, however, and some diabetics carry it in a kit. Glucagon reverses the effects of insulin and causes the blood sugar to rise – whereupon the child regains consciousness. He must then be sure to eat some carbohydrate to maintain the blood sugar level.

Hyperglycaemia is treated with insulin injections. The patient may be dehydrated and need intravenous fluids, so admission to hospital is often necessary.

Drowning

Children can drown in remarkably small amounts of water and do not need to be at the seaside or swimming pool to do so. The garden pond, paddling pool and bath are all hazards if your child is left unattended.

- A drowning child may be found lying face down in the water, not breathing. Don't be put off by this – children have been known to recover after periods of submersion in water if resuscitation procedures are carried out immediately.
- Lift him out of the water, preferably with his head lower than the rest of his body to drain as much fluid from the body as possible and prevent further inhalation of the water.
- Lay him on his back and assess his condition as quickly as you can.
- If he is not breathing but has a good pulse, artificial ventilation should be started.
- If he is not breathing and has no discernible pulse, artificial ventilation will need to be combined with chest compression; call for help and follow the 'ABC' procedure set out on pp. 377–8.
- Continue resuscitation until professional help arrives.
- It is also important to keep the casualty warm by removing any cold wet clothing and wrapping him in a blanket. If he is conscious and alert, give him a warm drink. However, even if recovery occurs fairly quickly, your child should still be sent to hospital because of the irritant effects of water entering the lungs which may subsequently affect breathing.

NB If someone appears to be in difficulty in the water, make a thorough assessment of the conditions and any other help available before jumping in to rescue him, otherwise you may run the risk of becoming a casualty yourself.

Electric shock

Young children are inquisitive and electric sockets look very interesting. It is therefore wise to keep them covered to prevent your child getting an electric shock by poking something inside.

If a child receives an electric shock, the damage may vary from a sharp tingling feeling at best to cardiac arrest at worst. Depending on how the shock was sustained, there may be a burn at the site of contact, and internal damage.

TREATMENT IN THE HOME   Electric shocks occurring in the home are from low voltage current and can be treated in the following way:

- The first thing to do is to switch off the electricity, as long as you can get to the socket or switch off the mains easily. Do not touch your child until you have done this.
- If your child is still in contact with the current and you have been unable to switch it off, do not touch him directly but use an insulated rod – a wooden broom, for example – to disengage him from the electrical apparatus. Do not use anything metal or anything that is wet. Make sure that you are not standing in any water which will conduct the current – instead stand on a thick rubber mat or large book, or quickly put on rubber boots. If these measures are not possible and the situation is grave, tug on the casualty's clothing to drag him free, providing that it is dry and therefore will not conduct the current to you.
- Once he is free of the electric current, check to see whether he is breathing and has a pulse. If not, start artificial ventilation and chest compression as necessary (see CPR, pp. 377–8). Electric burns should be cooled with water – again only when you are sure you are safe and that the current has been switched off.

HIGH VOLTAGE SHOCK   High voltage electrical injury is much more serious and usually occurs in the open near power lines, live electric rails or generating stations. It is important to call the emergency services immediately and not to go anywhere near the casualty until you know for sure that the power has been turned off by the authorities. Once you are sure it is safe to approach, assess the casualty, who is likely to need CPR (see pp. 377–8) until an ambulance or a doctor arrives.

Epileptic fit

- MINOR CONVULSION – PETIT MAL This is usually just a brief 'absence' with a dazed look and requires little intervention other than protecting the sufferer from any danger if he is in an unfamiliar place.
- MAJOR CONVULSION – TONIC-CLONIC SEIZURE OR GRAND MAL This is the classical fit in which the sufferer loses consciousness, falls to the ground jerking his limbs. He may bite his tongue or wet himself during the fit and will be rather dazed for a while afterward. The fit rarely lasts more than a few minutes and rarely requires treatment other than ensuring the child is placed safely in the recovery position (see p. 379). He should not be restrained in any way – though can be supported with pillows if necessary. Nothing should be placed in his mouth either.

If the fit is prolonged, rectal diazepam may need to be given to stop it. The drug comes in a special formulation and packaging for this purpose and parents can be instructed how and when to use it. If the child continues to fit despite treatment, or if this is a first fit in an adult or child, he should be taken to hospital for further treatment, observation and investigation (see also Epilepsy, p. 351).

Eye injuries

Eye injuries are painful and potentially serious and usually need expert assessment and treatment. If the eye has been splashed by a chemical, wash it out with clean water and take your child directly to casualty.

If you suspect a penetrating eye injury or foreign body in the eye do not touch the eye at all. Ask your child to keep his eyes still, cover the injured eye with a clean pad and then bandage both eyes, explaining what you are doing to your child for reassurance. Then get him to hospital immediately.

Fainting

Fainting occurs when the blood pressure drops suddenly, reducing the blood flow to the brain and causing a brief loss of consciousness. The most common cause of this is the pooling of blood in the legs if you have been standing still for a long period – particularly in warm weather. Severe pain, fright and other unpleasant stimuli can also cause fainting.

DIAGNOSIS It is important to differentiate a simple faint from other causes of unconsciousness, such as hypoglycaemia, heart attack, stroke or head injury. Someone who has fainted usually appears to be pale and has a slow pulse but is breathing normally. Recovery is also rapid.

TREATMENT When someone faints, he slumps to the ground and rectifies the problem of blood flow to the brain by bringing the head to the same level as the rest of the body and increasing the circulation to it. After a few seconds, consciousness returns, though the person may be confused and wobbly for a time.

The best treatment for a person who 'feels faint' or has fainted is to put his head between his knees if he is sitting down or to raise his legs above the level of his head if he is lying on the ground.

Foreign bodies

Children have a tendency to stick things in their ears, up their noses and sometimes inside the vagina or rectum. The first sign of a foreign body may be a nasty smelling discharge from the nose, ear or vagina.

It is best not to try to remove the object yourself but to seek medical help since trying to get it out is more likely to drive the offending object further in. The doctor at your surgery or casualty department will have special instruments for removing objects from narrow body passages (see also Choking, p. 384).

One possible exception to this advice is that of an insect in a child's ear. This will probably float out if the child lies on his side and a stream of warm water is poured into the ear from a jug. Alternatively, the ear can be gently syringed out at the surgery.

Swallowed foreign bodies such as buttons or small coins generally pass through the digestive tract with no problem and appear at the other end a day or so later. If, however, your child has swallowed something sharp, large or dangerous, go to the hospital casualty department, as X-rays may need to be taken to locate the object. Depending on size and position, some swallowed objects can be removed by a gastroscope, a flexible instrument passed through the mouth while the child is sedated or anaesthetized.

Head injury

A child with a head injury may be conscious, drowsy or unconscious. He may also pass from one state to another rapidly, so needs monitoring all the time. Signs of serious injury include loss of consciousness, unequal pupil size and discharge of clear fluid from the nose or ear. Even if your child seems all right at first after a severe bump on the head, keep a close eye on him as the signs of severe head injury may not happen for some time after the event.

- If he is unconscious or drowsy, place in the recovery position (p. 379) and send for help. If at any time he stops breathing and has no pulse start CPR (see pp. 377–8).
- Get your child to hospital as soon as possible for a skull X-ray, and neurological observation and investigation. If you suspect a fractured skull, control any bleeding from a scalp wound, but do not apply pressure to the injured area. Superficial head wounds bleed alarmingly, even though the injury itself may not be serious, and may have to be stitched.

Heat exhaustion

This is best avoided by keeping out of the sun during the hottest part of the day, drinking plenty of fluids, wearing powerful sunscreens and a large hat to protect the head. Children should be encouraged to play quietly in the shade rather than rush about in the sun when it is very hot.

DIAGNOSIS Your child may have heatstroke if he is irritable, complains of a headache and looks and feels very hot and flushed. If left untreated he may become confused and will at some stage lose consciousness.

TREATMENT Take your child indoors into a cool room and undress him. He should be cooled by tepid sponging and taken to hospital for further assessment. Severe heat exhaustion may cause dehydration and your child may need to have fluids through a drip.

Nosebleeds

These are common in childhood and rarely severe – though they may be distressing to both parents and child. They may happen spontaneously when your child has a bad cold, when one of the tiny vessels inside the nose ruptures, or they can be caused by a blow to the nose, perhaps by a hard ball. Another cause is nose picking – a common habit in children.

- When a nose bleed occurs as the result of a head injury, you should take your child to hospital straight away – the treatment below can be carried out on the journey.

TREATMENT
- Sit your child down; tilt his head slightly forward.
- Squeeze the soft part of the nose to stop the bleeding; your child should breathe through his mouth while this is done.

- The pressure can be released after about 10 minutes to see if the bleeding has stopped. If it has, it is sensible for your child to rest quietly for a time rather than rush about and risk starting the bleeding again.
- Do not let your child blow his nose or fiddle with it for a couple of hours after a nose bleed to avoid disturbing the clot.
- If the bleeding has not stopped after 10 minutes' pressure, repeat for a further 10 minutes. If,

however, your child is obviously pale and unwell, take him to the doctor or nearest casualty.

If your child has frequent nose bleeds your doctor may refer him to a specialist ENT (ear, nose and throat) surgeon for treatment. This may involve cauterizing the prominent vessels inside the nose to prevent further bleeding. Very rarely, nosebleeds can be the first sign of a bleeding disorder or more serious condition.

Poisoning

The problem with poisoning is that parents frequently do not know what, if anything, their child has taken and the child may be too ill or too young to tell you. Tablets, kitchen cleansers and garden chemicals are all common hazards and should be kept out of reach or locked away (see pp. 168–72). Teach your children never to eat any berries or fungi they might find and not to eat plant leaves.

TREATMENT If you know your child has eaten or drunk something poisonous take him to hospital straight away even if there are no apparent ill-effects at the time. If, however, you find your child unconscious and you suspect poisoning, call for help as soon as possible after checking to see if he is breathing and you can feel a pulse. If not, start artificial ventilation and chest compression as necessary (see CPR pp. 377–8). If he is breathing spontaneously and has a good pulse, place him in the recovery position (see p. 379) as he may vomit; the recovery position is designed to prevent him from inhaling any vomit. Then call for help.

- CORROSIVE CHEMICALS: If a corrosive chemical has been swallowed do not give your child anything to drink and do not try to make him vomit. Instead check his breathing regularly as the chemical may irritate the airways and obstruct breathing (in which case artificial ventilation may be necessary) and get him to hospital immediately.
- DRUGS OR MEDICINES: If your child appears well but you suspect an overdose or accidental poisoning with drugs or medicines, try to find out what he has taken and take your child to hospital as soon as possible for further treatment. Generally speaking it is better not to try and make him sick – unless you live in a very remote area miles from a

hospital. Try to get advice over the telephone. Your child may vomit anyway, particularly in the car on the way to hospital. Once in casualty, your child may be made to vomit under supervision or may need a stomach washout. Some drugs have specific antidotes while others require careful monitoring and treatment in an intensive care unit until the drug is excreted.

Shock

Shock is the general term for the condition in which the blood pressure drops and the casualty ultimately loses consciousness. Someone suffering from shock may become very pale and shaky, with low blood pressure, and may feel faint. There are many causes of shock – most of which involve either failure of the heart to pump blood around the circulation (as in a heart attack) or loss of blood volume so that there is not enough pressure in the circulation (as with major injury and bleeding).

TREATMENT Lay the person suffering from shock flat with his legs raised above the level of his head. Any obvious bleeding should be stopped if possible and urgent help should be summoned. Watch him closely and start artificial ventilation and chest compression, if necessary. See also Anaphylaxis (p. 377) and CPR (pp. 377–8).

Unconsciousness

There are many causes of unconsciousness ranging from head injury, infection of the brain and meninges, uncontrolled diabetes, electrocution, drowning, stroke, heart attack and major injury with excessive blood loss. For the person giving first aid, the treatment is the same irrespective of the cause. If the casualty is breathing and has a good pulse, place him in the recovery position (see p. 379). Check that he is not in immediate danger from his surroundings and that his condition is stable. Call for help.

If he is not breathing, begin artificial ventilation. If the casualty does not have a discernible pulse, start chest compression as well (see CPR, pp. 377–8). Continue to resuscitate until help arrives, or the child improves, with a good pulse and is breathing spontaneously.

The following is a list of useful organizations: some are large national charities, others are small local groups run by volunteers. Information may be provided over the phone, in the form of leaflets or in person by attending a counselling session or a self-help group.

Some of these organizations have separate branches in Northern Ireland, Scotland and Wales – these are listed where appropriate. Many can put you in touch with a local branch.

GENERAL INFORMATION AND SUPPORT

ACAS (Advisory, Conciliation and Arbitration Service)
Clifton House, 83 Euston Road
London NW1 2RB
(0171) 396 5100
Advice and information on maternity leave and such matters as unfair dismissal.

Active Birth Centre
25 Bickerton Road, London N19 5JT
(0171) 561 9006
Information and advice.

Association of Breastfeeding Mothers
26 Herschell Close, London SE26 4TH
(0181) 778 4796
Advice line for breastfeeding mothers and those with breastfeeding problems. Also runs support groups.

Association for Improvements in the Maternity Services (AIMS)
40 Kingswood Avenue, London NW6 6LS
(0181) 960 5585

Scotland
40 Leamington Terrace, Edinburgh EH10 4JL
(0131) 229 6259

Voluntary group offering support and advice on parents' rights and choices in maternity care.

Association for Post-Natal Illness (APNI)
25 Jerdan Place, London SW6 1BE
(0171) 386 0868
Network of volunteers, all of whom have recovered from postnatal illness, offering information, support and encouragement.

Caesarean Support Network
c/o Sheila Tunstall, 2 Hurst Park Drive
Huyton, Liverpool L36 1TF
(0151) 480 1184
Information and support for those who have had or will have a caesarean delivery. Can put you in touch with someone local who has had a caesarean and understands the problems.

Child
Caledonian House, 98 The Centre
Feltham, Middlesex
(01424) 732361
Self-help organization for people with fertility problems. Helplines for specific problems such as IVF, ectopic pregnancies, miscarriages etc.

Child Poverty Action Group (CPAG)
4th Floor, 1–5 Bath Street
London EC1V 9PY
(0171) 253 3406
Information on benefits.

Citizens Advice Bureau (CAB)
Free and confidential advice on topics including maternity rights, debts, housing, employment, legal problems as well as personal difficulties. Look in your phone book for your local branch.

CRY-SIS
BM CRY-SIS, London WC1N 3XX
(0171) 404 5011

Scotland
21 Falkland Gardens, Edinburgh EH12 6UW
(0131) 334 5317

Self-help and support group for parents of excessively crying, sleepless or demanding babies and young children. National network of volunteers, who may or not have been parents of such babies.

DSS Helpline
(0800) 393539
A helpful organization run by people with considerable knowledge of and experience in both tax and national insurance.

Equal Opportunities Commission
Overseas House, Quay Street
Manchester M3 3HN
(0161) 833 9244
Information and advice on issues of discrimination and equal opportunities.

Family Fund
PO Box 50, York YO1 22X
(01904) 621115
A government fund administered by the Rowntree Trust, which gives cash grants to families caring for severely disabled children under 16.

Family Health Services Authorities (FHSAs)
If you are new to an area your FHSA can give you a list of local doctors with whom you may be able to register, including those with a special interest in pregnancy, childbirth and family health. Look in the phone book under your local health authority.

Northern Ireland
Central Services Agency for Health and Personal Social Services (CSA)
25 Adelaide Street, Belfast BT2 8FH
(01232) 321313

Family Welfare Association
501–505 Kingsland Road, London E8 4AU
(0171) 254 6251
National charity providing free counselling for those who are experiencing relationship difficulties and advice on many other family-related problems.

Gingerbread
49 Wellington Street, London WC2E 7BN
(0171) 240 0953

Scotland
Gingerbread Scotland
304 Maryhill Road, Glasgow G20 7YE
(0141) 353 0953

Northern Ireland
Gingerbread Northern Ireland
169 University Street, Belfast BT7 1HR
(01232) 231417

Wales
Gingerbread Wales
Room 16, Albion Chambers, Swansea SA1 1RN
(01792) 648728

Countrywide network of local groups providing advice and support for lone parents on everything from child care to returning to work and benefits.

Health Search Scotland
The Priory, Canaan Lane
Edinburgh EH10 4SG
(0131) 452 8666
Information on local self-help groups in Scotland.

Homestart
2 Salisbury Road, Leicester LE1 7QR
(01533) 554988
Offers support, friendship and help for families temporarily under stress in their own homes. You can refer yourself, or may be referred by your health visitor, midwife or any other health professional.

Independent Midwives Association
Nightingale Cottage, Shamblehurst Lane
Botley, Hampshire SO3 2BY
(01703) 694429
Offers advice, support and information to women considering a home birth and full care to those women who book a member for a home birth.

Institute for Complementary Medicine
PO Box 194, London SE16 1QZ
(0171) 237 5165
Charity providing information on complementary medicine and referrals to qualified practitioners.

KIDS
80 Waynflete Square, London W1D 6UD
(0181) 969 2817
A small national organization set up to help families with children with special needs. Contact their head office to find out if KIDS operates in your area.

Labour Relations Agency
Windsor House, 9–15 Bedford Street
Belfast BT2 7NU
(01232) 321442
Advice on maternity rights in Northern Ireland.

Life
Life House, Newbold Terrace
Leamington Spa, Warwickshire CV32 4EA
(01926) 421587
Advice and information on pregnancy,
miscarriage, abortion and stillbirth.

MAMA (Meet-a-mum) Association
Cornerstone House, 14 Willes Road
Croydon, CR0 2XX
(0181) 655 0357
Support groups for new mums and for
mothers suffering from postnatal depression.

Maternity Alliance
15 Britannia Street London WC1X 9JM
(0171) 837 1265
Advice on employment and maternity rights
for expectant mothers.

**National Association for Maternal and Child
Welfare**
1st Floor, 40–42 Osnaburgh Street
London NW1 3ND
(0171) 383 4115
Telephone helpline offering advice on child
care.

National Childbirth Trust (NCT)
Alexandra House, Oldham Terrace
London W3 6NH
(0181) 992 8637
Charity with branches nationwide. Runs
antenatal classes to help expectant mothers
with labour, breathing and offers information
on the different birth positions. Also offers
help with breastfeeding.

National Council for One Parent Families
255 Kentish Town Road, London NW5 2LX
(0171) 267 1361

Scotland
Scottish Council for Single Parents
13 Gayfield Square, Edinburgh EH1 3NX
(0131) 556 3899

Provides information on all aspects of coping
alone. Also runs local groups.

**National Society for the Prevention of
Cruelty to Children (NSPCC)**
42 Curtain Road, London EC2A 3NH
(0171) 825 2500

Northern Ireland
16 Rosemary Street, Belfast BT1 1QD
(01232) 240311

Publishes a range of free booklets, and offers
counselling and advice to those who feel they
may be in danger of harming a child. Aims to
protect children from abuse and neglect.

Parentline
Endway House, The Endway
Hadleigh, Essex SS7 2AN
(01702) 559900
Support for parents of children of any age
under stress. Confidential telephone helplines
are manned by trained parents.

Parents Advice Centre
Room 1, Bryson House
28 Bedford Street, Belfast BT2 7FE
(01232) 238800
Confidential, 24-hour advice service offering
support and guidance to parents under stress.

Parents Anonymous
6–9 Manor Gardens, London N7 6LA
(0171) 263 8918
Helpline for parents who feel they can't cope
or might abuse their children.

Parents at Work
45 Beech Street, Barbican
London EC2Y 8AD
(0171) 628 3578
Rights and options for all working parents.
Also aims to promote the development of
workplace nurseries.

Patients' Association
8 Guilford Street, London WC1N 1DT
(0171) 242 3460
Advice for people who are experiencing
difficulties with their doctor.

Relate: Marriage Guidance
Herbert Gray College
Little Church Street, Rugby CV21 3AP
(01788) 573241
Professional family relationship counsellors
nationwide. Sliding scale of fees based on an
ability to pay.

Relate Northern Ireland
76 Dublin Road, Belfast BT2 7HP
(01232) 323454
A confidential counselling service for people
with relationship problems.

**Shelter: the National Campaign for the
Homeless**
88 Old Street, London EC1V 9HU
(0171) 253 0202

Northern Ireland
165 University Street, Belfast BT7 1HR
(01232) 247752

Wales
25 Walter Road, Swansea SA1 5NN
(01792) 469400

Information and advice on all housing matters,
including tenants' rights, grants etc.

Social Security
For general advice on all social security
benefits, Income Support, pensions etc., call
Freeline Social Security on 0800 666555

Social Services
Your area office will give you information on
benefits, housing employment, childcare and
useful organizations. See phone book under
the name of your local authority.

**Twins and Multiple Births Association
(TAMBA)**
PO Box 30, Little Sutton
S. Wirral L66 1TH
(0151) 348 0020
Helpline: (01732) 868000
(7pm-11pm weekdays; 10am-11pm weekends)
Advice on all aspects of twins from pregnancy
to breastfeeding to sleep problems.

Women's Aid Federation
PO Box 391, Bristol BS99 7WS
(0117) 963 3542

Northern Ireland
129 University Street, Belfast BT7 1HP
(01232) 249041

Scotland
Scottish Women's Aid
12 Torpichen Street
Edinburgh EH3 8IQ
(0131) 221 0401

Advice, support and refuge to women who
have been abused.

ALCOHOL, SMOKING AND DRUG ABUSE

Alcohol Concern
Waterbridge House, 32–36 Loman Street
London SE1 0EE
(0171) 928 7377

Wales
Alcohol Concern Wales
4 Dock Chambers, Bute Street
Cardiff CF1 6AG
(01222) 488000

Scotland
Scottish Council on Alcohol
166 Buchanan Street, Glasgow G1 2NH
(0141) 333 9677

Northern Ireland
Council on Alcohol
40 Elmswood Avenue, Belfast BT9 6AZ
(01232) 664434

Information on alcohol-related problems and
where you can get help locally.

Dunlewy Substance Advice Centre
1a Dunlewy Street, Belfast BT13 2QU
(01232) 324197
Offers help and counselling on alcohol, drug
and solvent abuse.

**SCODA (The Standing Conference on Drug
Abuse)**
Waterbridge House, 32–34 Loman Street
London SE1 0EE
(0171) 430 2341

Scotland
Scottish Drug Forum
5 Oswald Street, Glasgow G1 4QR
(0141) 221 1175

Information on local treatment and services
for drug users and their families.

Smokers' Quitline
(0800) 002200

Ulster Cancer Foundation
40 Eglantine Place, Belfast BT9 6DX
(01232) 663281/2/3
Carries out cancer research and education
programmes in Northern Ireland. Gives
information on the dangers of smoking.

CHILD CARE

Daycare Trust/National Childcare Campaign
Wesley House, 4 Wild Court
London WC2B 4AU
(0171) 405 5617/8
Advice on obtaining suitable daycare.

National Childminding Association
8 Masons Hill, Bromley BR2 9EY
(0181) 464 6164

Scotland
Scottish Childminding Association
Room 15, Stirling Business Centre
Wellgreen, Stirling SK8 2DZ
(01786) 445377

Northern Ireland
Northern Ireland Childminding Association
17a Court Street, Newtownards
Co Down BT23 3NX
(01247) 811015

Association for parents, childminders and
others who have an interest in daycare and
wish to see standards improve.

New Ways to Work
309 Upper Street, London N1 2TY
(0171) 226 4026
Information on flexible working hours and job
sharing.

Working for Childcare
77 Holloway Road, London N7 8JZ
(0181) 700 0281
Advice and information for employers, trades
unions and parents on developing childcare
facilities at work.

EDUCATION AND SCHOOLING

British Dyslexia Association
(01734) 668271
Offers a helpline which is open 10am–5pm
Mondays to Fridays. They can also send you
an information pack.

BTEC
Central House, Upper Woburn Place
London WC1H 0HH
(0171) 413 8400

The Child Accident Prevention Trust
18-20 Farringdon Lane, London EC1R 3AU
(0171) 608 3828
An educational charity which researches and
provides information on child safety.

City & Guilds
76 Portland Place, London W1N 4AA
(0171) 2942468

**The Independent Schools Information
Service (ISIS)**
56 Buckingham Gate, London SW1E 6AG
(0171) 630 8793
Provides a handbook giving information on
independent schools.

Kidscape
(0171) 730 3300
Publishes a 'Stop Bullying' leaflet and operates
a Parents Bullying Line on Mondays and
Wednesdays 9am–5pm.

Lucid Systems
26 Tunis Sreet, Sculcoates Lane
Hull HU5 1EZ
(01482) 465589
Information for parents with dyslexic children.

National Association for Gifted Children
Park Campus, Boughton Green Road
Northampton, NN2 7AL
(01604) 792300

**The National Association of Toy and Leisure
Libraries**
68 Churchway, London NW1 1LT
(0171) 387 9592
Provides support for toy libraries, advice on
toys and a range of publications relating to
child development.

The Parents' Charter Unit
Department for Education
Sanctuary Buildings, Great Smith Street
London SW1P 3BT
(0171) 925 6155

Preschool Learning Alliance
69 Kings Cross Road, London WC1X 9LL
(0171) 833 0991
Can provide information about preschool
playgroups in your area. Formerly known as
the Preschool Playgroups Association.

**Royal Society for the Prevention of Accidents
(ROSPA)**
Cannon House, The Priory
Queensway, Birmingham B4 6BS
(0121) 200 2461

RSA Examinations Board
Progress House, Westwood Way
Coventry CV4 8HS
(01203) 470033

Scottish Education Department
New St Andrew's House
Edinburgh EH1 3TG
(0131) 244 4440

Secretary of State
Admissions Team, Schools 1B
Department for Education
Great Smith Street, London SW1P 3BT

You can write to the Secretary of State if you
want to proceed with an appeal against a
school's decision not to admit your child.

*The following organizations may be useful in
giving advice on finding a qualified teacher for
your child.*

The Amateur Swimming Association
Harold Fern House, Derby Square
Loughborough Leicestershire LE11 0AL
(01509) 230431

British Amateur Gymnastics Association
Lilleshall Hall, Shropshire
(01952) 820330

Incorporated Society of Musicians
10 Stratford Place, London W1N 9AE
(0171) 629 4413

Sports Council
16 Upper Woburn Place, London WC1H 0QP
(0171) 388 1277

FAMILY PLANNING

Family Planning Association
27 Mortimer Street, London W1N 7RJ
(0171) 636 7866

Northern Ireland
113 University Street, Belfast BT7 1HP
(01232) 325488

Wales
4 Museum Place, Cardiff CF1 3BG
(01222) 644034

Information on all aspects of family planning
and contraception.

Family Planning Brook Advisory Centres
Brook Central Office, 153a East Street
London SE17 2SD
(0171) 708 1234
Advice and practical help with contraception
and unplanned pregnancies. Free and
confidential.

Marie Stopes Clinic
Marie Stopes House
108 Whitfield Street, London W1P 6BE
(0171) 388 0662
Registered charity providing family planning,
women's health centres, pregnancy testing and
counselling. A charge is made to cover costs.

ILLNESS, DISABILITY AND SPECIAL NEEDS

**AFASIC (Association for All Speech Impaired
Children)**
347 Central Markets, Smithfield
London EC1A 9NH
(0171) 236 3632
Campaigns and provides advice and
information service etc. for children with
speech and language disorders.

**Association for Spina Bifida and
Hydrocephalus (ASBAH)**
ASBAH House, 42 Park Road
Peterborough PE1 2UQ
(01733) 555988

Scotland
Scottish Spina Bifida Association
190 Queensferry Road, Edinburgh EH4 2BW
(0131) 332 0743

Northern Ireland
**Northern Ireland Spina Bifida and
Hydrocephalus Association**
75 New Row, Coleraine BT52 1EJ
(01265) 51522
Information and counselling for parents.

BLISS
17–21 Emerald Street, London WC1N 3QL
(0171) 831 9393
Provides support and information to parents
with a baby in special care.

British Chiropractic Association
Equity House, 59 Whitley Street
Reading RG2 0EG
(01734) 757557
Publishes an annual register of members. Call
0800 212618 for your nearest chiropractor.

British Diabetic Association
10 Queen Anne Street, London W1M 0BD
(0171) 323 1531

Northern Ireland
31 Grange Park, Belfast BT17 0AN
(01232) 610630

National charity which offers advice and
support.

Children's Liver Disease Foundation
138 Digbeth Street, Birmingham B5 6DR
(0121) 643 7282
Offers information on various aspects of the
disease. Can provide leaflets.

Cleft Lip and Palate Association (CLAPA)
1 Eastwood Gardens, Kenton
Newcastle-upon-Tyne NE3 3DQ
(0191) 285 9396
Gives support to parents of children with cleft
lip and/or palate.

Contact a Family
170 Tottenham Court Road, LondonW1P 0HA
(0171) 383 3555
Links families who have children with
disabilities or special needs through self-help
groups.

Council for Disabled Children
8 Wakley Street, London EC1V 7QE
(0171) 843 6000
Details of organizations offering help for
children and families with special disabilities.

Cystic Fibrosis Trust
Alexandra House, 5 Blyth Road
Bromley BR1 3RS
(0181) 464 7211

Northern Ireland
1 Circular Road East, Cultra
Co Down BT18 0HA
(01247) 272781

Wales
3 Aberfour, Newport, Gwent NP9 9QA
(01633) 277663

Scotland
Inverallan, 26 West Argyle Street
Helensburgh, Dunbartonshire G84 8DB
(01436) 676791

Information and support for parents of
children with cystic fibrosis. Local groups.

Disability Information Trust
Mary Marlborough Centre
Nuffield Orthopaedic Centre
Headington, Oxford OX3 7LD
(01865) 227592
Assesses and tests equipment for people with
disabilities.

Down's Syndrome Association
155 Mitcham Road, Tooting
London SW17 9PG
(0181) 682 4001

Scotland
Scottish Down's Syndrome Association
158 Balgreen Road, Edinburgh EH11 3AU
(0131) 313 4225

Northern Ireland
3rd Floor, Bryson House
28 Bedford Street, Belfast BT2 7FE
(01232) 243266

Support for parents of children with Down's
Syndrome. Runs a 24-hour helpline.

Endometriosis Society
33 Belgrave Sqaure, London SW1
(0171) 235 4137
Provides information about the disease.

Haemophilia Society
123 Westminster Bridge Road
London SE1 7HR
(0171) 928 2020

Northern Ireland
67 Woodvale Road, Belfast BT13 3BM

Practical help for families affected by the
disease.

**MENCAP (Royal Society for Mentally
Handicapped Children and Adults)**
MENCAP National Centre
123 Golden Lane, London EC1Y 0RT
(0171) 454 0454

Scotland
**Scottish Society for the Mentally
Handicapped**
7 Buchanan Street, Glasgow G1 3HL
(0141) 226 4541

Northern Ireland
Segal House, 44 Annadale Avenue
Belfast BT7 3JH
(01232) 691351

Advice and information for parents with
mentally handicapped children.

Meningitis Research Foundation
13 High Street, Thornbury, Bristol BS12 2AC
(01454) 413344

Northern Ireland
29 Springwell Street, Belfast BT43 6AT
(01266) 652060

Counselling for bereaved parents and families
and support for parents with children in
hospital.

National Aids Helpline
(0800) 567123
Confidential, free helpline which is available
24 hours a day. Information in other languages
is available as follows: *Bengali* on Tuesday
6pm–10pm on (0800) 371132; *Punjabi* on
Wednesday 6pm–10pm on (0800) 371133;
Gujerati on Wednesday 6pm–10pm on (0800)
371134; *Urdu* on Wednesday 6pm–10pm on
(0800) 371135; *Hindi* on Wednesday
6pm–10pm on (0800) 371136; *Arabic* on
Tuesday 6pm–10pm on (0800) 282447;
Cantonese on Monday 6pm–10pm on (0800)
371137.

**National Association for the Welfare of
Children in Hospital (NAWCH)**
Argyle House, 29–31 Euston Road
London NW1 2SD
(0171) 833 2041

Scotland
Action for Sick Children
15 Smith Place, Edinburgh EH6 8HT
(0131) 553 6553

Advice and emotional support for families
with sick children. Local groups.

National Deaf Children's Society
15 Dufferin Street, London EC1Y 8PD
(0171) 250 0123
Advice and information on all aspects of
childhood deafness. Supports parents through
self-help groups.

National Eczema Society
163 Eversholt Street, London NW1 1BU
(0171) 388 4097
Advice and support for eczema sufferers.

SCOPE
12 Park Crescent, London W1N 4EQ
(0171) 636 5020
Provides a range of services for people with
cerebral palsy and their families.

**SENSE (National Deaf-Blind and Rubella
Association)**
11–13 Clifton Terrace, London N4 3SR
(0171) 272 7774
Advice and support for families of deaf–blind
and rubella handicapped children.

Sickle Cell Society
54 Station Road, Harlesden
London NW10 4UA
(0181) 961 7795
Information and counselling.

Toxoplasmosis Trust
165 Gray's Inn Road, London WC1X 8UD
(0171) 713 9000
Information and counselling for pregnant
women with toxoplasmosis and parents of
infected children.

LOSS AND BEREAVEMENT

England and Wales
**Foundation for the Study of Infant Deaths
(Cot Death Research and Support)**
14 Halkin Street, London SW1X 7DP
(0171) 235 1721

Northern Ireland
**Friends of the Foundation for the Study of
Infant Deaths**
7 Glennan Avenue, Belfast BT17 9HT
(01232) 622688

Scotland
Scottish Cot Death Trust
Royal Hospital for Sick Children
Yorkhill, Glasgow G3 8SJ
(0141) 357 3946

Provides information and support for parents
who are coping with sudden infant death. Can
put you in touch with local groups and other
bereaved parents and provides advice on
prevention. Responsible for the 'Back to Sleep'
campaign.

**SAFTA (Support after Termination for
Abnormality)**
73 Charlotte Street, London W1P 1LB
(0171) 631 0285
Self-help charity offering support to parents
who have had a termination due to a
diagnosed foetal abnormality. Support given
by parents who have also terminated a
pregnancy in such circumstances.

**Stillbirth and Neonatal Death Society
(SANDS)**
28 Portland Place, London W1N 4DE
(0171) 436 5881
National network of support groups for
bereaved parents.

INDEX

The publishers would like to thank the following for helping with photography:
Akosua Adom; Ben Alexander; Husnara Begum; Chelsea and Jade Bess; Hal and Anabel Briggs;
Rosie Callery; Sandra Chambers; Niccy Cowen; Ben Dawes; James, Simon and Joanna Drayson;
Julia Eastell; Julie and Liam Fitzgerald; Xanthe and Robert Gwyn Palmer; Rosy and Angus
Halfyard; Sophie and Melanie Hoare; Fran Hollywood; Alexander Jesson; Henri Lanson; Jason and
Lucy Lubbock; Josh and Connor Lynch; Daisy and Anne King; Jamie MacIntyre; Jamille Malcolm;
Shannon and Debbie Mitchell; Oliver, Max and Sally Nield; Linda Ogden; Oscar Price; Ben,
Joe and Cindy Richards; Victoria Salentino; Ben and Edward Sanderson; Max Schofield; Sebastian
and Rosemary Tusa; Nigel Waters; Armand Weeresinge; Nicholas West; Caitlin and Jenny Wheeler;
Jack and Emma Windsor; Julia Yelland.

Thank you to the following for kind permission to reproduce photographs:
page 23 Custom Medical Stock Photo/Science Photo Library;
pages 42-43 Collections/Sandra Lousada.

Thank you to the following experts who were consulted on sections of the book:
Clare Brown, Information Services Co-ordinator, CHILD; Professor Geoffrey Chamberlain, Head
of Obstetrics and Gynaecology, St George's Medical School, London; Mary Daly, The Health
Visitors Association; Clare Delpach, Director of the Association for Post Natal Illness; Joanie
Diamavicius, Director of Support for Termination around Fetal Abnormality; Foresight;
Gingerbread; Ruth Grigg and Jane Owen, Medical Information Officer, The Family Planning
Association; Sarah Harvey, former midwife and health visitor; Dr David Haslam, GP, patron of
CRY-SIS, Chairman of the Examining Board of the Royal College of General Practitioners;
The Miscarriage Association; Professor Peter Hepper, Department of Psychiatry, Queens University,
Belfast; Annette Spence, Psychosexual Counsellor, and Fran Godfrey, Advice Sister, Marie Stopes
Clinics; Sheila Tunstall, The Caesarean Support Network; Professor James Walker, Department of
Obstetrics and Gynaecology, St James Hospital, Leeds.